# FIAT Uno Owners Workshop Manual

## Peter G Strasman

**Models covered**
FIAT Uno 45, 55, 60, 70 and 1.4, including Turbo ie
and special/limited editions
903 cc, 999 cc, 1108 cc, 1116 cc, 1299 cc, 1301 cc and
1372 cc petrol engines with manual transmissions

*Does not cover Selecta, Fiorino type vans, Diesel engine or
1.1 ie S model*

(923-4U6)       ABCDE
                FGHIJ
                KL

                2

**Haynes Publishing Group**
Sparkford Nr Yeovil
Somerset BA22 7JJ England

**Haynes Publications, Inc**
861 Lawrence Drive
Newbury Park
California 91320 USA

## Acknowledgements

Thanks are due to Champion Spark Plug who supplied the illustrations showing spark plug conditions, to Holt Lloyd Limited who supplied the illustrations showing bodywork repair, and to Duckhams Oils who provided lubrication data. Certain other illustrations are the copyright of the FIAT Motor Company (UK) Limited and are used with their permission. Thanks are also due to Sykes-Pickavant, who provided some of the workshop tools, and all those people at Sparkford who assisted in the production of this manual.

A book in the **Haynes Owners Workshop Manual Series**

Printed by J. H. Haynes & Co. Ltd., Sparkford, Nr Yeovil, Somerset BA22 7JJ, England

**ISBN 1 85010 717 3**

**British Library Cataloguing in Publication Data**
A catalogue record for this book is available from the British Library

We take great pride in the accuracy of information given in this manual, but vehicle manufacturers make alterations and design changes during the production run of a particular vehicle of which they do not inform us. No liability can be accepted by the authors or publishers for loss, damage or injury caused by any errors in, or omissions from, the information given.

# Restoring and Preserving our Motoring Heritage

Few people can have had the luck to realise their dreams to quite the same extent and in such a remarkable fashion as John Haynes, Founder and Chairman of the Haynes Publishing Group.

Since 1965 his unique approach to workshop manual publishing has proved so successful that millions of Haynes Manuals are now sold every year throughout the world, covering literally thousands of different makes and models of cars, vans and motorcycles.

A continuing passion for cars and motoring led to the founding in 1985 of a Charitable Trust dedicated to the restoration and preservation of our motoring heritage. To inaugurate the new Museum, John Haynes donated virtually his entire private collection of 52 cars.

Now with an unrivalled international collection of over 210 veteran, vintage and classic cars and motorcycles, the Haynes Motor Museum in Somerset is well on the way to becoming one of the most interesting Motor Museums in the world.

A 70 seat video cinema, a cafe and an extensive motoring bookshop, together with a specially constructed one kilometre motor circuit, make a visit to the Haynes Motor Museum a truly unforgettable experience.

Every vehicle in the museum is preserved in as near as possible mint condition and each car is run every six months on the motor circuit.

Enjoy the picnic area set amongst the rolling Somerset hills. Peer through the William Morris workshop windows at cars being restored, and browse through the extensive displays of fascinating motoring memorabilia.

From the 1903 Oldsmobile through such classics as an MG Midget to the mighty 'E' Type Jaguar, Lamborghini, Ferrari Berlinetta Boxer, and Graham Hill's Lola Cosworth, there is something for everyone, young and old alike, at this Somerset Museum.

## Haynes Motor Museum

*Situated mid-way between London and Penzance, the Haynes Motor Museum is located just off the A303 at Sparkford, Somerset (home of the Haynes Manual) and is open to the public 7 days a week all year round, except Christmas Day and Boxing Day.*

# About this manual

## Its aim

The aim of this manual is to help you get the best value from your vehicle. It can do so in several ways. It can help you decide what work must be done (even should you choose to get it done by a garage), provide information on routine maintenance and servicing, and give a logical course of action and diagnosis when random faults occur. However, it is hoped that you will use the manual by tackling the work yourself. On simpler jobs it may even be quicker than booking the car into a garage and going there twice, to leave and collect it. Perhaps most important, a lot of money can be saved by avoiding the costs a garage must charge to cover its labour and overheads.

The manual has drawings and descriptions to show the function of the various components so that their layout can be understood. Then the tasks are described and photographed in a step-by-step sequence so that even a novice can do the work.

## Its arrangement

The manual is divided into thirteen Chapters, each covering a logical sub-division of the vehicle. The Chapters are each divided into Sections, numbered with single figures, eg 5; and the Sections into paragraphs (or sub-sections), with decimal numbers following on from the Section they are in, eg 5.1, 5.2, 5.3 etc.

It is freely illustrated, especially in those parts where there is a detailed sequence of operations to be carried out. There are two forms of illustration: figures and photographs. The figures are numbered in sequence with decimal numbers, according to their position in the Chapter – eg Fig. 6.4 is the fourth drawing/illustration in Chapter 6. Photographs carry the same number (either individually or in related groups) as the Section or sub-section to which they relate.

There is an alphabetical index at the back of the manual as well as a contents list at the front. Each Chapter is also preceded by its own individual contents list.

References to the 'left' or 'right' of the vehicle are in the sense of a person in the driver's seat facing forwards.

Unless otherwise stated, nuts and bolts are removed by turning anti-clockwise, and tightened by turning clockwise.

Vehicle manufacturers continually make changes to specifications and recommendations, and these, when notified, are incorporated into our manuals at the earliest opportunity.

**We take great pride in the accuracy of information given in this manual, but vehicle manufacturers make alterations and design changes during the production run of a particular vehicle of which they do not inform us. No liability can be accepted by the authors or publishers for loss, damage or injury caused by any errors in, or omissions from, the information given.**

# Introduction to the FIAT Uno

The Fiat Uno is a well designed and constructed car having an excellent power-to-weight ratio.

The car is very economical, but still offers good performance with excellent body interior space.

Attractive features include the options available for four- or five-speeds or three- or five-door bodywork.

All essential accessories, except a radio, are fitted as standard and a sunroof is optionally available.

From the home mechanic's point of view all repair and servicing operations are straightforward without the need for special tools. Spare parts are immediately available at moderate cost.

Fiat Uno SX

# General dimensions, weights and capacities

*For information applicable to later models, see Supplement at end of manual*

## Dimensions

| | |
|---|---|
| Overall length | 3644 mm (143.6 in) |
| Overall width | 1555 mm (61.3 in) |
| Height | 1432 mm (56.4 in) |
| Wheelbase | 2362 mm (93.1 in) |
| Front track | 1340 mm (52.8 in) |
| Rear track | 1300 mm (51.2 in) |

## Weights (kerb)

| | |
|---|---|
| Uno 45: | |
| Three-door | 700 kg (1543 lb) |
| Five-door | 710 kg (1566 lb) |
| Uno 55: | |
| Three-door | 730 kg (1610 lb) |
| Five-door | 740 kg (1632 lb) |
| Uno 70: | |
| Three-door | 740 kg (1632 lb) |
| Five-door | 750 kg (1654 lb) |
| Uno SX: | |
| Three-door | 770 kg (1698 lb) |
| Five-door | 780 kg (1720 lb) |

## Capacities

| | |
|---|---|
| Fuel tank | 42.0 litre (9.25 gal) |
| Engine oil (with filter change): | |
| 903 cc engine | 3.42 litre (6.0 pint) |
| 1116 and 1301 cc engines | 4.10 litre (7.2 pint) |
| Transmission | 2.40 litre (4.2 pint) |
| Steering box | 140.0 cc |
| Driveshaft CV joints | 125.0 cc |
| Cooling system: | |
| 903 cc engine | 4.6 litre (8.1 pint) |
| 1116 cc engine | 6.0 litre (10.6 pint) |
| 1301 cc engine | 6.2 litre (10.9 pint) |

# Jacking, towing and wheel changing

To avoid repetition, the procedure for raising the vehicle, in order to carry out work under it, is not included before each relevant operation described in this Manual.

It is to be preferred, and it is certainly recommended, that the vehicle is positioned over an inspection pit or raised on a lift. Where these facilities are not available, use ramps or jack up the vehicle strictly in accordance with the following guide. Once the vehicle is raised, supplement the jack with axle stands.

### Jacking

The jack supplied with the car should only be used to change a wheel. Do not use this jack when overhaul or repair work is being carried out; employ a hydraulic or screw jack and supplement it with axle stands.

Jacking points are located under the sills for use with the jack supplied.

To raise the front end with a garage jack, locate the the jack under the transmission lower mounting, just below and slightly to the rear of the transmission oil drain plug. Protect the mounting by placing a block of wood between the jack head and the mounting.

To raise the rear of the car, the jack should be placed under the spare wheel housing as far to the rear as possible. Place a wooden bearer between the jack head and the housing.

### Towing

When being towed, use the left-hand front towing eye.

When towing another vehicle, use the rear towing eye adjacent to the exhaust tailpipe.

When being towed, remember that the brake pedal will require heavier pressure due to lack of servo assistance. Always turn the ignition key to MAR to retain the steering in the unlocked position.

### Wheel changing

With the car on firm level ground, apply the handbrake fully. Remove the hub cap or wheel trim, if fitted.

Release, but do not remove, the bolts. Chock the front and rear of the opposite roadwheel and then raise the car using the sill jack supplied with the car if it is being done at the roadside. Alternatively use a workshop jack supplemented with axle stands.

Remove the wheel bolts, change the wheel and screw in the bolts finger tight. It is recommended that the bolt threads are smeared with multi-purpose grease. Lower the car, remove the jack and tighten the wheel bolts to the specified torque. Refit any wheel trim that was removed.

**Spare wheel and jack stowage**

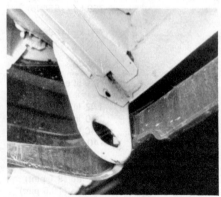

**Front tow hook**

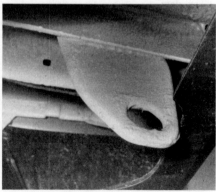

**Rear tow hook**

# Buying spare parts and vehicle identification numbers

*Buying spare parts*

Spare parts are available from many sources, for example, FIAT garages, other garages and accessory shops, and motor factors. Our advice regarding spare parts is as follows:

*Officially appointed FIAT garages* – This is the best source of parts which are peculiar to your car and otherwise not generally available (eg complete cylinder heads, internal gearbox components, badges, interior trim etc). It is also the only place at which you should buy parts if your vehicle is still under warranty; non-FIAT components may invalidate the warranty. To be sure of obtaining the correct parts it will always be necessary to give the partsman your car's engine number, chassis number and number for spares, and if possible, to take the old part along for positive identification. Many parts are available under a factory exchange scheme – any parts returned should always be clean. It obviously makes good sense to go straight to the specialists on your car for this type of part for they are best equipped to supply you. They will also be able to provide their own FIAT service manual for your car should you require one.

*Other garages and accessory shops* – These are often very good places to buy material and components needed for the maintenance of your car (eg oil filters, spark plugs, bulbs, drivebelts, oils and grease, touch-up paint, filler paste etc). They also sell accessories, usually have convenient opening hours, charge lower prices and can often be found not far from home.

*Motor factors* – Good factors stock all of the more important components which wear out relatively quickly (eg clutch components, pistons, valves, exhaust systems, brake pipes/seals/shoes and pads etc). Motor factors will often provide new or reconditioned components on a part exchange basis – this can save a considerable amount of money.

*Vehicle identification numbers*

Modifications are a continuing and unpublicised process in vehicle manufacture quite apart from major model changes. Spare parts manuals and lists are compiled upon a numerical basis, the individual vehicle numbers being essential to correct identification of the component required.

The *chassis type and number plate* is located on the wing valance under the bonnet. The *identification data plate* is located on the radiator top rail. The *engine type and number* is stamped on the cylinder block. The *paintwork colour code* is given on a label stuck to the inner surface of the tailgate.

**Engine number on 1116 cc engine**

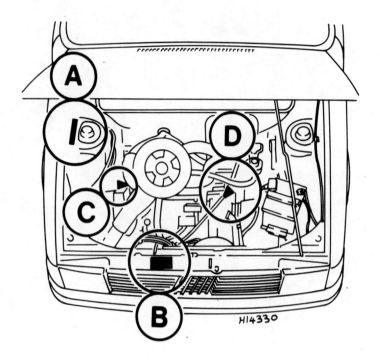

H14330

**Location of under-bonnet identification numbers and plates**

A   Chassis type and number
B   Manufacturer's plate
C   Engine number (903 cc)
D   Engine number (1116 cc and 1301 cc)

**Manufacturer's plate legend**

A   Name of manufacturer
B   Approval number
C   Vehicle identification number
D   Chassis serial number
E   Maximum laden weight
F   Maximum laden weight (vehicle plus trailer)
G   Maximum front axle weight
H   Maximum rear axle weight
I   Engine type
L   Body type
M   Spares reference
N   Diesel models only (smoke coefficient)

| | A | | |
|---|---|---|---|
| | B | | |
| C | ✪ | | D |
| | E | | Kg |
| | F | | Kg |
| 1→ | G | | Kg |
| 2→ | H | | Kg |
| MOTORE – ENGINE | | I | |
| VERSIONE – VERSION | | L | |
| NPER RICAMBI – N° FOR SPARES | | M | N |

H14331

# General repair procedures

Whenever servicing, repair or overhaul work is carried out on the car or its components, it is necessary to observe the following procedures and instructions. This will assist in carrying out the operation efficiently and to a professional standard of workmanship.

## Joint mating faces and gaskets

Where a gasket is used between the mating faces of two components, ensure that it is renewed on reassembly, and fit it dry unless otherwise stated in the repair procedure. Make sure that the mating faces are clean and dry with all traces of old gasket removed. When cleaning a joint face, use a tool which is not likely to score or damage the face, and remove any burrs or nicks with an oilstone or fine file.

Make sure that tapped holes are cleaned with a pipe cleaner, and keep them free of jointing compound if this is being used unless specifically instructed otherwise.

Ensure that all orifices, channels or pipes are clear and blow through them, preferably using compressed air.

## Oil seals

Whenever an oil seal is removed from its working location, either individually or as part of an assembly, it should be renewed.

The very fine sealing lip of the seal is easily damaged and will not seal if the surface it contacts is not completely clean and free from scratches, nicks or grooves. If the original sealing surface of the component cannot be restored, the component should be renewed.

Protect the lips of the seal from any surface which may damage them in the course of fitting. Use tape or a conical sleeve where possible. Lubricate the seal lips with oil before fitting and, on dual lipped seals, fill the space between the lips with grease.

Unless otherwise stated, oil seals must be fitted with their sealing lips toward the lubricant to be sealed.

Use a tubular drift or block of wood of the appropriate size to install the seal and, if the seal housing is shouldered, drive the seal down to the shoulder. If the seal housing is unshouldered, the seal should be fitted with its face flush with the housing top face.

## Screw threads and fastenings

Always ensure that a blind tapped hole is completely free from oil, grease, water or other fluid before installing the bolt or stud. Failure to do this could cause the housing to crack due to the hydraulic action of the bolt or stud as it is screwed in.

When tightening a castellated nut to accept a split pin, tighten the nut to the specified torque, where applicable, and then tighten further to the next split pin hole. Never slacken the nut to align a split pin hole unless stated in the repair procedure.

When checking or retightening a nut or bolt to a specified torque setting, slacken the nut or bolt by a quarter of a turn, and then retighten to the specified setting.

## Locknuts, locktabs and washers

Any fastening which will rotate against a component or housing in the course of tightening should always have a washer between it and the relevant component or housing.

Spring or split washers should always be renewed when they are used to lock a critical component such as a big-end bearing retaining nut or bolt.

Locktabs which are folded over to retain a nut or bolt should always be renewed.

Self-locking nuts can be reused in non-critical areas, providing resistance can be felt when the locking portion passes over the bolt or stud thread.

Split pins must always be replaced with new ones of the correct size for the hole.

## Special tools

Some repair procedures in this manual entail the use of special tools such as a press, two or three-legged pullers, spring compressors etc. Wherever possible, suitable readily available alternatives to the manufacturer's special tools are described, and are shown in use. In some instances, where no alternative is possible, it has been necessary to resort to the use of a manufacturer's tool and this has been done for reasons of safety as well as the efficient completion of the repair operation. Unless you are highly skilled and have a thorough understanding of the procedure described, never attempt to bypass the use of any special tool when the procedure described specifies its use. Not only is there a very great risk of personal injury, but expensive damage could be caused to the components involved.

# Tools and working facilities

## Introduction

A selection of good tools is a fundamental requirement for anyone contemplating the maintenance and repair of a motor vehicle. For the owner who does not possess any, their purchase will prove a considerable expense, offsetting some of the savings made by doing-it-yourself. However, provided that the tools purchased meet the relevant national safety standards and are of good quality, they will last for many years and prove an extremely worthwhile investment.

To help the average owner to decide which tools are needed to carry out the various tasks detailed in this manual, we have compiled three lists of tools under the following headings: *Maintenance and minor repair*, *Repair and overhaul*, and *Special*. The newcomer to practical mechanics should start off with the *Maintenance and minor repair* tool kit and confine himself to the simpler jobs around the vehicle. Then, as his confidence and experience grow, he can undertake more difficult tasks, buying extra tools as, and when, they are needed. In this way, a *Maintenance and minor repair* tool kit can be built-up into a *Repair and overhaul* tool kit over a considerable period of time without any major cash outlays. The experienced do-it-yourselfer will have a tool kit good enough for most repair and overhaul procedures and will add tools from the *Special* category when he feels the expense is justified by the amount of use to which these tools will be put.

It is obviously not possible to cover the subject of tools fully here. For those who wish to learn more about tools and their use there is a book entitled *How to Choose and Use Car Tools* available from the publishers of this manual.

## Maintenance and minor repair tool kit

The tools given in this list should be considered as a minimum requirement if routine maintenance, servicing and minor repair operations are to be undertaken. We recommend the purchase of combination spanners (ring one end, open-ended the other); although more expensive than open-ended ones, they do give the advantages of both types of spanner.

*Combination spanners - 10, 11, 12, 13, 14 & 17 mm*
*Adjustable spanner - 9 inch*
*Spark plug spanner (with rubber insert)*
*Spark plug gap adjustment tool*
*Set of feeler gauges*
*Brake bleed nipple spanner*
*Screwdriver - 4 in long x $^1/4$ in dia (flat blade)*
*Screwdriver - 4 in long x $^1/4$ in dia (cross blade)*
*Combination pliers - 6 inch*
*Hacksaw (junior)*
*Tyre pump*
*Tyre pressure gauge*
*Oil can*
*Fine emery cloth (1 sheet)*
*Wire brush (small)*
*Funnel (medium size)*

## Repair and overhaul tool kit

These tools are virtually essential for anyone undertaking any major repairs to a motor vehicle, and are additional to those given in the *Maintenance and minor repair* list. Included in this list is a comprehensive set of sockets. Although these are expensive they will be found invaluable as they are so versatile - particularly if various drives are included in the set. We recommend the $^1/2$ in square-drive type, as this can be used with most proprietary torque wrenches. If you cannot afford a socket set, even bought piecemeal, then inexpensive tubular box spanners are a useful alternative.

The tools in this list will occasionally need to be supplemented by tools from the *Special* list.

*Sockets (or box spanners) to cover range in previous list*
*Reversible ratchet drive (for use with sockets)*
*Extension piece, 10 inch (for use with sockets)*
*Universal joint (for use with sockets)*
*Torque wrench (for use with sockets)*
*'Mole' wrench - 8 inch*
*Ball pein hammer*
*Soft-faced hammer, plastic or rubber*
*Screwdriver - 6 in long x $^5/16$ in dia (flat blade)*
*Screwdriver - 2 in long x $^5/16$ in square (flat blade)*
*Screwdriver - 1$^1/2$ in long x $^1/4$ in dia (cross blade)*
*Screwdriver - 3 in long x $^1/8$ in dia (electricians)*
*Pliers - electricians side cutters*
*Pliers - needle nosed*
*Pliers - circlip (internal and external)*
*Cold chisel - $^1/2$ inch*
*Scriber*
*Scraper*
*Centre punch*
*Pin punch*
*Hacksaw*
*Valve grinding tool*
*Steel rule/straight-edge*
*Allen keys*
*Selection of files*
*Wire brush (large)*
*Axle-stands*
*Jack (strong trolley or hydraulic type)*

## Special tools

The tools in this list are those which are not used regularly, are expensive to buy, or which need to be used in accordance with their manufacturers' instructions. Unless relatively difficult mechanical jobs are undertaken frequently, it will not be economic to buy many of these tools. Where this is the case, you could consider clubbing together with friends (or joining a motorists' club) to make a joint purchase, or borrowing the tools against a deposit from a local garage or tool hire specialist.

The following list contains only those tools and instruments freely available to the public, and not those special tools produced by the vehicle manufacturer specifically for its dealer network. You will find occasional references to these manufacturers' special tools in the text of this manual. Generally, an alternative method of doing the job without the vehicle manufacturers' special tool is given. However, sometimes, there is no alternative to using them. Where this is the case and the relevant tool cannot be bought or borrowed, you will have to entrust the work to a franchised garage.

*Valve spring compressor*
*Piston ring compressor*
*Balljoint separator*
*Universal hub/bearing puller or slide hammer*
*Impact screwdriver*
*Micrometer and/or vernier gauge*
*Dial gauge*
*Stroboscopic timing light*
*Dwell angle meter/tachometer*
*Universal electrical multi-meter*
*Cylinder compression gauge*
*Lifting tackle*
*Trolley jack*
*Light with extension lead*

## Buying tools

For practically all tools, a tool factor is the best source since he will have a very comprehensive range compared with the average garage or accessory shop. Having said that, accessory shops often offer excellent quality tools at discount prices, so it pays to shop around.

There are plenty of good tools around at reasonable prices, but always aim to purchase items which meet the relevant national safety standards. If in doubt, ask the proprietor or manager of the shop for advice before making a purchase.

## Care and maintenance of tools

Having purchased a reasonable tool kit, it is necessary to keep the tools in a clean serviceable condition. After use, always wipe off any dirt, grease and metal particles using a clean, dry cloth, before putting the tools away. Never leave them lying around after they have been used. A simple tool rack on the garage or workshop wall, for items such as screwdrivers and pliers is a good idea. Store all normal wrenches and sockets in a metal box. Any measuring instruments, gauges, meters, etc, must be carefully stored where they cannot be damaged or become rusty.

Take a little care when tools are used. Hammer heads inevitably become marked and screwdrivers lose the keen edge on their blades from time to time. A little timely attention with emery cloth or a file will soon restore items like this to a good serviceable finish.

## Working facilities

Not to be forgotten when discussing tools, is the workshop itself. If anything more than routine maintenance is to be carried out, some form of suitable working area becomes essential.

It is appreciated that many an owner mechanic is forced by circumstances to remove an engine or similar item, without the benefit of a garage or workshop. Having done this, any repairs should always be done under the cover of a roof.

Wherever possible, any dismantling should be done on a clean, flat workbench or table at a suitable working height.

Any workbench needs a vice: one with a jaw opening of 4 in (100 mm) is suitable for most jobs. As mentioned previously, some clean dry storage space is also required for tools, as well as for lubricants, cleaning fluids, touch-up paints and so on, which become necessary.

Another item which may be required, and which has a much more general usage, is an electric drill with a chuck capacity of at least 5/16 in (8 mm). This, together with a good range of twist drills, is virtually essential for fitting accessories such as mirrors and reversing lights.

Last, but not least, always keep a supply of old newspapers and clean, lint-free rags available, and try to keep any working area as clean as possible.

*Spanner jaw gap comparison table*

| Jaw gap (in) | Spanner size |
|---|---|
| 0.250 | 1/4 in AF |
| 0.276 | 7 mm |
| 0.313 | 5/16 in AF |
| 0.315 | 8 mm |
| 0.344 | 11/32 in AF; 1/8 in Whitworth |
| 0.354 | 9 mm |
| 0.375 | 3/8 in AF |
| 0.394 | 10 mm |
| 0.433 | 11 mm |
| 0.438 | 7/16 in AF |
| 0.445 | 3/16 in Whitworth; 1/4 in BSF |
| 0.472 | 12 mm |
| 0.500 | 1/2 in AF |
| 0.512 | 13 mm |
| 0.525 | 1/4 in Whitworth; 5/16 in BSF |
| 0.551 | 14 mm |
| 0.563 | 9/16 in AF |
| 0.591 | 15 mm |
| 0.600 | 5/16 in Whitworth; 3/8 in BSF |
| 0.625 | 5/8 in AF |
| 0.630 | 16 mm |
| 0.669 | 17 mm |
| 0.686 | 11/16 in AF |
| 0.709 | 18 mm |
| 0.710 | 3/8 in Whitworth; 7/16 in BSF |
| 0.748 | 19 mm |
| 0.750 | 3/4 in AF |
| 0.813 | 13/16 in AF |
| 0.820 | 7/16 in Whitworth; 1/2 in BSF |
| 0.866 | 22 mm |
| 0.875 | 7/8 in AF |
| 0.920 | 1/2 in Whitworth; 9/16 in BSF |
| 0.938 | 15/16 in AF |
| 0.945 | 24 mm |
| 1.000 | 1 in AF |
| 1.010 | 9/16 in Whitworth; 5/8 in BSF |
| 1.024 | 26 mm |
| 1.063 | 1 1/16 in AF; 27 mm |
| 1.100 | 5/8 in Whitworth; 11/16 in BSF |
| 1.125 | 1 1/8 in AF |
| 1.181 | 30 mm |
| 1.200 | 11/16 in Whitworth; 3/4 in BSF |
| 1.250 | 1 1/4 in AF |
| 1.260 | 32 mm |
| 1.300 | 3/4 in Whitworth; 7/8 in BSF |
| 1.313 | 1 5/16 in AF |
| 1.390 | 13/16 in Whitworth; 15/16 in BSF |
| 1.417 | 36 mm |
| 1.438 | 1 7/16 in AF |
| 1.480 | 7/8 in Whitworth; 1 in BSF |
| 1.500 | 1 1/2 in AF |
| 1.575 | 40 mm; 15/16 in Whitworth |
| 1.614 | 41 mm |
| 1.625 | 1 5/8 in AF |
| 1.670 | 1 in Whitworth; 1 1/8 in BSF |
| 1.688 | 1 11/16 in AF |
| 1.811 | 46 mm |
| 1.813 | 1 13/16 in AF |
| 1.860 | 1 1/8 in Whitworth; 1 1/4 in BSF |
| 1.875 | 1 7/8 in AF |
| 1.969 | 50 mm |
| 2.000 | 2 in AF |
| 2.050 | 1 1/4 in Whitworth; 1 3/8 in BSF |
| 2.165 | 55 mm |
| 2.362 | 60 mm |

# Safety first!

Professional motor mechanics are trained in safe working procedures. However enthusiastic you may be about getting on with the job in hand, do take the time to ensure that your safety is not put at risk. A moment's lack of attention can result in an accident, as can failure to observe certain elementary precautions.

There will always be new ways of having accidents, and the following points do not pretend to be a comprehensive list of all dangers; they are intended rather to make you aware of the risks and to encourage a safety-conscious approach to all work you carry out on your vehicle.

## Essential DOs and DON'Ts

**DON'T** rely on a single jack when working underneath the vehicle. Always use reliable additional means of support, such as axle stands, securely placed under a part of the vehicle that you know will not give way.

**DON'T** attempt to loosen or tighten high-torque nuts (e.g. wheel hub nuts) while the vehicle is on a jack; it may be pulled off.

**DON'T** start the engine without first ascertaining that the transmission is in neutral (or 'Park' where applicable) and the parking brake applied.

**DON'T** suddenly remove the filler cap from a hot cooling system – cover it with a cloth and release the pressure gradually first, or you may get scalded by escaping coolant.

**DON'T** attempt to drain oil until you are sure it has cooled sufficiently to avoid scalding you.

**DON'T** grasp any part of the engine, exhaust or catalytic converter without first ascertaining that it is sufficiently cool to avoid burning you.

**DON'T** allow brake fluid or antifreeze to contact vehicle paintwork.

**DON'T** syphon toxic liquids such as fuel, brake fluid or antifreeze by mouth, or allow them to remain on your skin.

**DON'T** inhale dust – it may be injurious to health (see *Asbestos* below).

**DON'T** allow any spilt oil or grease to remain on the floor – wipe it up straight away, before someone slips on it.

**DON'T** use ill-fitting spanners or other tools which may slip and cause injury.

**DON'T** attempt to lift a heavy component which may be beyond your capability – get assistance.

**DON'T** rush to finish a job, or take unverified short cuts.

**DON'T** allow children or animals in or around an unattended vehicle.

**DO** wear eye protection when using power tools such as drill, sander, bench grinder etc, and when working under the vehicle.

**DO** use a barrier cream on your hands prior to undertaking dirty jobs – it will protect your skin from infection as well as making the dirt easier to remove afterwards; but make sure your hands aren't left slippery. Note that long-term contact with used engine oil can be a health hazard.

**DO** keep loose clothing (cuffs, tie etc) and long hair well out of the way of moving mechanical parts.

**DO** remove rings, wristwatch etc, before working on the vehicle – especially the electrical system.

**DO** ensure that any lifting tackle used has a safe working load rating adequate for the job.

**DO** keep your work area tidy – it is only too easy to fall over articles left lying around.

**DO** get someone to check periodically that all is well, when working alone on the vehicle.

**DO** carry out work in a logical sequence and check that everything is correctly assembled and tightened afterwards.

**DO** remember that your vehicle's safety affects that of yourself and others. If in doubt on any point, get specialist advice.

**IF,** in spite of following these precautions, you are unfortunate enough to injure yourself, seek medical attention as soon as possible.

## Asbestos

Certain friction, insulating, sealing, and other products – such as brake linings, brake bands, clutch linings, torque converters, gaskets, etc – contain asbestos. *Extreme care must be taken to avoid inhalation of dust from such products since it is hazardous to health.* If in doubt, assume that they *do* contain asbestos.

## Fire

Remember at all times that petrol (gasoline) is highly flammable. Never smoke, or have any kind of naked flame around, when working on the vehicle. But the risk does not end there – a spark caused by an electrical short-circuit, by two metal surfaces contacting each other, by careless use of tools, or even by static electricity built up in your body under certain conditions, can ignite petrol vapour, which in a confined space is highly explosive.

Always disconnect the battery earth (ground) terminal before working on any part of the fuel or electrical system, and never risk spilling fuel on to a hot engine or exhaust.

It is recommended that a fire extinguisher of a type suitable for fuel and electrical fires is kept handy in the garage or workplace at all times. Never try to extinguish a fuel or electrical fire with water.

**Note:** *Any reference to a 'torch' appearing in this manual should always be taken to mean a hand-held battery-operated electric lamp or flashlight. It does NOT mean a welding/gas torch or blowlamp.*

## Fumes

Certain fumes are highly toxic and can quickly cause unconsciousness and even death if inhaled to any extent. Petrol (gasoline) vapour comes into this category, as do the vapours from certain solvents such as trichloroethylene. Any draining or pouring of such volatile fluids should be done in a well ventilated area.

When using cleaning fluids and solvents, read the instructions carefully. Never use materials from unmarked containers – they may give off poisonous vapours.

Never run the engine of a motor vehicle in an enclosed space such as a garage. Exhaust fumes contain carbon monoxide which is extremely poisonous; if you need to run the engine, always do so in the open air or at least have the rear of the vehicle outside the workplace.

If you are fortunate enough to have the use of an inspection pit, never drain or pour petrol, and never run the engine, while the vehicle is standing over it; the fumes, being heavier than air, will concentrate in the pit with possibly lethal results.

## The battery

Never cause a spark, or allow a naked light, near the vehicle's battery. It will normally be giving off a certain amount of hydrogen gas, which is highly explosive.

Always disconnect the battery earth (ground) terminal before working on the fuel or electrical systems.

If possible, loosen the filler plugs or cover when charging the battery from an external source. Do not charge at an excessive rate or the battery may burst.

Take care when topping up and when carrying the battery. The acid electrolyte, even when diluted, is very corrosive and should not be allowed to contact the eyes or skin.

If you ever need to prepare electrolyte yourself, always add the acid slowly to the water, and never the other way round. Protect against splashes by wearing rubber gloves and goggles.

When jump starting a car using a booster battery, for negative earth (ground) vehicles, connect the jump leads in the following sequence: First connect one jump lead between the positive ( + ) terminals of the two batteries. Then connect the other jump lead first to the negative (–) terminal of the booster battery, and then to a good earthing (ground) point on the vehicle to be started, at least 18 in (45 cm) from the battery if possible. Ensure that hands and jump leads are clear of any moving parts, and that the two vehicles do not touch. Disconnect the leads in the reverse order.

## Mains electricity and electrical equipment

When using an electric power tool, inspection light etc, always ensure that the appliance is correctly connected to its plug and that, where necessary, it is properly earthed (grounded). Do not use such appliances in damp conditions and, again, beware of creating a spark or applying excessive heat in the vicinity of fuel or fuel vapour. Also ensure that the appliances meet the relevant national safety standards.

## Ignition HT voltage

A severe electric shock can result from touching certain parts of the ignition system, such as the HT leads, when the engine is running or being cranked, particularly if components are damp or the insulation is defective. Where an electronic ignition system is fitted, the HT voltage is much higher and could prove fatal.

# Routine maintenance

*For information applicable to later models, see Supplement at end of manual*

Maintenance is essential for ensuring safety and desirable for the purpose of getting the best in terms of performance and economy from the car. Over the years the need for periodic lubrication has been greatly reduced if not totally eliminated. This has unfortunately tended to lead some owners to think that because no such action is required the items either no longer exist or will last forever. This is certainly not the case; it is essential to carry out regular visual examinations as comprehensively as possible in order to spot any possible defects at an early stage before they develop into major and expensive repairs.

## Every 250 miles (400 km), weekly, or before a long journey

Check engine oil level
Check brake reservoir fluid level
Check tyre pressures
Check operation of all lights and horn
Top up washer fluid reservoirs, adding a screen wash such as Turtle Wax High Tech Screen Wash, and check operation of washers and wipers
Check coolant level
Check battery electrolyte level

## Every 6000 miles (10 000 km) or six months, whichever comes first

Check tyre tread wear (Chapter 7, Section 7)
Renew engine oil and filter (Chapter 1, Section 2)
Check disc pads for wear (Chapter 8, Section 3)
Check carburettor idle speed and mixture adjustments (Chapter 3)
Check drivebelt tension (Chapter 2, Section 8)
Check contact points and dwell angle (mechanical breaker distributors) (Chapter 4, Section 3)

## Every 12 000 miles (20 000 km) or 12 months, whichever comes first

Check clutch adjustment (Chapter 5, Section 2)
Check handbrake travel (Chapter 8, Section 16)
Lubricate controls, hinges and locks
Check headlamp beam alignment (Chapter 9, Section 17)
Check seat belts for fraying (Chapter 12, Section 23)
Check front wheel alignment (Chapter 10, Section 8)
Check exhaust system for corrosion (Chapter 3, Section 19)
Check suspension bushes for wear (Chapter 11, Section 2)
Check balljoints for wear (Chapter 10, Section 2)
Check driveshaft and steering rack gaiters for splits (Chapters 7 and 10)
Check transmission oil level (Chapter 6, Section 2)
Check rear brake shoe linings for wear (Chapter 8, Section 4)
Check and adjust valve clearances (903 cc) (Chapter 1, Sections 5 and 26)
Renew spark plugs (Chapter 4, Section 11)
Renew contact breaker points and adjust dwell angle (mechanical breaker distributors) (Chapter 4, Section 3)
Check and adjust ignition timing (Chapter 4, Section 4)
Renew air cleaner element (Chapter 3, Section 2)

## Every 24 000 miles (40 000 km) or two years, whichever comes first

Renew transmission oil (Chapter 6, Section 2)
Renew coolant anti-freeze mixture (Chapter 2, Section 3)
Check for underbody corrosion and clean out door and sill drain holes (Chapter 12, Section 2)
Renew brake hydraulic fluid (Chapter 8, Section 12)

## Every 36 000 miles (60 000 km) or three years, whichever comes first

Renew the timing belt – 1116 and 1299/1301 cc (Chapter 1, Section 28)

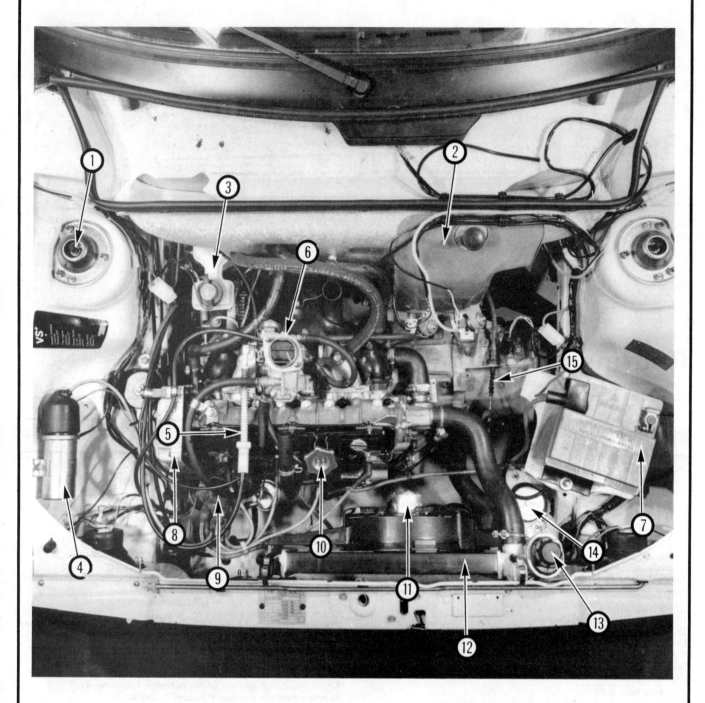

**Engine compartment (air cleaner removed for clarity) on 55S model**

| 1 Strut upper mounting | 5 Throttle cable | 9 Distributor | 13 Coolant expansion tank |
| 2 Washer fluid reservoir | 6 Carburettor | 10 Oil filler cap | 14 Front mounting |
| 3 Brake fluid reservoir | 7 Battery | 11 Radiator electric cooling fan | 15 Clutch operating cable |
| 4 Ignition coil | 8 Timing belt cover | 12 Radiator | |

**View of front end from below on 55S model**

1 Tie-rod end
2 Track control arm
3 Lower mounting
4 Gearchange control rods

5 Exhaust pipe
6 Driveshafts
7 Transmission

8 Sump drain plug
9 Disc caliper
10 Front mounting

11 Horns
12 Radiator
13 Oil filter

**View of rear end from below**

1  Suspension trailing arm
2  Fuel tank filler hose
3  Rear axle beam
4  Rear silencer
5  Spring seat
6  Expansion box
7  Handbrake cable
8  Fuel tank support strap
9  Fuel tank
10  Handbrake cable adjuster

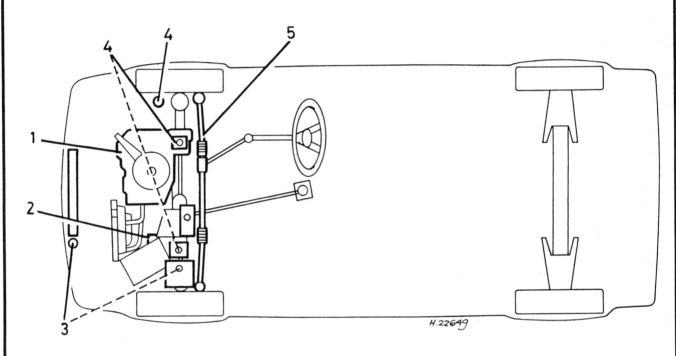

H.22649

# Recommended lubricants and fluids

| Component or system | Lubricant type/specification | Duckhams recommendation |
| --- | --- | --- |
| **1 Engine** | Multigrade engine oil, viscosity SAE 15W/40, meeting API-SG or CCMC G2/G3 specification (or equivalent multigrade engine oil with viscosity rating suitable for ambient temperature in which vehicle is operated – see owner's handbook) | Duckhams Hypergrade |
| **2 Transmission:**<br>1372 cc Turbo ie model<br>All other models | FIAT ZC 80/S gear oil<br>FIAT ZC 90 gear oil | Duckhams Hypoid 80<br>Duckhams Gear Oil 90Z* |
| **3 Cooling system** | Ethylene glycol based antifreeze | Duckhams Universal Antifreeze and Summer Coolant |
| **4 Brake and clutch hydraulic system(s)** | Hydraulic fluid to DOT 3 or 4, or SAE J1703C | Duckhams Universal Brake and Clutch Fluid |
| **5 Driveshaft CV joints and steering rack** | Lithium based molybdenum disulphide grease | Duckhams LBM 10 |
| **General greasing** | Multi-purpose lithium based grease | Duckhams LB10 |

*This is the latest recommendation for topping-up or for oil changes. However, this oil is only available in bulk; a multigrade engine oil such as Duckhams Hypergrade will mix fully with it, and may safely be used if wished

# Conversion factors

**Length (distance)**

| | | | | | | |
|---|---|---|---|---|---|---|
| Inches (in) | X | 25.4 | = Millimetres (mm) | X | 0.0394 | = Inches (in) |
| Feet (ft) | X | 0.305 | = Metres (m) | X | 3.281 | = Feet (ft) |
| Miles | X | 1.609 | = Kilometres (km) | X | 0.621 | = Miles |

**Volume (capacity)**

| | | | | | | |
|---|---|---|---|---|---|---|
| Cubic inches (cu in; in³) | X | 16.387 | = Cubic centimetres (cc; cm³) | X | 0.061 | = Cubic inches (cu in; in³) |
| Imperial pints (Imp pt) | X | 0.568 | = Litres (l) | X | 1.76 | = Imperial pints (Imp pt) |
| Imperial quarts (Imp qt) | X | 1.137 | = Litres (l) | X | 0.88 | = Imperial quarts (Imp qt) |
| Imperial quarts (Imp qt) | X | 1.201 | = US quarts (US qt) | X | 0.833 | = Imperial quarts (Imp qt) |
| US quarts (US qt) | X | 0.946 | = Litres (l) | X | 1.057 | = US quarts (US qt) |
| Imperial gallons (Imp gal) | X | 4.546 | = Litres (l) | X | 0.22 | = Imperial gallons (Imp gal) |
| Imperial gallons (Imp gal) | X | 1.201 | = US gallons (US gal) | X | 0.833 | = Imperial gallons (Imp gal) |
| US gallons (US gal) | X | 3.785 | = Litres (l) | X | 0.264 | = US gallons (US gal) |

**Mass (weight)**

| | | | | | | |
|---|---|---|---|---|---|---|
| Ounces (oz) | X | 28.35 | = Grams (g) | X | 0.035 | = Ounces (oz) |
| Pounds (lb) | X | 0.454 | = Kilograms (kg) | X | 2.205 | = Pounds (lb) |

**Force**

| | | | | | | |
|---|---|---|---|---|---|---|
| Ounces-force (ozf; oz) | X | 0.278 | = Newtons (N) | X | 3.6 | = Ounces-force (ozf; oz) |
| Pounds-force (lbf; lb) | X | 4.448 | = Newtons (N) | X | 0.225 | = Pounds-force (lbf; lb) |
| Newtons (N) | X | 0.1 | = Kilograms-force (kgf; kg) | X | 9.81 | = Newtons (N) |

**Pressure**

| | | | | | | |
|---|---|---|---|---|---|---|
| Pounds-force per square inch (psi; lbf/in²; lb/in²) | X | 0.070 | = Kilograms-force per square centimetre (kgf/cm²; kg/cm²) | X | 14.223 | = Pounds-force per square inch (psi; lbf/in²; lb/in²) |
| Pounds-force per square inch (psi; lbf/in²; lb/in²) | X | 0.068 | = Atmospheres (atm) | X | 14.696 | = Pounds-force per square inch (psi; lbf/in²; lb/in²) |
| Pounds-force per square inch (psi; lbf/in²; lb/in²) | X | 0.069 | = Bars | X | 14.5 | = Pounds-force per square inch (psi; lbf/in²; lb/in²) |
| Pounds-force per square inch (psi; lbf/in²; lb/in²) | X | 6.895 | = Kilopascals (kPa) | X | 0.145 | = Pounds-force per square inch (psi; lbf/in²; lb/in²) |
| Kilopascals (kPa) | X | 0.01 | = Kilograms-force per square centimetre (kgf/cm²; kg/cm²) | X | 98.1 | = Kilopascals (kPa) |
| Millibar (mbar) | X | 100 | = Pascals (Pa) | X | 0.01 | = Millibar (mbar) |
| Millibar (mbar) | X | 0.0145 | = Pounds-force per square inch (psi; lbf/in²; lb/in²) | X | 68.947 | = Millibar (mbar) |
| Millibar (mbar) | X | 0.75 | = Millimetres of mercury (mmHg) | X | 1.333 | = Millibar (mbar) |
| Millibar (mbar) | X | 0.401 | = Inches of water (inH₂O) | X | 2.491 | = Millibar (mbar) |
| Millimetres of mercury (mmHg) | X | 0.535 | = Inches of water (inH₂O) | X | 1.868 | = Millimetres of mercury (mmHg) |
| Inches of water (inH₂O) | X | 0.036 | = Pounds-force per square inch (psi; lbf/in²; lb/in²) | X | 27.68 | = Inches of water (inH₂O) |

**Torque (moment of force)**

| | | | | | | |
|---|---|---|---|---|---|---|
| Pounds-force inches (lbf in; lb in) | X | 1.152 | = Kilograms-force centimetre (kgf cm; kg cm) | X | 0.868 | = Pounds-force inches (lbf in; lb in) |
| Pounds-force inches (lbf in; lb in) | X | 0.113 | = Newton metres (Nm) | X | 8.85 | = Pounds-force inches (lbf in; lb in) |
| Pounds-force inches (lbf in; lb in) | X | 0.083 | = Pounds-force feet (lbf ft; lb ft) | X | 12 | = Pounds-force inches (lbf in; lb in) |
| Pounds-force feet (lbf ft; lb ft) | X | 0.138 | = Kilograms-force metres (kgf m; kg m) | X | 7.233 | = Pounds-force feet (lbf ft; lb ft) |
| Pounds-force feet (lbf ft; lb ft) | X | 1.356 | = Newton metres (Nm) | X | 0.738 | = Pounds-force feet (lbf ft; lb ft) |
| Newton metres (Nm) | X | 0.102 | = Kilograms-force metres (kgf m; kg m) | X | 9.804 | = Newton metres (Nm) |

**Power**

| | | | | | | |
|---|---|---|---|---|---|---|
| Horsepower (hp) | X | 745.7 | = Watts (W) | X | 0.0013 | = Horsepower (hp) |

**Velocity (speed)**

| | | | | | | |
|---|---|---|---|---|---|---|
| Miles per hour (miles/hr; mph) | X | 1.609 | = Kilometres per hour (km/hr; kph) | X | 0.621 | = Miles per hour (miles/hr; mph) |

**Fuel consumption\***

| | | | | | | |
|---|---|---|---|---|---|---|
| Miles per gallon, Imperial (mpg) | X | 0.354 | = Kilometres per litre (km/l) | X | 2.825 | = Miles per gallon, Imperial (mpg) |
| Miles per gallon, US (mpg) | X | 0.425 | = Kilometres per litre (km/l) | X | 2.352 | = Miles per gallon, US (mpg) |

**Temperature**

Degrees Fahrenheit = (°C x 1.8) + 32          Degrees Celsius (Degrees Centigrade; °C) = (°F - 32) x 0.56

*\*It is common practice to convert from miles per gallon (mpg) to litres/100 kilometres (l/100km), where mpg (Imperial) x l/100 km = 282 and mpg (US) x l/100 km = 235*

# Fault diagnosis

## Introduction

The vehicle owner who does his or her own maintenance according to the recommended schedules should not have to use this section of the manual very often. Modern component reliability is such that, provided those items subject to wear or deterioration are inspected or renewed at the specified intervals, sudden failure is comparatively rare. Faults do not usually just happen as a result of sudden failure, but develop over a period of time. Major mechanical failures in particular are usually preceded by characteristic symptoms over hundreds or even thousands of miles. Those components which do occasionally fail without warning are often small and easily carried in the vehicle.

With any fault finding, the first step is to decide where to begin investigations. Sometimes this is obvious, but on other occasions a little detective work will be necessary. The owner who makes half a dozen haphazard adjustments or replacements may be successful in curing a fault (or its symptoms), but he will be none the wiser if the fault recurs and he may well have spent more time and money than was necessary. A calm and logical approach will be found to be more satisfactory in the long run. Always take into account any warning signs or abnormalities that may have been noticed in the period preceding the fault – power loss, high or low gauge readings, unusual noises or smells, etc – and remember that failure of components such as fuses or spark plugs may only be pointers to some underlying fault.

The pages which follow here are intended to help in cases of failure to start or breakdown on the road. There is also a Fault Diagnosis Section at the end of each Chapter which should be consulted if the preliminary checks prove unfruitful. Whatever the fault, certain basic principles apply. These are as follows:

**Verify the fault.** This is simply a matter of being sure that you know what the symptoms are before starting work. This is particularly important if you are investigating a fault for someone else who may not have described it very accurately.

**Don't overlook the obvious.** For example, if the vehicle won't start, is there petrol in the tank? (Don't take anyone else's word on this particular point, and don't trust the fuel gauge either!) If an electrical fault is indicated, look for loose or broken wires before digging out the test gear.

**Cure the disease, not the symptom.** Substituting a flat battery with a fully charged one will get you off the hard shoulder, but if the underlying cause is not attended to, the new battery will go the same way. Similarly, changing oil-fouled spark plugs for a new set will get you moving again, but remember that the reason for the fouling (if it wasn't simply an incorrect grade of plug) will have to be established and corrected.

**Don't take anything for granted.** Particularly, don't forget that a 'new' component may itself be defective (especially if it's been rattling round in the boot for months), and don't leave components out of a fault diagnosis sequence just because they are new or recently fitted. When you do finally diagnose a difficult fault, you'll probably realise that all the evidence was there from the start.

## Electrical faults

Electrical faults can be more puzzling than straightforward mechanical failures, but they are no less susceptible to logical analysis if the basic principles of operation are understood. Vehicle electrical wiring exists in extremely unfavourable conditions – heat, vibration and chemical attack – and the first things to look for are loose or corroded connections and broken or chafed wires, especially where the wires pass through holes in the bodywork or are subject to vibration.

All metal-bodied vehicles in current production have one pole of the battery 'earthed', ie connected to the vehicle bodywork, and in nearly all modern vehicles it is the negative (–) terminal. The various electrical components – motors, bulb holders etc – are also connected to earth, either by means of a lead or directly by their mountings. Electric current flows through the component and then back to the battery via the bodywork. If the component mounting is loose or corroded, or if a good path back to the battery is not available, the circuit will be incomplete and malfunction will result. The engine and/or gearbox are also earthed by means of flexible metal straps to the body or subframe; if these straps are loose or missing, starter motor, generator and ignition trouble may result.

Assuming the earth return to be satisfactory, electrical faults will be due either to component malfunction or to defects in the current supply. Individual components are dealt with in Chapter 9. If supply wires are broken or cracked internally this results in an open-circuit, and the easiest way to check for this is to bypass the suspect wire temporarily with a length of wire having a crocodile clip or suitable connector at each end. Alternatively, a 12V test lamp can be used to verify the presence of supply voltage at various points along the wire and the break can be thus isolated.

If a bare portion of a live wire touches the bodywork or other earthed metal part, the electricity will take the low-resistance path thus formed back to the battery: this is known as a short-circuit. Hopefully a short-circuit will blow a fuse, but otherwise it may cause burning of the insulation (and possibly further short-circuits) or even a fire. This is why it is inadvisable to bypass persistently blowing fuses with silver foil or wire.

## Spares and tool kit

Most vehicles are supplied only with sufficient tools for wheel changing; the *Maintenance and minor repair* tool kit detailed in *Tools and working facilities*, with the addition of a hammer, is probably sufficient for those repairs that most motorists would consider attempting at the roadside. In addition a few items which can be fitted without too much trouble in the event of a breakdown should be carried.

Carrying a few spares can save you a long
walk!

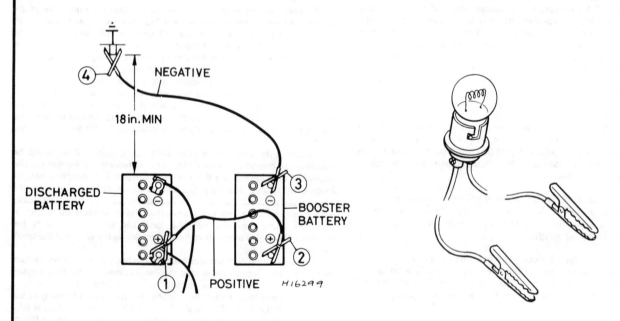

Jump start lead connections for negative earth vehicles –
connect leads in order shown

Simple test lamp is useful for tracing electrical faults

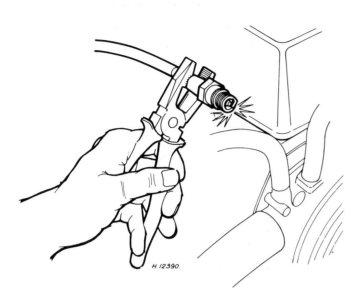

**Crank engine and check for spark. Note use of insulated tool**

Experience and available space will modify the list below, but the following may save having to call on professional assistance:

*Spark plugs, clean and correctly gapped*
*HT lead and plug cap – long enough to reach the plug furthest from the distributor*
*Distributor rotor, condenser and contact breaker points*
*Drivebelt(s) – emergency type may suffice*
*Spare fuses*
*Set of principal light bulbs*
*Tin of radiator sealer and hose bandage*
*Exhaust bandage*
*Roll of insulating tape*
*Length of soft iron wire*
*Length of electrical flex*
*Torch or inspection lamp (can double as test lamp)*
*Battery jump leads*
*Tow-rope*
*Ignition water dispersant aerosol*
*Litre of engine oil*
*Sealed can of hydraulic fluid*
*Emergency windscreen*
*Worm drive clips*

If spare fuel is carried, a can designed for the purpose should be used to minimise risks of leakage and collision damage. A first aid kit and a warning triangle, whilst not at present compulsory in the UK, are obviously sensible items to carry in addition to the above.

When touring abroad it may be advisable to carry additional spares which, even if you cannot fit them yourself, could save having to wait while parts are obtained. The items below may be worth considering:

*Clutch and throttle cables*
*Cylinder head gasket*
*Alternator brushes*
*Tyre valve core*

One of the motoring organisations will be able to advise on availability of fuel etc in foreign countries.

## Engine will not start

### Engine fails to turn when starter operated

Flat battery (recharge, use jump leads, or push start)

Battery terminals loose or corroded
Battery earth to body defective
Engine earth strap loose or broken
Starter motor (or solenoid) wiring loose or broken
Ignition/starter switch faulty
Major mechanical failure (seizure)
Starter or solenoid internal fault (see Chapter 9)

### Starter motor turns engine slowly

Partially discharged battery (recharge, use jump leads, or push start)
Battery terminals loose or corroded
Battery earth to body defective
Engine earth strap loose
Starter motor (or solenoid) wiring loose
Starter motor internal fault (see Chapter 9)

### Starter motor spins without turning engine

Flat battery
Starter motor pinion sticking on sleeve
Flywheel gear teeth damaged or worn
Starter motor mounting bolts loose

### Engine turns normally but fails to start

Damp or dirty HT leads and distributor cap (crank engine and check for spark) – try moisture dispersant such as Holts Wet Start
Dirty or incorrectly gapped distributor points (if applicable)
No fuel in tank (check for delivery at carburettor)
Excessive choke (hot engine) or insufficient choke (cold engine)
Fouled or incorrectly gapped spark plugs (renew or adjust)
Other ignition system fault (see Chapter 4)
Other fuel system fault (see Chapter 3)
Poor compression (see Chapter 1)
Major mechanical failure (eg camshaft drive)

### Engine fires but will not run

Insufficient choke (cold engine)
Air leaks at carburettor or inlet manifold
Fuel starvation (see Chapter 3)
Ignition fault (see Chapter 4)

## Engine cuts out and will not restart

### Engine cuts out suddenly – ignition fault

Loose or disconnected LT wires
Wet HT leads or distributor cap (after traversing water splash)
Coil or condenser failure (check for spark)
Other ignition fault (see Chapter 4)

### Engine misfires before cutting out – fuel fault

Fuel tank empty
Fuel pump defective or filter blocked (check for delivery)
Fuel tank filler vent blocked (suction will be evident on releasing cap)
Carburettor needle valve sticking
Carburettor jets blocked (fuel contaminated)
Other fuel system fault (see Chapter 3)

### Engine cuts out – other causes

Serious overheating
Major mechanical failure (eg camshaft drive)

## Engine overheats

### Ignition (no-charge) warning light illuminated

Slack or broken drivebelt – retension or renew (Chapter 2)

### Ignition warning light not illuminated

Coolant loss due to internal or external leakage (see Chapter 2)

Thermostat defective
Low oil level
Brakes binding
Radiator clogged externally or internally
Electric cooling fan not operating correctly
Engine waterways clogged
Ignition timing incorrect or automatic advance malfunctioning
Mixture too weak

**Note:** *Do not add cold water to an overheated engine or damage may result*

## Low engine oil pressure

### Gauge reads low or warning light illuminated with engine running

Oil level low or incorrect grade
Defective gauge or sender unit
Wire to sender unit earthed
Engine overheating
Oil filter clogged or bypass valve defective
Oil pressure relief valve defective
Oil pick-up strainer clogged
Oil pump worn or mountings loose
Worn main or big-end bearings

**Note:** *Low oil pressure in a high-mileage engine at tickover is not necessarily a cause for concern. Sudden pressure loss at speed is far more significant. In any event, check the gauge or warning light sender before condemning the engine.*

## Engine noises

### Pre-ignition (pinking) on acceleration

Incorrect grade of fuel
Ignition timing incorrect
Distributor faulty or worn
Worn or maladjusted carburettor
Excessive carbon build-up in engine

### Whistling or wheezing noises

Leaking vacuum hose
Leaking carburettor or manifold gasket
Blowing head gasket ·

### Tapping or rattling

Incorrect valve clearances
Worn valve gear
Worn timing belt
Broken piston ring (ticking noise)

### Knocking or thumping

Unintentional mechanical contact (eg fan blades)
Worn drivebelt
Peripheral component fault (generator, water pump etc)
Worn big-end bearings (regular heavy knocking, perhaps less under load)
Worn main bearings (rumbling and knocking, perhaps worsening under load)
Piston slap (most noticeable when cold)

# Chapter 1 Engine

*For modifications, and information applicable to later models, see Supplement at end of manual*

**Contents**

**Specifications**

*903 cc engine*

**Type** ............................................................................. Four cylinder in-line, liquid cooled, overhead valve. Transversely mounted with end-on transmission

**General**

Bore .................................................................................. 65.0 mm (2.56 in)
Stroke ............................................................................... 68.0 mm (2.68 in)
Displacement .................................................................... 903 cc (55 cu in)
Compression ratio:
    900 models .................................................................. 9.0 : 1
    900 ES models ............................................................ 9.7 : 1
Maximum power (DIN) ....................................................... 33.1 kW at 5600 rev/min (45 bhp)
Maximum torque (DIN):
    900 models .................................................................. 68 Nm at 3000 rev/min (49 lbf ft)
    900 ES models ............................................................ 69 Nm at 3000 rev/min (51 lbf ft)
Compression pressure ....................................................... 9.3 to 10.35 bar (135 to 150 lbf/in²)
Maximum pressure difference between cylinders ............... 0.69 bar (10 lbf/in²)
Firing order ....................................................................... 1 – 3 – 4 – 2 (No. 1 at crankshaft pulley end)

**Cylinder block and crankcase**

Material ............................................................................. Cast-iron
Bore diameter ................................................................... 65.000 to 65.050 mm (2.5591 to 2.5610 in)
Diameter of camshaft bearing bores in crankcase timing gear end:
    Grade B ....................................................................... 50.505 to 50.515 mm (1.9882 to 1.9886 in)
    Grade C ....................................................................... 50.515 to 50.525 mm (1.9886 to 1.9890 in)
    Grade D ....................................................................... 50.705 to 50.715 mm (1.9960 to 1.9964 in)
    Grade E ....................................................................... 50.715 to 50.725 mm (1.9964 to 1.9968 in)
Centre ............................................................................... 46.420 to 46.450 mm (1.8275 to 1.8287 in)
Flywheel end ..................................................................... 35.921 to 35.951 mm (1.4142 to 1.4154 in)
Maximum cylinder bore taper ............................................ 0.015 mm (0.0006 in)
Maximum cylinder bore ovality .......................................... 0.015 mm (0.0006 in)

## Pistons and piston rings

| | |
|---|---|
| Piston diameter: | |
|     Grade A | 64.940 to 64.950 mm (2.5566 to 2.5570 in) |
|     Grade C | 64.960 to 64.970 mm (2.5574 to 2.5578 in) |
|     Grade E | 64.980 to 64.990 mm (2.5582 to 2.5586 in) |
| Oversizes | 0.2, 0.4, 0.6 mm (0.008, 0.016, 0.024 in) |
| Piston clearance in cylinder bore | 0.050 to 0.070 mm (0.0020 to 0.0028 in) |
| Piston ring groove width: | |
|     Top | 1.785 to 1.805 mm (0.0703 to 0.0711 in) |
|     Second | 2.015 to 2.035 mm (0.0793 to 0.0801 in) |
|     Bottom | 3.975 to 3.977 mm (0.1566 to 0.1567 in) |
| Piston ring thickness: | |
|     Top | 1.728 to 1.740 mm (0.0680 to 0.0685 in) |
|     Second | 1.978 to 1.990 mm (0.0779 to 0.0784 in) |
|     Bottom | 3.925 to 3.937 mm (0.1545 to 0.1550 in) |
| Piston ring groove clearance: | |
|     Top | 0.045 to 0.077 mm (0.0018 to 0.0030 in) |
|     Second | 0.025 to 0.057 mm (0.0010 to 0.0022 in) |
|     Bottom | 0.020 to 0.052 mm (0.0008 to 0.0020 in) |
| Piston ring end gap: | |
|     Top | 0.25 to 0.45 mm (0.0098 to 0.0177 in) |
|     Second | 0.20 to 0.35 mm (0.0078 to 0.0137 in) |
|     Bottom | 0.20 to 0.45 mm (0.0078 to 0.0177 in) |
| Oversize piston rings | 0.2, 0.4, 0.6 mm (0.008, 0.016, 0.024 in) |
| Gudgeon pin diameter: | |
|     Grade 1 | 19.970 to 19.974 mm (0.7862 to 0.7863 in) |
|     Grade 2 | 19.974 to 19.978 mm (0.7863 to 0.7865 in) |
|     Grade 3 | 19.978 to 19.982 mm (0.7865 to 0.7866 in) |
| Oversize | 0.2 mm (0.008 in) |

## Crankshaft

| | |
|---|---|
| Journal diameter | 50.785 to 50.805 mm (1.9994 to 2.0002 in) |
| Standard main bearing shell thickness | 1.832 to 1.837 mm (0.0721 to 0.0723 in) |
| Undersizes | 0.254, 0.508, 0.762, 1.016 mm (0.010, 0.020. 0.030, 0.040 in) |
| Crankshaft endfloat | 0.06 to 0.26 mm (0.0024 to 0.0102 in) |
| Crankpin diameter | 39.985 to 40.005 mm (1.5741 to 1.5750 in) |
| Standard big-end shell bearing thickness | 1.807 to 1.813 mm (0.0712 to 0.0714 in) |
| Undersizes | 0.254, 0.508, 0.762, 1.016 mm (0.010, 0.020, 0.030, 0.040 in) |

## Camshaft

| | |
|---|---|
| Diameter of camshaft journals: | |
|     Timing end | 37.975 to 38.000 mm (1.4951 to 1.4961 in) |
|     Centre | 43.348 to 43.373 mm (1.7079 to 1.7088 in) |
|     Flywheel end | 30.975 to 31.000 mm (1.2194 to 1.2205 in) |
| Bush reamed diameters: | |
|     Timing gear end* | 38.025 to 38.050 mm (1.4971 to 1.4981 in) |
|     Centre | 43.404 to 43.424 mm (1.7088 to 1.7096 in) |
|     Flywheel end | 31.026 to 31.046 mm (1.2215 to 1.2223 in) |
| *Supplied reamed to size | |
| Cam lift | 5.1 mm (0.201 in) |
| Outside diameter of cam follower | 13.982 to 14.000 mm (0.5505 to 0.5512 in) |
| Oversizes | 0.05 to 0.010 mm (0.002 to 0.004 in) |
| Cam follower running clearance | 0.010 to 0.046 mm (0.0004 to 0.0018 in) |

## Cylinder head and valves

| | |
|---|---|
| Material (cylinder head) | Light alloy |
| Maximum distortion | 0.05 mm (0.002 in) |
| Valve guide bore in head | 12.950 to 12.977 mm (0.5099 to 0.5109 in) |
| Valve guide outside diameter | 13.010 to 13.030 mm (0.5122 to 0.5130 in) |
| Valve guide oversizes | 0.5, 0.10, 0.25 mm (0.002, 0.004, 0.010 in) |
| Inside diameter of valve guide (reamed) | 7.022 to 7.040 mm (0.2765 to 0.2772 in) |
| Guide fit in head (interference) | 0.033 to 0.080 mm (0.0013 to 0.0032 in) |
| Valve stem diameter | 6.982 to 7.000 mm (0.2748 to 0.2756 in) |
| Maximum clearance (valve stem to guide) | 0.022 to 0.058 mm (0.0009 to 0.0023 in) |
| Valve seat angle | 44°55′ to 45°05′ |
| Valve face angle | 45°25′ to 45°35′ |
| Valve head diameter: | |
|     Inlet | 29.0 mm (1.1417 in) |
|     Exhaust | 26.0 mm (1.0236 in) |
| Contact band (valve to seat) | 1.3 to 1.5 mm (0.0512 to 0.0591 in) |
| Valve clearance: | |
|     Inlet | 0.15 mm (0.006 in) |
|     Exhaust | 0.20 mm (0.008 in) |
|     For timing check | 0.60 mm (0.024 in) |

Valve timing:
Inlet valve:
Opens ........................................................ 7° BTDC
Closes ........................................................ 36° ABDC
Exhaust valve:
Opens ........................................................ 38° BBDC
Closes ........................................................ 5° ATDC

## Lubrication system

Oil pump type ................................................ Gear, driven by shaft from camshaft
Tooth tip to body clearance ............................... 0.05 to 0.14 mm (0.0020 to 0.0055 in)
Gear endfloat ................................................ 0.020 to 0.105 mm (0.0008 to 0.0041 in)
Oil pressure at normal operating temperature and average road/
engine speed ................................................ 2.94 to 3.92 bar (42 to 57 lbf/in²)
Oil capacity (with filter change) .......................... 3.42 litre (6.0 pint)
Oil type/specification ...................................... Multigrade engine oil, viscosity SAE 15W/40 (Duckhams Hypergrade)
Oil filter .................................................... Champion C101

## Torque wrench settings

| | Nm | lbf ft |
|---|---|---|
| Cylinder head bolts: | | |
| Stage 1 | 30 | 22 |
| Stage 2 | 59 | 43.5 |
| Camshaft sprocket bolt | 49 | 36 |
| Main bearing cap bolts | 69 | 51 |
| Big-end bearing cap bolts | 41 | 30 |
| Crankshaft pulley nut | 98 | 72 |
| Flywheel bolts | 44 | 32 |
| Rocker pedestal nuts | 39 | 29 |
| Engine mounting bracket bolts | 25 | 18 |
| Engine mounting centre nuts | 49 | 36 |
| Exhaust manifold nuts | 20 | 15 |
| Spark plugs | 25 | 18 |
| Temperature sender switch | 49 | 36 |
| Driveshaft to hub nuts | 272 | 200 |
| Hub carrier to strut clamp bolts | 49 | 36 |
| Roadwheel bolts | 86 | 63 |
| Brake caliper mounting bolts | 53 | 39 |
| Tie-rod end balljoint nuts | 34 | 25 |
| Driveshaft inboard boot retainer bolts | 9 | 7 |

### *1116 cc and 1301 cc engine*

Type .......................................................... Four cylinder in-line, liquid cooled single overhead camshaft. Transversely mounted with end-on transmission

## General

| | 1116 cc | 1301 cc |
|---|---|---|
| Bore | 80.0 mm (3.15 in) | 86.4 mm (3.40 in) |
| Stroke | 55.5 mm (2.19 in) | 55.5 mm (2.19 in) |
| Displacement | 1116 cc (68.08 cu in) | 1301 cc (79.36 cu in) |
| Compression ratio | 9.2 : 1 | 9.1 : 1 |
| Maximum power (DIN) | 40.5 kW (55 bhp) at 5600 rev/min | 50 kW (68 bhp) at 5700 rev/min |
| Maximum torque (DIN) | 86.3 Nm (64 lbf ft) at 2900 rev/min | 100 Nm (74 lbf ft) at 2900 rev/min |

Compression pressure (bore wear test) ................... 10.35 to 11.73 bar (150 to 170 lbf/in²)
Pressure difference between cylinders ................... 0.96 bar (14 lbf/in²)
Firing order ................................................ 1 – 3 – 4 – 2 (No. 1 at crankshaft pulley end)

## Cylinder block and crankcase

Material ...................................................... Cast-iron
Bore diameter:
1116 cc .................................................... 80.000 to 80.050 mm (3.152 to 3.154 in)
1301 cc .................................................... 86.400 to 86.450 mm (3.404 to 3.406 in)
Maximum cylinder bore taper ............................. 0.015 mm (0.0006 in)
Maximum cylinder bore ovality ........................... 0.015 mm (0.0006 in)

## Pistons and piston rings

Piston diameter – 1116 cc:
Grade A ................................................... 79.940 to 79.950 mm (3.1496 to 3.1500 in)
Grade C ................................................... 79.960 to 79.970 mm (3.1504 to 3.1508 in)
Grade E ................................................... 79.980 to 79.990 mm (3.1512 to 3.1516 in)
Piston diameter – 1301 cc:
Grade A ................................................... 86.320 to 86.330 mm (3.4010 to 3.4014 in)
Grade C ................................................... 86.340 to 86.350 mm (3.4018 to 3.4022 in)
Grade E ................................................... 86.360 to 86.370 mm (3.4025 to 3.4030 in)
Oversizes .................................................... 0.2, 0.4, 0.6 mm (0.008, 0.016, 0.023 in)
Piston clearance in cylinder bore:
1116 cc .................................................... 0.050 to 0.070 mm (0.0020 to 0.0027 in)
1301 cc .................................................... 0.070 to 0.090 mm (0.0027 to 0.0035 in)

Piston ring groove width – 1116 cc:
    Top ............................................................ 1.535 to 1.555 mm (0.1442 to 0.1461 in)
    Second ........................................................ 2.015 to 2.035 mm (0.0794 to 0.0802 in)
    Bottom ........................................................ 3.957 to 3.977 mm (0.1559 to 0.1567 in)
Piston ring groove width – 1301 cc:
    Top ............................................................ 1.535 to 1.555 mm (0.0605 to 0.0613 in)
    Second ........................................................ 2.030 to 2.050 mm (0.0800 to 0.0808 in)
    Bottom ........................................................ 3.967 to 3.987 mm (0.1563 to 0.1571 in)
Piston ring thickness:
    Top ............................................................ 1.478 to 1.490 mm (0.0582 to 0.0587 in)
    Second ........................................................ 1.978 to 1.990 mm (0.0779 to 0.0784 in)
    Bottom ........................................................ 3.925 to 3.937 mm (0.1546 to 0.1551 in)
Oversizes ............................................................ 0.2, 0.4, 0.6 mm (0.008, 0.016, 0.023 in)
Piston ring groove clearance – 1116 cc:
    Top ............................................................ 0.045 to 0.077 mm (0.0018 to 0.0030 in)
    Second ........................................................ 0.025 to 0.057 mm (0.0010 to 0.0022 in)
    Bottom ........................................................ 0.020 to 0.052 mm (0.0008 to 0.0020 in)
Piston ring groove clearance – 1301 cc:
    Top ............................................................ 0.045 to 0.077 mm (0.0018 to 0.0030 in)
    Second ........................................................ 0.040 to 0.072 mm (0.0016 to 0.0028 in)
    Bottom ........................................................ 0.030 to 0.062 mm (0.0012 to 0.0024 in)
Piston ring end gap – 1116 cc:
    Top ............................................................ 0.30 to 0.45 mm (0.0012 to 0.0018 in)
    Second ........................................................ 0.20 to 0.35 mm (0.008 to 0.014 in)
    Bottom ........................................................ 0.20 to 0.35 mm (0.008 to 0.014 in)
Piston ring end gap – 1301 cc:
    Top ............................................................ 0.30 to 0.45 mm (0.012 to 0.016 in)
    Second ........................................................ 0.30 to 0.50 mm (0.012 to 0.020 in)
    Bottom ........................................................ 0.25 to 0.40 mm (0.010 to 0.016 in)
Gudgeon pin diameter – 1116 cc:
    Grade 1 ...................................................... 21.970 to 21.974 mm (0.8656 to 0.8658 in)
    Grade 2 ...................................................... 21.974 to 21.978 mm (0.8658 to 0.8659 in)
    Grade 3 ...................................................... 21.978 to 21.982 mm (0.8659 to 0.8661 in)
Gudgeon pin diameter – 1301 cc:
    Grade 1 ...................................................... 21.991 to 21.994 mm (0.8664 to 0.8666 in)
    Grade 2 ...................................................... 21.994 to 21.997 mm (0.8666 to 0.8667 in)
Oversize ............................................................ 0.2 mm (0.008 in)

## Crankshaft

Journal diameter ................................................ 50.785 to 50.805 mm (1.9994 to 2.0002 in)
Standard main bearing shell thickness .................... 1.825 to 1.831 mm (0.0719 to 0.0721 in)
Undersizes ........................................................ 0.254, 0.508, 0.762, 1.016 mm (0.010, 0.020, 0.030, 0.040 in)
Crankshaft endfloat ............................................ 0.06 to 0.26 mm (0.0024 to 0.0102 in)
Crankpin diameter .............................................. 45.498 to 45.518 mm (1.7926 to 1.7934 in)
Standard big-end shell bearing thickness ................ 1.531 to 1.538 mm (0.0603 to 0.0606 in)
Undersizes ........................................................ 0.254, 0.508, 0.762, 1.016 mm (0.010, 0.020, 0.030, 0.040 in)

## Camshaft

Number of bearings ............................................ 5
Diameter of camshaft journals:
    No. 1 (timing end) ........................................ 29.944 to 29.960 mm (1.1798 to 1.1804 in)
    No. 2 .......................................................... 47.935 to 47.950 mm (1.8886 to 1.8892 in)
    No. 3 .......................................................... 48.135 to 48.150 mm (1.8965 to 1.8971 in)
    No. 4 .......................................................... 48.335 to 48.350 mm (1.9044 to 1.9050 in)
    No. 5 .......................................................... 48.535 to 48.550 mm (1.9122 to 1.9129 in)
Cam lift ............................................................ 8.8 mm (0.3467 in)
Camshaft bearing diameters in carrier:
    No. 1 .......................................................... 29.990 to 30.014 mm (1.1816 to 1.1825 in)
    No. 2 .......................................................... 47.980 to 48.005 mm (1.8904 to 1.8913 in)
    No. 3 .......................................................... 48.180 to 48.205 mm (1.8982 to 1.8992 in)
    No. 4 .......................................................... 48.380 to 48.405 mm (1.9062 to 1.9072 in)
    No. 5 .......................................................... 48.580 to 48.605 mm (1.9141 to 1.9150 in)
Outside diameter of cam follower ......................... 36.975 to 36.995 mm (1.4568 to 1.4576 in)
Cam follower running clearance ............................ 0.005 to 0.050 mm (0.0002 to 0.0020 in)

## Cylinder head and valves

Head material .................................................... Light alloy
Maximum distortion ............................................ 0.05 mm (0.002 in)
Valve guide bore in head ..................................... 13.950 to 13.977 mm (0.5496 to 0.5507 in)
Valve guide outside diameter ............................... 14.040 to 14.058 mm (0.5532 to 0.5539 in)
Valve guide oversizes ......................................... 0.05, 0.10, 0.25 mm (0.002, 0.004, 0.010 in)
Inside diameter of valve guide (reamed) ................. 8.022 to 8.040 mm (0.3161 to 0.3168 in)
Valve guide fit in cylinder head (interference) .......... 0.063 to 0.108 mm (0.0025 to 0.0043 in)
Valve stem diameter ........................................... 7.974 to 7.992 mm (0.3142 to 0.3149 in)
Maximum clearance (valve stem to guide) ............... 0.030 to 0.066 mm (0.0012 to 0.0026 in)

| | |
|---|---|
| Valve face angle .................................................................................. | 45° 25′ to 45° 35′ |
| Valve seat angle .................................................................................. | 44° 55′ to 45° 05′ |
| Valve head diameter: | |
| Inlet .......................................................................................... | 35.850 to 36.150 mm (1.4125 to 1.4243 in) |
| Exhaust ..................................................................................... | 30.850 to 31.450 mm (1.2155 to 1.2391 in) |
| Contact band (valve to seat) ................................................................ | 1.3 to 1.5 mm (0.0512 to 0.0591 in) |
| Valve clearance: | |
| Inlet .......................................................................................... | 0.40 mm (0.0158 in) |
| Exhaust ..................................................................................... | 0.50 mm (0.0197 in) |
| For timing check ....................................................................... | 0.80 mm (0.0315 in) |
| Valve clearance adjusting shim thicknesses ............................................ | 3.25 to 4.70 mm (0.128 to 0.185 in), in increments of 0.05 mm (0.002 in) |
| Valve timing: | |
| Inlet valve: | |
| Opens ................................................................................. | 7° BTDC |
| Closes ................................................................................ | 35° ABDC |
| Exhaust valve: | |
| Opens ................................................................................. | 37° BBDC |
| Closes ................................................................................ | 5° ATDC |

## Auxiliary shaft

| | |
|---|---|
| Bearing internal diameter (reamed): | |
| No 1 (timing belt end) ................................................................. | 35.664 to 35.684 mm (1.4052 to 1.4059 in) |
| No 2 ........................................................................................ | 32.000 to 32.020 mm (1.2608 to 1.2616 in) |
| Shaft journal diameter: | |
| No. 1 (timing belt end) ................................................................ | 35.593 to 35.618 mm (1.4024 to 1.4033 in) |
| No 2 ........................................................................................ | 31.940 to 31.960 mm (1.2584 to 1.2592 in) |

## Lubrication system

| | |
|---|---|
| Oil pump type ..................................................................................... | Gear driven from auxiliary shaft |
| Tooth tip to body clearance ................................................................. | 0.110 to 0.180 mm (0.0043 to 0.0071 in) |
| Gear endfloat ..................................................................................... | 0.020 to 0.105 mm (0.0008 to 0.0041 in) |
| Oil pressure at normal operating temperature and average road/ engine speed .......................................................................................... | 3.43 to 4.9 bar (50 to 71 lbf/in²) |
| Oil capacity (with filter change) .......................................................... | 4.05 litre (7.1 pint) |
| Oil type/specification ......................................................................... | Multigrade engine oil, viscosity SAE 15W/40 (Duckhams Hypergrade) |
| Oil filter ............................................................................................ | Champion C106 |

## Torque wrench settings

| | Nm | lbf ft |
|---|---|---|
| Cylinder head bolts: | | |
| Stage 1 ..................................................................................... | 20 | 15 |
| Stage 2 ..................................................................................... | 40 | 30 |
| Stage 3 ..................................................................................... | Turn through 90° | Turn through 90° |
| Stage 4 ..................................................................................... | Turn through 90° | Turn through 90° |
| Camshaft carrier to cylinder head ........................................................ | 20 | 15 |
| Main bearing cap bolts ....................................................................... | 80 | 59 |
| Big-end cap nuts ................................................................................. | 51 | 38 |
| Flywheel mounting bolts ...................................................................... | 83 | 61 |
| Camshaft sprocket bolt ....................................................................... | 83 | 61 |
| Belt tensioner bolt .............................................................................. | 44 | 32 |
| Exhaust manifold nuts ......................................................................... | 28 | 21 |
| Auxiliary shaft sprocket bolt ................................................................ | 83 | 61 |
| Flexible mounting bracket bolts ............................................................ | 59 | 44 |
| Flexible mounting centre nuts .............................................................. | 49 | 36 |
| Oil pressure switch ............................................................................. | 32 | 24 |
| Spark plugs ....................................................................................... | 25 | 18 |
| Roadwheel bolts ................................................................................. | 86 | 63 |
| Driveshaft/hub nuts ............................................................................ | 272 | 200 |
| Tie-rod end balljoint nuts .................................................................... | 34 | 25 |
| Brake caliper mounting bolts ............................................................... | 53 | 39 |
| Front strut lower clamp bolts ............................................................... | 49 | 36 |
| Driveshaft inboard boot retainer bolts ................................................... | 9 | 7 |
| Crankshaft pulley nut .......................................................................... | 98 | 72 |

## PART 1 GENERAL

### 1 Description

1   The Uno may be powered by one of three engines depending upon the particular model.

*903 cc*

2   This is of four cylinder overhead valve type with a light alloy cylinder head and a cast-iron block and crankcase.

3   A three bearing crankshaft is used and the chain-driven camshaft runs in three steel backed white metal bearings.

4   The light alloy pistons are fitted with two compression and one oil

control ring. The gudgeon pin is an interference fit in the small end of the connecting rod.

5   Lubrication is provided by an oil pump within the sump pan and both the pump and the distributor are driven from a gear on the camshaft. Pressurised oil passes through a cartridge type oil filter. An oil pressure relief valve is incorporated in the oil pump. The engine oil is independent of the transmission lubricant.

*1116 cc and 1301 cc*

6   These engines are of single overhead camshaft type, the camshaft being driven by a toothed belt.

7   The difference in engine capacity is achieved by increasing the cylinder bore on the 1301 cc engine.

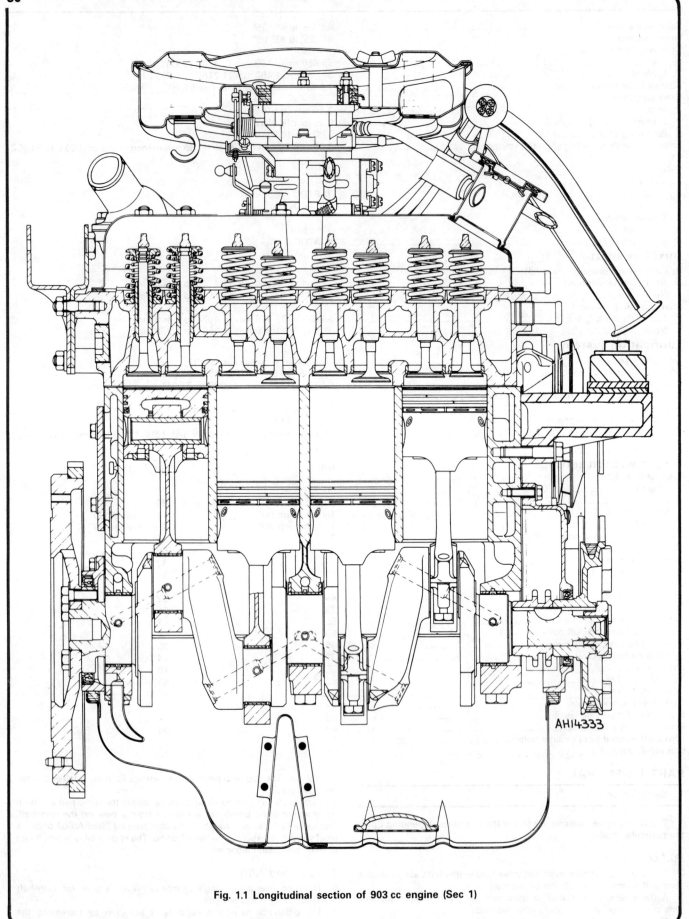

Fig. 1.1 Longitudinal section of 903 cc engine (Sec 1)

AH14333

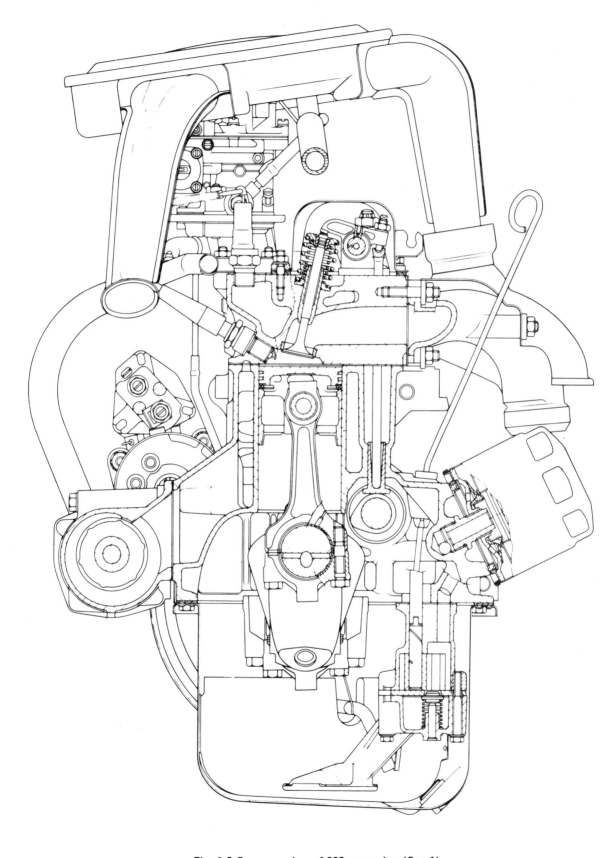

Fig. 1.2 Cross-section of 903 cc engine (Sec 1)

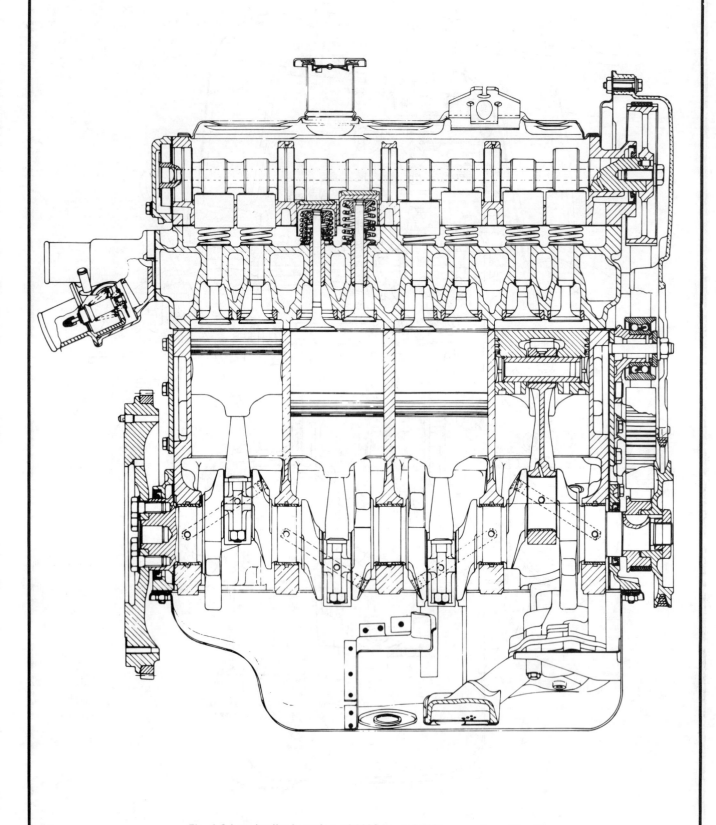

Fig. 1.3 Longitudinal section of 1116 cc and 1301 cc engines (Sec 1)

# Are your plugs trying to tell you something?

**Normal.**
Grey-brown deposits, lightly coated core nose. Plugs ideally suited to engine, and engine in good condition.

**Heavy Deposits.**
A build up of crusty deposits, light-grey sandy colour in appearance.
Fault: Often caused by worn valve guides, excessive use of upper cylinder lubricant, or idling for long periods.

**Lead Glazing.**
Plug insulator firing tip appears yellow or green/yellow and shiny in appearance.
Fault: Often caused by incorrect carburation, excessive idling followed by sharp acceleration. Also check ignition timing.

**Carbon fouling.**
Dry, black, sooty deposits.
Fault: over-rich fuel mixture.
Check: carburettor mixture settings, float level, choke operation, air filter.

**Oil fouling.**
Wet, oily deposits. Fault: worn bores/piston rings or valve guides; sometimes occurs (temporarily) during running-in period.

**Overheating.**
Electrodes have glazed appearance, core nose very white – few deposits. Fault: plug overheating. Check: plug value, ignition timing, fuel octane rating (too low) and fuel mixture (too weak).

**Electrode damage.**
Electrodes burned away; core nose has burned, glazed appearance. Fault: pre-ignition. Check: for correct heat range and as for 'overheating'.

**Split core nose.**
(May appear initially as a crack). Fault: detonation or wrong gap-setting technique. Check: ignition timing, cooling system, fuel mixture (too weak).

# WHY DOUBLE COPPER IS BETTER FOR YOUR ENGINE.

Unique Trapezoidal Copper Cored Earth Electrode — 50% Larger Spark Area — Copper Cored Centre Electrode

Champion Double Copper plugs are the first in the world to have copper core in both centre <u>and</u> earth electrode. This innovative design means that they run cooler by up to 100°C – giving greater efficiency and longer life. These double copper cores transfer heat away from the tip of the plug faster and more efficiently. Therefore, Double Copper runs at cooler temperatures than conventional plugs giving improved acceleration response and high speed performance with no fear of pre-ignition.

**TRAPEZOIDAL COPPER CORED EARTH ELECTRODE**
NEW TRAPEZOIDAL COPPER CORED EARTH ELECTRODE / CONVENTIONAL SOLID NICKEL ALLOY EARTH ELECTRODE
50% INCREASE IN SPARK AREA

**EARTH ELECTRODE TEMPERATURE VS ENGINE SPEED**
SOLID NICKEL EARTH ELECTRODE
COPPER CORED EARTH ELECTRODE
TEMPERATURE / ENGINE SPEED

Champion Double Copper plugs also feature a unique trapezoidal earth electrode giving a 50% increase in spark area. This, together with the double copper cores, offers greatly reduced electrode wear, so the spark stays stronger for longer.

 **FASTER COLD STARTING**

 **FOR UNLEADED OR LEADED FUEL**

 **ELECTRODES UP TO 100°C COOLER**

 **BETTER ACCELERATION RESPONSE**

 **LOWER EMISSIONS**

 **50% BIGGER SPARK AREA**

**THE LONGER LIFE PLUG**

**Plug Tips/Hot and Cold.**
Spark plugs must operate within well-defined temperature limits to avoid cold fouling at one extreme and overheating at the other.
Champion and the car manufacturers work out the best plugs for an engine to give optimum performance under all conditions, from freezing cold starts to sustained high speed motorway cruising.
Plugs are often referred to as hot or cold. With Champion, the higher the number on its body, the hotter the plug, and the lower the number the cooler the plug.

**Plug Cleaning**
Modern plug design and materials mean that Champion no longer recommends periodic plug cleaning. Certainly don't clean your plugs with a wire brush as this can cause metal conductive paths across the nose of the insulator so impairing its performance and resulting in loss of acceleration and reduced m.p.g.
However, if plugs are removed, always carefully clean the area where the plug seats in the cylinder head as grit and dirt can sometimes cause gas leakage.
Also wipe any traces of oil or grease from plug leads as this may lead to arcing.

**CHAMPION**
DOUBLE COPPER

This photographic sequence shows the steps taken to repair the dent and paintwork damage shown above. In general, the procedure for repairing a hole will be similar; where there are substantial differences, the procedure is clearly described and shown in a separate photograph.

First remove any trim around the dent, then hammer out the dent where access is possible. This will minimise filling. Here, after the large dent has been hammered out, the damaged area is being made slightly concave.

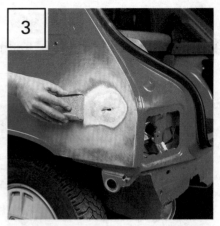

Next, remove all paint from the damaged area by rubbing with coarse abrasive paper or using a power drill fitted with a wire brush or abrasive pad. 'Feather' the edge of the boundary with good paintwork using a finer grade of abrasive paper.

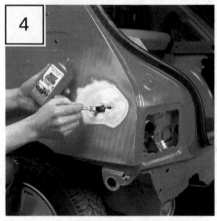

Where there are holes or other damage, the sheet metal should be cut away before proceeding further. The damaged area and any signs of rust should be treated with Turtle Wax Hi-Tech Rust Eater, which will also inhibit further rust formation.

*For a large dent or hole* mix Holts Body Plus Resin and Hardener according to the manufacturer's instructions and apply around the edge of the repair. Press Glass Fibre Matting over the repair area and leave for 20-30 minutes to harden. Then ...

... brush more Holts Body Plus Resin and Hardener onto the matting and leave to harden. Repeat the sequence with two or three layers of matting, checking that the final layer is lower than the surrounding area. Apply Holts Body Plus Filler Paste as shown in Step 5B.

*For a medium dent*, mix Holts Body Plus Filler Paste and Hardener according to the manufacturer's instructions and apply it with a flexible applicator. Apply thin layers of filler at 20-minute intervals, until the filler surface is slightly proud of the surrounding bodywork.

*For small dents and scratches* use Holts No Mix Filler Paste straight from the tube. Apply it according to the instructions in thin layers, using the spatula provided. It will harden in minutes if applied outdoors and may then be used as its own knifing putty.

Use a plane or file for initial shaping. Then, using progressively finer grades of wet-and-dry paper, wrapped round a sanding block, and copious amounts of clean water, rub down the filler until glass smooth. 'Feather' the edges of adjoining paintwork.

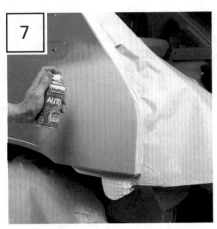

Protect adjoining areas before spraying the whole repair area and at least one inch of the surrounding sound paintwork with Holts Dupli-Color primer.

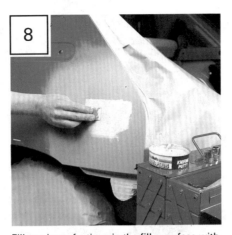

Fill any imperfections in the filler surface with a small amount of Holts Body Plus Knifing Putty. Using plenty of clean water, rub down the surface with a fine grade wet-and-dry paper – 400 grade is recommended – until it is really smooth.

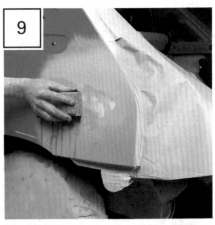

Carefully fill any remaining imperfections with knifing putty before applying the last coat of primer. Then rub down the surface with Holts Body Plus Rubbing Compound to ensure a really smooth surface.

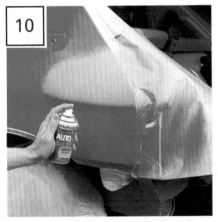

Protect surrounding areas from overspray before applying the topcoat in several thin layers. Agitate Holts Dupli-Color aerosol thoroughly. Start at the repair centre, spraying outwards with a side-to-side motion.

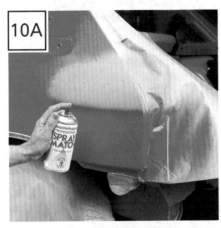

If the exact colour is not available off the shelf, local Holts Professional Spraymatch Centres will custom fill an aerosol to match perfectly.

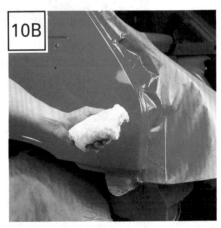

To identify whether a lacquer finish is required, rub a painted unrepaired part of the body with wax and a clean cloth.

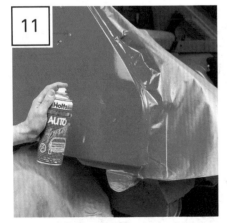

If *no* traces of paint appear on the cloth, spray Holts Dupli-Color clear lacquer over the repaired area to achieve the correct gloss level.

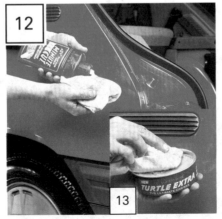

The paint will take about two weeks to harden fully. After this time it can be 'cut' with a mild cutting compound such as Turtle Wax Minute Cut prior to polishing with a final coating of Turtle Wax Extra.

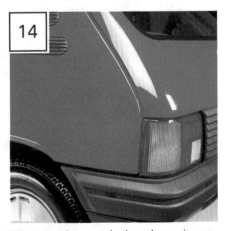

When carrying out bodywork repairs, remember that the quality of the finished job is proportional to the time and effort expended.

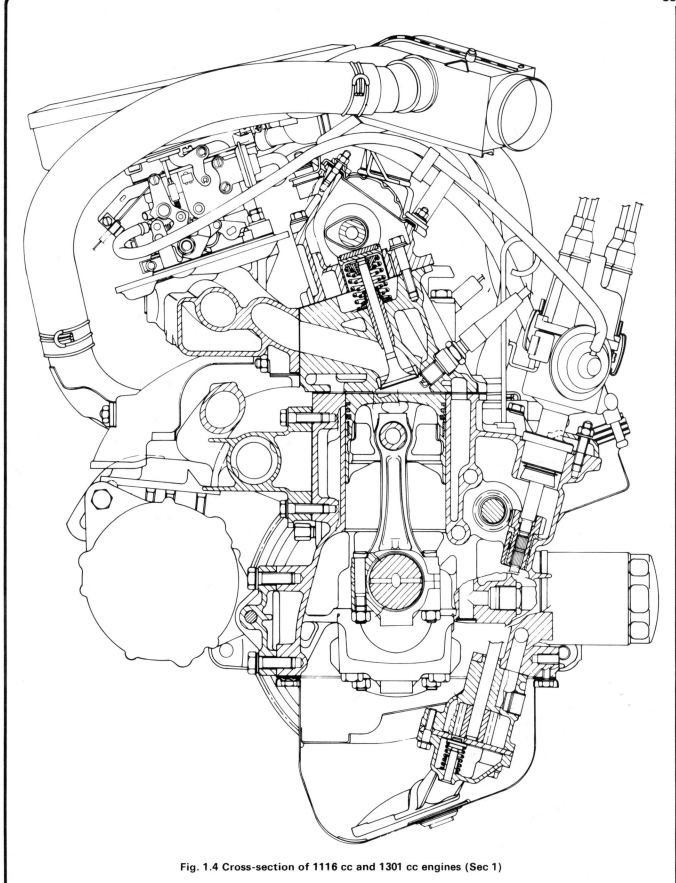

Fig. 1.4 Cross-section of 1116 cc and 1301 cc engines (Sec 1)

8 The cylinder head is of light alloy while the cylinder block and crankcase are of cast-iron construction.

9 A five bearing crankshaft is used and the camshaft runs in a similar number of bearings, but as these are in-line bored directly in the camshaft carrier, no repair is possible.

10 The pistons are of light alloy with two compression and one oil control ring. The gudgeon pin is an interference fit in the small end of the connecting rod.

11 An auxiliary shaft, driven by the timing belt is used to drive the distributor. oil pump and fuel pump.

12 The oil pump is located within the sump pan and incorporates a pressure relief valve.

13 Pressurised oil passes through a cartridge type oil filter.

14 The crankshaft main bearings are supplied under pressure from drillings in the crankcase from the main oil gallery whilst the connecting rod big-end bearings are lubricated from the main bearings by oil forced through the crankshaft oilways. The camshaft bearings are fed from a drilling from the main oil gallery. The cams and tappets are lubricated by oil mist from outlets in the camshaft bearings.

15 The cylinder walls, pistons and gudgeon pins are lubricated by oil splashed up by the crankshaft webs. An oil pressure warning light is fitted to indicate when the pressure is too low.

### All engines

16 The engine is mounted transversely with the transmission at the front of the car.

17 The engine oil is independent of the transmission lubricant.

## 2 Engine oil and filter

1 The engine oil level should be checked at the weekly service (see Routine Maintenance). Preferably check the level cold, first thing in the morning or if the engine has been running, allow at least ten minutes to elapse after switching off to permit the oil to drain.

2 Withdraw the dipstick, wipe it clean on non-fluffy material, re-insert it and then withdraw it for the second time (photo).

3 The oil level should be between the MIN and MAX marks. If not, top up with specified oil to the MAX mark. Pour the oil slowly through the filler orifice on the rocker cover. To raise the oil level from MIN to MAX will require approximately 1.1 litre (2.0 pints) (photos).

4 At the intervals specified in Routine Maintenance the oil and filter should be renewed.

5 Have the engine at normal operating temperature, remove the oil filler cap.

6 Place a suitable container under the sump pan. Unscrew and remove the oil drain plug and allow the oil to drain (photo).

7 While the oil is draining, unscrew and discard the oil filter. To unscrew the filter, a filter or chain wrench will normally be required. If

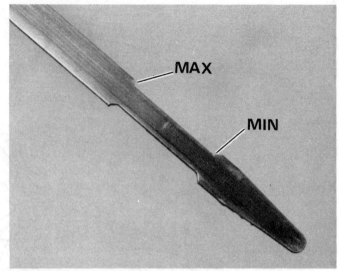

2.3A Typical dipstick markings

2.3B Topping up engine oil (1116 cc)

2.2 Withdrawing engine oil dipstick (1116 cc)

2.6 Engine sump drain plug

such a tool is not available, drive a long screwdriver through the oil filter casing and use it as a lever to unscrew the filter cartridge.

8  Smear the rubber sealing ring of the new oil filter with oil and screw it into position using hand pressure only (photo).

9  Refit the drain plug and refill the engine with the correct quantity and grade of oil.

10  Start the engine. It will take two or three seconds for the oil warning lamp to go out. This is normal and is due to the time taken for the new filter to fill with oil.

11  Switch off, check for leaks and check the oil level, topping up if necessary.

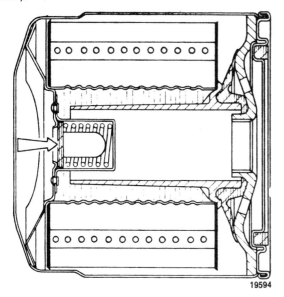

Fig. 1.5 Sectional view of oil filter. Bypass valve arrowed (Sec 2)

2.8 Screwing on the oil filter (903 cc)

## 3  Crankcase ventilation system

1  This system is designed to draw oil fumes and blow-by gas (which has passed the piston rings) from the crankcase and draw it into the intake manifold when it will then be burned during the normal combustion process.

2  Regularly check the security of the system hoses which run from the rocker cover or crankcase breather unit (photo).

3.2 Crankcase vent hose (1116 cc)

3  Periodically, detach the hoses and clean them out with paraffin and a brush or rag pull through.

4  Evidence of sludge or emulsified oil within the hoses or inside the oil filler cap will indicate that the engine is running too cool particularly if the car is used mainly for short journeys where the engine never reaches full working temperature.

## 4  Major operations possible without removing engine from car

1  The following work can be carried out without the need to remove the engine from the car.

### 903 cc engine

*Valve clearances – checking and adjusting*
*Timing chain and sprockets – removal and refitting*
*Cylinder head – removal and refitting*
*Sump pan – removal and refitting*
*Pistons/connecting rods – removal and refitting*
*Oil pump – removal and refitting*
*Engine mountings – renewal*

### 1116 cc and 1301 cc engines

*Valve clearances – checking and adjusting*
*Camshaft and camshaft carrier – removal and refitting*
*Timing belt – removal and refitting*
*Cylinder head – removal and refitting*
*Sump pan – removal and refitting*
*Oil pump – removal and refitting*
*Pistons/connecting rods – removal and refitting*
*Engine mountings – renewal*

## PART 2  903 CC ENGINE

## 5  Valve clearances – adjustment

1  Adjust the valves when the engine is cold.

2  Unbolt and remove the rocker cover.

3  It is important that the clearance is set when the cam follower of the valve being adjusted is on the heel of the cam (ie; opposite the peak). This can be done by carrying out the adjustments in the following order, which also avoids turning the crankshaft more than necessary.

4  Turn the crankshaft either using a spanner on the pulley nut or by raising a front roadwheel, engaging a gear (3rd or 4th) and turning the

wheel in the forward direction of travel. It will be easier to turn the engine if the spark plugs are first removed.

| Valve fully open | Check and adjust |
|------------------|------------------|
| *Valve No. 8 EX* | *Valve No. 1 EX* |
| *Valve No. 6 IN* | *Valve No. 3 IN* |
| *Valve No. 4 EX* | *Valve No. 5 EX* |
| *Valve No. 7 IN* | *Valve No. 2 IN* |
| *Valve No. 1 EX* | *Valve No. 8 EX* |
| *Valve No. 3 IN* | *Valve No. 6 IN* |
| *Valve No. 5 EX* | *Valve No. 4 EX* |
| *Valve No. 2 IN* | *Valve No. 7 IN* |

5   Count the valves from the timing cover end of the engine.
6   Remember, the inlet and exhaust valve clearances are different.
7   Insert the appropriate feeler gauge between the end of the valve stem and the rocker arm. It should be a stiff sliding fit (photo).
8   If the clearance is incorrect, release the rocker arm adjuster screw locknut using a ring spanner. Turn the adjuster screw using a small open-ended spanner, but tie something to it in case it is inadvertently dropped through one of the pushrod holes.
9   Once the clearance is correct, tighten the locknut without moving the position of the adjuster screw.
10  Repeat the operations on the remaining seven valves.
11  Re-check all the clearances. Make sure that the rocker cover gasket is in good condition and fit the rocker cover.

## 6   Timing chain and sprockets – removal and refitting

1   Remove the alternator drivebelt as described in Chapter 2.
2   Unscrew and remove the crankshaft pulley nut. To prevent the crankshaft rotating, either select a gear and have an assistant apply the footbrake hard or remove the starter motor and lock the ring gear teeth with a large cold chisel or screwdriver.
3   Disconnect the hoses from the fuel pump.

5.7 Adjusting a valve clearance

4   Unbolt and remove the fuel pump with spacer and rod.
5   Support the engine on a hoist or under the sump and disconnect and remove the right-hand mounting. Then unscrew and remove the timing cover bolts. The base of the cover is secured by the front two sump pan studs. Unbolt and lower the front end of the sump. Avoid breaking the gasket. Remove the timing cover.
6   Undo and remove the camshaft sprocket securing bolt; this will also release the fuel pump drive cam from the end of the camshaft. Note the timing marks on the camshaft and crankshaft sprockets.

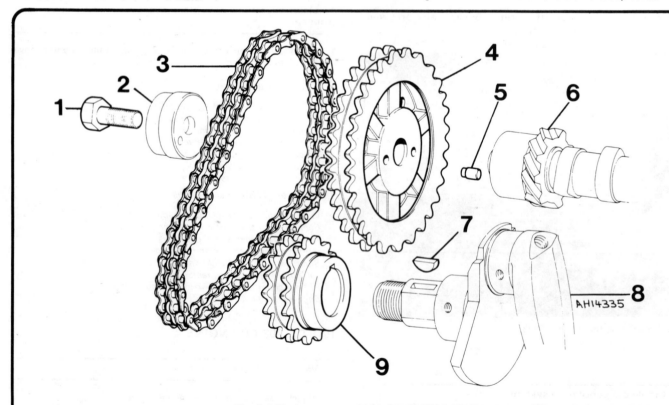

Fig. 1.6 Timing chain and sprockets (Sec 6)

| | | | |
|---|---|---|---|
| *1   Sprocket retaining bolt* | *4   Camshaft sprocket* | *6   Camshaft* | *8   Crankshaft* |
| *2   Fuel pump eccentric cam* | *5   Sprocket locating dowel* | *7   Woodruff key* | *9   Crankshaft sprocket* |
| *3   Timing chain* | | | |

7 Using two tyre levers, carefully ease the two sprockets forwards away from the crankcase. Lift away the two sprockets and timing chain.

8 Remove the Woodruff key from the crankshaft nose with a pair of pliers and note how the channel in the pulley is designed to fit over it. Place the Woodruff key in a container as it is a very small part and can easily become lost. The camshaft sprocket is located on the camshaft by a dowel peg.

*Refitting*

9 Fit the Woodruff key to the front of the crankshaft.

10 Tap the crankshaft sprocket onto the front of the crankshaft.

11 Turn the sprocket so that the Woodruff key is uppermost.

12 Turn the camshaft until it is in such a position that if the sprocket was fitted the dimple timing mark on the sprocket would be nearest to and in alignment with, the one on the crankshaft sprocket.

13 Engage the timing chain with the teeth of the crankshaft sprocket. Then locate the camshaft sprocket within the upper loop of the chain in such a way that when the sprocket is pushed onto the camshaft, the timing marks will be in alignment. Make sure that the self-tensioning links are on the inside of the chain against the cylinder block (photos).

14 Place the camshaft sprocket onto the camshaft so that its positioning dowel engages.

15 Secure the camshaft sprocket by fitting the special cam, that drives the fuel pump, on its locating dowel. Fit the camshaft sprocket retaining bolt (photo).

16 Tighten the sprocket bolt to the specified torque.

17 If the timing cover oil seal showed signs of leaking before engine overhaul the old seal should be removed and a new one fitted.

18 Using a screwdriver, carefully remove the old oil seal, working from the rear of the cover. Fit the new seal making sure it is inserted squarely, and tap home with a hammer.

19 Lubricate the oil seal with engine oil.

20 With all traces of old gasket and jointing compound removed from the timing cover and cylinder block mating faces, smear a little grease onto the timing cover mating face and fit a new gasket in position.

21 Fit the timing cover to the cylinder block and finger tighten the securing bolts, and spring washer. Ensure that the fuel pump pushrod bush is in place in the cover.

22 Wipe the hub of the pulley and carefully place into position on the crankshaft. It should locate on the Woodruff key. It may be necessary to adjust the position of the timing cover slightly in order to centralise the oil seal relative to the pulley hub.

23 Tighten the timing cover securing bolts in a diagonal and progressive manner.

24 Tighten the crankshaft pulley nut to the specified torque again holding the crankshaft against rotation as previously described (paragraph 2) this Section.

25 Refit the fuel pump and alternator drivebelt.

6.13B Timing mark alignment

6.13C Self-tensioning links on inside of chain

6.13A Fitting the sprockets and timing chain

6.15 Fitting fuel pump drive cam and sprocket bolt

## 7  Cylinder head – removal and refitting

1   For safety reasons, disconnect the battery negative lead.
2   Refer to Chapter 2 and drain the cooling system.
3   Refer to Chapter 3 and remove the carburettor, air cleaner and spacer block.
4   Undo and remove the five nuts and washers securing the exhaust manifold and hot air ducting to the cylinder head.
5   Detach the cable from the temperature indicator sender unit.
6   Refer to Chapter 4 and disconnect the distributor LT lead and the coil HT lead.
7   Refer to Chapter 2 and remove the thermostat housing from the cylinder head.
8   Disconnect the coolant hoses from the cylinder head.
9   Note the electrical connections to the rear of the alternator and disconnect them.
10  Disconnect the mounting and adjuster link bolts and remove the alternator from the engine.
11  Unscrew the four nuts securing the rocker cover to the top of the cylinder head and lift away the spring washers and metal packing pieces. Remove the rocker cover and cork gasket.
12  Unscrew the four rocker pedestal securing nuts in a progressive manner. Lift away the four nuts and spring washers and ease the valve rocker assembly from the cylinder head studs.
13  Remove the pushrods, keeping them in the relative order in which they were removed. The easiest way to do this is to push them through a sheet of thick paper or thin card in the correct sequence.
14  Unscrew the cylinder head securing bolts half a turn at a time in the reverse order to that shown in Fig. 1.7; don't forget the one within the inlet manifold. When all the bolts are no longer under tension they may be unscrewed from the cylinder head one at a time. This will also release a section of the cooling system pipe secured by two of the bolts. All the bolts have washers.
15  The cylinder head may now be lifted off. If the head is jammed, try to rock it to break the seal. Under no circumstances try to prise it apart from the cylinder block with a screwdriver or cold chisel as damage may be done to the faces of the head or block. If the head will not readily free, turn the crankshaft. The compression generated in the cylinders will often break the gasket joint. If this fails to work, strike the head sharply with a plastic headed hammer, or with a wooden hammer, or with a metal hammer with an interposed piece of wood to cushion the blows. Under no circumstances hit the head directly with a metal hammer as this may cause the casting to fracture. Several sharp taps with the hammer, at the same time pulling upwards, should free the head. Lift the head off and place on one side.
16  The cylinder head may now be decarbonised or dismantled, refer to Section 17.

### Refitting

17  After checking that both the cylinder block and cylinder head mating surfaces are perfectly clean, generously lubricate each cylinder with engine oil.
18  Always use a new cylinder head gasket as the old gasket will be compressed and not capable of giving a good seal.
19  Never smear grease on the gasket as, when the engine heats up, the grease will melt and may allow compression leaks to develop.
20  The cylinder head gasket cannot be fitted incorrectly due to its asymmetrical shape, but the word ALTO should be uppermost in any event (photo).
21  The locating dowels should be refitted to the front right and left-hand side cylinder head securing bolt holes.
22  Carefully fit the cylinder head gasket to the top of the cylinder block.
23  Lower the cylinder head onto the gasket, taking care not to move the position of the gasket.
24  Screw in the cylinder head bolts finger tight, remembering the bolt within the intake manifold and the metal coolant pipe which is held by the two cylinder head bolts adjacent to the coolant temperature sender unit (photos).
25  Tighten the cylinder head bolts in two stages, in the specified sequence to the torque given in Specifications.
26  With the cylinder head in position, fit the pushrods in the same order in which they were removed. Ensure that they locate properly in the stems of the tappets and lubricate the pushrod ends before fitment (photo).
27  Unscrew the rocker arm adjuster screws as far as they will go.

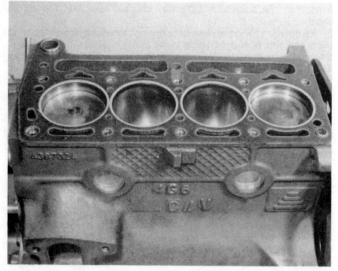

7.20 Cylinder head gasket

7.24A Cylinder head bolt in intake manifold

7.24B Cylinder head bolts holding coolant pipe

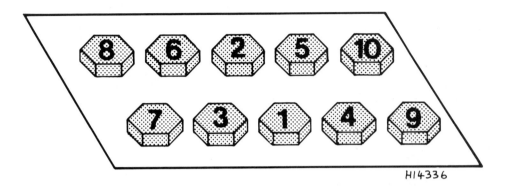

**Fig. 1.7 Cylinder head bolt tightening sequence (Sec 7)**

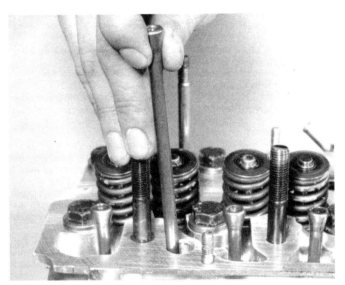

7.26 Fitting a pushrod

7.31 Fitting the rocker cover

28  Fit the rocker gear over the four studs in the cylinder head and lower onto the cylinder head. Make sure the ball ends of the rockers locate in the cups of the pushrods.

29  Fit the four nuts and washers to the rocker shaft pedestal studs and tighten in a progressive manner to the torque wrench setting given in the Specifications.

30  Adjust the valve clearances as described in Section 5.

31  Fit the exhaust manifold, thermostat housing and alternator, also the rocker cover (photo).

32  Fit the carburettor, air cleaner and distributor (Chapter 4).

33  Reconnect all hoses and electrical leads, including the battery.

34  Refill the cooling system.

## 8  Sump pan – removal and refitting

1  Drain the engine oil.

2  Unscrew and remove the four nuts and twelve bolts and lift away the sump pan. If it has stuck on the gasket carefully tap the side of the mating flange to break the seal. Remove the gasket and clean away any pieces of gasket cement which are adhering to the flanges.

3  Remove the sealing strips from the recesses at either end of the sump pan.

### Refitting

4  Fit the new sealing strips and if necessary, trim their ends until they are just proud of the sump pan flange (photo).

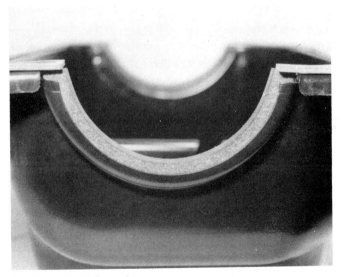

8.4 Sump pan sealing strip

5  Using thick grease, stick the gasket side strips to the crankcase.
6  Apply a blob of jointing compound at the points of overlap of the side gaskets and strips.
7  Offer up the sump pan, screw in and tighten the bolts and nuts progressively (photos).
8  Refill the engine with oil.

8.7A Fitting the sump pan

8.7B Sump pan nut, bolts and washers

## 9  Pistons/connecting rods – removal and refitting

1  Remove the cylinder head as described in Section 7.
2  Remove the sump pan as described in Section 8.
3  Undo and remove the big-end cap retaining bolts and keep them in their respective order for correct refitting.
4  Check that the connecting rod and big-end bearing cap assemblies are correctly marked. Normally the numbers 1 – 4 are stamped on adjacent sides of the big-end caps and connecting rods, indicating which cap fits on which rod and which way round the cap fits. The numbers are located on the sides of the rod and cap furthest away from the camshaft.
5  If numbers are not evident, then use a sharp file to make mating marks across the rod/cap joint. One line for connecting rod No. 1, two for connecting rod No. 2 and so on. This will ensure that there is no

confusion later as it is most important that the caps go back in the correct position on the connecting rods from which they were removed. No. 1 piston should be at the crankshaft pulley end of the engine.
6  If the big-end caps are difficult to remove they may be gently tapped with a soft-faced hammer.
7  To remove the shell bearings, press the bearing opposite the groove in both the connecting rod and the connecting rod caps and the bearings will slide out easily.
8  Keep the shells with their original cap or rod if the bearings are not being renewed.
9  Withdraw the pistons and connecting rods upwards and ensure that they are kept in the correct order for replacement in the same bore.
10  If the cylinder has a wear ridge at its upper end then this may make it difficult to remove the piston. In this event, relieve the sharp edge of the ridge by scraping.
11  Dismantling the pistons is described in Section 18, paragraph 17.
12  Lay the piston and connecting rod assemblies in the correct order ready for refitting into their respective bores.
13  With a wad of clean non-fluffy rag wipe the cylinder bores clean.
14  Position the piston rings so that their gaps are 120° apart and then lubricate the rings.
15  Wipe clean the connecting rod half of the big-end bearing and the underside of the shell bearing. Fit the shell bearing in position with its locating tongue engaged with the corresponding groove in the connecting rod.
16  Fit a piston ring compressor to the top of the piston, making sure it is tight enough to compress the piston rings.
17  Using a piece of fine wire double check that the little jet hole in the connecting rod is clean.
18  The pistons, complete with connecting rods, are fitted to their bores from above. The number stamped on the connecting rod must face away from the camshaft with the arrow on the piston crown pointing towards the timing cover.
19  With the base of the piston ring compressor resting on the cylinder block, apply the wooden handle of a hammer to the piston crown, strike the hammer head with the hand and drive the piston/rod into its bore (photo).
20  Draw the rod, complete with shell bearing down onto its crankpin.
21  Generously lubricate the crankpin journals with engine oil, and turn the crankshaft so that the crankpin is in the most advantageous position for the connecting rod to be drawn into it.
22  Wipe clean the connecting rod bearing cap and back of the shell bearing and fit the shell bearing in position ensuring that the locating tongue at the back of the bearing engages with the locating groove in the connecting rod cap.
23  Generously lubricate the shell bearing and offer up the connecting rod bearing cap to the connecting rod (photo).
24  Screw in the big-end bolts and tighten to the specified torque (photo).
25  Refit the sump pan (Sec 8) and the cylinder head (Sec 7).
26  Refill the engine with oil and coolant.

9.19 Fitting a piston/connecting rod

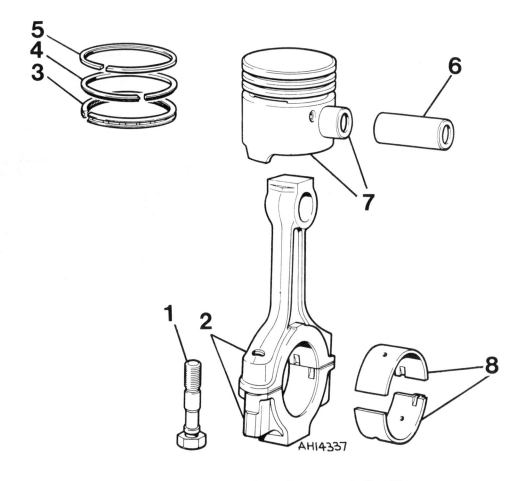

**Fig. 1.8 Piston/connecting rod components (Sec 9)**

1  Bolt
2  Connecting rod
3  Oil control ring
4  Compression ring (stepped at base)
5  Compression ring (marked TOP)
6  Gudgeon pin
7  Piston/gudgeon pin
8  Big-end shell bearings

9.23 Big-end cap

9.24 Tightening a big-end bolt

## 10 Oil pump – removal and refitting

1   Remove the sump pan as described in Section 8.
2   Unscrew the two bolts which hold the oil pump housing to the
underside of the crankcase and withdraw the pump. Remove and
discard the pump flange gasket.

### Refitting

3   Stick a new gasket to the oil pump location on the underside of the
crankcase (photo).

10.5 Tightening an oil pump bolt

10.3 Oil pump gasket

10.4 Fitting the oil pump

4   Locate the oil pump driveshaft in the oil pump and then offer up the
complete assembly to the crankcase so that the gear teeth on the
driveshaft mesh with those on the camshaft (photo).
5   Fit the securing bolts (photo).
6   Fit the sump pan and refill the engine with oil.

## 11 Engine mountings – renewal

1   The engine/transmission flexible mountings can be removed if the
power unit is supported under the sump pan or gearbox with a jack or a
hoist is attached to the engine lifting lugs and the weight of the power
unit just taken.
2   Unscrew the mounting bracket bolts and remove the mounting.
3   Fit the new mounting and remove the lifting gear.
4   In the unlikely event of all the mountings requiring renewal at the
same time, renew them one at a time, never disconnect all the
mountings together.

## 12 Engine – method of removal

1   The engine/transmission should be removed downwards and
withdrawn from under the front of the car which will have to be raised
sufficiently high to provide clearance.

## 13 Engine/transmission – removal and separation

1   Open the bonnet, disconnect the windscreen washer tube.
2   Mark the hinge positions on the underside of the bonnet using
masking tape and then with the help of an assistant to support its
weight unbolt the bonnet and remove it to a safe place.
3   Disconnect the battery negative lead.
4   Drain the cooling system and engine oil.
5   Disconnect the leads from the rear of the alternator, the starter
motor and the oil pressure switch also the coolant temperature switch.
6   Disconnect the HT lead from the ignition coil and the LT lead from
the distributor. Disconnect the transmission earth strap.
7   Remove the air cleaner.
8   Disconnect the clutch cable from the release lever at the
transmission.
9   Disconnect the speedometer drive cable by unscrewing the knurled
nut from the transmission.
10  Disconnect the leads from the reversing lamp switch.
11  Disconnect the coolant hoses from the cylinder head and coolant
pump.
12  Disconnect the fuel inlet hose from the fuel pump. Plug the hose.
13  Disconnect the throttle and choke controls from the carburettor.
14  Disconnect the heater hoses from the engine.

Fig. 1.9 Coolant temperature switch (Sec 13)

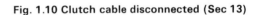

reversing switch cables

Fig. 1.10 Clutch cable disconnected (Sec 13)

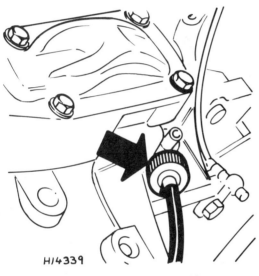

Fig. 1.11 Speedometer drive cable at transmission (Sec 13)

Fig. 1.12 Coolant hoses at thermostat housing (Sec 13)

Fig. 1.13 Coolant hose at rear of coolant pump (Sec 13)

Fig. 1.14 Fuel inlet hose disconnected from pump (Sec 13)

15 Disconnect the fuel return hose from the carburettor.
16 Disconnect the exhaust downpipe from the manifold.
17 Raise the front end of the car and support it securely on axle stands. Remove the roadwheels.
18 Unscrew the driveshaft to hub nuts. These are very tight and a long knuckle bar will be required when unscrewing them. Have an assistant apply the brakes hard to prevent the hub turning.
19 Working under the car, remove the protective shields and disconnect the exhaust system mountings and withdraw it to the rear.
20 Disconnect the forward ends of the gearchange rods by prising their sockets from the ballstuds.

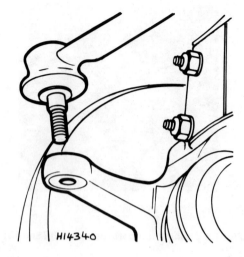

Fig. 1.17 Tie-rod end balljoint disconnected (Sec 13)

Fig. 1.15 Fuel return hose disconnected from carburettor (Sec 13)

13.22 Hub carrier strut clamp

Fig. 1.16 Gearchange rods disconnected (Sec 13)

21 Unscrew the nuts on the steering tie-rod end balljoints and using a suitable 'splitter' tool separate the balljoints from the steering arms. Unbolt the brake calipers and tie them up out of the way.
22 Unscrew and remove the bolts which secure the hub carriers to the U-clamps at the base of the suspension struts (photo).
23 Pull the tops of the hub carriers from the clamps and release the driveshafts from the hub carriers.
24 Tie the driveshafts in a horizontal plane with lengths of wire.
25 Support the engine on a hoist or use a trolley jack under the engine/transmission and remove the bottom mounting and then the upper left and right-hand ones (photo).
26 Carefully lower the power unit to the floor and withdraw it from under the car.
27 External dirt and grease should now be removed using paraffin and a stiff brush or a water-soluble solvent.
28 Unbolt and remove the engine mounting brackets and the starter motor.

Fig. 1.18 Hub carrier detached from strut clamp (Sec 13)

13.25 Right-hand engine mounting

Fig. 1.19 Left-hand flexible mounting (Sec 13)

AH14341

Fig. 1.20 Flywheel housing cover plate removed (Sec 13)

29 Unbolt and remove the cover plate and gearchange ball stud strut from the lower front face of the flywheel housing.
30 With the engine resting squarely on its sump pan unscrew the flywheel housing connecting bolts noting the location of any lifting lugs and hose and wiring brackets.
31 Support the weight of the transmission and withdraw it in a straight line from the engine.

## 14 Engine – dismantling (general)

1 Stand the engine on a strong bench at a suitable working height. Failing this, it can be dismantled on the floor, but at least stand it on a sheet of hardboard.
2 During the dismantling process, the greatest care should be taken to keep the exposed parts free from dirt. As the engine is stripped, clean each part in a bath of paraffin.
3 Never immerse parts with oilways in paraffin, e.g. the crankshaft, but to clean, wipe down carefully with a paraffin dampened rag. Oilways can be cleaned out with a piece of wire. If an air line is available, all parts can be blown dry and the oilways blown through as an added precaution.
4 Re-use of old gaskets is false economy and can give rise to oil and water leaks, if nothing worse. To avoid the possibility of trouble after the engine has been reassembled always use new gaskets throughout.
5 Do not throw the old gaskets away as it sometimes happens that an immediate replacement cannot be found and the old gasket is then very useful as a template. Hang up the gaskets on a suitable nail or hook as they are removed.
6 To strip the engine, it is best to work from the top downwards. The engine oil sump provides a firm base on which the engine can be supported in an upright position. When the stage is reached where the pistons are to be removed, turn the engine on its side. Turn the block upside down to remove the crankshaft.
7 Wherever possible, replace nuts, bolts and washers finger-tight from wherever they were removed. This helps avoid later loss and muddle. If they cannot be replaced then lay them out in such a fashion that it is clear from where they came.

## 15 Engine – removing ancillary components

1 Before dismantling the engine, remove the engine ancillary components.

> *Carburettor (Chapter 3)*
> *Thermostat housing (Chapter 2)*
> *Alternator (Chapter 9)*
> *Coolant pump (Chapter 2)*
> *Distributor (Chapter 4)*
> *Exhaust manifold (Chapter 3)*
> *Fuel pump (Chapter 3)*
> *Oil filter cartridge (Section 2 this Chapter)*
> *Clutch (Chapter 5)*

## 16 Engine – complete dismantling

1 Unbolt and remove the rocker cover.
2 Unscrew the rocker pedestal securing nuts and lift away the rocker assembly.
3 Remove the pushrods, keeping them in their original fitted order.
4 Remove the cylinder head as described in Section 7. Remove the dipstick and guide tube.
5 Turn the engine on its side and unbolt and remove the sump pan.
6 Remove the piston/connecting rods as described in Section 9.
7 Unscrew and remove the crankshaft pulley nut. To prevent the crankshaft rotating while this is done, either jam the flywheel ring gear or place a block between a crankshaft counterweight and the inside of the crankcase.
8 Unbolt and remove the timing cover.
9 Remove the timing chain and sprockets as described in Section 6.
10 Unbolt and remove the oil pump as described in Section 10.
11 Unscrew and remove the camshaft front bearing lockscrew noting that the chamfer on the bearing is on the inboard side.
12 Withdraw the camshaft, taking great care not to damage the bearings with the cam lobes.
13 Lift out the cam followers and keep them in their originally fitted sequence.
14 Unbolt and remove the flywheel. Jam the ring gear teeth to prevent rotation.
15 Remove the engine rear plate.
16 Turn the cylinder block so that it is standing upside down.

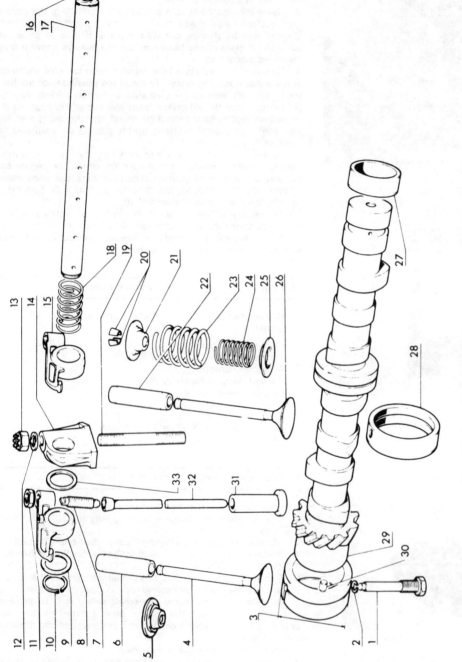

**Fig. 1.21 Camshaft and rocker gear components (Sec 16)**

1  Camshaft bush lockbolt
2  Washer
3  Camshaft front bearing
4  Exhaust valve
5  Spring cap
6  Valve guide
7  Adjuster screw
8  Rocker arm
9  Thrust washer

10  Circlip
11  Locknut
12  Washer
13  Locknut
14  Pedestal
15  Rocker arm
16  Plug
17  Rocker shaft

18  Coil spring
19  Stud
20  Split collets
21  Spring cap
22  Valve guide
23  Outer valve spring
24  Inner valve spring
25  Spring seat

26  Inlet valve
27  Camshaft bearing
28  Camshaft bearing
29  Camshaft
30  Locating dowel
31  Cam follower
32  Pushrod
33  Washer

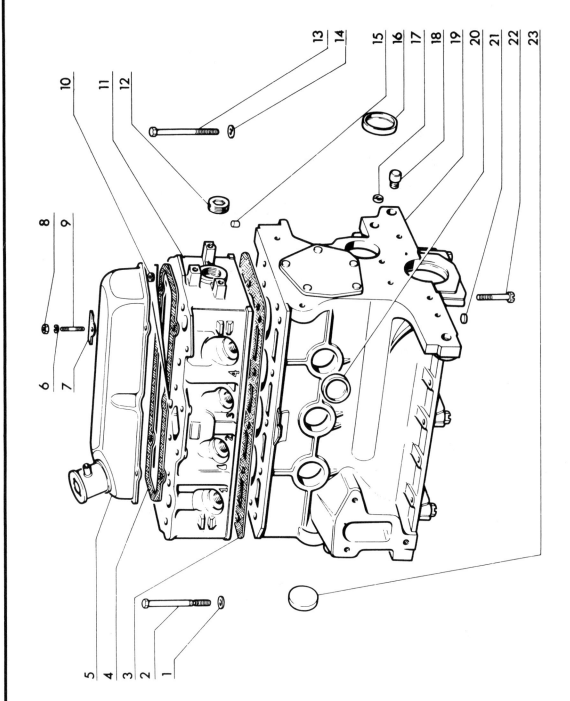

**Fig. 1.22 Cylinder head, block and crankcase (Sec 16)**

| | | | |
|---|---|---|---|
| 1 | Washer | 11 | Cylinder head |
| 2 | Cylinder head bolt | 12 | Plug |
| 3 | Gasket | 13 | Cylinder head bolt |
| 4 | Rocker cover gasket | 14 | Washer |
| 5 | Rocker cover | 15 | Dowel |
| 6 | Washer | 16 | Plug |
| 7 | Plate | 17 | Plug |
| 8 | Nut | 18 | Dowel |
| 9 | Stud | 19 | Block/crankcase |
| 10 | Plug | 20 | Plug |
| | | 21 | Plug |
| | | 22 | Bolt |
| | | 23 | Plug |

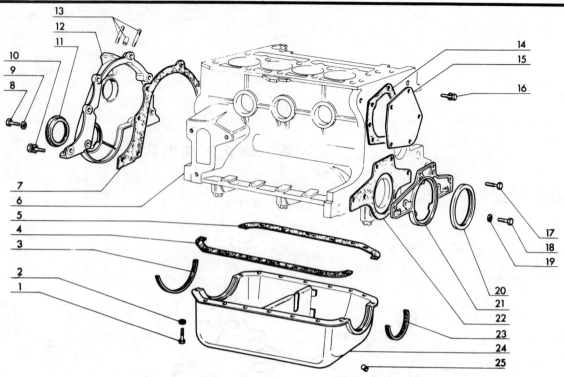

**Fig. 1.23 Timing cover, sump pan and oil seals (Sec 16)**

| | | |
|---|---|---|
| 1 Sump pan bolt | 8 Bolt | 14 Gasket | 20 Crankshaft rear oil seal |
| 2 Washer | 9 Washer | 15 Cover plate | 21 Oil seal carrier |
| 3 Sealing strip | 10 Bolt and washer | 16 Bolt and washer | 22 Gasket |
| 4 Side gasket | 11 Crankshaft front oil seal | 17 Bolt | 23 Sealing strip |
| 5 Side gasket | 12 Timing cover | 18 Bolt | 24 Sump pan |
| 6 Block/crankcase | 13 Fuel pump studs and bush | 19 Washer | 25 Drain plug |
| 7 Gasket | | | |

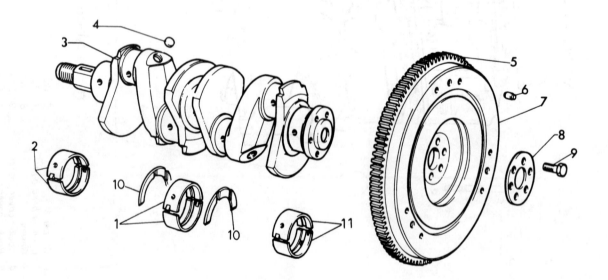

**Fig. 1.24 Crankshaft and flywheel (Sec 16)**

| | | | |
|---|---|---|---|
| 1 Centre main bearing shells | 4 Plug | 7 Flywheel | 10 Thrust washers |
| 2 Front main bearing shells | 5 Starter ring gear | 8 Thrust plate | 11 Rear main bearing shells |
| 3 Crankshaft | 6 Dowel | 9 Bolt | |

17 Unbolt and remove the crankshaft rear oil seal carrier. Note the sump fixing studs.

18 The main bearing caps should be marked 1, 2 and 3 but if they are not, centre punch them and note which way round they are located.

19 Unscrew the main bearing cap bolts progressively.

20 Remove the bearing caps and half shells. If the shell bearings are to be used again, keep them with their respective caps.

21 Note the semi-circular thrust washers on either side of the centre main bearing which control crankshaft endfloat.

22 Lift the crankshaft from the crankcase.

23 Remove the bearing shells from the crankcase and mark them as to position if they are to be used again.

## 17 Cylinder head – dismantling and decarbonising

1 The exhaust manifold and rocker gear will have been removed from the cylinder head during removal (see Section 7).

2 The valves should now be removed using a universal valve spring compressor.

3 Compress the first valve spring and extract the split cotters. If the valve spring refuses to compress, do not apply excessive force, but remove the compressor and place a piece of tubing on the spring retainer and strike it a sharp blow to release the collets from the valve stem. Refit the compressor and resume operations when the collets should come out.

4 Gently release the compressor, take off the spring retaining cap, the valve spring and the spring seat. Remove the valve. Keep the valve with its associated components together and in numbered sequence so that they can be returned to their original positions.

5 A small box with divisions is useful for this purpose. Remove and discard the valve stem oil seals.

6 Remove the other valves in a similar way.

7 Bearing in mind that the cylinder head is of light alloy construction and is easily damaged use a blunt scraper or rotary wire brush to clean all traces of carbon deposits from the combustion spaces and the ports. The valve head stems and valve guides should also be freed from any carbon deposits. Wash the combustion spaces and ports down with paraffin and scrape the cylinder head surface free of any foreign matter with the side of a steel rule, or a similar article.

8 If the engine is installed in the car, clean the pistons and the top of the cylinder bores. If the pistons are still in the block, then it is essential that great care is taken to ensure that no carbon gets into the cylinder bores as this could scratch the cylinder walls or cause damage to the piston and rings. To ensure this does not happen, first turn the crankshaft so that two of the pistons are at the top of their bores. Stuff rag into the other two bores or seal them off with paper and masking tape. The waterways should also be covered with small pieces of masking tape to prevent particles of carbon entering the cooling system and damaging the coolant pump.

9 Press a little grease into the gap between the cylinder walls and the two pistons which are to be worked on. With a blunt scraper carefully scrape away the carbon from the piston crown, taking care not to scratch the aluminium. Also scrape away the carbon from the surrounding lip of the cylinder wall. When all carbon has been removed, scrape away the grease which will now be contaminated with carbon particles, taking care not to press any into the bores. To assist prevention of carbon build-up the piston crown can be polished with a metal polish. Remove the rags or masking tape from the other two cylinders and turn the crankshaft so that the two pistons which were at the bottom are now at the top. Place rag in the cylinders which have been decarbonised, and proceed as just described.

10 Examine the head of the valves for pitting and burning, especially the heads of the exhaust valves. The valve seatings should be examined at the same time. If the pitting on the valve and seat is very slight, the marks can be removed by grinding the seats and valves together with coarse, and then fine, valve grinding paste.

11 Where bad pitting has occurred to the valve seats it will be necessary to recut them and fit new valves. This latter job should be entrusted to the local agent or engineering works. In practice it is very seldom that the seats are so badly worn. Normally it is the valve that is too badly worn for refitting, and the owner can easily purchase a new set of valves and match them to the seats by valve grinding.

12 Valve grinding is carried out as follows. Smear a trace of coarse carborundum paste on the seat face and apply a suction grinder tool to the valve head. With a semi-rotary motion, grind the valve head to its seat, lifting the valve occasionally to redistribute the grinding paste. When a dull matt even surface is produced on both the valve seat and the valve, wipe off the paste and repeat the process with fine carborundum paste, lifting and turning the valve to redistribute the paste as before. A light spring placed under the valve head will greatly ease this operation. When a smooth unbroken ring of light grey matt finish is produced, on both valve and valve seat faces, the grinding operation is complete. Carefully clean away every trace of grinding compound, take great care to leave none in the ports or in the valve guides. Clean the valve seats with a paraffin soaked rag, then with a clean rag, and finally, if an air line is available, blow the valves, valve guides and valve ports clean.

13 Check that all valve springs are intact. If any one is broken, all should be renewed. Check the free height of the springs against new ones. If some springs are not within specifications, replace them all. Springs suffer from fatigue and it is a good idea to renew them even if they look serviceable.

14 Check that the oil supply holes in the rocker arms are clear.

15 The cylinder head can be checked for warping either by placing it on a piece of plate glass or using a straight-edge and feeler blades. If there is any doubt or if its block face is corroded, have it re-faced by your dealer or motor engineering works.

16 Test the valves in their guides for side to side rock. If this is any more than almost imperceptible, new guides must be fitted. Again this is a job for your dealer as a special tool is required to ensure the correct installation depth and the cylinder head must be warmed to 80° C (176° F) before fitting the guides.

17 Commence reassembly by oiling the stem of the first valve and pushing it into its guide which should have been fitted with a new oil seal (photos).

18 Fit the spring seat. Fit the valve spring so that the closer coils are towards the cylinder head and then fit the spring retaining cap.

19 Compress the valve spring and locate the split cotters in the valve stem cut-out (photo).

20 Gently release the compressor, checking to see that the collets are not displaced.

21 Fit the remaining valves in the same way.

22 Tap the end of each valve stem with a plastic or copper-faced hammer to settle the components.

23 The cylinder head is now ready for refitting as described in Section 7.

17.17A Valve stem oil seal

17.17B Inserting a valve into its guide

17.19 Fitting split collets

## 18 Examination and renovation

1  With the engine stripped down and all parts thoroughly clean, it is now time to examine everything for wear. The following items should be checked and where necessary renewed or renovated as described in the following Sections.

### Cylinder block and crankcase

2  Examine the casting carefully for cracks especially around the bolt holes and between cylinders.
3  The cylinder bores must be checked for taper, ovality, scoring and scratching. Start by examining the top of the cylinder bores. If they are at all worn, a ridge will be felt on the thrust side. This ridge marks the limit of piston ring travel. The owner will have a good indication of bore wear prior to dismantling by the quantity of oil consumed and the emission of blue smoke from the exhaust especially when the engine is cold.
4  An internal micrometer or dial gauge can be used to check bore wear and taper against the Specifications, but this is a pointless operation if the engine is obviously in need of reboring due to excessive oil consumption.
5  Your engine reconditioner will be able to re-bore the block for you and supply the correct oversize pistons to give the correct running clearance.
6  If the engine has reached the limit for reboring then cylinder liners can be fitted, but here again this is a job for your engine reconditioner.
7  To rectify minor bore wear it is possible to fit proprietary oil control rings. A good way to test the condition of the engine is to have it at normal operating temperature with the spark plugs removed. Screw a compression gauge (available from most motor accessory stores) into the first plug hole. Hold the accelerator fully depressed and crank the engine on the starter motor for several revolutions. Record the reading. Zero the tester and check the remaining cylinders in the same way. All four compression figures should be approximately equal and within the tolerance given in the Specifications. If they are all low, suspect piston ring or cylinder bore wear. If only one reading is down, suspect a valve not seating.

### Crankshaft and bearings

8  Examine the crankpin and main journal surfaces for signs of scoring or scratches. Check the ovality of the crankpins at different positions with a micrometer. If more than 0.001 inch (0.025 mm) out of round, the crankpins will have to be reground. They will also have to be reground if there are any scores or scratches present. Also check the journals in the same fashion.

Fig. 1.25 Checking a crankpin (Sec 18)

9  Wear in a crankshaft can be detected while the engine is running. Big-end bearing and crankpin wear is indicated by distinct metallic knocking, particularly noticeable when the engine is pulling from low engine speeds. Low oil pressure will also occur.
10  Main bearing and journal wear is indicated by engine rumble increasing in severity as the engine speed increases. Low oil pressure will again be an associated condition.
11  Crankshaft grinding should be carried out by specialist engine reconditioners who will supply the matching undersize bearing shells to give the required running clearance.
12  Inspect the connecting rod big-end and main bearing shells for signs of general wear, scoring, pitting and scratching. The bearings should be matt grey in colour.
13  If a copper colour is evident, then the bearings are badly worn and the surface material has worn away to expose the underlay. Renew the bearings as a complete set.

14 At the time of major overhaul it is worthwhile renewing the bearing shells as a matter of routine even if they appear to be in reasonably good condition.

15 Bearing shells can be identified by the marking on the back of the shell. Standard sized shells are usually marked STD or 0.00. Undersized shells are marked with the undersize such as 0.25 mm.

### Connecting rods

16 Check the alignment of the connecting rods visually. If you suspect distortion, have them checked by your dealer or engine reconditioner on the special jig which he will have.

17 The gudgeon pin is an interference fit in the connecting rod small-end and removal or refitting and changing a piston is a job best left to your dealer or engine reconditioner due to the need for a press and jig and careful heating of the connecting rod.

18.20 Using feeler blades to fit piston rings

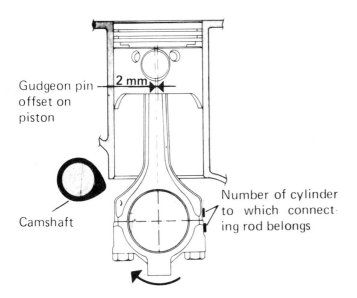

**Fig. 1.26 Piston/connecting rod relationship (Sec 18)**

18.22 Piston ring marking

### Pistons and piston rings

18 If the cylinders have been rebored, then the reconditioner will supply the oversize pistons and rings and the gudgeon pins. Give the job of fitting the new pistons to the connecting rods to him.

19 If the original piston rings or just new rings are to be fitted to the original pistons, use great care to remove and fit the rings as they are easily broken if expanded too much. Always remove and fit rings from the crown end.

20 If three old feeler blades are slid behind the piston rings and located at equidistant points, the rings may be removed or fitted without their dropping into the wrong grooves and will reduce the chance of breakage (photo).

21 If the original pistons are being refitted, make sure that the ring grooves and their oil return holes are cleaned out and freed from carbon. A piece of piston ring is a useful tool for this purpose.

22 The three pistons rings are as follows:

*Top* – Thinner compression, marked TOP
*Second* – Thicker compression, step at base
*Bottom* – Oil control (photo)

23 If proprietary wear control rings are to be fitted to overcome bore wear, fit them strictly in accordance with the manufacturer's instructions.

24 Always check the piston ring groove clearance and end gap. Both clearances should be checked with a feeler gauge. Check the end gap when the ring has been pushed squarely down the cylinder bore for two or three inches (photos).

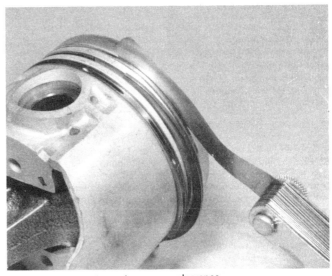

18.24A Checking piston ring groove clearance

18.24B Checking piston ring end gap

18.32 Camshaft bearing

25 If new rings are being used and the cylinder bores have not been rebored, always make sure that the top compression ring has been stepped to prevent it contacting the bore wear ridge.

### Flywheel

26 Check the clutch mating surface of the flywheel. If it is deeply scored (due to failure to renew a worn driven plate) then it may be possible to have it surface ground provided the thickness of the flywheel is not reduced too much.
27 If lots of tiny cracks are visible on the surface of the flywheel then this will be due to overheating caused by slipping the clutch or 'riding' the clutch pedal.
28 With a pre-engaged type of starter motor it is rare to find the teeth of the flywheel ring gear damaged or worn but if they are, then the ring gear will have to be renewed.
29 To remove the ring gear, drill a hole between the roots of two teeth taking care not to damage the flywheel and then split the ring with a sharp cold chisel.
30 The new ring gear must be heated to between 180 and 220°C (356 and 428°F) which is very hot, so if you do not have facilities for obtaining these temperatures, leave the job to your dealer or engine reconditioner.
31 Where such facilities are available, then the ring gear should be either pressed or lightly tapped gently onto its register and left to cool naturally, when the contraction of the metal on cooling will ensure that it is a secure and permanent fit. Great care must be taken not to overheat the ring gear, as if this happens its temper will be lost. A clutch input shaft pilot bearing is not fitted on this engine.

### Camshaft

32 Examine the camshaft bearings for wear, scoring or pitting. If evident then the bearings will have to be renewed. The three bearings are of different sizes and they can be removed and new ones fitted using a bolt, nut and distance pieces. When drawing a new bearing into position, make sure that the oil hole is correctly aligned with the one in the crankcase. The centre and rear bearings require reaming after fitting, the bearing at the timing chain end is supplied ready reamed (photo).
33 The camshaft itself should show no marks or scoring on the journal or cam lobe surfaces. Where evident, renew the camshaft or have it reprofiled by a specialist reconditioner.
34 Check the teeth of the camshaft sprocket for wear. Renew the sprocket if necessary.

### Cam followers

35 Examine the bearing surface of the cam followers which are in contact with the camshaft. Any indentations or cracks must be rectified by renewal. Clean sludge and dirt from the cam followers and check their fit in their bores. Side to side rock is unusual except at very high mileage.

### Timing chain

36 Examine the teeth on both the crankshaft sprocket and the camshaft sprocket for wear. Each tooth forms an inverted 'V' with the sprocket periphery and if worn, the side of each tooth under tension will be slightly concave in shape when compared with the other side of the tooth, ie; one side of the inverted 'V' will be concave when compared with the other. If any sign of wear is present the sprockets must be renewed.
37 Examine the links of the chain for side slackness and particularly check the self-tensioning links for freedom of movement. Renew the chain if any slackness is noticeable when compared with a new chain. It is a sensible precaution to renew the chain at about 60 000 miles (96 000 km) and at a lesser mileage if the engine is stripped down for a major overhaul.

### Cylinder head

38 This is covered in Section 17.

### Rockers and rocker shaft

39 Thoroughly clean out the rocker shaft. As it acts as the oil passages for the valve gear, clean out the oil holes and make sure they are quite clear. Check the shaft for straightness by rolling it on a flat surface. If it is distorted, renew it.
40 The surface of the shaft should be free from any wear ridges caused by the rocker arms. If it is not, the shaft will have to be renewed. Blocked shaft oil holes often contribute to such wear.
41 Check the rocker arms for wear of the rocker bushes, for wear at the rocker arm face which bears on the valve stem, and for wear of the adjusting ball ended screws. Wear in the rocker arm bush can be checked by gripping the rocker arm tip and holding the rocker arm in place on the shaft, noting if there is any lateral rocker arm shake. If any shake is present, and the arm is very loose on the shaft, remedial action must be taken. It is recommended that a worn rocker arm be taken to your local FIAT agent or automobile engineering works to have the old bush drawn out and a new bush fitted (photo).
42 Check the tip of the rocker arm where it bears on the valve head, for cracking or serious wear on the case hardening. If none is present the rocker arm may be refitted. Check the pushrods for straightness by rolling them on a flat surface.

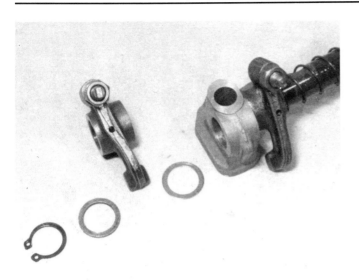

18.41 Rocker components

### Oil pump

43 Unscrew the four securing bolts which connect the two halves of the pump body.

44 Clean all the components in a bath of paraffin and dry them.

45 Inspect the gears for wear or damage and then check for wear in the following way.

46 Insert a feeler blade between the tooth peak and the body. This should be between 0.05 and 0.14 mm (0.0019 and 0.0055 in).

47 Now place a straight-edge across the body flange and check for gear endfloat. This should be between 0.020 and 0.105 mm (0.0008 and 0.0041 in). Where the clearances exceed the specified limits, renew the pump.

48 Check that the oil pressure relief valve spring is in good condition and not deformed.

### Oil seals and gaskets

49 It is recommended that all gaskets and oil seals are renewed at major engine overhaul. Sockets are useful for removing or refitting oil seals. An arrow is moulded onto some seals to indicate the rotational direction of the component which it serves. Make sure that the seal is fitted the correct way round to comply with the arrow.

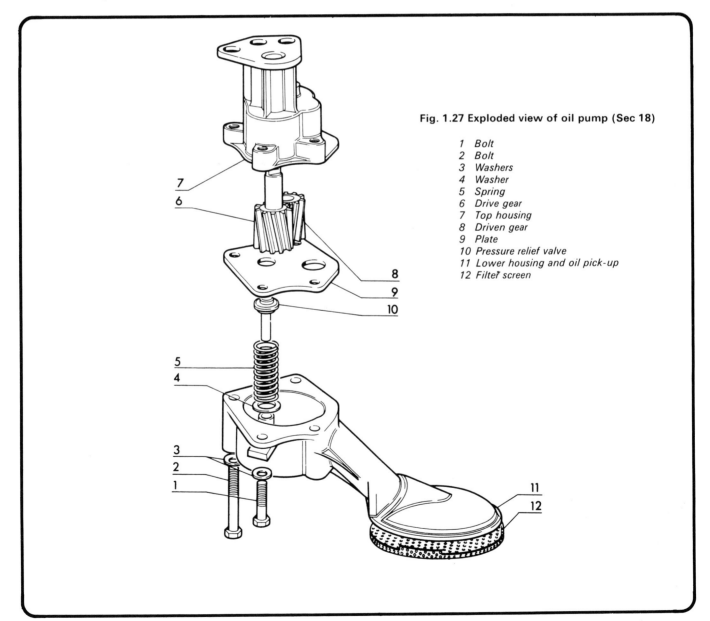

**Fig. 1.27 Exploded view of oil pump (Sec 18)**

1 Bolt
2 Bolt
3 Washers
4 Washer
5 Spring
6 Drive gear
7 Top housing
8 Driven gear
9 Plate
10 Pressure relief valve
11 Lower housing and oil pick-up
12 Filter screen

## 19 Engine – reassembly (general)

1 To ensure maximum life with minimum trouble from a rebuilt engine, not only must every part be correctly assembled, but everything must be spotlessly clean, all the oilways must be clear, locking washers and spring washers must always be fitted where indicated and all bearing and other working surfaces must be thoroughly lubricated during assembly. Before assembly begins renew any bolts or studs whose threads are in any way damaged; whenever possible use new spring washers.

2 Apart from your normal tools, a supply of non-fluffy rag, an oil can filled with engine oil, a supply of new spring washers, a set of new gaskets and a torque wrench should be gathered together.

## 20 Engine – complete reassembly

### Crankshaft and main bearings

1 With the cylinder block inverted on the bench, wipe out the crankcase shell bearing seats and fit the half shells so that their tabs engage in the notches (photo).

2 Stick the semi-circular thrust washers either side of the centre bearing in the crankcase using thick grease. Make sure that the oil grooves are visible when the washers are fitted (photo).

3 If the original bearing shells are being refitted, make sure that they are returned to their original positions.

4 Liberally oil the bearing shells and lower the crankshaft into position. Make sure that it is the correct way round (photos).

5 Wipe out the main bearing caps and fit the bearing shells into them.

6 Oil the crankshaft journals and fit the main bearing caps, the correct way round and in proper sequence (photo).

7 Replace the main bearing cap bolts and screw them up finger-tight.

8 Test the crankshaft for freedom of rotation. Should it be very stiff to turn, or possess high spots, a most careful inspection must be made, preferably by a skilled mechanic with a micrometer to trace the cause of the trouble. It is very seldom that any trouble of this nature will be experienced when fitting the crankshaft.

9 Tighten the main bearing bolts to the specified torque wrench settings (photo).

10 Using a dial gauge or feeler blades inserted between a thrust washer and the crankshaft, check the crankshaft endfloat. If it exceeds the specified limit, the thrust washers can be changed for thicker ones (photo).

11 Bolt on the crankshaft rear oil seal carrier using a new gasket. The carrier should have been fitted with a new oil seal and the seal lips greased (photos).

12 Fit the engine rear plate (photo).

20.2 Crankshaft thrust washer

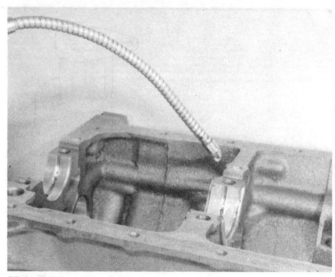

20.4A Oiling main bearing shells

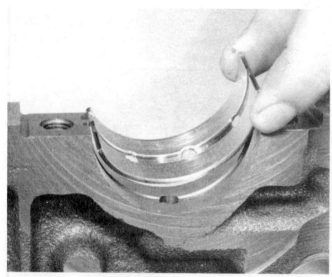

20.1 Fitting a main bearing shell

20.4B Lowering crankshaft into position

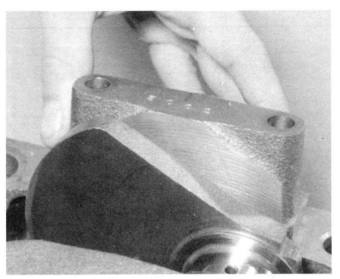

20.6 Fitting a main bearing cap

20.9 Tightening main bearing cap bolts

20.10 Checking crankshaft end float

20.11A Crankshaft rear oil seal carrier and gasket

20.11B Crankshaft oil seal and carrier fitted

20.12 Engine rear plate

*Flywheel*

13 Offer the flywheel to the crankshaft. With pistons No. 1 and 4 at TDC, the dimple on the flywheel must be uppermost.

14 Screw in and tighten the bolts to the specified torque. The crankshaft may be held against rotation by either jamming the starter ring gear or placing a block of wood between one of the crankshaft webs and the inside of the crankcase (photo).

20.16A Fitting camshaft

20.14 Tightening flywheel bolts

20.16B Camshaft front bearing

*Camshaft*

15 Oil the cam followers and return them to their original positions (photo).

16 Oil the camshaft bearings and insert the camshaft, taking great care not to damage the bearings with the cam lobes. Fit the front bearing, chamfer inwards (photos).

17 Screw in the camshaft front bearing lockscrew (photo).

*Oil pump*

18 Refit the oil pump as described in Section 10.

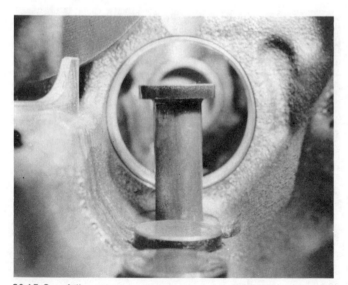

20.15 Cam followers

20.17 Camshaft front bearing lockscrew

## Timing chain and sprockets

19 Fit the timing chain and sprockets as described in Section 6. Fit the Woodruff key to the crankshaft nose.

20 Using a new gasket, fit the timing chain cover, but leave the bolts finger tight (photo).

21 Apply grease to the lips of the timing cover oil seal and then push the crankshaft pulley into position.

22 Move the timing cover if necessary so that the pulley hub is centralised in the oil seal and then tighten the cover bolts.

23 Screw on the crankshaft pulley nut and tighten to the specified torque. Hold the crankshaft against rotation either by jamming the starter ring gear or by placing a block of wood between a crankshaft web and the inside of the crankcase (photo).

20.20 Timing cover

20.23 Tightening crankshaft pulley nut

## Piston/connecting rods

24 Fit these as described in Section 9.

## Sump pan

25 Fit the sump pan as described in Section 8.

## Cylinder head

26 Stand the engine upright and fit the cylinder head as described in Section 7.

27 Insert the pushrods in their original fitted order.

28 With the rocker arm adjuster screws fully unscrewed, locate the rocker gear and screw on the fixing nuts.

29 Adjust the valve clearances as described in Section 5.

30 Locate a new gasket in position and fit the rocker cover (photo).

31 Screw on a new oil filter (Section 2).

20.30 Rocker cover nut and thrust plate

## 21 Engine – refitting ancillary components

1 Refer to Chapter 5 and refit the clutch, making sure to centralise the driven plate.

2 Fit the coolant pump as described in Chapter 2. Fit the thermostat housing if it was removed noting the air cleaner mounting bracket on the housing studs.

3 Fit the alternator and drivebelt as described in Chapter 9.

4 Refer to Chapter 3 and fit the exhaust manifold and hot air collector, the carburettor and spacer and the fuel pump.

5 Fit the distributor as described in Chapter 4. Fit the oil dipstick guide tube (photos).

21.5A Dipstick guide tube

21.5B Dipstick guide tube support

## 22 Engine/transmission – reconnection

1 Support the weight of the transmission and offer it squarely to the engine. The splined input shaft should pass easily through the hub of the driven plate, provided the plate has been centralised as described in Chapter 5. It may be necessary to align the splines with the hub grooves, in which case have an assistant turn the crankshaft pulley nut. The alignment dowels will make the connection stiff, so drawing the engine and transmission together with two connecting bolts will ease it.
2 Once the engine and transmission are fully engaged, insert and tighten all the connecting bolts. Locate the lifting eyes.
3 Bolt on the flywheel housing cover plate and the mounting brackets.
4 Bolt on the starter motor.

## 23 Engine/transmission – refitting

1 The refitting operations are reversals of those described in Section 13.

2 Observe the following special points.
3 Tighten the engine mounting and front suspension (disconnected) bolts to the specified torque when the hoist has been removed and the weight of the car is again on its roadwheels.
4 Fill the cooling system.
5 Fill the engine with oil.
6 Replenish lost transmission oil.
7 Reconnect the battery.
8 Adjust the clutch pedal as described in Chapter 5.

## 24 Engine – initial start-up after overhaul or major repair

1 Make sure that the battery is fully charged and that all lubricants, coolant and fuel are replenished.
2 If the fuel system has been dismantled it will require several revolutions of the engine on the starter motor to pump the petrol up to the carburettor.
3 Turn the carburettor throttle speed screw through one complete turn to increase the idle speed in order to offset the initial stiffness of new engine internal components.
4 As soon as the engine fires and runs, keep it going at a fast idle speed and bring it up to normal working temperature.
5 As the engine warms up there will be odd smells and some smoke from parts getting hot and burning off oil deposits. The signs to look for are leaks of water or oil which will be obvious.
6 Check also the exhaust pipe and manifold connections as these do not always 'find' their exact gas tight position until the warmth and vibration have acted on them and it is almost certain that they will need tightening further. This should be done, of course, with the engine stopped.
7 When normal running temperature has been reached, adjust the engine idle speed as described in Chapter 3.
8 Stop the engine and wait a few minutes to see if any lubricant or coolant is dripping out when the engine is stationary.
9 Road test the car to check that the timing is correct and that the engine is giving the necessary smoothness and power. Do not race the engine – if new bearings and/or pistons have been fitted it should be treated as a new engine and run in at a reduced speed for the first 500 km (300 miles).
10 After the first 1500 km (900 miles) the cylinder head bolts must be re-torqued in the following way (engine cold).
11 Remove the air cleaner and rocker cover. Unscrew the first bolt (Fig. 1.7) through a quarter turn and then tighten it to final stage 2 torque (see Specifications).
12 Repeat on the remaining bolts, one at a time.
13 Check and adjust the valve clearances (Section 5).
14 Refit the rocker cover and air cleaner.

## 25 Fault diagnosis – 903 cc (ohv) engine

| Symptom | Reason(s) |
| --- | --- |
| **Engine fails to turn when starter control operated** | |
| No current at starter motor | Flat or defective battery |
| | Loose battery leads |
| | Defective starter solenoid or switch or broken wiring |
| | Engine earth strap disconnected |
| | |
| Current at starter motor | Jammed starter motor drive pinion |
| | Defective starter motor |
| | |
| **Engine turns but will not start** | |
| No spark at spark plug | Ignition leads or distributor cap damp or wet |
| | Ignition leads to spark plugs loose |
| | Shorted or disconnected low tension leads |
| | Dirty, incorrectly set, or pitted contact breaker points |
| | Faulty condenser |
| | Defective ignition switch |
| | Ignition leads connected wrong way round |
| | Faulty coil |
| | Contact breaker point spring earthed or broken |

| Symptom | Reason(s) |
| --- | --- |
| No fuel at carburettor float chamber or at jets | No petrol in petrol tank<br>Vapour lock in fuel line (in hot conditions or at high altitude)<br>Blocked float chamber needle valve<br>Fuel pump filter blocked<br>Choked or blocked carburettor jets<br>Faulty fuel pump |
| **Engine stalls and will not restart**<br>Excess of petrol in cylinder or carburettor flooding | Too much choke allowing too rich a mixture to wet plugs<br>Float damaged or leaking or needle not seating<br>Float lever incorrectly adjusted |
| No spark at spark plug | Ignition failure – sudden<br>Ignition failure – misfiring precedes total stoppage<br>Ignition failure – in severe rain or after traversing water splash |
| No fuel at jets | No petrol in petrol tank<br>Petrol tank breather choked<br>Sudden obstruction in carburettor<br>Water in fuel system |
| **Engine misfires or idles unevenly**<br>Intermittent spark at spark plug | Ignition leads loose<br>Battery leads loose on terminals<br>Battery earth strap loose on body attachment point<br>Engine earth lead loose<br>Low tension leads on coil loose<br>Low tension lead to distributor loose<br>Dirty or incorrectly gapped plugs<br>Dirty, incorrectly set, or pitted contact breaker points<br>Tracking across inside of distributor cover<br>Ignition too retarded<br>Faulty coil |
| Fuel shortage at engine | Mixture too weak<br>Air leak in carburettor<br>Air leak at inlet manifold to cylinder head, or inlet manifold to carburettor |
| **Lack of power and poor compression**<br>Mechanical wear | Burnt out valves<br>Sticking or leaking valves<br>Weak or broken valve springs<br>Worn valve guides or stems<br>Worn pistons and piston rings |
| Fuel/air mixture leaking from cylinder | Burnt out exhaust valves<br>Sticking or leaking valves<br>Worn valve guides and stems<br>Weak or broken valve springs<br>Blown cylinder head gasket (accompanied by increase in noise)<br>Worn pistons and piston rings<br>Worn or scored cylinder bore |
| Incorrect adjustments | Ignition timing wrongly set<br>Contact breaker points incorrectly gapped<br>Incorrect valve clearances<br>Incorrectly set spark plugs<br>Carburation too rich or too weak |
| Carburation and ignition faults | Dirty contact breaker points<br>Fuel filter blocked<br>Air filter blocked<br>Distributor automatic advance and retard mechanisms not functioning correctly<br>Faulty fuel pump giving top and fuel starvation |
| **Excessive oil consumption** | Excessively worn valve stems and valve guides<br>Worn piston rings<br>Worn pistons and cylinder bores<br>Excessive piston ring gap allowing blow-by<br>Piston oil return holes choked |

| Symptom | Reason(s) |
|---|---|
| **Oil being lost due to leaks** | Leaking oil filter gasket<br>Leaking rocker cover gasket<br>Leaking timing gear cover gasket<br>Leaking sump gasket<br>Loose sump plug |
| **Unusual noises from engine**<br>Excessive clearances due to mechanical wear | Worn valve gear (noisy tapping from rocker box)<br>Worn big-end bearing (regular heavy knocking)<br>Worn timing chain and gears (rattling from front of engine)<br>Worn main bearings (rumbling and vibration)<br>Worn crankshaft (knocking, rumbling and vibration) |
| Pinking on acceleration | Fuel octane rating too low<br>Ignition timing over-advanced<br>Carbon build-up in cylinder head<br>Valve timing incorrect (after rebuild)<br>Mixture too weak<br>Overheating |

## PART 3 – 1116 CC AND 1301 CC ENGINES

### 26 Valve clearances – checking and adjusting

*This should only be required if the valves have been renewed or ground in, or at high mileages when noise or poor engine performance indicates that a check is necessary.*

*It is important that each valve clearance is set correct, otherwise the timing will be wrong and engine performance poor. If there is no clearance at all, the valve and its seat will soon burn. Always set the clearances with the engine cold.*

1 Remove the camshaft cover. Jack-up a front wheel and engage top gear so that by turning the wheel, the crankshaft can be rotated.
2 Each valve clearance must be checked when the high point of the cam is pointing directly upward away from the cam follower.
3 Check the clearances in the firing order 1-3-4-2, No 1 cylinder being at the timing belt end of the engine. This will minimise the amount of crankshaft rotation required.
4 Insert the appropriate feeler blade between the heel of the cam and the cam follower shim of the first valve. If necessary alter the thickness of the feeler blade until it is a stiff, sliding fit. Record the thickness, which will, of course, represent the valve clearance for this particular valve (photo).

5 Turn the crankshaft, check the second valve clearance and record it.
6 Repeat the operations on all the remaining valves, recording their respective clearances.
7 Remember that the clearance for inlet and exhaust valves differs – see Specifications. Counting from the timing cover end of the engine, the valve sequence is:

| | |
|---|---|
| *Inlet* | 2-3-6-7 |
| *Exhaust* | 1-4-5-8 |

8 Clearances which are incorrect will mean the particular shim will have to be changed. To remove the shim, turn the crankshaft until the high point of the cam is pointing directly upward. The cam follower will now have to be depressed so that the shim can be extracted. Special tools (A60642 and A87001) are available from your Fiat dealer to do the job, otherwise you will have to make up a forked lever to locate on the rim of the cam follower. This must allow room for the shim to be prised out by means of the cut-outs provided in the cam follower rim (photo).
9 Once the shim is extracted, establish its thickness and change it for a thicker or thinner one to bring the previously recorded clearance within specification. For example, if the measured valve clearance was 1.27 mm (0.05 in) too great, a shim *thicker* by this amount will be required. Conversely, if the clearance was 1.27 mm (0.05 in) too small, a shim *thinner* by this amount will be required.
10 Shims have their thickness (mm) engraved on them; although the engraved side should be fitted so as not to be visible, wear still occurs

26.4 Checking a valve clearance

26.8 Removing a shim from a cam follower

26.10 Shim engraved mark

and often obliterates the number. In this case, measuring their thickness with a metric micrometer is the only method to establish their thickness (photo).

11 In practice, if several shims have to be changed, they can often be interchanged, so avoiding the necessity of having to buy more new shims than is necessary.

12 If more than two or three valve clearances are found to be incorrect, it will be more convenient to remove the camshaft carrier for easier removal of the shims.

13 Where no clearance can be measured, even with the thinnest available shim in position, the valve will have to be removed and the end of its stem ground off squarely. This will reduce its overall length by the minimum amount to provide a clearance. This job should be entrusted to your dealer as it is important to keep the end of the valve stem square.

14 On completion, refit the camshaft cover and gasket.

## 27 Camshaft and camshaft carrier – removal and refitting

1 Disconnect the battery.
2 Remove the air cleaner (see Chapter 3).
3 Disconnect the fuel filter hose from the fuel pump and tie it back, out of the way.
4 Identify and then disconnect any electrical leads which must be moved away to enable the camshaft cover to be withdrawn.
5 Identify and disconnect any vacuum hoses which must be moved away to enable the camshaft cover to be withdrawn.
6 Unscrew the securing nuts and remove the camshaft cover.
7 Turn the crankshaft pulley nut until No. 4 piston is at TDC. This can be established as described in Section 28.
8 Unbolt and remove the timing belt cover.
9 Check that the timing mark on the camshaft sprocket is aligned with, and adjacent to the pointer on the timing belt cover backplate.
10 Restrain the timing belt with the hand and release but do not remove the camshaft sprocket bolt. Release the belt tensioner pulley by slackening the pulley centre nut. Push the timing belt evenly from the sprockets, noting which way round the belt is fitted if it is to be completely removed. The lettering on the belt is normally legible from the crankshaft pulley end of the engine when the belt is as originally fitted.
11 Unbolt the camshaft carrier and lift it sufficiently from the cylinder head to break the seal of the mating faces. **Note:** *It is important not to allow the cam followers to fall out;* they must be retained in their original locations. This can be done if the carrier is raised very slowly, until the fingers can be inserted to prise the cam followers onto their respective valve spring retainers. It is unlikely that the valve clearance adjusting shims will be displaced from their recesses in the cam followers because of the suction of the lubricating oil, but watch that

this does not happen; the shims must also be retained in their originally fitted sequence.

12 Remove the previously loosened camshaft sprocket bolt and take the sprocket from the camshaft.

13 Unbolt and remove the camshaft end cover with its gasket. Withdraw the camshaft (photos).

14 Refitting is a reversal of the removal process, but observe the following points.

15 Use new gaskets.

16 Retain the cam followers and shims in their bores in the camshaft carrier with thick grease; they must not be allowed to drop out when the carrier is lowered onto the cylinder head.

17 If the crankshaft or camshaft have been moved from their set positions, re-align the sprocket timing mark with the pointer on the belt cover and the crankshaft pulley or flywheel with the TDC mark. This must be observed otherwise the valves may impinge upon the piston crowns when the camshaft lobes compress any of the valve springs during bolting down of the carrier.

18 Screw in the carrier bolts and tighten them to the specified torque (photo).

19 Refit and tension the timing belt as described in Section 28.

20 Refit the camshaft cover and gasket.

21 Refit the hose and air cleaner.

22 Reconnect the battery.

27.13A Removing camshaft end cover

27.13B Withdrawing camshaft from carrier

27.18 Tightening a camshaft carrier bolt

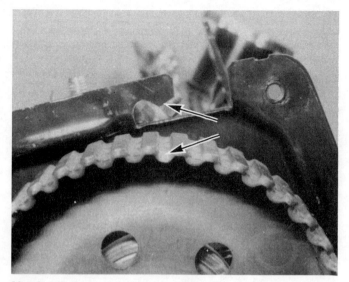

28.4 Camshaft sprocket alignment marks

## 28 Timing belt – renewal

1   Set No. 4 piston at TDC. Do this by turning the crankshaft pulley nut or by jacking up a front roadwheel, engaging a gear and turning the wheel until the mark on the flywheel is opposite to the TDC mark on the flywheel bellhousing aperture. Remove No. 4 spark plug, place a finger over the plug hole and feel the compression being generated as the crankshaft is rotated and the piston rises up the cylinder bore.

2   On some models the TDC marks on the crankshaft pulley and belt cover may be visible and can be used instead.

3   Remove the alternator drivebelt (Chapter 2, Section 8). Unbolt and remove the timing belt cover.

4   Check that the timing mark on the camshaft sprocket is aligned with the pointer on the belt cover backing plate (photo).

5   Slacken the nut in the centre of the tensioner pulley and push in on the support to release the tension on the belt, then retighten the nut. Slide the drivebelt off the pulleys.

6   Check that the crankshaft and camshaft pulleys have not been moved from their previously aligned positions.

7   To check that the auxiliary shaft sprocket has not moved, take off the distributor cap and check that the contact end of the rotor arm is aligned with No. 4 HT lead contact in the cap.

8   Fit the new belt. Start at the crankshaft drive pulley and, taking care not to kink or strain the belt, slip it over the camshaft pulley. The camshaft may have to be turned slightly to mesh the pulley with the teeth on the belt. Fit the belt on the tensioner pulley last; if this is difficult, do not lever or force the belt on, recheck the belt (photo).

9   Release the tensioner nut and rotate the crankshaft through two complete revolutions. Retighten the nut. The belt tension may be checked by twisting it through 90° with the finger and thumb. It should just turn through this angle without undue force.

**Note:** *The above procedure serves only as a rough guide to setting the belt tension – having it checked by a FIAT dealer at the earliest opportunity is recommended.*

10   Refit the timing belt cover (photo). Fit and tension the alternator drivebelt (Chapter 2, Section 8).

Fig. 1.28 TDC marks at front of engine (Sec 28)

28.8 Slipping timing belt onto tensioner pulley

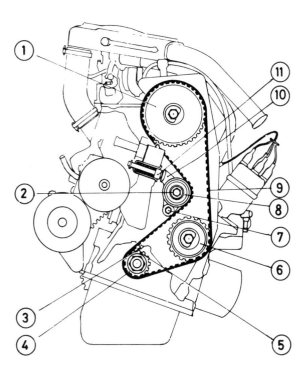

**Fig. 1.29 Timing belt arrangement (Sec 28)**

1  Camshaft sprocket
2  Tensioner pulley locknut
3  Timing mark on crankshaft front oil seal retainer
4  Crankshaft sprocket
5  Crankshaft sprocket timing mark

6  Auxiliary shaft sprocket
7  Tensioner bracket bolt
8  Tensioner pulley
9  Timing belt
10  Tensioner bracket
11  Tensioner spring

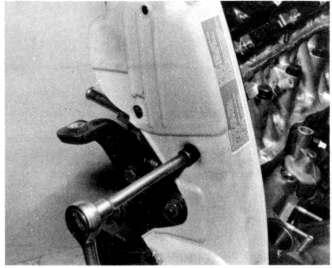

28.10 Tightening timing belt cover nut

## 29 Cylinder head – removal and refitting

1  Drain the cooling system (see Chapter 2).
2  Disconnect the battery.
3  Disconnect and plug the carburettor fuel hoses.

4  Disconnect the throttle and choke linkage from the carburettor.
5  Disconnect the HT leads from the spark plugs.
6  Disconnect the brake servo vacuum hose from the intake manifold.
7  Disconnect the coolant hoses from the thermostat housing.
8  Disconnect the crankcase ventilation system hoses from the rocker cover and carburettor.
9  Unbolt and remove the timing belt cover.
10  Release the timing belt tensioner pulley bolt, then lever the pulley against the spring plunger and retighten the bolt to retain the tensioner pulley in the non-tensioned position. Slip the belt from the camshaft sprocket.
11  Disconnect the coolant hoses from the carburettor and intake manifold.
12  Disconnect the exhaust downpipes from the manifold.
13  If a crowfoot type wrench is available, the cylinder head nuts and bolts can be removed and the complete cylinder head camshaft carrier assembly withdrawn (photo).

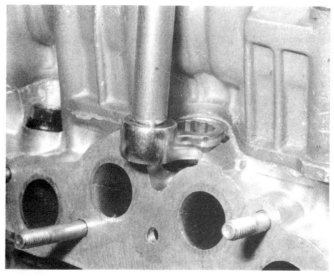

29.13 Using a crowfoot type wrench on a cylinder head bolt

14  If this type of wrench is not available however, remove the carrier first as described in Section 27.
15  If a crowfoot is available, unscrew the cylinder head nuts and bolts evenly and progressively starting with the centre ones and working towards both ends.
16  Rock the cylinder head by gripping the manifolds. **Note:** *Do not insert a lever in the gasket joint to prise the head from the block.*
17  Pull the head off the studs and remove it to the bench. Remove and discard the old cylinder head gasket.
18  Unbolt and remove the hot air collecting shield for the air cleaner from the exhaust manifold. The exhaust and inlet manifolds can now be unbolted. The carburettor may remain on the inlet manifold.
19  Overhaul and decarbonising of the cylinder head is described in Section 39.
20  Refitting is a reversal of the removal process, but make sure the crankshaft and camshaft timing marks are set as described in Section 28 to avoid the valve heads digging into the piston crowns when the head is refitted.
21  Always use new gaskets. The cylinder head gasket must be fitted (ALTO visible) so that the oil pressure hole in the block is central in the copper ringed cut-out in the gasket (photos). Make sure that the gasket surfaces on head and block are perfectly clean and free from oil, otherwise the heat sealing (polymerisation) process of the gasket cannot take place.
22  Tighten the cylinder head nuts and bolts to the specified torque, in the sequence shown in Fig. 1.30. Follow the procedure very carefully owing to the special type (ASTADUR) of gasket used which hardens in use. Always keep a new cylinder head gasket in its nylon cover until just before it is required for use.
23  Oil the cylinder head bolts and washers and allow them to drain for thirty minutes.

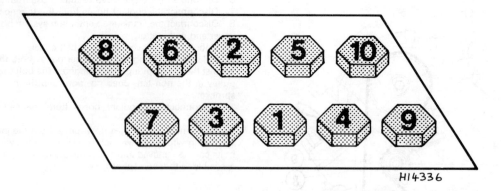

Fig. 1.30 Cylinder head bolt tightening sequence (Sec 29)

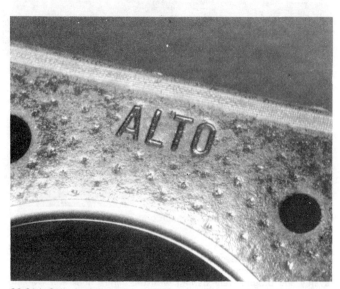

29.21A Cylinder head gasket top face marking

29.21B Cylinder head gasket in position – cylinder block drain plug arrowed

29.21C Lowering cylinder onto block

24  Tighten the bolts in the following stages:

| | |
|---|---|
| Stage 1 | 20 Nm (15 lbf ft) |
| Stage 2 | 40 Nm (30 lbf ft) |
| Stage 3 | Through 90° |
| Stage 4 | Through 90° (photo) |

Retightening the bolts after a running-in mileage is not required.
25  Fit the timing belt (Section 28).
26  Check the valve clearances (Section 26) after the camshaft carrier has been fitted (Section 27).
27  Bolt on the camshaft carrier cover.
28  Reconnect all hoses, leads and controls.
29  Reconnect the battery and refill the cooling system.

## 30  Sump pan – removal and refitting

1   Position the car over an inspection pit or raise the front wheels on ramps.
2   Disconnect the battery.
3   Drain the engine oil. Unbolt and remove the flywheel housing lower cover plate.
4   Unbolt the sump pan and remove it together with its gasket.
5   Refitting is a reversal of removal. Always use a new gasket locating

29.24 Tightening a cylinder head bolt through 90° using a protractor

30.5 Locating the sump pan gasket

31.3 Bolting on the oil pump

it on clean mating flanges and tighten the fixing bolts evenly and progressively (photo).

6    Fill the engine with oil and reconnect the battery.

## 31  Oil pump – removal and refitting

1    Remove the sump pan as described in the preceding Section.
2    Unbolt the oil pump and withdraw it complete with driveshaft.
3    Use a new gasket when refitting the pump and prime the pump by pouring engine oil through the pick-up filter screen (photo).

## 32  Pistons/connecting rod – removal and refitting

1    Remove the sump pan and the oil pump as described in Sections 30 and 31.
2    The big-end bearing shells can be renewed without having to remove the cylinder head if the caps are unbolted and the piston/connecting rod pushed gently about one inch up the bore (the crankpin being at its lowest point). If these shells are worn, however, the main bearing shells will almost certainly be worn as well. In this case, the engine should be removed for complete overhaul including crankshaft removal.
3    To remove the piston/connecting rods, remove the cylinder head as described in Section 29.
4    Grip the oil pick-up pipe and twist or rock it from its hole in the crankcase. It is an interference fit in the hole.
5    Unscrew the nuts from the big-end caps, then remove the caps with their bearing shells. The caps and their connecting rods are numbered 1, 2, 3 and 4 from the timing cover end of the engine. The numbers are adjacent at the big-end cap joint and on the side of the crankcase furthest from the auxiliary shaft.
6    If the bearing shells are to be used again, tape them to their respective big-end caps.
7    Push each connecting rod/piston assembly up the bore and out of the cylinder block. There is one reservation; if a wear ridge has developed at the top of the bores, remove this by careful scraping before trying to remove the piston/rod assemblies. The ridge will otherwise prevent removal or break the piston rings during the attempt.
8    If the connecting rod bearing shells are to be used again, tape the shells to their respective rods.
9    Dismantling the piston/connecting rod is described in Section 18.

### Refitting
10    Fit the new shells into the connecting rod and caps, ensuring the surfaces on which the shells seat, are clean and dry.
11    Check that the piston ring gaps are evenly spaced at 120° intervals. Liberally oil the rings and the cylinder bores.
12    Fit a piston ring clamp to compress the rings.
13    Insert the piston/connecting rod into the cylinder bore, checking that the rod assembly is correct for that particular bore. The cap and rod

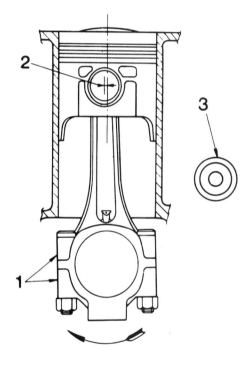

**Fig. 1.31 Piston/connecting rod assembly diagram (Sec 32)**

*1    Matching numbers*
*2    Gudgeon pin offset*
*3    Auxiliary shaft*
*Arrow indicates direction of rotation of crankshaft viewed from timing belt end*

matching numbers must be furthest away from the auxiliary shaft (Fig. 1.31).
14    Push the piston into the bore until the piston ring clamp is against the cylinder block and then tap the crown of the piston lightly to push it out of the ring clamp and into the bore (photo).
15    Oil the crankshaft journal and fit the big-end of the connecting rod to the journal. Fit the big-end cap and nuts, checking that the cap is the right way round (photo).
16    Tighten the big-end nuts to the specified torque. The correct torque is important as the nuts have no locking arrangement. After tightening each big-end, check the crankshaft rotates smoothly (photo).
17    Refit the oil pick-up pipe, the cylinder head, oil pump and sump pan, all as described earlier.
18    Refill the engine with oil and coolant.

32.14 Fitting piston into cylinder bore

32.15 Fitting a big-end cap

32.16 Tightening a big-end cap nut

## 33 Engine mountings – renewal

1 Three engine/transmission flexible mountings are used.
2 To renew a mounting, support the weight of the engine/transmission on a hoist or jack and unbolt and remove the mounting.
3 In the unlikely event of all three mountings requiring renewal at the same time, only disconnect them and renew them one at a time.

## 34 Engine – method of removal

1 The engine complete with transmission should be removed by lowering it to the floor and withdrawing it from under the front of the car which will have been raised to provide adequate clearance.

## 35 Engine/transmission – removal and separation

1 Open the bonnet, disconnect the windscreen washer tube.
2 Mark the hinge positions on the underside of the bonnet and then with the help of an assistant to support its weight unbolt and remove the bonnet to a safe place.
3 Disconnect the battery negative lead.
4 Drain the cooling system and the engine and transmission oils.
5 Remove the air cleaner.
6 From the rear of the alternator disconnect the electrical leads.
7 Disconnect the leads from the starter motor, oil pressure and coolant temperature switches, also the oil temperature switch.
8 Disconnect the LT lead from the distributor and the HT lead from the ignition coil.
9 Disconnect the clutch cable from the release lever at the transmission. Also disconnect the speedometer drive cable (knurled ring).
10 Pull the leads from the reversing lamp switch.
11 Disconnect all coolant hoses from the engine. Also disconnect the brake servo hose from the intake manifold.
12 Disconnect the choke and throttle controls from the carburettor.
13 Disconnect the inlet hose from the fuel pump and plug the hose.
14 Disconnect the fuel return hose from the carburettor.
15 Disconnect the coolant hoses from the carburettor throttle block.
16 Raise the front of the car and remove the front roadwheels.
17 Unscrew and remove the driveshaft to hub nuts. These are very tight and a long knuckle bar will be required when unscrewing them. Have an assistant apply the brake pedal hard to prevent the hub from turning.
18 Working under the car, remove the inner wing protective shields and then disconnect the exhaust downpipe from the manifold.
19 Disconnect the exhaust pipe sections by removing the socket clamp just forward of the rear axle beam. Remove the front section.
20 Disconnect the forward ends of the gearchange rods by prising their sockets from the ballstuds.
21 Unscrew the nuts on the steering tie-rod end balljoints and then

using a suitable 'splitter' tool, separate the balljoints from the steering arms.
22 Unbolt the front brake hose support clips from the suspension struts and then remove the bolts which secure the hub carriers to the U-clamps at the base of the suspension struts.
23 Pull the tops of the hub carriers down and then outwards and push the driveshafts from them.
24 Unbolt the driveshaft inboard boot retainers and then remove the driveshafts from the transmission.
25 Support the engine on a hoist or use a trolley jack under the engine/transmission. Remove the bottom mounting and then the upper left and right-hand ones.
26 Lower the power unit to the floor by pushing it to the left-hand side to clear the right-hand mounting bracket and then swivel the gearbox towards the rear of the car. Withdraw the engine/transmission from under the car.
27 External dirt and grease should now be removed using paraffin and a stiff brush or a water-soluble solvent.
28 Unbolt and remove the engine mounting brackets and the starter motor.
29 Unbolt and remove the cover plate with the gearchange ball stud strut from the lower front face of the flywheel housing.
30 With the engine resting squarely on its sump pan, unscrew the flywheel housing connecting bolts, noting the location of any lifting lugs and hose and wiring clips.
31 Support the weight of the transmission and withdraw it in a straight line from the engine.

## 36 Engine – dismantling (general)

Refer to Section 14, Part 2

## 37 Engine ancillary components – removal

Refer to Section 15, Part 2 and also remove the intake manifold.

## 38 Engine – complete dismantling

1 Have the engine resting squarely and supported securely on the work surface.
2 Unbolt and remove the timing belt cover.
3 Grip the now exposed timing belt with the hands and loosen the camshaft sprocket.
4 Release the timing belt tensioner pulley centre bolt, then slip the belt from the pulley and sprockets to remove it. Note which way round the belt is fitted, usually so that the lettering on the belt can be read from the crankshaft pulley end of the engine.
5 Remove the camshaft sprocket.
6 Unbolt and remove the camshaft timing belt cover backing plate.

7   Unbolt and remove the camshaft carrier cover.
8   Unbolt the camshaft carrier and lift it off very slowly, at the same time pushing the cam followers and their shims down with the fingers securely onto their respective valve springs. It is easy to remove the camshaft carrier too quickly with some of the cam followers stuck in it and as the carrier is lifted away, the cam followers will fall out. If this happens, the valve clearances will be upset as the cam followers and shims cannot be returned, with any certainty, to their original positions. Keep the cam followers and shims in their originally fitted order.
9   Unscrew and remove the cylinder head bolts and nuts, grip the manifold, rock the head and remove the complete cylinder head/manifold/carburettor assembly. Remove and discard the cylinder head gasket.
10  Unbolt the coolant pump from the side of the cylinder block and remove it complete with coolant distribution pipe. Remove the crankcase breather.
11  Remove the distributor/oil pump driveshaft. This is simply carried out by inserting a finger into the hole vacated by the distributor and wedging it in the hole in the end of the driveshaft. Lift the shaft out of mesh with the auxiliary shaft. Where the distributor is driven by the camshaft, a cover plate retains the oil pump driveshaft in position.
12  Unbolt and remove the sprocket from the end of the auxiliary shaft. The sprocket is held to the shaft with a Woodruff key.
13  Unbolt the auxiliary shaft retainer and withdraw the shaft from the crankcase.
14  Unscrew and remove the crankshaft pulley nut. This is very tight and the flywheel starter ring gear will have to be jammed with a cold chisel or a suitably bent piece of steel to prevent the crankshaft rotating.
15  Withdraw the crankshaft sprocket, which is located by the Woodruff key.
16  Unbolt the front engine mounting bracket from the cylinder block, together with the timing belt cover screw anchor bush. Unbolt and remove the timing belt tensioner pulley.
17  Unscrew the flywheel securing bolts. The starter ring gear will again have to be jammed to prevent the crankshaft rotating as the bolts

are unscrewed. Mark the flywheel position in relation to the crankshaft mounting flange, then remove it.
18  Unbolt the front and rear crankshaft oil seal retainer bolts from the crankcase and the sump. Remove the oil seal retainers.
19  Turn the engine on its side, extract the remaining sump bolts and remove the sump. If it is stuck, try tapping it gently with a soft-faced hammer. If this fails, cut all round the sump-to-gasket flange with a sharp knife. Do not try prising with a large screwdriver; this will only distort the sump mating flange.
20  With the sump removed, unbolt and remove the oil pump.
21  Grip the oil pick-up pipe and twist or rock it from its hole in the crankcase. It is an interference fit in the hole.
22  Remove the piston/connecting rods as described in Section 32.
23  Before unbolting the main bearing caps, note that they are marked with one, two, three or four notches. No 5 main bearing cap is unmarked. Note that the notches are nearer the auxiliary shaft side.
24  Unbolt and remove the main bearing caps. If the bearing shells are to be used again, tape them to their respective caps. The bearing shell at the centre position is plain, the others have a lubricating groove.
25  Carefully, lift the crankshaft from the crankcase, noting the thrust washers at No 5 main bearing. These control the crankshaft endfloat.

## 39 Cylinder head – dismantling and decarbonising

1   The operations are similar to those described for the ohv engine in Section 17 in respect of decarbonising and valve grinding.
2   To remove a valve, use a valve spring compressor to compress the first valve and then extract the split collets (photo).
3   Release the valve spring compressor.
4   Withdraw the valve spring cap and the double valve springs (photos).
5   Remove the valve (photo).
6   Remove the spring seat (photo).
7   Discard the valve stem oil seal and fit a new one (photo).

39.2 Valve spring compressor and split collets

39.4A Valve spring cap

39.4B Double valve springs

39.5 Removing a valve

39.6 Valve spring seat

39.7 Valve stem oil seal

8   Remove the remaining valves in a similar way and keep the components in their originally fitted sequence.
9   Reassembly is a reversal of removal. Refit the components to their original positions, but renew the valve springs if their free length is less than that of a new spring or if the springs have been in operation for more than 80 000 km (50 000 miles).
10  The original valve clearance adjusting shims will no longer provide the correct clearances if the valves have been ground in or the seats recut. Only where dismantling of a valve was carried out to renew a spring is there any purpose in returning the shims to their original locations. Try to obtain the loan of eight thin shims from your dealer and insert them into the tappets (cam followers) before assembling the cam followers to the carrier, where they should be retained with thick grease (photo).
11  Fit the camshaft carrier, complete with cam followers and shims to the cylinder head.
12  Adjust the valve clearances as described in Section 26.

39.10 Cam followers fitted to camshaft carrier

### 40  Examination and renovation

1   The procedures are similar to those described in Section 18 covering the following:

*Cylinder block and crankcase*
*Crankshaft and bearings*
*Pistons and piston rings*
*Flywheel*

2   The following additional items must also be examined.

#### Oil pump

3   Carefully, clamp the pump housing in a vice, shaft downwards.
4   Take off the pump cover, with the suction pipe. This will release the oil pressure relief valve inside. Also inside is a filter.
5   Remove the internal cover plate.
6   Take out the driveshaft and the gears.
7   Clean and examine all the parts. Measure the clearances against the Specifications. The end clearance is measured by putting a straight-edge across the cover face.
8   The oil pump should only need replacements after very long mileage, when the rest of the engine is showing great signs of wear.
9   The length of a new gear can be measured against the old gear to see if a new gear will restore the end clearance to the Specifications. Otherwise the housing must be changed.
10  The driven gear shaft is mounted in the housing with an interference fit. If there is any slackness, a new housing (which will come with shaft fitted) must be used.
11  The oil pump shares its drive with the distributor.

#### Camshaft, cam followers and shims

12  The camshaft journals and cams should be smooth, without grooves or scores.
13  Wear in the camshaft carrier bearings can only be rectified by renewal of the carrier.
14  Cam follower wear is usually very small and when they show slackness in their bores, it is probably the light alloy of the camshaft carrier which has worn.
15  Always measure the thickness of the valve clearance shims using a metric micrometer. Any grooving or wear marks in the shims should be rectified by renewal with ones of similar thickness.

#### Auxiliary shaft

16  The shaft journals, the fuel pump eccentric, and the drivegear for the distributor and oil pump should be smooth and shiny. If not, the shaft will have to be renewed.
17  The bushes should still be tight in the cylinder block, their oil holes lined up with those in the block.
18  Measure the bearing clearance. If excessive, the bushes will have to be renewed. They are a press fit, and require reaming with a special reamer after fitting. This is a job best done by a Fiat agent with the special tools.
19  Ensure the new bushes are fitted with the oil holes lined up.
20  Also check the driven gear and its bush.
21  It is recommended a new oil seal is fitted in the endplate. Hold the shaft in a vice, and remove the pulley. Fit the new oil seal in the endplate, lips inwards.

#### Timing belt tensioner

22  Check the bearing revolves smoothly and freely, and has no play. Do not immerse it in cleaning fluid, as it is partially sealed. Wipe the outside, and then smear in some new general purpose grease.
23  The action of the spring will have been felt when the belt was taken off. It should be cleaned, and oiled, to prevent seizure through dirt and rust.
24  Note the circlip on the engine right-hand mounting bracket. This retains the timing belt tensioner plunger.

### 41  Engine – reassembly (general)

Refer to Section 19, Part 2

### 42  Engine – complete reassembly

#### Crankshaft and main bearings

1   Fit the bearing shells to their crankcase seats and to their caps. The seatings and backs of the shells must be spotlessly clean, otherwise tight

42.1 Main bearing shells

spots will occur when the crankshaft is fitted. The centre bearing shell is plain (photo).

2   Fit the thrust washer halves to their locations at No 5 bearing, noting that the oil grooves in the washers face outwards (photo).

3   Oil the surfaces of the bearing shells liberally and lower the crankshaft into position (photo).

4   Fit the main bearing caps to their correct locations, the correct way round (numerical chisel marks towards the auxiliary shaft). The rear cap is unmarked. Tighten the cap bolts to the specified torque (photos).

5   Check that the crankshaft rotates smoothly and freely.

6   At this stage, the crankshaft endfloat should be checked. Prise the crankshaft fully in one direction and measure the gap between the machined face of the flywheel mounting flange and the crankcase. Now push the shaft in the opposite direction and measure again. Ideally, a dial gauge should be used for these measurements, but feeler blades will

serve as a reasonable alternative. The difference between the two dimensions (feeler blades) or the total movement of the crankshaft (dial gauge) should be within the specified tolerance. If it is not, the thrust washers at No 5 main bearing will have to be changed for thicker ones; this will require taking out the crankshaft again to reach them.

7   Fit new oil seals to the retainers and, using new gaskets, bolt the retainers to the front and rear ends of the crankshaft, having first filled the oil seal lips with grease (photos).

*Pistons/connecting rods*

8   The refitting operations are described in Section 32.

*Auxiliary shaft*

9   Lubricate the auxiliary shaft bearings and fit the shaft into the crankcase (photo).

42.2 Crankshaft thrust washers

42.3 Lowering crankshaft into position

42.4A Number one main bearing cap

42.4B Tightening a main bearing cap bolt

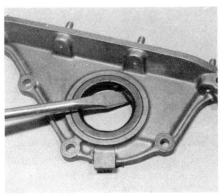
42.7A Removing oil seal from carrier

42.7B Front oil seal carrier

42.7C Rear oil seal carrier

42.9 Fitting the auxiliary shaft

10 Fit a new seal to the endplate and fit the plate to the crankcase, using a new gasket (photos).

11 Fit the belt sprocket and partially tighten its bolt. Then, using an oil filter strap wrench or similar device to hold the sprocket against rotation, tighten the bolt to the specified torque. Take care not to damage the teeth of the sprocket, which is of fibre construction (photo).

*Oil sump, sump pan and breather*

12 Fit the oil drain pipe by tapping it into place, squarely in its hole in the crankcase. Tighten its retaining bolt (photo).

13 Bolt up the oil pump, using a new gasket at its mounting flange (photo).

14 Fit the sump (using a new gasket) and tighten the securing screws to the specified torque. Note the reinforcement washers (photo).

15 Insert the oil pump/driveshaft into the distributor hole. This does not have to be specially positioned as the distributor is splined to the shaft and can be set by moving its location in the splines (refer to Chapter 4) (photo).

16 Push the breather into its crankcase recess and tighten its securing bolt (photos).

42.11 Tightening camshaft sprocket bolt. Note sprocket locking device

42.10A Auxiliary shaft end plate and gasket

42.12 Tightening oil drain pipe bolt

42.10B Tightening auxiliary shaft end plate bolt

42.13 Locating oil pump and gasket

42.14 Tightening sump pan bolt

42.16B Crankcase breather and retaining bolt

42.15 Fitting oil pump driveshaft

*Flywheel, crankshaft sprocket and pulley*
17 Make sure that the flywheel-to-crankshaft mounting flange surfaces are clean. Although the bolt holes have unequal distances between them, it is possible to fit the flywheel in one of two alternative positions at 180° difference. Therefore if the original flywheel is being refitted, align the marks made before removal.
18 If a new flywheel is being fitted, or if alignment marks were not made before dismantling, set No 1 position at TDC (crankshaft front Woodruff key pointing vertically). Fit the flywheel to its mounting flange so that its timing dimple is uppermost and in alignment with the relative position of the TDC mark on the flywheel housing inspection window.
19 Insert the bolts and tighten them to the specified torque, jamming the ring gear to prevent the flywheel turning. Fit the engine endplate (photo).
20 Fit the timing belt sprocket to the front end of the crankshaft (photo).
21 Fit the crankshaft pulley and the nut; tighten it to the specified torque, again jamming the starter ring gear to prevent the crankshaft from rotating (photo).

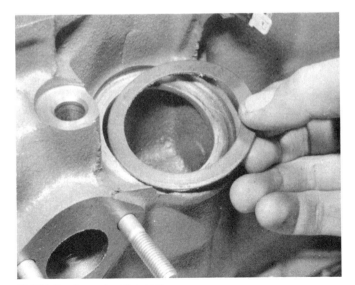

42.16A Crankcase breather seal

42.19 Tightening flywheel bolts

42.20 Fitting crankshaft timing belt sprocket

42.24A Belt cover rear plate

42.21 Crankshaft pulley and nut

42.24B Belt cover mounting stud

*Cylinder head*
22 Refitting is described in Section 29.

*Camshaft carrier and camshaft*
23 Refitting is described in Section 27.

*Timing belt and tensioner*
24 Refitting is described in Section 28, but make sure that the belt cover rear plate is bolted into position. If the engine mounting bracket was removed, bolt it into position complete with the tensioner plunger to provide spring pressure to the belt pulley (photos).

*Valve clearances*
25 Check the valve clearances as described in Section 26.
26 Using new gaskets, bolt on the camshaft carrier cover plate and the inlet and exhaust manifolds using new gaskets. Fit the exhaust manifold hot air collector plate (photo).
27 Locate the engine rear plate on its dowels by sliding it behind the flywheel (photo).

42.24C Engine mounting bracket with belt tensioner plunger (arrowed)

42.26 Tightening a camshaft carrier cover nut

44.1 Offering transmission to engine

42.27 Engine rear plate

44.2 Lifting lug at bellhousing bolt

## 43 Engine ancillaries – refitting

1   Bolt on the carburettor (Chapter 3).
2   Fit the coolant pump and thermostat housing (Chapter 2).
3   Fit the alternator and tension the drivebelt (Chapters 9 and 2).
4   Fit the distributor (Chapter 4).
5   Fit the fuel pump (Chapter 3)
6   Fit the clutch (Chapter 5)
7   Fit a new oil filter cartridge (Section 2 of this Chapter).

## 44 Engine/transmission – reconnection and refitting

1   Offer the transmission to the engine making sure that the clutch has been centralised as described in Chapter 5 (photo).
2   Draw the engine and transmission together by screwing in the connecting bolts. Refit lifting lugs and hose and wiring clips (photo).
3   Bolt the lower cover plate to the face of the flywheel housing.
4   Bolt the starter motor into position.
5   Bolt the mounting brackets into place.

6   Place the engine/transmission on the floor ready for raising by hoist or jack into the engine compartment.
7   Raise the car and position it over the engine/transmission.
8.  Hoist or jack the power unit upwards until the left and right-hand mountings can be connected (photos).
9   Remove the lifting mechanism and connect the bottom mounting (photos).
10 Connect the inboard ends of the driveshafts with the transmission and the outboard ends with the hub carriers.
11 Reconnect the hub carriers with the clamps at the base of the suspension struts. Tighten the fixing bolts to the specified torque.
12 Bolt the brake flexible hose support clips to the suspension struts.
13 Reconnect the tie-rod end balljoints tightening the nuts to the specified torque.
14 Reconnect the gearchange rods. The easiest way to do this is to force the sockets onto the ball studs using a pair of self-locking grips (photo).
15 Refit the exhaust system and reconnect the downpipe to the manifold (photo).
16 Screw on the driveshaft nuts and tighten them to the specified torque. Have an assistant apply the brake pedal hard to prevent the driveshaft from turning.

44.8A Raising engine/transmission into engine compartment

44.8B Left-hand engine mounting

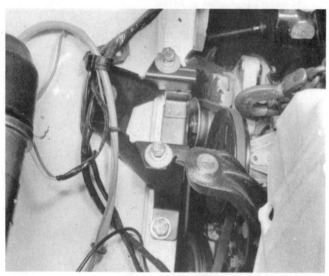

44.8C Right-hand engine mounting brackets

44.8D Right-hand mounting bolted up

44.9A Engine/transmission lower mounting

44.9B Lower mounting attachment bolts

44.14 Connecting a gearchange rod ball cup

44.21A Heater hose at manifold

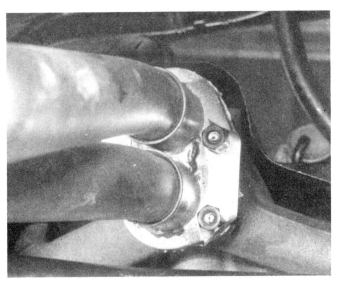

44.15 Exhaust downpipe flange nuts

44.21B Brake servo hose at manifold

17  Refit the front roadwheels and lower the car to the floor.
18  Reconnect the carburettor fuel and coolant hoses.
19  Unplug the fuel hose and connect it to the pump.
20  Reconnect the choke and throttle controls to the carburettor.
21  Reconnect the coolant and heater hoses to the engine. Also reconnect the brake servo hose to the intake manifold (photos).
22  Reconnect the leads to the reversing lamp switch. Reconnect the transmission earth lead (photos).
23  Reconnect the clutch cable and adjust as described in Chapter 5.
24  Reconnect the speedometer drive cable to the transmission and tighten the knurled retaining ring.
25  Reconnect the low tension lead to the distributor and the high tension lead to the ignition coil.
26  Reconnnect the electrical leads to the starter motor, the oil pressure and temperature switches and the coolant temperature switch.
27  Connect the leads to the alternator.
28  Refit the air cleaner.
29  Refill the cooling system. Refill the engine with oil.
30  Reconnect the battery.
31  Refit the bonnet and connect the windscreen washer tube.
32  Fit the inner wing protective shields (photo).

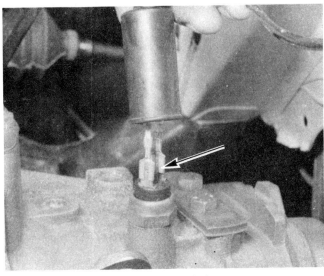

44.22A Reversing lamp switch on transmission

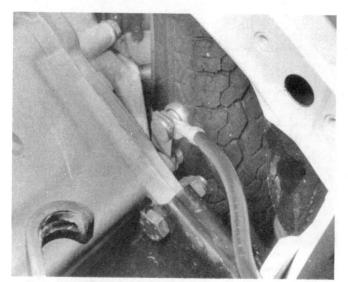

44.22B Transmission earth lead

44.26A Oil pressure warning switch

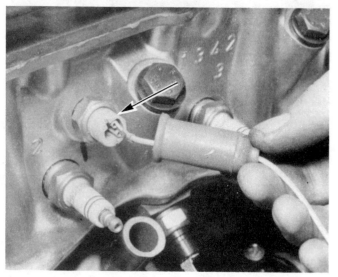

44.26B Coolant temperature switch

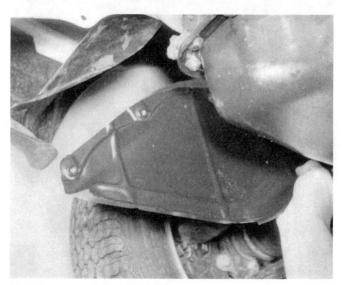

44.32 Inner wing protective shield

## 45 Engine – initial start-up after major overhaul

1   If new bearings and rings have been fitted, it is likely that the engine will be stiff to turn so make sure the battery is well charged.

2   Switch on the ignition and check that appropriate warning lights come on.

3   Start up the engine. If it refuses to start, refer to the Fault Diagnosis Section in the Introduction to this Manual.

4   Watch the oil pressure warning light and alternator charging indicator light. If there is no charge or if the oil pressure warning light does not go out after a second or two, having had time to fill the new oil filter, switch off and recheck.

5   If the warning lights go out, set the engine to run on fast idle and check the engine for leaks.

6   Check the coolant level; it will probably go down as air locks are filled.

7   Keep the engine running at a fast idle and bring it up to normal working temperature. As the engine warms up, there will be some odd smells and smoke from parts getting hot and burning off oil deposits.

8   When the engine running temperature has been reached, adjust the idling speed, as described in Chapter 3. Check and, if necessary, adjust the ignition timing using a stroboscope (see Chapter 4).

9   Stop the engine and wait a few minutes; check to see if there are any coolant or oil leaks.

10   Road test the car to check that the engine is running with the correct smoothness and power. If it does not, refer to the Fault Diagnosis Section in the Introduction of this Manual. Do not race the engine. If new bearings and/or pistons and rings have been fitted, it should be treated as a new engine and run it at reduced speed for at least 800 km (500 miles).

11   After 800 km (500 miles) change the engine oil and filter.

## 46 Fault diagnosis – 1116 cc and 1301 cc (ohc) engine

| Symptom | Reason(s) |
| --- | --- |
| Engine fails to turn when starter operated | Battery discharged<br>Battery terminals loose or corroded<br>Battery earth to body defective<br>Engine/transmission earth strap broken or loose<br>Disconnected or broken wire in starter circuit<br>Ignition/starter switch defective<br>Starter pinion jammed in mesh with flywheel gear<br>Starter motor or solenoid defective (see Chapter 9)<br>Major mechanical failure (seizure) or long disuse (piston rings rusted to bores) |
| Engine turns slowly and fails to start | Battery discharged<br>Battery terminals loose or corroded<br>Battery or engine earth strap loose<br>Starter motor connections loose<br>Oil in engine/transmission too thick<br>Starter motor defective |
| Engine turns normally but will not start | Fuel tank empty<br>Damp or dirty HT leads, distributor cap or plug bodies<br>Broken, loose or disconnected LT leads<br>Contact breaker points dirty or incorrectly gapped<br>Other ignition fault (see Chapter 4)<br>Other fuel system fault (see Chapter 3)<br>Valve timing incorrect (after rebuild) |
| Engine fires but will not run | Insufficient choke (cold engine)<br>Fuel starvation or tank empty<br>Ignition fault (see Chapter 4)<br>Other fuel system fault (see Chapter 3) |
| Difficult starting when cold | Insufficient choke<br>Fouled or incorrectly gapped spark plugs<br>Damp or dirty HT leads, distributor cap or spark plug bodies<br>Dirty or maladjusted contact breaker points<br>Other ignition fault or timing maladjustment (see Chapter 4)<br>Fuel system or emission control fault (see Chapter 3)<br>Poor compression (may be due to incorrect valve clearances, burnt or sticking valves, blown head gasket, worn or damaged pistons, rings or bores)<br>Incorrect valve timing (after rebuild) |
| Difficult starting when hot | Incorrect use of manual choke<br>Fuel line vapour lock (especially in hot weather or at high altitudes)<br>Incorrect ignition timing<br>Other fuel system or emission control fault (see Chapter 3)<br>Poor compression (see above) |
| Engine slow to warm up | Choke linkage maladjusted<br>Air cleaner temperature control unit defective<br>Thermostat stuck open (see Chapter 2)<br>Other fuel system fault (see Chapter 3) |
| Engine idles roughly | Carburettor incorrectly adjusted<br>Other fuel system fault (see Chapter 3)<br>Spark plugs fouled or incorrectly gapped. Ignition timing incorrect<br>Incorrect valve clearances<br>Widely differing cylinder compressions<br>Other ignition fault (see Chapter 4)<br>Low battery voltage (charging fault) |
| Engine lacks power | Ignition timing incorrect<br>Air cleaner choked<br>Valve clearances incorrect<br>Brake binding<br>Poor compression<br>Other fuel system fault (see Chapter 3)<br>Other ignition system fault (see Chapter 4)<br>Carbon build-up in cylinder head |

| Symptom | Reason(s) |
| --- | --- |
| Engine misfires throughout speed range | Defective or fouled spark plug<br>Loose, cracked or defective HT lead<br>Maladjusted, sticking or burnt valves<br>Ignition timing incorrect<br>Blown head gasket<br>Fuel contaminated<br>Other ignition fault (see Chapter 4)<br>Other fuel system fault (see Chapter 3) |
| Poor engine braking | High idle speed<br>Other fuel system fault (see Chapter 3)<br>Low compression |
| Pre-ignition (pinking) during acceleration | Incorrect grade of fuel being used<br>Ignition timing overadvanced<br>Engine overheated<br>Excessive carbon build-up<br>Other ignition fault (see Chapter 4)<br>Fuel system fault (see Chapter 3) |
| Engine runs on after switching off | Idle speed too high<br>Incorrect type of spark plug<br>Overheating<br>Excessive carbon build-up<br>Other emission control fault (see Chapter 3) |
| Low oil pressure (verify accuracy of sender before dismantling engine!) | Oil level low<br>Engine overheating<br>Incorrect grade of oil in use<br>Oil filter clogged or bypass valve stuck<br>Pressure relief valve stuck or defective<br>Oil pick-up strainer clogged or loose<br>Main or big-end bearings worn<br>Oil pump worn or mountings loose |
| Excessive oil consumption | Overfilling<br>Leaking gaskets or drain plug washer<br>Valve stem oil seals worn, damaged or missing after rebuild<br>Valve stems and/or guides worn<br>Piston rings and/or bores worn<br>Piston oil return holes clogged |
| Oil contaminated with water | Excessive cold running<br>Leaking head gasket<br>Cracked block or head |
| Oil contaminated with fuel | Excessive use of choke<br>Worn piston rings and/or bores |
| Unusual mechanical noises | Unintentional mechanical contact (eg fan blade)<br>Worn drivebelt<br>Worn valvegear (tapping noises from top of engine) or incorrect clearance<br>Peripheral component fault (generator, coolant pump)<br>Worn big-end bearings (regular heavy knocking, perhaps less under load)<br>Worn main bearings (rumbling and knocking, perhaps worsening under load)<br>Small-end bushes or gudgeon pins worn (light metallic tapping)<br>Piston slap (most noticeable when engine cold) |

**Note**: *When investigating starting and uneven running faults, do not be tempted into snap diagnosis. Start from the beginning of the check procedure and follow it through. It will take less time in the long run. Poor performance from an engine in terms of power and economy is not normally diagnosed quickly. In any event, the ignition and fuel systems must be checked first before assuming any further investigation needs to be made.*

# Chapter 2 Cooling and heating systems

*For modifications, and information applicable to later models, see Supplement at end of manual*

## Contents

## Specifications

**System type** ........................................ 'No loss' with radiator and integral expansion tank. Electric cooling fan, belt-driven coolant pump, thermostat on cylinder head

### General

Radiator fan cuts in ................................................ 90 to 94°C (194 to 201°F)
Radiator fan switches off ........................................... 85 to 89°C (185 to 192°F)
Thermostat opens:
   903 cc engine ................................................ 85 to 89°C (185 to 192°F)
   1116 cc and 1301 cc engines ................................. 83 to 87°C (181 to 188.6°F)
Fully open:
   903 cc ...................................................... 100°C (212°F)
   1116 cc and 1301 cc ......................................... 95°C (203°F)
Expansion tank pressure cap rating .................................. 0.78 bar (11 lbf/in²)

### Coolant

Capacity:
   903 cc ...................................................... 4.6 litre (8.1 pint)
   1116 cc ..................................................... 6.0 litre (10.6 pint)
   1301 cc ..................................................... 6.2 litre (10.9 pint)
Type ............................................................... Ethylene glycol based antifreeze (Duckhams Universal Antifreeze and Summer Coolant)

### Torque wrench settings

| | Nm | lbf ft |
|---|---|---|
| Temperature sender switch | 49 | 36 |
| Coolant pump mounting bolts | 34 | 25 |
| Alternator adjuster and mountings nuts | 49 | 36 |

## 1 Description and maintenance

1 The cooling system consists of a front-mounted radiator with built-in expansion tank, a coolant pump (belt-driven from the crankshaft pulley) and a thermostatically-controlled electric cooling fan.

2 In order to assist rapid warm-up, a thermostat is located in a housing at the left-hand end of the cylinder head. The hose connections to the thermostat housing vary according to model.
3 The heater is supplied with coolant from the engine and incorporates a matrix and blower with the necessary controls.
4 The throttle valve plate block of the carburettor is coolant-heated as a means of improving fuel atomisation.

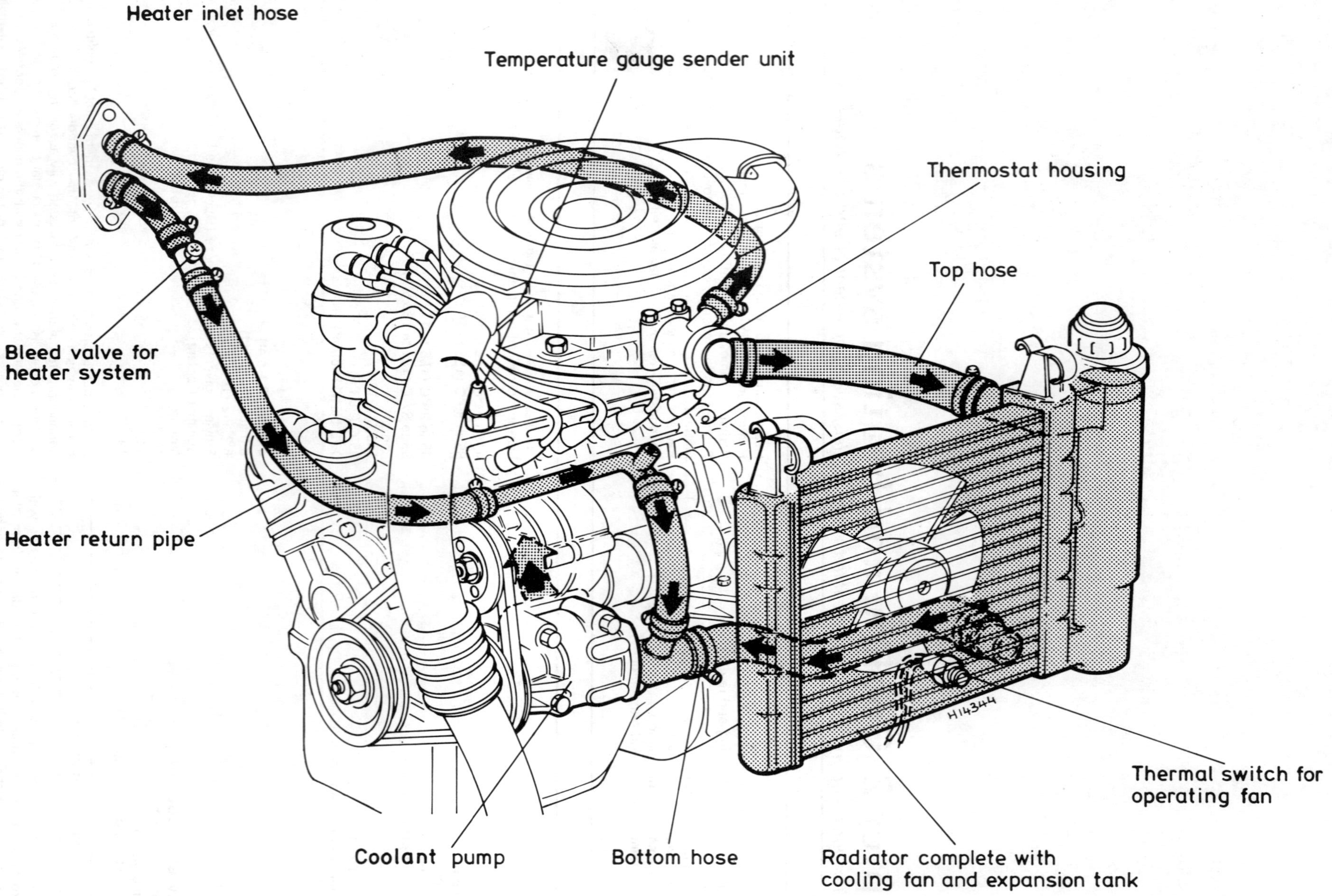

Thermal switch for operating fan

Thermostat housing

Top hose

Radiator complete with cooling fan and expansion tank

Temperature gauge sender unit

Bottom hose

Coolant pump

Heater inlet hose

Bleed valve for heater system

Heater return pipe

Fig. 2.1 Cooling system on 903 cc engine (Sec 1)

5 Maintenance is minimal as in theory no coolant should ever be lost from the expansion tank. Regularly check that the coolant level is between 50.0 and 70.0 mm (1.97 and 2.8 in) above the MIN mark on the tank with the engine cold. The need for regular topping up will indicate a leak somewhere in the system. If one cannot be found, suspect an internal leak in the engine although this is usually confirmed by a rise in the engine oil level and water on the dipstick (photo). Any topping-up should be done using an antifreeze mixture (see Section 3), not plain water.

6 Avoid unscrewing the expansion tank cap when the engine is hot, but if this must be done, cover the cap with a cloth to avoid scalding by escaping steam.

7 Periodically, check the condition of all coolant hoses and tighten the clips.

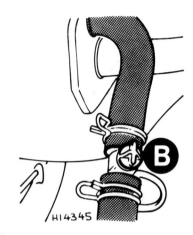

Fig. 2.2 Plug (B) in heater hose (Sec 2)

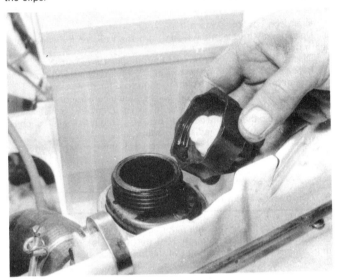

1.5 Expansion tank cap

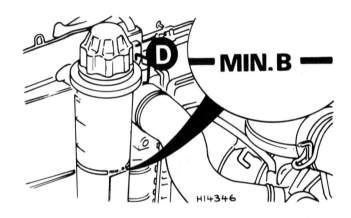

Fig. 2.3 Plug (D) in expansion tank (Sec 2)

## 2 Cooling system – draining, flushing and refilling

1 Set the heater temperature lever to maximum.

2 Unscrew the cap from the expansion tank.

3 Disconnect the radiator bottom hose and unscrew the cylinder block drain plug (1116 cc and 1301 cc engines) and allow the coolant to drain. Refer to photo 29.21B, page 64.

4 If the system is in good condition with no sign of rust or dirt in the drained coolant, then it may be refilled immediately. If the system has been neglected and the antifreeze has not been regularly renewed and there is evidence of rust and sediment in the drained liquid then flush the system through with a cold water hose.

5 If the radiator should appear to be clogged, it may be necessary to remove it (Section 7) invert it and reverse flush it using a cold water hose. If, after a reasonable period the water still does not run clear, the radiator should be flushed with a good proprietary cleaning system such as Holts Radflush or Holts Speedflush. Minor leaks from the radiator can be cured using Holts Radweld. Extensive damage should be repaired by a specialist or the unit exchanged for a new or reconditioned radiator.

6 Reconnect the bottom hose and screw in the drain plug.

7 Remove the plug (B) (Fig. 2.2) from the bleed hole in the heater hose.

8 Remove the plug (D) (Fig. 2.3) from the bleed hole in the expansion tank.

9 Pour antifreeze mixture slowly into the filler neck of the expansion tank until it is seen to come out of the expansion tank plug hole. Screw in the plug.

10 Add further coolant until it is seen to dribble out of the hole in the heater hose. Screw in the plug.

11 Top up the expansion tank to the specified level and screw on the tank cap.

12 Start the engine and run it until the cooling fan cuts in. Switch off, allow to cool and top up if necessary to the specified mark on the expansion tank.

## 3 Coolant mixtures

1 In cold climates, antifreeze is needed for two reasons. In extreme cases, if the coolant in the engine freezes solid it could crack the cylinder block or head. But also in cold weather, with the circulation restricted by the thermostat, and any warm water that *is* getting to the radiator being at the top, the bottom of the radiator could freeze, and so block circulation completely, making the coolant trapped in the engine boil.

2 The antifreeze should be mixed in the proportions advocated by the makers, according to the climate. There are two levels of protection. The first cuts risk of damage, as the antifreeze goes mushy before freezing. The second, valid all year round, is the corrosion protection it offers – see below. The normal proportion in a temperate climate to provide maximum protection against freezing and corrosion is 50% antifreeze and 50% water.

3 Use only ethylene glycol based antifreeze and preferably soft water.

4 Antifreeze should be left in through the summer. It has an important secondary function, to act as an inhibitor against corrosion. In the cooling system are many different metals, in particular the aluminium of the cylinder head. In contact with the coolant this sets up electrolytic corrosion, accentuated by any dirt in the system. This corrosion can be catastrophically fast.

5 After about two years, the effectiveness of the antifreeze's inhibitor is used up. It must then be discarded, and the system refilled with new coolant.

6 In warm climates free from frost, an inhibitor should be used. Again, a reputable make giving full protection must be chosen and renewed every two years. Inhibitors with dyes are useful for finding leaks, and on some makes the dye shows when the inhibiting ability is finished.

### 4 Thermostat – removal, testing and refitting

1 The thermostat assembly is mounted on the flywheel end of the cylinder block.
2 Unfortunately, the thermostat/housing is a complete unit and failure of the thermostat will necessitate the purchase of the complete component (photo).
3 If the thermostat/housing is removed from the engine, it can be suspended in water and the water heated to check out its opening temperature. Movement of the thermostat valve can be observed to some extent through the openings in the housing.
4 When refitting, always use a new gasket at its mounting face (photo).

### 5 Radiator fan thermostatic switch – removal, checking and refitting

1 Drain the cooling system.
2 If the thermostatic switch is being removed because the fan is not operating and the switch is suspect, check the fan fuse first, before removing the switch.
3 To remove the switch, disconnect the leads from the terminals and unscrew the switch.
4 Connect a test bulb and battery across the switch terminals and then immerse the sensing part of the switch in a container of water. Heat the water and, using a thermometer, check the temperature of the water when the bulb lights up, indicating the switch is functioning. The switch should operate at approximately 194°F (90°C). Allow the water to cool and check that the switch cuts out at 185°F (85°C). Renew a faulty switch.

5 Refitting of the switch is the reverse of the removal procedure. Always fit a new O-ring on the switch.

### 6 Radiator fan – removal and refitting

1 Disconnect the electrical leads from the radiator fan motor.
2 Unbolt the fan mounting struts from the radiator and lift the complete assembly away.
3 Refitting is a reversal of removal.

### 7 Radiator – removal and refitting

1 Drain the cooling system.
2 Disconnect the electrical leads from the radiator fan motor and thermostatic switch.
3 Disconnect the coolant hoses from the radiator (photos).
4 Release the clips from the top of the radiator and withdraw the radiator complete with fan from the engine compartment (photos).
5 The radiator is of combined plastic/metal construction and any repair should be left to specialists. In an emergency however, minor leaks from the radiator may be cured by using a radiator sealant such as Holts Radweld, with the radiator *in situ*.
6 Refitting is a reversal of removal. Fill the cooling system as described in Section 2.

### 8 Drivebelt – tensioning and renewal

1 The drivebelt for the alternator and coolant pump is correctly tensioned if it deflects through 10.0 mm (0.39 in) under moderate thumb pressure at the mid point of the longest run of the belt.
2 To tighten the belt, release the mounting and adjuster nuts on the

4.2 Thermostat housing

4.4 Fitting thermostat housing (1116 cc engine)

7.3A Radiator top hose

7.3B Radiator hose to thermostat housing

7.4A Radiator fixing clip

7.4B Removing radiator/fan assembly

alternator and prise the alternator away from the engine. Tighten the nuts when the belt is taut and then re-check the tension as previously described. Never over-tension a belt or the coolant pump or alternator bearings may be damaged.

3   Check the condition of the belt at regular intervals. If frayed or cracked, renew it in the following way.

4   Release the alternator mounting and adjuster nuts and push the alternator fully in towards the engine. Slip the belt off the pulleys. If this is difficult, turn the crankshaft pulley using a spanner on its retaining nut while pressing the belt over the edge of the pulley rim. Use this method to fit the new belt after first having engaged it with the coolant pump and alternator pulley grooves.

5   Tension the belt as previously described.

6   The tension of a new belt should be checked and adjusted after the first few hundred miles of running.

### 9   Coolant pump – removal, overhaul and refitting

**Note:** *The design of the pump differs between the 903 cc and the other two engines, but the removal, overhaul and refitting operations are essentially similar.*

1   To gain access to the coolant pump, open the bonnet and remove the air cleaner.

2   Slacken the alternator pivot and adjustment nuts, push the alternator in towards the engine and slip the drivebelt from the coolant pump pulley. Unplug and remove the alternator.

3   Drain the cooling system as previously described.

4   Disconnect the hoses from the coolant pump, also the metal coolant transfer pipe (photo).

5   Unscrew and remove the coolant pump securing bolts, and lift the pump from the engine. Peel away and discard the old gasket.

6   Clean away external dirt.

7   The pump is likely to need overhaul for worn or noisy bearings, or if the gland is leaking. There is a drain hole between the gland and the bearings to prevent contamination of the bearing grease by leaks, and possible damage to the bearings. Gland leaks are usually worse when the engine is not running. Once started, a leak is likely to get worse quickly, so should be dealt with soon. Worn bearings are likely to be noted first due to noise. To check them, the pulley should be rocked firmly, when any free movement can be felt despite the belt. But if the bearings are noisy, yet there is not apparently any free play, then the belt should be removed so the pump can be rotated by hand to check the smoothness of the bearings.

8   Dismantling and assembly of the pump requires the use of a press, and it is preferable to fit a new pump.

9.4 Coolant distribution tube at rear of pump

9   For those having the necessary facilities, overhaul can be carried out as follows.

10 Remove the retaining nuts and separate the two halves of the pump.

11 The pump shaft is an interference fit in the impeller, bearings, and pulley boss. How the pump is dismantled depends on whether only the gland needs renewing or the bearings as well, and what puller or press is available to get everything apart.

12 Assuming complete dismantling is required, proceed as follows. Supporting it close in at the boss, press the shaft out of the pulley. Pull the impeller off the other end of the shaft.

13 Take out the bearing stop screw.

14 From the impeller end, press the shaft with the bearings out of the cover half of the housing.

15 Press the shaft out of the bearings, take off the spacer, the circlip, and the shouldered ring.

16 Do not immerse the bearings in cleaning fluid. They are 'sealed'.

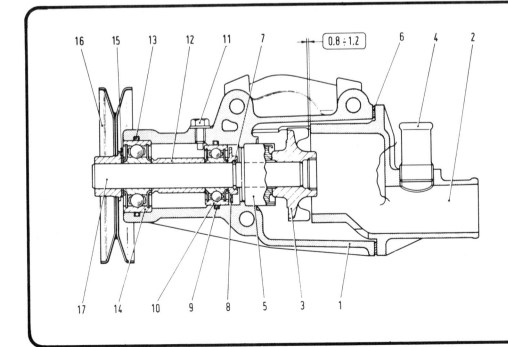

**Fig. 2.4 Sectional view of 903 cc engine coolant pump (Sec 9)**

1   Pump body
2   Pump cover
3   Impeller
4   Connector for hose from outlet to pump
5   Seal
6   Gasket
7   Circlip
8   Bearing shoulder washer
9   Inner seal
10  Inner bearing
11  Bearing retainment screw and lock washer
12  Spacer
13  Outer seal
14  Outer bearing
15  Lock washer
16  Pulley
17  Pump shaft

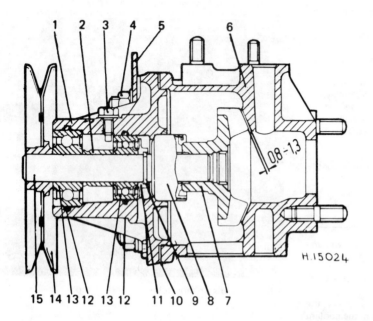

**Fig. 2.5 Sectional view of 1116 cc and 1301 cc engine coolant pump (Sec 9)**

1  Pump cover
2  Bearing spacer
3  Bearing stop screw
4  Cover nuts
5  Lifting bracket
6  Housing
7  Impeller
8  Gland (seal)
9  Circlip
10  Gasket
11  Shouldered ring
12  Grommets
13  Bearing
14  Pulley
15  Shaft

Liquid will get in, but a thorough clean will be impracticable, and it will be impossible to get new grease in.

17  Check all the parts, get a new gland, two new grommets, (1116 cc and 1301 cc) and a new gasket. Scrape all deposits out of the housing and off the impeller.

18  To reassemble, start by inserting the new grommets (1116 cc and 1301 cc) in the grooves by each bearing. Fit the circlip to the shaft, then the shouldered ring, bearings and spacer. Fit the shaft and bearing assembly into the cover. Fit the stop screw. Press on the pulley.

19  Fit the new gland (seal), seating it in its location in the cover. Press the impeller onto the shaft. The impeller must be put on part way, and then the housing held in place to see how far the impeller must go down the shaft to give the correct clearance, which is 0.8 to 1.3 mm (0.03 to 0.05 in) as shown in Figs. 2.4 and 2.5.

20  The impeller clearance can be checked through the coolant passage in the side of the pump.

21  Refitting is a reversal of the removal process, but use a new flange gasket and tension the drivebelt as described in Section 8 (photo).

22  Refill the cooling system.

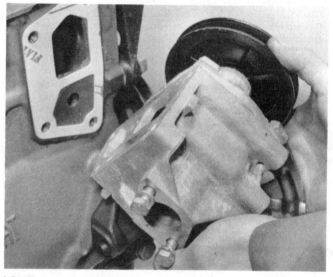

9.21 Fitting coolant pump (1116 cc engine)

## 10  Cooling system sensors

1  A coolant temperature sender switch is located in the cylinder head (above No. 1 spark plug) on 903 cc engines and adjacent to No. 2 spark plug on 1116 cc and 1301 cc engines.

2  The switch operates the coolant temperature gauge and an excessive temperature warning lamp.

3  On some models, a level sensor is screwed into the side of the expansion tank. This sensor consists of a pair of reed switches within a capsule which are kept closed by the strong magnetic flux generated by the hydrostatic force inspired by the action of the coolant against the float.

4  If the coolant level drops then the magnetic flux is weakened and the switches open.

5  In the event of a fault developing, before assuming that the cause is the sensor, check all connecting wiring.

## 11  Heating and ventilation system – description

1  The heater is centrally mounted under the facia and is of fresh air type.

Fig. 2.6 Checking impeller clearance (Sec 9)

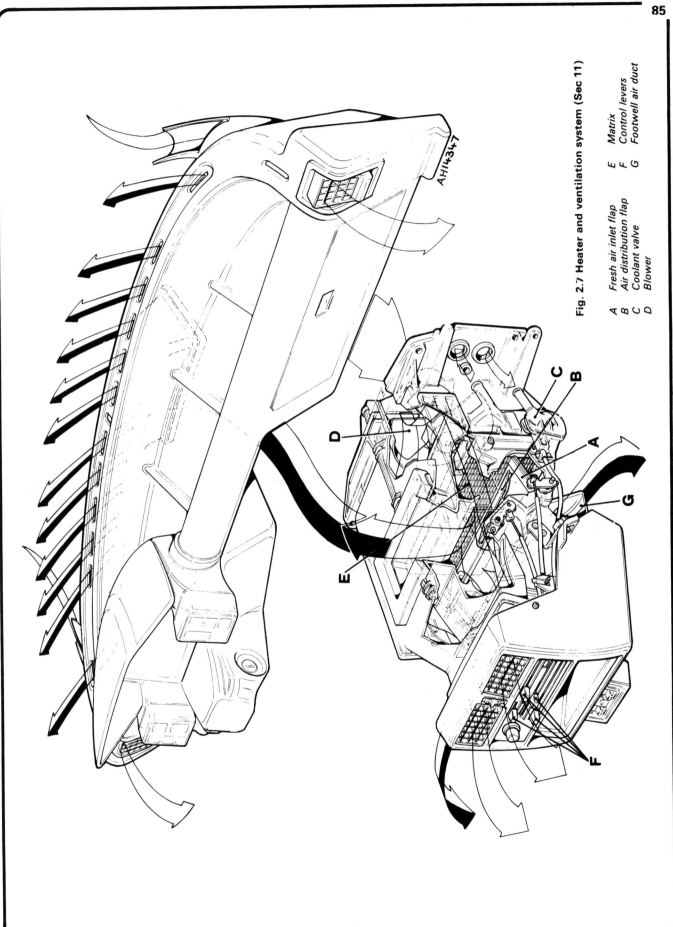

AH14347

**Fig. 2.7 Heater and ventilation system (Sec 11)**

A  Fresh air inlet flap
B  Air distribution flap
C  Coolant valve
D  Blower
E  Matrix
F  Control levers
G  Footwell air duct

2   Air is drawn in through the grille at the base of the windscreen. It then passes through the coolant heated matrix when it can then be distributed through selective outlets according to the setting of the control levers.

3   A booster fan is provided for use when the car is stationary or is travelling too slowly to provide sufficient air ram effect.

4   Fresh air outlets are provided at each end and centrally on the facia panel.

## 12 Heater unit – removal and refitting

1   Drain the cooling system.

2   Disconnect the heater hoses at the engine compartment rear bulkhead.

3   Working within the car under the facia panel, disconnect the leads from the heater blower by pulling the connecting plug apart.

4   If a radio is fitted, disconnect the aerial, earth, speaker and power leads from it.

5   Pull off the knobs from the control levers (photo).

6   Extract the screws and take off the control indicator plate (photos). Disconnect the leads from the cigar lighter and carefully detach the fibre optic which provides the panel illumination.

7   Unscrew and remove the screws which hold the console to the heater unit and withdraw the console.

12.6B Removing heater control panel escutcheon

12.5 Pulling off heater control lever knob

12.8A Heater coolant valve and control cable

12.6A Heater control panel screw

12.8B Heater flap valve cables

8 The control cables can be disconnected from the arms of the control flap valves (photos).
9 Unscrew the single screw from the upper face of the facia panel. This screw secures the upper part of the heater casing (photo).
10 Unscrew the mounting nuts which hold the heater to the bulkhead (photo).
11 Lower the heater to the floor, taking care not to allow coolant to spill on the carpet.
12 Refitting is a reversal of removal. Fill the cooling system.

## 13 Heater – dismantling, overhaul and reassembly

1 Remove the heater from the car as described in the preceding Section.
2 The control lever mounting platform can be removed after extracting its fixing screws.
3 The coolant control valve can be removed after extracting its fixing nuts.

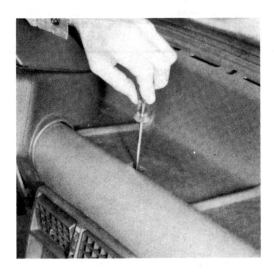

Fig. 2.8 Extracting heater upper fixing screw (Sec 12)

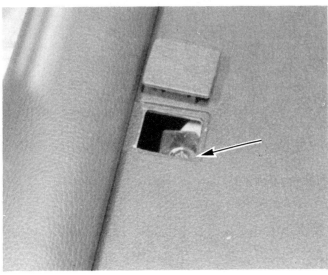

12.9 Heater upper fixing screw

12.10 Heater lower mounting bolt

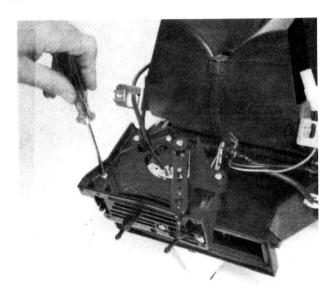

Fig. 2.9 Control lever platform screw (Sec 13)

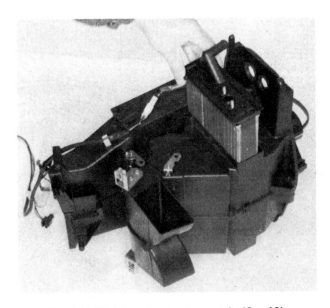

Fig. 2.10 Withdrawing heater matrix (Sec 13)

4   Unscrew the screws which hold the heater matrix in the casing and then slide the matrix from its location.

5   If the matrix is leaking, do not attempt a repair, but obtain a new one. These are usually obtainable on an exchange basis from radiator repairers.

6   The heater casing can be separated after prising off the clips and removing the bolts. The blower motor/fan can then be lifted out.

7   Reassembly is a reversal of dismantling, but set the cables to give complete range of travel between open and closed positions of the flap valve or coolant valve concerned.

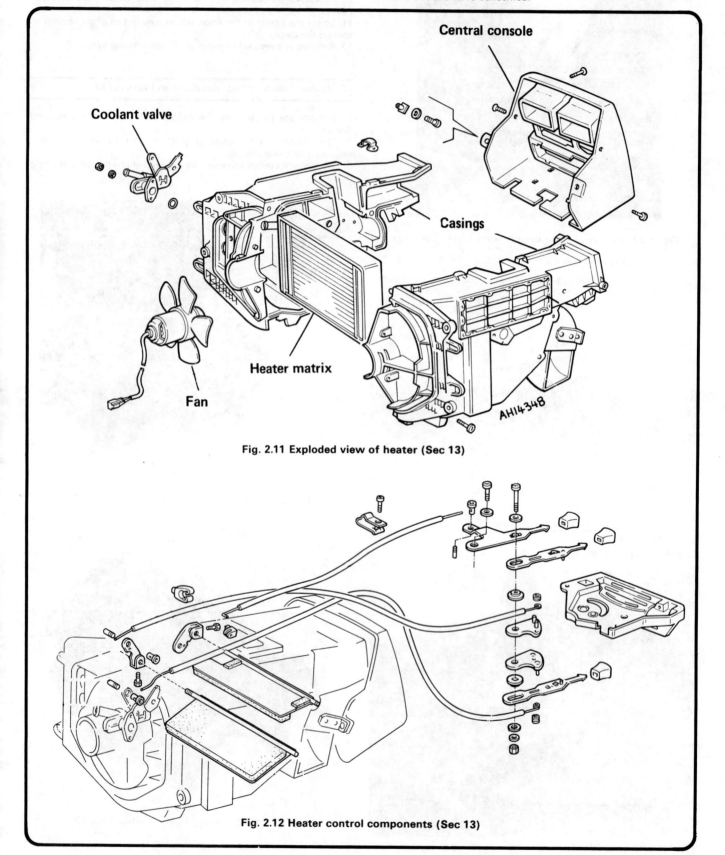

Fig. 2.11 Exploded view of heater (Sec 13)

Fig. 2.12 Heater control components (Sec 13)

**14 Fault diagnosis – cooling and heating**

| Symptom | Reason(s) |
| --- | --- |
| Overheating | Insufficient coolant in system |
| | Pump ineffective due to slack drivebelt |
| | Radiator blocked either internally or externally |
| | Kinked or collapsed hose causing coolant flow restriction |
| | Thermostat not working properly |
| | Engine out of tune |
| | Ignition timing retarded or auto advance malfunction |
| | Cylinder head gasket blown |
| | Engine not yet run-in |
| | Exhaust system partially blocked |
| | Engine oil level too low |
| | Brakes binding |
| Engine running too cool | Faulty, incorrect or missing thermostat |
| Loss of coolant | Loose hose clips |
| | Hoses perished or leaking |
| | Radiator leaking |
| | Filler/pressure cap defective |
| | Blown cylinder head gasket |
| | Cracked cylinder block or head |
| Heater gives insufficient output | Engine overcooled (see above) |
| | Heater matrix blocked |
| | Heater controls maladjusted or broken |
| | Heater control valve jammed or otherwise defective |

# Chapter 3 Fuel system

*For modifications, and information applicable to later models, see Supplement at end of manual*

## Contents

## Specifications

| System type | Rear mounted fuel tank, mechanically-operated fuel pump, downdraught carburettor |
| --- | --- |

### Air cleaner element
| | |
| --- | --- |
| 903 cc (45) and 1116 cc (55) engine | Champion W121 |
| 1116 cc (60) and 1299/1301 cc (70) engines | Champion W136 |

### Fuel tank
| | |
| --- | --- |
| Capacity | 42.0 litre (9.25 gal) |
| Octane rating | Leaded 97 RON minimum (see Supplement for use of unleaded petrol) |

### Fuel filter
| | |
| --- | --- |
| | Champion L101 |

### Carburettor – calibration (dimensions in mm)
**Weber 32 ICEV 50/250/1**

| | |
| --- | --- |
| Application | 903 cc engine |
| Venturi | 22 |
| Auxiliary venturi | 3.5 |
| Main jet | 1.12 |
| Air bleed | 1.70 |
| Emulsion tube | F89 |
| Idle jet | 0.47 |
| Air idle jet | 1.60 |
| Pump jet | 0.40 |
| Pump outlet | 0.40 |
| Superfeed jet | 0.80 |
| Superfeed mixture jet | 2.50 |
| Fuel inlet needle valve | 1.50 |
| Anti-syphon device | 1.00 |
| Idle mixture adjustment hole | 1.50 |
| Float setting (fuel level) | 10.5 to 11.0 |
| Float setting (travel/stroke) | 45.0 |
| Fast idle (throttle valve gap) | 0.75 to 0.80 |
| Accelerator pump delivery (ten strokes) | 4.0 to 5.5 cc |

### Solex C32 DISA 11

| | |
|---|---|
| Application | 903 cc engine |
| Venturi | 23 |
| Auxiliary venturi | 3.4 |
| Main jet | 1.20 |
| Air bleed jet | 1.35 |
| Emulsion tube | B03 |
| Idle jet | 0.525 |
| Air idle jet | 1.20 |
| Pump jet | 0.50 |
| Pump outlet | 0.45 |
| Fuel inlet needle valve | 1.60 |
| Anti-syphon device | 2.0 |
| Idle mixture adjustment hole | 1.10 |
| Float setting (fuel level) | 2.0 to 3.0 |
| Fast idle (throttle valve gap) | 0.90 to 1.0 |
| Accelerator pump delivery (ten strokes) | 2.5 to 4.5 cc |

### Weber 32 ICEE/250

| | |
|---|---|
| Application | 903 cc ES engine |
| Venturi | 22 |
| Auxiliary venturi | 3.5 |
| Main jet | 1.07 |
| Air bleed jet | 1.60 |
| Emulsion tube | F89 |
| Idle jet | 0.47 |
| Air idle jet | 1.60 |
| Pump jet | 0.40 |
| Pump outlet | 0.45 |
| Superfeed jet | 0.85 |
| Superfeed mixture jet | 2.50 |
| Fuel inlet needle valve | 1.50 |
| Anti-syphon device | 1.00 |
| Idle mixture adjustment hole | 1.50 |
| Float setting (fuel level) | 10.5 to 11.0 |
| Fast idle (throttle valve plate gap) | 0.75 to 0.80 |
| Accelerator pump delivery (ten strokes) | 4.0 to 5.5 cc |

### Solex C 32 DISA/14

| | |
|---|---|
| Application | 903 cc ES engine |
| Venturi | 23 |
| Auxiliary venturi | 3.4 |
| Main jet | 1.20 |
| Air bleed jet | 1.30 |
| Emulsion tube | B03 |
| Idle jet | 0.525 |
| Idle air jet | 1.20 |
| Pump jet | 0.70 |
| Pump outlet | 0.45 |
| Fuel inlet needle valve | 1.60 |
| Anti-syphon device | 2.0 |
| Idle mixture adjustment hole | 1.20 |
| Float setting (fuel level) | 2.0 to 3.0 |
| Fast idle (throttle valve plate gap) | 0.90 to 1.0 |
| Accelerator pump delivery (ten strokes) | 2.5 to 4.5 cc |

### Weber 32 ICEV 51/250

| | |
|---|---|
| Application | 1116 cc engine |
| Venturi | 22 |
| Auxiliary venturi | 3.5 |
| Main jet | 1.15 |
| Air bleed jet | 1.90 |
| Emulsion tube | F74 |
| Idle jet | 0.47 |
| Air idle jet | 1.55 |
| Pump jet | 0.40 |
| Pump outlet | 0.45 |
| Superfeed jet | 0.90 |
| Superfeed mixture jet | 2.50 |
| Fuel inlet needle valve | 1.50 |
| Anti-syphon device | 1.00 |
| Idle mixture adjustment hole | 1.50 |
| Float setting (fuel level) | 10.5 to 11.0 |
| Float setting (travel/stroke) | 45.0 |
| Fast idle (throttle valve plate gap) | 0.85 to 0.90 |
| Accelerator pump delivery (ten strokes) | 3.2 to 5.2 cc |

## Solex C 32 DISA/12

| | |
|---|---|
| Application | 1116 cc engine |
| Venturi | 22 |
| Auxiliary venturi | 3.4 |
| Main jet | 1.22 |
| Air bleed jet | 2.0 |
| Emulsion tube | 86 |
| Idle jet | 0.57 |
| Air idle jet | 1.40 |
| Pump jet | 0.45 |
| Pump outlet | 0.50 |
| Superfeed jet | 1.15 |
| Superfeed mixture jet | 2.0 |
| Fuel inlet needle valve | 1.60 |
| Anti-syphon device | 1.60 |
| Idle mixture adjustment hole | 1.70 |
| Float setting (fuel level) | 2.0 to 3.0 |
| Fast idle (throttle valve plate gap) | 0.90 to 1.0 |
| Accelerator pump delivery (ten strokes) | 3.0 to 4.0 cc |

## Weber 30/32 DMTR 90/250

| | | |
|---|---|---|
| Application | 1301 cc engine | |
| | **Primary** | **Secondary** |
| Venturi | 19 | 23 |
| Auxiliary venturi | 3.5 | 5 |
| Main jet | 0.87 | 0.95 |
| Air bleed jet | 1.85 | 1.75 |
| Emulsion tube | F43 | F38 |
| Idle jet | 0.50 | 0.50 |
| Air idle jet | 1.10 | 0.70 |
| Pump jet | 0.45 | – |
| Pump outlet | 0.40 | – |
| Superfeed jet | – | 0.80 |
| Superfeed mixture jet | – | 2.00 |
| Fuel inlet needle valve | 1.50 | |
| Anti-syphon device | 1.0 | – |
| Idle mixture adjustment hole | 1.50 | – |
| Float setting (fuel level) | 6.75 to 7.25 | |
| Fast idle (throttle valve plate gap) | 0.90 to 0.95 | |
| Accelerator pump delivery (ten strokes) | 8.5 to 12.5 cc | |

## Solex C 30/32 CIC/1

| | | |
|---|---|---|
| Application | 1301 cc engine | |
| | **Primary** | **Secondary** |
| Venturi | 19 | 23 |
| Auxiliary venturi | 3.2 | 4 |
| Main jet | 1.15 | 1.27 |
| Air bleed jet | 2.30 | 2.0 |
| Emulsion tube | 95 | 95 |
| Idle jet | 0.50 | 0.50 |
| Air idle jet | 1.20 | 1.60 |
| Pump jet | 0.50 | – |
| Pump outlet | 0.45 | – |
| Fuel inlet needle valve | 1.60 | |
| Anti-syphon device | 1.80 | – |
| Idle mixture adjustment hole | 1.60 | – |
| Float setting (fuel level) | 6.5 to 7.5 | |
| Fast idle (throttle valve plate gap) | 0.90 to 1.0 | |
| Accelerator pump delivery (ten strokes) | 7.5 to 9.5 cc | |

## Engine idle speed

| | |
|---|---|
| At normal operating temperature | 800 to 850 rev/min |

## CO percentage at idle

| | |
|---|---|
| CO percentage at idle | 3.5 maximum |

## Torque wrench settings

| | Nm | lbf ft |
|---|---|---|
| Exhaust manifold nuts (903 cc) | 20 | 15 |
| Exhaust and intake manifold nuts (1116 cc, 1301 cc) | 28 | 20 |
| Fuel pump nuts | 28 | 20 |
| Carburettor mounting nuts | 25 | 18 |

## 1   Description and maintenance

1   The fuel system consists of a rear-mounted fuel tank, a mechanically-operated fuel pump and a carburettor and air cleaner.
2   On all engines except the 1301 cc a single venturi downdraught carburettor is fitted. On the 1301 cc version, a dual barrel carburettor is fitted.
3   Maintenance consists of periodically checking the condition and security of the fuel hoses to the pump and carburettor. The fuel pump cannot be cleaned or repaired and in the event of a fault developing, the pump must be renewed.
4   On ES versions, an electronic fuel cut-out device is fitted which reduces fuel consumption on overrun, see Chapter 9, Section 33.

## 2   Air cleaner – servicing, removal and refitting

1   The air cleaner air intake draws air either from the front of the car or from the outside of the exhaust manifold according to ambient temperature (photo).

2.5 Air cleaner cover

2.1 Air cleaner hot air intake

2.6 Removing air cleaner element

2   At an ambient temperature of 13°C (55°F) and above, the SUN symbol should align with the intake spout arrow head. Remove the cover nuts and turn the cover.
3   At an ambient temperature lower than this, move the air cleaner cover until the SNOWFLAKE symbol aligns with the intake spout arrow head.
4   At the intervals specified in Routine Maintenance renew the air cleaner filter element.
5   To do this, remove the cover nuts and take off the cover (photo).
6   Take out the filter element and discard it. Wipe out the air cleaner casing (photo).
7   Locate the new element and refit the cover aligning the appropriate symbols.

### 903 cc engine

8   To remove the air cleaner from the 903 cc engine, unscrew the nuts and take off the cover. Lift out the filter element.
9   Unbolt the air cleaner casing from the carburettor flange and from the bracket on the rocker cover. Disconnect the vent hose (photo).
10 Disconnect the warm and cool air intake hoses from their collecting points and lift the air cleaner from the engine.

2.9 Crankcase vent hose at air cleaner

## 1116 cc and 1301 cc engines

11  Removal of the air cleaner from the 1116 cc engine is similar to that described for the 903 cc engine, but having a cylinder head support bracket (photos).
12  The air cleaner on the 1301 cc engine is mounted on the four flange studs of the carburettors, their nuts being accessible after the air cleaner lid has been removed and the filter element extracted.
13  Refitting of all types of air cleaner is a reversal of removal.

## 3  Fuel pump – removal and refitting

1  On 903 cc engines, the fuel pump is mounted on the side of the timing chain cover and is driven by a pushrod from an eccentric on the front of the camshaft.
2  On the 1116 cc and 1301 cc engines, the fuel pump is mounted on the side of the crankcase and is driven by a pushrod from an eccentric on the auxiliary shaft.
3  The removal of both types of pump is carried out in a similar way.
4  Disconnect the fuel inlet hose from the pump and plug the hose (photo).

3.4 Fuel pump

2.11A Air cleaner mounting studs (1116 cc)

5  Disconnect the fuel outlet hose from the pump.
6  Unscrew the pump fixing bolt and remove it together with spacer, pushrod and gaskets (photos).
7  Refitting is a reversal of removal. Make sure that a new gasket is located on each side of the spacer.
8  The gasket on the inboard side of the spacer should always be 0.3 mm thick, but gaskets for the outboard side are available in thicknesses 0.3, 0.7 and 1.2 mm, as a means of adjusting the fuel pump pressure. The standard fuel pressure is 0.176 bar (2.55 lbf/in²). If the pressure is too high a thicker gasket should be used, if too low, fit a thinner one.

## 4  Fuel level transmitter – removal and refitting

1  The transmitter is accessible after having removed the small cover panel from the floor of the car under the rear seat (tipped forward) with the floor covering peeled back (photo).

2.11B Air cleaner mounting bracket and pipe clip

3.6A Fuel pump on mounting studs

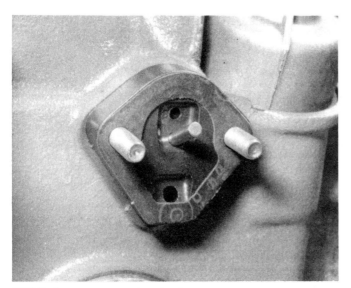

3.6B Fuel pump spacer and pushrod

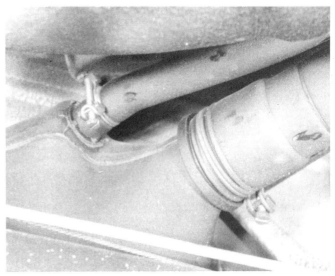

5.3 Fuel tank filler and vent hoses

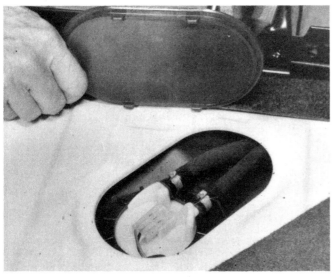

4.1 Fuel tank transmitter

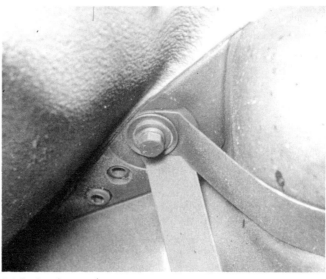

5.4 Fuel tank mounting straps

2   Disconnect the fuel flow and return hoses and the electrical leads from the transmitter.
3   Unscrew the securing ring and lift the transmitter from the tank.
4   Refitting is a reversal of removal. Use a new rubber sealing ring.

## 5   Fuel tank – removal and refitting

1   It is preferable to remove the fuel tank when it has only a very small quantity of fuel in it. If this cannot be arranged, syphon out as much fuel as possible into a suitable container which can be sealed.
2   The tank is mounted just forward of the rear axle.
3   Disconnect the filler hose and the breather hose from the tank (photo).
4   Unscrew the mounting bolts from the support straps and lower the tank using a jack with a block of wood as an insulator. Release the handbrake cable from its support bracket on the side of the tank (photo).
5   Once the tank has been lowered sufficiently far, disconnect the fuel

supply and return hoses, breather hose and sender unit leads and remove the tank from the car.
**Warning**: *Never attempt to solder or weld a fuel tank yourself; always leave fuel tank repairs to the experts. Never syphon fuel into a container in an inspection pit. Fuel vapour is heavier than air and can remain in the pit for a considerable time.*
6   If the tank contains sediment or water, clean it out by using several changes of paraffin and shaking vigorously. In order to avoid damage to the sender unit, remove this before commencing operations.
7   Finally allow to drain and rinse out with clean fuel.
8   Refit by reversing the removal operations.
9   On 1984 and later models, the fuel tank is of plastic construction.

## 6   Carburettors – general

1   The need to completely overhaul a carburettor is rare. A carburettor can normally be kept in good working order if the top cover is removed and the fuel mopped out of the fuel bowl. Individual jets can be

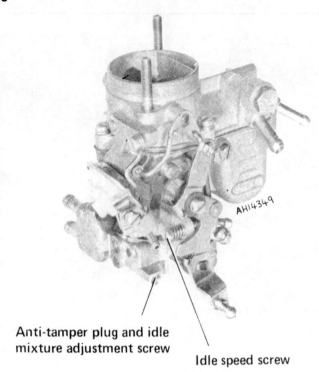

Anti-tamper plug and idle
mixture adjustment screw

Idle speed screw

Fig. 3.1 Weber 32 ICEV 50/250 carburettor (Sec 6)

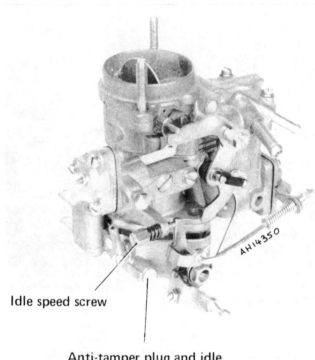

Idle speed screw

Anti-tamper plug and idle
mixture adjustment screw

Fig. 3.2 Solex C32 DISA 11 carburettor (Sec 6)

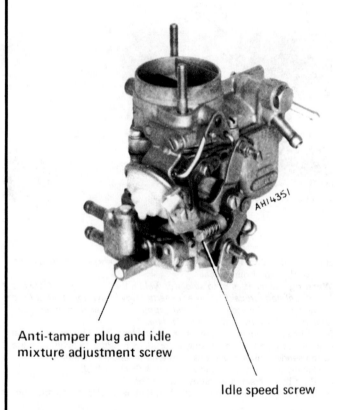

Anti-tamper plug and idle
mixture adjustment screw

Idle speed screw

Fig. 3.3 Weber 32 ICEV 51/250 carburettor (Sec 6)

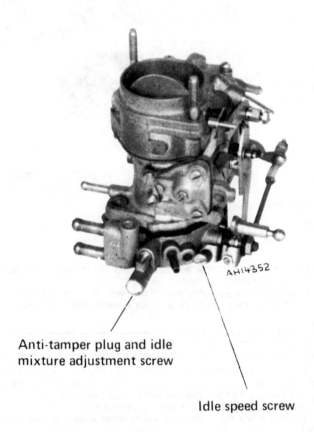

Anti-tamper plug and idle
mixture adjustment screw

Idle speed screw

Fig. 3.4 Solex C32 DISA 12 carburettor (Sec 6)

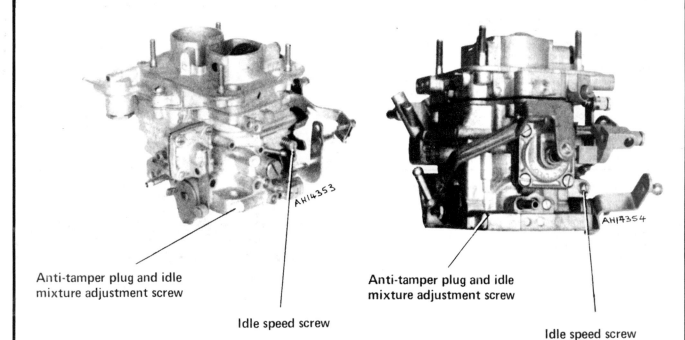

Anti-tamper plug and idle
mixture adjustment screw

Idle speed screw

**Fig. 3.5 Weber 30/32 DMTR 90/250 carburettor (Sec 6)**

Anti-tamper plug and idle
mixture adjustment screw

Idle speed screw

**Fig. 3.6 Solex C30/32 CIC/1 carburettor (Sec 16)**

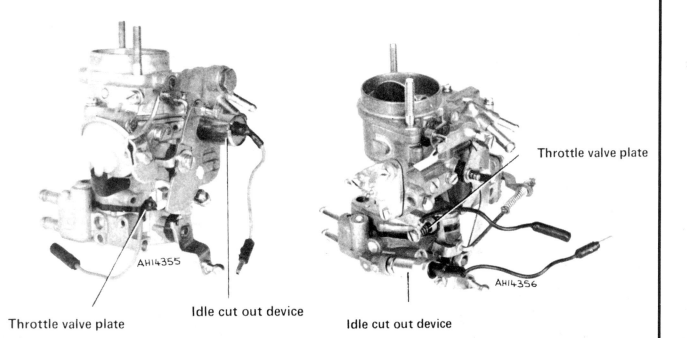

Throttle valve plate

Idle cut out device

Throttle valve plate

Idle cut out device

**Fig. 3.7 Weber 32 ICEE/250 carburettor (Sec 6)**

**Fig. 3.8 C32 DISA 14 carburettor (Sec 6)**

removed and blown through. *Never probe them with wire or their calibration will be ruined.*
2   Take the opportunity to check the jet sizes and other components against those listed in the Specifications in case a previous owner has substituted some of incorrect calibration.
3   When the stage is reached where the valve plate spindle bushes have worn, then the carburettor should be renewed complete.
4   When reassembling the carburettor, use new gaskets which can be obtained in a repair pack.

## 7   Carburettor idle speed and mixture – adjustment

1   All carburettors have their mixture adjustment set in production. The screw is fitted with a tamperproof cap.
2   Under normal circumstances, only the idle speed screw need be adjusted to set the engine idle speed to the specified level.
3   Before attempting to adjust the idle speed or mixture, it is important to have the ignition and valve clearances correctly set and the engine at normal operating temperature with the air cleaner fitted.
4   Where the mixture must be adjusted, prise out the tamperproof plug and turn the mixture screw in to weaken or out to enrich the mixture until the engine runs smoothly without any tendency to 'hunt'.
5   Ideally an exhaust gas analyser should be used to make sure that the CO level is within the specified range.
6   Once the mixture has been correctly set, re-adjust the idle speed screw.

## 8   Carburettor – removal and refitting

1   Remove the air cleaner.
2   Disconnect the flow and return fuel hoses from the carburettor and plug them.
3   Disconnect the coolant hoses from the carburettor throttle valve plate block. Provided the cooling system is cold and not under pressure there should be almost no loss of coolant. Tie the hoses up as high as possible with a piece of wire.
4   Disconnect the vacuum and vent hoses from the carburettor.
5   Disconnect the throttle and choke controls from the carburettor.
6   Unscrew the mounting flange nuts and lift the carburettor from the intake manifold (photo).
7   Refitting is a reversal of removal. Use a new flange gasket and make sure that the fuel return hose is routed above the air cleaner intake.

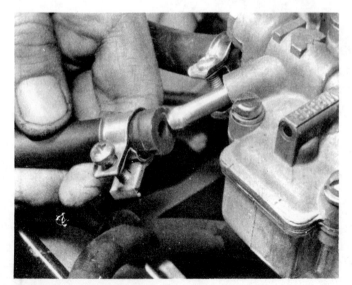

8.2 Fuel hose at carburettor

8.6 Carburettor mounting flange nut

## 9   Carburettor (Weber 32 ICEV 50/250/1) – servicing and adjustment

1   The carburettor top cover with float may be removed without the need to withdraw the carburettor from the manifold. The other adjustments described will require removal of the carburettor.
2   Unscrew the filter plug from the top cover, clean the filter screen and refit it.
3   Extract the top cover fixing screws, lift the cover and tilt it to unhook it from the diaphragm capsule link rod.
4   Access to the fuel inlet needle valve is obtained by carefully tapping out the float arm pivot pin. Take care, the pivot pin pillars are very brittle.
5   Check that the needle valve body is tight otherwise fuel can bypass the needle valve and cause flooding.

### Float adjustment

6   Reassemble and check the float setting. Do this by holding the top cover vertically so that the float hangs down under its own weight. Measure dimension (A) (Fig. 3.10) which should be between 10.50 and 11.10 mm (0.41 to 0.44 in) with the gasket in position. If necessary, bend the float arm tab to adjust.
7   Now check the float travel which should be 45.0 mm (1.77 in). If adjustment is required, bend the end of the float arm.

### Accelerator pump stroke

8   Using a twist drill as a gauge, open the throttle valve plate through 3.5 mm (0.138 in).
9   Turn the nut on the accelerator pump rod until it just makes contact with the pump control lever.

### Fast idle adjustment

10  With the choke valve plate fully closed by means of the control lever, the throttle valve plate should be open (dimension A) (Fig. 3.12) between 0.75 and 0.80 mm (0.030 and 0.032 in). Adjust if necessary by means of the screw and locknut.

### Anti-flooding device

11  This consists of a diaphragm capsule and link rod.
12  The condition of the diaphragm can be checked by applying a vacuum source to the hole in the throttle valve plate block. The vacuum pressure will drop if there is a leak.
13  Actuate the choke valve plate lever fully and depress the control lever of the anti-flooding device to simulate operating vacuum.

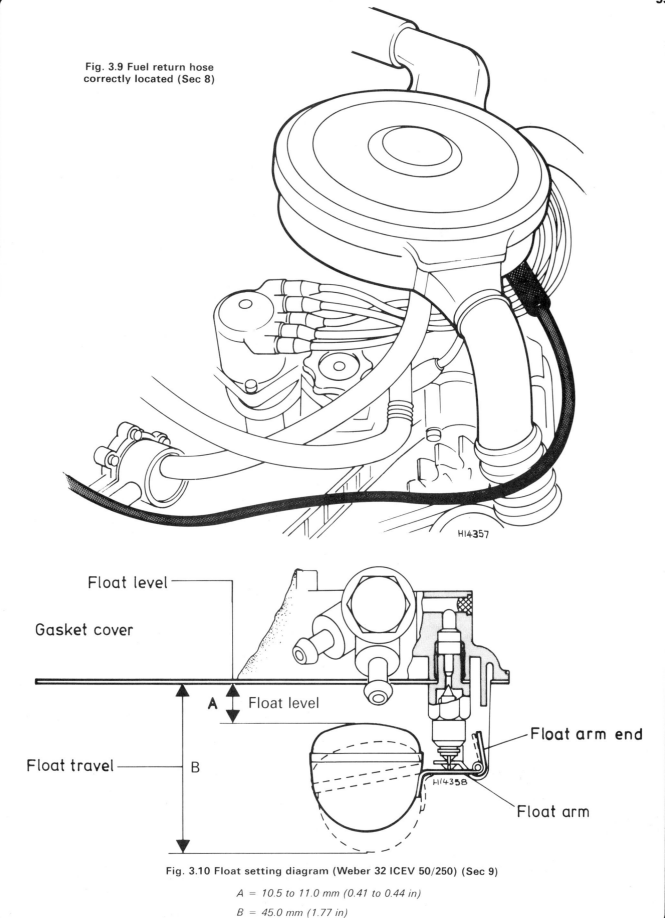

Fig. 3.9 Fuel return hose
correctly located (Sec 8)

H14357

Float level

Gasket cover

Float level

**A**

Float arm end

Float travel

B

Float arm

H14358

Fig. 3.10 Float setting diagram (Weber 32 ICEV 50/250) (Sec 9)

*A = 10.5 to 11.0 mm (0.41 to 0.44 in)*

*B = 45.0 mm (1.77 in)*

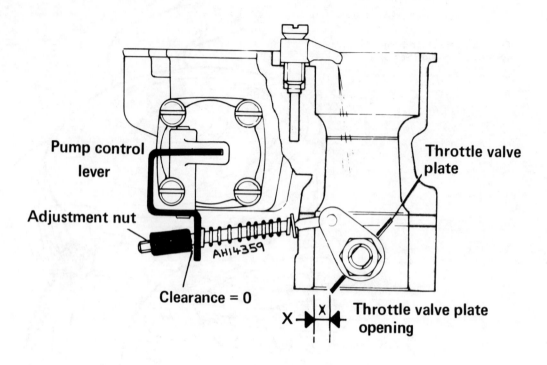

**Fig. 3.11 Accelerator pump setting diagram (Weber 32 ICEV 50/250) (Sec 9)**

*X = 3.5 mm (0.138 in)*

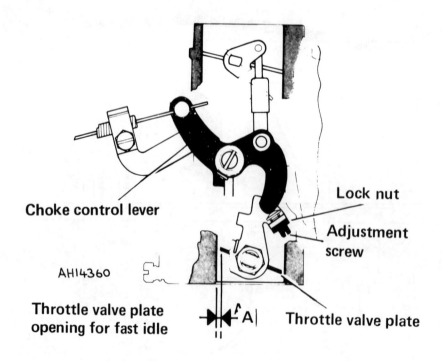

**Fig. 3.12 Fast idle adjustment diagram (Weber 32 ICEV 50/250) (Sec 19)**

*A = 0.75 to 0.80 mm (0.030 to 0.032 in)*

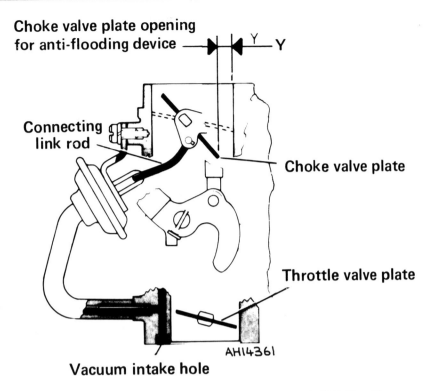

**Choke valve plate opening for anti-flooding device**

Y — Y

**Connecting link rod**

**Choke valve plate**

**Throttle valve plate**

AH14361

**Vacuum intake hole**

Fig. 3.13 Anti-flooding device (Weber 32 ICEV 50/250) (Sec 9)

*Y = 3.75 to 4.25 mm (0.148 to 0.167 in)*

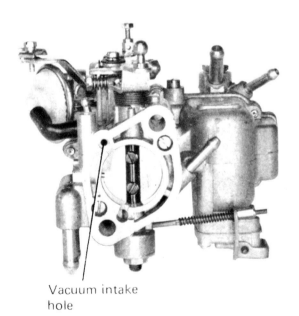

Vacuum intake hole

Fig. 3.14 Anti-flooding device vacuum intake (Weber 32 ICEV 50/250) (Sec 9)

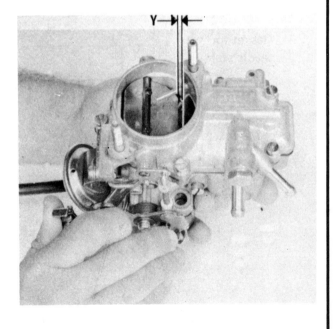

Y

Fig. 3.15 Choke valve gap opening (Weber 32 ICEV 50/250) (Sec 9)

*Y = 3.75 to 4.25 mm (0.148 to 0.167 in)*

14 There should be a gap (T) (Fig. 3.15) between the edge of the choke valve plate and the wall of the carburettor throat of between 3.75 and 4.25 mm (0.148 and 0.167 in). Any adjustment that may be needed should be carried out by bending the link rod.

## 10 Carburettor (Solex C32 DISA 11) – servicing and adjustment

1   The carburettor top cover with float may be removed without the need to withdraw the carburettor from the manifold. The other adjustments described will require removal of the carburettor.
2   Extract the top cover fixing screws, disconnect the small externally mounted tension spring and take off the the top cover.
3   Access to the fuel inlet needle valve is obtained by carefully tapping out the float arm pivot pin. Take care, the pivot pin pillars are very brittle.
4   Check that the needle valve body is tight otherwise fuel can bypass the needle valve and cause flooding.

### Float adjustment

5   Reassemble and check the float setting. Do this by inverting the top cover so that the weight of the float fully depresses the ball of the needle valve. The distance (A) (Fig. 3.16) between the float and the surface of the top cover flange gasket should be between 2.0 and 3.0 mm (0.079 and 0.118 in). If adjustment is required, alter the thickness of the washer under the needle valve.

### Accelerator pump

6   Fill the carburettor float chamber and then operate the throttle valve plate lever several times to prime the pump.
7   Position a test tube under the accelerator pump jet and give ten full strokes of the throttle lever, pausing between each stroke to allow fuel to finish dripping.
8   The total volume of fuel collected should be between 2.5 and 4.5 cc. Adjust the nut on the pump control and if necessary to increase or decrease the volume of fuel ejected.

### Fast idle adjustment

9   With the choke valve plate fully closed, the throttle valve plate should be open to give a dimension (X) (Fig. 3.18) of between 0.90 and 1.0 mm (0.035 to 0.039 in). Use a twist drill of suitable diameter to measure the gap. If necessary, adjust by means of the screw and locknut.

### Anti-flooding device

10 Close the choke valve plate by means of the control lever. At the same time, push the lean out valve rod towards the valve.
11 There should be a gap (X) (Fig. 3.19) between the edge of the choke valve plate and the carburettor throat of between 4.75 and 5.25 mm (0.187 to 0.207 in). Adjust if necessary by means of the screw and locknut on the lean out valve.

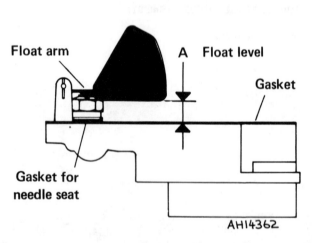

AH14362

Fig. 3.16 Float setting diagram (Solex C32 DISA 11) (Sec 10)

A = 2.0 to 3.0 mm (0.079 to 0.118 in)

Fig. 3.17 Adjusting accelerator pump rod (Solex C32 DISA 11) (Sec 10)

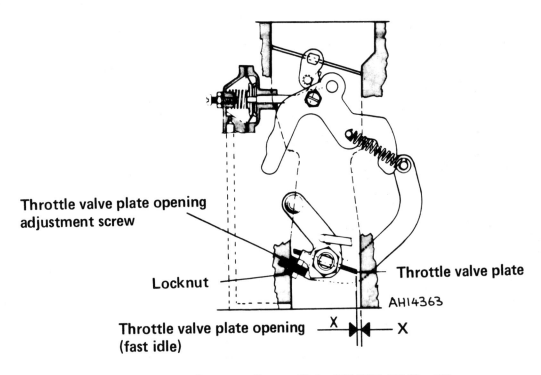

Throttle valve plate opening
adjustment screw

Locknut

Throttle valve plate

AHI4363

Throttle valve plate opening
(fast idle)

X ◄ ► X

Fig. 3.18 Fast idle adjustment diagram (Solex C32 DISA 11) (Sec 10)

*X = 0.90 to 1.0 mm (0.035 to 0.039 in)*

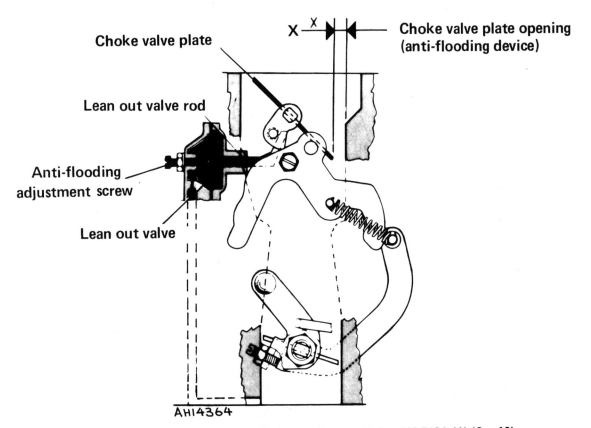

X ◄ ► X

Choke valve plate opening
(anti-flooding device)

Choke valve plate

Lean out valve rod

Anti-flooding
adjustment screw

Lean out valve

AHI4364

Fig. 3.19 Anti-flooding device adjustment diagram (Solex C32 DISA 11) (Sec 10)

*X = 4.75 to 5.25 mm (0.187 to 0.207 in)*

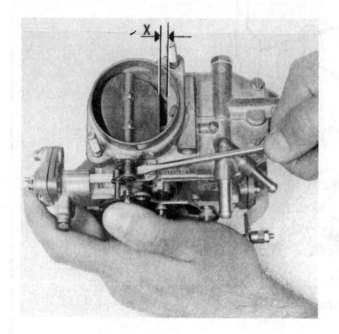

Fig. 3.20 Moving lean out valve rod (Solex C32 DISA 11)
(Sec 10)

X = 4.75 to 5.25 mm (0.187 to 0.207 in)

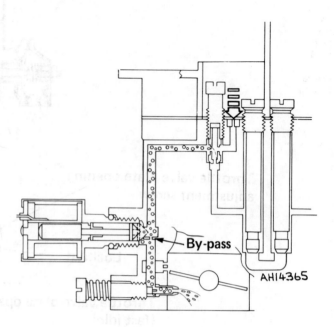

Fig. 3.21 Sectional view of fuel cut-off switch (Solex C32
DISA 14) (Sec 11)

## 11 Carburettors (Weber 32 ICEE/250 and Solex C32 DISA 14) – description and adjustment

1   One of these carburettors is used on 903 cc ES engines. They are very similar to the Weber 32 ICEV 50/250 and Solex C32 DISA 11 already described in this Chapter except that a fuel cut-out solenoid valve is fitted in association with the Digiplex ignition system (see Chapters 4 and 9).
2   The solenoid valve cuts off the supply of fuel to the carburettor whenever the accelerator pedal is released during overrun conditions.
3   A fuel cut-out device control unit receives information regarding engine speed from the static ignition control unit.
4   A throttle butterfly switch relays information that the accelerator pedal is in the released state.
5   At certain minimum idle speeds during deceleration, the fuel cut-out solenoid valve is re-energised so that engine idling is maintained without the tendency to cut out.
6   The Solex type control unit varies the fuel cut-out point according to the deceleration value.

*Fault testing*

7   Should a fault develop, connect a test lamp between the fuel cut-out solenoid switch and a good earth.
8   Connect a reliable tachometer to the engine in accordance with the maker's instructions.
9   Start the engine and raise its speed to between 3000 and 4000 rev/min, then fully release the accelerator pedal.
10   The test lamp should only go out during the period when the accelerator pedal is released. Should the test lamp remain on all the time, or never come on, check the throttle switch earth and the solenoid switch connections.
11   Disconnect the multi-plug from the control unit. Switch on the ignition and check that a test lamp connected between contact 7 of the multi-plug and earth will illuminate. If it does not, there is an open circuit from connection 15/54 of the fuel cut-off switch.
12   Switch off the ignition and check for continuity between contact 3 of the multiplug and earth. An ohmmeter will be required for this test.
13   If there is no continuity (ohmmeter shows infinity), check all the system earth connections. Also check that the wiring plug under the control unit is properly connected.

14   Finally, check the engine speed signal. To do this, a tachometer must be connected to the single socket under the control unit within the engine compartment.
15   If the tachometer registers correctly then this confirms that the electronic ignition control unit is functioning, if the tachometer does not register, renew the ignition control unit.
16   If a replacement carburettor is to be fitted, only fit the Solex assembly including the control module, even if a Weber was originally fitted.

## 12 Carburettor (Weber 32 ICEV 51/250) – servicing and adjustment

1   This carburettor, fitted to 1116 cc engines, is very similar to the unit described in Section 9.
2   The fast idle adjustment procedure is identical, but note that dimension (A) (Fig. 3.12) should be between 0.85 and 0.90 mm (0.033 and 0.035 in).
3   The choke valve plate gap (Y) (Fig. 3.13) should be between 5.5 and 6.5 mm (0.22 and 0.26 in) and if adjustment is required, bend the stop on the control lever.

## 13 Carburettor (Solex C32 DISA 12) – servicing and adjustment

1   This carburettor is an alternative to the Weber fitted to 1116 cc engines.
2   The adjustments described in Section 9 apply.

## 14 Carburettor (Weber 30/32 DMTR 90/250) – servicing and adjustment

1   The carburettor top cover with float may be removed without the need to withdraw the carburettor from the manifold. The other adjustments described in this Section will require removal of the carburettor.
2   Extract the top cover fixing screws and lift away the top cover with float. Access to the fuel inlet needle valve is as described in Section 9 paragraphs 4 and 5.

*Float adjustment*

3  Hold the cover vertically so that the floats hang down under their own weight. Measure the distance between the float and the surface of the gasket on the top cover. This should be between 6.75 and 7.25 mm (0.27 and 0.29 in).
4  Bend the float arm if necessary to adjust the setting.

*Primary valve plate opening*

5  With the throttle valve plate control lever in contact with the stop, the primary valve plate should be open (dimension X Fig. 3.22) between 6.45 and 6.95 mm (0.25 and 0.27 in). If adjustment is required, carefully bend the lever stop.

*Primary and secondary valve plate openings*

6  With the throttle control lever fully actuated the valve plate gaps (X and Y Fig. 3.24) should be:

$X = 13.5$ to $14.5$ mm ($0.53$ to $0.57$ in)
$Y = 14.5$ to $15.5$ mm ($0.57$ to $0.61$ in)

*Fast idle*

7  Close the choke valve plate fully and check the gap (A) (Fig. 3.25) between the edge of the throttle valve plate and the carburettor throat.

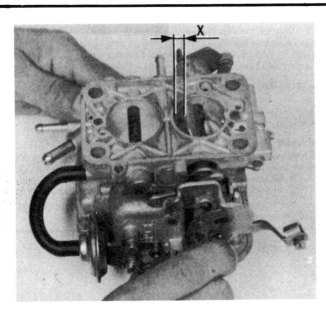

Fig. 3.22 Primary valve plate opening (Weber 30/32 DMTR 90/250) (Sec 14)

$X = 6.45$ to $6.95$ mm ($0.25$ to $0.27$ in)

Fig. 3.24 Throttle valve plate openings (Weber 30/32 DMTR 90/250) (Sec 14)

$X$ (primary) $= 13.5$ to $14.5$ mm ($0.53$ to $0.57$ in)
$Y$ (secondary) $= 14.5$ to $15.5$ mm ($0.57$ to $0.61$ in)

Fig. 3.23 Bending throttle lever stop (Weber 30/32 DMTR 90/250) (Sec 14)

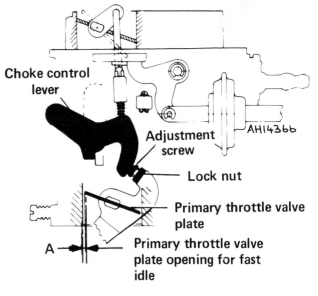

Fig. 3.25 Fast idle adjustment diagram (Weber 30/32 DMTR 90/250) (Sec 14)

$A = 0.90$ to $0.95$ mm ($0.035$ to $0.037$ in)

The gap should be between 0.90 and 0.95 mm (0.035 and 0.037 in), a twist drill is useful for measuring this.

8   If adjustment is required, carry this out using the screw and locknut.

### Anti-flooding device (mechanically-operated)

9   With the choke control pulled fully out, it should be possible to open the choke valve plate to give a gap (X) of between 7.0 and 7.5 mm (0.28 and 0.30 in). If adjustment is required, carefully bend the stop on the control lever (Fig. 3.26).

### Anti-flooding device (automatic)

10  Pull the choke control fully out and hold the control lever, on the anti-flooding device, depressed. There should be a gap (Y) (Fig. 3.27) between the edge of the choke valve plate and the carburettor wall of between 3.75 and 4.25 mm (0.15 and 0.17 in). If adjustment is required, turn the adjuster screw provided.

### 15  Carburettor (Solex C30-32 (CIC/1) – servicing and adjustment

1   The carburettor top cover with float may be removed without the need to withdraw the carburettor from the manifold.

2   The other adjustments described in this Section will require removal of the carburettor.

3   Extract the top cover fixing screws and lift away the top cover with float.

4   Refer to Section 9 paragraphs 4 and 5 for details of removal of the fuel inlet needle valve.

### Float adjustment

5   Invert the carburettor cover so that the weight of the floats depresses the ball of the needle valve.

6   Measure the distance between the float and the surface of the cover gasket. This should be between 6.5 and 7.5 mm (0.26 and 0.30 in). If adjustment is required, change the thickness of the needle valve washer or carefully bend the float arm.

### Accelerator pump

7   Refer to Section 10, paragraphs 6 and 7. The total volume of fuel collected should be between 7.5 and 9.5 cc. If the volume of fuel is incorrect, release the locknut and turn the adjuster screw on the pump lever then re-test the volume ejected.

### Fast idle

8   Operate the choke control lever to close the choke valve plate. The gap between the edge of the primary throttle valve plate and the venturi wall should be between 0.90 and 1.00 mm (0.035 and 0.039 in). If adjustment is required, turn the nut on the fast idle rod.

### Automatic anti-flooding device

9   The vacuum system of the device can be checked for leaks by applying a vacuum to the drilling in the carburettor throttle valve block. If vacuum cannot be maintained, renew the diaphragm.

### Choke valve plate automatic opening

10  Move the choke control lever to fully close the choke valve plate and then press the lean out valve rod. There should now be a gap (X) (Fig. 3.32) between the edge of the choke valve plate and the wall of the carburettor throat of between 4.75 and 5.25 mm (0.187 and 0.207 in).

11  Where adjustment is required, release the locknut and turn the screw on the lean out valve.

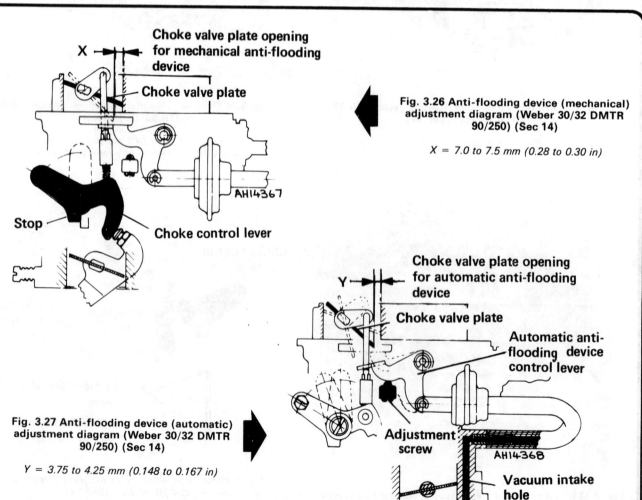

Fig. 3.26 Anti-flooding device (mechanical) adjustment diagram (Weber 30/32 DMTR 90/250) (Sec 14)

X = 7.0 to 7.5 mm (0.28 to 0.30 in)

Fig. 3.27 Anti-flooding device (automatic) adjustment diagram (Weber 30/32 DMTR 90/250) (Sec 14)

Y = 3.75 to 4.25 mm (0.148 to 0.167 in)

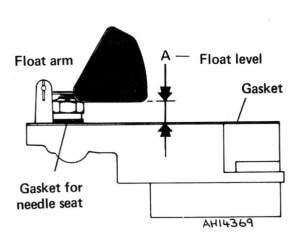

Float arm

A — Float level

Gasket

Gasket for needle seat

AH14369

Fig. 3.28 Float setting diagram (Solex C30-32 CIC/1) (Sec 15)

*A = 6.5 to 7.5 mm (0.26 to 0.30 in)*

Fig. 3.29 Adjusting accelerator pump stroke (Solex C30-32 CIC/1) (Sec 15)

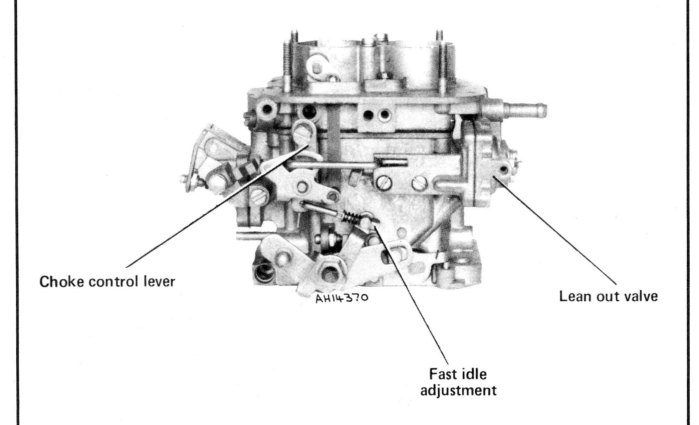

Choke control lever

Lean out valve

AH14370

Fast idle adjustment

Fig. 3.30 Fast idle screw on Solex C30-32 CIC/1 (Sec 15)

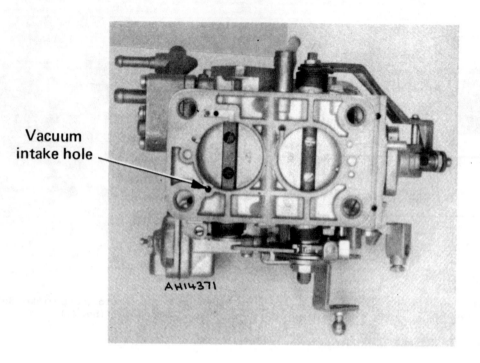

**Fig. 3.31 Vacuum drilling for automatic anti-flooding device (Solex C30-32 CIC/1) (Sec 15)**

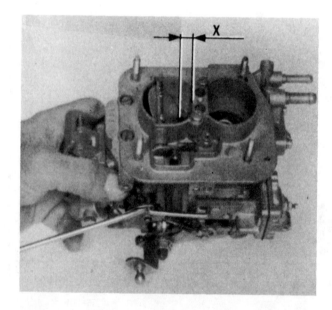

**Fig. 3.32 Choke valve plate setting (Solex C30-32 CIC/1) (Sec 15)**

*X = 4.75 to 5.25 mm (0.187 to 0.207 in)*

## 16 Economy meter

1   This device is fitted to ES (energy saving) models. It is essentially a vacuum gauge to advise the driver with regard to economical throttle opening related to engine and road speed. The point of change to a higher gear can also be deduced from this gauge. The latter facility is provided by an LED (light emitting diode).
2   Fault testing of the system is described in Chapter 9.

## 17 Accelerator cable – adjustment and renewal

1   The socket type cable end fitting is detached from the carburettor throttle lever simply by prising it off the ball stud.
2   Adjustment can be carried out by releasing the locknut and turning the end fitting. With the accelerator pedal fully depressed, check that full throttle can be obtained at the carburettor.
3   To renew the cable, prise off the end fitting from the carburettor throttle lever.
4   Slip the cable sleeve from its retaining bracket (photo).
5   Working inside the car under the facia panel, slip the cable from the fork at the top of the accelerator pedal arm (photo).
6   Withdraw the cable through the engine compartment bulkhead.
7   Fit the new cable by reversing the removal operations, adjust as described in paragraph 2.

17.4 Throttle cable sleeve and bracket

17.5 Accelerator pedal

18.3 Extracting choke control lever screw

## 18 Choke control cable – removal and refitting

1  Remove the air cleaner.
2  Release the choke outer cable clamp and the inner cable from the swivel on the choke control lever (photo).
3  The choke control is of lever type. To remove it, extract its hinge screw, accessible when the lever is pulled upwards (photo).
4  Withdraw the choke cable assembly until the inner cable can be released from the hand control lever and the choke warning lamp lead unplugged.
5  Withdraw the cable assembly through the engine compartment rear bulkhead.
6  Fit the new cable by reversing the removal operations. Before tightening the inner cable pinch screw at the carburettor, hold the choke valve plate open and pull the control lever out 2.0 or 3.0 mm, then tighten the screw. This will provide just enough free movement to ensure that when the control is pushed fully in the choke valve plate

will remain fully open even with engine movement slightly stretching the cable.

## 19 Manifolds and exhaust system

1  The intake manifold on 903 cc engines is integral with the cylinder head.
2  On the other engines, the intake and exhaust manifolds are mounted on the same side of the cylinder head.
3  A hot air collector plate is fitted over the exhaust manifold from where the air cleaner draws air when in the winter setting.
4  When fitting a manifold, thoroughly clean the cylinder head and manifold mating surfaces, use a new gasket and tighten nuts to the specified torque (photos).
5  The exhaust system on 903 cc models is of single downpipe, single silencer two section type.

18.2 Choke cable at carburettor

19.4A Manifold gasket

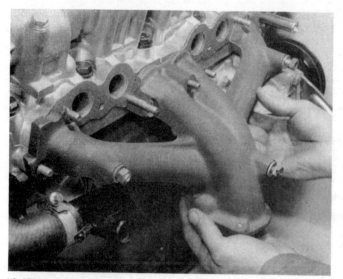

19.4B Fitting exhaust manifold

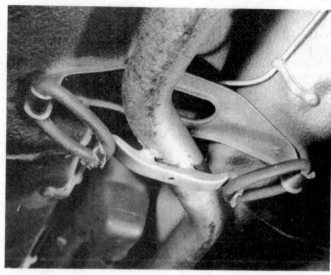

19.7A Exhaust pipe support rings

19.4C Fitting intake manifold complete with carburettor

19.7B Exhaust tailpipe mounting

6    On 1116 cc and 1301 cc models, the exhaust system is of dual downpipe, two silencer, two section type.

7    The exhaust system is flexibly mounted (photo). Holts Flexiwrap and Holts Gun Gum exhaust repair systems can be used for effective repairs to exhaust pipes and silencer boxes, including ends and bends. Holts Flexiwrap is an MOT approved permanent exhaust repair. Holts Firegum is suitable for the assembly of all exhaust system joints.

8    Do not attempt to separate the sections of the exhaust system, while in position in the car. Unbolt the pipe from the manifold and, using a screwdriver, prise off the flexible suspension rings. Provided the car is then raised on jacks, ramps or placed over an inspection pit, the complete exhaust system can be withdrawn from under the car.

9    If only one section is to be renewed, it is far easier to separate once the complete system is out of the car.

10  When refitting, grease the pipe sockets and fit the clamps loosely until the suspension rings are connected and the downpipe bolted up (using a new copper gasket). Check the attitude of the sections with regard to each other and the adjacent parts of the underbody. Fully tighten the clamps and downpipe flange nuts, remembering to bend up the lockplate tabs on 1116 cc and 1301 cc models (photo).

11  On the larger engined models, it may be necessary to raise the vehicle at the rear and support it on axle stands so that the rear suspension hangs down and is fully extended. This will allow sufficient clearance between the axle and the body for the exhaust system to be withdrawn.

19.10 Exhaust pipe socket clamp

## 20  Fault diagnosis – fuel system

*Unsatisfactory engine performance and excessive fuel consumption are not necessarily the fault of the fuel system or carburettor. In fact they more commonly occur as a result of ignition and timing faults. Before acting on the following it is necessary to check the ignition system first. Even though a fault may lie in the fuel system it will be difficult to trace unless the ignition is correct. The faults below, therefore, assume that this has been attended to first (where appropriate).*

| Symptom | Reason(s) |
| --- | --- |
| Smell of petrol when engine is stopped | Leaking fuel lines or unions<br>Leaking fuel tank |
| Smell of petrol when engine is idling | Leaking fuel line unions between pump and carburettor<br>Overflow of fuel from float chamber due to wrong level setting, ineffective needle valve or punctured float |
| Excessive fuel consumption for reasons not covered by leaks or float chamber faults | Worn jets<br>Over-rich setting<br>Sticking mechanism<br>Dirty air cleaner element |
| Difficult starting, uneven running, lack of power, cutting out | One or more jets blocked or restricted<br>Float chamber fuel level too low or needle valve sticking<br>Fuel pump not delivering sufficient fuel<br>Induction leak |
| Difficult starting when cold | Choke control<br>Insufficient use of manual choke<br>Weak mixture |
| Difficult starting when hot | Excessive use of manual choke<br>Accelerator pedal pumped before starting<br>Vapour lock (especially in hot weather or at high altitude)<br>Rich mixture |
| Engine does not respond properly to throttle | Faulty accelerator pump<br>Blocked jet(s)<br>Slack in accelerator cable |
| Engine idle speed drops when hot | Incorrect air cleaner intake setting<br>Overheated fuel pump |
| Engine runs on | Idle speed too high |

# Chapter 4 Ignition system

*For modifications, and information applicable to later models, see Supplement at end of manual*

## Contents

## Specifications

### System type
Except ES engines ................................................................... Battery, coil mechanical breaker distributor
ES engines ............................................................................... Marelli Digiplex electronic with breakerless distributor

### Firing order ........................................... 1 – 3 – 4 – 2 (No. 1 cylinder at crankshaft pulley end)

### *Mechanical breaker distributor*
#### General
Type .......................................................................................... Marelli or Ducellier
Contact breaker points gap ...................................................... 0.37 to 0.43 mm (0.015 to 0.017 in)
Condenser capacity .................................................................. 0.20 to 0.25 µF
Dwell angle .............................................................................. 52 to 58°
Rotor rotational direction ......................................................... Clockwise
Ignition timing (dynamic):
  903 cc engine ...................................................................... 5° BTDC at idle
  1116 and 1301 cc engines .................................................. 10° BTDC at idle
Centrifugal advance:
  903 cc engine ...................................................................... Between 30 and 34° max
  1116 and 1301 cc engines .................................................. Between 22 and 24° max
Vacuum advance ...................................................................... Between 10 and 14° max

### Ignition coil
Primary winding resistance at 20°C (68°F) .............................. Between 2.6 and 3.3 ohms depending upon make of coil
Secondary winding resistance at 20°C (68°F) .......................... Between 6745 and 12 000 ohms depending upon make of coil

### *Marelli Digiplex electronic ignition*
#### General
Rotor arm resistance ................................................................ 1000 ohms
Advance range .......................................................................... Between 6 to 10° and 47 to 51°

### Engine speed sensor
Resistance on flywheel ............................................................. 612 to 748 ohms
Sensor to flywheel tooth gap .................................................... 0.25 to 1.3 mm (0.0099 to 0.0512 in)

### TDC sensor

Resistance on pulley ................................................................ 612 to 748 ohms
Sensor to pulley tooth gap ..................................................... 0.4 to 1.0 mm (0.016 to 0.039 in)

### Ignition coil

Primary winding resistance at 20°C (68°F) ........................... 0.310 to 0.378 ohms
Secondary winding resistance at 20°C (68°F) ...................... 3330 to 4070 ohms

*All systems*
### Spark plugs

Type ........................................................................................ Champion RN9YCC or RN9YC
Electrode gap .......................................................................... 0.8 mm (0.031 in)

### HT leads

903 cc (45) ............................................................................. Champion LS-07
1116, 1299 and 1301 cc (55, 60 and 70) ............................. Champion LS-05

### Torque wrench setting

|  | Nm | lbf ft |
|---|---|---|
| Spark plugs | 25 | 18 |

---

### 1 General description

On all models except the 903 ES engine version, a mechanical contact breaker type distributor is fitted.

On 45 Super ES models which have the 903 ES engine, an electronic (Digiplex) ignition system is used which incorporates a breakerless distibutor.

*Mechanical contact breaker system*

For the engine to run correctly, it is necessary for an electrical spark to ignite the fuel/air mixture in the combustion chamber at exactly the right moment in relation to engine speed and load. The ignition system is based on feeding low tension voltage from the battery to the coil where it is converted to high tension voltage. The high tension voltage is powerful enough to jump the spark plug gap in the cylinders under high compression pressures, providing that the system is in good condition and that all adjustments are correct.

The ignition system is divided into two circuits, the low tension (LT) circuit and the high tension (HT) circuit.

The low tension (sometimes known as the primary) circuit consists of the battery, the lead to the ignition switch, the lead from the ignition switch to the low tension or primary coil windings, and the lead from the low tension coil windings to the contact breaker points and condenser in the distibutor.

The high tension circuit consists of the high tension or secondary coil windings, the heavy ignition lead from the centre of the coil to the centre of the distributor cap, the rotor arm, and the spark plug leads and spark plugs.

The system functions in the following manner: High tension voltage is generated in the coil by the interruption of the low tension circuit. The interruption is effected by the opening of the contact breaker points in this low tension circuit. High tension voltage is fed from the centre of the coil via the carbon brush in the centre of the distributor cap to the rotor arm of the distributor.

The rotor arm revolves at half engine speed inside the distributor cap, and each time it comes in line with one of the four metal segments in the cap, which are connected to the spark plug leads, the opening of the contact breaker points causes the high tension voltage to build up, jump the gap from the rotor arm to the appropriate metal segment, and so via

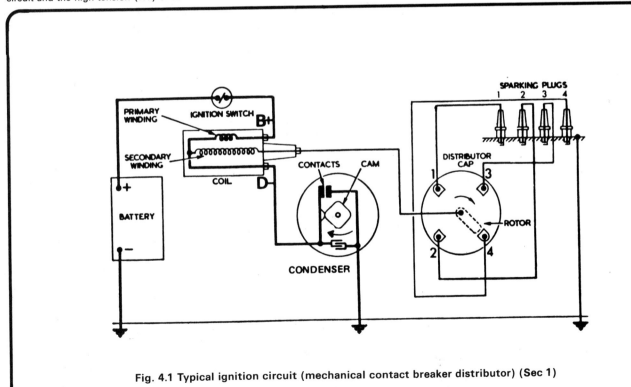

Fig. 4.1 Typical ignition circuit (mechanical contact breaker distributor) (Sec 1)

the spark plug lead to the spark plug, where it finally jumps the spark plug gap before going to earth.

The ignition timing is advanced and retarded automatically, to ensure the spark occurs at just the right instant for the particular load at the prevailing engine speed.

The ignition advance is controlled mechanically, and by vacuum. The mechanical governor mechanism consists of two weights, which move out from the distributor shaft as the engine speed rises, due to centrifugal force. As they move outwards, they rotate the cam relative to the distributor shaft, and so advance the spark. The weights are held in position by two springs and it is the tension of the springs which is largely responsible for correct spark advancement.

The vacuum advance is controlled by a diaphragm capsule connected to the carburettor venturi. The vacuum pressure varies according to the throttle valve plate opening and so adjusts the ignition advance in accordance with the engine requirements.

### Digiplex ignition system

This electronic system eliminates the mechanical contact breaker and centrifugal advance mechanism of conventional distributors and uses an electronic control unit to provide advance values according to engine speed and load. No provision is made for adjustment of the ignition timing.

Information relayed to the control unit is provided by two magnetic sensors which monitor engine speed and TDC directly from the engine crankshaft.

A vacuum sensor in the control unit converts intake manifold vacuum into an electric signal.

The control unit selects the optimum advance angle required and a closed magnetic circuit resin coil guarantees a spark owing to the low primary winding resistance.

Five hundred and twelve advance values are stored in the control unit memory to suit any combination of engine operating conditions.

No maintenance is required to the distributor used on this system.

### Distributor drive

The mechanical breaker type distributor on 903 cc engines and the Digiplex type distributor on 903 cc ES engines are mounted on the cylinder head and driven from a gear on the camshaft through a shaft which also drives the oil pump.

The distributor on 1116 cc and 1301 cc engines is mounted on the crankcase and is driven from a gear on the auxiliary shaft as is also the oil pump.

### 2  Mechanical contact breaker – points servicing

1   At the intervals specified in Routine Maintenance, prise down the clips on the distributor cap and place the cap with high tension leads to one side.

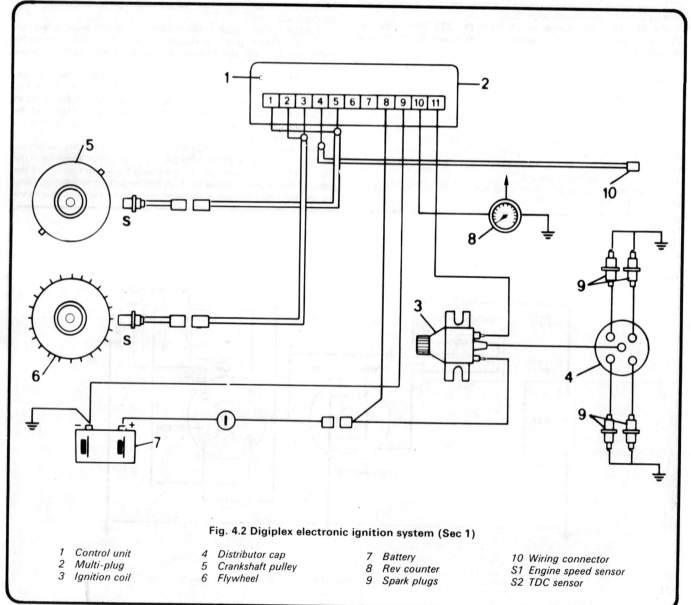

Fig. 4.2 Digiplex electronic ignition system (Sec 1)

| | | | |
|---|---|---|---|
| 1 Control unit | 4 Distributor cap | 7 Battery | 10 Wiring connector |
| 2 Multi-plug | 5 Crankshaft pulley | 8 Rev counter | S1 Engine speed sensor |
| 3 Ignition coil | 6 Flywheel | 9 Spark plugs | S2 TDC sensor |

2  Pull off the rotor.
3  Remove the spark shield. Mechanical wear of the contact breaker reduces the gap. Electrical wear builds up a 'pip' of burned metal on one of the contacts. This prevents the gap being measured for re-adjustment, and also spoils the electric circuit.

### Ducellier type distributor

4  To remove the contact breaker movable arm, extract the clip and take off the washer from the top of the pivot post.
5  Extract the screw and remove the fixed contact arm.
6  Clean the points by rubbing the surfaces on a fine abrasive such as an oil stone. The point surface should be shaped to a gentle convex curve. All the 'pip' burned onto one contact must be removed. It is not necessary to go on until all traces of the crater have been removed from the other. There is enough metal on the contacts to allow this to be done once. At alternate services, fit new points. Wash debris off cleaned points, and preservatives off new ones.
7  Now the distributor should be lubricated. This lubrication is important for the correct mechanical function of the distributor, but excess lubrication will ruin the electrical circuits, and give difficult starting.
8  Whilst the contact breaker is off, squirt some engine oil into the bottom part of the distributor, onto the centrifugal advance mechanism below the plate.
9  Wet with oil the felt pad on the top of the distributor spindle, normally covered by the rotor arm.
10  Put just a drip of oil on the pivot for the moving contact.
11  Smear a little general purpose grease onto the cam, and the heel of the moving contact breaker.
12  Refit the contact points and then set the gap in the following way.
13  Turn the crankshaft by applying a spanner to the pulley nut or by jacking up a front wheel, engaging top gear and turning the roadwheel in the forward direction of travel. Keep turning until the plastic heel of the movable contact arm is on the high point of a cam lobe on the distributor shaft.
14  Set the points gap by moving the fixed contact arm until the specified feeler blades are a sliding fit. Tighten the fixed contact arm screw.
15  Check the contact end of the rotor arm. Remove any slightly burnt deposits using fine abrasive paper. Severe erosion will necessitate renewal of the rotor.
16  Wipe out the distributor cap and check for cracks or eroded contacts (photo). Renew if evident or if the carbon brush is worn.
17  Refit the spark shield, rotor and distributor cap.
18  Setting the contact breaker gap with a feeler blade must be regarded as a means of ensuring that the engine will start. For optimum engine performance, the dwell angle must be checked and adjusted as described in Section 3.

### Marelli type distributor

19  Open the points with a finger nail and inspect their condition. If they are badly eroded or burned, then they must be renewed. The contact points can only be renewed complete with carrier plate as an assembly.
20  Release the low tension leads from the terminals on the distributor body (photo).
21  Extract the screws which hold the vacuum advance capsule to the distributor body. Tilt the capsule and release its link rod from the contact breaker carrier plate (photo).
22  Prise out the E-clip from the top of the contact breaker carrier and then withdraw the contact assembly from the top of the distributor shaft. Note the washers above and below the contact assembly (photos).
23  Fit the new contact assembly by reversing the removal operations.
24  Although the points gap is normally set in production, check it using feeler blades when the plastic heel of the movable arm is on a high point of the shaft cam. Adjust if necessary by inserting an Allen key (3.0 mm) into the socket-headed adjuster screw.
25  Carry out the operations described in paragraphs 14 to 17 in this Section.

2.20 Marelli distributor

2.16 Interior of distributor cap showing carbon brush

2.21 Extracting vacuum diaphragm unit screw

2.22A Marelli contact breaker E-clip

**Fig. 4.4 Adjusting Marelli type contact breaker points gap
(Sec 2)**

## 3  Dwell angle – checking

*The dwell angle is the number of degrees through which the
distributor cam turns between the instants of closure and opening of
the contact breaker points.*

1   Connect a dwell meter in accordance with the maker's instruction.
The type of meter that operates with the engine running is to be
preferred; any variation in contact breaker gap, caused by wear in the
distributor shaft or bushes, or the height of the distributor cam peaks, is
evened out when using this.
2   The correct dwell angle is given in the Specifications at the
beginning of this Chapter. If the angle is too large, increase the contact
points gap. If the angle is too small, reduce the points gap. Only very
slight adjustments should be made to the gap before re-checking.
3   On Ducellier distributors, adjustment of the dwell angle can only be
carried out by switching off the ignition, removing the distributor cap,
rotor and spark shield and adjusting the points gap.
4   Re-check once the engine is running. Adjustment may have to be
carried out several times to obtain the correct dwell angle.
5   On Marelli distributors, adjustment of the points gap (dwell angle)
is carried out with the engine running by inserting a 3.0 mm Allen key
in the hole provided in the distributor body.
6   Always check and adjust the dwell angle before timing the ignition
as described in Section 4.

## 4  Ignition timing

1   Timing the ignition on engines with mechanical breaker distributors is carried out in the following way.
2   Disconnect the vacuum hose from the distributor diaphragm
capsule (photo).
3   Have the engine at normal operating temperature and idling with a
stroboscope connected in accordance with the manufacturer's
instructions.
4   Point the stroboscope at the timing marks on the flywheel and the
index on the aperture on the flywheel housing. The mark on the
flywheel should be opposite to the BTDC mark on the index specified
for your particular engine. Alternatively, use the notch on the
crankshaft pulley and the marks on the timing belt cover (photo), but
this will necessitate removal of the wheel arch shield.
5   If the marks are not in alignment, release the distributor clamp plate
and turn the distributor gently until they are (photo).
6   Tighten the clamp plate nut, switch off the ignition, reconnect the
vacuum hose and remove the stroboscope.
7   If there is any difficulty in seeing the timing marks clearly, highlight
them by painting with quick-drying white paint.

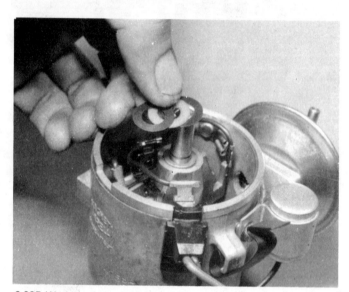

2.22B Washers above contact breaker

**Fig. 4.3 Marelli contact breaker (Sec 2)**

4.2 Distributor vacuum hose

4.5 Distributor clamp plate nut

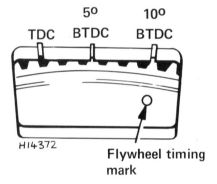

Fig. 4.5 Flywheel housing timing marks (Sec 4)

4.4 Ignition timing marks on belt cover

## 5 Condenser (capacitor) – removal, testing and refitting

*The purpose of the condenser (sometimes known as the capacitor) is to ensure that when the contact breaker points open there is no sparking across them which would weaken the spark and cause rapid deterioration of the points.*

*The condenser is fitted in parallel with the contact breaker points. If it develops a short circuit, it will cause ignition failure as the points will be prevented from interrupting the low tension circuit.*

1 If the engine becomes very difficult to start (or begins to misfire whilst running) and the breaker points show signs of excessive burning, suspect the condenser has failed with open circuit. A test can be made by separating the points by hand with the ignition switched on. If this is accompanied by a bright spark at the contact points, it is indicative that the condenser has failed.

2 Without special test equipment, the only sure way to diagnose condenser trouble is to replace a suspected unit with a new one and note if there is any improvement.

3 To remove the condenser from the distributor, take out the screw which secures it to the distributor body and disconnect its leads from the terminals.

4 When fitting the condenser, it is vital to ensure that the fixing screw is secure. The lead must be secure on the terminal with no chance of short circuiting.

## 6 Distributor – removal and refitting

1 Remove the spark plug from No. 4 cylinder and then turn the crankshaft either by applying a spanner to the pulley nut or by jacking up a front wheel, engaging top gear and turning the wheel in the forward direction of travel.

2 Place a finger over the plug hole and feel the compression being generated as the piston rises up the cylinder bore.

3 Alternatively, if the rocker cover is off, check that the valves on No. 1 cylinder are closed.

4 Continue turning the crankshaft until the flywheel and flywheel housing (BTDC) ignition timing marks are in alignment. Number 4 piston is now in firing position.

5 Remove the distributor cap and place it to one side complete with high tension leads.

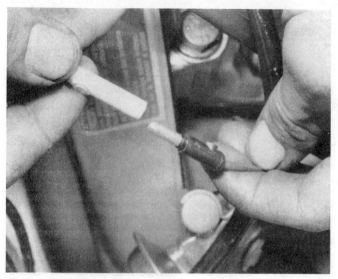

6.6 Distributor LT connection

7 Pick out the lubrication pad from the recess in the top of the distributor shaft. Unscrew the screw now exposed.

8 Mark the relationship of the cam to the counterweight pins and then remove the cam assembly.

9 There is no way to test the bob weight springs other than by checking the performance of the distributor on special test equipment, so if in doubt, fit new springs anyway. If the springs are loose where they loop over the posts, it is more than possible that the post grooves are worn. In this case, the various parts which include the shaft will need renewal. Wear to this extent would mean that a new distributor is probably the best solution in the long run. Be sure to make an exact note of both the engine number and any serial number on the distributor when ordering.

10 If the mainshaft is slack in its bushes or the cam on the spindle, allowing sideways play, it means that the contact points gap setting can only be a compromise; the cam position relative to the cam follower on the moving point arm is not constant. It is not practical to re-bush the distributor body unless you have a friend who can bore and bush it for you. The shaft can be removed by driving out the roll pin from the retaining collar at the bottom. (The collar also acts as as oil slinger to prevent excess engine oil creeping up the shaft).

*Marelli*

11 With the distributor removed from the engine, take off the spark shield and rotor.

12 Remove the contact breaker and carrier as described in Section 2.

6 Disconnect the distributor vacuum hose and low tension lead (photo).

7 Mark the distributor pedestal mounting plinth in relation to the crankcase. Also mark the contact end of the rotor in relation to the rim of the distributor body.

8 Unbolt the clamp plate and withdraw the distributor.

9 Refit by having No. 4 piston at its firing position and the distributor rotor and pedestal marks aligned, then push the distributor into position, mating it to the splined driveshaft.

10 If a new distributor is being fitted then of course alignment marks will not be available to facilitate installation in which case, hold the unit over its mounting hole and observe the following.

*903 cc engine:* Distributor cap high tension lead sockets pointing towards alternator and at 90° to centre line of rocker cover. Contact end of rotor arm pointing towards No. 4 contact in distributor cap (when fitted).

*1116 cc and 1301 cc engine:* Distributor vacuum unit pointing downwards at 135° to rear edge of timing belt cover. Contact end of rotor arm pointing towards No. 4 contact in distributor cap (when fitted).

11 Tighten the distributor clamp bolt, reconnect the vacuum hose and the low tension leads. Refit the distributor cap. Screw in the spark plug.

12 Check the ignition timing as described in Section 4.

7.13 Marelli distributor centrifugal weights and springs

13 Refer to paragraphs 9 and 10 for details of counterweight springs and shaft bushes (photo).

*Reassembly*

14 This is a reversal of dismantling. On Ducellier distributors, make sure that the advance toothed segment is returned to its original setting otherwise the advance curves for your particular engine will be upset.

## 7 Distributor (mechanical breaker type) – overhaul

*Ducellier*

1 The cap must have no flaws or cracks and the HT terminal contacts should not be severely corroded. The centre spring-loaded carbon contact is renewable. If in any doubt about the cap, buy a new one.

2 The rotor deteriorates minimally, but with age the metal conductor tip may corrode. It should not be cracked or chipped and the metal conductor must not be loose. If in doubt, renew it. Always fit a new rotor if fitting a new cap.

3 With the distributor removed as described in the preceding Section, take off the rotor and contact breaker.

4 To remove the contact breaker movable arm, extract the clip and take off the washer from the top of the pivot post.

5 Extract the screw and remove the fixed contact arm.

6 Carefully note and record the setting of the advance toothed segment and then remove the spring clip and vacuum capsule fixing screws and withdraw the capsule with link rod.

## 8 Ignition coil (mechanical breaker ignition)

1 Coils normally last the life of a car. The most usual reason for a coil to fail is after being left with the ignition switched on but the engine not running. There is then constant current flowing, instead of the

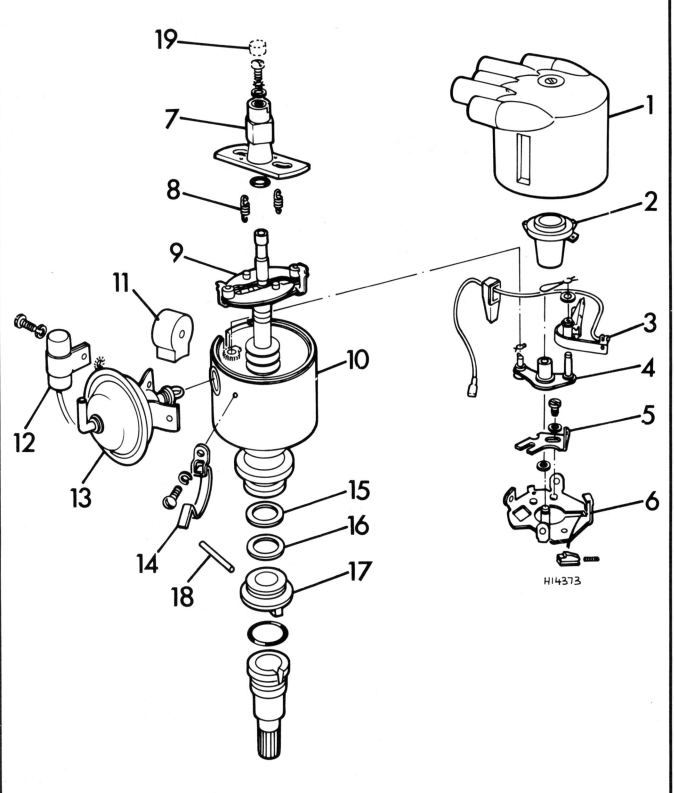

**Fig. 4.6 Exploded view of typical Ducellier distributor**
**(Sec 7)**

| | | | |
|---|---|---|---|
| 1 Cap | 6 Contact breaker baseplate | 10 Body | 15 Thrust washer |
| 2 Rotor | 7 Cam assembly | 11 LT insulator | 16 Spacer washer |
| 3 Movable breaker arm | 8 Centrifugal advance weight | 12 Condenser | 17 Driving dog |
| 4 Vacuum advance link | control springs | 13 Vacuum capsule | 18 Retaining pin |
| 5 Fixed contact breaker arm | 9 Driveshaft and plate | 14 Cap retaining spring | 19 Felt pad |

8.1 Ignition coil

intermittent flow when the contact breaker is opening. The coil then overheats, and the insulation is damaged (photo).

2   If the coil seems suspect after fault finding, the measurement of the resistance of the primary and secondary windings (usually an ohmmeter) can establish its condition. If an ohmmeter is not available, it will be necessary to try a new coil.

## 9   Digiplex (electronic) ignition – location of components and precautions

1   The main components of this system are located within the engine compartment as shown.
2   On cars equipped with this system, it is important that the following precautions are observed.
3   Never start the engine if the battery leads are loose.
4   Do not stop the engine by pulling off a battery lead.
5   Remove the control unit if ambient temperature (paint drying oven) is above 80°C (176°F).
6   Never connect or disconnect the multi-plug at the control unit unless the ignition is switched off.
7   Disconnect the battery negative lead before carrying out electric body welding.

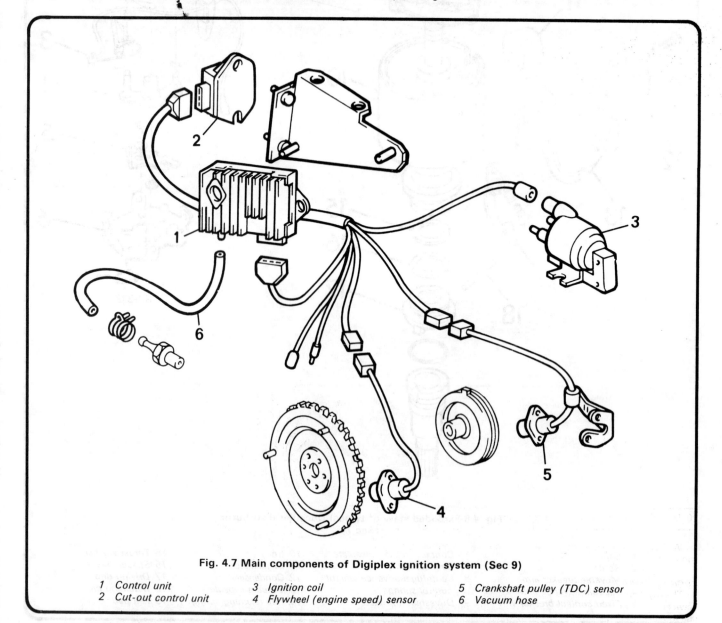

Fig. 4.7 Main components of Digiplex ignition system (Sec 9)

| | | |
|---|---|---|
| 1   Control unit | 3   Ignition coil | 5   Crankshaft pulley (TDC) sensor |
| 2   Cut-out control unit | 4   Flywheel (engine speed) sensor | 6   Vacuum hose |

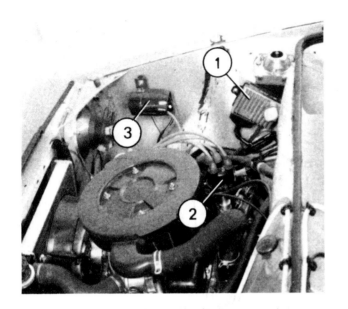 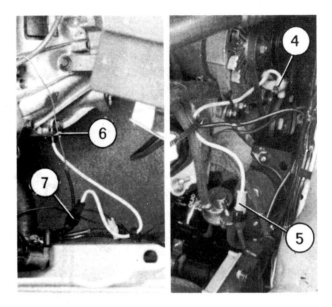

**Fig. 4.8 Location of Digiplex ignition system components (Sec 9)**

| | | | |
|---|---|---|---|
| 1 Control unit | 3 Ignition coil | 5 Wiring connector plug | 7 Wiring connector plug |
| 2 Distributor | 4 TDC sensor | 6 Engine speed sensor | |

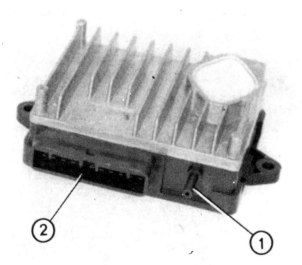

**Fig. 4.9 Digiplex control unit (Sec 9)**

1 Vacuum hose connector    2 Multi-plug socket

---

## 10 Digiplex (electronic) ignition – checks and adjustments

1 Without special equipment, any work on the system components should be restricted to the following.

### Engine speed sensor
2 The gap between the sensor and the teeth of the flywheel should be between 0.25 and 1.3 mm (0.0099 to 0.0512 in). Any deviation will be due to mechanical damage to the sensor, no adjustment being possible.

### TDC sensor
3 The gap between the sensor and one of the TDC reference marks on the crankshaft pulley should be between 0.4 and 1.0 mm (0.016 to 0.039 in).
4 Any deviation will be due to the sensor plate becoming loose. To reposition it will necessitate setting No. 1 piston at TDC which can only be carried out accurately by your dealer using special tools.

### Supply circuit and continuity of coil primary winding
5 Connect a test lamp between contacts 11 and 9 of the multi-plug having first pulled it from the control unit.
6 Switch on the ignition, the test lamp should come on. If it does not, either the connection at the positive pole of the control unit or the coil primary winding is open.

### Control unit earth
7 Connect a test lamp between contacts 8 and 9 of the multi-plug having first pulled it from the control unit. Switch on the ignition, the test lamp should come on. If it does not, improve the earth connection.

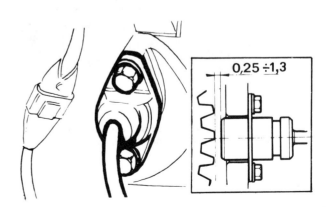

**Fig. 4.10 Engine speed sensor gap (Sec 10)**

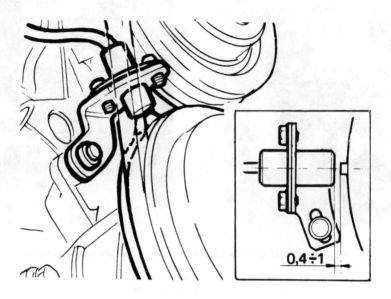

Fig. 4.11 TDC sensor gap (Sec 10)

Fig. 4.12 Test lamp connected between terminals 11 and 9 of control unit multi-plug (Sec 10)

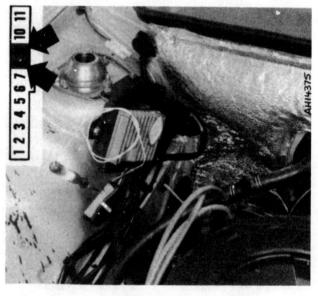

Fig. 4.13 Test lamp connected between terminals 8 and 9 of control unit multi-plug (Sec 10)

## 11 Spark plugs

1   The correct functioning of the spark plugs is vital for the correct running and efficiency of the engine. It is essential that the plugs fitted are appropriate for the engine, and the suitable type is specified at the beginning of this chapter. If this type is used and the engine is in good condition, the spark plugs should not need attention between scheduled replacement intervals. Spark plug cleaning is rarely necessary and should not be attempted unless specialised equipment is available as damage can easily be caused to the firing ends.

2   At the specified intervals, the plugs should be renewed. The condition of the spark plug will also tell much about the overall condition of the engine.

3   If the insulator nose of the spark plug is clean and white, with no deposits, this is indicative of a weak mixture, or too hot a plug. (A hot plug transfers heat away from the electrode slowly – a cold plug transfers it away quickly.)

4   If the tip of the insulator nose is covered with sooty black deposits, then this is indicative that the mixture is too rich. Should the plug be black and oily, then it is likely that the engine is fairly worn, as well as the mixture being too rich.

5   The spark plug gap is of considerable importance, as, if it is too large or too small the size of the spark and its efficiency will be seriously impaired. The spark plug gap should be set to the gap shown in the Specifications for the best results.

6   To set it, measure the gap with a feeler gauge, and then bend open, or close, the outer plug electrode until the correct gap is achieved. The centre electrode should never be bent as this may crack the insulation and cause plug failure, if nothing worse.

7   When fitting new plugs, check that the plug seats in the cylinder head are quite clean. Refit the leads from the distributor in the correct firing order, which is 1-3-4-2; No 1 cylinder being the one nearest the flywheel housing (903 cc) or timing belt (1116 or 1301 cc). The distributor cap is marked with the HT lead numbers to avoid any confusion. Simply connect the correctly numbered lead to its respective spark plug terminal (photo).

11.7 Distributor cap HT lead markings

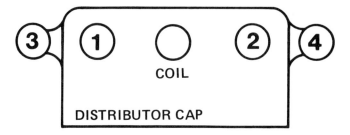

Fig. 4.14 Spark plug connections on 903 cc engine (Sec 11)

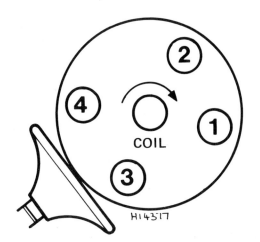

Fig. 4.15 Spark plug connections on 1116 cc and 1301 cc engines (Sec 11)

## 12 Ignition switch – removal and refitting

1   Access to the steering column lock/ignition switch is obtained after removing the steering wheel and column shrouds (Chapter 10) and the column switch unit (Chapter 9).

2   In the interest of safety, disconnect the battery negative lead and the ignition switch wiring plug (photo).

3   Insert the ignition key and turn to the STOP position (photo).

4   Pull the two leads from the switch.

5   Turn the ignition key to MAR.

6   Using a screwdriver depress the retaining tabs (1) (Fig. 4.16) and release the ignition switch.

7   Set the switch cam (2) so that the notches (3) are in alignment.

8   Insert the switch into the steering lock and engage the retaining tabs.

9   Turn the ignition key to STOP and connect the two leads.

10  Reconnect the battery and refit the steering wheel, switch and shrouds.

11  Removal and refitting of the steering column lock is described in Chapter 10.

**Note:** *The ignition key is removable when set to the STOP position and all electrical circuits will be off. If the interlock button is pressed, the key can be turned to the PARK position in order that the parking lamps can be left on and the steering lock engaged, but the key can be withdrawn.*

12.2 Ignition switch and lock

12.3 Ignition key positions

1 AVV (Start)
2 Park (Parking lights on)
3 Stop (Lock)
4 MAR (Ignition)

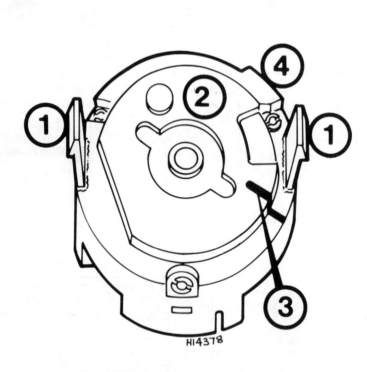

HI4378

Fig. 4.16 Typical ignition switch (Sec 12)

1 Retaining tabs
2 Switch cam
3 Alignment notches
4 Locating projection

**Fault diagnosis overleaf**

## 13 Fault diagnosis – ignition system

| Symptom | Reason(s) |
| --- | --- |
| *Mechanical breaker type* | |
| Engine fails to start | Loose battery connections |
| | Discharged battery |
| | Oil in contact points |
| | Disconnected ignition leads |
| | Faulty condenser |
| Engine starts and runs but misfires | Faulty spark plug |
| | Cracked distributor cap |
| | Cracked rotor arm |
| | Worn advance mechanism |
| | Incorrect spark plug gap |
| | Incorrect contact points gap |
| | Faulty condenser |
| | Faulty coil |
| | Incorrect timing |
| | Poor engine/transmission earth connections |
| Engine overheats, lacks power | Seized distributor weights |
| | Perforated vacuum pipe |
| | Incorrect ignition timing |
| *Digiplex (electronic) type* | |
| Engine fails to start | Excessive gap on TDC sensor |
| | TDC or engine speed sensor short circuited or earthed |
| | Defective ignition control unit |
| | Control unit multi-plug contacts corroded |
| | Defective coil |
| Engine lacks power, high fuel consumption | Incorrect ignition advance |
| | TDC sensor incorrectly set |
| | Distributor vacuum hose blocked |

# Chapter 5 Clutch

*For modifications, and information applicable to later models, see Supplement at end of manual*

## Contents

## Specifications

### System ...................................................................

Single dry plate, diaphragm spring with cable actuation. Ball type, grease-sealed release bearing

### Pedal height (by cable adjustment)

903 cc engine ...................................................................... 10.0 to 15.0 mm (0.39 to 0.59 in) below brake pedal
1116 and 1301 cc engines .................................................... 0 to 5.0 mm (0 to 0.20 in) below brake pedal

### Driven plate diameter

903 cc engine ...................................................................... 170.0 mm (6.7 in)
1116 and 1301 cc engines .................................................... 181.5 mm (7.15 in)

### Torque wrench settings

| | Nm | lbf ft |
|---|---|---|
| Clutch cover bolts | 16 | 12 |
| Release fork lockbolt | 26 | 19 |

## 1  General description

The clutch is of single dry plate type with a diaphragm spring pressure plate.

The unit consists of a steel cover, dowelled and bolted to the flywheel and contains the pressure plate, diaphragm spring and fulcrum rings.

The clutch disc is free to slide along the splined input shaft of the gearbox and is held in position between the flywheel and the pressure plate by the pressure of the pressure plate spring. Friction lining material is riveted to the clutch disc, and it has a spring-cushioned hub to absorb transmission shocks.

The release mechanism consists of an operating arm and bearing which is actuated by a cable.

## 2  Clutch – adjustment

1  This is carried out at the transmission end of the clutch operating cable.

2  The clutch pedal does not have any free play as the release bearing is in constant light contact with the fingers of the diaphragm spring.

3  The height of the clutch pedal should be maintained so that its pedal pad surface is as specified.

4  Carry out the adjustment by releasing the locknut on the cable end fitting and turning the adjuster nut (photo).

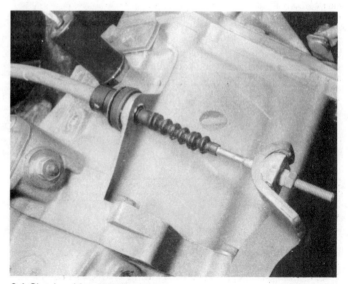

2.4 Clutch cable at release lever

## 3 Clutch cable – renewal

1   Unscrew the nuts from the cable end fitting at the release lever on the transmission.
2   Disconnect the cable from the release lever and from its support bracket.
3   Working inside the car, pull out the split pin from the top of the clutch pedal, remove the washer and disconnect the cable from the pedal.
4   Withdraw the cable through the bulkhead.
5   Fit the new cable by reversing the removal operations, use a new split pin at the pedal connection.
6   Adjust as described in Section 2.

## 4 Clutch pedal – removal and refitting

1   Slacken the clutch cable adjustment by unscrewing the nuts at the release lever.
2   Disconnect the clutch cable from the pedal by pulling out the split pin and taking off the washer.
3   Push the pedal pivot shaft out of its retaining spring clip until both the brake and clutch pedals are free.
4   Apply grease to the pedal bushes before reassembling.
5   Use a new split pin when reconnecting the clutch cable to its pedal.
6   Adjust as described in Section 2.

## 5 Clutch – removal

1   The clutch is accessible normally only if the transmission is removed from the car, as described in Chapter 6. Alternatively, if the engine/transmission is being removed for major overhaul, the clutch is accessible once the transmission has been separated from the engine; refer to Chapter 1.
2   Unscrew the clutch cover securing bolts evenly and progressively, until the spring pressure is relieved. Remove the bolts completely and lift the clutch cover from the flywheel. Take care to catch the driven plate, which is sandwiched between the pressure plate and the flywheel.

## 6 Clutch – inspection

1   Inspect the driven plate. If the friction linings have worn down – or nearly down – to the rivet heads, it should be renewed complete. *Do not waste your time trying to rivet new linings into place; this seldom proves satisfactory.*
2   Check the clutch pressure plate/cover assembly. If the driven plate contact surfaces on the pressure plate or flywheel are scored, grooved or tiny hair cracks are evident (caused by overheating), the flywheel should be reground or renewed and the clutch pressure plate/cover renewed. The latter are usually available as a factory reconditioned assembly. *Never dismantle the clutch assembly*; special jigs and tools are needed to reset it, even if the necessary spare parts were available.
3   Check the tips of the diaphragm spring fingers. If these are stepped as a result of contact with the clutch release bearing, then again, a new cover assembly is the only remedy.

## 7 Clutch release mechanism

**Note:** *The clutch release bearing should be renewed at the same time as the clutch assembly is being renewed.*
    *Renewal of the clutch release bearing is unlikely to be required at other times, unless as a result of reference to the Fault Diagnosis Section, the symptoms indicate it being necessary.*
1   Extract the securing clips and withdraw the release bearing from its hub on the oil seal retainer within the clutch bellhousing (photo).
2   If the bearing is noisy or rough when turned with the fingers, or its spring finger contact area is grooved, the bearing must be renewed.

7.1 Clutch release bearing and fork

3   Examine the release lever pivot shaft bushes for wear. If they are worn, they can be extracted and new ones fitted. If they are in good condition, it is worth removing the pivot shaft, after releasing its lockbolt, and applying a little high melting point grease to the bushes.
4   The release bearing is grease-sealed for life. Refit by reversing the removal operations, making sure that the retaining spring clips are secure on completion.

## 8 Clutch – refitting

1   To refit the clutch, locate the driven plate against the flywheel so that the projecting hub (which contains the torsion coil springs) is away from the flywheel (photo).
2   Position the clutch cover assembly on its locating dowels. Screw in the retaining bolts no more than finger tight, to allow the driven plate to slide.

8.1 Offering up clutch driven plate and cover

3   The clutch driven plate must now be centralised. This cannot be carried out in the usual way – by using an alignment tool or old input shaft to engage in the centre of the flywheel – as the crankshaft rear mounting flange does not incorporate a bush or bearing. A piece of tubing is the best alternative to solve the problem of centralising. Obtain a piece of tubing, the outside diameter of which provides a sliding fit in the tips of the fingers of the diaphragm spring in the clutch cover. The internal diameter of the tubing should be such that the end of the tubing will engage centrally on the chamfer of the driven plate's splined hub.

4   Hold the tool in position, so it centralises the driven plate on the flywheel. Then start to tighten the clutch cover bolts evenly and progressively, until the driven plate is just nipped between the pressure plate and the flywheel. Withdraw the tool. Note that if the cover bolts are tightened too much, the diaphragm spring fingers will grip the alignment tool and prevent its withdrawal.

5   Fully tighten the clutch cover bolts. Confirmation of alignment can be made by viewing the splined hub through the circle of diaphragm spring finger tips; it should appear to be concentric with them (photo).

8.5 Tightening a clutch cover bolt

## 9   Fault diagnosis – clutch

| Symptom | Reason(s) |
| --- | --- |
| Difficulty in engaging gear (grinding) | Clutch cable adjustment incorrect<br>See under Clutch spin |
| Judder when taking up drive | Engine/transmission mountings loose or worn<br>Driven plate linings contaminated or worn<br>Pressure plate loose or defective |
| *Clutch spin (failure to disengage) so that gears cannot be meshed | Incorrect release bearing to pressure plate clearance<br>Rust on splines (may occur after vehicle standing idle for long periods)<br>Damaged or misaligned pressure plate assembly<br>Cable stretched or broken |
| Clutch slip (increase in engine speed does not increase road speed) | Incorrect cable adjustment<br>Driven plate linings worn or contaminated<br>Pressure plate defective |
| Noise evident when clutch pedal depressed | Release arm pivots unlubricated<br>Release bearing worn, loose or unlubricated<br>Worn or damaged pressure plate |
| Noise evident as clutch pedal released | Distorted driven plate<br>Broken or weak driven plate cushion coil springs<br>Incorrect pedal adjustment<br>Weak or broken clutch pedal return spring<br>Distorted or worn input shaft<br>Release bearing loose on retainer hub |

*This condition may also be due to the driven plate being rusted to the flywheel or pressure plate. It is possible to free it by applying the handbrake, depressing the clutch pedal, engaging top gear and operating the starter motor. If really badly corroded, then the engine will not turn over, but in the majority of cases the driven plate will free. Once the engine starts, rev it up and slip the clutch several times to clear the rust deposits.*

# Chapter 6 Transmission

*For modifications, and information applicable to later models, see Supplement at end of manual*

**Contents**

**Specifications**

## Type

| | |
|---|---|
| 45 and 55 Comfort | Four forward and reverse |
| 45, 55 and 70 Super | Five forward and reverse |

## Ratios

| | |
|---|---|
| 1st | 3.909 : 1 |
| 2nd | 2.055 : 1 |
| 3rd | 1.342 : 1 |
| 4th | 0.964 : 1 |
| 5th | 0.780 : 1 (0.830 : 1 on 45S) |
| Reverse | 3.615 : 1 |

## Final drive ratios

| | |
|---|---|
| Models 45 and 45S | 4.071 : 1 |
| Model ES | 3.867 : 1 |
| Models 55, 55S and 70S | 3.733 : 1 |

## Lubrication

| | |
|---|---|
| Oil capacity | 2.4 litres (4.2 pints) |
| Oil type/specification | FIAT ZC90 gear oil (Duckhams Gear Oil 90Z*) |

*\* This is the latest recommendation for topping-up or for oil changes. However, this oil is only available in bulk; a multigrade engine oil such as Duckhams Hypergrade will mix fully with it, and may safely be used if wished*

| Torque wrench settings | Nm | lbf ft |
|---|---|---|
| Flywheel housing to engine bolts | 78 | 57 |
| Starter motor mounting bolts | 25 | 18 |
| Selector fork lockbolts | 18 | 13 |
| Mainshaft nut | 118 | 87 |

## Torque wrench settings (cont'd)

| | Nm | lbf ft |
|---|---|---|
| Secondary shaft nut | 118 | 87 |
| Crownwheel bolts | 69 | 51 |
| Filler and drain plugs | 46 | 34 |
| Differential side bearing cover bolts | 25 | 18 |
| Rear cover bolts | 25 | 18 |
| Gearcase to flywheel housing bolts | 45 | 33 |
| Gear engagement lever pressed steel cover bolts | 25 | 18 |
| Intermediate plate bolts (five-speed) | 25 | 18 |
| Driveshaft inboard boot retainer bolts | 9 | 7 |
| Front driveshaft/hub nut | 272 | 200 |
| Roadwheel bolts | 86 | 63 |

## 1 General description

The transmission (gearbox and final drive) is mounted transversely in line with the engine.

Depending upon the model, four or five forward speeds and reverse are provided.

All forward gears have synchromesh, 1st and 2nd having baulk ring type while 3rd, 4th and 5th have Porsche spring segment synchronisers.

The gearchange control is of floor-mounted type operating through rod linkage.

## 2 Maintenance

1   At the intervals specified in Routine Maintenance and with the transmission cold and the car standing on level ground, unscrew and remove the oil filler/level plug. If oil just starts to dribble out then the oil level is correct. If it does not, add oil of the correct grade to bring it up to level. Refit the plug.

2   At the intervals specified in Routine Maintenance the transmission oil should be renewed.

3   Drain the oil hot by removing the filler/level plug and drain plug. When the oil has ceased dripping, refit the drain plug and refill with the correct grade and quantity of oil. Screw in and tighten the filler/level plug (photos).

## 3 Gearchange lever and linkage – removal and refitting

1   Working under the car, unscrew the nuts which secure the gaiter at the base of the control lever (photo).

2.3A Transmission drain plug

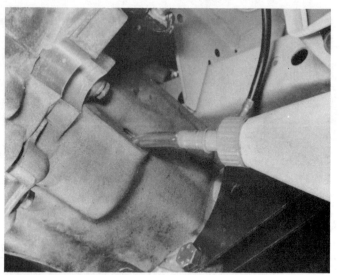

2.3B Filling transmission

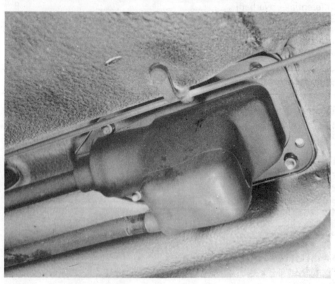

3.1 Gearchange control lever lower gaiter

2   The linkage can now be dismantled by unscrewing the self-locking nuts or by extracting the spring clips from the pivots.

3   Working inside the car, pull the rubber boot up the gear lever and then withdraw the lever upwards.

4   To disconnect the control rod from the relay lever, prise the socket from the ball stud.

5   The plastic bushes in the ends of the control rods may be renewed, using a press or by drawing them out with a bolt, nut and distance pieces.

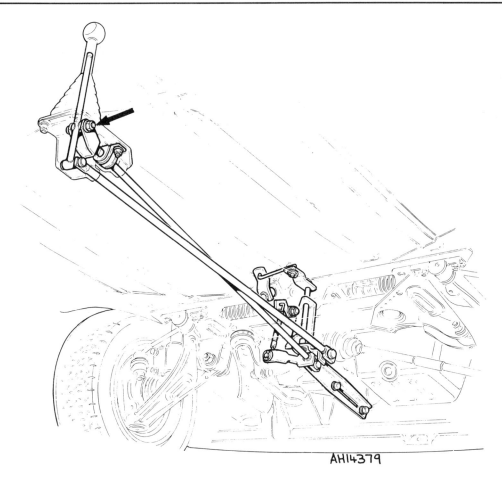

**Fig. 6.1 Gearchange control rods (Sec 3)**

*Apply Loctite 242 to threads (arrowed)*

6   Reconnection and refitting are reversals of separation and removal. The easiest way to reconnect the socket on the link rod to the relay lever ball stud is to use a pair of self-locking grips.

## 4   Transmission – removal and refitting

1   Disconnect the battery negative lead and then disconnect the earth lead from the transmission.
2   Unscrew the knurled ring and disconnect the speedometer drive cable from the transmission.
3   Unscrew the nuts and disconnect the clutch cable from the release lever on the transmission.
4   Pull the leads from the reversing lamp switch.
5   Unbolt the starter motor, pull it away from the bellhousing and support it within the engine compartment.
6   Raise the front of the car and remove the front roadwheels.
7   Release the driveshaft to hub nuts. These are very tight so use a long bar to unscrew them and have an assistant apply the brakes hard to prevent the hubs from turning.
8   Drain the transmission oil if the unit is to be dismantled.
9   Raise the front end sufficiently high so that there is adequate clearance for the transmission to be withdrawn from under the car. Support securely.
10   Support the weight of the engine either by attaching a hoist or by placing a jack and block of wood under the sump pan. An alternative idea is shown in Fig. 6.2.
11   Disconnect the exhaust downpipe from the manifold.
12   Remove protective shields (if fitted).
13   Disconnect the gearchange rods from the transmission.
14   Disconnect the engine and transmission upper mountings.

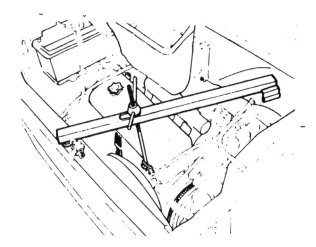

**Fig. 6.2 Method of supporting weight of engine during removal of transmission (Sec 4)**

15   Disconnect the lower mounting and unbolt the complete mounting assembly from the transmission casing.
16   Unscrew and remove the bellhousing to engine connecting bolts.
17   Unbolt the cover plate and gearchange rod support strut from the face of the bellhousing.
18   Partially unscrew the tie-rod end ball-stud nuts and then using a suitable balljoint 'splitter' tool, disconnect the tie-rod balljoint from the steering arms on the hub carrriers.

19 Unbolt the front brake hose support clips from the suspension struts.

20 Remove the bolts from the U-shaped clamps at the base of the suspension struts and separate the hub carriers from the struts.

21 Pull the tops of the hub carriers outwards and push the driveshafts out of them.

22 Unbolt the driveshaft inboard boot retainers and withdraw the driveshafts from the transmission.

23 Withdraw the transmission from the engine and lower it to the floor. If you are working unaided, then the transmission can be supported and lowered using a trolley jack.

24 Refitting is a reversal of removal, but if the clutch has been disturbed, make sure that it is centralised as described in Chapter 5.

25 Use new driveshaft nuts and after tightening them to the specified torque, stake them into the shaft grooves.

26 Adjust the clutch (Chapter 5).

27 Fill the transmission with the correct grade and quantity of oil.

## 5 Transmission – removal of main assemblies

1 With the transmission removed, clean away external dirt and grease using paraffin and a stiff brush or a water soluble solvent.

2 Remove the clutch release bearing from the bellhousing (Chapter 5).

3 Disconnect the gearchange selector link rod end relay lever.

4 Unscrew the bolts which connect the bellhousing and gearcase. Note that one bolt is inside the bellhousing.

5 Unbolt the detent spring plate and extract the springs and balls. The blue painted spring is at the reverse lamp switch end.

6 Stand the gearbox upright on the bellhousing flange.

7 Unbolt the rear cover to expose the 5th speed gears and synchromesh (five-speed) or shaft circlips (four-speed).

8 Unbolt the pressed steel cover to expose the gear bias springs.

9 Unscrew the nut and withdraw the gear engagement lever from the reverse spring cap. Note the master spline so that the lever can only be fitted in one position. Also note that the closer coiled spring is on the right-hand side.

10 Unbolt the gear selector lever from its dog. It will only go in one position as the shaft has a square shank.

11 Using an Allen key, extract the lock screw and pull out the speedo. driven gear.

12 Unscrew and remove the reverse lamp switch.

### Four-speed units

13 Extract the circlips from the ends of the shafts. These are difficult to remove due to the pressure exerted on them by the Belleville washers. Compress the washers by using a clamp. Such a clamp can be made up from a short length of tubing which has a cut-out for access to the circlip and of suitable diameter to bear on the Belleville washers. A roadwheel or bellhousing to engine connecting bolt has suitable threads for the internally threaded gearshaft so use one of these as part of the clamp. Remove the bearing circlip from the end of the mainshaft (photos).

### Five-speed units

14 On five-speed units, lock two gears simultaneously by moving the selector dogs with a screwdriver inserted through the bias spring aperture.

15 Relieve the staking on the shaft nuts and unscrew them (normal RH thread).

16 Unscrew the 5th speed selector fork lock bolt.

17 From the mainshaft pull off 5th speed gear, the synchromesh unit selector fork and gear bush.

18 Pull 5th speed gear from the secondary shaft.

19 Remove the intermediate plate if required although this is not essential.

20 Pull the gearcase upwards and at the same time have an assistant tap the ends of the shafts downwards with a plastic or copper-faced hammer which will release the bearings and allow the casing to be removed.

21 Unbolt the reverse idler lockplate and draw out reverse idler gear and shaft, reverse selector shaft and fork or 5th/reverse selector shaft as applicable (four- or five-speed unit).

22 Unscrew the selector fork lock bolts and withdraw 1st/2nd and 3rd/4th selector shafts. Remove the selector forks.

5.13A Locating Belleville washers and circlips (4-speed)

5.13B One method of compressing Belleville washers (4-speed)

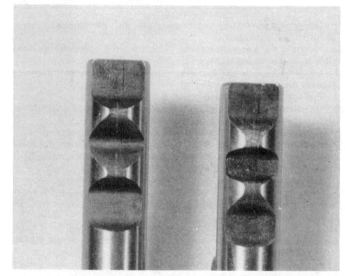

5.23 Selector shaft notches

23 Note that the 1st/2nd selector fork is closest to the bellhousing. Also note that the three adjacent shaft notches are furthest away from the bellhousing (photo).

24 Retrieve the large interlock plungers from the casing passages, also the smaller one from its hole in the 3rd/4th selector shaft.

25 Withdraw both shaft/geartrains simultaneously meshed together.

26 Lift out the final drive/differential.

27 Remove the small magnet from the casing.

28 If necessary, remove the bearings from the casing, using a puller or tubular drift.

29 If necessary, the differential flanges can be unbolted to renew the oil seal (photo).

## 6  Inspection of components

1   Check all the components for signs of damage. All the gear teeth should be smooth and shiny, without any chips. The ball and rollers of the bearings should be unblemished.

2   The tracks of the final drive taper roller bearings, still in the casing, should be a smooth, even colour without any mark. Should either the rollers or the tracks be marked at all, the complete bearing must be renewed. In this case, the outer tracks must be extracted from the casing, and the rollers and the inner tracks pulled off the differential cage halves.

3   Check the synchromesh baulk rings for signs of wear. Check their fit in their respective gears. If the gears are being renewed, the synchromesh units should also be renewed. One point easy to miss in examining the gears is fracture of the small ends of the teeth that are on the outside of the synchro-ring, and are an extension of the teeth for the dog clutch to engage. If any of these are chipped, the gear must be renewed.

4   On Porsche type synchro. units, the stop plates can be renewed if the circlip is extracted. You will require a strong pair of circlip pliers for this job. A repair kit is available.

5   On baulk ring type synchros. the baulk ring should be very stiff to turn when pressed onto the gear cone. If it does not provide good braking characteristics, renew it.

5.29 Differential flange

6   The condition of synchro. units will be obvious before dismantling by evidence of 'crunchy' gearchanges or if the synchro. can be easily 'beaten' during all but the slowest of gearchanges.

7   Check the casings for cracks. If there are leaks at a plug, it must be renewed. This must be tapped carefully into place, sufficient to expand it but not enough to distort it too much.

8   Renew seals and gaskets at each dismantling.

9   Check the movement of the selector rods in their bores in the casing. They should move freely but without appreciable sideplay. Inspect the sliding surfaces of the selector forks for wear or damage.

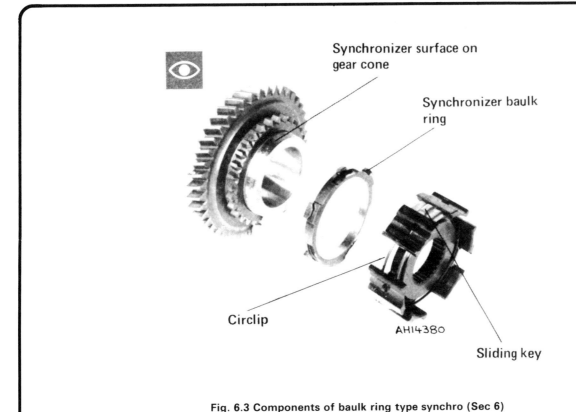

Synchronizer surface on gear cone

Synchronizer baulk ring

Circlip

AH14380

Sliding key

**Fig. 6.3 Components of baulk ring type synchro (Sec 6)**

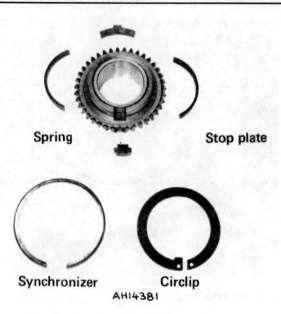

Spring        Stop plate

Synchronizer       Circlip

AHI4381

**Fig. 6.4 Components of Porsche type synchro (Sec 6)**

---

### 7 Shaft geartrains – overhaul

---

#### Secondary shaft

1  Only the bearing can be renewed on this shaft. Use a press or puller to remove and refit it (photo).

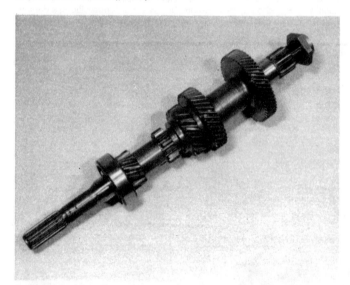

7.1 Secondary shaft (5-speed)

#### Mainshaft

2  All components can be removed from the mainshaft using hand pressure only, with the exception of the bearing, for which a puller will be required (photo).
3  Keep the dismantled components in the exact order and same way round as they were originally fitted.
4  With all the components clean and renewed (where necessary) and lightly lubricated, assemble the mainshaft in the following sequence.
5  Slide on the 1st speed gear bush (photo).
6  Fit the 1st speed gear (photo).
7  Fit the 1st/2nd synchro sleeve/reverse gear with baulk rings. The sleeve groove must be towards the shaft pinion gear (photos).

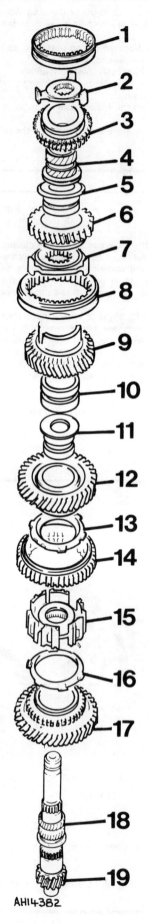

**Fig. 6.5 Exploded view of mainshaft (Sec 7)**

1  5th speed synchro sleeve
2  Synchro hub
3  5th speed gear
4  5th speed gear bush
5  4th speed gear bush
6  4th speed gear
7  3rd/4th synchro hub
8  3rd/4th synchro sleeve
9  3rd speed gear
10  3rd speed gear bush
11  2nd speed gear bush
12  2nd speed gear
13  2nd speed synchro baulk ring
14  1st/2nd synchro sleeve with reverse gear
15  1st/2nd synchro hub
16  Synchro baulk ring
17  1st speed gear
18  1st speed gear bush
19  Pinion (final drive) gear

AHI4382

7.2 Mainshaft (5-speed)

7.5 1st speed gear bush on mainshaft

7.6 1st speed gear on mainshaft

7.7A 1st/2nd synchro sleeve with reverse gear

7.7B Fitting baulk ring to mainshaft

7.8 Fitting 2nd speed gear to mainshaft

7.9A 2nd speed gear bush

7.9B 3rd speed gear bush

7.9C 3rd speed gear

7.10A 3rd/4th synchro hub

7.10B 3rd/4th synchro sleeve

7.11 4th speed gear and bush

8   Fit 2nd speed gear (photo).
9   Warm and fit 2nd and 3rd gear bushes followed by 3rd speed gear (photos).
10   Fit 3rd/4th synchro hub so that the completely circular oil groove is towards 3rd speed gear. Fit 3rd/4th synchro sleeve (photos).
11   Warm and fit the bush together with 4th speed gear (photo).
12   The shafts are now ready for assembling into the casing as described in Section 9.

## 8   Differential – overhaul

1   The speedometer drivegear is an integral part of the differential casing unit and it cannot be removed.
2   Unscrew the crownwheel bolts and separate the two halves of the differential case and the crownwheel. The lockplate for the pinion shaft will also be released. Remove the planet gears (photos).
3   Take out the bevel side gears and thrust washers (photo).
4   Remove the tapered roller bearings only if they are to be renewed.
5   Reassembly is a reversal of the dismantling procedure. Tighten the bolts in diagonal sequence to the specified torque. If new bearings are being fitted, drive them into place carefully and evenly, applying the drift to the inner tracks. Set the preload of these bearings as described in Section 9.

## 9   Transmission – reassembly

1   As work proceeds, oil the components liberally with gear oil.
2   Fit the shaft bearings to the casings (photos).
3   Fit the magnet (photo).

8.2A Crownwheel bolts

8.2B Differential planet gear pinion shaft lockplate

8.2C Differential dismantled

8.2D Removing differential planet gears

8.3 Differential side gear and thrust washer

9.2A Shaft bearings in casing

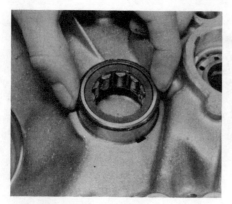

9.2B Shaft bearing in casing

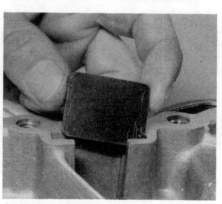

9.3 Fitting magnet

9.4 Differential/final drive in casing

9.5 Fitting geartrains

9.6 Using a magnet to fit interlock plunger

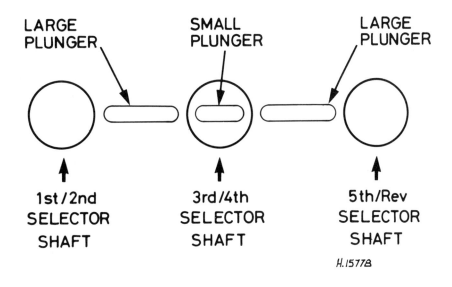

LARGE PLUNGER     SMALL PLUNGER     LARGE PLUNGER

1st/2nd SELECTOR SHAFT     3rd/4th SELECTOR SHAFT     5th/Rev SELECTOR SHAFT

H.15778

**Fig. 6.6 Selector shaft plungers (Sec 9)**

4  Lower the differential/final drive into position, with speedo. drivegear uppermost (photo).

5  Mesh the geartrains together and fit them simultaneously into the casing (photo).

6  Locate the selector shaft interlock plungers in the casing as shown in Fig. 6.6. A pencil magnet is useful for this (photo).

7  Locate the 1st/2nd and 3rd/4th selector forks in their synchro. sleeve grooves.

8  Fit the 1st/2nd and 3rd/4th selector shafts passing them through the holes in the forks. Make sure that the small interlock plunger is in its hole in the 3rd/4th selector shaft (photo).

9  Screw in and tighten the fork locking bolts (photos).

10  Fit a new O-ring to the reverse idler shaft and fit the shaft and reverse idler gear (photo).

11  Fit the reverse selector fork (photo).

12  Fit 5th/reverse selector shaft.

13  Fit the reverse idler shaft lockplate (photo).

14  Bolt reverse selector fork to its shaft (photo).

15  If the differential bearings have been renewed, the bearing preload must now be calculated and adjusted by means of shims. This sounds very complicated, but in fact means that when the bearing cover is bolted down, it must exert just enough pressure to give the bearings the specified preload.

9.8 Interlock plunger in 3rd/4th selector shaft

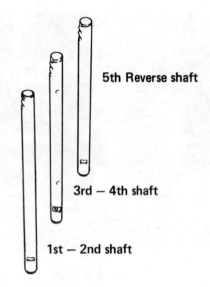

5th Reverse shaft

3rd — 4th shaft

1st — 2nd shaft

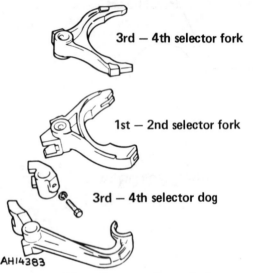

3rd — 4th selector fork

1st — 2nd selector fork

3rd — 4th selector dog

AHI4383

5th — Reverse selector fork

Fig. 6.7 Selector shafts and forks (Sec 9)

9.9A Tightening 3rd/4th selector fork lock bolt

9.9B Tightening 1st/2nd selector fork lock bolt

9.10 Reverse idler gear and shaft O-ring arrowed

9.11 Reverse selector fork

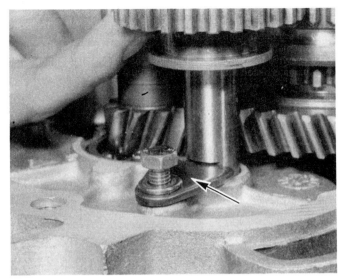

9.13 Reverse idler shaft lockplate and bolt

9.14 Tightening reverse selector fork lock bolt

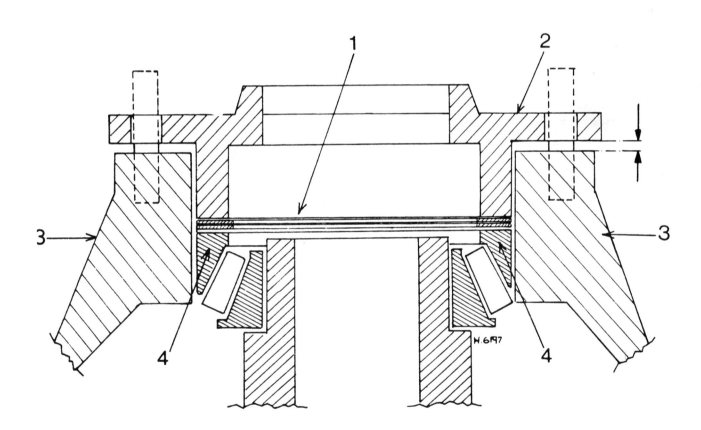

**Fig. 6.8 Location of differential bearing preload adjusting shims (Sec 9)**

1 Shims      2 Bearing cover plate      3 Final drive housing      4 Bearing outer track

16 To do this work, a suitable depth gauge will be required. First, measure the depth of the bearing cover recess. Second, measure the projection of the cover's machined section (O-ring removed). Subtract one dimension from the other and add 0.08 mm (0.003 in). This is the thickness of the shim required. Where a depth gauge is not available, shims can be inserted into the housing recess until, when the bearing cover plate is fitted (and resting under its own weight), there is a gap between the plate and the edge of the bearing recess of between 0.08 and 0.12 mm (0.003 and 0.005 in). This method is not so accurate and will require the purchase of unnecessary shims.

17 If necessary, fit a new oil seal to the differential bearing cover.

18 Fit a new O-ring to the bearing cover and bolt it down, using a new paper gasket.

19 Lower the casing over the geartrains. Use a piece of tubing if necessary to tap the casing down around the shaft bearings. Always use a new flange gasket.

20 Screw in and tighten the casing bolts, noting the one inside the bellhousing (photo).

9.20 Casing bolt inside bell housing

9.22 Fitting 5th speed gear to secondary shaft

*Five-speed units*
21  Bolt on the intermediate plate, if removed.
22  Fit 5th speed gear to the secondary shaft (photo).
23  Fit 5th speed gear, the synchro unit, the selector fork and the gear bush as an assembly to the mainshaft. Note the Belleville washer on the synchro hub (photo).
24  Select two gears simultaneously to lock up the geartrains. This is done by pushing up 1st/2nd selector shaft by means of its dog, then pushing down 5th/reverse fork.
25  Screw on two new shaft nuts, tighten to the specified torque and stake the nuts into the shaft grooves (photos).
26  Return the gears to neutral and then fit the 5th/reverse fork lock bolt (photo).

9.23 5th speed gear, fork and synchro being fitted to mainshaft

Fig. 6.9 Fitting the intermediate plate (Sec 9)

9.25A Tightening secondary shaft nut

9.25B Staking shaft nut

9.27 Method of compressing Belleville washers and circlip

9.26 5th speed selector fork lock bolt

9.28A Speedo driven gear

*Four-speed units*
27 Fit the two Belleville washers, concave sides towards each other. Compress the washers as described for dismantling (Section 5) using a clamp and fit the circlip (photo).

*All units*
28 Fit the speedometer driven gear and its lock screw. Screw in the reverse lamp switch (photos).
29 Reassemble the gear engagement lever, reverse spring cap and coil springs. It is recommended that the gear engagement components with their coil springs are assembled by passing a long screwdriver through them. The gear engagement shaft can then be pushed into place, displacing the screwdriver (photos).
30 Bolt on the pressed steel cover noting the 5th speed gear resistor spring. Always use a new cover gasket (photos).
31 Using a new gasket, bolt on the rear cover (photo).
32 Fit the detent balls and springs and bolt on the retaining plate (photos).
33 Reconnect the gearcasing and bellhousing.
34 Fit the gearchange selector link rod (photos).
35 Fit the clutch release bearing into the bellhousing.

9.28B Speedo/driven gear lockscrew

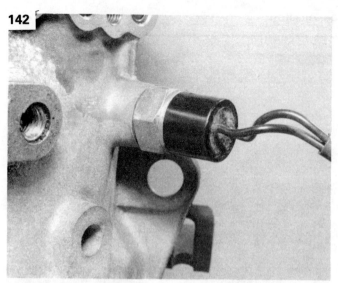

9.28C Reverse lamp switch

9.29A Fitting gear engagement lever

9.29B Gear engagement lever shaft nut

9.29C Gear selector lever and fixing nut

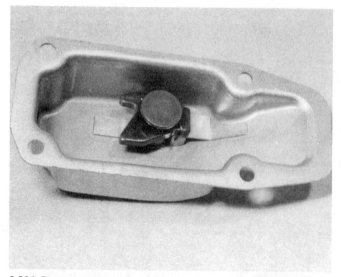

9.30A Pressed steel cover and 5th gear pawl and resistor spring

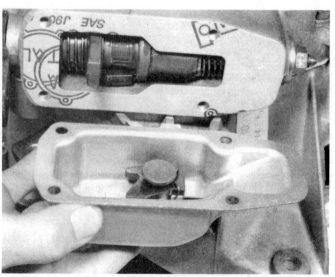

9.30B Fitting pressed steel cover and gasket

9.31 Fitting end cover and gasket

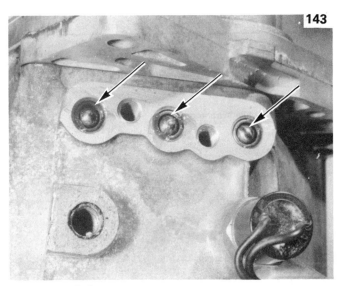

9.32A Detent balls

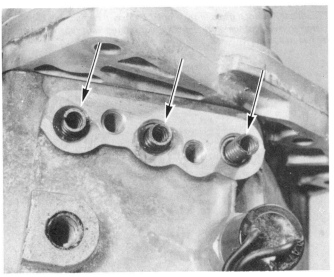

9.32B Detent springs

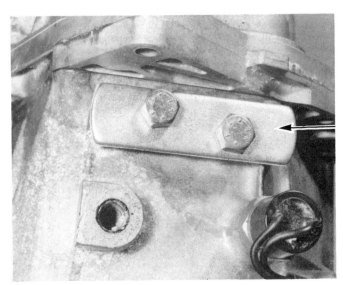

9.32C Detent spring retaining plate

9.34A Selector link rod

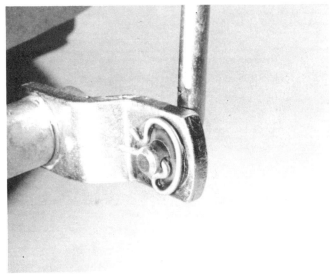

9.34B Selector link rod securing clip

## 10 Fault diagnosis – transmission

| Symptom | Reason(s) |
| --- | --- |
| Weak or ineffective synchromesh | Synchro baulk rings worn, split or damaged |
| | Synchromesh units worn, or damaged |
| Jumps out of gear | Gearchange mechanism worn |
| | Synchromesh units badly worn |
| | Selector fork badly worn |
| Excessive noise | Incorrect grade of oil in gearbox or oil level too low |
| | Gearteeth excessively worn or damaged |
| | Intermediate gear thrust washers worn allowing excessive end play |
| | Worn bearings |
| Difficulty in engaging gears | Clutch pedal adjustment incorrect |
| Noise when cornering | Wheel bearing or driveshaft fault |
| | Differential fault |

**Note:** *It is sometimes difficult to decide whether it is worthwhile removing and dismantling the gearbox for a fault which may be nothing more than a minor irritant. Gearboxes which howl, or where the synchromesh can be 'beaten' by a quick gearchange, may continue to perform for a long time in this state. A worn gearbox usually needs a complete rebuild to eliminate noise because the various gears, if re-aligned on new bearings, will continue to howl when different wearing surfaces are presented to each other. The decision to overhaul therefore, must be considered with regard to time and money available, relative to the degree of noise or malfunction that the driver has to suffer.*

# Chapter 7
# Driveshafts, hubs, roadwheels and tyres

*For modifications, and information applicable to later models, see Supplement at end of manual*

## Contents

## Specifications

### Driveshafts

Type ............................................................................ Solid with CV joint at outboard end and tripode (spider) joint at inboard end

Lubrication ................................................................. Inboard joint from transmission oil, outboard joint with 125 cc of lithium based molybdenum disulphide grease (Duckhams LBM 10).

### Hub bearings

Type ............................................................................ Lubricant sealed, double track ball

### Roadwheels

Type ............................................................................ Pressed steel or (SX option) – light alloy
Size ............................................................................. 4.50 J x 13

### Tyres

Type ............................................................................ Radial ply
Size:
    45 Comfort and Super and 55 Comfort ................... 135 SR 13
    55 and 70 Super ...................................................... 155/70 SR 13
    SX ............................................................................ 165/65 R 13
Pressures (cold):     **Front and rear**
    Average load ............................................................ 1.9 bar (28 lbf/in²)
    Fully loaded ............................................................. 2.2 bar (32 lbf/in²)

### Torque wrench settings

| | Nm | lbf ft |
|---|---|---|
| Driveshaft inboard boot flange retainer bolts | 9 | 7 |
| Driveshaft/hub nut | 272 | 200 |
| Front hub bearing ring nut | 58 | 43 |
| Track control arm to hub carrier balljoint nut | 49 | 36 |
| Rear hub nut | 220 | 160 |
| Roadwheel bolts | 86 | 63 |
| Front strut to hub carrier U-clamp bolts | 49 | 36 |

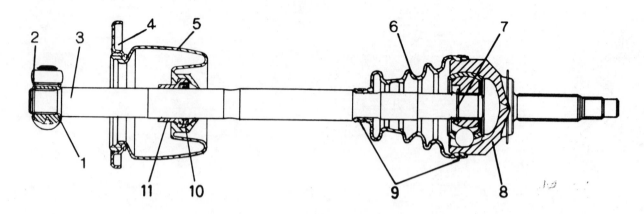

**Fig. 7.1 Typical driveshaft (Sec 1)**

| | | | |
|---|---|---|---|
| 1 | Inboard Tripode type joint | 4 | Boot retaining flange |
| 2 | Circlip | 5 | Boot |
| 3 | Driveshaft | 6 | Boot |

| | | | |
|---|---|---|---|
| 7 | Circlip | 9 | Boot clamping rings |
| 8 | Constant velocity (CV) joint | 10 | Integral oil seal |
| | | 11 | Oil seal retainer |

## 1 Description and maintenance

1 The driveshafts transmit the power from the transmission final drive to the front roadwheels.

2 The shafts are of open type having a tripode type joint at the inboard end and a ball and cage type constant velocity joint at the outboard end.

3 The tripode joints are located in the bevel side gears of the differential, and are lubricated by the transmission oil. The constant velocity joints are packed for life with molybdenum disulphide grease.

4 Provided the rubber boots are in good condition and keep out the dirt, the constant velocity joints last well, though on cars used in towns or hills, with a high proportion of driving hard in low gears, they are unlikely to last as long as the rest of the transmission. The tripode joints should last the life of the transmission.

5 Maintenance is virtually unnecessary except to check occasionally the security of the flange connecting screws on the inboard boot.

6 Inspection is the more important task, and this must be carried out frequently. First, check the flexible boots for splits or cuts. Immediately any defect is observed, the boot must be removed, the lubricant renewed and a new boot fitted (see Section 3).

7 Wear in the constant velocity (CV) joints is usually indicated by a clicking noise. Wear in the shaft-to-hub splines and in the inboard tripode joints is unlikely to occur unless the hub nut has been loose or the joint boot split and has been allowed to operate in this condition over an extended period.

## 2 Driveshaft – removal and refitting

1 Drain the transmission oil into a suitable container.

2 Loosen off the front roadwheel bolts on the side concerned, then raise the car at the front and support it on axle stands. Remove the front roadwheel.

3 Have an assistant apply the footbrake firmly while the driveshaft-to-hub nut is loosened. A socket and long knuckle bar will be needed for this; the nut is very tight. Unscrew and remove the nut.

4 Unbolt the hydraulic flexible hose support clip from the lower part of the suspension strut. This will provide more freedom of movement for the hose when the hub carriers are pulled out.

5 Using a suitable balljoint separator, disconnect the tie-rod and balljoint from the steering arm at the base of the suspension strut.

6 Remove the bolts which hold the hub carrier to the U-clamp at the base of the suspension strut.

7 Tap the hub carrier downwards out of the strut clamp, then pull the top outwards.

8 Press or tap the driveshaft out of the hub carrier. If the shaft has to be tapped, screw on the nut a few turns to protect the threads, and use a plastic-faced hammer (photo).

9 Support the driveshaft and unbolt the inboard boot retaining flange. Withdraw the shaft from the differential/final drive (photo).

10 Refitting is the reversal of the removal process.

11 Fit the thrust washer and then tighten a new driveshaft/hub nut to the specified torque wrench setting and stake the nut into the shaft groove (photos).

12 Check and top up the transmission oil.

2.8 Removing driveshaft from hub carrier

2.9 Driveshaft inboard boot retainer

### 3 Driveshaft boot – renewal

1 A split driveshaft joint boot can be renewed after removing the joint as described in Section 4.

2 The CV joint must be packed with 125 cc of the specified grease before fitting the boot.

3 New boot clamps must be fitted to the outboard boot and a new seal and bush to the inboard boot (photos).

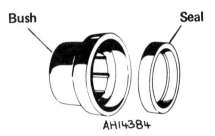

Fig. 7.2 Oil seal and bush located in inboard boot of driveshaft (Sec 3)

2.11A Hub thrust washer

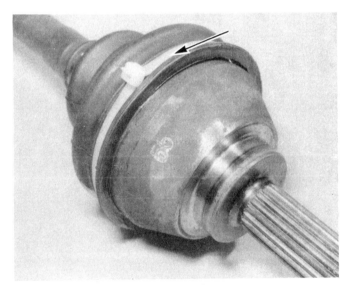

3.3A Cable tie used as driveshaft boot clip

2.11B Hub nut

3.3B Metal type boot clip

## 4 Driveshaft joints – overhaul

### Outboard (constant velocity) joint

1   The joint can be withdrawn from the shaft, once the rubber boot has been peeled back and the securing circlip extracted (photo).
2   If the joint is worn, a complete new joint should be fitted, individual spares not being available.
3   Fit the flexible boot, pack 125 cc of specified grease into the joint, pull the boot over the joint and fit the clips. Plastic wiring retaining straps of ratchet type are suitable for this purpose.

### Inboard (tripode) joint

4   Push back the dust excluding boot to expose the spider (photo).
5   Extract the circlip using circlip pliers then pull the spider from the shaft. If necessary use a small puller (photo).
6   Fit the new spider to the shaft then engage a new circlip in the shaft groove.
7   Apply transmission oil to the joint. Pull the boot into position, taking care not to damage the boot oil seal.
8   If a new seal has been fitted, make sure that the seal lips are filled with grease.

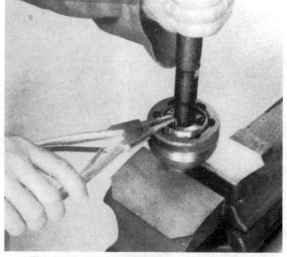

**Fig. 7.4 Extracting CV joint circlip (Sec 4)**

4.1 CV joint (circlip arrowed)

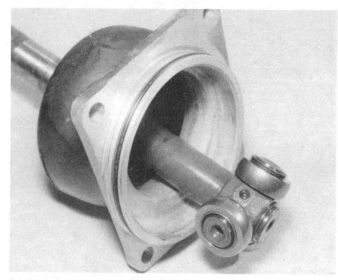

4.4 Tripode joint

**Fig. 7.3 Peeling back driveshaft CV joint boot (Sec 4)**

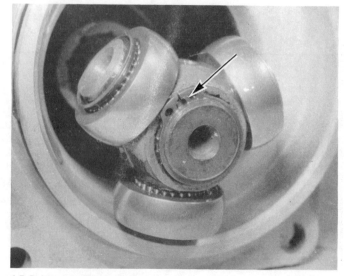

4.5 Spider (circlip arrowed)

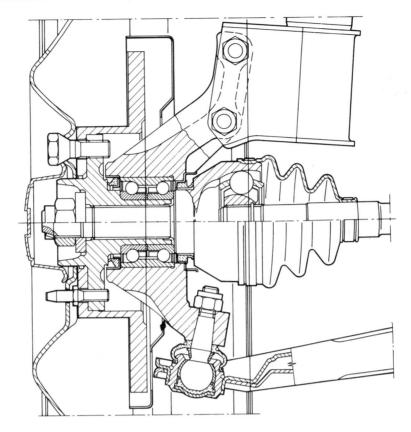

Fig. 7.5 Sectional view of front hub (Sec 5)

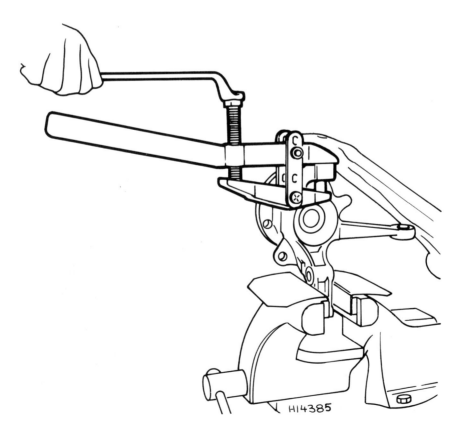

H14385

Fig. 7.6 Using a balljoint 'splitter' tool to separate track rod balljoint from hub carrier (Sec 5)

### 5  Front hub bearings – renewal

1  Normally, the front wheels should run silently especially during cornering. When a roadwheel is raised, and gripped at top and bottom, it should show no evidence of rock due to worn bearings. The bearings are sealed for life. No additional lubrication being required.
2  The bearings are a press fit in the hub carrier and the force required to remove them will destroy them.
3  Remove the hub carrier as described in Chapter 11.
4  Unbolt and remove the brake disc and disc shield as described in Chapter 8.
5  Unscrew the nut from the track control arm balljoint and then using a suitable 'splitter' tool, disconnect the balljoint from the hub carrier.
6  Grip the hub carrier in the jaws of a vice and attach a slide hammer

to the hub then withdraw the hub.
7  Remove the bearing inner track from the hub, if it has remained attached to it.
8  Relieve the staking on the bearing ring nut which is screwed into the hub carrier and then unscrew and remove the nut.
9  Press the bearing assembly from the hub carrier.
10  Press the bearing into the hub carrier, applying pressure only to the outer track.
11  Screw in a new bearing ring nut and tighten to the specified torque. Stake the ring nut as shown (Fig. 7.9).
12  Support the bearing inner track and press the hub into the carrier.
13  Reconnect the track control arm to the hub carrier and refit the disc shield and the brake disc.
14  Refit the hub carrier to the car as described in Chapter 11.

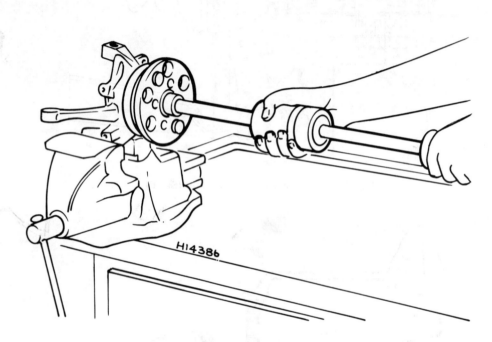

H14386

**Fig. 7.7 Removing hub from carrier (Sec 7)**

**Fig. 7.8 Front hub bearing (Sec 5)**

**Fig. 7.9 Front hub bearing ring nut staking point (arrowed) (Sec 5)**

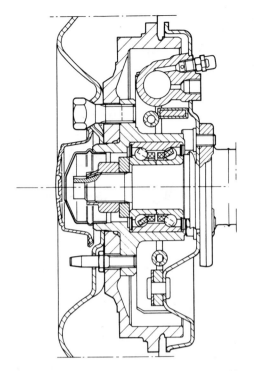

Fig. 7.10 Sectional view of rear hub (Sec 6)

Fig. 7.11 Unscrewing rear hub nut (Sec 6)

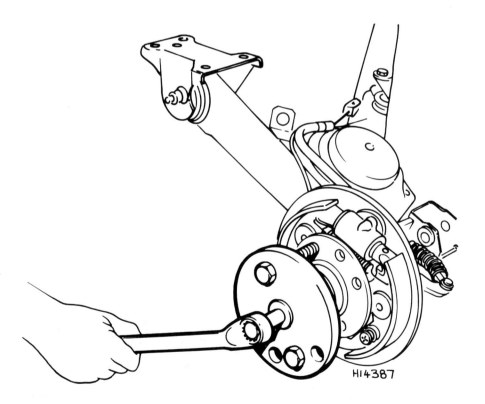

Fig. 7.12 Using an extractor to remove rear hub from stub axle (Sec 6)

### 6  Rear hub bearings – renewal

1  Raise the rear of the car and remove the roadwheel.
2  Remove the brake drum as described in Chapter 8.
3  Relieve the staking and unscrew and remove the hub nut.
4  Using a suitable puller, withdraw the hub from the stub axle.
5  Although the bearing/hub is an assembly, it often happens that the inboard section of the bearing inner track remains on the stub axle. In order to remove it, refer to Chapter 8 and disconnect the handbrake cable from the shoe lever and the hydraulic pipe from the wheel cylinder.
6  Unscrew the bolts which hold the brake backplate to the axle flange then withdraw the brake assembly.
7  Using a claw type puller or a sharp cold chisel, remove the bearing track from the stub axle.
8  If the bearing came apart during removal of the hub or the reason for removal was worn bearings then the complete bearing/hub will have to be renewed as an assembly; separate components are not supplied. The bearing is sealed for life and requires no additional lubrication.
9  Refit the brake assembly, reconnect the hydraulic pipe and the handbrake cable.
10  Locate the hub on the stub axle and apply a tubular drift to the

bearing inner track and drive the hub home. Fit the thrust washer (photo).
11  Screw on the new hub nut and tighten to the specified torque. Stake the nut into the shaft groove (photo).
12  Refit the brake drum, dust cap and roadwheel. Lower the car to the floor (photo).
13  Bleed the brake hydraulic circuit as described in Chapter 8.

Fig. 7.13 Rear hub with bearing (Sec 6)

6.10 Rear hub thrust washer

6.11 Rear hub nut

6.12 Rear hub dust cap

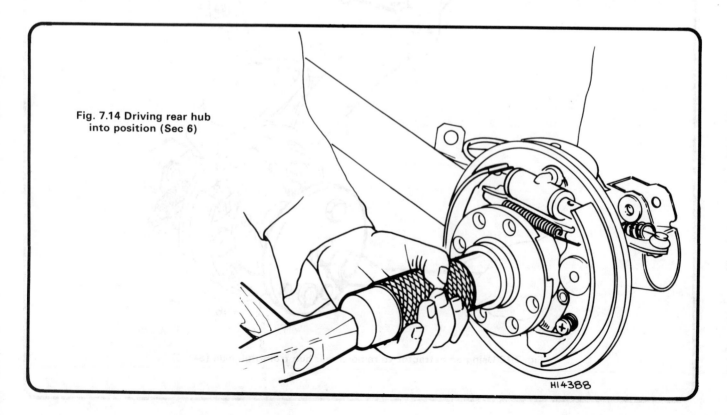

Fig. 7.14 Driving rear hub into position (Sec 6)

HI4388

### 7 Roadwheels and tyres

**Note:** *The repair of a punctured tubeless tyre by the fitting of an inner tube should not be attempted, even if temporary*

1 The roadwheels are of pressed steel type, using bolts to retain them to the hub flanges. No hub caps are fitted to Comfort models, but hub caps or wheel trims are used on Super versions (photo).

2 Periodically, remove the wheels, clean the inside and outside, and make good any rusty patches.

3 Keep the wheel retaining bolts lightly greased and tighten them to the specified torque after fitting the wheel.

4 Keep the tyres inflated to specified pressure and inspect the treads and sidewalls regularly for cuts, blisters or damage (photo).

5 If the wheels and tyres have been balanced on the car, they should not be moved from their original positions, nor their location on the hub be altered; paint one bolt hole on the wheel, and the matching one on the hub flange, before removing the wheel or the original balance will be lost at time of refitting.

6 If the wheels have been balanced on the car, they may be moved to even out the tread wear. With the radial tyres fitted as original equipment, however, only move them from front to rear and rear to front on the same side of the car. *Do not change them from side to side.*

7 If the spare wheel is introduced into the tyre rotational scheme, mark it as to which side it is fitted and from which side the 'new' spare came from. Keep the wheels to that side of the car in future movements.

8 It is recommended that the wheel is re-balanced after a puncture is repaired and at halfway through the life of the tyre (perhaps 15 000 miles (24 000 km) approximately) when loss of tread rubber due to wear may have altered the original balance.

9 Tyre tread wear characteristics are illustrated. Apart from those shown, if parts of the tread are scooped out or flattened, this may be caused by out of balance wheels or repeated heavy brake applications, causing the wheels to lock (photo).

10 Bulges or blisters on the tyre sidewalls may be caused by striking kerbs or mounting the kerb at anything more than a walking pace.

11 Scrubbing the tyres can occur where the roadwheel steering angles are incorrect on steering lock. This may be due to the lengths of the tie-rods being unequal.

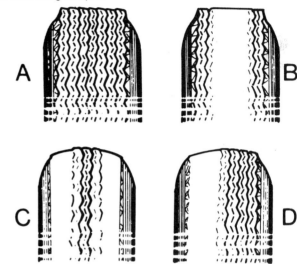

**Fig. 7.15 Tyre wear patterns and causes (Sec 7)**

A 'Feathering' due to incorrect toe-in
B Over inflation
C Under inflation
D Wear due to incorrect camber, worn wheel bearings or fast cornering

7.1 Removing a hub cap

7.4 Checking a tyre pressure

7.9 Checking tyre tread depth

## 8 Fault diagnosis – driveshafts and hubs

| Symptom | Reason(s) |
| --- | --- |
| Knock or clunk when taking up drive | Loose driveshaft-to-hub nut<br>Loose driveshaft flange bolts<br>Worn final drive-to-shaft splines<br>Worn shaft-to-hub splines<br>Worn CV or tripode joint |
| Clicking or knocking, especially when cornering | Worn or damaged CV joint |
| Vibration (check wheel balance first) | Bent driveshaft<br>Worn driveshaft/hub bearings<br>Worn CV joint<br>Loose hub mountings |
| Noise when cornering | Worn hub bearings |
| Roadwheel rock when gripped top<br>and bottom with wheel raised | Worn bearings<br>Incorrectly tightened hub nut<br>Loose roadwheel bolts |

# Chapter 8 Braking system

*For modifications, and information applicable to later models, see Supplement at end of manual*

## Contents

## Specifications

**System type** .................................................................... Dual-circuit hydraulic with servo unit and pressure regulating valve. Discs front, drums rear. Handbrake mechanical to rear wheels.

### Disc brakes
| | |
|---|---|
| Type | Single cylinder, sliding caliper |
| Disc diameter | 227.0 mm (8.94 in) |
| Disc thickness | 10.7 to 10.9 mm (0.42 to 0.43 in) |
| Minimum regrind thickness | 9.0 mm (0.35 in) |
| Minimum wear thickness of pad friction material | 1.5 mm (0.06 in) |
| Caliper cylinder diameter | 48.0 mm (1.89 in) |

### Drum brakes
| | |
|---|---|
| Type | Single cylinder, with automatic adjusters |
| Drum internal diameter | 185.24 to 185.53 mm (7.30 to 7.31 in) |
| Maximum regrind diameter | 187.0 mm (7.37 in) |
| Minimum shoe lining friction material thickness | 1.5 mm (0.06 in) |
| Cylinder diameter | 19.05 mm (0.75 in) |

**Master cylinder bore diameter** .................................. 19.05 mm (0.75 in)

**Vacuum servo diameter** ........................................... 158.5 mm (6.0 in)

**Hydraulic fluid type/specification** ........................................ Hydraulic fluid to DOT 3 or 4, or SAE J1703C (Duckhams Universal Brake and Clutch Fluid)

**System capacity** ........................................................... 0.33 litre (0.58 pint)

| Torque wrench settings | Nm | lbf ft |
|---|---|---|
| Caliper mounting bracket bolts ............................................ | 53 | 39 |
| Rear wheel cylinder mounting bolts ...................................... | 10 | 7 |
| Pressure regulating valve mounting bolts ............................ | 20 | 15 |
| Master cylinder mounting nuts ............................................ | 25 | 18 |
| Rear brake backplate bolts ................................................ | 20 | 15 |

## 1  General description

The braking system is of four wheel hydraulic type with discs on the front wheels and drums on the rear.

The hydraulic system is of dual-circuit type and incorporates a pressure regulator valve to limit pressure to the rear brakes during heavy braking to prevent rear wheel lock up.

A vacuum servo unit is fitted to some models.

The handbrake is mechanically operated on the rear wheels.

## 2  Maintenance

1   At the weekly service check, inspect the fluid level in the master cylinder reservoir. Topping up should only be required at very infrequent intervals and should only be necessary owing to the need for extra fluid in the hydraulic system caused by wear of the friction material of the disc pads and shoe linings.

2   The need for frequent or regular topping up will be due to a leak in

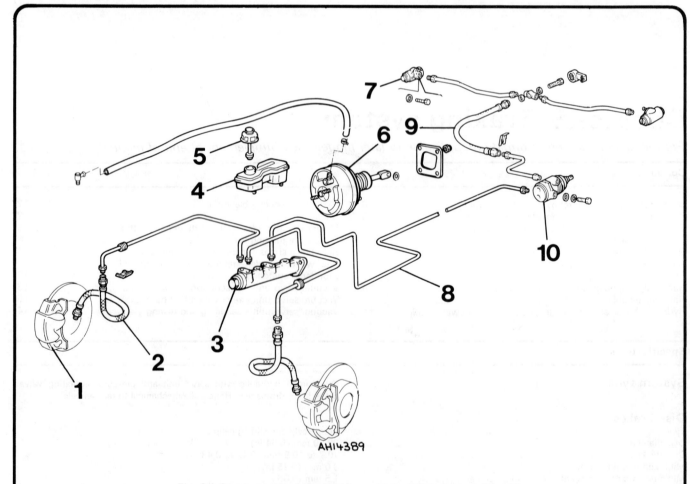

**Fig. 8.1 Components of the braking system (LHD shown) (Sec 1)**

| | | | |
|---|---|---|---|
| 1  Caliper | 4  Fluid reservoir | 7  Rear wheel cylinder | 9   Hose |
| 2  Hose | 5  Cap and fluid level sensor | 8  Pipeline | 10  Pressure regulating valve |
| 3  Master cylinder | 6  Vacuum servo unit | | |

the system, probably from a hydraulic cylinder seal or a flexible hose. Correct the problem immediately.

3  Use only clean new fluid for topping up. It must be of the specified type and have been stored in a closed container and not have been shaken for at least 24 hours (photo).

4  At regular intervals, check the hoses and pipelines for condition. Adjust the handbrake if the lever travel becomes excessive. Check the condition and security of the brake servo vacuum hose. All these operations are described later in this Chapter.

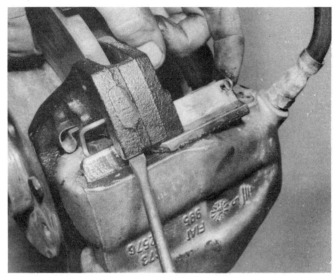

3.2B Removing a locking block

2.3 Fluid reservoir cap and float for warning switch

friction material on each pad (photo). If it is 1.5 mm (0.06 in) or less, renew the pads.

5  Withdraw the pads and the anti-rattle springs.

6  Brush away any dust and dirt from the caliper, taking care not to inhale the dust – this contains asbestos and is thus potentially injurious to health.

7  As the new pads are thicker than the old ones, the caliper piston must be depressed into its cylinder to accommodate them. This will cause the fluid level to rise in the reservoir. Anticipate this by syphoning some out beforehand, but take care not to let it drip onto the paintwork – it acts as an effective paint stripper!

8  Refit the anti-rattle springs, the pads (friction lining-to-disc), the cylinder body, the locking blocks and their retaining clips (photos).

9  Refit the roadwheel and apply the footbrake hard, several times, to bring the pads into contact with the brake disc.

10 Renew the pads on the opposite brake. The pads should always be renewed in axle sets.

11 Top up the fluid reservoir.

## 3  Disc pads – inspection and renewal

1  Jack up the front of the car and remove the roadwheels.

2  Extract the spring clips and slide out the locking blocks (photos).

3  On SX versions, carefully disconnect the wear sensor lead connecting plug.

4  Lift the caliper body from the disc and inspect the thickness of the

3.2A Removing a disc pad locking block clip

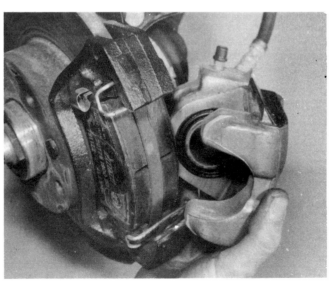

3.4 Removing the caliper unit

3.8A Disc pad and anti-rattle spring

3.8B Cylinder body located on caliper bracket

7   Before removing the brake shoes, note the way in which the shoes are positioned, with respect to leading and trailing ends (the end of the shoe not covered by lining material). Note also into which holes in the shoe web the return springs are connected. Sketch the shoes or mark the holes on the new shoes with quick drying paint if you are doubtful about remembering (photo).

4.7 Rear brake assembly

8   Undo the steady springs by depressing and rotating their caps a quarter turn to disengage the slot from the pin. On later models a U-shaped steady spring is used. Depress and slide it out.
9   Rotate the hub until the cut-outs in its rear flange face are in alignment with the shoe self-adjusters.
10 Pivot the trailing shoe on the self-adjuster post and disengage the ends of the shoe from the slot in the wheel cylinder tappet and from the lower anchor block.
11 Work the shoe up the self-adjuster pivot post until the self-adjuster boss enters the cut-out in the hub flange. The shoe can now be withdrawn (photo).

## 4   Rear brake shoes – inspection and renewal

1   Jack up the rear of the car and remove the roadwheels.
2   Fully release the handbrake.
3   Unscrew and remove the drum securing bolts. One of these is a long locating spigot for the roadwheel.
4   Pull off the drum. If it is tight, clean off the rust at its joint with the hub flange, and apply a little penetrating fluid. Two bolts may be screwed into the drum securing bolt holes if necessary and the drum thus eased off the hub. The securing bolt holes are tapped for this purpose.
5   Brush away all the dust and dirt from the shoes and operating mechanism, taking care not to inhale it.
6   The friction linings fitted as original equipment are of the bonded type and the rivet heads normally used as a guide to wear are not, of course, fitted. However, if the thickness of the friction linings is down to 1.5 mm (0.06 in) or less, the shoes must be renewed. Always purchase new or factory relined brake shoes.

4.11 Rear hub showing cut-outs on rear face for shoe self-adjuster bosses

12  Once off the self-adjuster post, the pull-off spring tension is eased, as the shoe can move towards the other, so the springs can be unhooked.
13  Remove the leading shoe in a similar way.
14  The new shoes will already be fitted with new self-adjusters.
15  Fit the new shoes to their self-adjuster posts, making sure that the handbrake shoe lever is correctly located. Engage the ends of the shoes.
16  Using a wooden or plastic-faced mallet, tap the shoes inwards against the friction of their self-adjuster coil springs. This will have the effect of reducing the overall diameter of the shoes to facilitate fitting of the shoe return springs and to allow the brake drum to slide over them.
17  Using pliers, reconnect the upper (longer) and lower shoe return springs.
18  Hold the steady pins in position from the rear of the backplate. Fit the small coil springs and the retaining cap, again using pliers to grip the cap and to depress and turn it to engage the pin. On later models fit the U-shaped springs.
19  Before refitting the drum, clean it out and examine it for grooves or scoring (refer to Section 8).
20  Fit the drum and the roadwheel.
21  Apply the brakes two or three times to position the shoes close to the drum.
22  Renew the shoes on the opposite brake in a similar way.
23  The handbrake should be automatically adjusted by the action of the shoe adjuster. If the handbrake control lever has excessive travel, refer to Section 16 for separate adjusting instructions.

### 5  Caliper – removal, overhaul and refitting

**Note:** *Purchase a repair kit in advance of overhaul*
1  Jack up the front roadwheel and remove it.
2  Brush away all dirt from the caliper assembly and the flexible pipe, particularly the fixing bracket and union at the car end of the flexible pipe.
3  Have ready a container suitable to catch the brake fluid, and sheets of clean newspaper on which to put parts.
4  Take out the spring clips and locking blocks, and take the caliper off the support bracket.
5  Disconnect the hydraulic flexible pipe at the under wing support bracket and cap both pipe ends. It may help to prevent loss of fluid if the vent in the reservoir cap is sealed with adhesive tape, to create a vacuum.
6  Remove the caliper to the bench or other work surface, and clean it thoroughly with hydraulic fluid or methylated spirit.
7  Depress the piston until the dust excluding boot can be removed.
8  Now apply air pressure to the flexible hose and eject the piston. Quite a low pressure is required for this, such as can be generated with a hand or foot operated pump.
9  Pick out the piston seal from its groove in the cylinder. Use a sharp probe, but take care to avoid scratching the cylinder bore.
10  Examine the surface of the piston and cylinder bore. If either is corroded, scored or shows metal-to-metal rubbed areas, the complete assembly should be renewed.

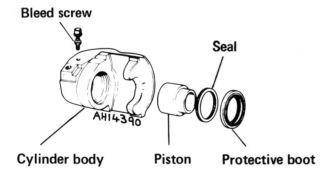

**Fig. 8.2 Exploded view of caliper (Sec 5)**

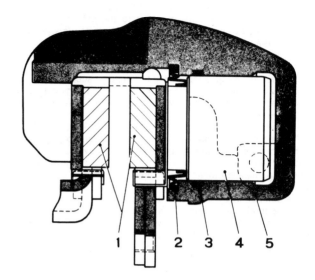

**Fig. 8.3 Sectional view of caliper (Sec 5)**

1  *Pads*
2  *Dust excluder*
3  *Piston seal*
4  *Piston*
5  *Cylinder body*

11  If the components are in good condition, discard the oil seals, clean the piston and cylinder and fit the new seal for the piston. This is included in the repair kit. Use the fingers only to manipulate it into its groove.
12  Lubricate the piston with clean hydraulic fluid and insert it partially into the cylinder.
13  Fit the new dust excluding boot to its projecting end, push the piston fully into the cylinder and engage the dust excluder with the rim of the cylinder.
14  Refit the caliper, reconnect the flexible hose, then bleed the front hydraulic circuit (refer to Section 12).

### 6  Brake disc – inspection, renovation or renewal

1  Whenever the front disc pads are being checked for wear, take the opportunity to inspect the discs for deep scoring or grooving. After a high mileage the disc may become reduced in thickness away from the extreme outer edge of the disc. If this wear is rapid, it is possible that the friction pads are of too hard a type.
2  If the disc has evidence of many tiny cracks, these may be caused by overheating due to a seized caliper piston in the 'applied' position.
3  The foregoing conditions may be corrected by regrinding the disc provided that the thickness of the disc is not reduced below that specified by such action. Alternatively, fit a new disc.
4  To remove a disc, take off the caliper and pads as described in Sections 3 and 5. Tie the caliper up, out of the way.
5  Knock back the tabs of the lockplates and unbolt the caliper support bracket from the hub carrier.
6  Unscrew and remove the two bolts which hold the disc assembly to the hub. One of these bolts is for wheel locating purposes.
7  Pull the disc from the hub.
8  Refitting is a reversal of the removal process. If the disc has excessive run-out, repositioning it in relation to the hub may bring it within tolerance by cancelling out the run-out characteristics in the hub and disc, once the most suitable fitted position has been found.

### 7  Rear wheel cylinder – removal, overhaul and refitting

**Note:** *Purchase a repair kit in advance of overhaul*
1  If fluid seepage is observed from the ends of the rear wheel cylinder when the brake drum has been removed, the seals are leaking and immediate action must be taken.

2 Although the cylinder can be dismantled without taking it from the backplate, this is not recommended due to the possibility of under wing dirt and mud dropping onto the components as work proceeds.

3 Remove the brake shoes, as described in Section 4.

4 Disconnect the hydraulic line from the wheel cylinder and cap the open end of the pipe. It may help to reduce the loss of fluid if the vent hole in the reservoir cap is taped over to create a vacuum.

5 Unscrew and remove the setscrews which hold the cylinder to the backplate and withdraw the cylinder. Prise off the rubber dust excluding boots.

6 Apply gentle air pressure from a hand or foot operated pump to eject the pistons and spring. Alternatively, tap the end of the cylinder on a piece of hardwood and the pistons should move out.

7 Inspect the piston and cylinder bore surfaces for scoring, corrosion or evidence of metal-to-metal rubbing areas. If these are found, discard the assembly and purchase a new one.

8 If the components are in good condition, note which way round the lips are fitted, then discard the seals and boots and wash the pistons and cylinder bore in clean hydraulic fluid or methylated spirit.

9 Manipulate the new seals into position, using the fingers only for this job.

10 Dip the pistons in clean hydraulic fluid and insert them with the coil spring and washers into the cylinder.

11 Fit the new dust excluding boots.

12 Refit the wheel cylinder to the backplate, reconnect the hydraulic pipe, then refit the shoes, the drum and the roadwheel.

13 Bleed the rear hydraulic circuit as described in Section 12.

## 8 Brake drum – inspection, renovation or renewal

1 Whenever the rear brake linings are being checked for wear, take the opportunity to inspect the internal surfaces of the brake drums.

2 If the drums are grooved or deeply scored, they may be reground, provided that their new internal diameter will not then exceed the specified dimension. If it will, or the drum is cracked, it must be renewed.

3 Removal and refitting of a brake drum is described in Section 4.

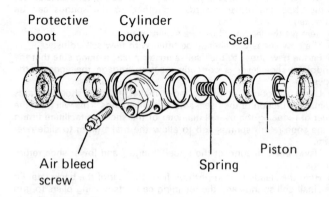

**Fig. 8.4 Exploded view of a rear wheel cylinder (Sec 7)**

## 9 Master cylinder – removal, overhaul and refitting

**Note:** *Purchase a repair kit in advance of overhaul.*

1 The master cylinder is mounted on the front face of the brake vacuum servo unit (55 and 70 models) or directly to the bulkhead (45 models).

2 Cover the front wings with polythene sheeting or similar material, in case hydraulic fluid spills onto the paintwork of the car during removal of the cylinder.

3 Detach the leads from the terminals on the reservoir cap, then unscrew and remove the cap and float.

4 Unscrew the pipe unions and prise the pipes carefully away from the master cylinder. Cap the open ends of the pipes and catch any fluid leaking from the master cylinder in a suitable container.

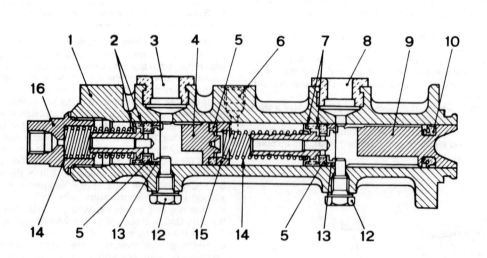

**Fig. 8.5 Sectional view of master cylinder (Sec 9)**

| | | | |
|---|---|---|---|
| 1 Cylinder body | 5 Seal | 9 Primary piston | 14 Springs |
| 2 Spring and cup | 6 Fluid outlet to front brakes | 10 Seal | 15 Seal |
| 3 Inlet from reservoir | 7 Spring and cup | 12 Stop bolts | 16 End plug and fluid outlet to |
| 4 Secondary piston | 8 Inlet from reservoir | 13 Spacer | rear brakes |

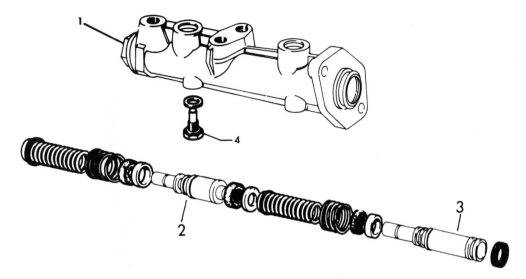

**Fig. 8.6 Exploded view of master cylinder (Sec 9)**

| 1 Cylinder body | 2 Secondary piston | 3 Primary piston | 4 Stop bolt |
|---|---|---|---|

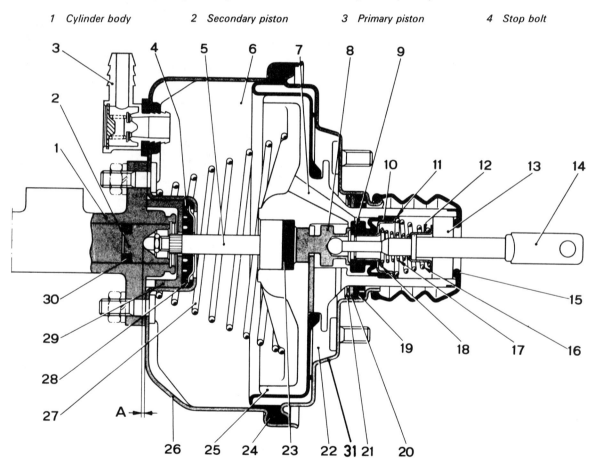

**Fig. 8.7 Sectional view of vacuum servo unit (Sec 9)**

| | | | |
|---|---|---|---|
| 1 Master cylinder | 8 Plunger | 16 Return spring | 24 Diaphragm |
| 2 Master cylinder primary piston | 9 Seal centraliser | 17 Valve spring | 25 Vacuum piston |
| 3 Non-return valve | 10 Valve | 18 Valve cup | 26 Front shell |
| 4 Front seal | 11 Spring cup | 19 Rear seal | 27 Return spring |
| 5 Pushrod | 12 Spring cup | 20 Seal | 28 Cup |
| 6 Front chamber | 13 Filter | 21 Cup | 29 Guide bush |
| 7 Vacuum port | 14 Pushrod | 22 Rear chamber | 30 Seal |
| | 15 Dust excluding boot | 23 Backing plate | 31 Rear shell |

*A = Projection of pushrod above vacuum cylinder face*

5   Unscrew the mounting nuts and withdraw the master cylinder from the bulkhead or from the servo unit.
6   Clean away all external dirt and tip out the fluid from the reservoir and cylinder body.
7   The fluid reservoirs need not be removed from the master cylinder but if they are, renew the rubber sealing collars when refitting.
8   Grip the master cylinder in a vice, then unscrew and remove the end plug. Catch the coil spring.
9   Using a thin rod, apply pressure to the end of the primary piston then unscrew and remove the two stop bolts and sealing washers.
10  The internal piston assemblies with seals and springs can now be pushed out of the cylinder body. Keep all the components in their originally fitted sequence and note in which direction the seal lips are located.
11  Inspect the surfaces of the piston and cylinder bore. If scoring, corrosion or metal-to-metal rubbing areas are evident, renew the master cylinder complete.
12  If the components are in good condition, discard the oil seals and manipulate the new ones into position, using the fingers only.
13  Refit by reversing the removal operations; apply pressure to the piston ends so that the stop bolts can be fitted, then tighten the end plug. Make sure that the grooves in the pistons engage in the stop bolts.
14  Before refitting the master cylinder to the servo, measure the projection of the servo piston pushrod. When the master cylinder is fitted, there must be a clearance (see A in Fig. 8.7) between the end of the pushrod and the primary piston end face of between 0.825 and 1.025 mm (0.03 and 0.04 in). A depth gauge will be required for these measurements, the reference point being the mating surfaces of the master cylinder and the vacuum servo.
15  Alter the adjusting screw on the servo as necessary and lock it by applying locking fluid to the threads on completion.
16  Bolt the master cylinder to the vacuum servo or bulkhead, then reconnect the pipelines and reservoir cap leads.
17  Bleed the complete hydraulic system, as described in Section 12.

## 10  Pressure regulating valve

1   The pressure regulating valve is a load proportioning valve which restricts the hydraulic pressure to the rear brakes according to car weight during heavy applications of the brake pedal. This prevents the rear wheels locking.

2   A faulty or non-operational valve should be renewed complete, no repair being possible.
3   To remove the valve, unscrew the pipe unions and disconnect the hydraulic pipes from the valve. Cap the ends of the pipes to prevent loss of fluid.
4   Unbolt the valve mounting bracket, withdraw it and disconnect the tension spring (photo).
5   Refit the new valve and then adjust it in the following way.
6   Have the car standing on a level floor.
7   The car should be normally loaded (kerb weight) with fuel, oil, spare wheel etc: Load the luggage compartment immediately behind the seat back with:

*65 kg (143 lbs) on three-door models or*
*55 kg (121 lbs) on five-door models*

10.4 Pressure regulating valve bracket and tension spring

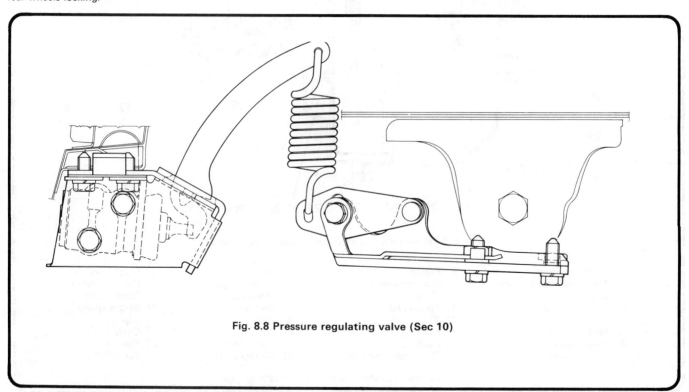

Fig. 8.8 Pressure regulating valve (Sec 10)

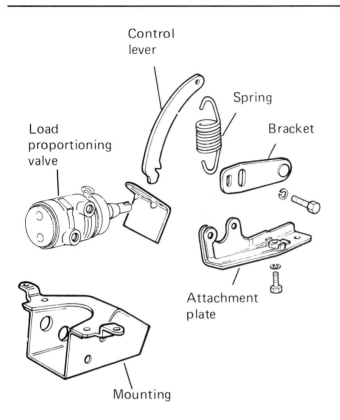

Fig. 8.9 Components of the pressure regulating valve (Sec 10)

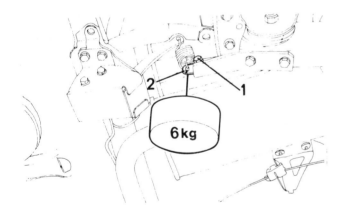

**Fig. 8.10 Weight attachment point for pressure regulating valve adjustment (Sec 10)**

*1 Fixing bolt*        *2 Bracket eye*

8   Refer to Fig. 8.10 and slacken the valve bracket securing bolt (1).
9   Attach a 6.0 kg (13.2 lb) weight to the bracket eye (2) as shown and then tighten the bracket securing bolt.
10  Bleed the braking system if a new valve has been fitted. Bleeding will not of course be required if only adjustment has been carried out to an existing valve.

## 11  Hydraulic hoses and pipes – inspection and renewal

*Flexible hoses*

1   Periodically, all brake pipes, pipe connections and unions should be completely and carefully examined.

2   First examine for signs of leakage where the pipe unions occur. Then examine the flexible hoses for signs of chafing and fraying and, of course, leakage. This is only a preliminary part of the flexible hose inspection, as exterior condition does not necessarily indicate the interior condition, which will be considered later.
3   Flexible hoses are always mounted at both ends in a rigid bracket attached to the body or a sub-assembly. To remove them, it is necessary first of all to unscrew the pipe unions of the rigid pipes which go into them. The hose ends can then be unclipped from the brackets. The mounting brackets, particularly on the body frame, are not very heavy gauge and care must be taken not to wrench them off (photo).
4   With the flexible hose removed, examine the internal bore. If it is blown through first, it should be possible to see through it. Any specks of rubber which come out, or signs of restriction in the bore, mean that the inner lining is breaking up and the pipe must be renewed.
5   When refitting the flexible hoses check they cannot be under tension, or rub, when the wheels are at the full range of suspension or steering movement.
6   Bleed the system (see Section 12) on completion.

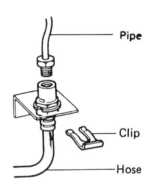

**Fig. 8.11 Typical hydraulic hose connection (Sec 11)**

11.3 Front hydraulic hose bracket

*Rigid pipes*

7   Inspect the condition of the braking system rigid pipelines at frequent intervals. They must be cleaned off and examined for any signs of dents (or other percussive damage) and rust and corrosion. Rust and corrosion should be scraped off and, if the depth of pitting in the pipes is significant, they will need renewal. This is particularly likely in those areas underneath the car body and along the rear axle where the pipes are exposed to the full force of road and weather conditions.

8   Rigid pipe removal is usually straightforward. The unions at each end are undone, the pipe and union pulled out, and the centre sections of the pipe removed from the body clips where necessary. Underneath the car, exposed unions can sometimes be very tight. As one can use only an open-ended spanner and the unions are not large, burring of the flats is not uncommon when attempting to undo them. For this reason, a self-locking grip wrench (Mole) is often the only way to remove a stubborn union.

9   Rigid pipes which need renewal can usually be purchased at any garage where they have the pipe, unions and special tools to make them up. All they need to know is the total length of the pipe, the type of flare used at each end with the union, and the length and thread of the union. Fiat is metric, remember.

10  Fitting your new pipes is a straightforward reversal of the removal procedure. If the rigid pipes have been made up, it is best to get all the sets bends in them before trying to fit them. Also, if there are any acute bends ask your supplier to put these in for you on a tube bender. Otherwise, you may kink the pipe and thereby restrict the bore area and fluid flow.

11  Bleed the system (see Section 12) on completion.

## 12  Hydraulic system – bleeding

1   If the master cylinder or the pressure regulating valve has been disconnected and reconnected then the complete system (both circuits) must be bled.

2   If a component of one circuit has been disturbed then only that particular circuit need be bled.

3   The two disc brakes comprise the front circuit and the two rear brakes the rear circuit.

4   Unless the pressure bleeding method is being used, do not forget to keep the fluid level in the master cylinder reservoir topped up to prevent air from being drawn into the system which would make any work done worthless.

5   Before commencing operations, check that all system hoses and pipes are in good condition with all unions tight and free from leaks.

6   Take great care not to allow hydraulic fluid to come into contact with the vehicle paintwork as it is an effective paint stripper. Wash off any spilled fluid immediately with cold water.

7   As the system on 55 and 70 models incorporates a vacuum servo, destroy the vacuum by giving several applications of the brake pedal in quick succession. The car should be loaded with enough weight to actuate the pressure regulating valve before bleeding commences.

### Bleeding – two man method

8   Gather together a clean glass jar and a length of rubber or plastic tubing which will be a tight fit on the brake bleed screws (photo).

9   Engage the help of an assistant.

10  Push one end of the bleed tube onto the first bleed screw and immerse the other end of the glass jar which should contain enough hydraulic fluid to cover the end of the tube.

11  Open the bleed screw one half a turn and have your assistant depress the brake pedal fully then slowly release it. Tighten the bleed screw at the end of each pedal downstroke to obviate any chance of air or fluid being drawn back into the system.

12  Repeat this operation until clean hydraulic fluid, free from air bubbles, can be seen coming through into the jar.

13  Tighten the bleed screw at the end of a pedal downstroke and remove the bleed tube. Bleed the remaining screws in a similar way.

### Bleeding – using a one way valve kit

14  There are a number of one-man, one-way brake bleeding kits available from motor accessory shops. It is recommended that one of these kits is used wherever possible as it will greatly simplify the bleeding operation and also reduce the risk of air or fluid being drawn back into the system quite apart from being able to do the work without the help of an assistant.

15  To use the kit, connect the tube to the bleedscrew and open the screw one half a turn.

16  Depress the brake pedal fully and slowly release it. The one-way valve in the kit will prevent expelled air from returning at the end of each pedal downstroke. Repeat this operation several times to be sure of ejecting all air from the system. Some kits include a translucent container which can be positioned so that the air bubbles can actually be seen being ejected from the system.

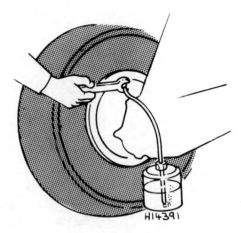

**Fig. 8.12 Bleeding a rear wheel cylinder (Sec 12)**

12.8 Caliper bleed screw with dust cap fitted

17  Tighten the bleed screw, remove the tube and repeat the operations on the remaining brakes.

18  On completion, depress the brake pedal. If it still feels spongy repeat the bleeding operations as air must still be trapped in the system.

### Bleeding – using a pressure bleeding kit

19  These kits too are available from motor accessory shops and are usually operated by air pressure from the spare tyre.

20  By connecting a pressurised contained to the master cylinder fluid reservoir, bleeding is then carried out by simply opening each bleed screw in turn and allowing the fluid to run out, rather like turning on a tap, until no air is visible in the expelled fluid.

21  By using this method, the large reserve of hydraulic fluid provides a safeguard against air being drawn into the master cylinder during bleeding which often occurs if the fluid level in the reservoir is not maintained.

22  Pressure bleeding is particularly effective when bleeding 'difficult' systems or when bleeding the complete system at time of routine fluid renewal.

## All methods

23 When bleeding is completed, check and top up the fluid level in the master cylinder reservoir.

24 Check the feel of the brake pedal. If it feels at all spongy, air must still be present in the system and further bleeding is indicated. Failure to bleed satisfactorily after a reasonable period of the bleeding operation, may be due to worn master cylinder seals.

25 Discard brake fluid which has been expelled. It is almost certain to be contaminated with moisture, air and dirt making it unsuitable for further use. Clean fluid should always be stored in an airtight container as it absorbs moisture readily (hygroscopic) which lowers its boiling point and could affect braking performance under severe conditions.

## 13 Vacuum servo unit – description

*A vacuum servo unit is fitted into the brake hydraulic circuit on 55 and 70 models in series with the master cylinder, to provide assistance to the driver when the brake pedal is depressed. This reduces the effort required by the driver to operate the brakes under all braking conditions.*

The unit operates by vacuum obtained from the induction manifold and comprises basically a booster diaphragm and non-return valve. The servo unit and hydraulic master cylinder are connected together so that the servo unit piston rod acts as the master cylinder pushrod. The driver's braking effort is transmitted through another pushrod to the servo unit piston and its built-in control system. The servo unit piston does not fit tightly into the cylinder, but has a strong diaphragm to keep its edges in constant contact with the cylinder wall, so assuring an air tight seal between the two parts. The forward chamber is held under vacuum conditions created in the inlet manifold of the engine and, during periods when the brake pedal is not in use, the controls open a passage to the rear chamber so placing it under vacuum conditions as well. When the brake pedal is depressed, the vacuum passage to the rear chamber is cut off and the chamber opened to atmospheric pressure. The consequent rush of air pushes the servo piston forward in the vacuum chamber and operates the main pushrod to the master cylinder.

The controls are designed so that assistance is given under all conditions and, when the brakes are not required, vacuum in the rear chamber is established when the brake pedal is released. All air from the atmosphere entering the rear chamber is passed through a small air filter.

Under normal operating conditions, the vacuum servo unit is very reliable and does not require overhaul except at very high mileages. In this case, it is far better to obtain a service exchange unit, rather than repair the original unit.

It is emphasised that the servo unit assists in reducing the braking effort required at the foot pedal and in the event of its failure, the hydraulic braking system is in no way affected except that the need for higher pressures will be noticed.

## 14 Vacuum servo unit – servicing and testing

1 Regularly, check that the vacuum hose which runs between the servo unit and the inlet manifold is in good condition and is a tight fit at both ends.

2 If broken or badly clogged, renew the air filter which is located around the brake pedal push rod. Access to this is obtained by disconnecting the pushrod from the cross-shaft or pedal arm, withdrawing the pushrod, dust excluding boot and end cap.

3 If the new filter is cut diagonally from its centre hole, future renewal can be carried out without the need for disconnection of the pushrod.

4 If the efficiency of the servo unit is suspect, it can be checked out in the following way.

5 Run the engine, then switch off the ignition. Depress the footbrake pedal; the distinctive in-rush of air into the servo should be clearly heard. It should be possible to repeat this operation several times before the vacuum in the system is exhausted.

6 Start the engine and have an assistant apply the footbrake pedal and hold it down. Disconnect the vacuuum hose from the servo. There should not be any in-rush of air into the servo through the connecting stub. If there is, the servo diaphragm is probably faulty. During this test,

expect the engine to idle roughly, unless the open end of the hose to the inlet manifold is plugged. Reconnect the hose.

7 With the engine off, depress the brake pedal fully. Start the engine with the brake pedal still depressed; the pedal should be felt to go down fractionally.

8 If the results of these tests are not satisfactory, remove the unit and fit a new one as described in the next Section.

## 15 Vacuum servo unit – removal and refitting

1 Syphon as much fluid as possible out of the master cylinder reservoir.

2 Disconnect electrical leads from the terminals in the reservoir cap then uncouple the rigid pipelines from the master cylinder body. Be prepared to catch leaking fluid and plug the open ends of the pipelines.

3 The master cylinder can be unbolted now from the servo unit, or detached later when the complete assembly is withdrawn.

4 Working inside the car, disconnect the servo pushrod from the pedal then remove the servo mounting nuts.

5 Withdraw the servo assembly into the engine compartment, then remove it to the bench. If the master cylinder is still attached, cover the wings with protective sheeting, in case brake fluid is spilled during removal.

6 Refitting is a reversal of the removal process, but adjust the pushrod clearance as described in Section 9. On completion of refitting, bleed the complete hydraulic system as described in Section 12. **Note:** *Where the help of an assistant is available, the servo pushrod need not be disconnected from the pedal. The rod is a sliding fit in the servo and the servo can be simply pulled off the rod. Refitting without having disconnected the rod from the pedal can be difficult unless the help of an assistant is available.*

## 16 Handbrake – adjustment

*Adjustment is normally automatic, by the movement of the rear brake shoes on their automatic adjusters.*

*However, owing to cable stretch, supplementary adjustment is occasionally required at the control lever adjuster nut. The need for this adjustment is usually indicated by excessive movement of the control lever when fully applied.*

1 The rear brakes should be fully applied when the handbrake control lever has been pulled over four or five notches.

2 If adjustment is required, release the locknut and turn the adjuster nut on the handbrake primary rod (photo).

3 Raise the rear roadwheels and check that they turn freely when the handbrake lever is fully released.

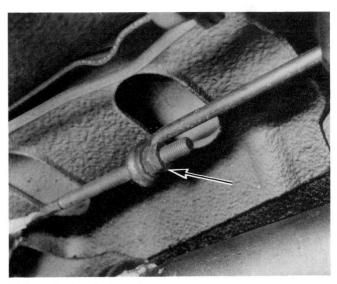

16.2 Handbrake adjuster nuts

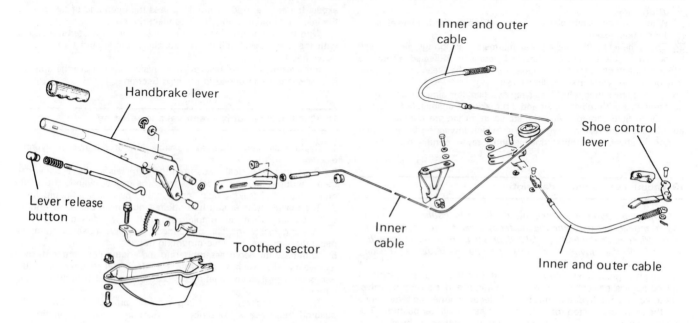

**Fig. 8.13 Handbrake components (Sec 17)**

## 17 Handbrake cable – renewal

1   There are two cables, either of which may be renewed independently.
2   Disconnect the cable, which is to be renewed, from the shoe lever at the brake backplate.
3   Disconnect the longer cable from the primary link or rod and release the cable from its retainers. On later models with a plastic fuel tank, a cable bracket is moulded into the side of the tank (photo).
4   Disconnect the shorter cable from the pivot lever at the pulley on the rear axle (photo).
5   Refit the new cables by reversing the removal operations and then adjust as described in the preceding Section.

17.4 Handbrake cable pulley

## 18 Brake pedal – removal and refitting

1   The operations are described in conjunction with the clutch pedal in Chapter 5, Section 4.
2   The brake pedal pushrod will slide out of the servo unit as the pedal is withdrawn.

## 19 Stop lamp switch

1   The brake stop lamp switch is of plunger type acting on the pedal arm.
2   Adjust the position of the switch by turning the locknuts until the stop lamps illuminate when the pedal arm is depressed through 1.0 mm (0.039 in).

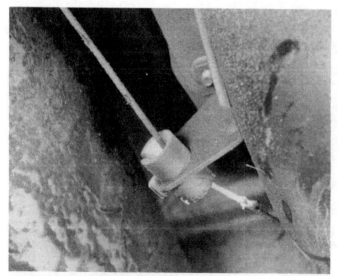

17.3 Handbrake cable guide on fuel tank

**20 Fault diagnosis – braking system**

| Symptom | Reason(s) |
|---|---|
| Excessive pedal travel | Pads or shoes excessively worn |
| | Incorrect pedal or servo pushrod adjustment |
| | Automatic adjusters faulty |
| | Seized wheel cylinder or caliper piston |
| | Master cylinder seals worn |
| Pedal feels spongy or soggy | Air in hydraulic system |
| | Low fluid level |
| | Loose connections |
| | Flexible hose perished |
| | Defective wheel cylinder or caliper seal |
| Pedal feels springy | New pads or linings not bedded-in |
| | Master cylinder mounting loose |
| Excessive effort required to stop car | Worn or contaminated linings or pads |
| | Incorrect grade of lining or pad material |
| | Servo vacuum hose leaking or disconnected |
| | Faulty servo or non-return valve (55 or 70 models) |
| | Seized caliper or wheel cylinder piston |
| | One circuit defective on dual circuit hydraulic system |
| Brakes pull to one side | Friction linings contaminated on one side of car |
| | Seized hydraulic piston on one side of car |
| | Different types of linings fitted on different sides of car, or new linings on one side only |
| | Seized automatic adjuster on one side of car |
| Pedal vibrates when brakes applied | Discs or drums distorted |
| | Friction linings excessively worn |
| | Loose backplate or caliper mounting bolts |
| | Wear in steering or suspension components |
| Brakes drag | Handbrake linkage overadjusted or seized |
| | Seized caliper or wheel cylinder piston |
| Brakes squeal | Drums or discs rusty or damp (temporary fault – no action necessary) |
| | Dust or grit in brake drums |
| | Linings excessively worn |

# Chapter 9 Electrical system

*For modifications, and information applicable to later models, see Supplement at end of manual*

## Contents

## Specifications

**System type** ................................................... 12 negative earth, battery alternator and pre-engaged starter

**Battery**

| | |
|---|---|
| Except 70S | 30 Ah |
| 70S | 40 Ah |

**Alternator**

| | |
|---|---|
| Type | Marelli, Valeo or Bosch 45A, 55A or 65A, with integral voltage regulator |
| Nominal voltage | 14 V |
| Minimum brush (wear) length | 6.0 mm (0.236 in) |

**Starter motor**

| | |
|---|---|
| Type | Marelli, Bosch or Femsa pre-engaged |
| Nominal power | 0.8 kW or 1.0 kW |
| Armature shaft endfloat | 0.1 to 0.5 mm (0.0039 to 0.0197 in) |
| Minimum brush (wear) length | 10.0 mm (0.39 in) |

## Fuses

| Fuse number | Circuit protected | Fuse rating (A) |
|---|---|---|
| 1 | Stop lamps, direction indicator lamps, instrument panel warning lamps, tachometer economy gauge, check control system | 10 |
| 2 | Windscreen wiper and washer, rear screen wiper/washer, check system panel illumination | 20 |
| 3 | Left front parking, right rear tail lamp, cigar lighter illumination, heater control and clock, digital clock illumination | 7.5 |
| 4 | Right front parking lamp and left rear tail lamp, instrument panel illumination and rear number plate lamp | 7.5 |
| 5 | Left-hand dipped headlamp, rear foglamps | 10 |
| 6 | Right-hand dipped headlamp | 10 |
| 7 | Left-hand headlamp (main beam) | 10 |
| 8 | Right-hand headlamp (main beam) | 10 |
| 9 | Engine cooling fan and horn (Comfort) | 25 |
| 10 | Heater booster fan, digital clock map reading lamp | 20 |
| 11 | Heated tailgate glass | 20 |
| 12 | Courtesy lamps, cigar lighter, radio power feed, disc pad sensors, economy gauge (ES models) | 10 |
| 13 | Hazard warning lamps | 10 |
| 14 | Spare (Comfort), Horn (Super) | 20 |

## Bulbs

| | Wattage |
|---|---|
| Headlamp | 40/45 or Halogen H4 60/55 |
| Front parking | 5 |
| Side repeater | 5 |
| Tail | 5 |
| Stop | 21 |
| Reversing | 21 |
| Rear foglamp | 21 |
| Direction indicator | 21 |
| Rear number plate | 5 |
| Courtesy lamp (roof) | 10 |
| Courtesy lamp (pillar) | 5 |
| Warning and indicator | Wedge base |

## Wiper blades

| | |
|---|---|
| Front | Champion X-4801 (19 in) or X-4503 (18 in) |
| Rear | Champion X-3303 |

## Torque wrench settings

| | Nm | lbf ft |
|---|---|---|
| Alternator mounting and adjustment nuts | 50 | 37 |
| Starter motor bolts | 48 | 35 |

## 1  General description

The electrical system is of 12 volt negative earth type and employs a belt-driven alternator and a pre-engaged type starter motor.

The models in the range are all adequately equipped with electrical accessories, while SX versions also have power windows and centralised door locking plus a check control system (Section 34).

## 2  Battery – inspection, charging, removal and refitting

1  The battery is of maintenance-free type and under normal circumstances, no topping up will be required, but regularly check that the electrolyte level is between the minimum and maximum lines on the translucent battery casing.

2  If the electrolyte level does drop below the minimum line, suspect a leak in the battery casing or that the alternator is overcharging. If the latter is the case, rectify the alternator fault and then prise out the two rectangular plugs from the top of the battery and top up with distilled or purified water.

3  Always keep the battery terminals clean and smear them with petroleum jelly to prevent corrosion. If corrosion has occurred, it may be neutralised by applying sodium bicarbonate or household ammonia.

4  The battery will normally be kept fully charged by the alternator, but it is possible for the battery to become discharged if the daily mileage is very low with much use being made of the starter and electrical accessories.

5  When the battery begins to deteriorate with age it may also require a boost from a mains charger.

6  Disconnect both battery leads before connecting the mains charger.

7  To remove the battery from the car, first disconnect the leads from the battery terminals (earth first) and then unscrew the securing clamp from the casing projection at the base of the casing (photo).

8  Lift the battery from its mounting platform. Refitting is a reversal of removal. Reconnect the earth cable last.

2.7 Battery clamp

## 3  Alternator – maintenance and precautions

*To avoid damage to the alternator, the following precautions should be observed.*

1  Disconnect the leads from the battery before connecting a mains charger to the battery terminals.
2  Never stop the engine by pulling off one of the battery leads.
3  Disconnect the battery if electric welding is to be carried out on the vehicle.
4  If using booster cables from another battery to start the car, make sure that they are connected positive to positive and negative to negative.
5  Maintenance consists of keeping the outside of the alternator clean, the electrical connections secure and the drivebelt correctly tensioned, see Chapter 2, Section 8.

## 4  Alternator – removal and refitting

**Note:** *Depending on the model, access to the alternator from above may be poor in which case it will be necessary to work from the underside of the vehicle, through the right-hand wheel arch (after removing the roadwheel and the lower undershield). Refer to Chapter 13 for details*

1  Disconnect the leads from the rear of the alternator.
2  Release the mounting and adjuster link nuts and push the alternator as far as it will go in towards the engine (photos).
3  Slip the drivebelt from the pulley.
4  Remove the mounting and adjuster bolts and lift the alternator from the brackets on the engine. Remove downwards on 1116 cc and 1301 cc models.
5  Refitting is a reversal of removal, tension the drivebelt as described in Chapter 2, Section 8.

## 5  Alternator – overhaul

1  Overhaul of the alternator should be limited to renewal of the brushes. If the unit has covered a high mileage, it will be found more economical to exchange it for a new or factory-reconditioned one, rather than renew worn components on the original unit.

### Brush renewal (Marelli alternator)

2  Unscrew the nuts and take off the rear cover.
3  Unscrew the two small bolts and withdraw the brush holder (photos).
4  Fit the new brush holder which is supplied complete with brushes, by reversing the removal operations.

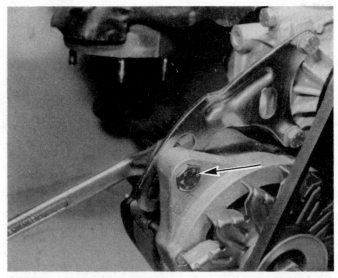

4.2B Alternator adjuster bolt

5.3A Alternator brush holder bolt

4.2A Alternator mounting

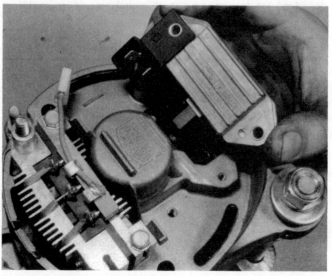

5.3B Removing alternator brush holder

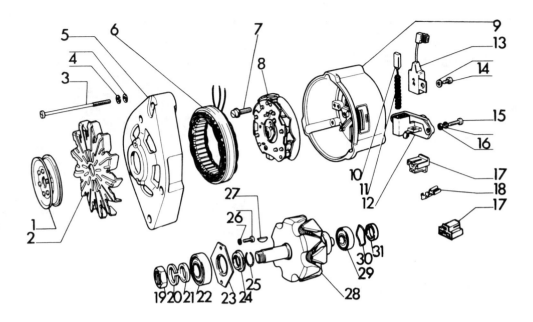

**Fig. 9.1 Exploded view of typical alternator (Sec 5)**

| | | | | | | |
|---|---|---|---|---|---|---|
| 1 | Pulley | 9 | Body | 17 | Plug socket | 25 | Spring washer |
| 2 | Fan | 10 | Brush | 18 | Suppressor | 26 | Screw and washer |
| 3 | Bolts | 11 | Spring | 19 | Shaft nut | 26 | Screw and washer |
| 4 | Washers | 12 | Brush holder | 20 | Spring washer | 27 | Key |
| 5 | Drive-end bracket | 13 | Condenser | 21 | Thrust ring | 28 | Rotor |
| 6 | Stator windings | 14 | Screws and washers | 22 | Bearing | 29 | Bearing |
| 7 | Plate screw | 15 | Screws and washers | 23 | Retainer plate | 30 | Backing washer |
| 8 | Diode plate (rectifier pack) | 16 | Screws and washers | 24 | Thrust ring | 31 | Shield (where applicable) |

*Brush renewal (Bosch alternator)*

5  Where applicable, remove the radio suppression condenser (capacitor) from the rear end frame (one screw and washer, and a plug-in connection).

6  Undo the two screws which retain the brush holder to the rear frame of the alternator, then ease the holder out of the alternator. Inspect the brushes and if worn below the specified minimum length, they must be renewed.

7  Disconnect the brush leads by unsoldering or carefully cutting them.

8  When soldering the new brush leads, do not allow solder to run down them or their flexibility will be ruined. Gripping the leads with a pair of pliers to act as a heat sink will prevent heat transfer to the internal components of the alternator.

9  When inspecting or renewing brushes, check the surface of the slip rings. Clean them with solvent or if they are very discoloured, use very fine glasspaper.

## 6  Voltage regulator

1  This is of integral type and is part of the brushholder assembly.

2  No provision is made for adjustment or overhaul.

## 7  Starter motor – description and testing

1  The starter motor may be one of two different makes. Both are of pre-engaged type.

2  This type of starter motor incorporates a solenoid mounted on top of the starter motor body. When the ignition switch is operated, the solenoid moves the starter drive pinion, through the medium of the shift lever, into engagement with the flywheel starter ring gear. As the solenoid reaches the end of its stroke, and with the pinion by now

partially engaged with the flywheel ring gear, the main fixed and moving contacts close and engage the starter motor to rotate the engine.

3  This pre-engagement of the starter drive does much to reduce the wear on the flywheel ring gear associated with inertia type starter motors.

4  If the starter fails, some fault-finding can be done with it still on the car. Check the ignition warning light comes on, and does not go out when the starter is switched on. If it goes out, the fault is probably in the battery. If it stays bright, get an assistant to work the switch, whilst listening to the starter. Listen to find out if the solenoid clicks into position. If it does not, pull off the solenoid wire, and check it with a test bulb. If the wire is live when the key is turned, but the solenoid does not move, take off the starter and remove it to the bench for overhaul.

## 8  Starter motor – removal and refitting

1  Disconnect the battery negative lead.

2  Disconnect the lead from the starter motor (photo).

3  Unscrew the fixing bolts and withdraw the starter motor, downwards on 1116 cc and 1301 cc models (photo).

4  Refitting is a reversal of the removal procedure.

## 9  Starter motor – overhaul

1  As with the alternator, the operations should normally be limited to renewal of the brushes. If the unit has covered a high mileage it will usually be more economical to purchase a new or factory-reconditioned one rather than renew several components of the original unit.

8.2 Starter motor connections

8.3 Removing starter motor

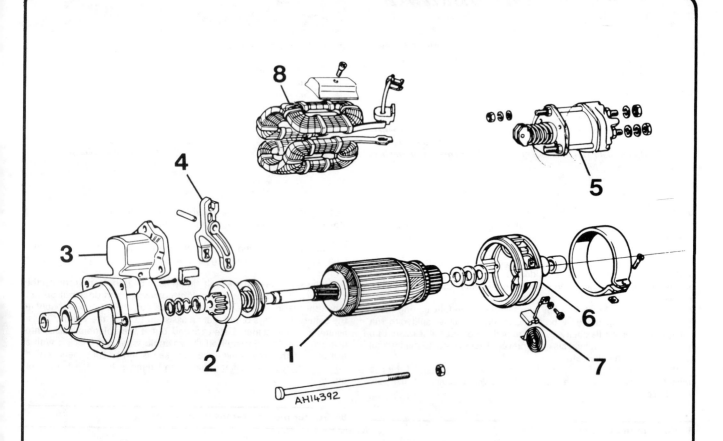

Fig. 9.2 Exploded view of typical starter motor (Sec 9)

1  Armature
2  Drive pinion/clutch
3  Drive end bracket
4  Shift lever
5  Solenoid
6  Brush endplate
7  Brush
8  Field windings

2  Owing to the possibility that a fault can develop in the starter motor solenoid or drive assembly, full dismantling procedures are given later in this Section.

### Brush – renewal

3  Slide off the cover band.
4  Using a hooked piece of wire, pull up the springs so that the brushes can be withdrawn and their lengths checked for wear. If they have worn below the specified minimum length, renew them by extracting the brush lead connecting screws (photo).

### Solenoid

5  Disconnect the field connecting wire from the solenoid.
6  Unscrew the bolts which hold the solenoid to the end-frame.
7  Unscrew the yoke tie-rod nuts.
8  Withdraw the solenoid and yoke off the armature and from the drive end bracket. Note the steel and fibre washers and the shims on the armature shaft (photo).
9  Extract the split pin and tap out the engagement lever pivot pin.
10 Pull the rubber packing piece from the drive end bracket.
11 Withdraw the armature with solenoid plunger, coil spring and engagement lever.

9.4 Starter motor brush partly withdrawn

9.8 Starter motor dismantled

12 Clean the commutator with a fuel soaked rag or very fine glass paper. *Do not undercut the mica insulators on the commutator.*

### Drive

13 To remove the drive assembly from the armature shaft, use a piece of tubing to tap the stop collar down the shaft to expose the snap ring. Remove the snap ring and stop collar and slide the drive assembly from the shaft.
14 Refitting is a reversal of removal, but use a new snap ring to secure the drive to the armature shaft.

### 10  Fuses and relays

1  The fuse box is located under the left-hand side of the facia panel and is held in place by two hand screws (photo).
2  The fuses and the circuits protected are identified by symbols. Refer also to Specifications.
3  If a fuse blows, always renew it with one of identical rating. If the new fuse blows immediately, find the cause before renewing the fuse for the second time. This is usually due to defective wiring insulation causing a short circuit.
4  Never substitute a piece of wire or other makeshift device for a proper fuse.
5  Various relays are plugged into the fuse block and include those for the heated rear screen, heater and horns.
6  On cars fitted with power-operated front windows and centralised door locking, the fuses and relays for these circuits are mounted separately under the right-hand side of the facia panel.
7  The relay (flasher unit) for the direction indicators and hazard warning lamps is located on the lower part of the steering column combination switch and is accessible after removing the column shroud.

10.1 Fuse block (later models)

1  *Horn relay*
2  *Heated tailgate window relay*

### 11  Steering column combination switch

1  Disconnect the battery negative lead.
2  Remove the steering column shrouds.
3  The switch can be removed without having to take off the steering wheel, but for clarity, the photographs show the wheel removed.
4  Unscrew the switch clamp nuts, disconnect the wiring plug and remove the switch from the steering column (photo).
5  Refitting is a reversal of removal, but make sure that the activating projections on the steering wheel hub engage correctly with the switches.

11.4 Unscrewing steering column switch clamp nut

1   Direction indicator flasher unit (relay)

13.4 Switch panel screw

## 12 Courtesy lamp switch

1   These are located in and secured to the body pillars with a single screw (photo).
2   Disconnect the battery negative lead.
3   Extract the switch screw and withdraw the switch.
4   If the leads are to be disconnected, tape them to the pillar to prevent them from slipping inside.
5   Refitting is a reversal of removal. Apply petroleum jelly to the switch contacts to prevent corrosion.

12.1 Courtesy lamp switch

## 13 Rocker and push-button switches

1   These are mounted in panels on each side of the instrument panel.
2   Disconnect the battery negative lead.
3   Prise off the instrument panel hood cover. This is held in place by

clips. The careful use of a screwdriver will assist in releasing them (see Section 21).
4   Extract the switch panel fixing screws. These compress spring clips which in turn secure the switch panel (photo).
5   Withdraw the switch panel until the wiring plugs can be disconnected. Record the location of the plugs before disconnecting them. Carefully release the fibre optic filaments (photos).
6   A push-button switch can be removed by compressing its retaining tabs and pushing it from the panel.
7   A rocker switch can be removed if its knob is pulled off and the switch sections withdrawn from the panel.
8   Reassembly and refitting of both types of switches are reversals of removal and dismantling.

## 14 Tailgate contacts

1   Contact blocks are used to transmit power to the heated tailgate window and to the wiper motor.
2   The block on the tailgate or the body may be released by prising their ends with a screwdriver (photos).

13.5A Withdrawing switch panel

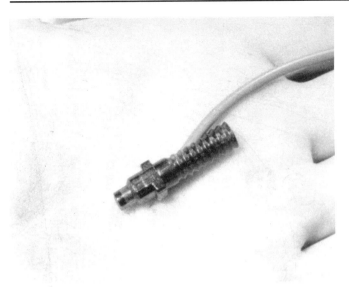

13.5B Switch panel fibre optic

## 15 Horns

1   These are mounted close to the engine/transmission left-hand mounting below the radiator.
2   Apart from keeping the connecting leads secure, no maintenance or adjustment is required.

## 16 Headlamp bulb – renewal

1   Open the bonnet and pull off the plug and the rubber cover from the rear of the headlamp (photo).
2   Prise back the spring bulbholder clips and withdraw the combined bulb and holder (photos).
3   Refit the new bulb. Avoid fingering it if it is of halogen type. Should the fingers touch the bulb, wipe it with a rag soaked in methylated spirit to remove any residual grease.
4   Turn the bulbholder until the pip on its flange engages in the cut-out in the rim of the reflector.
5   Snap back the spring retaining clips, refit the rubber cover and reconnect the plug.

14.2A Tailgate contact block

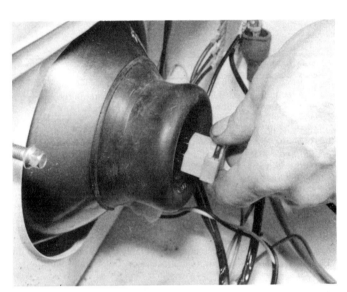

16.1 Headlamp plug and rubber cover

14.2B Body contact block

16.2A Headlamp bulbholder spring clips

16.2B Headlamp halogen type bulb

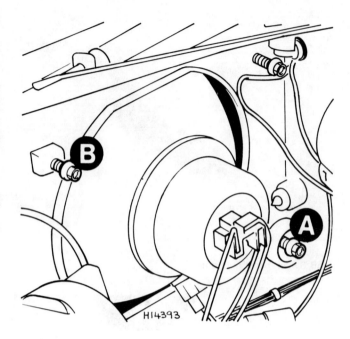

H14393

**Fig. 9.3 Headlamp beam adjustment screws (Sec 17)**

A    *Vertical*                                    B    *Horizontal*

## 17 Headlamp beam – alignment

1    It is recommended that the headlamp beams are aligned by your dealer or a service station having optical setting equipment.
2    Where an owner wishes to do the job himself, proceed in the following way.
3    Have the car standing on a level floor with the tyres correctly inflated and square to a wall, at a distance of 10.0 m (32.8 ft) from it.
4    Mark the wall to correspond with the centres of the headlamps.
5    Switch to dipped beams when the brightest parts of the light pattern should be below the marks on the wall by an amount equal to one tenth of the distance between the floor and the mark on the wall.
6    Adjust the beams as necessary by turning the adjuster screws (A) vertical or (B) horizontal, which are located at the rear of the headlamp.
7    Holts Amber Lamp is useful for temporarily changing the headlight colour to conform with the normal usage on Continental Europe.

## 18 Headlamp – removal and refitting

1    Open the bonnet and extract the two headlamp mounting screws from the top rail (photo).

2    Pull the headlamp unit forward off its ballstud and then disconnect the wiring plug (photo).
3    Refitting is a reversal of removal.

## 19 Exterior lamps – bulb renewal

### Front parking lamp

1    The bulbholder is located in the headlamp reflector.
2    Open the bonnet, push and twist the bulbholder from its location (photo).
3    The wedge base type bulb is simply pulled from its holder.

18.1 Headlamp upper fixing screw

18.2 Withdrawing headlamp

19.2 Front parking lamp bulb

## Front direction indicator lamp

4  Extract the screws and remove the lens (photo).
5  Depress and twist the bayonet fitting type bulb from its holder.

## Side repeater lamp

6  This bulb may be renewed in one of two ways. Either partially remove the underwing protective shield and reach up under the front wing and pull the holder out of the lamp body or depress the lamp retaining tab and withdraw the lamp from outside the wing. The tab is very brittle (photo).
7  Remove the bulb from the holder.

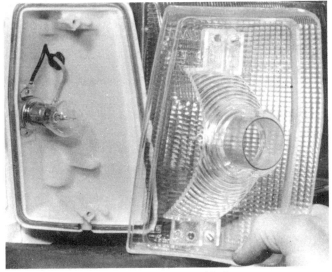

19.4 Front direction indicator lamp lens and bulb

19.6 Side repeater lamp

## Rear lamp cluster

8  Open the tailgate.
9  Gently prise up the clips on the top surface of the lens. Pull the upper part of the lens outwards and release it from the lower fixings (photo).
10  The individual lamp bulbs may be renewed, all of them being of bayonet fitting type (photo).

19.9 Rear lamp lens upper clip

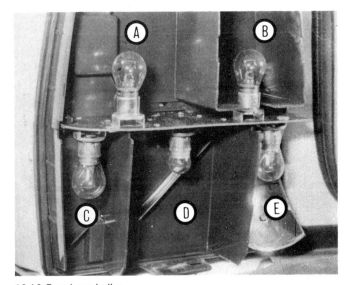

19.10 Rear lamp bulbs

A   Direction indicator
B   Reversing
C   Stop
D   Tail
E   Fog

## Rear number plate lamp

11  Insert a screwdriver blade in the lens slot and prise it from the bulb holder. Withdraw the bulb.
12  If preferred, the complete lamp may be removed from the bumper by reaching up under the bumper and squeezing the lamp retaining tabs (photo).

## 20  Interior lamps – bulb renewal

### Courtesy lamp

1  The lamp lenses, whether roof or pillar mounted, are removed by prising off using a screwdriver inserted under one end (photo).
2  The festoon type bulb is pulled from its spring contacts.

19.12 Rear number plate lamp withdrawn

### Instrument panel lamps

3   Remove the instrument panel hood cover as described in the next Section. The panel lighting bulbs may be renewed without further dismantling, but access to the warning and indicator bulbs can only be obtained if the instrument panel is partially withdrawn as described in the next Section (photo).
4   Pull out the appropriate bulbholder and withdraw the wedge base type bulb.
5   Fit the new bulb, the holder, instrument panel and hood cover.

### 21  Instrument panel – removal and refitting

1   Disconnect the battery negative lead.
2   Remove the instrument panel hood cover. The easiest way to do this is to insert the fingers at the sides, and pull the hood sharply upwards off its retaining clips.

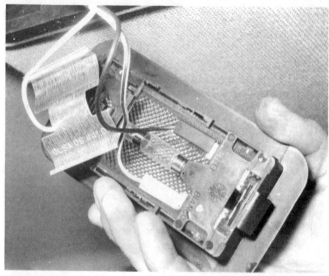

20.1 Interior roof lamp withdrawn

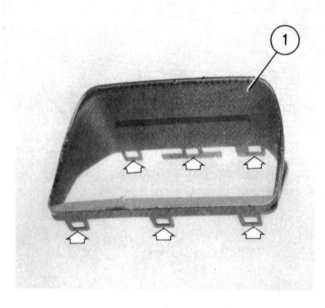

Fig. 9.4 Instrument hood cover (1) (Sec 21)

20.3 Instrument panel warning lamp

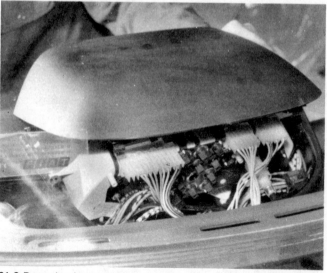

21.2 Removing instrument panel hood cover

3  Extract the two fixing screws from the instrument panel and pull it towards you until the speedometer drive cable can be disconnected by squeezing its plastic retaining ring (photo).
4  Disconnect the wiring plugs and record their exact locations.
5  Remove the instrument panel upwards (photo).
6  Refitting is a reversal of removal.

21.3 Removing instrument panel screw

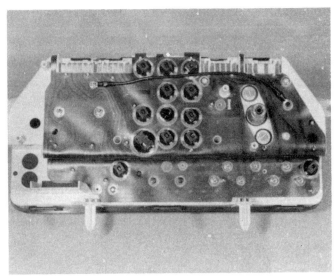

22.3 Rear view of instrument panel

5  On models equipped with a check control system (see Section 34), the speedometer cannot be removed until the control unit has first been withdrawn.
6  On ES versions, the speedometer cannot be removed until the economy gauge control unit has been removed.

## 23 Speedometer drive cable – renewal

1  Remove the instrument panel hood cover as described in Section 21.
2  Disconnect the speedometer cable from the speedometer by squeezing the plastic retaining ring (photo).
3  Working at the transmission, disconnect the speedometer cable by unscrewing the knurled retaining ring (photo).
4  Withdraw the cable through the bulkhead grommet.
5  Refit the new cable assembly by reversing the removal operations.

21.5 Instrument panel and steering wheel removed

## 22 Instrument panel – dismantling

1  With the instrument panel removed from the car, individual instruments may be removed in the following way.
2  Pull off the speedometer trip device knob.
3  Remove the instrument hood cover by gently releasing the plastic clips (Fig. 9.4) (photo).
4  The speedometer is secured by two screws for its metal casing and one screw for its plastic casing (photo). Other instruments are held to the panel by nuts.

23.2 Speedometer cable connector at head

23.3 Speedometer cable connector at transmission

24.4 Windscreen wiper arm nut

## 24 Windscreen wiper blade and arm – removal and refitting

1   The wiper blade can be removed once the arm has been pulled away from the glass and locked in position.
2   Depress the small tab (A) and push the U-shaped carrier out of the hook (B) of the wiper arm. The blade can then be withdrawn, passing the wiper arm hook through the slot (C) in the blade stretcher (Fig. 9.5).
3   Before removing the wiper arm, it is worthwhile sticking a strip of masking tape on the screen to indicate the setting of the arm and blade as a guide to refitting.

4   Flip up the plastic cover and unscrew the arm retaining nut. Pull off the arm from the splined drive spindle (photo).
5   Refitting is a reversal of removal.

## 25 Windscreen wiper motor – removal and refitting

1   Open the bonnet and disconnect the battery negative lead.
2   Remove the wiper arm and blade as previously described.
3   Prise off the sealing cover from around the drive spindle and then unscrew the drive spindle bezel nut.

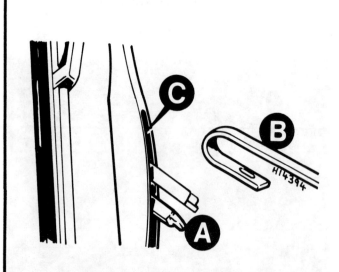

Fig. 9.5 Windscreen wiper blade fixing (Sec 24)

A    Tab                          C    Blade slot
B    Wiper arm

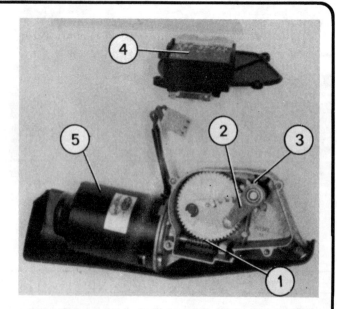

Fig. 9.6 Windscreen wiper motor components (Sec 25)

1   Gears                        4   Intermittent control unit
2   Crank arm                    5   Motor yoke
3   Shaft gear

4 Pull back the weathersealing strip from above the wiper motor location and remove the two screws which are exposed (photo).
5 Withdraw the motor/gearbox with protective cover from under the lip of the upper bulkhead. Disconnect the wiring plug (photos).
6 Refitting is a reversal of removal.

## 26 Tailgate wiper blade and arm – removal and refitting

1 Pull the wiper arm from the glass until it locks.
2 With the thumb nail pull down the tab to release the peg (B) from the hole (A) (Fig. 9.7). Pull the blade from the arm.
3 To remove the arm, flip up the plastic cover and remove the nut exposed. Pull the arm from the drive spindle.
4 Refitting is a reversal of removal.

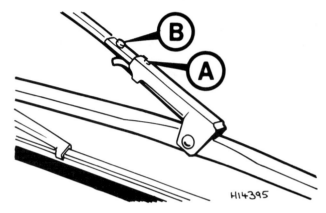

**Fig. 9.7 Tailgate wiper blade fixing (Sec 26)**

A  Hole                           B  Peg

## 27 Tailgate wiper motor – removal and refitting

1 Remove the blade and arm as previously described. Unscrew the drive spindle bezel nut.
2 Open the tailgate fully.
3 Unclip and remove the wiper motor cover.
4 Unscrew the mounting screws, withdraw the motor and disconnect the wiring plug (photo).
5 Refitting is a reversal of removal.

25.4 Removing windscreen wiper motor mounting screws

25.5A Windscreen wiper motor cover

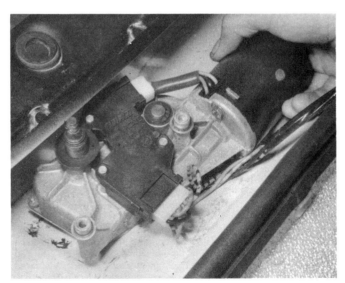

25.5B Removing windscreen wiper motor

27.4 Tailgate wiper motor

### 28 Washer system

1   The washer system for the windscreen and the tailgate operates from a bag type fluid reservoir within the engine compartment (photo).
2   The reservoir bag is fitted with two pumps, one for each system (photo).
3   Use screen cleaning fluid mixed in the recommended proportion in the washer fluid reservoir and in very cold weather add a small quantity of methylated spirit.
4   To clear a blocked washer jet nozzle or to adjust the wash jet glass-striking pattern, insert a pin part way into the jet nozzle.

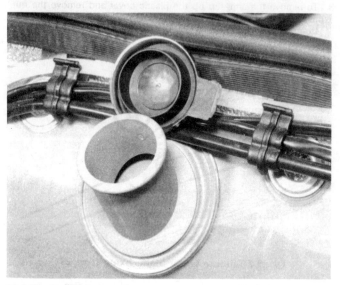

28.1 Washer fluid reservoir

28.2 Washer pumps

### 29 Heated tailgate window – precautions and repair

1   The heater element inside the tailgate glass should be treated with care.
2   Clean only with a damp cloth and wipe in the direction in which the filaments run. Avoid scratching with rings on the fingers, or by allowing luggage to rub on the glass. Never stick adhesive labels over the heater element.

3   Should one of the heater filaments be broken it can be repaired using one of the special silver paints available, but follow the manufacturer's instructions carefully.

### 30 Radio/cassette – fitting

1   In-car entertainment equipment is not provided as standard on the models covered by this Manual.
2   However, the centre console is designed to receive a radio set after removing the blanking plate behind which a power lead is already provided.
3   The ignition system and other electrical components are suppressed during production of the car and further suppression should not be required other than earthing the wiper motor.

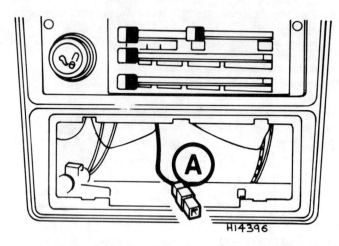

Fig. 9.8 Radio housing and power lead (A) (Sec 30)

#### Receiver

4   Fit the radio/cassette using the installation kit supplied with the equipment.
5   On Comfort models, fit an in-line fuse in the power feed. On Super models the radio supply is protected by fuse number 12.
6   Make sure that the radio is well earthed to a metal body component.

#### Aerial

7   The recommended locations for the aerial are towards the rear of the right-hand front wing or on the windscreen pillar.
8   Fitting instructions for Fiat aerials are supplied with them, but the following general advice will help if using non-Fiat equipment.
9   Motorised automatic aerials rise when the equipment is switched on and retract at switch-off. They require more fitting space and supply leads, and can be a source of trouble.
10  There is no merit in choosing a very long aerial as, for example, the type about three metres in length which hooks or clips on to the rear of the car, since part of this aerial will inevitably be located in an interference field. For VHF/FM radios the best length of aerial is about one metre. Active aerials have a transistor amplifier mounted at the base and this serves to boost the received signal. The aerial rod is sometimes rather shorter than normal passive types.
11  A large loss of signal can occur in the aerial feeder cable, especially over the Very High Frequency (VHF) bands. The design of feeder cable is invariably in the co-axial form, ie a centre conductor surrounded by a flexible copper braid forming the outer (earth) conductor. Between the inner and outer conductors is an insulator material which can be in solid or stranded form. Apart from insulation, its purpose is to maintain the correct spacing and concentricity. Loss of signal occurs in this insulator, the loss usually being greater in a poor quality cable. The quality of cable used is reflected in the price of the aerial with the attached feeder cable.
12  The capacitance of the feeder should be within the range 65 to 75 picofarads (pF) approximately (95 to 100 pF for Japanese and American

equipment), otherwise the adjustment of the car radio aerial trimmer may not be possible. An extension cable is necessary for a long run between aerial and receiver. If this adds capacitance in excess of the above limits, a connector containing a series capacitor will be required, or an extension which is labelled as 'capacity-compensated'.

13 Fitting the aerial will normally involve making a $^7/_8$ in (22 mm) diameter hole in the bodywork, but read the instructions that come with the aerial kit. Once the hole position has been selected, use a centre punch to guide the drill. Use sticky masking tape around the area for this helps with marking out and drill location, and gives protection to the paintwork should the drill slip. Three methods of making the hole are in use:

(a) Use a hole saw in the electric drill. This is, in effect, a circular hacksaw blade wrapped round a former with a centre pilot drill.

(b) Use a tank cutter which also has cutting teeth, but is made to shear the metal by tightening with an Allen key.

(c) The hard way of drilling out the circle is using a small drill, say $^1/_8$ in (3 mm), so that the holes overlap. The centre metal drops out and the hole is finished with round and half-round files.

14 Whichever method is used, the burr is removed from the body metal and paint removed from the underside. The aerial is fitted tightly ensuring that the earth fixing, usually a serrated washer, ring or clamp, is making a solid connection. *This earth connection is important in reducing interference.* Cover any bare metal with primer paint and topcoat, and follow by underseal if desired.

15 Aerial feeder cable routing should avoid the engine compartment and areas where stress might occur, eg under the carpet where feet will be located.

### Loudspeakers

16 A mono speaker may be located under the facia panel beneath the glovebox.

17 Provision is made for twin speakers within the door tidy bins or under the rear shelf mountings.

18 Speakers should be matched to the output stage of the equipment, particularly as regards the recommended impedance. Power transistors used for driving speakers are sensitive to the loading placed on them.

### Radio/cassette case breakthrough

19 Magnetic radiation from dashboard wiring may be sufficiently intense to break through the metal case of the radio/cassette player. Often this is due to a particular cable routed too close and shows up as ignition interference on AM and cassette play and/or alternator whine on cassette play.

20 The first point to check is that the clips and/or screws are fixing all parts of the radio/cassette case together properly. Assuming good earthing of the case, see if it is possible to re-route the offending cable – the chances of this are not good, however, in most cars.

21 Next release the radio/cassette player and locate it in different positions with temporary leads. If a point of low interference is found, then if possible fix the equipment in that area. This also confirms that local radiation is causing the trouble. If re-location is not feasible, fit the radio/cassette player back in the original position.

22 Alternator interference on cassette play is now caused by radiation from the main charging cable which goes from the battery to the output terminal of the alternator, usually via the + terminal of the starter motor relay.

23 Ignition breakthrough on AM and/or cassette play can be a difficult problem. It is worth wrapping earthed foil round the offending cable run near the equipment, or making up a deflector plate well screwed down to a good earth. Another possibility is the use of a suitable relay to switch on the ignition coil. The relay should be mounted close to the ignition coil; with this arrangement the ignition coil primary current is not taken into the dashboard area and does not flow through the ignition switch. A suitable diode should be used since it is possible that at ignition switch-off the output from the warning lamp alternator terminal could hold the relay on.

### VHF/FM broadcasts

24 Reception of VHF/FM in an automobile is more prone to problems than the medium and long wavebands. Medium/long wave transmitters are capable of covering considerable distances, but VHF transmitters are restricted to line of sight, meaning ranges of 10 to 50 miles, depending upon the terrain, the effects of buildings and the transmitter power.

25 Because of the limited range it is necessary to retune on a long journey, and it may be better for those habitually travelling long

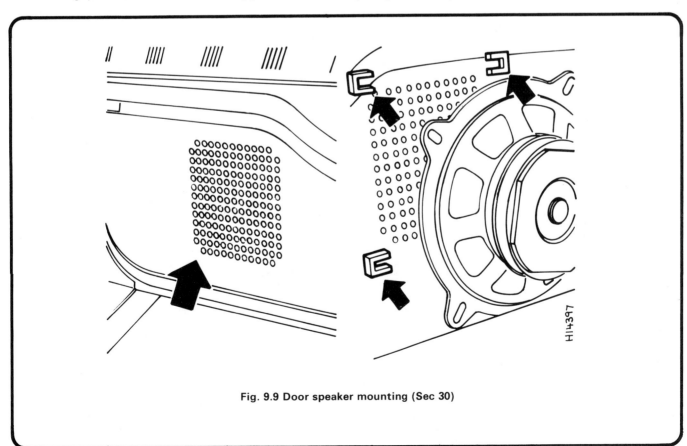

Fig. 9.9 Door speaker mounting (Sec 30)

H14398

**Fig. 9.10 Rear speaker mounting (Sec 30)**

distances or living in areas of poor provision of transmitters to use an AM radio working on medium/long wavebands.

26 For VHF/FM receiver installation the following points should be particularly noted:

(a) Earthing of the receiver chassis and the aerial mounting is important. Use a separate earthing wire at the radio, and scrape paint away at the aerial mounting.

(b) If possible, use a good quality roof aerial to obtain maximum height and distance from interference generating devices on the vehicle.

(c) Use of a high quality aerial downlead is important, since losses in cheap cable can be significant.

(d) The polarisation of FM transmissions may be horizontal, vertical, circular or slanted. Because of this the optimum mounting angle is at 45° to the vehicle roof.

*Citizens' Band radio (CB)*

27 In the UK, CB transmitter/receivers work within the 27 MHz and 934 MHz bands, using the FM mode. At present interest is concentrated on 27 MHz where the design and manufacture of equipment is less difficult. Maximum transmitted power is 4 watts, and 40 channels spaced 10 kHz apart within the range 27.60125 to 27.99125 MHz are available.

28 Aerials are the key to effective transmission and reception. Regulations limit the aerial length to 1.65 metres including the loading coil and any associated circuitry, so tuning the aerial is necessary to obtain optimum results. The choice of a CB aerial is dependent on whether it is to be permanently installed or removable, and the performance will hinge on correct tuning and the location point on the vehicle. Common practice is to clip the aerial to the roof gutter or to employ wing mounting where the aerial can be rapidly unscrewed. A popular solution is to use the 'magmount' – a type of mounting having a strong magnetic base clamping to the vehicle at any point, usually the roof.

29 Aerial location determines the signal distribution for both transmission and reception, but it is wise to choose a point away from the engine compartment to minimise interference from vehicle electrical equipment.

30 The aerial is subject to considerable wind and acceleration forces. Cheaper units will whip backwards and forwards and in so doing will alter the relationship with the metal surface of the vehicle with which it forms a ground plane aerial system. The radiation pattern will change correspondingly, giving rise to break-up of both incoming and outgoing signals.

31 Interference problems on the vehicle carrying CB equipment fall into two categories:

(a) Interference to nearby TV and radio receivers when transmitting.

(b) Interference to CB set reception due to electrical equipment on the vehicle.

32 Problems of break-through to TV and radio are not frequent, but can be difficult to solve. Mostly trouble is not detected or reported because the vehicle is moving and the symptoms rapidly disappear at the TV/radio receiver, but when the CB set is used as a base station any trouble with nearby receivers will soon result in a complaint.

33 It must not be assumed by the CB operator that his equipment is faultless, for much depends upon the design. Harmonics (that is, multiples) of 27 MHz may be transmitted unknowingly and these can fall into other user's bands. Where trouble of this nature occurs, low pass filters in the aerial or supply leads can help, and should be fitted in base station aerials as a matter of course. In stubborn cases it may be necessary to call for assistance from the licensing authority, or, if possible, to have the equipment checked by the manufacturers.

34 Interference received on the CB set from the vehicle equipment is, fortunately, not usually a severe problem. The precautions outlined previously for radio/cassette units apply, but there are some extra points worth noting.

35 It is common practice to use a slide-mount on CB equipment enabling the set to be easily removed for use as a base station, for example. Care must be taken that the slide mount fittings are properly earthed and that first class connection occurs between the set and slide-mount.

36 Vehicle suppliers in the UK are required to provide suppression of electrical equipment to cover 40 to 250 MHz to protect TV and VHF radio bands. Such suppression appears to be adequately effective at 27 MHz, but suppression of individual items such as alternators, clocks, stabilisers, flashers, wiper motors, etc, may still be necessary. The suppression capacitors and chokes available from auto-electrical suppliers for entertainment receivers will usually give the required results with CB equipment.

*Other vehicle radio transmitters*

37 Besides CB radio already mentioned, a considerable increase in the use of transceivers (ie combined transmitter and receiver units) has taken place in the last decade. Previously this type of equipment was fitted mainly to military, fire, ambulance and police vehicles, but a large business radio and radio telephone usage has developed.

38 Generally the suppression techniques described previously will suffice, with only a few difficult cases arising. Suppression is carried out to satisfy the 'receive mode', but care must be taken to use heavy duty chokes in the equipment supply cables since the loading on 'transmit' is relatively high.

## 31 Electrically-operated front door windows

1 The electrically-operated front door windows are controlled by switches on the centre console or in the door armrest (depending on model). The regulator motor and cable are located within the door cavity.

2 To gain access to the assembly, remove the door trim panel as described in Chapter 12.

3 Disconnect the wiring plug (1) (Fig. 9.11).

4 Release the bolts which connect the power lift to the glass mounting.

5 Remove the bolts which hold the lift assembly to the door.

6 The motor and glass mounting may be disconnected from the cable guide and sleeve and any faulty components renewed.

7 When refitting the assembly to the door, make sure that the window glass slides smoothly before fully tightening the cable guide bolts. Refer to Section 10 for details of system fuses and relays.

## 32 Central door locking system

1 The doors are locked simultaneously from the outside by turning the key in either direction.

2 The doors can be locked from inside the car in the following ways:

*All doors locked or unlocked – depress or lift a front door lock plunger knob.*

*One rear door locked or unlocked – depress or lift a rear door lock plunger knob.*

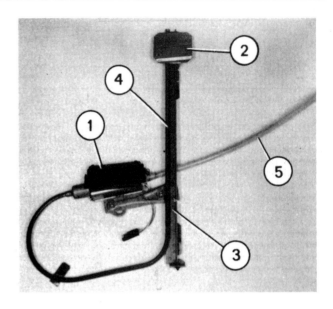

**Fig. 9.12 Power operated window components (Sec 31)**

| | | | |
|---|---|---|---|
| 1 | Electric motor | 4 | Cable |
| 2 | Glass mounting | 5 | Cable sleeve |
| 3 | Cable guide | | |

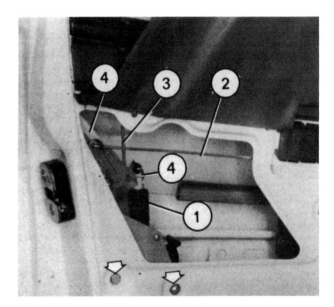

**Fig. 9.13 Central door locking system components (Sec 32)**

| | | | |
|---|---|---|---|
| 1 | Solenoid | 3 | Link rod |
| 2 | Lock relay lever | 4 | Exterior handle lever |

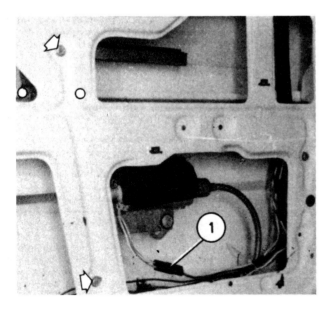

**Fig. 9.11 Power-operated window motor (Sec 31)**

*1 Connector plug*

3 The centralised door locking system can operate independently of the key.

4 To gain access to the lock solenoid and linkage, remove the front door trim panel as described in Chapter 12.

5 Disconnect the battery negative lead.

6 Disconnect the electrical wiring plugs from the solenoid within the door cavity.

7  Disconnect the solenoid from the lock lever by removing the clip.
8  Unscrew the two bolts which secure the solenoid to the door and remove it.
9  Renew the solenoid or switch as necessary.
10  Refitting is a reversal of removal.
11  Refer to Section 10 for details of system fuses and relays.

## 33 Economy gauge (Econometer)

1  This device is fitted to ES (energy saving) models and indicates to the driver the fuel consumption (in litres per 100 km) coupled with a needle which moves over coloured sections of a dial to make the driver aware that his method of driving is either conducive to high or low fuel consumption. Refer to Chapter 3, Section 16.
2  The device is essentially a vacuum gauge which also incorporates a warning lamp to indicate to the driver when a change of gear is required.
3  A fuel cut-out valve (see Chapter 3, Section 11) is used in conjunction with the economy gauge so that when the accelerator pedal is released during a pre-determined engine speed range, fuel supply to the engine is stopped, but resumes when the engine speed falls below the specified range.

### LED (light emitter diode)
4  The gearchange indicator will only light up at engine speeds in excess of 2000 rev/min for vacuum pressures up to 600 mm Hg in 1st, 2nd and 3rd speed gears and for vacuum pressures up to 676 mm Hg in 4th speed gear. The light will not come on if 5th speed gear is engaged or if the coolant temperature is below 55°C.
5  There is a two second delay in the light coming on to prevent it operating during rapid acceleration in a low gear.
6  If the LED light comes on during deceleration it should be ignored.

### Fault diagnosis
7  A faulty economy gauge should be checked in the following way.
8  Refer to Section 21 and remove the instrument panel.
9  Disconnect the economy gauge L connector and then connect a test lamp between the BN cable contact and earth. If the lamp comes on then the gauge supply circuit is not open. If the lamp does not come on, check all connections in the supply cable which comes from the interconnecting unit of the electrical system, also Fuse No 12.
10  Now connect a voltmeter between the white cable and earth. Check the voltage with the engine not running, but the ignition switched on. It should be between 0.7 and 0.9 volt. If the reading varies considerably from that specified, check the connections between the economy gauge and the fuel cut-out device control unit. If the fault cannot be rectified, renew the ignition control unit (Digiplex system, see Chapter 4).
11  Now check the closed throttle valve plate switch by connecting a voltmeter between the brown and BN cables of the L connector. With the valve plate open, there should be no reading, but with it open, voltage should be indicated.
12  Failure to conform as described will be due to a faulty earth in the switch or a faulty fuel cut-out device control unit.
13  A further test of the throttle valve plate switch may be carried out by disconnecting the multi-plug from the fuel cut-out device control unit.
14  Connect a test lamp to contact 4 (positive battery terminal). The lamp should come on, when the engine is idling or the accelerator released. If it does not, renew the throttle valve plate switch.
15  Connect a tachometer to the brown/white cable contact in the L connector and record the engine speed with the engine running. If no reading is obtained, renew the Digiplex ignition control unit which must be faulty.

## 34 Check control (warning module) system

1  This is fitted into the instrument panel of certain models to provide a means of checking the operation of many electrical circuits and other systems in the interest of safety. Sensors are used where appropriate.
2  The following components are not monitored by the system, but have separate warning lamps:

*Handbrake 'on'*
*Choke in use*
*Low engine oil pressure*
*Battery charge indicator*

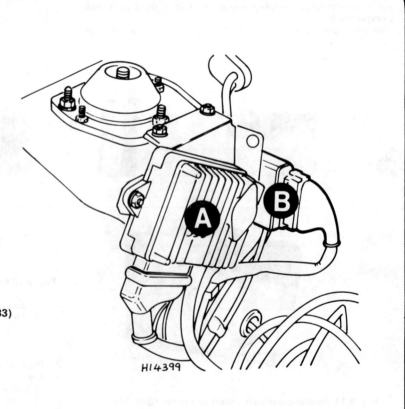

**Fig. 9.14 Location of control units (Sec 33)**

*A     Digiplex ignition system control unit*
*B     Fuel cut-out valve control unit*

H14399

GREEN – Signal

RED – General
warning light

AH14400

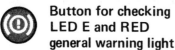
Button for checking
LED E and RED
general warning light

Fig. 9.15 Check system control panel (Sec 34)

A   Parking lamps              D   Door closure
B   Coolant level              E   Brake fluid level
C   Engine oil level           F   Disc pad wear

3   The multi-functional electronic device automatically checks the following functions whether the engine is running or not:

Coolant level
Disc pad wear
Door closure
Engine oil level
Front parking lamps
Rear foglamps
Stop lamps

4   The check information is stored by the system monitor until the engine is started when the display panel then indicates the situation by means of the LEDs (light emitter diodes) and the general lamp.
5   If all functions are in order, the green panel lamp will come on when the ignition key is turned and will go out after two to three seconds.
6   If some functions are not in order, then the red panel lamp will come on also the appropriate LED.

Sensors – checking
7   If a fault signal occurs which is subsequently found to be incorrect, first check the wiring connections between the sensors, lamp circuits and the control unit. Corrosion at the terminals may also be a contributary cause.
8   Never short circuit a sensor supply wire or the electronic module will be damaged.

Check control unit and monitor – removal and refitting
9   Remove the instrument panel as described in Section 21.
10  Unbolt the control unit housing from the instrument panel.
11  Access to the monitor can only be obtained after removing the

tachometer and the red and green general warning lamps. Unscrew the two monitor fixing bolts.

## 35  Clocks – setting

Quartz type
1   To set the hands, depress the knob and turn it.

Digital type
2   To set the clock, depress button A to display minutes and seconds and again to display hours and minutes.
3   To correct the hour setting, depress button C then button A and release it at the correct time. Depress button C three times to display hours and minutes.
4   To correct the minute setting, depress button C twice. Depress button A and release it when the correct time is shown. Depress button C twice to display hours and minutes.
5   To correct the second setting, depress button C three times. Depress button A and hold it depressed to zero the seconds then release the button. Depress button C to display the hours and minutes.
6   Switch D, Fig. 9.16 operates the map reading lamp fitted to SX models in conjunction with the digital clock.

## 36  Cigar lighter

1   This device can be operated without switching on the ignition.
2   Push in the knob and when it springs out it is ready for use.
3   The cigar lighter socket may be used as a power source provided the rating of the accessory does not exceed 100 Watts.

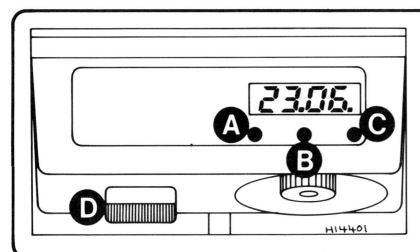

Fig. 9.16 Digital clock controls (Sec 35)

A   Control button – hour setting
B   Control button – display (ignition off)
C   Control button – minute setting
D   Map reading lamp switch

H14401

## 37 Fault diagnosis – electrical system

| Symptom | Reason(s) |
| --- | --- |
| No voltage at starter motor | Battery discharged <br> Battery defective internally <br> Battery terminals loose or earth lead not securely attached to body <br> Loose or broken connections in starter motor circuit <br> Starter motor switch or solenoid faulty |
| Voltage at starter motor – faulty motor | Starter brushes badly worn, sticking, or brush wires loose <br> Commutator dirty, worn or burnt <br> Starter motor armature faulty <br> Field coils earthed |
| Starter motor noisy or rough in engagement | Pinion or flywheel gear teeth broken or worn <br> Starter drive main spring broken <br> Starter motor retaining bolts loose |
| Alternator not charging* | Drivebelt loose and slipping, or broken <br> Brushes worn, sticking, broken or dirty <br> Brush springs weak or broken |

*If all appears to be well but the alternator is still not charging, take the car to an automobile electrician for checking of the alternator*

| Symptom | Reason(s) |
| --- | --- |
| Battery will not hold charge for more than a few days | Battery defective internally <br> Electrolyte level too low or electrolyte too weak due to leakage <br> Plate separators no longer fully effective <br> Battery plates severely sulphated <br> Drivebelt slipping <br> Battery terminal connections loose or corroded <br> Alternator not charging properly <br> Short in lighting circuit causing continual battery drain |
| Ignition light fails to go out, battery runs flat in a few days | Drivebelt loose and slipping, or broken <br> Alternator faulty |

**Failure of individual electrical equipment to function correctly is dealt with alphabetically below**

| Symptom | Reason(s) |
| --- | --- |
| Fuel gauge gives no reading | Fuel tank empty! <br> Electric cable between tank sender unit and gauge earthed or loose <br> Fuel gauge case not earthed <br> Fuel gauge supply cable interrupted <br> Fuel gauge unit broken |
| Fuel gauge registers full all the time | Electric cable between tank unit and gauge broken or disconnected |
| Horn operates all the time | Horn push either earthed or stuck down <br> Horn cable to horn push earthed |
| Horn fails to operate | Blown fuse <br> Cable or cable connection loose, broken or disconnected <br> Horn has an internal fault |
| Horn emits intermittent or unsatisfactory noise | Cable connections loose <br> Horn incorrectly adjusted |
| Lights do not come on | If engine not running, battery discharged <br> Light bulb filament burnt out or bulbs broken <br> Wire connections loose, disconnected or broken <br> Light switch shorting or otherwise faulty |
| Lights come on but fade out | If engine not running, battery discharged |
| Lights give very poor illumination | Lamp glasses dirty <br> Reflector tarnished or dirty <br> Lamps badly out of adjustment <br> Incorrect bulb with too low wattage fitted <br> Existing bulbs old and badly discoloured <br> Electrical wiring too thin not allowing full current to pass |
| Lights work erratically, flashing on and off, especially over bumps | Battery terminals or earth connections loose <br> Lights not earthing properly <br> Contacts in light switch faulty |

| Symptom | Reason(s) |
| --- | --- |
| Wiper motor fails to work | Blown fuse<br>Wire connections loose, disconnected or broken<br>Brushes badly worn<br>Armature worn or faulty<br>Field coils faulty |
| Wiper motor works very slowly and takes excessive current | Commutator dirty, greasy or burnt<br>Drive spindle binding or damaged<br>Armature bearings dry or unaligned<br>Armature badly worn or faulty |
| Wiper motor works slowly and takes little current | Brushes badly worn<br>Commutator dirty, greasy or burnt<br>Armature badly worn or faulty |
| Wiper motor works but wiper blade remains static | Drive spindle damaged or worn<br>Wiper motor gearbox parts badly worn |

# Chapter 10 Steering

## Contents

## Specifications

**Type** ................................................................. Rack and pinion with safety column

**Steering wheel diameter** .................................. 381.0 mm (15.0 in)

**Number of turns, lock-to-lock** ......................... 4

**Turning circle** ................................................. 9.4 m (30.84 ft)

**Steering angles of roadwheels**
Inner wheel ........................................................ 32° 58'
Outer wheel ....................................................... 39° 8'

**Front suspension steering angles**
Camber .............................................................. 0° 5' negative to 0° 55' positive
Castor ............................................................... 1° 40' to 2° 20' positive
Toe-in ............................................................... 0 to 2.0 mm (0 to 0.08 in)

**Rear suspension**
Camber .............................................................. 0° (non-adjustable)

**Rack lubricant**
Type .................................................................. Lithium based molybdenum disulphide grease (Duckhams LBM 10)
Capacity ............................................................ 140 cc

**Torque wrench settings**

| | Nm | lbf ft |
| --- | --- | --- |
| Steering wheel nut | 50 | 37 |
| Steering shaft coupling pinch-bolt | 27 | 20 |
| Steering gear mounting bolts | 24 | 18 |
| Tie-rod balljoint locknut | 35 | 26 |
| Tie-rod balljoint taper pin nut | 35 | 26 |
| Steering column upper mounting bolts | 5 | 3 |

## 1 Description and maintenance

1 The steering gear is of rack and pinion type with a universally-jointed column which incorporates a steering lock and ignition switch.
2 The steering wheel is of two spoke type on all models except the SX which has four spokes.
3 The system is maintenance-free except to check occasionally the tightness of the mounting bolts on the rack, column and universal joint pinch-bolts.
4 At the intervals specified in Routine Maintenance carefully inspect the rack gaiters for splits, particularly at the bottom of the vees, as a split here can often go unnoticed.
5 Check the tie-rod balljoints for wear. To do this, have an assistant turn the steering wheel repeatedly in both directions through an arc of about 10 or 15 degrees. Observe the balljoints for lost motion or slackness. If evident, renew the balljoint as described in Section 2.

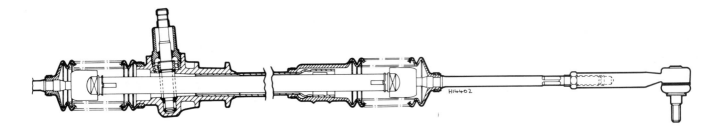

**Fig. 10.1 Sectional view of steering gear (Sec 1)**

## 2 Tie-rod end balljoint – renewal

1  Jack up the front of the car and remove the roadwheel from the side on which the balljoint is to be renewed.
2  Unscrew the tie-rod balljoint taper pin nut and, using a suitable extractor, separate the tie-rod balljoint from the eye of the steering arm (photo).
3  Release the locknut on the tie-rod, unscrewing it only just enough to be able to unscrew the tie-rod end from the tie-rod.
4  With the tie-rod end removed, wire brush the threads on the tie-rod without disturbing the position of the locknut; apply grease to the threads and screw on the new tie-rod end until the locknut can be tightened by turning it through the same amount of rotation it was given when unscrewed.
5  Reconnect the balljoint taper pin to the eye of the steering arm and tighten the retaining nut to the specified torque. *Never grease the taper pin or eye;* the pin will otherwise turn when the nut is tightened. If a taper pin is inclined to rotate when a nut is being tightened, apply pressure to the socket of the joint to force the taper pin into closer contact with the tapered hole in the eye. If a taper pin is pointing downward, a strong lever can be used to apply the extra pressure. Where the taper pin of a balljoint points upward, a jack placed under the joint socket will produce the desired result.
6  Although the careful fitting of the new tie-rod end will have approximately maintained the original front wheel alignment of the car, manufacturing differences alone of the new component make it essential to check the setting, as described in Section 8 and to adjust if necessary.

## 3 Steering rack gaiter – renewal

1  If lubricant is found to be leaking from the gaiters (at the ends of the housing), first check that the gaiter clips are secure.
2  If the lubricant is leaking from the gaiter through a split, the gaiter can be removed in the following way, without the necessity of withdrawing the gear from the car.
3  Remove the tie-rod end from the side concerned, as described in the preceding Section.
4  Release the gaiter clips; draw the gaiter from the rack housing and off the tie-rod.
5  If the gaiter has only just split, road dirt is unlikely to have entered and lubricant can be wiped away. If it is severely grit contaminated, the steering gear should be completely removed, the original lubricant flushed out and new lubricant pumped in.
6  If the gear does not have to be removed from the car, slide the new gaiter into position and secure it with the inboard clip.
7  The rack lubricant is molybdenum disulphide type grease.
8  When recharging the gaiter with this type of lubricant, give full steering lock to the side being replenished so that the extended section of the rack will take the grease into the housing as it returns.
9  Reconnect the tie-rod end to the tie-rod and the eye of the steering arm. Provided the locknut is tightened by only rotating it through the same distance by which it was loosened, the front wheel alignment (tracking) should not have been unduly disturbed. Even so, check the alignment as described in Section 8.

## 4 Steering wheel – removal and refitting

1  Disconnect the battery negative lead.
2  Set the steering wheel and the front roadwheels in the straight-ahead attitude. Prise out the hub plate (photo).
3  Unscrew and remove the steering wheel securing nut, then pull the wheel from the column shaft. If it is tight on its splines, tap it upward at the wheel rim, using the palms of the hands.
4  Refitting is a reversal of the removal process; make sure that the spokes of the wheel are in the lower part of the wheel.
5  Tighten the securing nut to the specified torque.

## 5 Steering column – removal, overhaul and refitting

1  Remove the steering wheel as previously described.
2  Extract the screws from the underside of the steering column upper shroud and then lift off the upper and lower shroud sections (photo). Where applicable, detach and remove the trim panel from the underside of the facia on the driver's side.
3  Disconnect the battery negative lead.
4  Disconnect the wiring plug for the steering column combination switch.
5  Unscrew the clamp nuts and pull the combination switch off the end of the steering shaft.
6  Unscrew the column upper mounting bracket bolts and lower the shaft/column tube to rest on the seat (photo).
7  Remove the pinch-bolt from the lower universal joint coupling and remove the shaft/column tube from the car.

2.2 Disconnecting a tie-rod end balljoint

4.2 Removing steering wheel hub plate

Fig. 10.2 Removing steering column shroud screws (Sec 5)

5.2 Removing steering column shrouds

Fig. 10.3 Unscrewing combination switch clamp nuts (Sec 5)

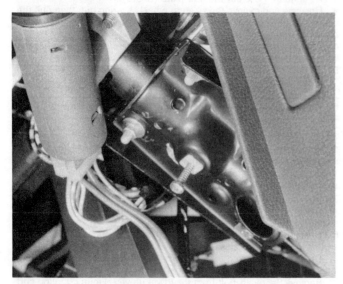

5.6 Steering column upper mounting

*Overhaul*
8   Remove the pinch-bolt from the upper universal joint and disconnect the lower shaft.
9   Grip the tube mounting flange in the jaws of a vice and relieve the staking at the base of the tube.
10  Using a plastic or copper-faced hammer, tap the shaft down out of the tube.
11  The lower bush will be ejected while the upper one should be prised out of the tube.
12  Reassemble the upper shaft into the tube by tapping new bushes into position.
13  Stake the lower end of the tube to retain the bush.

3   Disconnect the tie-rod end balljoints from the steering arms as described earlier in this Chapter.
4   Unscrew and remove the rack clamp mounting bolts and withdraw the steering gear from the car crossmember (photo).
5   Refitting is a reversal of removal, but on completion check the front wheel alignment as described in Section 8.

Fig. 10.4 Renewing steering shaft bushes (Sec 5)

6.4 Steering rack housing at pinion end

14  Reassembly is a reversal of removal, noting that the universal joint coupling pinch-bolts should pass smoothly through the grooves in the steering shaft.
15  Fit the steering wheel when the roadwheels are in the straight-ahead position.
16  Tighten all nuts and bolts to the specified torque. Reconnect the battery.

## 6  Steering rack – removal and refitting

1   Set the steering in the straight-ahead mode.
2   Working inside the car, disconnect the steering shaft lower coupling by unscrewing and removing the pinch-bolt (photo).

## 7  Steering gear – overhaul

1   A worn steering gear should not be overhauled, but a new or factory reconditioned unit fitted.
2   After a high mileage, the following adjustment may be needed however.

### Rack damper – adjustment
3   The slipper in the rack housing presses the rack into mesh with the pinion. This cuts out any backlash between the gears. Also, due to its pressure, it introduces some stiffness into the rack, which cuts out excessive reaction from the road to the steering wheel.
4   In due course, wear reduces the pressures exerted by the slipper. The pressure is controlled by the cover plate and a spring.
5   The need for resetting of the slipper is not easy to detect. On bumpy roads, the shock induced through the steering will give a feeling of play, and sometimes faint clonking can be heard. In extreme cases, free play in the steering may be felt, though this is rare. If the steering is compared with that of a new rack on another car, the lack of friction damping is quite apparent in the ease of movement of the steering wheel of the worn one.
6   Centralise the steering rack. Do this by counting the number of turns lock-to-lock and then turning the steering wheel from one lock through half the number of turns counted.
7   Take the cover plate off the damping slipper, remove the spring and shims, and refit the cover plate.
8   Screw in the cover plate bolts just enough to hold the slipper against the rack.
9   Measure the gap between the cover plate and the rack housing using feeler blades.
10  Select shims from the thicknesses available (0.10, 0.125 and 0.30 mm) to provide a shim pack thicker than the gap by between 0.05 and 0.13 mm.
11  Remove the cover plate, fit the spring and bolt on the cover plate with the selected shims.

6.2 Steering shaft coupling

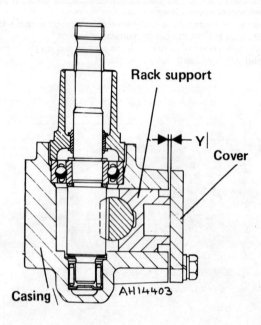

Fig. 10.5 Sectional view of rack damper (Sec 7)

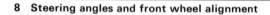

## 8 Steering angles and front wheel alignment

1 Accurate front wheel alignment is essential to provide good steering and roadholding characteristics and to ensure slow and even tyre wear. Before considering the steering angles, check that the tyres are correctly inflated, that the front wheels are not buckled, the hub bearings are not worn or incorrectly adjusted and that the steering linkage is in good order, without slackness or wear at the joints.

2 Wheel alignment consists of four factors:

*Camber*, is the angle at which the road wheels are set from the vertical when viewed from the front or rear of the vehicle. Positive camber is the angle (in degrees) that the wheels are tilted outwards at the top from the vertical.

*Castor*, is the angle between the steering axis and a vertical line when viewed from each side of the vehicle. Positive castor is indicated when the steering axis is inclined towards the rear of the vehicle at its upper end.

*Steering axis inclination*, is the angle when viewed from the front or rear of the vehicle between vertical and an imaginary line drawn between the upper and lower suspension strut mountings.

*Toe*, is the amount by which the distance between the front inside edges of the roadwheel rims differs from that between the rear inside edges.

3 If the distance between the front edges is less than that at the rear, the wheels are said to toe-in. If the distance between the front inside edges is greater than that at the rear, the wheels toe-out.

4 Camber and castor are set during production of the car and are not adjustable. Any deviation from specification will be due to collision damage or to gross wear in the components concerned.

5 To check the front wheel alignment, first make sure that the lengths of both tie-rods are equal when the steering is in the straight-ahead position. Measure between the locknut at the balljoint and the ball cup at the end of the rack housing by passing a thin rod under the rack of the gaiter. If adjustment is required, release the locknut and turn the tie-rod.

6 Obtain a tracking gauge. These are available in various forms from accessory stores or one can be fabricated from a length of steel tubing suitably cranked to clear the sump and bellhousing and having a setscrew and locknut at one end.

7 With the gauge, measure the distance between the two wheel inner rims (at hub height) at the rear of the wheel. Push the vehicle forward to rotate the wheel through 180° (half a turn) and measure the distance

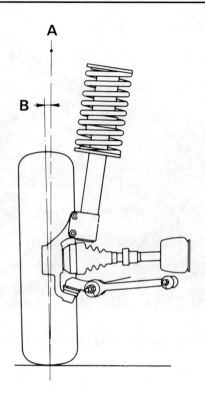

Fig. 10.6 Camber angle (Sec 8)

*A  Vertical line      B  Camber angle (positive)*

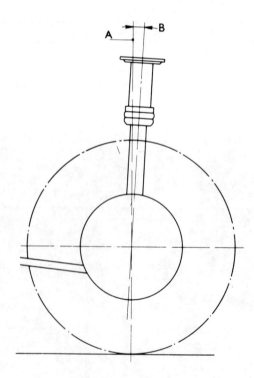

Fig. 10.7 Castor angle (Sec 8)

*A  Vertical line                    B  Castor angle (positive)*

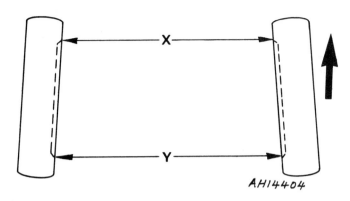

*AH14404*

**Fig. 10.8 Front wheel alignment diagram (Sec 8)**

*X   Front dimension*      *Y   Rear dimension*
                                        *Y - X = Toe-in*

between the wheel inner rims, again at hub height, at the front of the wheel. This last measurement should differ from (be less than) the first by the appropriate toe-in according to the Specification (see Specifications Section).

8   Where the toe-in is found to be incorrect, release the tie-rod balljoint locknuts and turn the tie-rods equally. Only turn them a quarter of a turn at a time before re-checking the alignment. Viewed from the centre line of the car, turning the tie-rod clockwise will decrease the toe-in.

9   Make sure that the gaiter outboard clip is released otherwise the gaiter will twist as the tie-rod is rotated.

10  Always turn both rods in the same direction when viewed from the centre line of the vehicle otherwise the rods will become unequal in length. This would cause the steering wheel spoke position to alter and cause problems on turns with tyre scrubbing.

11  On completion, tighten the tie-rod balljoint locknuts without altering their setting. Check that the balljoint is at the centre of its arc of travel and then retighten the gaiter clip.

## 9   Steering column lock – removal and refitting

1   Remove the steering wheel and column shrouds as described in Section 5, also the steering column combination switch.

2   Unscrew and remove the steering column mounting bolts and lower the column to expose the lock shear bolts.

3   Drill out the bolts or extract them using an extractor.

4   Refer to Chapter 4 for details of separation of the ignition switch from the lock section.

5   When fitting the new lock, tighten the shear bolts until their heads break off.

6   Bolt up the column, fit the combination switch, shrouds and steering wheel and tighten all nuts and bolts to the specified torque.

**Fig. 10.9 Steering column lock shear bolts (arrowed) (Sec 9)**

## 10 Fault diagnosis – steering

**Note:** *Before diagnosing steering faults, be sure that trouble is not due to incorrect or uneven tyre pressures, inappropriate tyre combinations, or braking system or suspension defects*

| Symptom | Reason(s) |
| --- | --- |
| Car pulls to one side | Incorrect steering geometry<br>Collision damage |
| Car wanders when driven straight-ahead | Play in steering gear<br>Wear in steering balljoints |
| Heavy or stiff steering | Lack of lubricant in steering gear or balljoints<br>Incorrect steering geometry<br>Collision damage |
| Play at steering wheel | Wear in steering rack or balljoints<br>Loose steering shaft coupling pinch-bolt or worn splines<br>Worn steering column/shaft universal joints |
| Vibration at steering wheel | Roadwheels out of balance or loose<br>Tyre damage<br>Loose driveshaft-to-hub nuts |
| Rattles from steering when traversing rough surfaces | Steering damper defective or in need of adjustment<br>Loose steering column mounting bolts<br>Loose steering column/shaft coupling pinch-bolts<br>Loose steering rack housing mounting bolts<br>Worn steering shaft bushes |
| Excessive or uneven tyre wear | Incorrect steering geometry<br>Worn steering components<br>Collision damage |

# Chapter 11 Suspension

*For modifications, and information applicable to later models, see Supplement at end of manual*

## Contents

## Specifications

### Front suspension
**Type** ........................................................................... Independent with MacPherson struts and coil springs

### Coil springs
Free height:
   903 cc models .......................................................... 334 mm (13.16 in)
   1116 and 1301 cc models ....................................... 342 mm (13.5 in)
Number of coils ............................................................ 4.25

### Rear suspension
**Type** ........................................................................... Beam axle, trailing arms, coil springs and double-acting gas-filled shock absorbers.

### Coil springs
Free height ................................................................... 246.5 mm (9.7 in)
Number of coils ............................................................ 2.75

### Torque wrench settings

| | Nm | lbf ft |
|---|---|---|
| **Front suspension** | | |
| Driveshaft/hub nut | 272 | 200 |
| Strut upper mounting nuts | 24 | 18 |
| Strut spindle nut | 60 | 44 |
| Strut base clamp bolts | 49 | 36 |
| Track control arm balljoint nuts | 49 | 36 |
| Track control arm inboard mounting bolts | 90 | 66 |
| Roadwheel bolts | 86 | 63 |
| Crossmember bolts | 60 | 44 |
| | | |
| **Rear suspension** | | |
| Trailing arm bracket to body bolts | 20 | 15 |
| Trailing arm pivot bolt | 70 | 52 |
| Shock absorber lower mounting bolt | 30 | 22 |
| Shock absorber upper mounting nuts | 12 | 9 |
| Shock absorber spindle nut | 30 | 22 |
| Roadwheel bolts | 86 | 63 |

## 1 General description

The front suspension is of independent MacPherson strut type.

The rear suspension consists of a beam axle with trailing arms, coil springs and double acting gas-filled telescopic shock absorbers.

Operations covering the hubs, roadwheels and tyres are described in Chapter 7.

## 2 Maintenance

1 Periodically check the tightness of all suspension nuts and bolts using a torque wrench.

2 At the intervals specified in Routine Maintenance inspect all suspension rubber bushes for deterioration or wear. Renew where necessary.

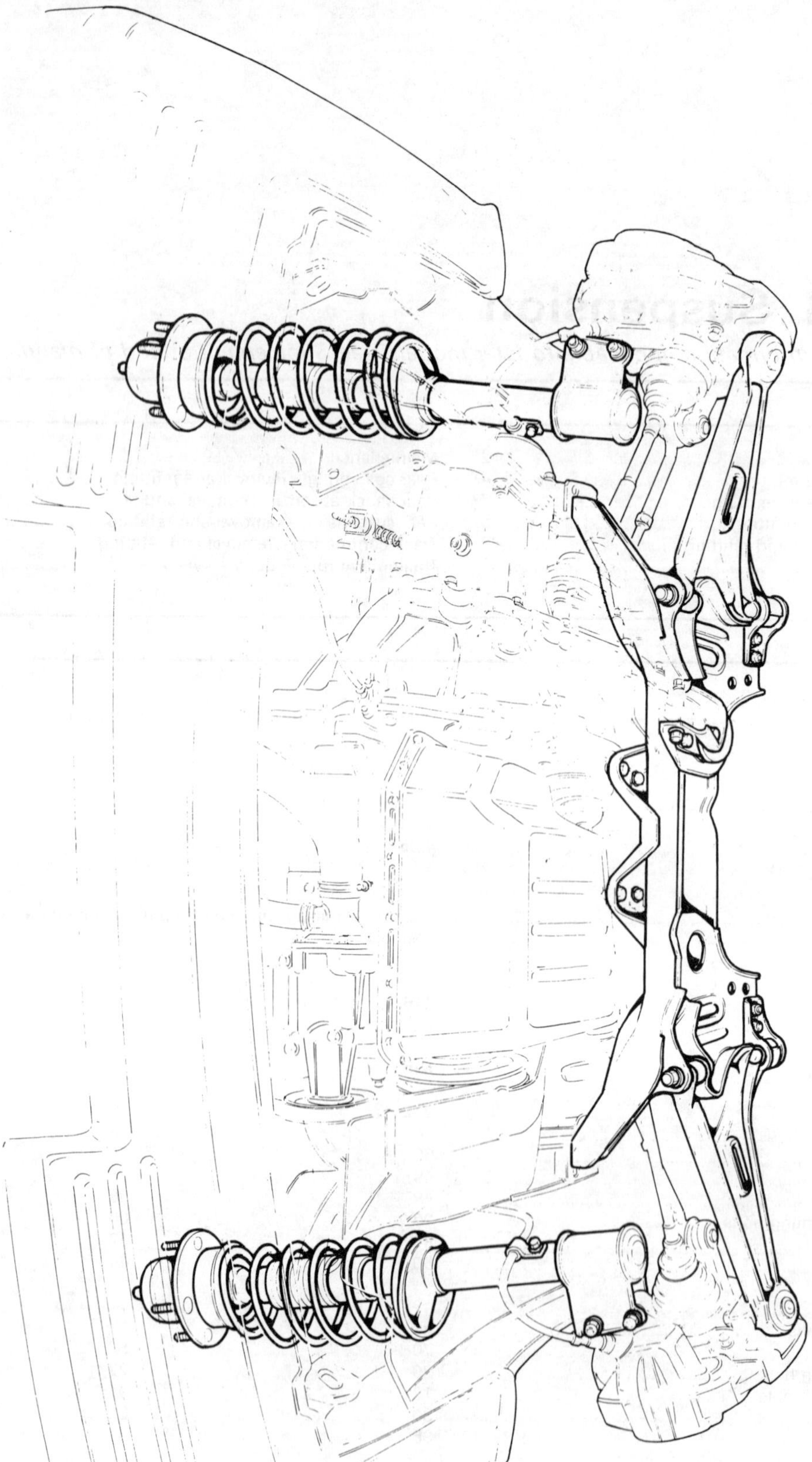

Fig. 11.1 Front suspension arrangement (Sec 1)

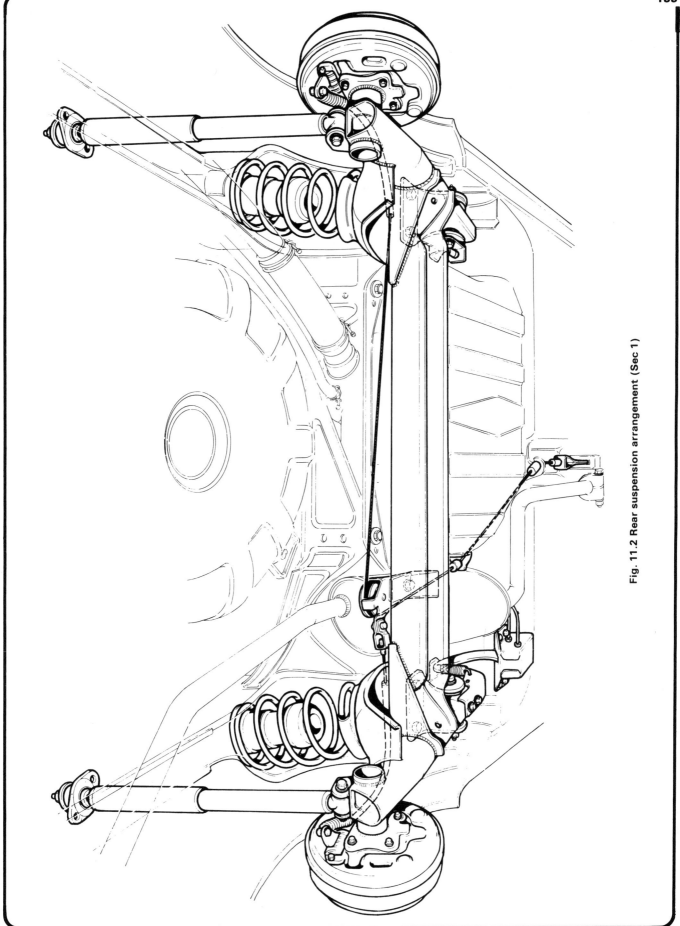

Fig. 11.2 Rear suspension arrangement (Sec 1)

3   Check for wear in the track control arm to hub carrier balljoint.
Do this by raising the roadwheel and prising the control arm down.
If the hub carrier is pulled outwards, any up and down movement
or slackness will necessitate renewal of the track control arm, although
it may be possible to obtain a balljoint repair kit from a motor factor.
4   A defective strut or shock absorber can usually be detected by the
tendency of the car to pitch badly when braking or cornering. However
the component can be tested more thoroughly in the following way.
5   Remove the strut and take off the coil spring or withdraw the rear
shock abosrber as described later in this Chapter.
6   Grip the strut or shock absorber lower mounting in the jaws of a
vice and then fully extend and contract the unit five or six times, with
the unit held in a vertical attitude. If there is any lack of resistance,

jerkiness or seizure, then the unit will have to be renewed, no repair
being possible. It is recommended that struts or shock absorbers are
renewed in pairs as axle sets, in order to maintain similar suspension
characteristics on both sides of the car.
7   Check for signs of hydraulic fluid leakage from around the front
strut spindle gland and also the condition of the dust excluding boot.
Oil leakage will mean a new unit, a split boot can be renewed after
having withdrawn the coil spring.

### 3   Front suspension strut – removal and refitting

1   Raise the front of the car, support it securely and remove the
roadwheel.

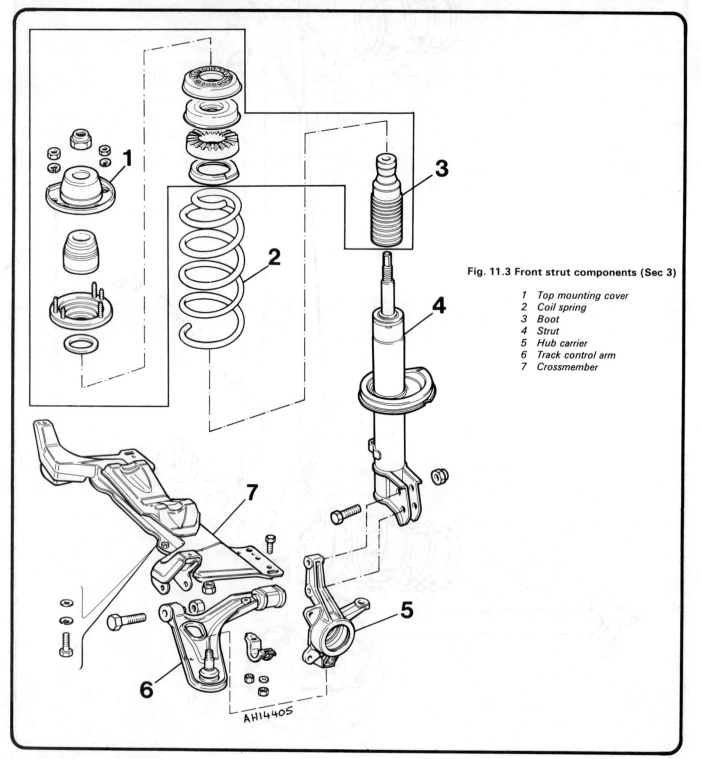

**Fig. 11.3 Front strut components (Sec 3)**

1   Top mounting cover
2   Coil spring
3   Boot
4   Strut
5   Hub carrier
6   Track control arm
7   Crossmember

AH14405

2   Release the brake hydraulic hose from the strut by unscrewing the retaining clip bolt.

3   Unscrew and remove the two bolts from the clamp at the bottom of the strut, push the hub carrier down out of the clamp (photo).

4   Open the bonnet. Unscrew and remove the domed reinforcement cover. Then remove the strut top mounting nuts from the turret. Do not attempt to unscrew the centre spindle nut (photos).

5   Withdraw the strut downwards and out from under the wing (photo).

6   Coil spring clamps must now be fitted. These are available from most motor stores or can be hired (photo).

7   Once the spring has been compressed to release its top coil from the strut upper mounting, hold the flats on the strut spindle and unscrew the spindle nut.

8   Take off the upper mounting components and the clamped coil spring. The clamps need not be removed if the spring is to be fitted to a new strut.

9   Commence reassembly by fitting the coil spring onto the strut. Make sure that the smaller coil is at the top and the lower coil is up against its end stop in the spring seat.

10  Check that the strut boot is in position.

11  Fit the upper mounting components and screw on the spindle nut.

12  Gently release the spring clamps and remove them.

3.4B Strut upper mounting nuts

3.3 Strut clamp bolt

3.5 Withdrawing a front strut

3.4A Strut reinforcement plate

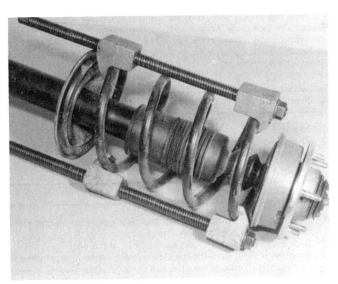

3.6 Spring clamps in position

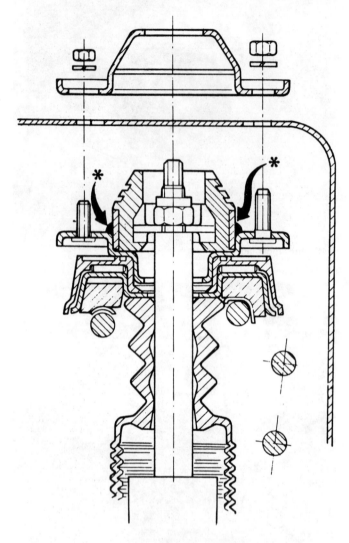

Fig. 11.4 Waterproof bead applied to strut with top cover
removed (Sec 3)

13  Refit the strut to the car by reversing the removal operations.
**Note:** *On cars built before 1985, when assembling the strut top
mounting, apply a bead of RTV sealant as shown in Figs. 11.4 and 11.5
to prevent the entry of water into the strut bearing. Later models are
fitted with a rubber seal.*

### 4  Front coil spring – removal and refitting

1  The operations are covered in the preceding Section.
2  The springs are colour coded according to model and a
replacement must be of identical type to the original.

### 5  Front hub carrier – removal and refitting

1  Disconnect the driveshaft from the hub carrier as described in
Chapter 7, Section 2, paragraphs 1 to 8.
2  Unbolt the brake caliper and tie it up out of the way.
3  Unscrew the nut from the track control arm balljoint taper pin and
then separate the balljoint from the hub carrier using a suitable 'splitter'
tool. If such a tool is not available, support the base of the brake disc
and drive the balljoint taper pin downwards, but screw on the nut to
protect the threads.

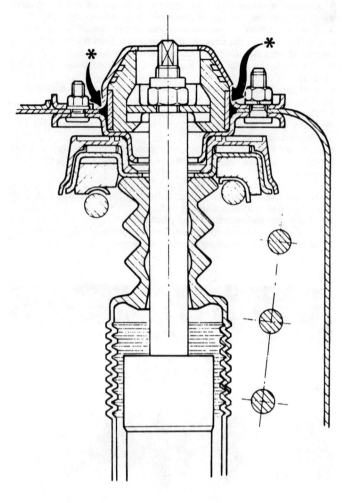

Fig. 11.5 Waterproof bead applied to strut with top cover in
position (Sec 3)

4  Remove the hub carrier.
5  Refitting is a reversal of removal, use a new driveshaft nut and
tighten all nuts and bolts to the specified torque. Stake the driveshaft
nut after tightening.

### 6  Track control arm – removal and refitting

1  Raise the front of the car and support it securely.
2  Unless a special tool is available to press the track control arm
balljoint from the hub carrier, the driveshaft will have to be
disconnected as described in Chapter 7, Section 2, paragraphs 1 to 8
to provide more space to enable the balljoint taper pin to be driven
from the hub carrier. This should now be done as described in the
preceding Section (photo).
3  Unbolt the inboard end of the track control arm. This is retained by
a pivot bolt and a clamp (photo).
4  As previously explained, a worn balljoint or flexible pivot bushes
will necessitate renewal of the track control arm complete. Note that
it may, however, be possible to obtain a replacement balljoint through
a motor factor.
5  Refitting is a reversal of removal. Tighten all nuts and bolts to the
specified torque. Use a new driveshaft nut and stake it into the
driveshaft groove after tightening.

6.2 Separating track control arm balljoint from hub carrier

Fig. 11.6 Steering rack mounting bolts (Sec 7)

6.3 Track control arm inboard fixing

Fig. 11.7 Front crossmember bolts (Sec 7)

## 7 Front crossmember – removal and refitting

1 Raise the front of the car, support securely with axle stands placed under the side-members or sill jacking points.
2 Remove the front roadwheels.
3 Unscrew the nuts from the tie-rod end balljoint taper pins and then using a balljoint 'splitter' tool disconnect the balljoints from the steering arms on the hub carrier.
4 Unscrew the bolts which hold the inboard track control arms to the body members, and also withdraw the pivot bolt from the body bracket.
5 Support the weight of the engine/transmission using a hoist or support bar across the top of the engine compartment as described in Chapter 6.
6 Disconnect the lower (central) engine/transmission flexible mounting from the floor pan.
7 Unscrew the steering rack mounting bolts and remove them. Leave the steering rack hanging loose.
8 Remove the front crossmember mounting bolts and manoeuvre it from the car.

9 Refitting is a reversal of removal. Tighten all nuts and bolts to the specified torque wrench settings and on completion, check the front wheel alignment as described in Chapter 10.

## 8 Rear shock absorber – removal and refitting

1 Open the tailgate and remove the cover from the shock absorber top mounting which is located within the luggage area (photo).
2 Hold the flats on the spindle with an open-ended spanner and then unscrew the self-locking nut.
3 Working under the car, disconnect the shock absorber lower mounting.
4 Withdraw the unit from under the wing.
5 The shock absorber can be tested as described in Section 2.
6 Refitting is a reversal of removal. Tighten mounting nuts and bolts to the specified torque.

8.1 Rear shock absorber upper mounting cover

## 9 Rear coil spring – removal and refitting

1 Raise the rear of the car and support it securely on axle stands placed under the side-members or sill jacking points.
2 Remove the roadwheel.
3 Place a jack under the brake drum and support the suspension trailing arm.
4 Disconnect the shock absorber lower mounting and then lower the trailing arm jack until the coil spring can be withdrawn.
5 Refitting is a reversal of removal. If the spring is being changed, make sure that it is of the same colour code as the original and that its lower coil is correctly located up against its stop in the spring pan.
6 Tighten the shock absorber lower mounting bolt to the specified torque.

## 10 Trailing arm rubber bush – renewal

1 A worn trailing arm rubber bush may be renewed in the following way.
2 Raise the rear of the car and support securely on axle stands placed under the body side-members or sill jacking points.
3 Remove the roadwheels.

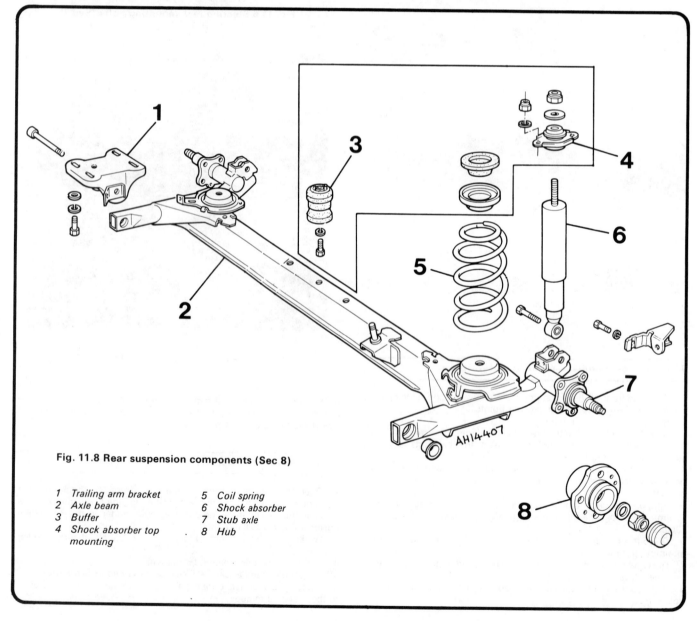

**Fig. 11.8 Rear suspension components (Sec 8)**

1  Trailing arm bracket
2  Axle beam
3  Buffer
4  Shock absorber top
   mounting

5  Coil spring
6  Shock absorber
7  Stub axle
8  Hub

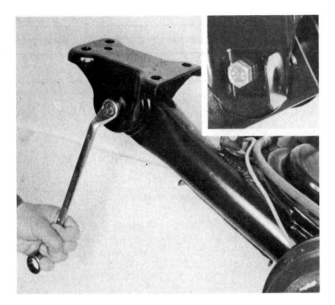

**Fig. 11.9 Removing trailing arm pivot bolt (Sec 10)**

**Fig. 11.10 Method of renewing trailing arm bush (Sec 10)**

4  Unscrew and remove both pivot bolts which hold the forward ends of the trailing arms to the body brackets.
5  Pull the trailing arms downward out of the body brackets.
6  A two-legged puller may be used to press the old bush out and to force the new one in. Smear the bush with soapy water or brake fluid to facilitate fitting.
7  Reconnect the trailing arms to the body brackets. Use jacks if necessary to push the arms upwards into the brackets.
8  Tighten the pivot bolts to the specified torque, but only when the car has been located with four occupants or the equivalent plus 40 kg (88 lb) of luggage.

## 11  Rear suspension – removal and refitting

1  Raise the rear of the car, support it securely and remove the rear road wheels.
2  Unhook the brake pressure regulating valve arm tension spring from its bracket.
3  Disconnect the handbrake cables from the brake backplate levers.
4  Disconnect the flexible brake hose at its junction with the rigid pipeline adjacent to the pressure regulating valve. Cap the open ends of hose and pipe.
5  Support the trailing arms and then disconnect the shock absorber upper mountings.
6  Unbolt the trailing arm forward end support brackets from the body, lower the complete rear suspension and withdraw it from under the car.
7  Refitting is a reversal of removal, but tighten the trailing arm pivot bolts to the specified torque only when the car is loaded with four occupants and 40 kg (88 lb) of luggage (photo).
8  Bleed the brakes as described in Chapter 8.

**Fig. 11.11 Handbrake cable and lever at brake backplate (Sec 11)**

11.7 One side of the rear suspension

**12 Fault diagnosis — suspension**

**Note:** *Before diagnosing suspension defects, be sure that trouble is not due to incorrect or uneven tyre pressures, in inappropriate combinations*

| Symptom | Reason(s) |
| --- | --- |
| Car pulls to one side | Worn or weak shock absorbers or struts on one side |
| Excessive roll on corners | Weak shock absorbers or struts |
|  | Coil spring weak or cracked |
| Car wanders or skips on rough surfaces | Defective shock absorbers or struts |
| Vibration and wheel wobble | Loose or defective shock absorbers or struts |
| Excessive or uneven tyre wear | Worn suspension components |

# Chapter 12 Bodywork

*For modifications, and information applicable to later models, see Supplement at end of manual*

## Contents

## Specifications

For dimensions, weights etc. refer to the Introductory Section of this Manual.

## 1  General description

The Uno is an all steel, welded Hatchback of unitary construction available in three- or five-door versions.

Various levels of trim and equipment are available depending upon model.

Factory fitted options include a sunroof, central door locking and electrically-operated front windows.

## 2  Maintenance – bodywork and underframe

1  The general condition of a vehicle's bodywork is the one thing that significantly affects its value. Maintenance is easy but needs to be regular. Neglect, particularly after minor damage, can lead quickly to further deterioration and costly repair bills. It is important also to keep watch on those parts of the vehicle not immediately visible, for instance the underside, inside all the wheel arches and the lower part of the engine compartment.

2  The basic maintenance routine for the bodywork is washing – preferably with a lot of water, from a hose. This will remove all the loose solids which may have stuck to the vehicle. It is important to flush these off in such a way as to prevent grit from scratching the finish. The wheel arches and underframe need washing in the same way to remove any accumulated mud which will retain moisture and tend to encourage rust. Paradoxically enough, the best time to clean the underframe and wheel arches is in wet weather when the mud is thoroughly wet and soft. In very wet weather the underframe is usually cleaned of large accumulations automatically and this is a good time for inspection.

3  Periodically, except on vehicles with a wax-based underbody protective coating, it is a good idea to have the whole of the underframe of the vehicle steam cleaned, engine compartment included, so that a thorough inspection can be carried out to see what minor repairs and renovations are necessary. Steam cleaning is available at many garages and is necessary for removal of the accumulation of oily grime which sometimes is allowed to become thick in certain areas. If steam cleaning facilities are not available, there are one or two excellent grease solvents available such as Holts Engine Cleaner or Holts Foambrite which can be brush applied. The dirt can then be simply hosed off. Note that these methods should not be used on vehicles with wax-based underbody protective coating or the coating will be removed. Such vehicles should be inspected annually, preferably just prior to winter, when the underbody should be washed down and any damage to the wax coating repaired using Holts Undershield. Ideally, a completely fresh coat should be applied. It would also be worth considering the use of such wax-based protection for injection into door panels, sills, box sections, etc, as an additional safeguard against rust damage where such protection is not provided by the vehicle manufacturer.

4  After washing paintwork, wipe off with a chamois leather to give an unspotted clear finish. A coat of clear protective wax polish, like the many excellent Turtle Wax polishes, will give added protection against chemical pollutants in the air. If the paintwork sheen has dulled or oxidised, use a cleaner/polisher combination such as Turtle Extra to restore the brilliance of the shine. This requires a little effort, but such dulling is usually caused because regular washing has been neglected. Care needs to be taken with metallic paintwork, as special non-abrasive cleaner/polisher is required to avoid damage to the finish. Always check that the door and ventilator opening drain holes and pipes are completely clear so that water can be drained out (photos). Bright work should be treated in the same way as paint work. Windscreens and windows can be kept clear of the smeary film which often appears, by the use of a proprietary glass cleaner like Holts Mixra. Never use any form of wax or other body or chromium polish on glass.

## 3  Maintenance – upholstery and carpets

Mats and carpets should be brushed or vacuum cleaned regularly to keep them free of grit. If they are badly stained remove them from the vehicle for scrubbing or sponging and make quite sure they are dry before refitting. Seats and interior trim panels can be kept clean by wiping with a damp cloth and Turtle Wax Carisma. If they do become stained (which can be more apparent on light coloured upholstery) use a little liquid detergent and a soft nail brush to scour the grime out of the grain of the material. Do not forget to keep the headlining clean in the same way as the upholstery. When using liquid cleaners inside

2.4A Door drain hole

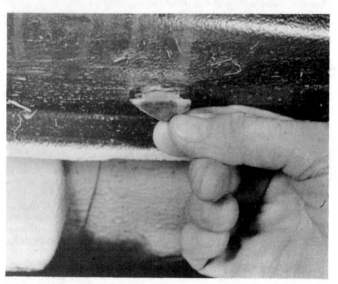

2.4B Sill drain with non-return valve

the vehicle do not over-wet the surfaces being cleaned. Excessive damp could get into the seams and padded interior causing stains, offensive odours or even rot. If the inside of the vehicle gets wet accidentally it is worthwhile taking some trouble to dry it out properly, particularly where carpets are involved. *Do not leave oil or electric heaters inside the vehicle for this purpose.*

## 4  Minor body damage – repair

*The colour bodywork repair photographic sequences between pages 32 and 33 illustrate the operations detailed in the following sub-sections.*
**Note**: *For more detailed information about bodywork repair, the Haynes Publishing Group publish a book by Lindsay Porter called The Car Bodywork Repair Manual. This incorporates information on such aspects as rust treatment, painting and glass fibre repairs, as well as details on more ambitious repairs involving welding and panel beating.*

### Repair of minor scratches in bodywork

If the scratch is very superficial, and does not penetrate to the metal of the bodywork, repair is very simple. Lightly rub the area of the scratch with a paintwork renovator like Turtle Wax New Color Back, or a very fine cutting paste like Holts Body + Plus Rubbing Compound, to remove loose paint from the scratch and to clear the surrounding bodywork of wax polish. Rinse the area with clean water.

Apply touch-up paint, such as Holts Dupli-Color Color Touch or a paint film like Holts Autofilm, to the scratch using a fine paint brush; continue to apply fine layers of paint until the surface of the paint in the scratch is level with the surrounding paintwork. Allow the new paint at least two weeks to harden: then blend it into the surrounding paintwork by rubbing the scratch area with a paintwork renovator or a very fine cutting paste, such as Holts Body + Plus Rubbing Compound or Turtle Wax New Color Back. Finally, apply wax polish from one of the Turtle Wax range of wax polishes.

Where the scratch has penetrated right through to the metal of the bodywork, causing the metal to rust, a different repair technique is required. Remove any loose rust from the bottom of the scratch with a penknife, then apply rust inhibiting paint, such as Turtle Wax Rust Master, to prevent the formation of rust in the future. Using a rubber or nylon applicator fill the scratch with bodystopper paste like Holts Body + Plus Knifing Putty. If required, this paste can be mixed with cellulose thinners, such as Holts Body + Plus Cellulose Thinners, to provide a very thin paste which is ideal for filling narrow scratches. Before the stopper-paste in the scratch hardens, wrap a piece of smooth cotton rag around the top of a finger. Dip the finger in cellulose thinners, such as Holts Body + Plus Cellulose Thinners, and then quickly sweep it across the surface of the stopper-paste in the scratch; this will ensure that the surface of the stopper-paste is slightly hollowed. The scratch can now be painted over as described earlier in this Section.

### Repair of dents in bodywork

When deep denting of the vehicle's bodywork has taken place, the first task is to pull the dent out, until the affected bodywork almost attains its original shape. There is little point in trying to restore the original shape completely, as the metal in the damaged area will have stretched on impact and cannot be reshaped fully to its original contour. It is better to bring the level of the dent up to a point which is about ⅛ in (3 mm) below the level of the surrounding bodywork. In cases where the dent is very shallow anyway, it is not worth trying to pull it out at all. If the underside of the dent is accessible, it can be hammered out gently from behind, using a mallet with a wooden or plastic head. Whilst doing this, hold a suitable block of wood firmly against the outside of the panel to absorb the impact from the hammer blows and thus prevent a large area of the bodywork from being 'belled-out'.

Should the dent be in a section of the bodywork which has a double skin or some other factor making it inaccessible from behind, a different technique is called for. Drill several small holes through the metal inside the area – particularly in the deeper section. Then screw long self-tapping screws into the holes just sufficiently for them to gain a good purchase in the metal. Now the dent can be pulled out by pulling on the protruding heads of the screws with a pair of pliers.

The next stage of the repair is the removal of the paint from the damaged area, and from an inch or so of the surrounding 'sound' bodywork. This is accomplished most easily by using a wire brush or abrasive pad on a power drill, although it can be done just as effectively by hand using sheets of abrasive paper. To complete the preparation for filling, score the surface of the bare metal with a screwdriver or the tang of a file, or alternatively, drill small holes in the affected area. This will provide a really good 'key' for the filler paste.

To complete the repair see the Section on filling and re-spraying.

### Repair of rust holes or gashes in bodywork

Remove all paint from the affected area and from an inch or so of the surrounding 'sound' bodywork, using an abrasive pad or a wire brush on a power drill. If these are not available a few sheets of abrasive paper will do the job just as effectively. With the paint removed you will be able to gauge the severity of the corrosion and therefore decide whether to renew the whole panel (if this is possible) or to repair the affected area. New body panels are not as expensive as most people think and it is often quicker and more satisfactory to fit a new panel than to attempt to repair large areas of corrosion.

Remove all fittings from the affected area except those which will act as a guide to the original shape of the damaged bodywork (eg headlamp shells etc). Then, using tin snips or a hacksaw blade, remove all loose metal and any other metal badly affected by corrosion. Hammer the edges of the hole inwards in order to create a slight depression for the filler paste.

Wire brush the affected area to remove the powdery rust from the surface of the remaining metal. Paint the affected area with rust inhibiting paint like Turtle Wax Rust Master; if the back of the rusted area is accessible treat this also.

Before filling can take place it will be necessary to block the hole in some way. This can be achieved by the use of aluminium or plastic mesh, or aluminium tape.

Aluminium or plastic mesh or glass fibre matting, such as the Holts Body + Plus Glass Fibre Matting, is probably the best material to use for a large hole. Cut a piece to the approximate size and shape of the hole to be filled, then position it in the hole so that its edges are below the level of the surrounding bodywork. It can be retained in position by several blobs of filler paste around its periphery.

Aluminium tape should be used for small or very narrow holes. Pull a piece off the roll and trim it to the approximate size and shape required, then pull off the backing paper (if used) and stick the tape over the hole; it can be overlapped if the thickness of one piece is insufficient. Burnish down the edges of the tape with the handle of a screwdriver or similar, to ensure that the tape is securely attached to the metal underneath.

### Bodywork repairs – filling and re-spraying

Before using this Section, see the Sections on dent, deep scratch, rust holes and gash repairs.

Many types of bodyfiller are available, but generally speaking those proprietary kits which contain a tin of filler paste and a tube of resin hardener are best for this type of repair, like Holts Body + Plus or Holts No Mix which can be used directly from the tube. A wide, flexible plastic or nylon applicator will be found invaluable for imparting a smooth and well contoured finish to the surface of the filler.

Mix up a little filler on a clean piece of card or board – measure the hardener carefully (follow the maker's instructions on the pack) otherwise the filler will set too rapidly or too slowly. Alternatively, Holts No Mix can be used straight from the tube without mixing, but daylight is required to cure it. Using the applicator apply the filler paste to the prepared area; draw the applicator across the surface of the filler to achieve the correct contour and to level the filler surface. As soon as a contour that approximates to the correct one is achieved, stop working the paste – if you carry on too long the paste will become sticky and begin to 'pick up' on the applicator. Continue to add thin layers of filler paste at twenty-minute intervals until the level of the filler is just proud of the surrounding bodywork.

Once the filler has hardened, excess can be removed using a metal plane or file. From then on, progressively finer grades of abrasive paper should be used, starting with a 40 grade production paper and finishing with 400 grade wet-and-dry paper. Always wrap the abrasive paper around a flat rubber, cork, or wooden block – otherwise the surface of the filler will not be completely flat. During the smoothing of the filler surface the wet-and-dry paper should be periodically rinsed in water. This will ensure that a very smooth finish is imparted to the filler at the final stage.

At this stage the 'dent' should be surrounded by a ring of bare metal, which in turn should be encircled by the finely 'feathered' edge of the good paintwork. Rinse the repair area with clean water, until all of the dust produced by the rubbing-down operation has gone.

Spray the whole repair area with a light coat of primer, either Holts Body + Plus Grey or Red Oxide Primer – this will show up any imperfections in the surface of the filler. Repair these imperfections with fresh filler paste or bodystopper, and once more smooth the surface with abrasive paper. If bodystopper is used, it can be mixed with cellulose thinners to form a really thin paste which is ideal for filling small holes. Repeat this spray and repair procedure until you are satisfied that the surface of the filler, and the feathered edge of the paintwork are perfect. Clean the repair area with clean water and allow to dry fully.

The repair area is now ready for final spraying. Paint spraying must be carried out in a warm, dry, windless and dust free atmosphere. This condition can be created artificially if you have access to a large indoor working area, but if you are forced to work in the open, you will have to pick your day very carefully. If you are working indoors, dousing the floor in the work area with water will help to settle the dust which would otherwise be in the atmosphere. If the repair area is confined to one body panel, mask off the surrounding panels; this will help to minimise the effects of a slight mis-match in paint colours. Bodywork fittings (eg chrome strips, door handles etc) will also need to be masked off. Use genuine masking tape and several thicknesses of newspaper for the masking operations.

Before commencing to spray, agitate the aerosol can thoroughly, then spray a test area (an old tin, or similar) until the technique is mastered. Cover the repair area with a thick coat of primer; the thickness should be built up using several thin layers of paint rather than one thick one. Using 400 grade wet-and-dry paper, rub down the surface of the primer until it is really smooth. While doing this, the work area should be thoroughly doused with water, and the wet-and-dry paper periodically rinsed in water. Allow to dry before spraying on more paint.

Spray on the top coat using Holts Dupli-Color Autospray, again building up the thickness by using several thin layers of paint. Start spraying in the centre of the repair area and then work outwards, with a side-to-side motion, until the whole repair area and about 2 inches of the surrounding original paintwork is covered. Remove all masking material 10 to 15 minutes after spraying on the final coat of paint.

Allow the new paint at least two weeks to harden, then, using a paintwork renovator or a very fine cutting paste such as Turtle Wax New Color Back or Holts Body + Plus Rubbing Compound, blend the edges of the paint into the existing paintwork. Finally, apply wax polish.

### 5 Major body damage – repair

1 Major repair to the body should be left to your Fiat dealer or specialist body repairer.
2 Special jigs and alignment gauges are required without which steering and suspension characteristics may be incorrect after the repairs are completed.

### 6 Radiator grille – removal and refitting

1 Open the bonnet.
2 Extract the single fixing screw from the centre of the grille slats (photo).
3 Release the retaining clips and withdraw the grille upwards from its lower spigot holes (photo).
4 Refitting is a reversal of removal.

### 7 Bonnet – removal and refitting

1 Open the bonnet and support it on its stay.
2 Pencil around the hinges on the underside of the bonnet or stick strips of masking tape around them as a guide to refitting (photo).
3 With the help of an assistant, support the weight of the bonnet, unbolt the hinges and lift the bonnet from the car.
4 Refitting is a reversal of removal, but do not fully tighten the hinge bolts until the bonnet has been gently closed and its alignment checked. If the gap between the bonnet and the front wings is not equal on both sides, release the hinge bolts and move the bonnet within the elongation provided at the bolt holes.

### 8 Bonnet lock and release

1 The bonnet lock is operated by a remote control lever inside the car through a cable (photo).
2 When closing the bonnet, the spring-loaded striker should enter the lock centrally. If it does not, release the lock bolts and slide the lock as necessary (photo).
3 Engagement of the striker in the lock should be adjusted for depth in order that the surface of the bonnet is level with the front wings. To do this, release the striker locknut and turn the striker in or out by inserting a screwdriver in its slot.
4 In conjunction with the striker adjustment, screw the bonnet rubber buffers in or out as necessary to provide secure rattle-free closure of the bonnet (photo).
5 If the lock must be removed, first withdraw the radiator grille as described in Section 6.

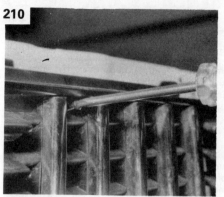

6.2 Grille screw

6.3 Grille clip

7.2 Bonnet hinge

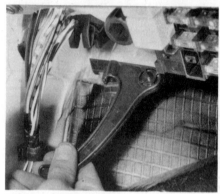

8.1 Bonnet release lever

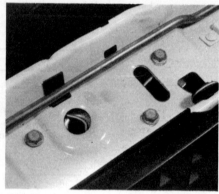

8.2 Bonnet lock

8.4 Bonnet buffer

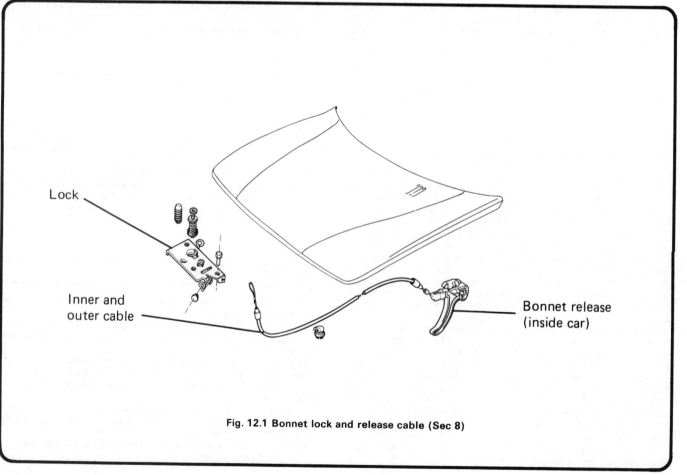

Lock

Inner and
outer cable

Bonnet release
(inside car)

Fig. 12.1 Bonnet lock and release cable (Sec 8)

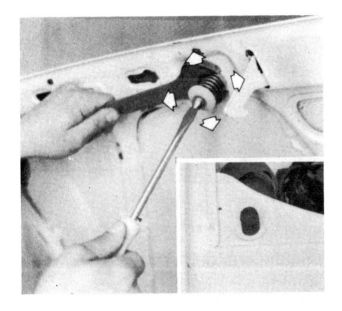

Fig. 12.2 Adjusting bonnet lock striker (Sec 8)

9.1A Front bumper upper fixing screw

9.1B Front bumper upper fixing screw

6   To renew the release cable, unclip and lower the release lever under the facia panel.
7   Disconnect the cable from the lever and then slip it from the lock operating arm. Withdraw the cable.
8   Refit the new cable by reversing the removal operations.

## 9  Front bumpers – removal and refitting

1   Remove the radiator grille as described in Section 6 to expose the two upper bumper fixing screws. Remove them (photos).
2   Working inside at the lower edge of the bumper remove the three fixing bolts.
3   Finally, unscrew the side bracket fixing bolts and lift the bumper away.
4   Refitting is a reversal of removal.

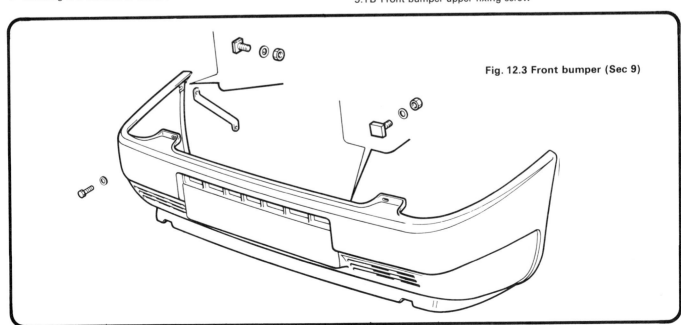

Fig. 12.3 Front bumper (Sec 9)

Fig. 12.4 Front bumper upper screws (Sec 9)

Fig. 12.5 Front bumper lower screws (Sec 9)

## 10 Front wing – removal and refitting

1   Remove the headlamp and front parking lamp as described in Chapter 9.
2   Withdraw the side repeater lamp and disconnect the leads.
3   Remove the front roadwheel.
4   Working under the wing, remove the fixing screw and withdraw the plastic protective shield (photos).
5   Unscrew the wing lower fixing screws at the front and rear ends.
6   Open the bonnet and support it. Then unscrew and remove the row of fixing screws from the inner top edge of the wing.

10.4B Removing wing shield

10.4A Unscrewing wing shield screw

7   The wing joints will have to be cut round with a sharp knife to release the mastic seal before the wing can be lifted away.
8   Clean the body mating flanges in readiness for fitting the new wing.
9   Apply a bead of mastic to the body flanges and offer the new wing into position.
10  Refit the fixing screws.
11  Apply protective coating to the underside of the wing and refinish the outer surface to match the bodywork.
12  Refit the headlamp, parking lamp and repeater lamp.
13  Fit the under wing shield and the roadwheel, close the bonnet.

## 11 Door trim panel – removal and refitting

1   Open the door and extract the three armrest fixing screws. Remove the armrest in a downward direction (photos).
2   Remove the screws from the door tidy bin (photo).
3   Push the door remote control escutcheon rearwards towards the door lock and remove it (photos).
4   Remove the window regulator handle spring clip. Do this by inserting a length of wire with a hooked end or by pulling a strip of rag between the handle and the door trim panel at its lower gap (photo).
5   Insert the fingers or a broad blade between the trim panel and the door and release the panel.
6   Remove the trim panel and the waterproof sheet (photo).

7   Refitting is a reversal of removal, but when refitting the window regulator handle locate its retaining spring clip fully and then simply locate the handle on its splined shaft and strike it sharply with the hand. Make sure that with the window fully closed, the angle of the regulator handle matches the one on the opposite door (photo).

## 12 Door – dismantling

1   Remove the trim panel as described in the preceding Section.

### Lock remote control handle
2   Slide the handle rearwards to disengage the tabs from the cut-outs.
3   Rotate the lock handle and disconnect it from the link rod.

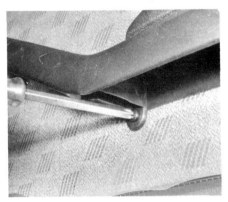
11.1A Removing an armrest screw

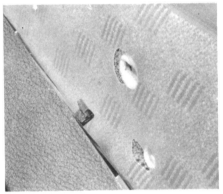
11.1B Removing armrest downward

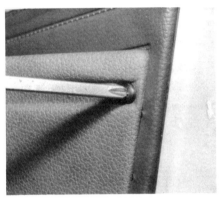
11.2 Door tidy bin screw

11.3A Removing remote control handle escutcheon

11.3B Remote control handle withdrawn

11.4 Window regulator handle removed

11.6 Removing door trim panel

11.7 Window regulator handle ready for fitting

12.7 Door glass mounting

## Door glass

4   Extract the screws from the glass mounting.
5   With the glass fully lowered, remove the weatherseal strips from the glass slot in the door.
6   Turn the glass very carefully and withdraw it from the door. A new glass is supplied complete with lower mounting.

## Window regulator

7   Extract the fixing screws (arrowed) (Fig. 12.9) and withdraw the regulator from the door through one of the larger lower apertures (photo).

## Door lock (three-door)

8   Extract the screw and remove the handle from the edge of the door.
9   Remove the glass guide channel fixing bolts and withdraw the channel from the door.
10  Extract the screws which hold the lock to the edge of the door and remove it.

Fig. 12.8 Removing door glass (Sec 12)

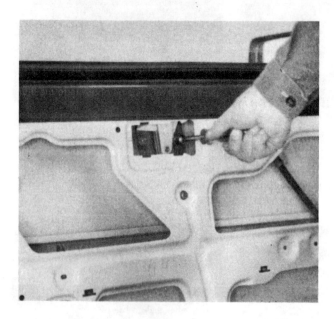

Fig. 12.6 Door glass mounting screw (Sec 12)

Fig. 12.9 Door window regulator fixing screws (Sec 12)

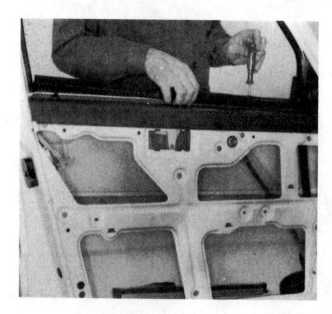

Fig. 12.7 Removing door weatherseal (Sec 12)

Fig. 12.10 Removing door window regulator (Sec 12)

Fig. 12.11 Removing door handle fixing screw (three-door model) (Sec 12)

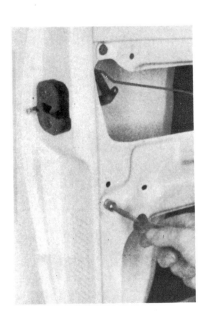

Fig. 12.12 Extracting glass guide channel screw (Sec 12)

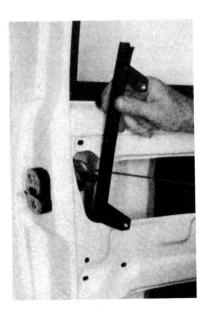

Fig. 12.13 Removing glass guide channel (Sec 12)

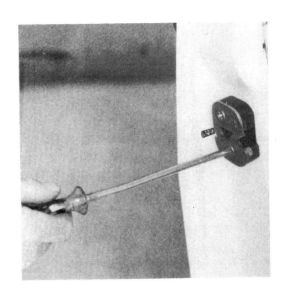

Fig. 12.14 Removing door lock fixing screw (Sec 12)

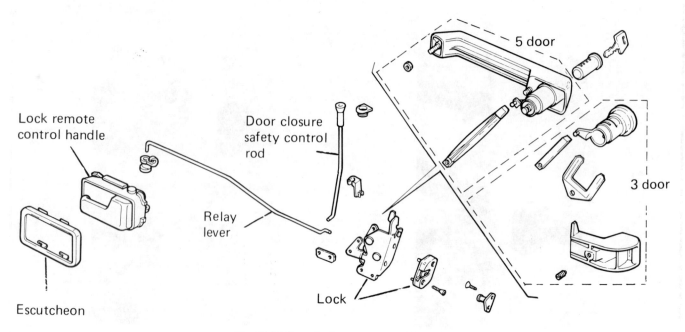

Fig. 12.15 Door lock components (Sec 12)

12.11 Door lock plunger rod

### Door lock (five-door)

11  Extract the screws which hold the lock to the door edge. Withdraw the lock and disconnect the lock plunger link rod (photo).
12  The exterior handle with cylinder lock can be removed by reaching into the door cavity and unscrewing the two fixing nuts.

### Refitting

13  This is a reversal of the removal operations. Oil and grease the lock and window regulator mechanism.

### 13  Door – removal and refitting

1  Open the door fully and support it under its lower edge on jacks or blocks covered with an insulating pad.

2  The door hinges are fixed to the doors with hexagonal headed bolts and to the body pillar with socket-headed bolts.
3  The door check is incorporated in the lower hinge (photo).
4  On cars equipped with door mounted speakers, central door locking or power operated windows, the electrical leads must be disconnected and withdrawn through the flexible duct before the door hinges are unbolted. Disconnection will require removal of the door trim panel as described in Section 11.
5  It is recommended that the door is unbolted from the hinge, leaving the hinge attached to the body pillar.
6  Refitting is a reversal of removal, but leave the bolts finger tight until the door has been gently closed and its alignment checked.
7  The door can be moved up and down or sideways using the travel provided by the elongated bolt holes.
8  If the door is not flush with the adjacent body panels then shims should be inserted under the hinges.
9  Adjust the striker to provide smooth positive closure (photo).

13.3 Door lower hinge

13.9 Door lock striker

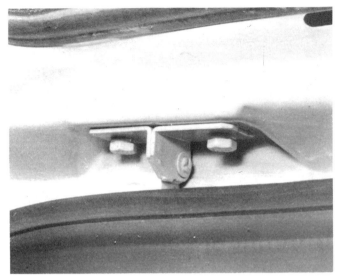

14.4 Tailgate hinge

## 14 Tailgate – removal and refitting

1   Open the tailgate and have an assistant support it.
2   From the upper ends of the struts, prise out the locking wedges from the ball cups and disconnect the struts (photo).
3   Disconnect the washer tube.
4   Unscrew the hinge mounting bolts from the tailgate and lift the tailgate from the car (photo).
5   Refitting is a reversal of removal, but if re-alignment is required, then the rear section of the roof lining will have to be removed and the hinge to body bolts released.
6   Adjust the position of the lock striker to provide smooth positive closure. The rubber buffers should be screwed in or out in conjunction with the adjustment of the striker (photos).
7   On some models, a remote control tailgate opening release lever is fitted. Removal and refitting of the cable is similar to that described in Section 8 (photo).

14.6A Tailgate lock

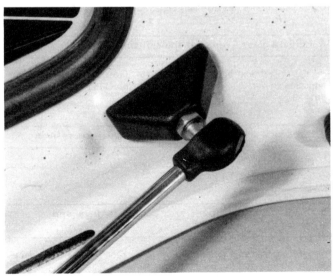

14.2 Tailgate strut ball cup

14.6B Tailgate striker

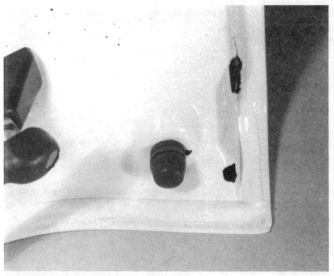

14.6C Tailgate rubber buffer

Fig. 12.16 Peeling back lip of windscreen glass weatherseal
(Sec 15)

14.7 Tailgate remote control release lever

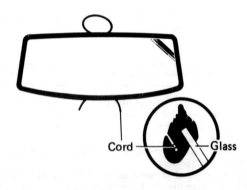

Fig. 12.17 Position of cord for fitting windscreen weatherseal
(Sec 15)

8   Tap the glass with the palm of the hand to settle it.
9   If the weatherseal is in good condition then it should prove
waterproof, but if there is any doubt, apply sealant with a gun between
the rubber and the glass and the rubber and the body flange.
10  Refit the mirror, tax disc and wiper.

## 16 Tailgate glass – removal and refitting

1   The operations are very similar to those described for the
windscreen, but disconnect the leads from the heater element
terminals.

## 17 Fixed side window (five-door) – removal and refitting

1   The operations are similar to those described for the windscreen in
Section 15.

## 18 Opening side window (three-door) – removal and refitting

1   Have an assistant support the glass and then extract the screws
from the hinges and the toggle type fastener.
2   Swivel the glass outwards and downwards to remove it.
3   Refitting is a reversal of removal.

## 15 Windscreen glass – removal and refitting

1   Remove the interior rear view mirror, the tax disc and the wiper
blade and arm.
2   If the glass is intact, go inside the car and pull the lip of the
weatherseal downwards off the body metal all along the top edge.
3   Push the glass outwards while an assistant stands outside ready to
catch it.
4   Clean the body flange and fit the weatherstrip to the glass.
5   Insert a length of strong cord in the body flange groove of the
weatherseal so that the ends of the cord cross over at the centre of the
bottom run and hang out a few inches.
6   Brush soapy water onto the edge of the body flange and then offer
the glass to the body so that the bottom edge of the rubber seal
engages over the metal flange.
7   With an assistant pressing on the outside of the glass, go inside and
pull the cords evenly. This will draw the lip of the weatherseal over the
body flange and seat the glass.

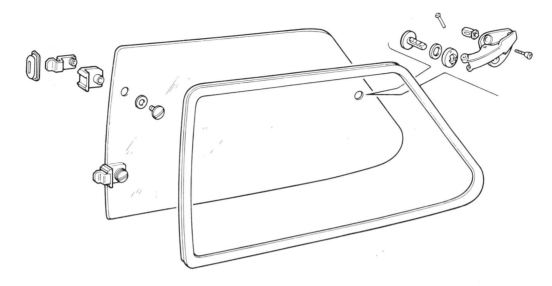

Fig. 12.18 Components of opening side window (Sec 18)

## 19 Front seat – removal and refitting

1   Unbolt the seat front anchorage clamps (photo).
2   Slide the seat fully rearwards out of its guide rails, but bend the end of the seat adjustment lever so that it passes over its stop.

19.1 Front seat mounting clamp

## 20 Rear seat – removal and refitting

1   The rear seat may be of one piece design or split (60/40) depending upon the model.
2   Either type of seat is easily removable once the hinge bolts have been unscrewed and removed (photo).

20.2 Rear seat mounting hinges

## 21 Centre console – removal and refitting

1   Pull the small black knobs from the heater control levers.
2   Extract the screws from both sides of the heater control panel, remove the panel. As the panel is withdrawn, disconnect the leads from the cigar lighter and take care not to damage the fibre optics.
3   From inside the glove box, prise out the lid stop block. Insert a screwdriver in the hole left by its removal and unscrew the console fixing screw (photo).
4   Reach up behind the facia panel on the side opposite to the glove box and unscrew the remaining console fixing screw.
5   Withdraw the console downwards and disconnect the fibre optics from their source.
6   Refitting is a reversal of removal.

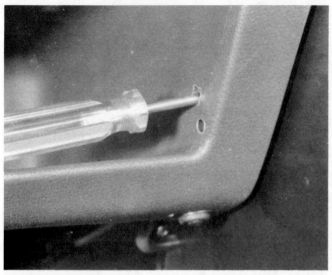

21.3 Removing screw (glovebox side) from centre console

22.5A Facia fixing screw inside glovebox

## 22 Facia panel – removal and refitting

1  Remove the instrument panel as described in Chapter 9.
2  Remove the steering wheel (Chapter 10).
3  Disconnect the choke control lever and cable from the facia panel as described in Chapter 3.
4  Remove the screws arrowed in Fig. 12.19.
5  Remove the facia fixing screws, their locations on the facia being shown in Fig. 12.20. Screw (3) is inside the glove box (photos).
6  Release the facia from the upper clips and withdraw it.
7  Refitting is a reversal of removal.

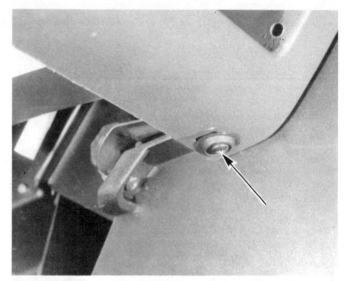

22.5B Facia panel lower mounting screw at centre console

**Fig. 12.19 Facia panel fixing screws (Sec 22)**

22.5C Facia panel lower mounting screw (left-hand side)

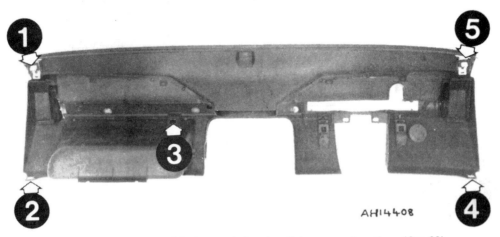

**Fig. 12.20 Rear view of facia panel showing fixing screw locations (Sec 22)**

*1 and 5 Clips*     *2, 3 and 4 Screws*

## 23 Seat belts

1 Seat belts are fitted as standard equipment to both the front and rear seats.
2 Regularly inspect the belts for fraying and if evident, renew the belt.
3 The front belt reel may be unbolted if the seat is pushed fully forward and the reel cover panel removed (photo).
4 The rear belt reels are located at each side of the luggage area (photo).
5 When removing or refitting a belt from its anchorage point, it is essential to maintain the original fitted sequence of spacer, washer and wave washer otherwise the belt anchor plate will not swivel (photo).

## 24 Rear view mirrors

### Interior
1 The mirror may be removed after extracting the fixing screws. The mirror is designed to break off if struck.

### Exterior
2 The mirror is remotely controlled. To remove the mirror, peel back the rubber cover from the control knob (photo).
3 Unscrew the ring nut using a C-spanner or similar (photo).
4 Withdraw the mirror from its mounting hole, the triangular trim plate will come with it. Refitting is a reversal of removal (photo).

23.3 Front seat belt lower mounting

23.4 Rear seat belt reel

23.5 Front seat belt upper mounting

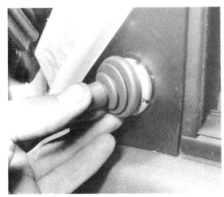

24.2 Exterior mirror control knob

24.3 Mirror ring nut and C-spanner

24.4 Withdrawing exterior mirror and trim plate

## 25 Grab handles

1   These are located above the door openings and can be removed if
the end covers are prised back on their hinges to expose the fixing
screws (photo).

## 26 Rear bumpers – removal and refitting

1   Refer to Chapter 9 and withdraw the number plate lamp.
Disconnect the leads.
2   Open the tailgate and three bumper fixing bolts from the top edge.
3   Working under the car, remove the two side and the three lower
edge fixing bolts.
4   Remove the bumper from the car.
5   Refitting is a reversal of removal.

## 27 Roof rack

1   As the car is not fitted with conventional type rain water gutters,
the Fiat roof rack should be used which incorporates clamps which
engage under the door arches. The doors are then closed on them.
2   On three-door models, the rear clamps fit into recesses provided
just above the rear side window weatherseals.

## 28 Sunroof – operation and maintenance

1   To unlock the sunroof, bring the control lever down and turn it
anti-clockwise. The glass sunroof will partially rise and then slide
rearwards.
2   A sliding louvre is provided to decrease noise and airflow.
3   On cars fitted with a sunroof, the interior lamps are of pillar-
mounted type.

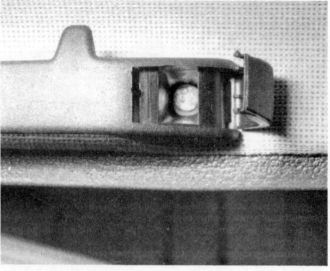

25.1 Grab handle screw

4   If the sunroof must be removed, prise out the screw caps using a
thin blade.
5   Extract the screws which hold the glass panel to the rails.
6   The sunroof channel water drain hoses should be kept clear. If the
hoses are to be cleared of obstruction remove the trim panels at the
sides of the front footwells and insert a length of curtain spring in the
bottom ends of the hoses.
7   The rear drain hoses are accessible once the parcels shelf supports
are removed and the trim panels unclipped.

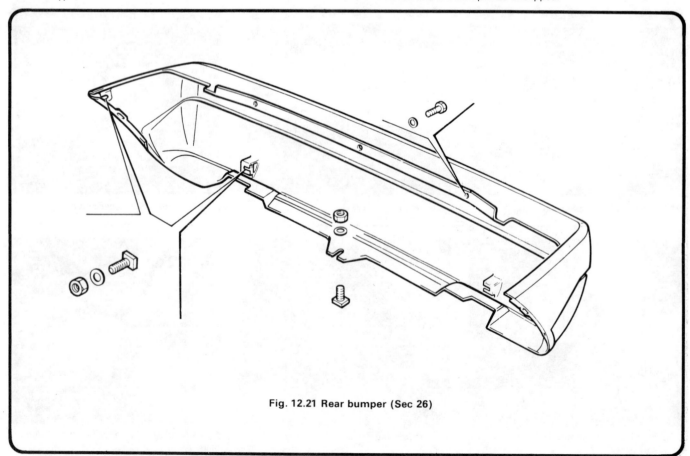

Fig. 12.21 Rear bumper (Sec 26)

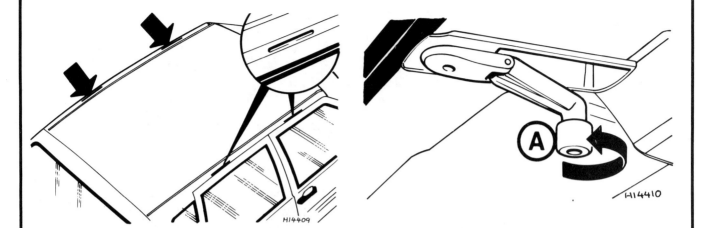

Fig. 12.22 Roof rack clamp locations (Sec 27)

Fig. 12.23 Sunroof control handle (A) (Sec 28)

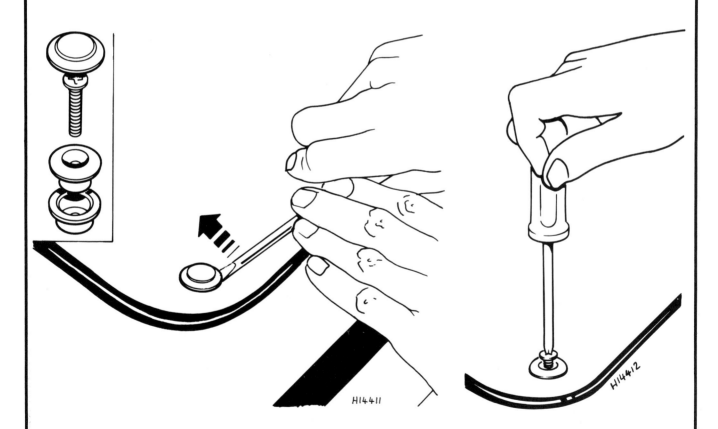

Fig. 12.24 Prising out sunroof glass panel screw caps (Sec 28)

Fig. 12.25 Extracting sunroof panel screw (Sec 28)

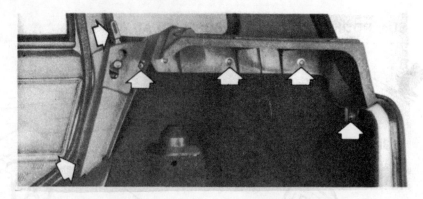

Fig. 12.26 Rear parcels shelf supports (Sec 28)

Fig. 12.27 Sunroof front drainhose routing at bodypillar (Sec 28)

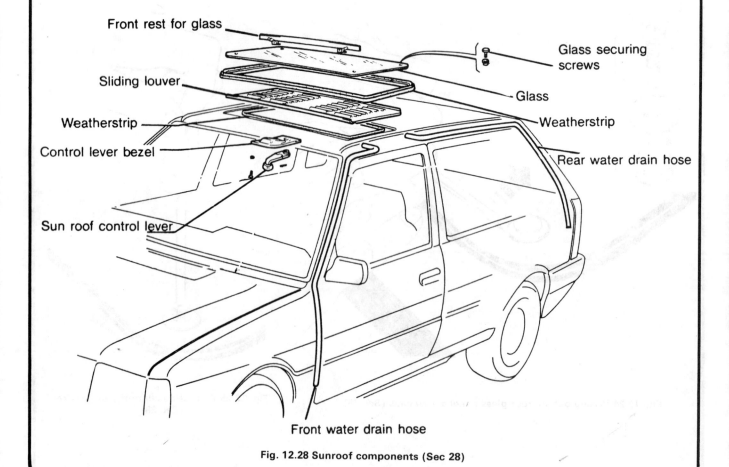

Front rest for glass

Glass securing screws

Sliding louver

Glass

Weatherstrip

Weatherstrip

Control lever bezel

Rear water drain hose

Sun roof control lever

Front water drain hose

Fig. 12.28 Sunroof components (Sec 28)

The 1301 cc Turbo ie model

The 1372 cc 70 SX ie model

# Chapter 13 Supplement:
# Revisions and information on later models

## Contents

## 1 Introduction

Since its introduction in 1983, the FIAT Uno has had a number of modifications and improvements including the fitting of a twin choke carburettor, low profile tyres, tinted windows and remotely-controlled central door locking.

The major mechanical change was the introduction of the FIRE (Fully Integrated Robotised Engine) on 45 and 45S models to be followed by a new 1108 cc 'FIRE' engine on the 60S model from 1989 on.

A 1301 cc Turbo ie engine model was available for a short period. This model had electronic fuel injection (ie) and a turbocharger to give added performance. To uprate the braking to suit, disc brakes were fitted to the rear in place of the original drum type brakes.

A 1372 cc engine model was introduced in 1989. In its basic form it is fitted with a single-point fuel injection system, as found on the SX model. A turbocharged multi-point fuel injection version of this engine was introduced at the same time. All fuel injection engines are fitted with electronically controlled engine management systems, the type being specific to the model.

Other modifications to the engine include a revised fuel and ignition system for later models to allow the use of 95 RON unleaded fuel and in some instances, a catalytic converter is fitted.

The 1372 cc engine models are fitted with a FIAT Tipo type manual transmission, the ratios differing according to model.

A new style instrument panel, switchgear and a revised facia layout was introduced in 1989.

In order to use this Supplement to the best advantage, it is suggested that it is referred to before the main Chapters of the Manual; this will ensure that any relevant information can be collated and absorbed into the procedures described in Chapters 1 to 12.

### Project vehicles

The vehicles used in the preparation of this supplement, and appearing in many of the photographic sequences were a 1986 Uno 45S FIRE, a 1988 1301 cc Uno Turbo ie and a 1991 1372 cc Uno SX ie.

## 2 Specifications

*The specifications below are supplementary to, or revisions of, those at the beginning of the preceding Chapters. Note that, for maximum accuracy, metric units should be used, as metric-only specifications are provided by the manufacturers.*

### Engine – 1299 cc (non-Turbo)
*All other Specifications as for 1301 cc engine in Chapter 1*

## General
Stroke .......................................................................................... 55.4 mm (2.18 in)

### Engine – 999 and 1108 cc
## General
Type ........................................................................................ FIRE (Fully Integrated Robotised Engine). Four-cylinder, in-line overhead camshaft. Transversely mounted with end-on transmission
Application .............................................................................. 45 and 45S
Bore ........................................................................................ 70.0 mm (2.8 in)
Stroke ..................................................................................... 64.9 mm (2.6 in)
Displacement ......................................................................... 999 cc (60.9 cu in)
Compression ratio:
  999 cc:
    Up to mid 1988 ............................................................... 9.8:1
    From mid 1988* ............................................................. 9.5:1
  1108 cc ............................................................................. 9.0:1
Maximum torque (DIN):
  999 cc:
    Up to mid 1988 ............................................................... 59 lbf ft (80 Nm) at 2750 rev/min
    From mid 1988* ............................................................. 57 lbf ft (78 Nm) at 2750 rev/min
  1108 cc ............................................................................. 64 lbf ft (87 Nm) at 2900 rev/min
Maximum power (DIN):
  999 cc ............................................................................... 45 bhp (34 kW) at 5000 rev/min
  1108 cc ............................................................................. 57 bhp (43 kW) at 5500 rev/min
Compression pressure (bore wear test) ................................ 10.35 to 11.73 bars (150 to 170 lbf/in²)
Maximum pressure difference between cylinders ................. 0.96 bars (14 lbf/in²)
Firing order ............................................................................ 1-3-4-2 (No 1 at timing belt end)

*\*95 RON (unleaded fuel) engines*

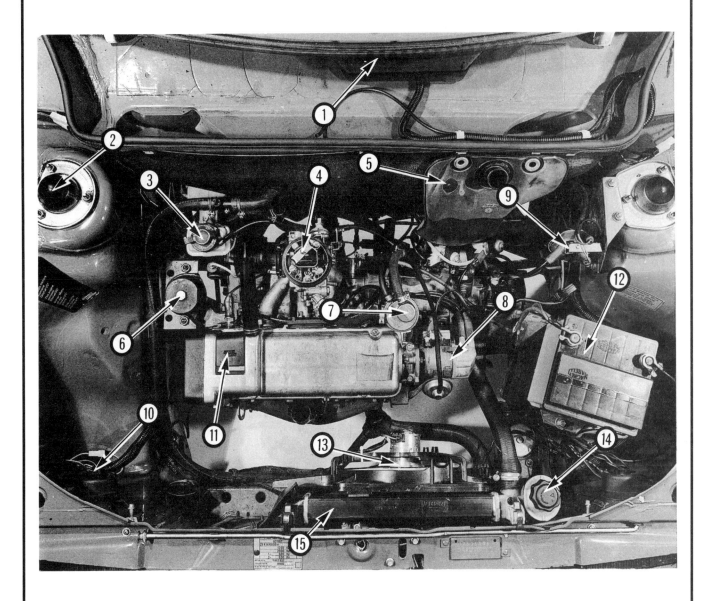

**View of engine compartment (air cleaner removed) on the 999 cc FIRE engined model**

1 Wiper motor cover
2 Suspension strut turret
3 Brake hydraulic fluid reservoir
4 Carburettor
5 Washer fluid reservoir
6 Right-hand engine mounting
7 Fuel pump
8 Ignition distributor
9 Ignition coil
10 Headlamp
11 Oil filler cap
12 Battery
13 Radiator cooling fan
14 Coolant filler/ expansion tank
15 Radiator

**View of front end from below on the 999 cc FIRE engined model**

1  Left hand front
   engine mounting
2  Transmission
3  Track control arm
4  Driveshaft
5  Left hand rear (lower)
   engine mounting
6  Gearchange rods
7  Exhaust pipe
8  Oil filter cartridge
9  Brake caliper
10 Sump pan drain plug

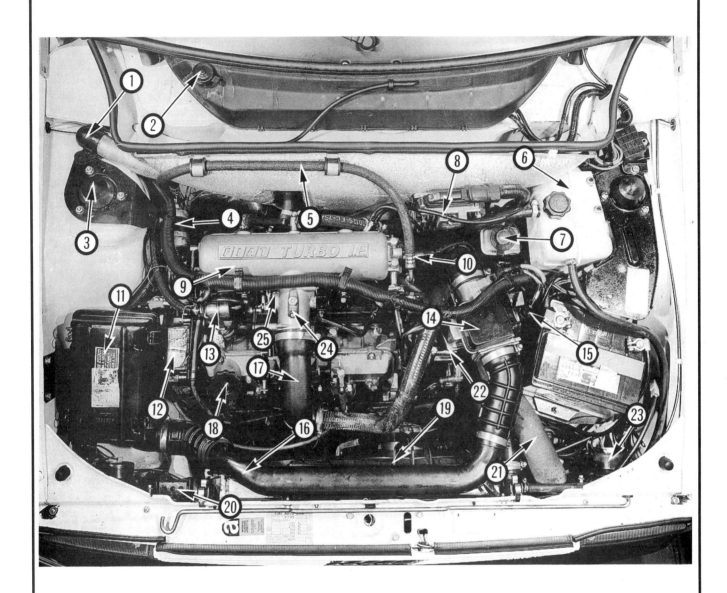

**View of engine compartment on the 1301 cc Turbo ie engined model**

1 Alternator air cooling intake
2 Washer fluid reservoir cap
3 Suspension strut turret
4 Secondary fuel filter
5 Fuel supply hose
6 Coolant expansion tank
7 Brake fluid reservoir cap

8 Ignition system ECU
9 Inlet manifold
10 Excessive pressure switch
11 Air cleaner
12 Timing belt cover
13 Fuel pressure regulator
14 Airflow meter

15 Throttle position switch
16 Air intake duct
17 Air intake to throttle valve
   housing
18 Engine oil filler cap
19 Radiator cooling fan
20 Headlamp dim-dip
   transformer

21 Intercooler air duct
22 Ignition distributor
23 Headlamp
24 Main idle speed adjusting
   screw
25 Base setting idle speed
   screw

**View of front end from below on the 1301 cc Turbo ie engined model**

| 1 | Anti-roll bar | 6 | Brake caliper | 11 | Engine oil drain plug | 16 | Oil filter cartridge |
|---|---|---|---|---|---|---|---|
| 2 | Exhaust pipe | 7 | Left-hand driveshaft | 12 | Auxiliary lamp | 17 | Oil pressure sender unit |
| 3 | Track control arm | 8 | Intermediate driveshaft | 13 | Horn | 18 | Engine oil cooler |
| 4 | Engine centre mounting | 9 | Right-hand driveshaft | 14 | Intercooler | 19 | Right-hand underwing shield |
| 5 | Gearchange rods | 10 | Transmission | 15 | Starter motor | 20 | Left-hand underwing shield |

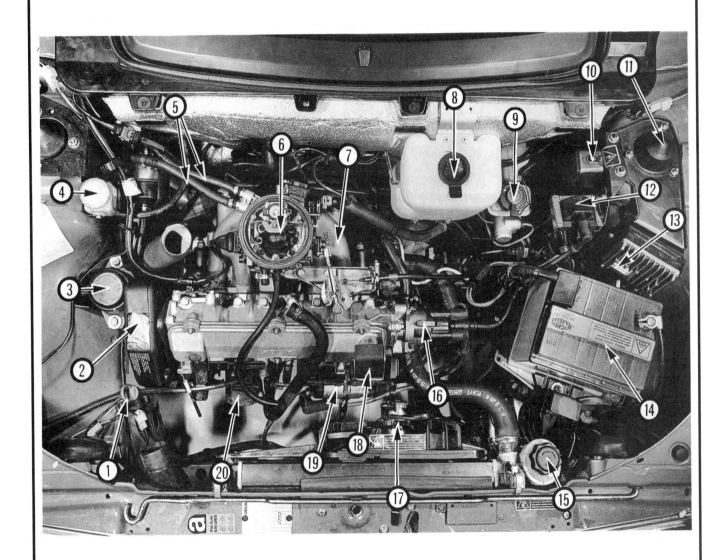

**View of engine compartment (air cleaner removed) on the 1372 cc ie engined model**

1 Engine oil level dipstick
2 Timing belt cover
3 Engine mounting (right-hand)
4 Clutch master cylinder fluid
　reservoir

5 Fuel supply and return hoses
6 Injection unit
7 Inlet manifold
8 Washer reservoir
9 Brake master cylinder and fluid
　reservoir

10 Injection system fuse/relay
　block
11 Suspension strut turret
12 Ignition coil
13 Ignition system ECU
14 Battery

15 Coolant filter expansion tank
16 Ignition distributor
17 Radiator cooling fan
18 Engine oil filler cap
19 Starter motor
20 Oil filter

**View of front end from below on the 1372 cc ie engined model**

| | | | |
|---|---|---|---|
| 1 | Oil filter | 5 | Transmission front mounting |
| 2 | Engine oil drain plug | 6 | Front fog lamp and adjuster |
| 3 | Starter motor | 7 | Driveshaft |
| 4 | Horns | 8 | Transmission rear mounting |

| | | | |
|---|---|---|---|
| 9 | Gearchange linkage | 13 | Tie-rod balljoint |
| 10 | Exhaust downpipe and system joint | 14 | Brake unit |
| 11 | Anti-roll bar | 15 | Driveshaft damper |
| 12 | Track control arm | 16 | Underwing shield |

## Cylinder block and crankcase

| | |
|---|---|
| Material | Cast-iron |
| Bore diameter | 70.000 to 70.050 mm (2.758 to 2.760 in) |
| Maximum cylinder bore taper | 0.015 mm (0.00059 in) |
| Maximum cylinder bore ovality | 0.015 mm (0.00059 in) |

## Pistons and piston rings

| | |
|---|---|
| Piston diameter: | |
| Grade A | 69.960 to 69.970 mm (2.7564 to 2.7568 in) |
| Grade B | 69.980 to 69.990 mm (2.7572 to 2.7576 in) |
| Grade C | 70.000 to 70.010 mm (2.7580 to 2.7584 in) |
| Oversize | 0.4 mm (0.016 in) |
| Weight difference between pistons | 5.0g (0.18 oz) |
| Piston clearance in cylinder bore | 0.030 to 0.050 mm (0.0012 to 0.0020 in) |
| Piston ring groove width: | |
| Top | 1.530 to 1.550 mm (0.0603 to 0.0611 in) |
| Second | 1.515 to 1.535 mm (0.0597 to 0.0605 in) |
| Bottom | 3.010 to 3.030 mm (0.1186 to 0.1194 in) |
| Piston ring thickness: | |
| Top | 1.478 to 1.490 mm (0.0582 to 0.0587 in) |
| Second | 1.478 to 1.490 mm (0.0582 to 0.0587 in) |
| Bottom | 2.975 to 2.990 mm (0.1172 to 0.1178 in) |
| Oversize available | 0.4 mm (0.016 in) |
| Piston ring groove clearance: | |
| Top | 0.040 to 0.072 mm (0.0016 to 0.0028 in) |
| Second | 0.025 to 0.057 mm (0.0010 to 0.0023 in) |
| Bottom | 0.020 to 0.055 mm (0.0008 to 0.0022 in) |
| Piston ring end gap: | |
| Top | 0.24 to 0.45 mm (0.0099 to 0.0177 in) |
| Second | 0.25 to 0.45 mm (0.0099 to 0.0177 in) |
| Bottom | 0.20 to 0.45 mm (0.0080 to 0.0177 in) |
| Gudgeon pin diameter | 19.970 to 19.974 mm (0.7862 to 0.7863 in) |
| Gudgeon pin clearance in piston | 0.008 to 0.016 mm (0.0003 to 0.0006 in) |

## Crankshaft

| | |
|---|---|
| Journal diameter | 43.990 to 44.000 mm (1.7332 to 1.7336 in) |
| Crankpin diameter | 37.988 to 38.008 mm (1.4967 to 1.4975 in) |
| Undersizes | 0.254, 0.508 mm (0.010, 0.020 in) |
| Main bearing shell thickness | 1.834 to 1.840 mm (0.0723 to 0.0725 in) |
| Big-end bearing shell thickness | 1.542 to 1.548 mm (0.0608 to 0.0610 in) |
| Thrust washer thickness | 2.310 to 2.360 mm (0.0910 to 0.0930 in) |
| Crankshaft endfloat | 0.055 to 0.265 mm (0.0022 to 0.0104 in) |

## Camshaft and cam followers

| | |
|---|---|
| Number of bearings | 3 |
| Diameter of camshaft bearing journals: | |
| 1 (timing belt end) | 24.000 to 24.015 mm (0.9456 to 0.9462 in) |
| 2 | 23.500 to 23.515 mm (0.9259 to 0.9265 in) |
| 3 | 24.000 to 24.015 mm (0.9456 to 0.9462 in) |
| Diameter of bearings in cylinder head: | |
| 1 (timing belt end) | 24.045 to 24.070 mm (0.9474 to 0.9484 in) |
| 2 | 23.545 to 23.570 mm (0.9277 to 0.9287 in) |
| 3 | 24.025 to 24.070 mm (0.9466 to 0.9484 in) |
| Camshaft bearing running clearance | 0.030 to 0.070 mm (0.0012 to 0.0028 in) |
| Cam lift: | |
| 999 cc | 7.1 mm (0.2797 in) |
| 1108 cc | 8.0 mm (0.3149 in) |
| Diameter of cam followers | 34.975 to 34.995 mm (1.3769 to 1.3788 in) |
| Diameter of cam follower housing in cylinder head | 35.000 to 35.025 mm (1.379 to 1.380 in) |
| Valve clearance shim thickness | 3.20 to 4.70 mm in increments of 0.05 mm (0.1261 to 0.1852 in increments of 0.0020 in) |

## Cylinder head and valves

| | |
|---|---|
| Head material | Light alloy |
| Maximum permissible distortion of gasket surface | 0.1 mm (0.0039 in) |
| Valve guide bore in head | 12.950 to 12.977 mm (0.5102 to 0.5113 in) |
| Valve guide outside diameter | 13.010 to 13.030 mm (0.5126 to 0.5134 in) |
| Valve guide oversizes | 0.05, 0.10, 0.25 mm (0.0020, 0.0039, 0.0099 in) |
| Inside diameter of valve guide (reamed) | 7.022 to 7.040 mm (0.2767 to 0.2774 in) |
| Valve guide fit in cylinder head (interference) | 0.033 to 0.080 mm (0.0012 to 0.0031 in) |
| Valve stem diameter: | |
| 999 cc | 6.970 to 7.000 mm (0.2746 to 0.2758 in) |
| 1108 cc | 6.982 to 7.000 mm (0.2748 to 0.2758 in) |
| Maximum clearance (valve stem-to-guide) | 0.022 to 0.052 mm (0.0009 to 0.0020 in) |
| Valve face angle | 45°25' to 45°35' |

## Cylinder head and valves (continued)

Valve seat angle ........................................................................... 44°55′ to 45°05′
Valve head diameter:
    Inlet .......................................................................................... 30.20 to 30.50 mm (1.1899 to 0.2017 in)
    Exhaust ..................................................................................... 27.20 to 27.50 mm (1.0717 to 1.0835 in)
Contact band (valve to seat) ........................................................ 2.0 mm (0.0788 in)
Valve clearance:
    Inlet .......................................................................................... 0.25 to 0.35 mm (0.0099 to 0.0138 in)
    Exhaust ..................................................................................... 0.35 to 0.45 mm (0.0138 to 0.0177 in)
Valve timing clearance:
    999 cc ....................................................................................... 1.0 mm (0.0394 in)
    1108 cc ..................................................................................... 0.70 mm (0.0275 in)

Valve timing:

|  | 999 cc | 1108 cc |
|---|---|---|
| Inlet valve: |  |  |
|   Opens | 1°BTDC | 2° BTDC |
|   Closes | 19° ABDC | 42°ABDC |
| Exhaust valve: |  |  |
|   Opens | 29° BBDC | 42° BBDC |
|   Closes | 9° ATDC | 2° ATDC |

## Lubrication system

Oil pump type ................................................................................ Gear driven from front of crankshaft
Tooth tip-to-body clearance ......................................................... 0.080 to 0.186 mm (0.0032 to 0.0073 in)
Gear endfloat ................................................................................ 0.025 to 0.056 mm (0.0010 to 0.0022 in)
Oil pressure at normal operating temperature and average road/engine
speed ............................................................................................ 3.4 to 4.9 bars (49 to 71 lbf/in$^2$)
Oil capacity (with filter change) ................................................... 3.8 litres (6.7 pints)
Oil filter ........................................................................................ Champion F107

## Torque wrench settings

| | Nm | lbf ft |
|---|---|---|
| Cylinder head bolts: | | |
|   Stage 1 | 30 | 22 |
|   Stage 2 | Turn through 90° | Turn through 90° |
|   Stage 3 | Turn through 90° | Turn through 90° |
| Main bearing cap bolts: | | |
|   Stage 1 | 39 | 29 |
|   Stage 2 | Turn through 90° | Turn through 90° |
| Manifold nuts | 27 | 20 |
| Big-end cap bolts | 41 | 30 |
| Flywheel bolts | 43 | 32 |
| Oil pump mounting bolts | 10 | 7 |
| Crankshaft rear oil seal retainer bolts | 10 | 7 |
| Camshaft bearing cap bolts: | | |
|   M8 | 19 | 14 |
|   M6 | 10 | 7 |
| Timing belt tensioner nut | 27 | 20 |
| Camshaft sprocket bolt | 68 | 50 |
| Camshaft cover screws | 8 | 6 |
| Crankshaft sprocket bolt | 79 | 58 |
| Crankshaft pulley bolts | 25 | 18 |
| Sump pan fixing screws | 10 | 7 |
| Oil pump backplate screws | 7 | 5 |
| Oil pressure switch | 31 | 23 |
| Coolant temperature switch | 25 | 18 |
| Engine mounting nuts: | | |
|   M10 | 57 | 42 |
|   M8 | 25 | 18 |
| Engine mounting to engine and transmission | 60 | 44 |
| Engine mounting bracket body | 25 | 18 |

## Engine – 1116 cc, 1299/1301 cc non-Turbo (1985-on)

### General – 1116 cc from mid 1988*

Compression ratio ........................................................................ 9.0:1
Maximum torque (DIN) .................................................................. 63 lbf ft (86 Nm) at 3000 rev/min
*95 RON unleaded fuel engine*

### Crankshaft

Journal diameter ........................................................................... 50.790 to 50.810 mm (1.9996 to 2.0004 in)
Crankpin diameter ........................................................................ 45.503 to 45.525 mm (1.7915 to 1.7923 in)

### Camshaft

Cam lift:
    1116 cc ..................................................................................... 8.8 mm (0.346 in)
    1299 and 1301 cc ..................................................................... 8.0 mm (0.315 in)

## Valve timing

| | 1116 cc | 1299 and 1301 cc |
|---|---|---|
| Inlet valve: | | |
| Opens | 7° BTDC | 9° BTDC |
| Closes | 35° ABDC | 31° ABDC |
| Exhaust valve: | | |
| Opens | 37° BBDC | 39° BBDC |
| Closes | 5° ATDC | 1° ATDC |

## *Engine – 1299/1301 cc Turbo ie*
*All Specifications as for 1301 cc engine in Chapter 1 except for the following*

## General
| | |
|---|---|
| Bore | 80.5 mm (3.17 in) |
| Stroke: | |
| 1299 cc | 63.8 mm (2.51 in) |
| 1301 cc | 63.9 mm (2.52 in) |
| Displacement | 1299 or 1301 cc (79.24 or 79.36 cu in) |
| Compression ratio: | |
| Up to mid 1988 | 8.1:1 |
| From mid 1988 (1301 cc) | 7.7:1 (95 RON unleaded fuel engine) |
| Maximum power (DIN) | 105 bhp (77 kW) at 5750 rev/min |
| Maximum torque (DIN) | 109 lbf ft (147 Nm) at 3200 rev/min |

## Cylinder block and crankcase
| | |
|---|---|
| Bore diameter | 80.500 to 80.550 mm (3.1693 to 3.1713 in) |

## Pistons and piston rings
| | |
|---|---|
| Piston diameter: | |
| Grade A | 80.450 to 80.460 mm (3.1673 to 3.1677 in) |
| Grade C | 80.470 to 80.480 mm (3.1681 to 3.1685 in) |
| Grade E | 80.490 to 80.500 mm (3.1689 to 3.1693 in) |
| Oversize | 0.4 mm ((0.0157 in) |
| Weight difference between pistons | 2.5 g (0.0875 oz) max |
| Piston clearance in cylinder bore | 0.040 to 0.060 mm (0.0016 to 0.0024 in) |
| Piston ring groove width: | |
| Top | 1.535 to 1.555 mm (0.0604 to 0.0612 in) |
| Second | 2.010 to 2.030 mm (0.0791 to 0.0799 in) |
| Bottom | 3.967 to 3.987 mm (0.1562 to 0.1570 in) |
| Piston ring thickness: | |
| Top | 1,478 to 1.490 mm (0.0582 to 0.0587 in) |
| Second | 1.978 to 1.990 mm (0.0779 to 0.0783 in) |
| Bottom | 3.922 to 3.937 mm (0.1544 to 0.1550 in) |
| Oversize | 0.4 mm (0.0157 in) |
| Piston ring groove clearance: | |
| Top | 0.045 to 0.077 mm (0.0018 to 0.0030 in) |
| Second | 0.020 to 0.072 mm (0.0008 to 0.0028 in) |
| Bottom | 0.030 to 0.085 mm (0.0012 to 0.0033 in) |
| Piston ring end gap: | |
| Top | 0.30 to 0.50 mm (0.0118 to 0.0197 in) |
| Second | 0.30 to 0.50 mm (0.0118 to 0.0197 in) |
| Bottom | 0.25 to 0.50 mm (0.0098 to 0.0197 in) |

## Crankshaft
| | |
|---|---|
| Journal diameter: | |
| Grade 1 | 50.785 to 50.795 mm (1.9994 to 1.9998 in) |
| Grade 2 | 50.775 to 50.785 mm (1.9990 to 1.9994 in) |
| Standard main bearing shell thickness: | |
| Grade 1 | 1.833 to 1.842 mm (0.0722 to 0.0725 in) |
| Grade 2 | 1.838 to 1.847 mm (0.0724 to 0.0727 in) |
| Undersizes | 0.254, 0.508 mm (0.0100, 0.0200 in) |
| Crankshaft endfloat | 0.055 to 0.265 mm (0.0022 to 0.0104 in) |
| Crankpin diameter: | |
| Grade A | 45.508 to 45.518 mm (1.7916 to 1.7920 in) |
| Grade B | 45.498 to 45.508 mm (1.7913 to 1.7916 in) |
| Standard big-end shell thickness: | |
| Grade A | 1.534 to 1.543 in (0.0604 to 0.0607 in) |
| Grade B | 1.539 to 1.548 mm (0.0606 to 0.0609 in) |
| Undersizes | 0.254, 0.508 mm (0.0100, 0.0200 in) |
| Crankshaft thrustwashers: | |
| Standard thickness | 2.310 to 2.360 mm (0.0909 to 0.0929 in) |
| Oversize | 2.437 to 2.487 mm (0.0959 to 0.0979 in) |

## Camshaft
| | |
|---|---|
| Cam lift | 8.0 mm (0.315 in) |

## Cylinder head and valves

| | |
|---|---|
| Inlet valve head diameter | 43.300 to 43.700 mm (1.7047 to 1.7205 in) |
| Valve clearance: | |
| Inlet | 0.35 to 0.45 mm (0.014 to 0.018 in) |
| Exhaust | 0.45 to 0.55 mm (0.018 to 0.022 in) |
| Valve timing: | |
| Inlet valve: | |
| Opens | 0° (TDC) |
| Closes | 40° ABDC |
| Exhaust valve: | |
| Opens | 30° BBDC |
| Closes | 10° ATDC |

## Torque wrench settings

| | Nm | lbf ft |
|---|---|---|
| Engine mounting bracket-to-transmission nut | 85 | 63 |
| Flexible mountings to brackets | 23 | 17 |
| Centre flexible mounting-to-engine bracket bolt | 85 | 63 |
| Centre flexible mounting to transmission bracket | 23 | 17 |
| Engine mounting bracket-to-body bolt | 48 | 35 |
| Mounting bracket to final drive casing | 95 | 70 |
| Centre flexible mounting to final drive casing bracket | 23 | 17 |
| Cylinder head bolts (ten): | | |
| Stage 1 | 20 | 15 |
| Stage 2 | 40 | 30 |
| Stage 3 | Turn through 90° | Turn through 90° |
| Stage 4 | Turn through 90° | Turn through 90° |
| Cylinder head bolts (four bolts adjacent to spark plug holes) | 30 | 22 |

## *Engine – 1372 cc ie and 1372 cc Turbo ie*

### General

| | |
|---|---|
| Bore | 80.5 mm (3.17 in) |
| Stroke | 67.4 mm (2.66 in) |
| Displacement | 1372 cc (83.7 cu in) |
| Compression ratio: | |
| 1372 cc ie | 9.2:1 |
| 1372 cc Turbo ie | 7.8:1 |
| Maximum power (DIN): | |
| 1372 cc ie | 72 bhp (54 kW) at 6000 rev/min |
| 1372cc Turbo ie | 116 bhp (87 kW) at 6000 rev/min |
| Maximum torque (DIN): | |
| 1372 cc ie | 78 lbf ft (106 Nm) at 3250 rev/min |
| 1372 cc Turbo ie | 119 lbf ft (161 Nm) at 3500 rev/min |

### Cylinder block and crankcase

| | |
|---|---|
| Material | Cast iron |
| Bore diameter | 80.500 to 80.550 mm (3.169 to 3.171 in) |
| Maximum allowable cylinder bore taper | 0.015 mm (0.00059 in) |
| Maximum allowable cylinder bore ovality | 0.015 mm (0.00059 in) |

### Pistons and piston rings

| | |
|---|---|
| Piston diameter – 1372 cc ie | |
| Grade A | 80.460 to 80.470 mm (3.1677 to 3.1681 in) |
| Grade C | 80.480 to 80.490 mm (3.1684 to 3.1688 in) |
| Grade E | 80.500 to 80.510 mm (3.1692 to 3.1696 in) |
| Piston diameter – 1372 cc Turbo ie: | |
| Grade A | 80.450 to 80.460 mm (3.1673 to 3.1677 in) |
| Grade C | 80.470 to 80.480 mm (3.1681 to 3.1684 in) |
| Grade E | 80.490 to 80.500 mm (3.1688 to 3.1692 in) |
| Oversize | 0.4 mm (0.015 in) |
| Weight difference between pistons | ± 2.5g (± 0.08 oz) |
| Piston clearance in cylinder bore: | |
| 1372 cc ie | 0.030 to 0.050 mm (0.0012 to 0.0020 in) |
| 1372 cc Turbo ie | 0.030 to 0.060 mm (0.0012 to 0.0023 in) |
| Piston ring groove width: | |
| Top | 1.535 to 1.555 mm (0.0604 to 0.0612 in) |
| Second – 1372 ie | 1.780 to 1.800 mm (0.0700 to 0.0708 in) |
| Second – 1372 Turbo ie | 2.010 to 2.030 mm (0.0791 to 0.0799 in) |
| Bottom | 1.780 to 1.800 mm (0.0700 to 0.0786 in) |
| Piston ring thickness: | |
| Top | 1.478 to 1.490 mm (0.0581 to 0.0586 in) |
| Second – 1372 cc ie | 1.728 to 1.740 mm (0.0680 to 0.0685 in) |
| Second – 1372 cc Turbo ie | 1.978 to 1.990 mm (0.0778 to 0.0783 in) |
| Bottom | 2.975 to 2.990 mm (0.1171 to 0.1177 in) |

## Pistons and piston rings (continued)

Piston ring-to-groove clearance:

| | |
|---|---|
| Top .................................................................................................. | 0.045 to 0.077 mm (0.0017 to 0.0030 in) |
| Second – 1372 cc ie ...................................................................... | 0.040 to 0.072 mm (0.0015 to 0.0028 in) |
| Second – 1372 cc Turbo ie............................................................ | 0.020 to 0.052 mm (0.0007 to 0.0020 in) |
| Bottom ............................................................................................. | 0.030 to 0.065 mm (0.0011 to 0.0025 in) |

Piston ring end gap:

| | |
|---|---|
| Top and second .............................................................................. | 0.30 to 0.45 mm (0.0118 to 0.0177 in) |
| Bottom ............................................................................................. | 0.20 to 0.50 mm (0.0078 to 0.0196 in) |

Gudgeon pin diameter:

| | |
|---|---|
| Grade 1 ............................................................................................ | 21.991 to 21.994 mm (0.8657 to 0.8659 in) |
| Grade 2 ............................................................................................ | 21.994 to 21.998 mm (0.8659 to 0.8660 in) |

## Crankshaft

Main journal diameter:

| | |
|---|---|
| Grade 1 ............................................................................................ | 50.790 to 50.800 mm (1.9996 to 1.9999 in) |
| Grade 2 ............................................................................................ | 50.780 to 50.790 mm (1.9992 to 1.9996 in) |

Crankpin diameter:

| | |
|---|---|
| Grade A ........................................................................................... | 45.513 to 45.523 mm (1.7918 to 1.7922 in) |
| Grade B ........................................................................................... | 45.503 to 45.513 mm (1.7916 to 1.7918 in) |
| Undersizes ............................................................................................... | 0.025 to 0.063 mm (0.0010 to 0.0024 in) |

Main bearing shell thickness:

| | |
|---|---|
| Grade A ........................................................................................... | 1.840 to 1.844 mm (0.0724 to 0.0726 in) |
| Grade B ........................................................................................... | 1.845 to 1.849 mm (0.0726 to 0.0728 in) |

Big-end bearing shell thickness:

| | |
|---|---|
| Grade A ........................................................................................... | 1.535 to 1.541 mm (0.0604 to 0.0606 in) |
| Grade B ........................................................................................... | 1.540 to 1.546 mm (0.0606 to 0.0608 in) |
| Thrustwasher thickness.......................................................................... | 2.310 to 2.360 mm (0.0910 to 0.0930 in) |
| Crankshaft endfloat................................................................................ | 0.055 to 0.265 mm (0.0022 to 0.0104 in) |

## Camshaft cam bearings and followers

| | |
|---|---|
| Number of bearings ............................................................................... | 5 |

Diameter of camshaft journals:

| | |
|---|---|
| No 1................................................................................................. | 29.444 to 29.960 mm (1.1592 to 1.1795 in) |
| No 2................................................................................................. | 47.935 to 47.950 mm (1.8872 to 1.8877 in) |
| No 3................................................................................................. | 48.135 to 48.150 mm (1.8950 to 1.8956 in) |
| No 4................................................................................................. | 48.335 to 48.350 mm (1.9029 to 1.9035 in) |
| No 5................................................................................................. | 48.535 to 48.550 mm (1.9108 to 1.9114 in) |

Diameter of bearings in cylinder head:

| | |
|---|---|
| No 1 – 1372 cc ie ........................................................................... | 29.900 to 30.014 mm (1.1771 to 1.1816 in) |
| No 1 – 1372 cc Turbo ie................................................................. | 29.969 to 30.014 mm (1.1798 to 1.1816 in) |
| No 2................................................................................................. | 47.980 to 48.005 mm (1.8889 to 1.8899 in) |
| No 3................................................................................................. | 48.180 to 48.205 mm (1.8968 to 1.8978 in) |
| No 4................................................................................................. | 48.380 to 48.405 mm (1.9047 to 1.9057 in) |
| No 5................................................................................................. | 48.580 to 48.605 mm (1.9125 to 1.9135 in) |
| Camshaft bearing running clearance ................................................... | 0.030 to 0.070 mm (0.0012 to 0.0028 in) |

Cam lift-inlet valves:

| | |
|---|---|
| 1372 cc ie ...................................................................................... | 8.8 mm (0.3464 in) |
| 1372 cc Turbo ie ........................................................................... | 9.5 mm (0.3740 in) |
| Cam lift – exhaust valves .................................................................... | 8.8 mm (0.3464 in) |
| Diameter of cam followers .................................................................. | 36.975 to 36.995 mm (1.4557 to 1.4564 in) |
| Diameter of cam follower housing's bearings in cylinder head ................ | 37.000 to 37.025 mm (1.4566 to 1.4576 in) |

Valve clearance shim thicknesses available (in increments
of 0.05 mm/0.002 in):

| | |
|---|---|
| 1372 cc ie ...................................................................................... | 3.25 to 4.70 mm (0.1279 to 0.1850 in) |
| 1372 cc Turbo ie ........................................................................... | 3.25 to 4.90 mm (0.1279 to 0.1929 in) |

## Cylinder head and valves

| | |
|---|---|
| Head material.......................................................................................... | Light alloy |
| Maximum allowable distortion of gasket face ...................................... | 0.1 mm (0.0039 in) |
| Valve guide bore diameter .................................................................... | 13.950 to 13.977 mm (0.5492 to 0.5502 in) |

Valve guide outside diameter:

| | |
|---|---|
| Inlet ................................................................................................ | 14.040 to 14.058 mm (0.5527 to 0.5534 in) |
| Exhaust – 1372 cc ie ..................................................................... | 14.040 to 14.058 mm (0.5527 to 0.5534 in) |
| Exhaust – 1372 cc Turbo ie............................................................ | 13.998 to 14.016 mm (0.5511 to 0.5518 in) |
| Valve guide oversizes ............................................................................ | 0.05, 0.10, 0.25 mm (0.0020, 0.0039, 0.0099 in) |
| Valve face angle .................................................................................... | 45°25′ to 45° 35′ |
| Valve seat angle .................................................................................... | 45° ± 5′ |

Valve head diameter:

Inlet valves:

| | |
|---|---|
| 1372 cc ie .............................................................................. | 37.35 to 37.65 mm (1.4704 to 1.4822 in) |
| 1372 cc Turbo ie.................................................................... | 35.85 to 36.15 mm (1.4114 to 1.4232 in) |

Exhaust valves:

| | |
|---|---|
| 1372 cc ie .............................................................................. | 30.85 to 31.15 mm (1.2145 to 1.2263 in) |
| 1372 cc Turbo ie.................................................................... | 32.85 to 33.45 mm (1.2933 to 1.3169 in) |

## Cylinder head and valves (continued)

Valve stem diameter:

| | |
|---|---|
| Inlet valves | 7.974 to 7.992 mm (0.3139 to 0.3146 in) |
| Exhaust valves: | |
|   1372 cc ie | 7.974 to 7.992 mm (0.3139 to 0.3146 in) |
|   1372 cc Turbo ie | 7.954 to 7.972 mm (0.3131 to 0.3138 in) |
| Valve stem-to-guide clearance | 0.030 to 0.066 mm (0.0011 to 0.0025 in) |
| Valve to seat contact face width | 2.0 mm (0.0788 in) |

Valve clearance:

| | |
|---|---|
| Inlet | 0.35 to 0.45 mm (0.0137 to 0.0177 in) |
| Exhaust | 0.45 to 0.55 mm (0.0177 to 0.0216 in) |
| Valve timing check clearance | 0.80 mm (0.031 in) |

Valve timing:

| | |
|---|---|
| Inlet valve – 1372 cc ie: | |
|   Opens | 7° BTDC |
|   Closes | 35° ABDC |
| Inlet valve – 1372 cc Turbo ie: | |
|   Opens | 14° BTDC |
|   Closes | 44° ABDC |
| Exhaust valve – 1372 cc ie: | |
|   Opens | 37° BBDC |
|   Closes | 5° ATDC |
| Exhaust valve – 1372 cc Turbo ie: | |
|   Opens | 36° BBDC |
|   Closes | 6° ATDC |

## Auxiliary shaft

Bearing journal diameters:

| | |
|---|---|
| Wide journal | 35.593 to 35.618 mm (1.4012 to 1.4022 in) |
| Narrow journal | 31.940 to 31.960 mm (1.2574 to 1.2582 in) |
| Shaft journal-to-bush running clearance: | |
|   Wide journal | 0.046 to 0.091 mm (0.0018 to 0.0035 in) |
|   Narrow journal | 0.040 to 0.080 mm (0.0015 to 0.0031 in) |

## Lubrication system

| | |
|---|---|
| Pump type | Pump operated from front of crankshaft. Oil pressure relief valve in front cover |
| Gear-to-body clearance | 0.110 to 0.180 mm (0.0043 to 0.0070 in) |
| Gear top face-to-cover clearance (endfloat) | 0.040 to 0.106 mm (0.0015 to 0.0041 in) |
| Drive to driven gear clearance | 0.30 mm (0.0118 in) |
| Oil pressure (at oil temperature of 100°C/212°F) | 3.4 to 4.9 bars (49 to 71 lbf/in²) |
| Oil capacity (with filter change) | 4.1 litres (7.2 pints) |
| Oil filter | Champion C106 |

## Torque wrench settings

| | Nm | lbf ft |
|---|---|---|
| Cylinder head bolts – M10: | | |
|   Stage 1 | 40 | 30 |
|   Stage 2 | Turn through 90° | Turn through 90° |
|   Stage 3 | Turn through 90° | Turn through 90° |
| Cylinder head bolts – M8 | 30 | 22 |
| Camshaft housing to lower cylinder head securing bolt | 20 | 15 |
| Connecting rod/big-end bearing cap nuts: | | |
|   1372 cc ie (M9) | 51 | 38 |
|   1372 cc Turbo ie (M8) | 51 | 38 |
| Main bearing cap bolts | 80 | 59 |
| Flywheel bolts | 83 | 62 |
| Camshaft sprocket bolt | 83 | 62 |
| Ignition distributor cover (in crankcase) bolt* | 25 | 18 |
| Auxiliary shaft sprocket bolt | 83 | 62 |
| Oil pump-to-crankcase bolt* | 25 | 18 |
| Water pump-to-crankcase bolt* | 25 | 18 |
| Sump-to-crankcase nut/bolt | 10 | 7 |
| Oil pressure switch | 32 | 24 |
| Oil temperature sender unit* | 50 | 37 |
| Oil pressure sender unit* | 37 | 28 |
| Crankshaft pulley nut | 197 | 145 |
| Oil pump shaft driven gear bolt (1372 cc ie only) | 83 | 61 |
| Turbine-to-exhaust manifold and head nut | 29 | 21 |
| Camshaft housing to inlet manifold bracket bolt | 25 | 18 |

*Turbo ie only

## Cooling system – 999 and 1108 cc
### General
Thermostat:
Begins to open .................................................................. 85 to 90°C (185 to 194°F)
Fully open .......................................................................... 100°C (212°F)
Coolant capacity...................................................................... 4.6 litres (8.1 pints)

### Torque wrench setting
| | Nm | lbf ft |
|---|---|---|
| Coolant pump mounting bolts | 8 | 6 |

## Cooling system – 1301 cc Turbo ie
### General
Radiator fan cut-in temperature:
1st speed ........................................................................... 86 to 90°C (187 to 194°F)
2nd speed .......................................................................... 90 to 94°C (194 to 201°F)
Radiator fan switch-off temperature:
1st speed ........................................................................... 81 to 85°C (178 to 185°F)
2nd speed .......................................................................... 85 to 89°C (185 to 192°F)
Thermostat opens .................................................................... 78 to 82°C (172 to 180°F)
Thermostat fully open ............................................................. 95°C (203°F)
Coolant capacity...................................................................... 6.9 litres (12.1 pints)

## Cooling system – 1372 cc
### General
Expansion tank pressure cap rating ..................................... 0.98 bar (14.2 lbf/in$^2$)
Thermostat opens .................................................................... 80 to 84°C (176 to 183°F)
Thermostat fully open ............................................................. 96°C (204°F)
Radiator fan switch:
Cut-in temperature ......................................................... 90 to 94°C (194 to 201°F)
Switch-off temperature.................................................. 85 to 89°C (185 to 192°F)
Coolant capacity:
1372 cc ie (without catalyst)........................................ 6.2 litres (10.9 pints)
1372 cc ie (with catalyst)............................................. 6.5 litres (11.4 pints)
1372 cc Turbo ie ............................................................ 7.7 litres (13.6 pints)
Coolant pump/alternator drivebelt tension ........................ Approximately 10 mm (0.4 in) deflection midway between crank-shaft and alternator pulleys under firm thumb pressure

### Torque wrench settings
| | Nm | lbf ft |
|---|---|---|
| Water pump to crankcase | 25 | 18 |
| Water pump cover | 15 | 11 |
| Coolant temperature sender unit | 27 | 20 |
| Fan thermostatic switch | 30 | 22 |
| Coolant temperature gauge sender unit – 1372 cc ie | 30 | 22 |
| Thermal valve (on inlet manifold): | | |
| M10 | 20 | 15 |
| M8 | 10 | 7 |

## Fuel system – general
### Air cleaner element
999 cc (45) and 1108 cc (60) FIRE ...................................... Champion U520
1372 cc ie (70 and 1.4)............................................................ Champion U533
1301/1372 cc Turbo ie ............................................................ Champion U522

### Fuel filter
999 cc (45) and 1108 cc (60) FIRE ...................................... Champion L101
1372 cc ie (70 and 1.4)............................................................ Champion L201
1301/1372 cc Turbo ie ............................................................ Champion L203

## Fuel system – carburettor calibration
### Weber 32 ICEV 61/250
Application .............................................................................. 903 cc
Venturi ..................................................................................... 22 mm
Auxiliary venturi..................................................................... 3.5 mm
Main jet ................................................................................... 1.10 mm
Air bleed jet ............................................................................ 1.80 mm
Emulsion tube......................................................................... F74
Idle jet ..................................................................................... 0.47 mm
Air idle jet ............................................................................... 1.60 mm
Pump jet .................................................................................. 0.40 mm
Pump outlet............................................................................. 0.40 mm
Full power jet .......................................................................... 0.50 mm
Needle valve ........................................................................... 1.50 mm
Idle mixture adjustment port................................................. 1.50 mm

## Weber 32 ICEV 61/250 (continued)

Float level (with gasket)........................................................ 10.75 mm
Accelerator pump capacity (for 10 strokes) ........................... 3.8 to 6.3 cc
Idle speed ............................................................................. 750 to 800 rev/min
Exhaust gas CO at idle ......................................................... 1.0 to 2.0%

## Weber 32 TLF 4/250

Application ............................................................................ 999 cc
Venturi diameter .................................................................. 22.0 mm
Main jet................................................................................ 105
Emulsion tube ...................................................................... F70
Air compensating jet ........................................................... 165
Idle jet.................................................................................. 47
Idle air bleed ....................................................................... 50/90
Accelerator pump jet ........................................................... 35
Pump discharge jet............................................................... 40
Needle valve......................................................................... 1.5 mm
Full power jet........................................................................ 50
Power feed jet....................................................................... 40
Float level ............................................................................ 26.75 to 27.25 mm
Fast idle (throttle valve plate gap)........................................ 0.65 to 0.75 mm
Anti-flooding device (choke valve plate gap)........................ 4.0 to 5.0 mm
Idle speed............................................................................. 750 to 800 rev/min
Exhaust gas CO at idle ......................................................... 1.0 to 2.0%

## Weber 32 TLF 4/252 (and 251)

Application ............................................................................ 999 cc
Venturi ................................................................................. 22 mm
Auxiliary venturi................................................................... 4.5 mm
Main jet................................................................................ 1.05 mm
Air bleed jet ......................................................................... 1.65 mm
Emulsion tube ...................................................................... F70
Idle jet.................................................................................. 0.47 mm
Air idle jet ............................................................................ 0.50 mm
Pump jet ............................................................................... 0.40 mm
Pump outlet.......................................................................... 0.40 mm
Full power jet........................................................................ 0.50 mm
Superfeed jet........................................................................ 0.40 mm
Superfeed mixture jet .......................................................... 3.00 mm
Needle valve......................................................................... 1.50 mm
Idle mixture adjustment port ............................................... 1.50 mm
Float level (with gasket)........................................................ 26.75 to 27.25 mm
Float travel .......................................................................... 33.7 to 34.7 mm
Accelerator pump capacity (for 10 strokes) ......................... 8 to 12 cc
Fast idle ............................................................................... 0.65 to 0.75 mm
Idle speed............................................................................. 750 to 800 rev/min
Exhaust gas CO at idle ......................................................... 1.0 to 2.0%

## Weber 32 TLF 27/251

Application ............................................................................ 1108 cc
Venturi ................................................................................. 22 mm
Auxiliary venturi................................................................... 4.5 mm
Main jet................................................................................ 1.05 mm
Air bleed jet ......................................................................... 1.65 mm
Emulsion tube ...................................................................... F70
Idle jet.................................................................................. 0.45 mm
Air idle jet ............................................................................ 0.50 mm
Pump jet ............................................................................... 0.40 mm
Pump outlet.......................................................................... 0.40 mm
Full power jet........................................................................ 0.55 mm
Superfeed jet........................................................................ 0.45 mm
Superfeed mixture jet .......................................................... 3.00 mm
Needle valve......................................................................... 1.50 mm
Idle mixture adjustment port ............................................... 1.50 mm
Float level (with gasket)........................................................ 26.75 to 27.25 mm
Float travel .......................................................................... 33.7 to 34.7 mm
Accelerator pump capacity (for 10 strokes) ......................... 8 to 10 cc
Idle speed............................................................................. 800 to 850 rev/min
Exhaust gas CO at idle ......................................................... 0.5 to 1.5%

## Weber 30/32 DMTE 30/150

Application ............................................................................ 1116 cc engine (95 RON unleaded engine)
Pull down capsule bush......................................................... 0.20 mm
Idle pull-down ...................................................................... 3.0 to 3.5 mm

## Weber 30/32 DMTE 30/150 (continued)

| | | |
|---|---|---|
| Needle valve | 1.50 mm | |
| Float level (with gasket fitted) | 6.5 to 7.5 mm | |
| Idle speed | 800 to 900 rev/min | |
| Exhaust gas CO at idle | 1.0 to 2.0% | |
| | **Primary** | **Secondary** |
| Main venturi | 19 | 23 |
| Secondary venturi | 4.5 | – |
| Main jet | 0.90 | 1.05 |
| Air correction jet | 2.10 | 1.80 |
| Emulsion tube | F30 | F30 |
| Idle jet | 0.47 | 0.40 |
| Idle air jet | 1.15 | 0.70 |
| Idle jet | 1.50 | – |
| Pump jet | 0.45 | – |
| Pump discharge | 0.40 | – |
| Full power jet | 0.40 | – |

## Weber 30/32 DMTE 10/150

| | | |
|---|---|---|
| Application | 1116 cc | |
| Float setting (fuel level) | 6.5 to 7.5 mm | |
| Excess fuel discharge orifice | 0.40 | |
| Needle valve | 1.5 mm | |
| Accelerator pump capacity (ten strokes) | 8.5 to 12.5 cc | |
| Throttle valve plate opening – fast idle (A) | 0.90 to 0.95 mm | |
| Primary valve plate opening (X) | 6.45 to 6.95 mm | |
| Primary and secondary valve plate openings: | | |
|     X | 13.5 to 14.5 mm | |
|     Y | 14.5 to 15.5 mm | |
| Anti-flooding device (mechanical – X) | 8.0 to 9.5 mm | |
| Anti-flooding device (automatic – Y) | 3.75 to 4.25 mm | |
| Idle speed | 800 to 900 rev/min | |
| Exhaust gas CO at idle | 0.5 to 1.5% | |
| | **Primary** | **Secondary** |
| Venturi diameter | 19.0 mm | 23.0 mm |
| Auxiliary venturi | 3.5 | 5 |
| Main jet | 90 | 95 |
| Air correction jet | 195 | 195 |
| Emulsion tube | F42 | F38 |
| Idle jet | 47 | 70 |
| Accelerator pump jet | 40 | 40 |

## Solex C 30/32 – CIC8

Application ................ 1116 cc

*All calibration as for the Weber 30/32 DMTE 10/150 except for the following:*

| | **Primary** | **Secondary** |
|---|---|---|
| Main jet | 100 | 100 |
| Air correction jet | 230 | 190 |
| Idle jet | 47.5 | 40 |
| Accelerator pump jet | 50 | 50 |
| Needle valve | 1.6 | 1.6 |

## Weber 30/32 DMTE 12/150

Application ................ 1299/1301 cc

*All calibration as for the Weber 30/32 DMTE 10/150 except for the following:*

| | **Primary** | **Secondary** |
|---|---|---|
| Main jet | 0.90 | 0.97 |
| Air correction jet | 2.20 | 1.75 |
| Idle jet | 45 | 70 |
| Accelerator pump jet | 45 | 45 |

## Torque wrench settings – 999 and 1108cc

| | **Nm** | **lbf ft** |
|---|---|---|
| Fuel pump mounting bolts | 8 | 6 |
| Exhaust pipe flange-to-manifold nuts | 18 | 13 |
| Exhaust bracket nuts and bolts | 23 | 17 |
| Inlet and exhaust manifold to cylinder head nuts | 27 | 20 |

## Torque wrench setting – all models

| | **Nm** | **lbf ft** |
|---|---|---|
| Rear exhaust pipe/silencer mounting bracket nut | 24 | 18 |

## *Fuel system – fuel injection (1301 cc Turbo ie)*
### General
| | |
|---|---|
| System type.................................................... | Bosch LE2-Jetronic fuel injection with turbocharger |
| Fuel pump..................................................... | Electric |
| Fuel pressure................................................ | 1.6 bars (23.2 lbf/in$^2$) |
| Fuel tank capacity......................................... | 50.0 litres (11.0 gallons) |
| Fuel octane rating ........................................ | 98 RON minimum (unleaded or leaded) |
| Idle speed..................................................... | 800 to 900 rev/min |
| Exhaust gas CO at idle ................................. | 0.5 to 1.5% |

### Torque wrench settings
| | Nm | lbf ft |
|---|---|---|
| Fuel pressure regulator nut ......................................... | 48 | 35 |
| Inlet manifold to cylinder head..................................... | 25 | 18 |
| Exhaust manifold to cylinder head............................... | 25 | 18 |
| Exhaust manifold to crankcase bracket......................... | 25 | 18 |
| Turbocharger-to-exhaust manifold-and-cylinder head nut ...................... | 28 | 21 |
| Coolant pipe union nut to turbocharger ...................... | 38 | 28 |
| Coolant pipe bolt to turbocharger................................ | 25 | 18 |

## *Fuel system – fuel injection (1372 cc ie and 1372 cc Turbo ie)*
### General
| | |
|---|---|
| System type: | |
|     1372 cc ie.............................................. | Bosch Mono-Jetronic (SPi) fuel injection. Catalyst on some models |
|     1372 cc Turbo ie ................................... | Bosch L3.1-Jetronic (MPi) fuel injection with turbocharger |
| Fuel pump..................................................... | Electric |
| Fuel pressure: | |
|     1372 cc ie without catalyst ................... | 0.8 to 1.2 bars (11.6 to 17.4 lbf/in$^2$) |
|     1372 cc ie with catalyst........................ | 1.0 to 1.2 bars (14.5 to 17.4 lbf/in$^2$) |
|     1372 cc Turbo ie ................................. | 6.0 bars (87 lbf/in$^2$) maximum |
| Fuel tank capacity: | |
|     1372 cc ie.......................................... | 42 litres (9.2 gallons) |
|     1372 cc Turbo ie ................................. | 50 litres (11 gallons) |
| Fuel octane rating: | |
|     1372 cc ie (without catalyst) ................ | 95 RON minimum (unleaded or leaded) |
|     1372 cc ie (with catalyst) .................... | 95 RON minimum (unleaded only) |
|     1372 cc Turbo ie ................................. | 95 RON minimum (unleaded or leaded) |
| Idle speed: | |
|     1372 cc ie.......................................... | 800 to 900 rev/min |
|     1372 cc Turbo ie ................................. | 800 to 850 rev/min |
| Exhaust gas CO at idle – 1372 cc Turbo ie...................... | 1.2 to 1.8% |

### Torque wrench settings
| | Nm | lbf ft |
|---|---|---|
| Inlet manifold to cylinder head..................................... | 25 | 18 |
| Exhaust manifold to cylinder head............................... | 25 | 18 |
| Exhaust rear pipe/silencer bracket nut ........................ | 24 | 17 |
| Exhaust manifold flange nut ......................................... | 18 | 13 |
| Turbo to exhaust manifold and cylinder head (1372 cc Turbo ie) ............. | 29 | 21 |

## *Ignition system – 'Breakerless' (999, 1108, 1116, 1299/1301 cc)*
### General
| | |
|---|---|
| System type..................................................... | Magnetic impulse generator electronic |
| Spark plug type............................................... | Champion RC9YCC or RC9YC |
| Spark plug electrode gap ................................ | 0.8 mm (0.031 in) |
| HT lead type (999 and 1108 cc)...................... | Champion LS-20 |

### Ignition timing (in relation to distributor type)
| | |
|---|---|
| At idle with vacuum hose disconnected and plugged: | |
|     Marelli SE101A and Ducellier 525473A..................... | 2° BTDC |
|     Marelli SE100EX, SE100CX and SE100NX ................. | 10° BTDC |
|     Marelli SE101G ...................................................... | 3° BTDC |
|     Marelli SE100SX ..................................................... | Not available |
| Centrifugal advance (maximum): | |
|     Marelli SE101A and Ducellier 525473A..................... | 26 to 30° BTDC |
|     Marelli SE100EX and SE100CX ................................ | 22 to 26° BTDC |
|     Marelli SE100NX ..................................................... | 18 to 22° BTDC |
|     Marelli SE101G ...................................................... | 23 to 27° BTDC |
|     Marelli SE100SX ..................................................... | 20 to 24° BTDC |
| Vacuum advance (maximum): | |
|     Marelli SE101A, Ducellier 525473A and Marelli SE101G...................... | 12 to 14° BTDC |
|     Marelli SE100NX ..................................................... | 14 to 16° BTDC |
|     Marelli SE100EX and SE100CX ................................ | 10 to 14° BTDC |
|     Marelli SE100SX ..................................................... | 13 to 17° BTDC |

## Component testing values

Magnetic impulse generator resistance:
    Models with Marelli distributors ............................................................ 758 to 872 ohms
    Models with the Ducellier distributor.................................................... 171 to 209 ohms
Ignition coil resistance at 20°C (68°F):
    Models with BA506A coil:
        Primary.......................................................................................... 0.756 to 0.924 ohms
        Secondary ..................................................................................... 3330 to 4070 ohms
    Models with BA506D coil:
        Primary.......................................................................................... 0.666 to 0.814 ohms
        Secondary ..................................................................................... 2970 to 3630 ohms

## Ignition system – Digiplex 2 (1372 cc ie)

### General

System type......................................................................................................... Marelli Digiplex 2 electronic
Spark plug type .................................................................................................. Champion RN9YCC or RN9YC
Spark plug electrode gap .................................................................................. 0.8 mm (0.031 in)

### Ignition timing

At 800 to 850 rpm............................................................................................... 2 to 6° BTDC
Maximum advance (at 4500 to 6200 rpm with 0.6 bar/8.7 lbf/in$^2$
vacuum)............................................................................................................... 44 to 48° BTDC

### Component testing values

Ignition coil:
    Primary resistance at 23°C (73°F) ................................................ 0.405 to 0.495 ohms
    Secondary resistance at 23°C (73°F)........................................... 4320 to 5280 ohms
Engine speed/TDC sensor:
    Resistance....................................................................................... 680 to 920 ohms
    Sensor-to-flywheel tooth gap ....................................................... 0.2 to 0.8 mm (0.008 to 0.031 in)

## Ignition system – Microplex (1301 cc Turbo ie)

### General

System type......................................................................................................... Marelli Microplex electronic
Spark plug type .................................................................................................. Champion RC7YCC or RC7YC
Spark plug electrode gap .................................................................................. 0.8 mm (0.031 in)
Rotor arm resistance......................................................................................... 800 to 1200 ohms

### Ignition timing

At idle with vacuum hose detached:
    Up to mid 1988 ............................................................................... 8 to 12° BTDC
    From mid 1988 ............................................................................... 8.5 to 11.5° BTDC
Maximum advance:
    Up to mid 1988 ............................................................................... 36 to 40° BTDC
    From mid 1988............................................................................... 32.5 to 35.5 BTDC

### Component testing values

Ignition coil:
    Primary winding resistance at 20°C (68°F)................................. 0.31 to 0.37 ohms
    Secondary winding resistance at 20°C (68°F)............................ 3330 to 4070 ohms
Engine speed sensor:
    Resistance....................................................................................... 612 to 748 ohms
    Sensor-to-flywheel tooth gap ....................................................... 0.25 to 1.3 mm (0.010 to 0.051 in)
TDC sensor:
    Resistance....................................................................................... 612 to 748 ohms
    Sensor-to-crankshaft pulley tooth gap ........................................ 0.4 to 1.0 mm (0.016 to 0.039 in)

## Ignition system – Microplex (1372 cc Turbo ie)

### General

System type......................................................................................................... Marelli Microplex electronic ignition
Spark plug type .................................................................................................. Champion RC7BYC4
Spark plug electrode gap .................................................................................. 0.9 mm (0.035 in)

### Ignition timing

At idle.................................................................................................................. 8° to 12° BTDC
Maximum advance (at 4000 to 6000 rpm with 0.377 bars/5.5 lbf/in$^2$
vacuum)............................................................................................................... 32° to 36° BTDC

### Component testing values

Ignition coil:
    Primary resistance at 20°C (68°F) ............................................... 0.40 to 0.49 ohms
    Secondary resistance at 20°C (68°F)........................................... 4320 to 5280 ohms

## Component testing values (continued)
Engine speed sensor:
    Resistance .................................................................................. 612 to 748 ohms
Sensor to flywheel teeth clearance ................................................ 0.25 to 1.3 mm (0.010 to 0.051 in)
TDC sensor:
    Resistance .................................................................................. 612 to 748 ohms
    Sensor to crankshaft pulley tooth gap ........................................ 0.4 to 1.0 mm (0.016 to 0.039 in)

## *Clutch*
### Pedal height
All later models ............................................................................... 136 to 146 mm (5.4 to 5.7 in)

### Driven plate diameter
903, 999 and 1301 cc ..................................................................... 170 mm (6.7 in)
1108 cc ........................................................................................... 180 mm (7.0 in)
1372 cc ie ....................................................................................... 181.5 mm (7.1 in)
1372 cc Turbo ie ............................................................................. 200 mm (7.8 in)

## *Transmission*
### General
Type number:
    903, 999, 1108 and 1372 cc ie ................................................. C.501.5.10
    1372 cc, Turbo ie ....................................................................... C.510.5.17

### Gear ratios – 903, 999, 1108 and 1372 cc ie
1st .................................................................................................. 3.909:1
2nd ................................................................................................. 2.055:1
3rd ................................................................................................. 1.344:1
4th ................................................................................................. 0.978:1
5th (999 and 1108 cc) .................................................................... 0.780:1
5th (903 and 1372 cc ie) ................................................................ 0.836:1
Reverse .......................................................................................... 3.727:1

### Gear ratios – 1372 cc Turbo ie
1st .................................................................................................. 3.909:1
2nd ................................................................................................. 2.267:1
3rd ................................................................................................. 1.440:1
4th ................................................................................................. 1.029:1
5th .................................................................................................. 0.875:1
Reverse .......................................................................................... 3.909:1

### Gear ratios – 1301 cc Turbo ie (without Antiskid)
1st .................................................................................................. 4.091:1
2nd ................................................................................................. 2.235:1
3rd ................................................................................................. 1.469:1
4th ................................................................................................. 1.043:1
5th .................................................................................................. 0.863:1
Reverse .......................................................................................... 3.714:1

### Gear ratios – 1301 cc Turbo ie (with Antiskid)
1st .................................................................................................. 3.909:1
2nd ................................................................................................. 2.267:1
3rd ................................................................................................. 1.440:1
4th ................................................................................................. 1.029:1
5th .................................................................................................. 0.875:1
Reverse .......................................................................................... 3.909:1

### Final drive ratios
903 cc ............................................................................................ 4.071:1
999 and 1108 cc ............................................................................. 3.733:1
1301 cc Turbo ie (without Antiskid) ............................................... 3.588:1
1301 cc Turbo ie (with Antiskid) .................................................... 3.562:1
1372 cc Turbo ie ............................................................................. 3.353:1

### Oil capacity
1301 cc Turbo ie ............................................................................. 2.9 litres (5.1 pints)
1372 cc Turbo ie ............................................................................. 2.0 litres (3.5 pints)
All other models ............................................................................. 2.4 litres (4.2 pints)

### Oil type/specification – 1372 cc Turbo ie ................... Fiat ZC 80/S gear oil (Duckhams Hypoid 80)

*Driveshafts, hubs, roadwheels and tyres*
**Roadwheels – Turbo ie**................................................................ 5½J x 13

### Tyres – Turbo ie
Size ......................................................................................................... 175/60 HR 13
Pressures:
    Front and rear, normal load.............................................................. 2.2 bars (32 lbf/in²)
    Front, full load.................................................................................. 2.3 bars (33 lbf/in²)
    Rear, full load .................................................................................. 2.5 bars (36 lbf/in²)
Spare wheel tyre size – 1372 cc Turbo ie .......................................... 5.50B x 13 FH
Spare wheel tyre pressure – 1372 cc Turbo ie ................................... 2.2 bars (32 lbf/in²)

### Tyres– 1372 cc ie with catalyst (1.4 ie S)
Size ......................................................................................................... 155/70 SR 13
Pressures:
    Front ................................................................................................ 2.0 bars (29 lbf/in²)
    Rear – normal load .......................................................................... 1.9 bars (28 lbf/in²)
    Rear – full load................................................................................. 2.2 bars (32 lbf/in²)

### Torque wrench settings – Turbo ie

| | Nm | lbf ft |
|---|---|---|
| Driveshaft flange connecting bolts | 43 | 32 |
| Intermediate shaft support to crankcase | 48 | 35 |
| Final drive output shaft bearing cover bolts | 24 | 18 |

*Braking system – 1301 and 1372 cc Turbo ie*
### General
System type........................................................................................... Four-wheel discs, ventilated front, solid rear. Vacuum servo. Pressure regulating valve on rear brakes
Master cylinder bore diameter ............................................................. 22.225 mm (0.88 in)
Vacuum servo diameter........................................................................ 177.8 mm (7.0 in)

### Front disc brakes
Disc diameter........................................................................................ 240.0 mm (9.45 in)
Disc thickness – new ........................................................................... 19.9 to 20.1 mm (0.78 to 0.79 in)
Disc thickness – minimum (refinishing) .............................................. 18.6 mm (0.73 in)
Disc thickness – minimum (wear limit) ............................................... 18.2 mm (0.72 in)
Minimum thickness of pad friction material ........................................ 1.5 mm (0.06 in)
Caliper cylinder diameter...................................................................... 48.0 mm (1.89 in)

### Rear disc brakes
Disc diameter........................................................................................ 227.0 mm (8.94 in)
Disc thickness – new ........................................................................... 10.7 to 10.9 mm (0.42 to 0.43 in)
Disc thickness – minimum (refinishing):
    1301 cc Turbo ie ............................................................................. 9.7 mm (0.38 in)
    1372 cc Turbo ie ............................................................................. 9.35 mm (0.37 in)
Disc thickness – minimum (wear limit) ............................................... 9.0 mm (0.35 in)
Minimum thickness of pad friction material ........................................ 1.5 mm (0.06 in)
Caliper cylinder diameter...................................................................... 34.0 mm (1.33 in)

### Torque wrench settings

| | Nm | lbf ft |
|---|---|---|
| Front caliper cylinder housing mounting bolts | 52 | 38 |
| Front caliper support bracket bolts | 52 | 38 |
| Front disc fixing bolts | 25 | 18 |
| Rear caliper support bracket bolts | 25 | 18 |
| Rear caliper cylinder housing mounting bolts | 52 | 38 |

*Braking system – 903, 999, 1108, 1116 and 1372 cc*
### General
    *The following items differ, or are additional to those specified in Chapter 8:*
Master cylinder bore diameter:
    903 cc, 999 cc, 1108 cc and 1116 cc........................................... 19.05 mm (0.750 in)
    1372 cc ie........................................................................................ 20.65 mm (0.813 in)
Vacuum servo diameter........................................................................ 152.4 mm (6.0 in)
Hydraulic push rod-to-master cylinder support plate clearance ............. 0.825 to 1.025 mm (0.032 to 0.040 in)

*Electrical system*
### Battery
Turbo ie engine models........................................................................ 45 Ah

## Fuses – 903, 999, 1116, 1299/1301 and 1301 cc Turbo ie

| Fuse no | Circuit protected | Rating (A) |
|---|---|---|
| 1 | LH tail, RH front parking, rear number plate, check panel | 7.5 |
| 2 | RH tail, LH front parking, cigar lighter illumination, clock light, heater control illumination, map reading lamp | 7.5 |
| 3 | RH headlamp main beam | 10 |
| 4 | LH headlamp main beam and warning light | 10 |
| 5 | Radiator cooling fan, econometer, horns | 25 |
| 6 | Cigar lighter, courtesy lamps, digital clock, stop-lamp switch, clock, radio | 10 |
| 7 | RH headlamp dipped beam | 10 |
| 8 | LH headlamp dipped beam, rear fog warning lamp and indicator | 10 |
| 9 | Heated rear screen and warning lamp | 20 |
| 10 | Instrument panel, stop-lamps, direction indicators, reversing lamps warning module | 10 |
| 11 | Heater fan, fan control illumination digital clock | 20 |
| 12 | Windscreen wiper, washer pump, rear screen wiper | 20 |
| 13 | Spare | |
| 14 | Hazard warning lamps and indicator | 10 |

Supplementary fuses at side of main fuse block:

| | | |
|---|---|---|
| A | Front foglamps | 20 |
| B | Coolant fan | 30 (Turbo ie) |
| C | Fuel injector cooling fan | 10 (Turbo ie) |
| D | Electric windows | 30 |
| E | Fuel pump | 10 (Turbo ie) |

## Fuses – later 903, 999, 1108, 1372 ie and 1372 cc Turbo ie

| Fuse no | Circuit protected | Rating (A) |
|---|---|---|
| 1 | LH tail, RH front parking, rear number plate, check panel | 7.5 |
| 2 | RH tail, LH front parking, cigar lighter illumination, clock light, heater control illumination, map reading lamp | 7.5 |
| 3 | RH headlamp main beam | 10 |
| 4 | LH headlamp main beam and warning light | 10 |
| 5 | Radiator cooling fan (except Turbo ie), horns | 25 |
| 6 | Cigar lighter, courtesy lamps, digital clock, stop-lamp switch, clock, radio | 10 |
| 7 | RH headlamp dipped beam | 10 |
| 8 | LH headlamp dipped beam | 10 |
| 9 | Rear fog lamp and warning lamp | 10 |
| 10 | Heated rear screen and warning lamp | 20 |
| 11 | Instrument panel, stop-lamps, direction indicators, reversing lamps, warning module and carburettor cut-off valve (FIRE model only) | 10 |
| 12 | Heater fan, heater/ventilation control illumination lights, digital clock light | 20 |
| 13 | Windscreen wiper, windscreen washer and pump, rear wiper/washer (where fitted) | 20 |
| 14 | Horns and relay | 20 |
| 15 | Hazard warning light and indicator light | 10 |

Supplementary fuses at side of main fuse block:

| | | |
|---|---|---|
| A | Electric windows (where applicable) | 30 |
| B | Central locking (where applicable) | 25 |
| C | Injector cooling fan (Turbo ie) | 10 |
| D | Headlamp washers (where applicable) | 20 |
| E | Foglamp and warning lamp | 20 |
| E | Dim-dip | 7.5 |
| F | | |
| G | Fuel pump (fuel injection models) | 10 |
| – | Heated Lambda sensor (where applicable) | 10 |

Supplementary fuses on steering column relay bracket:

| | | |
|---|---|---|
| Antiskid monitor circuit (where fitted) | | 10 |
| Antiskid supply circuit (where fitted) | | 25 |

## Steering and suspension

## General – 1301 cc Turbo ie

| | |
|---|---|
| Castor | 1°55' to 2°35' positive |
| Number of turns of steering wheel, lock-to-lock | 3.42 |
| Steering angles of roadwheels: | |
|   Inner wheel | 36°43' |
|   Outer wheel | 31°27' |

### Steering angles – later models
Camber ..................................................................................... –30' ± 30'
Castor ...................................................................................... 2°10' ± 15'
Toe-in ...................................................................................... 0 to 2.0 mm (0 to 0.8 in)

### Steering angles of roadwheels – 1372 cc Turbo ie
Inner wheel .............................................................................. 36°43'
Outer wheel ............................................................................. 31°27'

### Torque wrench settings – 1301 and 1372 cc Turbo ie

| | Nm | lbf ft |
|---|---|---|
| Anti-roll bar clamp bolts | 25 | 18 |
| Anti-roll bar end fixing nuts | 15 | 11 |

## *General dimensions, weights and capacities – later models*
### Dimensions
Overall length ......................................................................... 3689 mm (145.2 in)
Overall width:
    Base and Super models ...................................................... 1558 mm (61.3 in)
    SX and Turbo models ......................................................... 1562 mm (61.4 in)
Height (unladen):
    1372 cc (except Turbo) ...................................................... 1425 mm (56.10 in)
    1299/1301 cc (except Turbo) ............................................ 1420 mm (55.90 in)
    Turbo ................................................................................. 1405 mm (55.31 in)
    All other models ................................................................ 1415 mm (55.70 in)

### Weights (kerb)
**Note:** *3-door model weights are given. Add 15 kg (33 lb) to the following for 5-door models. Weight will also vary according to the model version.*
903cc ....................................................................................... 740 kg (1632 lb)
999 cc (45, 45 S and 45 SX) .................................................. 740 to 775 kg (1632 to 1709 lb)
1108 cc (60 S and 60 SX) ...................................................... 760 to 795 kg (1676 to 1753 lb)
1299/1301 cc (70 SX) ............................................................ 770 kg (1698 lb)
1301 cc Turbo ie ..................................................................... 845 kg (1863 lb)
1372 cc (1.4 ie S catalyst) ..................................................... 830 kg (1830 lb)
1372 cc ie (70 SX) ................................................................. 795 to 845 kg (1753 to 1863 lb)
1732 cc Turbo ie ..................................................................... 925 kg (2039 lb)

### Capacities
Fuel tank:
    1372 cc Turbo ie ............................................................... 50 litres (11 gallons)
    All other models ................................................................ 42 litres (9.2 gallons)
Engine oil (with filter change):
    903, 999 and 1108 cc ....................................................... 3.8 litres (6.7 pints)
    1116, 1299/1301 and 1372 cc ........................................... 4.1 litres (7.2 pints)
Transmission:
    1301 cc Turbo ie ............................................................... 2.9 litres (5.1 pints)
    1372 cc Turbo ie ............................................................... 2.0 litres (3.5 pints)
    All other engines ............................................................... 2.4 litres (4.2 pints)
Cooling system:
    903, 999 and 1108 cc ....................................................... 4.6 litres (8.1 pints)
    1116 and 1299/1301 cc, non-catalyst 1372 cc ie ............. 6.2 litres (10.9 pints)
    1372 cc ie with catalyst .................................................... 6.5 litres (11.4 pints)
    1301 cc Turbo ie ............................................................... 6.9 litres (12.1 pints)
    1372 cc Turbo ie ............................................................... 7.7 litres (13.6 pints)

### 3  Routine maintenance – all models from June 1991

The maintenance intervals for all models produced from June 1991 have been extended as shown below. The home mechanic, may however, prefer to continue following the original intervals given in *Routine maintenance* at the beginning of this Manual. Older and high-mileage vehicles, and those used under adverse conditions, should also receive attention more frequently.

#### *Every 250 miles (400 km), weekly or before a long journey*
Proceed as described for the earlier models at the start of this manual

#### *Every 6000 miles (10 000 km) or 12 months (whichever comes first)*
Renew the engine oil and oil filter (Turbo models only)

#### *Every 9000 miles (15 000 km) or twelve months (whichever comes first)*
Renew the engine oil and oil filter (non-Turbo models)
Renew the spark plugs and check the HT leads and connections (Turbo and models running on leaded fuel)
Check the condition of all coolant, fuel and hydraulic hoses and connections
Check the engine idle speed and CO emissions
Check the front brake disc pads for excessive wear. Where a pad wear warning light is fitted, check its operation
Check the tyre pressures and the condition of the tyres (including the spare)
Check the underbody condition

#### *Every 18 000 miles (30 000 km)*
Check/adjust the valve clearances
Check the condition and adjustment of drivebelts
Renew the air cleaner element

Renew the secondary fuel filter in the engine compartment (where applicable)

Renew the spark plugs and check the HT leads and connections (all non-Turbo models running on unleaded fuel)

Check the clutch adjustment (cable operated models)

Check the rear brake disc pads for excessive wear (where applicable)

### Every 28 000 miles (45 000 km)

Check the transmission oil level

### Every 37 000 miles (60 000 km)

Check the condition of the rear brake shoe linings

Check the condition of the timing belt

### Every 2 years

Renew the engine coolant

Renew the brake fluid

### Every 65 000 miles (105 000 km)

Renew the timing belt

### Every 74 500 miles (120 000 km)

Renew the manual transmission oil

---

## 4  Engine – 903 and 1299/1301 cc

### Sump pan sealing strips (903 cc engine) – modification

1    The design of the sealing strips which go between the sump pan and the main bearing caps has been changed. Make sure that the narrower side of the strip fits into the channel in the sump pan.

### 1299 cc engine – description

2    In April 1984, a 1299 cc engine was introduced, progressively replacing the 1301 cc units used previously. The new engine is identical to the 1031 cc engine described in Chapter 1, with the exception of having a slightly shorter stroke.

3    However, as of approximately September 1987, the 1299 cc unit was phased out, being progressively replaced by the 1301 cc engine used initially.

4    As mentioned above, the two engines are all but identical, so identification of the unit fitted should not be necessary in practice. Consult a FIAT dealer if in doubt.

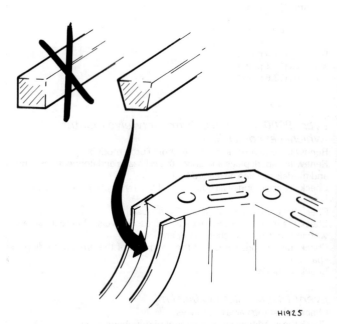

**Fig. 13.1 Correct method of fitting sump pan sealing strip (Sec 4)**

---

## 5   Engine – 999 and 1108 cc (FIRE)

## PART A: GENERAL

### Description

1    Both of these engine types are designated FIRE (Fully Integrated Robotised Engine), being largely manufactured and assembled by computer-controlled mechanical robots.

2    The engine is of oversquare design, having four cylinders and a belt-driven overhead camshaft.

3    The high torque of this engine enables higher gear ratios to be used with the result that fuel economy is exceptionally good.

4    The cylinder head is of light alloy, while the cylinder block is cast-iron.

5    The camshaft is supported in three bearings which have detachable caps.

6    Valve clearances are maintained by shims located in the cam followers (tappets).

7    The cylinder head is of crossflow type having the intake manifold (coolant-heated) and exhaust manifold on opposite sides.

8    The pistons have two compression rings and one oil control ring and are connected to the connecting rods by means of a gudgeon pin which is an interference fit in the rod small-end.

9    The crankshaft is supported in five main bearings. The upper section of the centre bearing shell retains semi-circular thrustwashers to control crankshaft endfloat.

10    The oil pump, which is of gear type, is mounted on the front end of the crankshaft and driven by it.

11    The flexible toothed timing belt drives the camshaft and the coolant pump from a sprocket on the front end of the crankshaft. The belt is tensioned by an eccentrically-mounted pulley.

12    The distributor and the fuel pump are driven from the flywheel end of the camshaft.

## PART B:
## OPERATIONS POSSIBLE WITH ENGINE IN CAR

### Valve clearances – adjustment

1    The operations are similar to those described in Chapter 1, Section 26, but note that the special tools referred to have different part numbers for the FIRE engine – 1860443000 and 1887001000 (photos).

2    Remember that the clearance for inlet and exhaust valves differs – see Specifications at the beginning of this Supplement.

3    Counting from the timing cover end of the engine, the valve sequence is as follows.

Inlet      2-4-5-7
Exhaust    1-3-6-8

5B.1A Checking a valve clearance

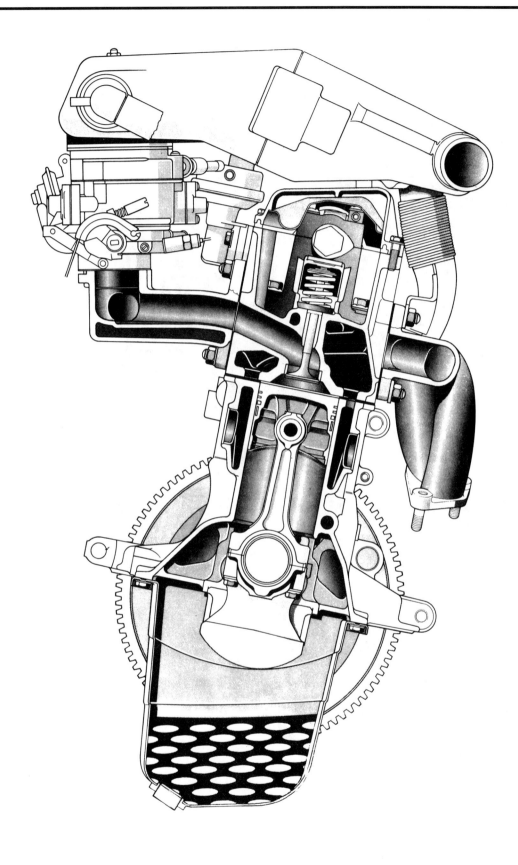

Fig. 13.2 Cross-section view of the 999 and 1108 cc engine (Sec 5A)

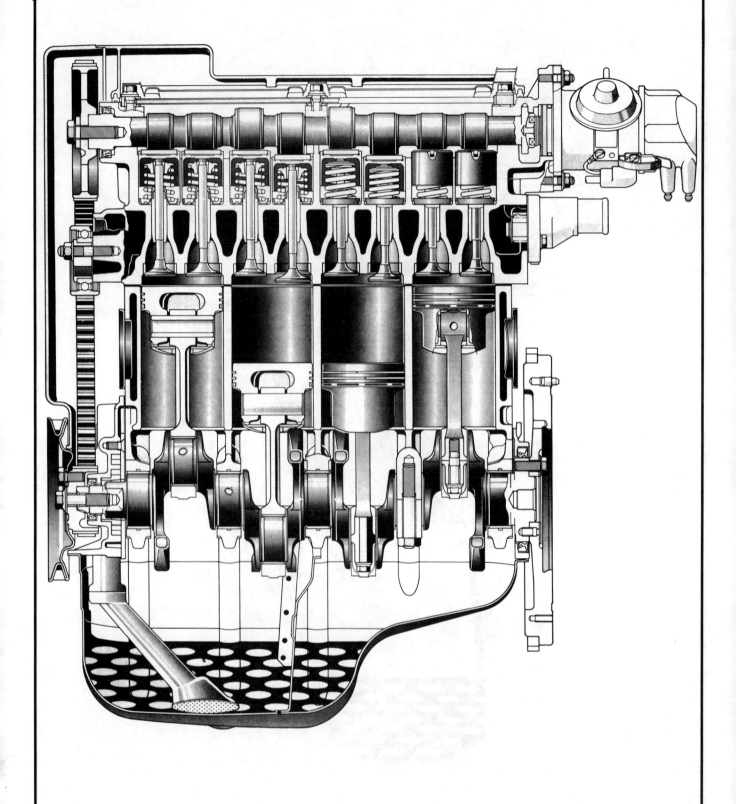

**Fig. 13.3 Longitudinal sectional view of the 999 and 1108 cc engine (Sec 5A)**

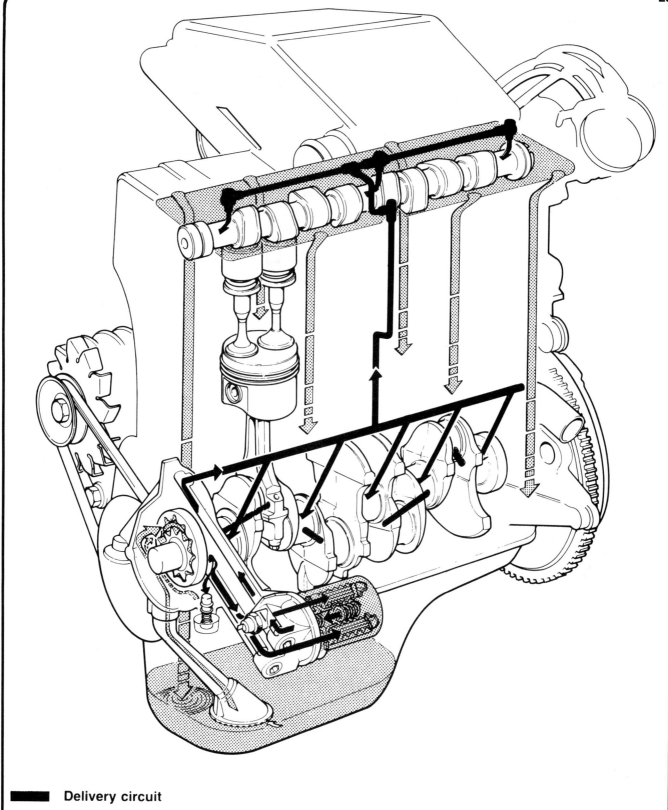

**Delivery circuit**

**Return circuit**

Fig. 13.4    999 and 1108 cc engine lubrication system (Sec 5A)

5B.1B Using a modified C-spanner and screwdriver to remove a shim

5B.6 Timing cover lower fixing bolt removal

## Timing belt – renewal

4   Remove the air cleaner.

5   Slacken and remove the alternator drivebelt, then remove the spark plugs.

6   Unbolt and remove the timing belt cover. Note the bolt located at the bottom of the cover, this can be easily overlooked (photo).

7   Unbolt and remove the crankshaft pulley (photo).

8   Turn the crankshaft sprocket bolt, or engage top gear and raise and turn a front roadwheel, until the camshaft sprocket TDC timing mark is aligned with the mark on the cylinder head and the crankshaft sprocket timing mark is aligned with the mark on the oil pump cover (photos).

9   Release the nut on the timing belt tensioner, move the pulley away from the belt and retighten the nut to hold the pulley in the retracted position (photo).

10   Slide the drivebelt from the sprockets.

11   When refitting the new belt, make sure that the sprocket timing marks are still in alignment and fit the belt so that the arrows on the belt point in the direction of engine rotation, and the lines of the belt coincide with the sprocket marks.

12   Engage the timing belt with the crankshaft sprocket first, then place it around the coolant pump sprocket and the camshaft sprocket (photo). Finally slip the belt around the tensioner pulley.

13   Release the tensioner nut and push the pulley against the belt until the belt is quite taut. Check that the sprocket timing marks have not moved out of alignment. If they have, reset them by moving them over the belt teeth.

14   Still applying force to the pulley, tighten its nut.

15   Turn the crankshaft through two complete turns in the normal direction of rotation and check that when the centre of the longest run of the belt is gripped between finger and thumb it can just be twisted through 90°. If increased tension is required to achieve this, release the tensioner nut and prise the pulley against the timing belt. **Note:** *The*

5B.7 Unscrewing the crankshaft pulley bolts

5B.8A Camshaft sprocket timing mark and cylinder head timing mark in alignment

5B.8B Crankshaft sprocket timing mark and oil pump cover alignment mark (arrowed)

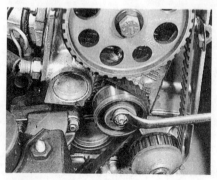

5B.9 Releasing the timing belt tensioner nut

5B.12 Fitting the timing belt

5B.20A Camshaft cover HT lead clip

5B.20B Removing the camshaft cover

5B.22A Unscrewing the camshaft sprocket bolt

5B.22B Camshaft sprocket bolt and washer

5B.22C Camshaft sprocket showing integral key (arrowed)

5B.23A Prising out the camshaft oil feed pipe stub

5B.23B Unscrewing the camshaft bearing/banjo union bolt

5B.23C Camshaft lubrication pipe

5B.23D Camshaft bearing cap showing short and long positioning dowels for correct fitting

*above procedure serves only as a rough guide to setting the belt tension – having it checked by a FIAT dealer at the earliest opportunity is recommended.*

16    Refit the timing belt cover, the crankshaft pulley, alternator drivebelt, spark plugs and the air cleaner.

## Camshaft – removal and refitting

17    Remove the air cleaner and the fuel pump as described in Section 9 of this Supplement.
18    Remove the distributor (Section 10).
19    Remove the timing belt cover.
20    Unbolt and remove the camshaft cover, having first disconnected the HT lead clip (photos).
21    Turn the crankshaft (by engaging top gear and raising and turning a front roadwheel) until No 4 piston is at TDC. The timing mark on the camshaft sprocket will be in alignment with the mark on the cylinder head.
22    Pass a rod through one of the holes in the camshaft sprocket to prevent it rotating and then unscrew the sprocket fixing bolt. Slip the sprocket from the camshaft and out of the loop of the belt (photos).
23    Mark the camshaft bearing caps as to position and then unbolt and remove the lubrication pipe (prise the oil feed stub out with a screw-

driver), unscrew the remaining bolts and take off the bearing caps (photos).
24    Lift the camshaft carefully from the cylinder head, checking that the valve clearance shims and cam followers are not withdrawn by the adhesion of the oil (photo).
25    If the shims and cam followers are to be removed, keep them in their originally fitted order (photos).
26    Refitting is a reversal of removal but use a new camshaft oil seal and camshaft cover gasket. Oil the camshaft bearings (photos).
27    Make sure that the timing belt is reconnected and tensioned as described previously.
28    Check the valve clearances.
29    Tighten all nuts and bolts to the specified torque.

## Cylinder head – removal and refitting

**Note:** *The cylinder head should be removed cold.*

30    Drain the cooling system.
31    Remove the air cleaner.
32    Disconnect the throttle and choke connections from the carburettor (photo).
33    Disconnect the fuel hoses from the fuel pump and the carburettor.

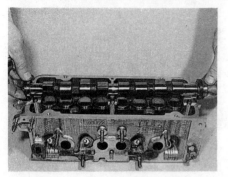
5B.24 Removing the camshaft

5B.25A Valve clearance shim showing thickness mark

5B.25B Removing a cam follower (tappet) with shim

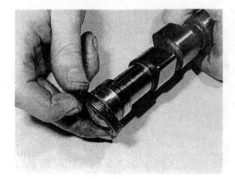
5B.26A Camshaft oil seal

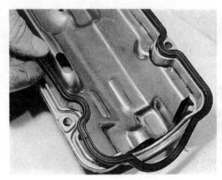
5B.26B Camshaft cover gasket

5B.32 Disconnecting the throttle cable

34   Disconnect the coolant and vacuum hoses from the cylinder head and inlet manifold (photo).
35   Disconnect the electrical lead from the coolant temperature switch, the LT leads from the distributor and the idle cut-off solenoid lead.
36   Remove the distributor cap, disconnect the plug leads and place the cap and leads to one side of the engine compartment.
37   Unbolt and remove the timing belt cover.
38   Set No 4 piston to TDC and then release the timing belt tensioner and slip the belt from the camshaft and coolant pump sprockets.
39   Unbolt and remove the inlet manifold, complete with carburettor.
40   Unbolt the exhaust manifold from the cylinder head and tie it to one side of the engine compartment; the downpipe bracket will have to be disconnected.

41   Unscrew the cylinder head bolts, a half turn at a time in the reverse order to that shown in Fig. 1.30 of Chapter 1. When the bolts are free, remove them with their washers.
42   Lift the cylinder head from the block. If it is stuck tight, insert pieces of wood into the exhaust or inlet ports and use them as levers to 'rock' the head off the block. On no account drive levers into the gasket joint or attempt to tap the head sideways as it is located on positioning dowels.
43   Remove and discard the cylinder head gasket and both manifold gaskets.
44   The cylinder head can be dismantled after removing the camshaft and cam followers as described in the preceding sub-Section.
45   Further dismantling and decarbonising are described in Chapter 1, Section 39. Note that single valve springs are used.
46   If the valves have been ground in, the valve clearances will require adjusting, as described previously. This should be done before the cylinder head is refitted to the engine.
47   Before refitting the assembled cylinder head, make sure that the head and block mating surfaces are perfectly clean, and that the block bolt holes have been cleared of any oil.
48   The camshaft sprocket timing mark must be aligned with the one on the cylinder head.
49   The new gasket should not be removed from its nylon cover until required for use. Fit the gasket dry to perfectly clean surfaces.
50   Place the gasket on the cylinder block so that the word ALTO can be read from above (photos).
51   Lower the cylinder head onto the block so that it locates on the positioning dowels (photo).
52   The cylinder head bolts must have clean threads, dipped in engine oil and allowed to drain for thirty minutes. Screw the bolts in finger-tight and then tighten them in the sequence shown in Fig. 1.30 of Chapter 1, and in the stages specified (see Specification) (photos).
53   Refit the inlet manifold and carburettor using a new gasket.
54   Reconnect the exhaust manifold using a new gasket. Tighten all nuts to the specified torque. Reconnect the exhaust downpipe bracket.
55   Reconnect the timing belt and tension it as described earlier.
56   Refit the timing belt cover and the distributor cap and camshaft cover.
57   Reconnect all hoses, electrical leads and controls.
58   Fit the air cleaner.
59   Fill and bleed the cooling system.

5B.34 Inlet manifold coolant hose (A) and brake servo vacuum hose (B)

5B.50A Cylinder head gasket

5B.50B Cylinder head gasket top surface marking

5B.51 Fitting the cylinder head

5B.52A Inserting a cylinder head bolt

5B.52B Typical disc for angular tightening of cylinder head bolts

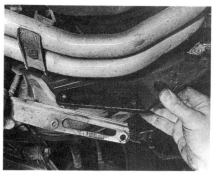

5B.61 Removing the flywheel housing cover plate

5B.62 Removing the sump pan

5B.63A Tightening a sump pan screw

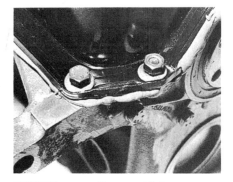

5B.63B Sump pan flange end fixing screw and nut

## Sump pan – removal and refitting

60    Drain the engine oil.
61    Unbolt and remove the cover plate from the lower part of the flywheel housing (photo). The two lower bolts retain the gearchange rod support strut.
62    Unscrew the sump pan securing screws and pull the sump pan downwards to remove it (photo). The joint sealant will require cutting with a sharp knife to release the pan. Clean away all old gasket material.
63    A bead 3.0 mm in diameter of RTV silicone instant gasket should be applied to the sump pan flange and then the pan offered up. Screw in the fixing screws and tighten to the specified torque. Note the flange end fixing screw nuts (photos).
64    Wait one hour before filling with engine oil.
65    Refit the flywheel housing cover plate.

## Oil pump – removal, checking and refitting

66    Drain the engine oil and remove the sump pan as described in the last sub-Section. Unscrew and remove the oil filter cartridge.

67    Remove the timing belt.
68    Lock the crankshaft against rotation either by placing a block of wood between a crankshaft web and the inside of the crankcase or by jamming the flywheel starter ring gear with a suitable tool.
69    Unscrew and remove the crankshaft sprocket bolt and take off the timing belt sprocket. If it is tight, use two screwdrivers to lever it off or use a two- or three-legged puller.
70    Unbolt and remove the oil pick-up/filter screen assembly. Note the sealing washer.
71    Extract the oil pump fixing bolts and withdraw the pump.
72    The oil pump incorporates a pressure relief valve which can be removed for examination by depressing the spring plunger and pulling out the keeper plate (photos).
73    If pump wear is suspected, check the gears in the following way. Extract the fixing screws and remove the rear cover plate. The screws are very tight and will probably require the use of an impact driver to release them (photo).
74    Check the clearance between the outer gear and the pump housing using feeler blades, and also the gear endfloat by placing a straight-

5B.72A Removing the oil pump relief valve keeper plate

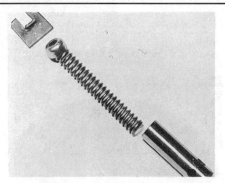

5B.72B Oil pump relief valve components

5B.73 Removing the oil pump rear cover plate screws

5B.74A Checking the oil pump gear-to-housing clearance

5B.74B Checking the oil pump gear endfloat

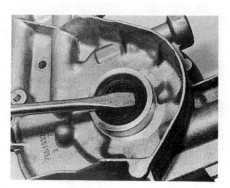

5B.77A Removing the oil pump seal

5B.77B Using a socket to fit the new oil pump oil seal

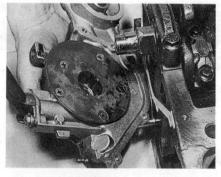

5B.78 Fitting the oil pump

edge across the pump body and checking the gap between the straight-edge and gear face. If the clearances are outside the specified tolerance, renew the oil pump complete (photos).

75   If the pump is unworn, refit the rear cover plate and tighten the screws fully.

76   Apply air pressure from a tyre pump to the oil pump oil ducts to clear any sludge or other material and then prime the pump by pouring clean engine oil into its intake duct at the same time turning the oil pump inner gear with the fingers.

77   Lever out the oil seal and drive a new one squarely into the oil pump casing (photos). Lubricate the oil seal lips.

78   Bolt the pump into position using a new joint gasket. Note one bolt is longer than the others (photo).

79   Bolt on the oil pick-up assembly using a new sealing washer.

80   Fit the crankshaft sprocket and tighten the bolt to specified torque.

81   Fit and tension the timing belt.

82   Fit the sump pan. Screw on a new oil filter cartridge. Wait for the specified period of time (one hour) and then fill the engine with oil.

83   Run the engine for a few minutes, then check and top up the oil level.

*Pistons/connecting rods – removal and refitting*

84   Remove the sump pan.

85   Unbolt and remove the oil pump pick-up/filter screen assembly.

86   The big-end bearing shells can be renewed without having to remove the cylinder head if the caps are unbolted and the piston/connecting rod pushed gently about one inch up the bore (the crankpin being at its lowest point). If these shells are worn, however, the main bearing shells will almost certainly be worn as well, necessitating a complete overhaul, including crankshaft removal.

87   To remove the piston/connecting rods, the cylinder head must be removed.

88   The big-end caps and their connecting rods are numbered 1, 2, 3 and 4 from the timing cover end of the engine. The numbers are located either side of the rod/cap joint on the engine oil dipstick tube side (photo).

89   Turn the crankshaft as necessary to bring the first connecting rod big-end crankpin to its lowest point, then unscrew the cap bolts and remove the cap and shell bearing.

90   Push the connecting rod/piston assembly up the bore and out of the cylinder block. There is one reservation; if a wear ridge has devel-

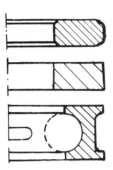

**Fig. 13.5 Piston ring arrangement on the 999 cc engine (Sec 5B)**

oped at the top of the bores, remove this by careful scraping before trying to remove the piston/rod assemblies. The ridge will otherwise prevent removal, or break the piston rings during the attempt.

91    Remove the remaining piston/connecting rods in a similar way. If the bearing shells are to be used again, tape them to their respective caps or rods.

92    Removal of the piston rings and separation of the piston from the connecting rod is covered in the next sub-Section.

93    Fit the bearing shells into the connecting rods and caps, ensuring that the recesses into which the shells seat are clean and dry.

94    Check that the piston ring gaps are evenly spaced at 120° intervals. Liberally oil the rings and the cylinder bores.

95    Fit a piston ring clamp to compress the rings, oiling the rings and the clamp interior surfaces liberally.

96    Insert the first piston/connecting rod into its cylinder bore. Make sure that the assembly is the correct one for its particular bore. The cap and rod matching numbers must be towards the engine oil dipstick guide tube and the arrow on the piston crown towards the timing belt (photo).

97    Push the piston into the bore until the piston ring clamp is against the cylinder block and then tap the crown of the piston lightly to push it out of the ring clamp and into the bore (photo).

98    Oil the crankshaft journal and fit the big-end of the connecting rod to the journal. Check that the bearing shells are still in position, then fit the big-end cap and bolts; check that the cap is the right way round (photo).

99    Tighten the big-end bolts to the specified torque (photo). The

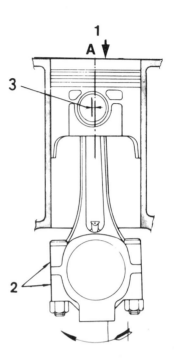

**Fig. 13.6 Piston/connecting rod correctly assembled –
999 and 1108 cc engine (Sec 5B)**

1    Piston grade (A) and directional arrow on piston crown
     (towards timing belt)
2    Rod/cap matching numbers
3    Gudgeon pin offset in piston (0.9 to 1.1 mm)
Arrow indicates crankshaft rotation direction

correct torque is important as the bolts have no locking arrangement. After tightening each big-end, check that the crankshaft rotates smoothly.

100    Repeat the operations on the remaining piston/rod assemblies.
101    Refit the oil pump pick-up assembly using a new sealing ring.
102    Refit the sump pan and the cylinder head as described in earlier sub-Sections.
103    Fill the engine with oil and coolant.

5B.88 Connecting rod and cap numbers

5B.96 Piston directional arrow

5B.97 Fitting a piston/connecting rod

5B.98 Fitting a big-end bearing cap

5B.99 Tightening a big-end cap bolt

5B.107A Left-hand front engine/transmission mounting

5B.107B Left-hand rear engine/transmission mounting

5B.107C Right-hand engine mounting

### Pistons/connecting rods – separation and piston ring renewal

104   If the piston/connecting rods have been removed in order to renew the piston rings, refer to Chapter 1, Section 18, but note that the piston rings should be fitted so that the word TOP is uppermost.

105   If new pistons are to be fitted, it is recommended that the gudgeon pins are removed and refitted by a FIAT dealer as the connecting rods must be carefully heated in order to be able to push the gudgeon pin out of the rod small-end, change the piston and push the pin back into position. Locating the gudgeon pin will require a special tool. The gudgeon pin is a sliding fit in the piston but an interference fit in the connecting rod.

106   Refer to Fig. 13.6 for the correct assembly of the piston and connecting rod.

### Engine/transmission mountings – renewal

107   Refer to Chapter 1, Section 33. Three mountings are used (photos).

## PART C: ENGINE REMOVAL AND DISMANTLING

### Method of removal – general

1   The engine, complete with transmission, should be removed upwards out of the engine compartment.

### Engine/transmission – removal and separation

2   Mark the position of the hinges on the underside of the bonnet and then, with the help of an assistant, unscrew the hinge bolts and lift the bonnet to a safe storage area.

3   Drain the coolant; a cylinder block drain plug is not fitted.

4   Drain the engine and transmission oils.

5   Disconnect the battery, negative lead first.

6   Remove the air filter.

7   Disconnect the radiator hoses from the engine (photos).

8   Disconnect the heater hose from the inlet manifold.

9   Disconnect the fuel inlet and return hoses from the fuel pump (photo).

10   Disconnect the brake servo vacuum hose from the inlet manifold.

5C.7A Radiator hose connection to coolant distribution tube

5C.7B Radiator hose at thermostat housing

5C.9 Fuel hose identification at pump: inlet hose (1), hose to carburettor (2), return hose (3)

5C.12 Choke cable connection at carburettor

5C.15 Ignition coil HT lead connection

5C.16 Coolant temperature switch

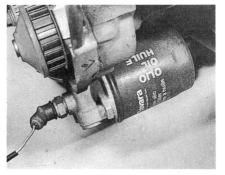

5C.18 Oil pressure switch

5C.19A Radiator retaining clip

5C.19B Radiator fan motor wiring connector

5C.19C Radiator fan cut-out thermostatic switch

5C.19D Removing the radiator/fan assembly

11   Disconnect the throttle cable from the carburettor.

12   Disconnect the choke cable (photo).

13   Disconnect the leads from the alternator.

14   Disconnect the battery earth lead from the transmission casing.

15   Disconnect the leads from the starter motor and the HT lead from the ignition coil (photo).

16   Disconnect the coolant temperature switch lead and the HT leads from the distributor (photo).

17   Disconnect the lead from the carburettor fuel cut-off (anti-diesel) solenoid valve.

18   Disconnect the lead from the oil pressure switch (photo).

19   Although not essential, removal of the radiator is recommended as a precaution against its damage during removal of the power unit. Disconnect the wiring plugs from the fan and thermostatic switches (photos).

20   Disconnect the leads from the reversing lamp switch on the transmission.

21   Disconnect the clutch cable from the release lever on the transmission.

22   Disconnect the speedometer cable from the transmission by unscrewing the knurled ring.

23   Working under the car, disconnect the exhaust downpipes from the manifold and the lower support bracket (photos).

24   Disconnect the gearchange rods from the levers on the transmission. One rod is retained by a spring clip, the other by a snap-on ball socket. Unbolt the gearchange rod support bracket from the cover plate on the flywheel housing (photos).

25   Remove the screws from the driveshaft inboard gaiter retaining plates (photos). Expect slight oil loss.

26   Disconnect the rear left-hand transmission mounting. Do this by unscrewing the two outer bolts **not** the centre one. The engine will incline to the rear once the mounting is released (photo).

27   Raise the front of the car and support it securely so that the front roadwheels hang free.

28   Remove the front roadwheels.

29   Unscrew the tie-rod end balljoint taper pin nuts, and then using a suitable 'splitter' tool, disconnect the balljoints from the eyes of the steering arms.

30   Unscrew the bolts from the clamps at the bottom of the front suspension struts, tilt the hub carriers outwards and partially disconnect the driveshaft inboard joints from the transmission.

31   Support the weight of the engine/transmission on a suitable hoist,

5C.23A Exhaust downpipe flange nuts

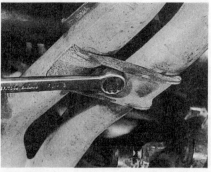

5C.23B Unscrewing the exhaust pipe lower support bracket bolt

5C.24A Gearchange rod connecting pin and spring clip

5C.24B Gearchange rod with ball socket connection

5C.24C Gearchange rod support bracket

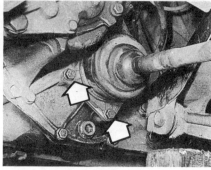

5C.25A Two of the left-hand driveshaft joint gaiter retaining plate screws (arrowed)

5C.25B Driveshaft joint gaiter withdrawn

5C.26 Left-hand rear (lower) transmission mounting disconnected

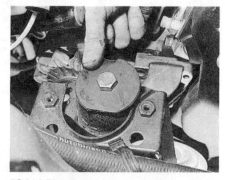

5C.31A Right-hand engine mounting disconnected

5C.31B Left-hand engine mounting and bracket

5C.32 Right-hand engine mounting brackets on body and engine

5C.34 Lifting out the engine and transmission

5C.39 Separating the engine and transmission

and then disconnect the right-hand and left-hand front engine/transmission mountings (photos).

32   Unbolt and remove the engine mounting brackets from the engine and the transmission (photo).

33   Raise the power unit slowly until the driveshafts release from the transmission and can be lowered to rest on the exhaust and bodymember.

34   Continue to raise the engine and the transmission until it can be removed from the engine compartment and placed on the work surface (photo).

35   Clean the exterior of the engine and transmission by steam cleaning or using a water soluble solvent.

36   Unbolt and remove the starter motor.

37   Unscrew the flywheel housing-to-engine flange bolts. Note the location of the engine lifting lug.

38   Unbolt and remove the lower cover plate from the flywheel housing.

39   Pull the transmission from the engine. it is located by two hollow dowels and one stud (photo).

## Dismantling – general

40   Refer to Chapter 1, Section 14.

## Complete dismantling

41   Unbolt and remove the camshaft cover.

42   Unbolt and remove the timing belt cover.

43   Remove the distributor (Section 10).

44   Remove the hot air collector and the exhaust manifold.

45   Release, disconnect and remove the coolant distribution pipe from the rear of the coolant pump.

46   Unscrew and discard the oil filter cartridge.

47   Unbolt the thermostat housing, discard the joint gasket.

48   Remove the fuel pump, together with its insulator block and actuating pushrod.

49   Remove the carburettor.

50   Remove the inlet manifold and discard the joint gasket.

51   Remove the alternator and its drivebelt and withdraw the engine oil dipstick.

52   Unbolt and remove the crankshaft pulley.

53   Unbolt and remove the timing belt tensioner.

54   Remove the timing belt.

55   Unbolt and remove the coolant pump.

56   Remove the cylinder head.

57   Remove and discard the cylinder head gasket.

58   Remove the clutch.

59   Lock the flywheel starter ring gear teeth and remove the crankshaft sprocket bolt and sprocket.

60   Unbolt and remove the sump pan, then the exhaust pipe support bracket (photos).

61   Prevent rotation of the crankshaft by locking the starter ring gear teeth and then unbolt and remove the flywheel. The flywheel can only be fitted in one position as it is located on a dowel.

62   Remove the engine rear plate. Note the small socket-headed screw which holds the timing index plate (photo).

63   Unbolt and remove the oil pump pick-up assembly, followed by the oil pump itself.

64   Turn the engine on its side and remove the piston/connecting rod assemblies.

65   Stand the engine on its cylinder block machined face, and then unbolt and remove the crankshaft rear oil seal retainer. Discard the gasket.

66   Note the markings on the main bearing caps. One line on the cap nearest the timing belt, then two, C for centre cap, then three and four (photo).

5C.60A Removing the sump pan

5C.60B Exhaust pipe support bracket attached to crankcase

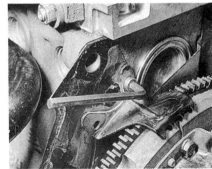

5C.62 Unscrewing socket-head screw from timing index plate

5C.66 Main bearing cap markings

5C.80 Timing belt tensioner

67    The caps will only fit one way round.
68    Unbolt the main bearing caps, removing them with the shell bearings.
69    Lift the crankshaft from the crankcase and remove the bearing half shells from the crankcase. If the shells are to be used again, keep them with their respective bearing caps.
70    The thrustwashers which control crankshaft endfloat are located in the crankcase, and retained by the turned-over edges of the centre main bearing shell.
71    The engine is now fully stripped.

*Examination and renovation*
72    The procedures for the following items are essentially as described in Chapter 1, Section 18.

   *Cylinder block and crankcase*
   *Crankshaft and bearings*
   *Flywheel*
   *Oil seals and gaskets*

**Cylinder head**
73    Using a straight-edge, check the cylinder head gasket surface for

distortion. If it exceeds the specified tolerance, it must be surface-ground by your dealer.
74    Refer to Chapter 1, Section 39, for dismantling and renovation operations. Note that single valve springs are fitted.
**Oil pump**
75    Checking operations are described in sub-Section B.
**Pistons and connecting rods**
76    Refer to sub-Section B.
77    If one or more connecting rods are changed, it is important that its weight is identical to that of the original. Use an accurate balance to weigh them and remove metal if necessary from the new rod in the areas indicated in Fig. 13.7.
**Camshaft and cam followers**
78    If the camshaft journals or bearings show any sign of wear or scoring, then the camshaft, or cylinder head, or both must be renewed.
79    The cam followers should be checked for ovality using a micrometer. Unless unworn they should be renewed.
**Timing belt tensioner and timing belt**
80    The tensioner is a lubricant-sealed pulley, and it should be tested for smooth and quiet operation by turning it with the fingers. Any evidence of roughness or rattle will indicate the need for a new assembly (photo).

Fig. 13.7 Metal removing areas (arrowed) on connecting rod –
999 and 1108 cc engine (Sec 5C)

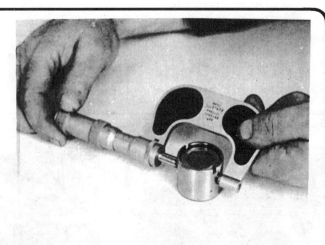

Fig. 13.8 Checking a cam follower for ovality – 999 and 1108 cc
engine (Sec 5C)

81   The timing belt should be inspected at regular intervals for correct adjustment and condition (see Section 3 or Routine maintenance at the beginning of the Manual). If there is evidence of worn teeth, cracking or fraying, or oil contamination, renew the belt. The vehicle manufacturers recommend that the belt is renewed whenever it is removed, and it should certainly be renewed at the intervals specified in Section 3 or the main Routine maintenance section at the beginning of this Manual as a precautionary measure against belt breakage and consequent expensive engine damage.

## PART D: ENGINE REASSEMBLY AND REFITTING

*Reassembly – general*
1   Refer to Chapter 1, Section 19.

*Complete reassembly*
2   With the cylinder block/crankcase standing on the work surface, fit the bearing half shells into their crankcase seats (photo). Make sure that the seats are perfectly clean as dirt or grit trapped under the shell will cause binding when the crankshaft is turned.
3   The centre bearing crankcase web incorporates the thrustwashers held by the lips of the bearing shell (photo).
4   Oil the shells and lower the crankshaft into the crankcase (photo).
5   Fit the bearing shells into the main bearing caps, again making sure that the shell seats are perfectly clean (photo).
6   Fit the main bearing caps in their numbered sequence and the correct way round (photo).
7   Clean the threads of the main bearing cap bolts, lightly oil them and screw them in finger-tight. Tighten all bolts progressively to the specified torque, then check that the crankshaft turns smoothly and evenly (photos).
8   Now check the crankshaft endfloat. Do this using a dial gauge or feeler blades inserted between the machined shoulder of a journal and the side of the bearing cap (photo). Move the crankshaft fully in one direction and then the other to ensure that full movement is obtained. If the endfloat is outside the specified tolerance and new bearing shells have been fitted, then a fault must have occurred during crankshaft regrinding.
9   Fit a new oil seal to the crankshaft rear oil seal retainer. Apply grease to the seal lips. A conventional gasket is not used at the oil seal joint face

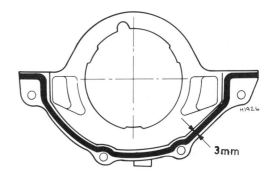

**Fig. 13.9 Application area for silicone gasket on crankshaft rear oil seal retainer (Sec 5D)**

but a 3.0 mm diameter bead of RTV silicone instant gasket must be applied to a clean surface as shown in Fig. 13.9 (photo).
10   Bolt the retainer into position. One hour at least must be allowed for the RTV to cure before oil contacts it.
11   Turn the engine on its side and fit the piston/connecting rods as described in sub-Section B.
12   Fit a new oil seal to the oil pump, oil the seal lips and bolt on the pump using a new joint gasket (photos).
13   Use a new sealing washer and fit the oil pick-up/filter screen assembly.
14   Fit the engine rear plate and then the flywheel on its mounting flange. Apply thread-locking fluid to (clean) bolt threads and screw in the bolts to the specified torque (photo). Hold the flywheel against rotation by locking the starter ring gear with a suitable tool.
15   Fit the sump pan as described in sub-Section B.
16   Fit the crankshaft sprocket so that the timing mark is visible. Lock the flywheel starter ring gear teeth, and screw in and tighten the sprocket bolt to the specified torque (photos).
17   Refit the clutch to the flywheel as described in Chapter 5. Make sure that the driven plate is centralised.
18   Fit the cylinder head.

5D.2 Main bearing shell in crankcase

5D.3 Crankshaft thrust-washer at centre bearing

5D.4 Fitting the crankshaft

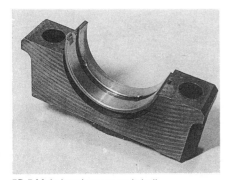

5D.5 Main bearing cap and shell

5D.6 Fitting a main bearing cap

5D.7A Initial tightening of a main bearing cap bolt

5D.7B Angle-tightening a main bearing cap bolt

5D.8 Checking crankshaft endfloat using a dial gauge

5D.9 Fitting crankshaft rear oil seal retainer

5D.12A Oil pump gasket

5D.12B Tightening an oil pump bolt

5D.14 Tightening a flywheel bolt

5D.16A Crankshaft sprocket showing integral key

5D.16B Tightening the crankshaft sprocket bolt

5D.20 Fitting the timing belt rear cover

5D.22 Crankshaft pulley installation

5D.23 Alternator and drivebelt

5D.25A Inlet manifold gasket

5D.25B Fitting the inlet manifold

5D.29 Oil filter cartridge and mounting base

5D.30 Coolant distribution pipe

5D.31 Exhaust manifold

5D.32 Air cleaner hot air collector plate

5D.38 Lifting eye on flywheel housing flange

19    Refit the coolant pump. A conventional gasket is not used at the joint face, but apply a continuous bead of RTV silicone instant gasket 3.0 mm in diameter to the pump mating surface. Allow at least one hour for curing before permitting coolant to contact it.

20    Fit the timing belt rear cover, then the timing belt tensioner and lock in its retracted position (photo).

21    Fit and tension the timing belt as described in sub-Section B.

22    Bolt on the crankshaft pulley (photo).

23    Refit the alternator and drivebelt (photo).

24    Refit the engine oil dipstick.

25    Using a new gasket, bolt on the inlet manifold, tightening the nuts to the specified torque (photos).

26    Refit the carburettor.

27    Fit the fuel pump, insulator block and actuating rod. Make sure that a new gasket is placed on each side of the pump insulator block.

28    Using a new gasket, bolt on the thermostat housing.

29    Oil the sealing ring of a new oil filter cartridge and screw it into position using hand pressure only (photo).

30    Refit the coolant distribution pipe to the rear of the coolant pump. Use a new seal (photo).

31    Using a new gasket, bolt on the exhaust manifold (photo).

32    Fit the hot air collector plate for the air cleaner (photo).

33    Refer to Section 10 and fit the distributor.

34    Bolt on the timing belt cover.

35    Fit the camshaft cover, using a new gasket unless the original one is in perfect condition.

## Engine/transmission – reconnection and refitting

36    Locate the engine in an upright position on wooden blocks to allow for the greater depth of the transmission flywheel housing when it is joined to the engine.

37    Make sure that the clutch driven plate has been centralised, offer the transmission to the engine and locate the flywheel housing on the single stud and dowels.

38    Tighten the connecting bolts to specified torque, having located the lifting eye (photo).

39    Bolt on the starter motor.

40    Refit the cover plate to the flywheel housing, but do not insert the lower bolts at this stage as they retain the support bracket for the gearchange rod.

41    The engine and transmission are now ready for refitting. The operations are a direct reversal of the operations described earlier, but observe the following points.

42    Have the engine/transmission perfectly horizontal and suspended on the hoist.

43    Lower it into position very slowly until it is possible to engage the driveshaft inboard joints with the transmission.

44    Continue lowering until the driveshafts can be fully engaged and the mountings reconnected. Remove the hoist.

45    Tighten all nuts and bolts to the specified torque. Note the method shown for connecting the gearchange rod ball socket using pliers (photo).

46    Refill the engine with oil and coolant and replenish the transmission oil.

## Initial start-up after major overhaul

47    Refer to Chapter 1, Section 45.

5D.45 Connecting ball socket type gearchange rod

## 6    Engine – 1301 cc Turbo ie

### PART A: GENERAL

#### Description

1    This engine is similar in design to the 1301 cc engine described in Chapter 1, but the fuel and ignition systems are different, and a turbocharger, oil cooler and intercooler are fitted.

2    Many dimensions and tolerances have been altered for this engine, and reference should be made to the Specifications at the beginning of this Supplement.

3    Operations which differ from those described in Chapter 1 are given in the following sub-Sections.

#### Lubrication system – description

4    The lubrication system differs from the non-Turbo 1301 cc engine in the following respects.

5    An oil cooler is fitted, which comprises a matrix with inlet and outlet hoses connected to the oil filter cartridge mounting base.

6    A thermostatic control switch is fitted, which diverts the oil flow through the matrix only at oil temperatures above 84°C (183°F). Note that a faulty switch will require renewal of the complete oil filter mounting base.

6A.9 Oil pressure sender unit

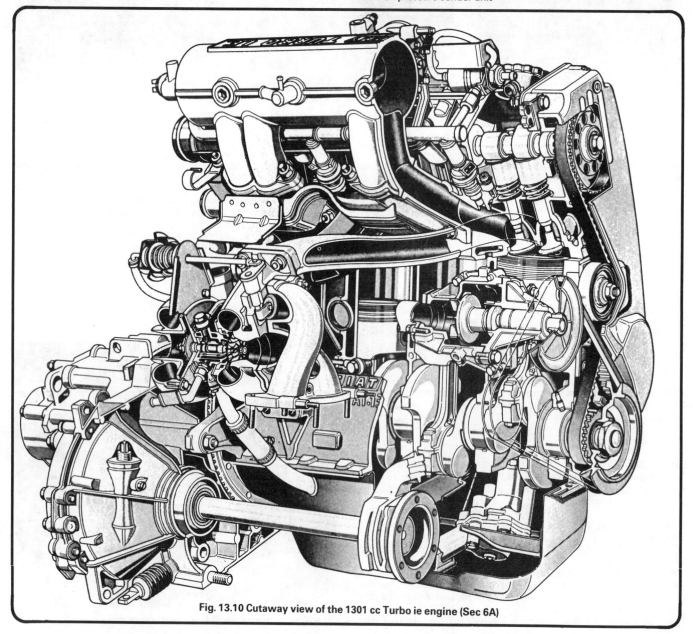

Fig. 13.10 Cutaway view of the 1301 cc Turbo ie engine (Sec 6A)

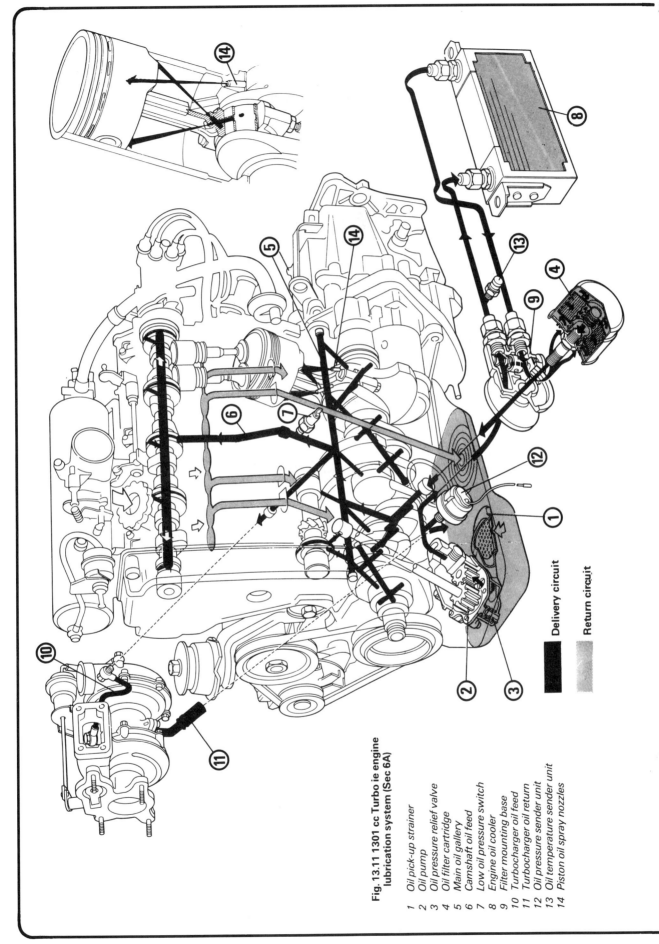

**Fig. 13.11 1301 cc Turbo ie engine lubrication system (Sec 6A)**

1  Oil pick-up strainer
2  Oil pump
3  Oil pressure relief valve
4  Oil filter cartridge
5  Main oil gallery
6  Camshaft oil feed
7  Low oil pressure switch
8  Engine oil cooler
9  Filter mounting base
10  Turbocharger oil feed
11  Turbocharger oil return
12  Oil pressure sender unit
13  Oil temperature sender unit
14  Piston oil spray nozzles

Delivery circuit

Return circuit

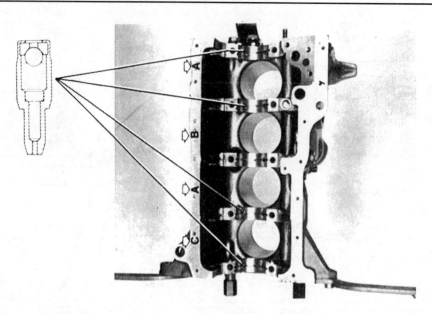

**Fig. 13.12 Piston oil spray nozzle locations – 1301 cc Turbo ie engine (Sec 6A)**

*Letters denote cylinder bore grade*

7 Special oil spray nozzles are located in the crankcase main bearing webs, to cool the underside of the pistons.
8 The ball-type valves in the nozzles open when the engine oil pressure reaches 1.2 bars (17.4 lbf/in²).
9 An oil pressure sender unit is screwed into the crankcase to operate the oil pressure gauge. In addition, a low oil pressure switch screwed into the camshaft oil gallery actuates a warning light on the instrument panel in the event of the pressure dropping dangerously low (photo).
10 Oil supply/return ducts provide the turbocharger lubrication.

## PART B:
## OPERATIONS POSSIBLE WITH ENGINE IN CAR
*Camshaft and camshaft carrier – removal and refitting*
1 Disconnect the battery, negative lead first.
2 Disconnect its leads and unbolt the distributor from the end of the camshaft, and place it to one side.
3 Disconnect the air intake hose from the throttle valve housing.
4 Disconnect the short throttle control cable from its sector.
5 Remove the throttle cable support bracket.
6 Disconnect the earth leads from the camshaft cover.
7 Refer to Section 9, Part C of this Supplement and remove the following components.

*Supplementary air valve*
*Inlet manifold with fuel pressure regulator and excess pressure safety switch*
*Injector cooling duct*

8 Disconnect the wiring plug from the Microplex ignition anti-knock sensor.
9 Carry out the operations described in Chapter 1, Section 27, paragraphs 4 to 12.
10 Refitting is a reversal of removal, referring to Section 28 of Chapter 1 for the timing belt refitting procedure, and to Chapter 1, Section 27, paragraphs 15 to 18.

*Cylinder head – removal and refitting*
11 Carry out the operations described in paragraphs 4 to 9 in the preceding sub-Section, then refer to Chapter 1, Section 29, but ignore all references to the carburettor.
12 Note the distributor mounting cover.
13 Four additional cylinder head bolts are used on these engines, adjacent to the spark plugs (photo). Note that their tightening torque differs from the other cylinder head bolts – see Specifications. These four bolts are tightened separately, after the ten main bolts (see Fig. 13.13).

*Piston rings*
14 The piston rings comprise two compression rings marked TOP, and an oil control ring.
15 Cross-sections and fitting details are shown in Fig. 13.14.

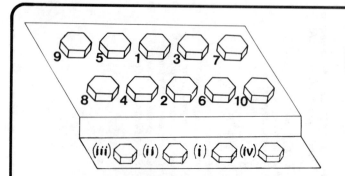

**Fig. 13.13 Cylinder head bolt tightening sequence on the 1301 cc Turbo ie engine (Sec 6B)**

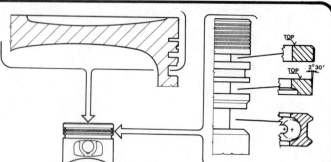

**Fig. 13.14 Piston ring arrangement on the 1301 cc Turbo ie engine (Sec 6B)**

6B.13 Two of the four additional cylinder head bolts (arrowed)

6B.16A Engine/transmission centre mounting

6B.16B Engine/transmission right-hand mounting

6B.19A Removing the TDC sensor

6B.19B Removing the timing belt

6B.20 Belt tensioner pulley locknut (arrowed)

6B.22 Distributor drive hole cover plate (arrowed)

6B.23 Oil cooler

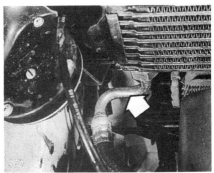

6B.24A Oil cooler pipe connection (arrowed)

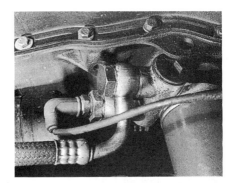

6B.24B Connections at oil filter cartridge mounting base

6B.25 Oil cooler mounting bolts (arrowed)

6C.27 Filling the engine with oil

## Engine mountings – renewal

16   The operations are essentially as described in Section 33 of Chapter 1, but note the design and fixings of the individual mountings used on the turbocharged engine (photos).

## Timing belt – renewal

17   The operations described in Chapter 1, Section 28 generally apply, but the following differences should be noted.

18   Remove the engine compartment right-hand shield. This is secured by plastic clips. To remove a clip, push out its centre pin.

19   The TDC sensor must be unbolted to provide room to remove and refit the timing belt, which can be carried out without having to remove the crankshaft pulley (photos).

20   The belt tensioner on later versions does not incorporate a spring, but is of eccentric centre bolt hole type. Have the pulley bolt released, and tension the belt by turning the pulley using a pin wrench or circlip pliers in the two holes provided. Keep the tension applied while the lockbolt is tightened. Turn the crankshaft through two complete turns, and then check the belt tension. With moderate finger and thumb pressure, the belt should just twist through 90° when gripped at the mid-point of its longest run (photo). **Note:** *This procedure serves only as a rough guide to setting the belt tension – having it checked by a FIAT dealer at the earliest opportunity is recommended.*

## Oil pump drivegear cover plate

21   Due to the fact that the distributor is driven from the end of the camshaft, the oil pump gear does not have an extension to drive the distributor, which would be the case if it was mounted on the crankcase.

22   The crankcase aperture is therefore covered by a plate and gasket, together with a wiring clip (photo).

## Engine oil cooler – removal and refitting

23   The oil cooler is mounted behind the front bumper/spoiler (photo).

24   Disconnect the oil flow and return hoses, either from the cooler or the oil filter cartridge mounting base. Be prepared for some leakage of oil (photos).

25   Unscrew the mounting bolts and remove the oil cooler heat exchanger (photo).

26   When refitting, make sure that the banjo union sealing washers are in good condition.

## PART C: ENGINE REMOVAL, DISMANTLING, REASSEMBLY AND REFITTING

### Engine/transmission – removal and separation

1   Refer to Chapter 1, Section 35, and carry out the operations described in paragraphs 1 to 11.

2   Disconnect the excessive air pressure switch from the inlet manifold.

3   Disconnect the ducts and remove the airflow meter.

4   Disconnect the leads from the spark plugs and the distributor LT connector, and unbolt and remove the distributor from the rear end of the camshaft carrier.

5   Disconnect the fuel return hose from the pressure regulator.

6   Disconnect the fuel inlet hose from the injector rail.

7   Disconnect the wiring plugs from the fuel injectors.

8   Disconnect the leads from the oil pressure sender unit, the low oil pressure switch and the coolant temperature switch.

9   Remove the hose/pipe assemblies from the intercooler.

10   Disconnect the throttle control rod at the balljoint.

11   Disconnect the hoses and ducts from the turbocharger and the mechanical bypass valve.

12   Disconnect the leads from the engine speed and anti-knock sensors.

13   Raise the front of the car and support it securely. As the engine/transmission will eventually be lowered to the floor, make sure that there is sufficient clearance under the front end for the assembly to be withdrawn. If the car is over an inspection pit, then the car need only be raised enough to lift the roadwheels from the floor.

14   Remove the front roadwheels.

15   Disconnect the transmission earth cable.

16   Working under the car, remove the engine shields from under the wheel arches.

17   Remove the engine oil cooler, and the intercooler.

18   Unscrew the fixing screws and disconnect the driveshafts from the flanges at the transmission final drive. The right-hand driveshaft will not release until the upper bolt on the suspension strut-to-hub carrier clamp has been removed, and the hub assembly tilted downwards.

19   Disconnect the exhaust downpipe from the manifold, and then remove the front section of the exhaust system.

20   Disconnect the coolant return pipe from the turbocharger.

21   Disconnect the gearchange control rods from the transmission selector rod. Do this by unscrewing the self-locking nut from the bolt which connects the clevis fork.

22   Attach suitable lifting gear to the engine lifting eyes, and take the weight of the engine/transmission.

23   Disconnect the left-front, centre-rear and the right-hand engine/transmission mountings. Do this by removing the bolts from the diamond-shaped mounting plates – there is no need to disturb the flexible mounting centre bolts.

24   Lower the engine/transmission to the floor and withdraw it from under the car.

25   Carry out the operations described in Chapter 1, Section 35, paragraphs 27 to 31.

### Engine dismantling and reassembly

26   The operations are essentially as described for the 1301 cc engine in Chapter 1, but reference must be made to Sections 9 and 10 of this Chapter for the procedures for removing and refitting the components of the fuel injection, turbocharger and ignition systems.

### Engine/transmission – reconnection and refitting

27   The operations are a reversal of those described in paragraphs 1 to 25, but otherwise the following (photo).

    (a)   Tighten all nuts and bolts to the specified torque.
    (b)   Use a new gasket at the exhaust downpipe-to-manifold flange.
    (c)   Check and adjust the clutch pedal travel.
    (d)   Refill the cooling system.
    (e)   Refill the engine and transmission with oil.
    (f)   Reconnect the battery, negative lead last.

### Initial start-up after major overhaul

28   Refer to Chapter 1, Section 45, but note that an oil pressure gauge is fitted to indicate oil pressure.

29   Check the ignition static timing as described in Section 10.

30   Check the engine idle speed and CO level as described in Section 9.

---

## 7   Engine – 1372 cc ie and 1372 cc Turbo ie

## PART A: GENERAL

### Description

1   The 1372 cc engine is similar in design to the OHC engine fitted to the FIAT Tipo variants. The engine is of four-cylinder, in-line, overhead camshaft type, mounted transversely at the front of the vehicle.

2   The crankshaft runs in five main bearings. Thrustwashers are fitted to the rear (flywheel end) main bearing in order to control crankshaft endfloat.

3   The connecting rods are attached to the crankshaft by horizontally-split shell-type big-end bearings. The pistons are attached to the connecting rods by fully-floating gudgeon pins which are secured by circlips. The aluminium alloy pistons are fitted with three piston rings: two compression rings and an oil control ring.

4   The camshaft is driven by a toothed belt and operates the valves via bucket and shim type cam followers. The camshaft is located in a separate housing on top of the cylinder head.

5   The inlet and exhaust valves are each closed by double valve springs, and operate in guides pressed into the cylinder head.

6   The auxiliary shaft, which is also driven by the toothed belt, drives the oil pump.

7   Lubrication is by means of a gear type pump which draws oil through a strainer located in the sump, and forces it through a full-flow filter into the engine oil galleries from where it is distributed to the crankshaft, camshaft and auxiliary shaft. The big-end bearings are supplied with oil via internal drillings in the crankshaft. The undersides

7A.11 Topping up the engine oil level – 1372 cc engine

7A.12A Engine sump drain plug – 1372 cc engine

7A.12B Engine oil filter removal using a strap wrench – 1372 cc engine

of the pistons are cooled by oil spray nozzles located in each main bearing location in the crankcase.

8    A crankcase ventilation system is employed, whereby piston blow-by gases are drawn via an oil separator into the air cleaner, from where they are drawn into the inlet manifold and re-burnt with fresh air/fuel mixture.

9    The 1372 cc ie engine is fitted with a Bosch Mono-Jetronic single point fuel injection (SPi) system, whilst the higher performance 1372 cc Turbo ie engine is fitted with a Bosch L3.1 Jetronic multi-point injection (MPi) system and turbocharger with intercooler and oil cooling.

## Maintenance

10    At the intervals specified in Section 3 or *Routine maintenance* at the beginning of this Manual, carry out the following tasks.

11    Check the engine oil level as follows. With the vehicle parked on level ground, and with the engine having been stopped for a few minutes, withdraw the oil level dipstick, wipe it on a clean rag, and re-insert it fully. Withdraw the dipstick again and read off the oil level relative to the MAX and MIN marks. The oil level should be between the marks. If the level is at or below the MIN mark, top up through the filler on the camshaft cover without delay (photo). The quantity of oil required to raise the level from MIN to MAX on the dipstick is approximately 1.0 litre (1.8 pints). Do not overfill.

12    Renew the engine oil and filter as described in Section 2 of Chapter 1 (photos).

13    Check and if necessary adjust the valve clearances as described in Part B of this Section.

14    Inspect the engine for signs of oil, coolant or fuel leaks and rectify as necessary.

15    Inspect the crankcase ventilation hose for blockage or damage. Clean or renew as necessary.

16    Check the condition and tension of the timing belt as described in Part B of this Section.

17    Renew the timing belt as described in Part B of this Section.

## PART B: OPERATIONS POSSIBLE WITH ENGINE IN CAR

### Valve clearances – checking and adjustment

1    It is important to ensure that the valve clearances are set correctly, as incorrect clearances will result in incorrect valve timing thus affecting engine performance.

2    The clearances must be checked and adjusted with the engine **cold**.

3    On the ie engine, refer to Section 9 in this Chapter for details and remove the air cleaner unit.

4    On the ie engine disconnect the crankcase ventilation hose from the injector unit and position the hose out of the way.

5    On Turbo ie engines, loosen off the clips and remove the air hose to the inlet manifold (above the camshaft cover).

6    On Turbo ie engines, disconnect the accelerator cable from the throttle housing and the support bracket on the camshaft cover.

7    Unscrew the securing nuts and washers and remove the camshaft cover, noting that on later models two of the nuts also secure the hose clip assembly. Recover the gasket.

8    Numbering from the front (timing belt) end of the engine, the exhaust valves are 1, 4, 5 and 8, and the inlet valves are 2, 3, 6 and 7.

9    Turn the engine clockwise using a suitable socket on the crankshaft pulley bolt, until the exhaust valve of No 1 cylinder (valve No 1) is fully

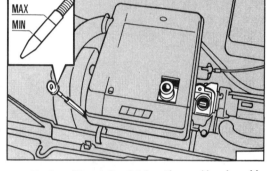

**Fig. 13.15 Engine oil level dipstick location and level markings on the 1372 cc ie and Turbo ie engines (Sec 7A)**

closed; ie the cam lobe is pointing directly upwards. Alternatively, the engine can be turned by jacking up one front corner of the vehicle and supporting it securely on an axle stand (apply the handbrake and chock the diagonally-opposite rear wheel before jacking), engaging top gear and turning the raised roadwheel in the forward direction of travel. In both cases, it will be easier to turn the engine if the spark plugs are removed, but this is done, take care not to allow dirt or other foreign matter to enter the spark plug holes.

10    Insert a feeler gauge of the correct thickness between the cam follower shim and the heel of the No 1 cam lobe (photo). If necessary, increase or reduce the thickness of the feeler gauge until it is a firm sliding fit. Record the thickness of the feeler gauge, which will represent the valve clearance for this particular valve.

11    Turn the crankshaft, and repeat the procedure for the remaining valves, recording their respective clearances. Note that the clearance for inlet and exhaust valves differs.

12    If a clearance is incorrect, the relevant cam follower shim must be removed, and a thicker or thinner shim must be fitted to achieve the correct clearance. To remove a shim proceed as follows.

13    Turn the crankshaft until the relevant cam lobe is pointing directly upwards.

14    The cam follower must now be depressed in order to extract the shim. FIAT special tool No 1860642000 is available for this purpose, but alternatively a suitable tool can be improvised (photo). The tool should locate on the rim of the cam follower, leaving enough room for the shim to be prised out by means of the cut-outs provided in the cam follower rim. Depress the cam follower by turning the crankshaft as described previously until the relevant cam lobe is pointing directly downwards, then fit the tool between the camshaft and the edge of the cam follower to retain the cam follower in the depressed position.

15    Ensure that the tool is securely located, as there is a risk of personal injury if the tool is dislodged whilst the cam follower is depressed, then turn the crankshaft until the relevant cam lobe is pointing directly upwards, leaving sufficient room to extract the shim (photo). A pair of angle-nosed pliers will greatly ease removal of the shim.

16    Once the shim has been extracted, establish its thickness. The thickness in mm should be stamped into the face of the shim, although it is possible for wear to obliterate the number, in which case the use of a metric micrometer is the only way to accurately establish the thickness.

17    Refer to the clearance recorded for the valve concerned. If the clearance recorded was larger than that specified, a thicker shim must

7B.10 Measuring a valve clearance (No 2 valve shown)

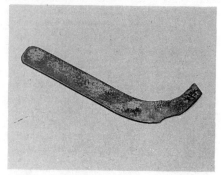

7B.14 Special tool for retaining cam follower in depressed position

7B.15 Removing a shim from a cam follower

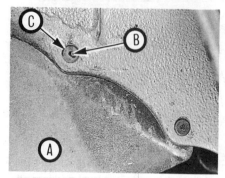

7B.27 Underwing shield (A) showing central compression pin (B) and retaining clip (C). Drive pin through clip to remove

7B.29 Slide back inspection cover in the timing case

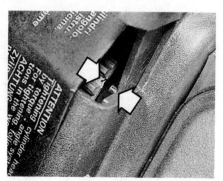

7B.30A Camshaft sprocket timing notch aligned with timing (TDC) pointer in timing case

be fitted, and if the clearance recorded was smaller than that specified, a thinner shim must be fitted. The required thickness of shim can be calculated as follows.

*Sample calculation – clearance too large:*
Desired clearance (A) ..............................................0.40 mm
Measured clearance (B) ...........................................0.45 mm
Difference (B – A) ..................................... + 0.05 mm
Original shim thickness .............................................3.40 mm
Required shim thickness............................ 3.40 + 0.05 = 3.45 mm

*Sample calculation – clearance too small:*
Desired clearance (A) ..............................................0.50 mm
Measured clearance (B) ...........................................0.35 mm
Difference (B – A) ...................................... –0.15 mm
Original shim thickness .............................................4.55 mm
Required shim thickness............................ 4.55 – 0.15 = 4.40 mm

18    Shims are available in thicknesses from 3.20 to 4.70 mm, in steps of 0.05 mm. Note that if several shims have to be changed, they can often be interchanged, thus avoiding the need by buy more new shims than are necessary.
19    The shims should be fitted to the cam followers with the stamped thickness marking against the face of the cam follower.
20    After fitting a shim, rotate the crankshaft as described previously until the relevant cam lobe is pointing directly downwards (resting on the shim), then carefully remove the tool used to retain the follower in the depressed position.
21    Re-check each relevant valve clearance after fitting the shim.
22    On completion, where applicable, lower the vehicle to the ground.
23    Refit the camshaft cover, using a new gasket.
24    On the ie engine, reconnect the hoses and refit the air cleaner unit.
25    On the Turbo ie engine, reconnect the air hose and the accelerator cable.

*Timing belt tensioner and sprockets – removal and refitting*

**Note:** *The timing belt must be renewed after removal: never refit a used*

*drivebelt. When fitting the new timing belt it will need to be correctly tensioned and to achieve this the manufacturers specify the use of special tools 1860745200 (18760745300 on Turbo model) and 1860745100. If these tools are not readily available, an approximate setting can be made, but in this instance it is strongly recommended that the car be taken to a FIAT dealer at the earliest opportunity to have the belt tension checked and correctly set using the recommended tools.*

26    Loosen off the front right-hand side wheel bolts, then raise and support the car at the front end on axle stands. Remove the front right-hand roadwheel.
27    Remove the underwing shield from the right-hand wheel arch to allow access to the lower timing cover and alternator fixings (photo).
28    Loosen off the retaining clips and detach the air intake pipe from the air filter.
29    Slide back the inspection cover from the upper end of the timing cover (photo).
30    Turn the engine over by hand to bring the TDC timing marks of the flywheel-to-bellhousing and the camshaft sprocket-to-rear cover projection into alignment. The crankshaft pulley also has a TDC timing mark and this should be positioned as shown (photos).
31    Loosen off the retaining and adjustment strap fixings, then pivot the alternator towards the engine.
32    Unscrew the upper retaining bolts securing the timing cover.
33    Loosen off the nut securing the alternator and its drivebelt relay, then detach and remove the alternator drivebelt.
34    Unscrew and remove the crankshaft pulley nut. Where the engine is in the car, prevent the crankshaft from turning by engaging top gear and having an assistant apply the brake pedal hard. Unscrew and remove the flywheel housing lower cover bolts and remove the cover. The flywheel ring gear can now be jammed with a suitable lever or implement to prevent the crankshaft from rotating. It should be noted that the pulley nut is tightened to a considerable torque and a strong socket, together with an L-bar and extension tube, will therefore be required to loosen and remove it (photo). Take care not to damage the gearbox/flywheel housing by jamming the flywheel at a weak point.
35    Withdraw the crankshaft pulley (photo).
36    Unscrew and remove the lower retaining bolts and remove the timing cover upwards from the vehicle.

7B.30B Crankshaft pulley and timing cover timing marks

7B.34 Crankshaft pulley nut removal

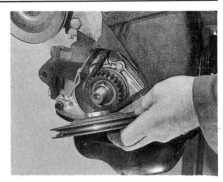

7B.35 Crankshaft pulley removal

7B.38A Timing belt tensioner removal

7B.38B The three sections of the timing belt tensioner

7B.41 Removing the crankshaft sprocket bolt, plain washer and thrustwasher

7B.43 Remove the crankshaft Woodruff key if it is loose

7B.45 Withdrawing the auxiliary shaft sprocket

7B.46 Tightening the auxiliary shaft sprocket bolt

37    Check that the previously mentioned timing marks are still in alignment. Loosen off the timing belt tensioner nut, then with the tension released, withdraw the timing belt from the sprockets.
38    To remove the drivebelt tensioner, undo the securing nut and withdraw the tensioner pulley unit noting that it is in three sections (photos).
39    If desired, the sprockets and the rear timing belt cover can be removed as follows, otherwise proceed to paragraph 49.
40    To remove the camshaft sprocket, a suitable tool must be used to hold the camshaft stationary as the sprocket bolt is loosened. A suitable tool can be improvised as shown in photo 7B.48 using two pieces of steel bar joined together by a pivot bolt, with suitable bolts through the ends of the steel bars to engage with the holes in the sprocket.
41    Unscrew the sprocket bolt, then recover the plain washer, and the thrustwasher which is bonded into a plastic sleeve (photo).
42    The sprocket can now be withdrawn from the end of the camshaft. If the sprocket is tight, carefully lever it from the camshaft using two screwdrivers, but take care not to damage the rear timing belt cover.

43    The crankshaft sprocket can be removed by simply pulling it from the end of the crankshaft after the pulley securing nut has been removed. Recover the Woodruff key from the end of the crankshaft if it is loose (photo).
44    To remove the auxiliary shaft sprocket, a suitable tool must be used to hold the sprocket stationary as the securing bolt is loosened (the bolt is extremely tight). In the workshop, a "scissors" style tool was improvised, using two pieces of steel bar joined together by a pivot bolt, with their ends bent through a right-angle to engage securely between the teeth on the sprocket – see photo 7B.46.
45    Unscrew the sprocket bolt, and recover the washer, then withdraw the sprocket from the end of the auxiliary shaft (photo). If the sprocket is tight, carefully lever it from the shaft using two screwdrivers.
46    Refit the auxiliary shaft sprocket, making sure that the lug on the end of the shaft engages with the hole in the sprocket, then tighten the securing bolt to the specified torque (ensure that the washer is in place under the bolt head). Prevent the sprocket from turning as during removal (photo).

7B.47 Refitting the crankshaft sprocket

7B.48 Tightening the crankshaft sprocket bolt

7B.50 Crankshaft at TDC with key and timing mark aligned (arrows)

47    Where applicable, refit the Woodruff key to the end of the crankshaft, then refit the crankshaft sprocket with the flanged side against the oil seal housing (photo).
48    Refit the camshaft sprocket to the end of the camshaft, making sure that the lug on the end of the shaft engages with the hole in the sprocket, then refit the thrustwasher, plain washer, and bolt, and tighten the bolt to the specified torque. Prevent the camshaft from turning as during removal (photo).
49    Refit the belt tensioner pulley assembly, ensuring that the washer is in place under the securing nut, but do not fully tighten the nut at this stage.
50    Before refitting the new timing belt into position, first ensure that the crankshaft and camshaft sprocket timing marks are still aligned as described in paragraph 30 (photo).
51    If the new timing belt has two timing marks on its outer face they must align with the corresponding marks on the crankshaft and camshaft sprockets. Do not distort or bend the belt any more than is necessary during its fitting or its structural fibres may be damaged.
52    Refit the belt around the sprockets and the tensioner pulley, starting at the crankshaft sprocket. One of the timing index marks must align with the scribed mark on the lower edge of the crankshaft sprocket (opposite the Woodruff key) whilst the second mark must align with the timing marks of the camshaft and rear timing belt cover (photos).
53    With the belt fitted over the sprockets and correctly aligned, temporarily refit the crankshaft pulley nut (tightening it to its full torque wrench setting) and then adjust the timing belt tension.

**Approximate setting**
54    The timing belt tension can be checked approximately by twisting it between the thumb and forefinger at the centre of the run between the auxiliary shaft sprocket and the camshaft sprocket. Using this method it should just be possible to twist the belt through 90° using moderate pressure.

55    To adjust the tension, loosen off the tensioner pulley nut then insert two rods (or screwdrivers) into position in the pulley holes and position a lever between them.
56    Gently lever the tensioner pulley in the required direction to set the tension as described, then initially tighten the pulley nut to lock the tensioner in the required position.
57    Remove the tools from the tensioner, recheck the tension and then tighten the tensioner pulley nut securely.
58    Rotate the crankshaft clockwise through two complete turns using a socket or spanner on the crankshaft pulley nut, then recheck the belt tension. To avoid the possibility of unscrewing the pulley nut, remove the spark plugs to enable the engine to be turned over easier.
59    If further adjustment is required, repeat the previously mentioned procedures. If in doubt, err on the slightly tight side when adjusting the tension. If the belt is set too loose, it may jump off the sprockets resulting in serious damage.
60    Remove the crankshaft pulley retaining nut, fit the timing belt cover, then refit and tighten the pulley nut to the specified torque setting.
61    Refit the remaining components in the reverse order of removal. Tighten the retaining nuts/bolts to the specified torque settings where given. Adjust the tension of the alternator drivebelt as described in Section 8.

**Adjustment using FIAT special tools**
62    Assemble the special tools and fit them to the belt tensioner pulley as shown in Fig. 13.16. When fitted, the tool rod must be as vertical as possible and it is important to note that no sliding weights must be attached to tool No. 1860745100.
63    Slacken the tensioner pulley nut, if not already done. Rotate the crankshaft clockwise through two complete turns using a socket or spanner on the crankshaft pulley nut. The special tool rod may move from the vertical as the engine is turned over, in which case the joint will

7B.52A Timing belt refitted over the sprockets and tensioner

7B.52B Timing belt mark aligned with scribed mark on crankshaft sprocket (arrows)

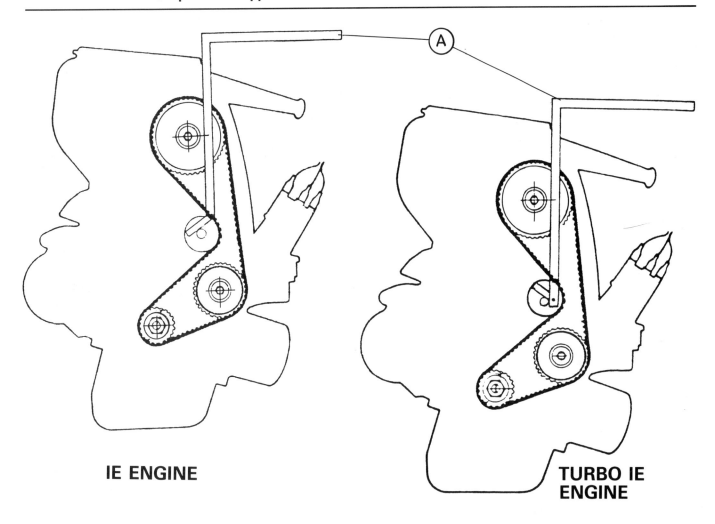

**IE ENGINE**

**TURBO IE ENGINE**

**Fig. 13.16 FIAT special tool No. 1860745100 (A) for timing belt adjustment shown fitted to the tensioner pulley – 1372 cc ie and Turbo ie engines (Sec 7B)**

*Use with adapter No. 1860745200 on 1372 cc ie engines and No. 1860745300 on 1372 cc Turbo ie engines*

need to be re-adjusted to return the rod to the vertical and the operation repeated.

64    With the two revolutions of the crankshaft completed, tighten the belt tensioner pulley nut securely and remove the special tools.

65    Remove the crankshaft pulley retaining nut, fit the timing belt cover, then refit and tighten the pulley nut to its specified torque setting.

66    Refit the remaining components in the reverse order of removal. Tighten the retaining nuts/bolts to the specified torque settings where given. Adjust the tension of the alternator drivebelt as described in Section 8.

### Camshaft front oil seal – renewal

67    The camshaft front oil seal may be renewed with the engine in the vehicle, and the camshaft *in situ,* as follows.

68    Remove the timing belt and the camshaft sprocket as described previously in this Section.

69    Punch or drill a small hole in the centre of the exposed oil seal. Screw in a self-tapping screw, and pull on the screw with pliers to extract the seal.

70    Clean the oil seal seat with a wooden or plastic scraper.

71    Lubricate the lips of the new seal with clean engine oil, and drive it into position until it is flush with the housing, using a suitable socket or tube. Take care not to damage the seal lips during fitting. Note that the seal lips should face inwards.

72    Refit the camshaft sprocket and the timing belt as described previously in this Section.

### Camshaft housing, camshaft and cam followers – removal and refitting

**Note:** *The engine must be cold when removing the camshaft housing. Do not remove the camshaft housing from a hot engine. New camshaft housing and camshaft cover gaskets must be used on refitting.*

73    If the engine is still in the vehicle, disconnect the battery negative lead.

74    Refer to paragraphs 3 to 7 in this part of this Section for details and remove the camshaft cover.

75    Remove the camshaft sprocket and timing belt as described previously in this Section.

76    Remove the three securing nuts and the single securing bolt, and withdraw the upper section of the rear timing belt cover.

77    Unscrew the camshaft housing securing bolts. There are seven bolts which are accessible from outside the camshaft housing, and five shorter bolts which are accessible from inside the housing (these bolts are normally covered by the camshaft cover). Note that each bolt is fitted with two washers (photo).

78    Carefully lift the camshaft housing from the cylinder head. Be prepared for the cam followers to drop from their bores in the camshaft housing as the camshaft housing is lifted, and ensure that the cam followers are identified for position so that they can be refitted in their original positions (this can be achieved by placing each cam follower over its relevant valve in the cylinder head).

79    Recover the gasket.

7B.77 Removing one of the camshaft housing shorter securing bolts

7B.82 Locating a new camshaft housing gasket on the cylinder head

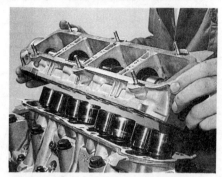

7B.84 Lowering the camshaft housing on to the cylinder head

7B.85 Tightening a camshaft housing securing bolt

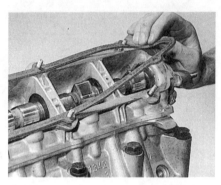

7B.89A Locate a new gasket on the camshaft housing ...

7B.89B ... and refit the camshaft cover

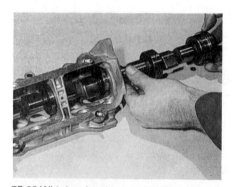

7B.93 Withdrawing the camshaft from its housing

7B.97A Prising out the camshaft front oil seal

7B.97B Inserting the new camshaft front oil seal

80    Removal of the camshaft from the housing, and inspection of the components is described in the following sub-Section.
81    Commence refitting by cleaning the gasket mating surfaces of the camshaft housing and cylinder head.
82    Locate a new gasket on the cylinder head, making sure that it is correctly positioned over the dowels (photo).
83    Ensure that the cam followers are correctly located over their relevant valves.
84    Liberally oil the cam follower bores in the camshaft housing, then carefully lower the housing over the cam followers, and onto the cylinder head (photo). Some manipulation will be required to engage the cam followers with their relevant bores in the camshaft housing.
85    Loosely refit all the camshaft housing securing bolts, ensuring that the washers are in place under their heads, then tighten them progressively to the specified torque, starting at the centre of the housing and working outwards in a spiral pattern (photo).
86    Refit the upper section of the rear timing belt cover.
87    Refit the camshaft sprocket and the timing belt as described previously in this Section.
88    Check the valve clearances as described earlier in this Section.

89    Refit the camshaft cover using a new gasket, and tighten the securing nuts, ensuring that the washers are in place (photos). Where applicable, ensure that the hose clip is in place before refitting the relevant camshaft cover securing nuts.
90    The remainder of the refitting procedure is a reversal of that given for removal.

*Camshaft housing, camshaft and cam followers – dismantling, inspection and reassembly*
91    With the camshaft housing removed from the cylinder head as previously described proceed as follows.
92    Unscrew the three securing bolts, and withdraw the blanking plate from the end of the camshaft housing. Recover the gasket.
93    The camshaft can now be carefully withdrawn from the blanking plate/distributor end of the camshaft housing, taking care not to damage the bearing journals (photo).
94    With the camshaft removed, examine the bearings in the camshaft housing, and the cam follower bores for signs of obvious wear or pitting. If evident, a new camshaft housing will probably be required.

95   The camshaft itself should show no signs of marks or scoring on the journal or cam lobe surfaces. If evident, renew the camshaft.

96   Examine the cam followers for signs of obvious wear, and for ovality, and renew if necessary.

97   It is advisable to renew the camshaft front oil seal as a matter of course if the camshaft has been removed. Prise out the old seal using a screwdriver, and drive in the new seal until it is flush with the housing, using a suitable socket or tube (photos).

98   Commence reassembly by liberally oiling the bearings in the housing, and the oil seal lip.

99   Carefully insert the camshaft into the housing from the blanking plate/distributor end, taking care to avoid damage to the bearings.

100   Refit the blanking plate using a new gasket.

101   Refit the camshaft housing as described previously in this Section.

### Cylinder head (1372 cc ie engine)– removal and refitting

**Note:** *The following instructions describe cylinder head removal and refitting leaving the camshaft, manifolds and associated items in situ in the head. If required, these items can be removed separately. When removing the cylinder head the engine must be cold – do not remove the head from a hot engine. A new cylinder head gasket and any associated gaskets must be used during reassembly. FIAT specify that the main cylinder head bolts should be renewed after they have been used (ie tightened) four times. If in any doubt as to the number of times that they have been used, renew them as a precaution against possible failure.*

102   Depressurise the fuel supply system as described in Section 9 of this Chapter.

103   Disconnect the battery negative lead.

104   Drain the engine coolant as described in Section 8.

105   Remove the air cleaner unit as described in Section 9.

106   Remove the timing belt as described previously in this Section.

107   Disconnect the crankcase ventilation hose from the cylinder head and the SPi injector unit.

108   Disconnect the accelerator cable at the engine end.

109   Detach the engine idle speed check actuator lead, the inlet manifold vacuum sensor lead, the coolant temperature sensor lead, the injector supply lead, the throttle position switch lead and the distributor cap (with HT leads). Position them out of the way.

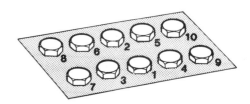

**Fig. 13.17 Cylinder head bolt tightening sequence on the 1372 cc ie and Turbo ie engines (Sec 7B)**

110   Disconnect the brake servo hose from the manifold.

111   Disconnect the coolant hoses from the thermostat and the inlet manifold.

112   Slowly release the fuel supply and return hose retaining clips and detach the hoses from the injector unit housing and connections. Catch any fuel spillage in a clean cloth and plug the hoses to prevent the ingress of dirt and further fuel loss.

113   Unbolt and detach the exhaust downpipe from the manifold.

114   Loosen off the cylinder head retaining bolts in a progressive manner, reversing the sequence shown in Fig. 13.17. When all of the bolts are loosened off, extract them and collect the washers.

115   Check that all fittings and associated attachments are clear of the cylinder head, then carefully lift the head from the cylinder block. If necessary tap the head lightly with a soft-faced mallet to free it from the block, but **do not** lever it free between the joint faces. Note that the cylinder head is located on dowels.

116   Recover the old cylinder head gasket and discard it.

117   Clean the cylinder head and block mating surfaces by careful scraping. Take care not to damage the cylinder head – it is manufactured in light alloy and is easily scored. Cover the coolant passages and other openings to prevent dirt and carbon from falling into them. Mop out all the oil from the cylinder head bolt holes – if oil is left in them, hydraulic pressure, caused when the bolts are refitted, could cause the block to crack.

118   If required the cylinder head can be dismantled and overhauled as described in paragraphs 129 to 131 of this Section.

7B.119 Locating a new cylinder head gasket on the cylinder block (engine shown on dismantling stand)

7B.120A Lower the cylinder head onto the block ...

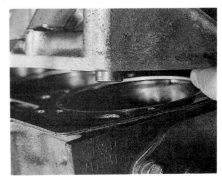

7B.120B ... and engage the positioning dowels in their holes

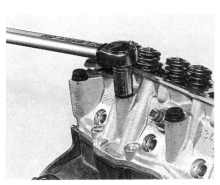

7B.121A Tighten main cylinder head bolts to specified torque ...

7B.121B ... and then through the specified angle

7B.122 Tighten the smaller cylinder head bolts to their specified torque setting

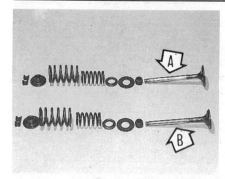

7B.130A Inlet (A) and exhaust (B) valves and associate components – 1372 cc engine

7B.130B Valve assembly – 1372 cc engine: insert valve into guide ...

7B.130C ... locate stem oil seal ...

7B.130D ... and drive it into position

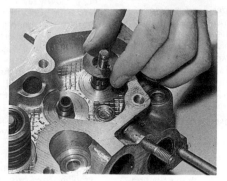

7B.130E Refit the flat washer ...

7B.130F ... locate the spring seat ...

7B.130G ... the inner spring ...

7B.130H ... the outer spring ...

7B.130I ... and cap

119   The new gasket must be removed from its protective packing just before it is fitted. Do not allow any oil or grease to come into contact with the gasket. Commence refitting the cylinder head by locating the new gasket on the cylinder block so that the word 'ALTO' is facing up (photo).

120   With the mating faces scrupulously clean, refit the cylinder head into position and engage it over the dowels. Refer to the note at the beginning of this part of the Section, then refit the ten main cylinder head bolts and washers. Screw each bolt in as far as possible by hand to start with. Do not fit the smaller (M8 x 1.25) bolts at this stage (photos).

121   The bolts must now be tightened in stages and in the sequence shown in Fig. 13.17. Refer to the specified torque wrench settings and tighten all bolts to the Stage 1 torque, then using a suitable angle gauge, tighten them to the second stage, then the third stage (photos).

122   With the main cylinder head bolts fully tightened, refit the five smaller (M8 x 1.25) bolts adjacent to the line of the spark plug holes and tighten them to their specified torque wrench setting (photo).

123   Reconnect the associated fittings to the cylinder head in the reverse order of removal. Ensure that the mating faces of the exhaust manifold-to-downpipe are clean and fit a new gasket when reconnecting.

124   Ensure that all wiring connections are cleanly and securely made.

125   Top up the engine oil and coolant levels as required on completion.

*Cylinder head (1372 cc Turbo ie engine) – removal and refitting*

126   Proceed as described in paragraphs 102 to 125 above for the non-Turbo model, but note the following differences.

127   The cylinder head cannot be removed and refitted with the manifolds and turbocharger fitted. It is therefore first necessary to detach and remove the inlet manifold, then the turbocharger and the exhaust manifold as described in Section 9.

128   The ignition distributor is mounted on the side of the engine, not the rear end of the cylinder head as on the 'ie' engine. It is therefore only necessary to disconnect the HT leads from the spark plugs.

*Cylinder head – inspection and renovation*

**Note:** *Refer to a dealer for advice before attempting to carry out valve grinding or seat recutting operations. These operations may not be possible for the DIY mechanic due to the fitment of hardened valve seats for use with unleaded petrol.*

129   Use a straight-edge to check the cylinder head gasket surface for distortion. If it exceeds the specified tolerance, it must be resurfaced by a FIAT dealer or automotive engineer.

130   Refer to Section 39 in Chapter 1 for the general details on dismantling and renovating operations on the cylinder head but note

7B.130J Compress spring and refit the split collets

7B.140 Driving a new crankshaft front oil seal into its housing

that there is a spring seat and a flat washer fitted between the cylinder head and the valve springs (photos).

*Crankshaft front oil seal – removal and renewal*

131    Remove the timing belt as described earlier in this Section. Note that as mentioned previously, the timing belt will need to be renewed during reassembly.

132    Referring to Fig. 13.18, loosen off the bolt indicated from the timing belt rear cover.

133    Drain the engine oil from the sump into a suitable container. Disconnect the lead from the engine oil level sensor in the sump.

134    Where applicable, unscrew and remove the bolts retaining the gear linkage mounting bracket and the clutch housing lower cover bolts. Remove the cover from the clutch housing.

135    Unscrew the sump retaining nuts and bolts, then lower and remove the sump.

136    Unscrew the timing belt rear cover retaining bolts.

137    Move the timing belt rear cover towards the front of the car to gain access to the retaining bolt and then unscrew and remove the three oil seal housing retaining bolts. Remove the crankshaft front oil seal housing.

138    Note the orientation of the seal in its housing prior to its removal.

Support the underside of the housing and carefully drive the old oil seal from the housing using a punch or a tubular drift of suitable diameter. An alternative method is to punch or drill a small hole in the face of the oil seal (but take care not to drill into the housing) and insert a self-tapping screw into the seal. Withdraw the seal by gripping the screw with pliers and pulling the seal from the housing. If necessary, fit a second screw into the seal on the opposite side to provide an even pull.

139    Clean the mating faces of the housing and the front of the crankcase using a suitable scraper.

140    Drive or press the new seal into position in the housing in the reverse order of removal, but ensure that it is correctly orientated as noted during removal (photo).

141    Refit the oil seal housing with a new gasket and tighten the retaining bolts to the specified torque setting (photos).

142    Refit the sump as described later in this Section using a new gasket. Tighten its retaining nuts and bolts to the specified torque. Refit the clutch cover and the gear linkage mounting bracket.

143    Fit the new timing belt, adjust its tension and refit the crankshaft pulley as described earlier in this Section.

144    Reconnect the remaining components that were detached during removal in the reverse order and top up the engine oil level to complete.

Fig. 13.18 Timing belt rear cover bolt (arrowed) – 1372 cc ie and Turbo ie engines (Sec 7B)

Fig. 13.19 Unscrew the bolts at the points indicated to release the gear linkage mounting bracket – 1372 cc ie and Turbo ie engines (Sec 7B)

7B.141A Refit the crankshaft front oil seal housing ...

7B.141B ... ensuring it is flush with the face of the cylinder block

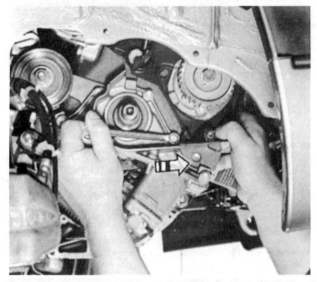

Fig. 13.20 Removing the timing belt rear cover on the 1372 ie and
Turbo ie engines (Sec 7B)

### Crankshaft rear oil seal – removal and renewal

145    If the engine is still in the car, disconnect the battery negative
lead.
146    Remove the flywheel as described in the next sub-Section.
147    Punch or drill a small hole in the rear face of the rear oil seal (but
take care not to drill into the housing) and insert a self-tapping screw into
the seal. Withdraw the seal by gripping the screw with pliers and pulling
it from the housing. If necessary, fit a second screw into the seal on the
opposite side to provide an even pull.
148    Clean the seal housing, then locate the new oil seal, ensuring that
it is correctly orientated, and drive it squarely into position.
149    Refit all disturbed components.

### Flywheel – removal, inspection and refitting

150    If not already done, remove the clutch as described in Chapter 5.
151    Prevent the flywheel from turning by jamming the ring gear teeth,
or by bolting a strap between the flywheel and the cylinder block.
152    Make alignment marks on the flywheel and the end of the
crankshaft, so that the flywheel can be refitted in its original position.
153    Unscrew the securing bolts and remove the washer plate, then
withdraw the flywheel. **Do not** drop it, it is very heavy.
154    With the flywheel removed, the ring gear can be examined for
wear and damage.
155    If the ring gear is badly worn or has missing teeth it should be
renewed. The old ring gear can be removed from the flywheel by

7B.158A Locate the flywheel, washer plate and bolts ...

7B.158B ... tighten the bolts to the specified torque

7B.165 Apply sealant to the front oil seal housing/cylinder block joint

cutting a notch between two teeth with a hacksaw and then splitting it with a cold chisel. Wear eye protection when doing this.

156 Fitting of a new ring gear requires heating the ring to a temperature of 80°C (176°F). Do not overheat, or the hard-wearing properties will be lost. The gear has a chamfered inner edge which should fit against the shoulder on the flywheel. When hot enough, place the gear in position quickly, tapping it home if necessary, and let it cool naturally without quenching in any way.

157 Ensure that the mating faces are clean, then locate the flywheel on the rear of the crankshaft, aligning the previously made marks on the flywheel and crankshaft.

158 Fit the washer plate, and insert the securing bolts, then prevent the flywheel from turning as described in paragraph 151 whilst the bolts

are tightened progressively to the specified torque setting in a diagonal sequence (photos).

159 If applicable, refit the clutch as described in Chapter 5.

### Sump – removal and refitting

160 Drain the engine oil from the sump as described in Chapter 1.

161 Disconnect the lead from the engine oil level sensor in the sump.

162 Unscrew and remove the bolts retaining the gear linkage mounting bracket (where applicable) and the clutch housing lower cover bolts. Remove the cover from the clutch housing.

163 Unscrew and remove the sump retaining bolts and nuts and lower the sump from the crankcase. Recover the gasket.

164 Clean all traces of old gasket from the sump, crankcase and both oil seal housing mating surfaces.

165 Commence reassembly by applying sealing compound (FIAT No. 5882442 or equivalent) to the joints between the crankshaft front and rear oil seal housings and the mating face of the crankcase (photo).

166 Locate the new gasket in position on the crankcase then fit the sump. As it is fitted it will need to be twisted to avoid fouling the oil pump unit. Refit the retaining bolts and nuts and tighten them to the specified torque (photos).

167 Check that the sump drain plug is refitted and fully tightened. If the engine is in the car, top up the engine oil level.

### Oil pump – removal, checking and refitting

168 Drain the engine oil and remove the sump as described in the previous sub-Section.

169 Unscrew the retaining bolts then withdraw the oil pump and intake pipe/filter from its location within the crankcase. Remove the gasket.

170 If oil pump wear is suspected, first check the cost and availability of new parts and the cost of a new pump. Then examine the pump as described below and decide whether renewal or repair is the best course of action.

171 Unscrew the three securing bolts and remove the oil pump cover (photo). Note that as the cover is removed, the oil pressure relief valve components will be released.

7B.166A Locate the new gasket ...

7B.166B ... refit the sump ...

7B.166C ... and insert the retaining bolts

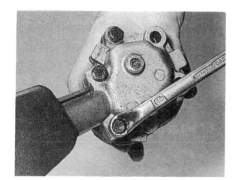

7B.171 Undo the oil pump cover bolts

7B.175 Correct alignment of scribed marks (arrowed) on gears

7B.176 Check gear-to-body clearance

7B.177 Checking the gear endfloat

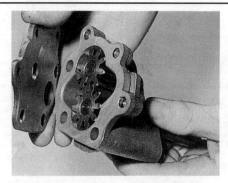

7B.179 Refitting the intermediate plate

7B.180A Locate pressure relief valve and spring on the intermediate plate

7B.180B Locate spring seat over boss within pump cover ...

7B.180C ... then fit the cover

172    Recover the oil pressure relief valve, spring and spring seat.
173    Lift the intermediate plate from the oil pump body.
174    The gears can now be removed from the oil pump body. Inspect them for obvious signs of wear or damage, and renew if necessary.
175    Commence reassembly by lubricating the gears with clean engine oil, and refitting them to the casing. Note that the scribed marks on the top faces of the gears should face each other with the gears installed (photo).
176    Using a feeler gauge, check that the clearance between the gears and the pump body is within the limits given in the Specifications (photo).
177    Using a straight-edge placed across the top of the pump body and the gears, and a feeler gauge, check that the gear endfloat is within the limits given in the Specifications (photo).
178    If either the gear-to-body clearance, or the gear endfloat is outside the specified limits, both gears should be renewed.
179    Locate the intermediate plate on the pump body (photo).
180    Place the pressure relief valve and spring over the pressure relief hole in the intermediate plate, and locate the spring seat over the boss in the pump cover, then refit the pump cover, ensuring that the pressure relief valve components seat correctly (photos).
181    Refit and tighten the pump cover securing bolts.
182    Thoroughly clean the mating faces of the pump and crankcase before refitting the pump. Prime the pump by injecting clean engine oil into it and turning it by hand.
183    Fit the pump using a new gasket, then insert the securing bolts and tighten them.
184    Refit the sump and top up the engine oil level.

### Pistons/connecting rods – removal and refitting

185    Remove the sump and the cylinder head as described previously in this Section.
186    The big-end caps and connecting rods normally have identification marks stamped into their sides, facing the coolant pump side of the cylinder block. If no marks are present, use a centre-punch to identify the bearing caps and the connecting rods for location.
187    Turn the crankshaft so that No 1 crankpin is at its lowest point, then unscrew the nuts and tap off the bearing cap. Keep the bearing

shells in the cap and the connecting rod if they are to be re-used, taping them in position if necessary to avoid loss.
188    Using the handle of a hammer, push the piston and connecting rod up the bore and withdraw it from the top of the cylinder block. Loosely refit the cap to the connecting rod.
189    Repeat the procedure given in paragraphs 187 and 188 on No 4 piston and connecting rod, then turn the crankshaft through half a turn and repeat the procedure on Nos 2 and 3 pistons and connecting rods.
190    The pistons and connecting rods and the big-end bearings can be examined and if necessary renovated as described later in this Section.
191    Commence refitting as follows.
192    Clean the backs of the bearing shells and the recesses in the connecting rods and big-end caps.
193    Lubricate the cylinder bores with engine oil.
194    Fit a ring compressor to No 1 piston, then insert the piston and connecting rod into No 1 cylinder. With No 1 crankpin at its lowest point, drive the piston carefully into the cylinder with the wooden handle of a hammer (photos). Leave enough space between the connecting rod and the crankshaft to allow the bearing shell to be fitted. The piston must be fitted with the cut-out in the piston crown on the auxiliary shaft side of the engine, and the cylinder identification marking on the connecting rod and big-end cap on the coolant pump side of the engine – see Fig. 13.21.
195    Slide the appropriate bearing shell into position in the connecting rod big-end, then pull the connecting rod firmly into position on the crankpin (photo).
196    Press the appropriate bearing shell into position in the big-end cap (photo).
197    Oil the crankpin, then fit the big-end bearing cap with the cylinder identification marking on the coolant pump side of the engine, and tighten the nuts to the specified torque setting (photos).
198    Check that the crankshaft turns freely.
199    Repeat the procedure in paragraphs 194 to 198 inclusive on the remaining pistons.
200    Refit the cylinder head and the sump.

### Pistons/connecting rods – examination and renovation

201    The procedures for inspecting and renovating the pistons and

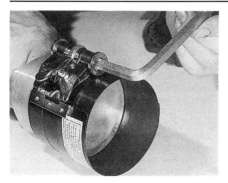

7B.194A Fitting a ring compressor to a piston

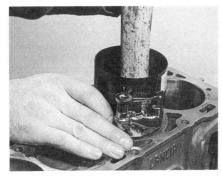

7B.194B Tapping a piston into its bore

7B.195 Assemble the shell bearing to the connecting rod ...

7B.196 ... and big-end bearing cap ...

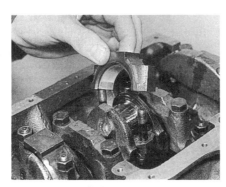

7B.197A ... then fit the cap ...

7B.197B ... and tighten the nuts to the specified torque

connecting rod assemblies are in general the same as that described for the smaller engines in Section 18 of Chapter 1. However, the following additional points should be noted.

202    When renewing a gudgeon pin, first check the fit in the piston. It should be possible to fit the gudgeon pin using hand pressure, but the pin should be a tight enough fit that it does not drop out under its own weight. Oversize gudgeon pins are available as spares if necessary. Use new circlips when refitting the pistons to the connecting rods.

203    Before fitting the pistons to their connecting rods, weigh each piston and check that their weights are all within 2.5 g of each other. If not, the heavier pistons must be lightened by machining metal from the underside of the small-end bosses. This operation must be entrusted to a FIAT dealer or engine reconditioning specialist.

204    The pistons should be fitted to the connecting rods so that the higher, flat side of the piston crown is on the side of the connecting rod with the stamped cylinder identification number, ie the gudgeon pin is offset towards the cylinder identification number – see Fig. 13.21.

205    The piston rings should be fitted with the word 'TOP' on each ring facing uppermost, or if no marks are visible, as noted during removal. If a stepped top compression ring is being fitted, fit the ring with the smaller diameter of the step uppermost. The ring end gaps should be off-set 120° from each other. Use two or three old feeler gauges to assist fitting, as during removal. Note that the compression rings are brittle, and will snap if expanded too far.

206    If new pistons are to be fitted, they must be selected from the grades available, after measuring the cylinder bores. Normally, the appropriate oversize pistons are supplied by the dealer when the block is rebored.

207    Whenever new piston rings are being installed, the glaze on the original cylinder bores should be removed using either abrasive paper or a glaze-removing tool in an electric drill. If abrasive paper is used, use strokes at 60° to the bore centre-line, to create a cross-hatching effect.

*Engine/transmission mountings – renewal*

208    The engine/gearbox assembly is suspended in the engine compartment on three mountings, two of which are attached to the gearbox, and one to the engine.

*Right-hand mounting*

209    Apply the handbrake, then jack up the front of the vehicle and support it securely on axle stands.

210    Suitable lifting tackle must now be attached to the engine in order to support it as the engine mounting is removed. No lifting brackets are provided, so care must be taken when deciding on an engine lifting point. In the workshop, a right-angled bracket was made up by bending a suitable piece of steel plate. The bracket was then bolted to the engine using the rear right-hand camshaft housing securing bolt with suitable packing washers.

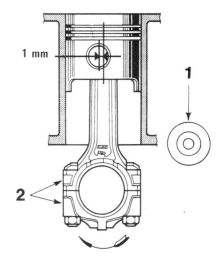

**Fig. 13.21 Correct orientation of piston and connecting rod in engine – 1372 cc ie and Turbo ie engines (Sec 7B)**

1    *Auxiliary shaft*
2    *Cylinder identification markings on connecting rod and big-end cap*

*Arrow denotes direction of engine rotation.*
*Note offset gudgeon pin*

211   Attach the lifting tackle to the bracket on the engine and just take the weight of the assembly.
212   Working under the vehicle, unbolt the engine mounting bracket from the cylinder block, and unbolt the mounting from the body, then withdraw the bracket/mounting assembly.
213   Unscrew the nut and through-bolt, counterholding the bolt with a second spanner or socket, and separate the mounting from the bracket.
214   Fit the new mounting to the bracket, and tighten the nut to the specified torque, while counterholding the through-bolt using a suitable spanner or socket.
215   Refit the mounting bracket to the cylinder block, and tighten the securing bolts to the specified torque.
216   Refit the mounting to the body and tighten the securing bolts to the specified torque.
217   Disconnect the lifting tackle from the engine, and remove the engine lifting bracket.
218   Lower the vehicle to the ground.

*Left-hand mountings*
219   Apply the handbrake, then jack up the front of the vehicle and support it securely on axle stands.
220   Suitable lifting tackle must now be attached to the gearbox lifting bracket in order to support the weight of the assembly as the mounting is removed.
221   Attach the lifting tackle to the bracket on the gearbox, and just take the weight of the assembly.
222   Working under the vehicle, unbolt the mounting bracket from the gearbox, and unbolt the mounting from the body, then withdraw the bracket/mounting assembly.
223   Proceed as described in paragraphs 213 and 214.
224   Refit the mounting bracket to the gearbox, and tighten the securing bolts to the specified torque.
225   Refit the mounting to the body and tighten the mounting bolts to the specified torque.
226   Disconnect the lifting tackle from the engine.
227   Lower the vehicle to the ground.

## PART C: ENGINE REMOVAL AND DISMANTLING
### *Method of removal – general*
1   The engine (complete with transmission) is disconnected and lowered downwards through the engine compartment, then withdrawn from the front underside of the car.

### *1372 cc engine/transmission – removal and separation*
2   Depressurize the fuel system as described in Section 9 of this Chapter.
3   Disconnect the battery negative lead.
4   Mark the position of the hinges on the underside of the bonnet, then with the aid of an assistant, unscrew the hinge bolts and lift the bonnet clear of the car. Store the bonnet in a safe area.
5   Drain the engine coolant.
6   Drain the engine and transmission oils.
7   Disconnect and remove the air filter.
8   Disconnect the coolant hoses from the engine, including the hose to the inlet manifold.

9   Detach the ignition coil (HT) lead from the distributor.
10   Compress the retaining clip and detach the engine idle speed actuator lead from the SPi unit (photo).
11   Disconnect the brake servo vacuum pipe from its connector on the inlet manifold.
12   Disconnect the throttle cable from the SPi unit.
13   Disconnect the engine speed sensor lead.
14   Release and detach the reversing light lead from the switch on the transmission (photo).
15   Before disconnecting the hydraulic hose from the clutch slave cylinder, remove the filler cap from the reservoir and place a piece of polythene sheet over the filler neck, then refit the cap; this will help prevent excess fluid loss. Once disconnected, plug the hose and its cylinder connection to prevent the ingress of dirt into the hydraulic system.
16   Disconnect the wiring connector from the alternator.
17   Position a clean rag under the fuel supply and return hose connections to the SPi unit, then slowly unscrew the hose clips to release the system pressure; catch fuel leakage in the rag and dispose of it safely. Detach the hoses and plug them to prevent ingress of dirt and any further fuel leakage. Position the hoses out of the way.
18   Detach the wiring connector from the engine coolant temperature sender unit (photo).
19   Release the retaining clip and detach the wiring connector from the throttle position switch. Also detach the associated earth leads from the cylinder head.
20   Release the retaining clip and detach the wiring connector from the fuel injector connection (photo).
21   Loosen off the front wheel bolts each side, then raise and support the car at the front end on axle stands. When raised, support at a height which will allow the engine and transmission to be withdrawn from the underside when fully disconnected. Ensure that the vehicle is securely supported before working underneath it.
22   Unscrew the wheel bolts and remove the front roadwheels.
23   Release the retaining clips and remove the underwing shield from the right- and left-hand front wheel arch.
24   Relieve the staking, then unscrew and remove the front hub nut using a socket and suitable extension. Repeat the procedure on the opposite front hub.
25   Unscrew the retaining nut and disconnect the tie-rod to steering arm balljoint using a suitable balljoint separator tool. Repeat the procedure on the other side.
26   Note the direction of fitting, then unscrew and remove the hub-to-strut retaining bolts and nuts on each side.
27   Unscrew and remove the anti-roll bar-to-track control arm retaining nuts each side.
28   Unscrew and remove the front brake caliper hydraulic pipe support bracket bolt each side.
29   Pull the wheel hub outwards and detach the driveshaft from it, noting that there may be a small amount of oil spillage as it is withdrawn. Repeat the procedure on the opposite side.
30   Disconnect the wiring connector from the engine oil level sensor lead.
31   Unscrew the retaining nuts to detach and remove the exhaust pipe front section or alternatively, remove the system complete.
32   Unscrew the knurled retaining nut and detach the speedometer cable from the transmission (photo).

7C.10 Engine idle speed actuator/SPi unit lead connection (arrowed)

7C.14 Reversing light switch and lead

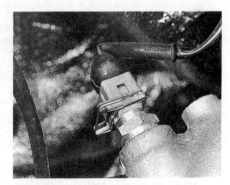
7C.18 Engine coolant temperature sender and wiring connector

7C.20 Fuel injector wiring connection

7C.32 Disconnecting the speedometer drive cable from the transmission

7C.33 Disconnect the transmission earth strap

Fig. 13.22 The underwing shield retaining clips (arrowed) on the 1372 cc ie and Turbo ie engines (Sec 7C)

Fig. 13.23 Engine oil level sensor wiring connector (arrowed) on the 1372 cc ie and Turbo ie engines (Sec 7C)

33   Unscrew the retaining nut and detach the earth strap from the transmission (photo).

34   Extract the split pin and detach the gear selector rod from the transmission pin. Disconnect the gear engagement and selector levers from the balljoints.

35   The weight of the engine will now need to be supported from above. Connect a suitable lift hoist and sling to the engine. When securely connected, take the weight of the engine/transmission unit so that the tension is relieved from the mountings.

36   Unscrew and remove the engine and transmission support mounting bolts at the points indicated (photos).

37   The engine/transmission unit should now be ready for removal from the vehicle. Check that all of the associated connections and fittings are disconnected from the engine and transmission and positioned out of the way. Enlist the aid of an assistant to help steady and guide the power unit down through the engine compartment as it is removed. If available, position a suitable engine trolley or crawler board under the engine/transmission so that when lowered, the power unit can be withdrawn from the front end of the vehicle and moved to the area where it is to be cleaned and dismantled.

38   Carefully lower the engine and transmission unit, ensuring that no fittings become snagged. Detach the hoist and withdraw the power unit from under the vehicle.

39   To separate the engine from the transmission, unbolt and remove the starter motor, then unscrew the retaining bolts and withdraw the transmission from the engine. As it is withdrawn, do not allow the weight of the engine or transmission to be taken by the input shaft.

40   To remove the clutch unit, refer to Chapter 5 for details.

*1372 cc Turbo ie engine/transmission – removal and separation*

41   The engine and transmission removal and refitting details for Turbo-engined models are similar to those described for the non-Turbo

Fig. 13.24 Disconnect the gear selector rod at the connection indicated on the 1372 cc ie and Turbo ie engines (Sec 7C)

models in the previous sub-Section, but the following differences should be noted.

42   To provide access for the disconnection of the turbo and related components, first remove the inlet manifold. Removal of the inlet manifold and the turbocharger is described in Section 9 of this Chapter.

43   The ignition distributor on the Turbo engine is driven from the auxiliary shaft and is mounted at the front of the engine, towards the timing cover end.

44   The right-hand driveshaft has a steady bearing and this will need to be unbolted and detached.

7C.36A Engine right-hand mounting

7C.36B Transmission rear mounting

7C.36C Transmission front mounting

Fig. 13.25 Gear engagement and selector lever balljoints (arrowed)
on the 1372 cc ie and Turbo ie engines (Sec 7C)

7C.53 Driving a new oil seal into the auxiliary shaft cover

### Engine dismantling – general

45    Refer to Chapter 1, Section 14 for details.

### Auxiliary shaft – removal, inspection and refitting

46    Remove the engine and transmission from the vehicle as described previously in this Section part.

47    Drain the engine oil and remove the sump as described in Part B of this Section.

48    Remove the oil pump as described in Part B of this Section.

49    Remove the timing belt and the auxiliary shaft sprocket as described in Part B of this Section.

50    Unscrew the three retaining bolts and remove the auxiliary shaft cover. Remove the gasket.

51    Withdraw the auxiliary shaft from the cylinder block.

52    Examine the shaft and its bearing bushes in the cylinder block for signs of excessive wear and/or damage and renew it if necessary. Bush renewal is described in paragraph 79 in this Section.

53    The cover gasket and the oil seal should always be renewed whenever the cover is removed. To renew the seal, support the cover on blocks of wood and drive out the old seal using a suitable drift inserted in the cut-out in the back of the cover. Clean the seal location in the housing. Drive the new seal into place using a suitable metal tube or socket (photo). The sealing lip must face towards the cylinder block. Smear the sealing lips with clean engine oil before installation.

54    Commence refitting by lubricating the auxiliary shaft journals with clean engine oil, then insert the shaft into the cylinder block (photo).

55    Refit the auxiliary shaft cover, using a new gasket, and tighten the securing bolts (photos).

7C.54 Inserting the auxiliary shaft into the cylinder block (rear timing belt cover removed)

7C.55A Refit the auxiliary shaft cover with a new gasket ...

7C.55B ... and tighten the securing bolts

7C.69 Identification notches on No 3 main bearing cap

7C.70 Measuring crankshaft endfloat using feeler gauge method

56   Refit the auxiliary shaft sprocket, timing belt, cover and crankshaft pulley as described in Part B of this Section.
57   Refit the engine and transmission with reference to Part D of this Section.

### Engine – complete dismantling

58   Detach and remove the following ancillary items. Where applicable, refer to the appropriate Chapter or Section within this Chapter for more detailed removal instructions.

   *Engine oil disptick*
   *Ignition distributor and HT leads*
   *Fuel pump*
   *Alternator*
   *Oil filter*
   *Oil vapour recovery unit*
   *Inlet and exhaust manifolds and associated fuel injection components (as applicable)*
   *Clutch unit*

59   Refer to Part B of this Section for details and remove the timing cover and drivebelt.
60   Refer to Part B of this Section for details and remove the cylinder head unit.
61   Refer to Part B of this Section for details and remove the flywheel.
62   Refer to the previous sub-Section for details and remove the auxiliary shaft.
63   Refer to Part B of this Section for details and remove the sump.
64   Refer to Part B of this Section for details and remove the oil pump unit.
65   Refer to Part B of this Section for details and remove the front and rear crankshaft oil seals.
66   Refer to Part B of this Section and remove the piston/connecting rod assemblies.
67   Refer to Part B of this Section for details and remove the crankshaft and main bearing assemblies.

### Crankshaft and main bearings – removal

68   Unscrew the securing bolts and remove the front and rear crankshaft oil seal housings. Recover the gaskets.
69   Check the main bearing caps for identification marks and if necessary use a centre-punch to identify them. Normally the caps have identifying notches cut into their top face nearest the timing belt end of the engine, with the exception of No 5 cap (flywheel end) which has no marking (photo).
70   Before removing the crankshaft, check that the endfloat is within the specified limits. Ideally a dial gauge should be used, but alternatively feeler gauges can be used as follows. Push the crankshaft as far as possible towards the timing end of the engine, and using a feeler gauge, measure the gap between the rear face of the flywheel mounting flange on the crankshaft and the outer face of the thrustwasher (photo). Now push the crankshaft as far as possible in the opposite direction and take

the same measurement again. The difference between the two measurements is the crankshaft endfloat. If the endfloat is outside the specified limits, new thrustwashers will be required.
71   Unscrew the bolts and tap off the main bearing caps complete with bearing shells. If the bearing shells are to be re-used, tape them to their respective caps.
72   Lift the crankshaft from the crankcase.
73   Extract the bearing shells from the crankcase, keeping them identified for location if they are to be re-used, and recover the thrustwashers from No 5 main bearing location.

### Engine components – examination and renovation

74   With the engine completely stripped, clean all the components and examine them for wear. Each part should be checked and where necessary renewed or renovated as described elsewhere in this Section. Renew main and big-end bearing shells as a matter of course, unless it is known that they have had little wear and are in perfect condition.
75   If in doubt as to whether to renew a component which is still just serviceable, consider the time and effort which will be incurred should the component fail at an early date. Obviously the age and expected life of the vehicle must influence the standards applied.
76   Gaskets, oil seals and O-rings must all be renewed as a matter of course. FIAT specify that the main cylinder head bolts should be renewed after they have been used (ie tightened) four times – if in any doubt as to the number of times the bolts have been used, renew them in any case as a precaution against possible failure.
77   Take the opportunity to renew the engine core plugs while they are easily accessible. Knock out the old plugs with a hammer and chisel or punch. Clean the plug seats, smear the new plugs with sealant and tap them squarely into position.
78   Clean and examine the cylinder block as described in paragraphs 2 to 7 of Section 18, Chapter 1.
79   If the auxiliary shaft bushes are excessively worn or are oval, they must be renewed. When the new bushes are installed, they may need to be reamed to suit. The renewal of the auxiliary shaft bushes is therefore best entrusted to an engine reconditioner or FIAT dealer. When the bushes are renewed, ensure that the oil hole in each bush is aligned with the oil channel in the cylinder block.

## PART D: ENGINE REASSEMBLY

### Reassembly – general

1   Refer to Chapter 1, Section 19.

### Crankshaft and main bearings – refitting

2   Ensure that the crankcase and crankshaft are thoroughly clean, and that the oilways are clear. If possible, blow through the oil drillings with compressed air, and inject clean engine oil into them.
3   Unless they are virtually new, the old main bearing shells should be renewed. Failure to do so is a false economy.

7D.6A No 3 main bearing shell is plain ...

7D.6B ... all others have oil groove

7D.7A Locate the thrustwashers ...

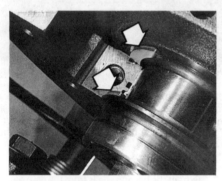

7D.7B ... sliding them into position each side
of the No 5 main bearing

7D.8 Locate the bearing shells into the main
bearing caps ...

4    If new bearing shells are being fitted, wipe away all traces of
protective grease.
5    Note that there is a tag on the back of each bearing shell, which
engages with a groove in the relevant seat in the crankcase or bearing
cap.
6    Wipe clean the bearing shell locations in the crankcase with a non-
fluffy rag, then lubricate them and fit the five upper halves of the bearing
shells to their seats. Note that the centre (No 3) bearing shell is plain,
whereas all the other shells have oil grooves (photos).
7    Fit the thrustwashers to the No 5 main bearing shell location, with
the grooved side of each washer facing away from the face of the
cylinder block – ie towards the thrust face of the crankshaft (photos).
8    Wipe the bearing shell locations in the bearing caps with a soft non-
fluffy rag, then fit the lower halves of the bearing shells to their seats.
Again, note that the centre (No 3) bearing shell is plain, whereas all the
other shells have oil grooves (photo).
9    Lubricate the crankshaft journals and the upper and lower main
bearing shells with clean engine oil (photo).
10    Carefully lower the crankshaft into the crankcase (photo). If necessary, seat the crankshaft using light taps with a rubber-faced hammer on
the crankshaft balance webs.
11    Lubricate the crankshaft main bearing journals again, the fit the

No 1 bearing cap. Fit the two securing bolts, and tighten them as far as
possible by hand.
12    Fit the No 5 bearing cap, and as before tighten the bolts as far as
possible by hand.
13    Fit the centre and then the intermediate bearing caps, and again
tighten the bolts as far as possible by hand.
14    Check that the markings on the bearing caps are correctly orientated as noted during dismantling – ie the identification grooves should
face towards the timing side of the engine, then working from the centre
cap outwards in a progressive sequence, finally tighten the bolts to the
specified torque (photo).
15    Check that the crankshaft rotates freely. Some stiffness is to be
expected with new components, but there should be no tight spots or
binding.
16    Check that crankshaft endfloat is within the specified limits, as
described in paragraph 70 of Part C in this Section.
17    Examine the condition of the front and rear crankshaft oil seals and
renew if necessary with reference to Part B of this Section. It is advisable
to renew the oil seals as a matter of course unless they are in perfect
condition.
18    Lubricate the oil seal lips with clean engine oil, then carefully fit the
front and rear oil seal housings using new gaskets.

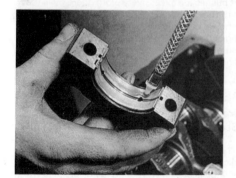

7D.9 ... and lubricate the shells

7D.10 Lower the crankshaft into position

7D.14 Tighten the main bearing cap bolts to
the specified torque setting

## Pistons and connecting rods – refitting
19    Refer to Part B of this Section.

## Oil pump – refitting
20    Refer to Part B of this Section.

## Sump – refitting
21    Refer to Part B of this Section.

## Flywheel – refitting
22    Refer to Part B of this Section. When the flywheel is bolted in position, refer to Chapter 5 for details and refit the clutch unit.

## Auxiliary shaft – refitting
23    Refer to Part C of this Section.

## Cylinder head – refitting
24    Refer to Part B of this Section. Note that this procedure describes cylinder head refitting complete with the camshaft housing assembly and manifolds as a complete unit. Details of refitting the camshaft housing (and followers) to the cylinder head will be found separately in Part B.

## Timing belt and covers – refitting
25    Refer to Part B of this Section.

## Engine/transmission – reconnection and refitting
**Note:** *A suitable hoist and lifting tackle will be required for this operation. New locktabs will be required for the exhaust downpipe-to-manifold nuts, and suitable exhaust assembly paste, such as Holts Firegum, will be required when reconnecting the downpipes to the exhaust manifold.*

26    Before attempting to reconnect the engine to the gearbox, check that the clutch friction disc is centralised as described in Chapter 5, Section 8. This is necessary to ensure that the gearbox input shaft splines will pass through the splines in the centre of the friction disc.
27    Check that the clutch release arm and bearing are correctly fitted, and lightly grease the input shaft splines.
28    Mate the engine and gearbox together, ensuring that the engine adapter plate is correctly located, and that the gearbox locates on the dowels in the cylinder block, then refit the engine-to-gearbox bolts and the single nut, but do not fully tighten them at this stage. Ensure that any brackets noted during removal are in place under the engine-to-gearbox bolts. **Do not** allow the weight of the gearbox to hang on the input shaft as it is engaged with the clutch friction disc.
29    Refit the starter motor, ensuring that the wiring harness bracket is in position on the top bolt.
30    Locate the engine/transmission unit at the front of the car and move it into position under the engine compartment. Attach the lifting sling and hoist as during removal.
31    Enlist the aid of an assistant to help steady the combined units as they are raised into position and to locate the mountings in the engine compartment.
32    Once they are located, tighten the mountings to the specified torque settings, then disconnect the lifting hoist and sling.
33    The remainder of the refitting and reconnection procedures are a reversal of the removal procedure described in Part C. For further details on reconnecting the suspension and driveshaft components, refer to Chapter 7 and Section 13 of this Chapter.
34    Ensure that the exhaust downpipe-to-manifold connection is clean and renew the gasket when reconnecting this joint. Use a smear of exhaust assembly paste on the joint faces. Use new lockwashers and tighten the flange nuts securely.
35    Ensure that all fuel and coolant connections are cleanly and securely made.
36    Ensure that all wiring connections are correct and securely made.
37    Top up the engine and transmission oil levels.
38    Refill the cooling system.
39    Check that all connections are securely made, then reconnect the battery negative lead.

## Initial start-up after major overhaul
40    Refer to Chapter 1, Section 45.

---

**8    Cooling system**

---

## PART A: 999 AND 1108 CC ENGINES
### Description
1    The operation and function of the cooling system is essentially as described in Chapter 2 but note the location of the various components and the routing of the coolant hoses in Fig. 13.26.

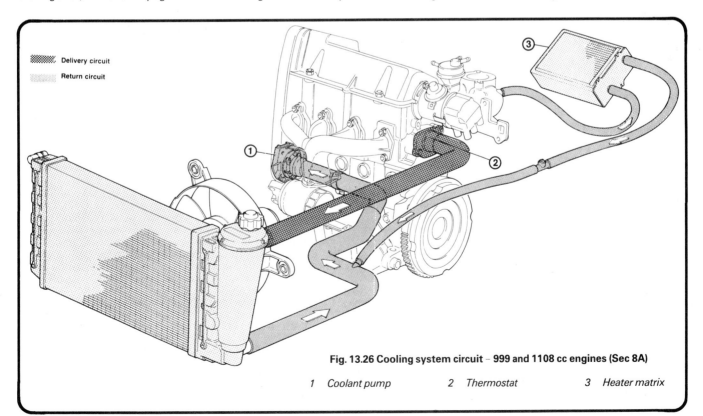

Fig. 13.26 Cooling system circuit – **999 and 1108 cc engines (Sec 8A)**

1    *Coolant pump*          2    *Thermostat*          3    *Heater matrix*

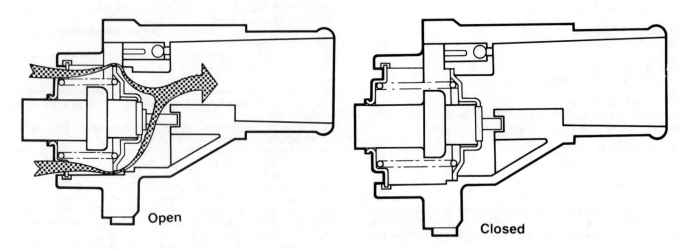

**Fig. 13.27 Cooling system thermostat in open and closed positions – 999 and 1108 cc engines (Sec 8A)**

8A.6 Thermostat housing (shown with distributor removed) on the 999 cc engine

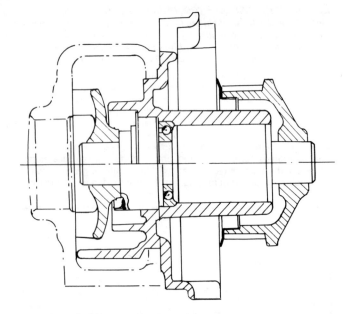

**Fig. 13.28 Sectional view of the coolant pump on the 999 and 1108 cc engines (Sec 8A)**

### Maintenance

2    Topping-up, draining and refilling procedures are as for 1116 and 1301 cc engines in Chapter 2, but note that the coolant capacity is different (see Specifications).

### Thermostat – removal and refitting

3    The thermostat is located on the left-hand end of the cylinder head, below the distributor.
4    The thermostat cannot be renewed independently of its housing and if faulty the complete assembly must be renewed.
5    Drain the cooling system.
6    Although the thermostat housing can be removed directly from the cylinder head, better access is provided if the distributor is first withdrawn as described in Section 10 of this Chapter (photo).
7    Disconnect the coolant hose from the thermostat housing and unscrew the housing flange bolts. Remove the assembly. Note that it may be necessary to tap it free with a plastic-faced or wooden mallet if stuck in place.
8    Remove the gasket and clean the mating surfaces.
9    Use a new gasket and bolt the assembly into position (photo).
10    Reconnect the coolant hose, then fill and bleed the cooling system.

### Coolant pump – removal and refitting

11    The coolant pump is located on the crankshaft pulley end of the

engine and is driven by the timing belt.
12    The pump cannot be repaired and must be regarded as disposable.
13    Drain the cooling system.
14    Remove the timing belt cover and then set No 1 piston to TDC. To achieve this, turn the crankshaft pulley bolt until the camshaft sprocket timing mark is aligned with the one on the cylinder head.
15    Release the belt tensioner and slip the timing belt off the camshaft and coolant pump sprockets.
16    Unbolt and remove the coolant pump and clean the mounting face of all old gasket material.
17    Apply a continuous bead of RTV silicone sealant (instant gasket) to the mounting face of the coolant pump and bolt it into position (photos).
18    Check that the camshaft sprocket and the crankshaft have not been moved and fit the timing belt to the camshaft and coolant pump sprockets. The pump sprocket does not require setting in any particular position before connecting the timing belt.
19    Tension the belt as described in Section 5B of this Chapter.
20    Fit the timing belt cover.
21    After allowing one hour for the gasket material to cure, refill and bleed the cooling system.

8A.9 Fitting the thermostat housing. Note the new gasket

8A.17A Fitting the coolant pump to the 999 cc engine

8A.17B Tightening the coolant pump bolts

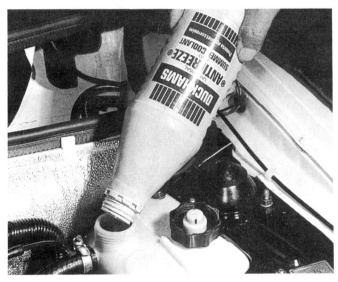

8B.4 Topping up the expansion tank with antifreeze on the 1301 cc engine

## PART B: 1301 CC TURBO IE ENGINE

### Description

1    The cooling system on this model has flow and return connections to the turbocharger, and is an essential means of cooling the turbo-charger.

2    The radiator cooling fan is of two-speed type, being controlled by a two-stage thermostatic switch screwed into the radiator side tank.

3    According to the coolant temperature level, the fan speed is regulated to provide the most effective cooling.

4    The remote cooling system expansion tank is mounted in the left-hand rear corner of the engine compartment (photo).

## PART C: 1372 CC IE AND 1372 CC TURBO IE ENGINES

### Description

1    The cooling system layout and components for the 1372 cc engines is shown in Figs. 13.29 and 13.30.

2    The system on each engine operates in essentially the same manner as that described for the other models in Chapter 2, but the location of components and the coolant hose routings differ according to model. The cooling system expansion tank location differs according to model, being either located on the side of the radiator or mounted separately on the side of the inner wing panel.

3    On Turbo models, the cooling system also assists in cooling the turbocharger.

### Maintenance

4    The maintenance procedures are essentially the same as those described for the other models in Chapter 2.

### Cooling system – draining, flushing and refilling

**Warning**: *Wait until the engine is cold before starting this procedure. Do not allow antifreeze to come into contact with your skin or painted surfaces of the vehicle. Rinse off spills immediately with plenty of water. Never leave antifreeze lying around in an open container or in a puddle in the driveway or on the garage floor. Children and pets are attracted by its sweet smell. Antifreeze is fatal if ingested.*

5    Disconnect the battery negative lead.

6    Working inside the vehicle, turn the heater temperature control knob fully to the right, which will fully open the heater coolant valve.

7    With the expansion tank cap removed, place a suitable container beneath the radiator bottom hose.

8    Loosen the clip and ease the bottom hose away from the radiator outlet (photo). Allow the coolant to drain into the container.

9    Reposition the container under the front of the cylinder block, and unscrew the cylinder block drain plug (photo). Allow the coolant to drain into the container.

10    Apply suitable sealant to the threads of the drain plug, then refit and tighten the plug.

11    Dispose of the drained coolant safely, or keep it in a covered container if it is to be re-used.

8C.8 Bottom hose connection to the radiator

8C.9 Cylinder block drain plug

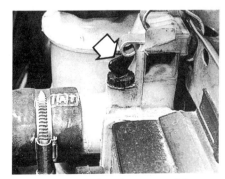

8C.14 Bleed screw location on top of the expansion tank (arrowed)

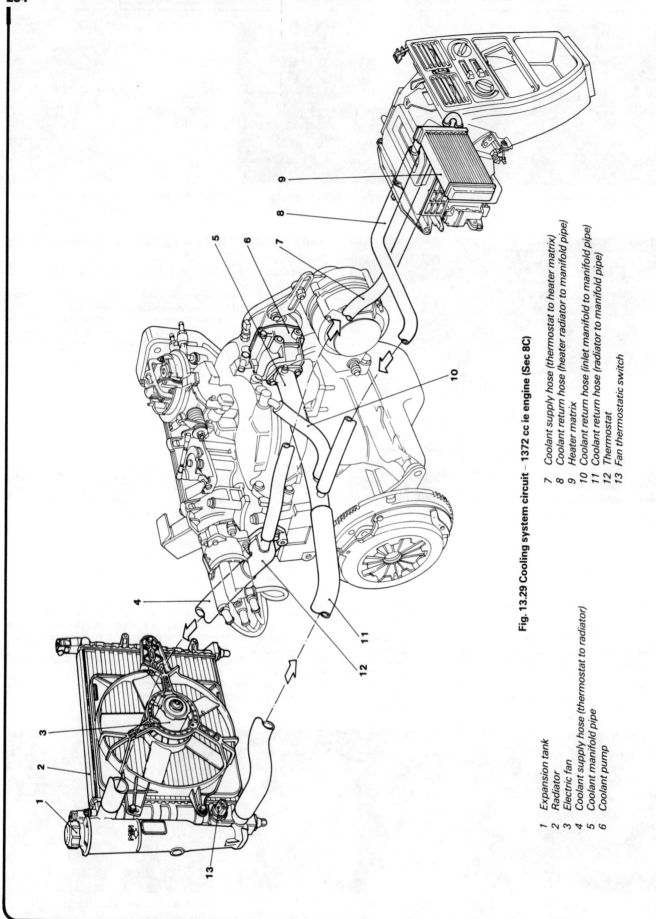

**Fig. 13.29 Cooling system circuit – 1372 cc ie engine (Sec 8C)**

1  Expansion tank
2  Radiator
3  Electric fan
4  Coolant supply hose (thermostat to radiator)
5  Coolant manifold pipe
6  Coolant pump
7  Coolant supply hose (thermostat to heater matrix)
8  Coolant return hose (heater radiator to manifold pipe)
9  Heater matrix
10  Coolant return hose (inlet manifold to manifold pipe)
11  Coolant return hose (radiator to manifold pipe)
12  Thermostat
13  Fan thermostatic switch

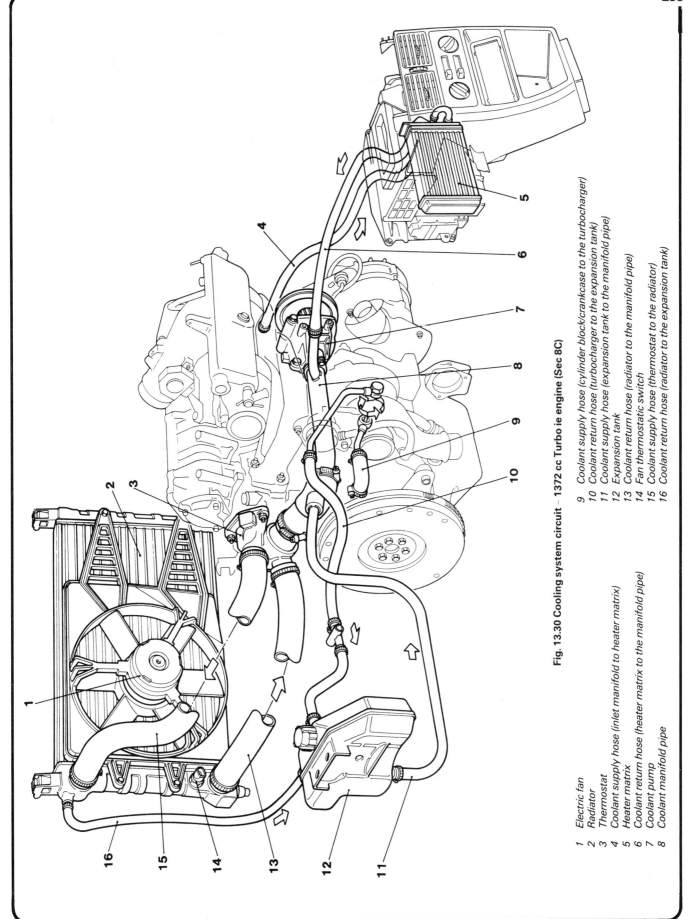

**Fig. 13.30 Cooling system circuit – 1372 cc Turbo ie engine (Sec 8C)**

1  Electric fan
2  Radiator
3  Thermostat
4  Coolant supply hose (inlet manifold to heater matrix)
5  Heater matrix
6  Coolant return hose (heater matrix to the manifold pipe)
7  Coolant pump
8  Coolant manifold pipe

9  Coolant supply hose (cylinder block/crankcase to the turbocharger)
10  Coolant return hose (turbocharger to the expansion tank)
11  Coolant supply hose (expansion tank to the manifold pipe)
12  Expansion tank
13  Coolant return hose (radiator to the manifold pipe)
14  Fan thermostatic switch
15  Coolant supply hose (thermostat to the radiator)
16  Coolant return hose (radiator to the expansion tank)

8C.21A Cooling fan and wiring connector

8C.21B Cooling fan switch wiring connector

8C.22 Cooling fan to radiator securing bolt

12   If required, the system can be flushed through as described in Section 2 of Chapter 2.
13   Before attempting to refill the cooling system, make sure that all hoses have been reconnected, that the hoses and clips are in good condition, and that the clips are tight. Also ensure that the cylinder block drain plug has been refitted and tightened. Note that an antifreeze mixture must be used all year round to prevent corrosion of the engine components – refer to Section 3, Chapter 2.
14   Open the bleed screw in the top of the expansion tank (photo).
15   Remove the expansion tank cap, and fill the system by slowly pouring the coolant into the expansion tank to prevent air locks from forming.
16   Top up the coolant until liquid free from air bubbles emerges from the radiator bleed screw orifice, then close the bleed screw.
17   Continue topping up until the coolant reaches the MAXimum mark on the expansion tank.
18   Start the engine and run it until it reaches normal operating temperature, then stop the engine and allow it to cool. Normal operating temperature is reached when the cooling fan cuts into operation. Feel the radiator top hose to ensure that it is hot. If cool, it indicates an air lock in the system.
19   Check for leaks, particularly around disturbed components. Check the coolant level in the expansion tank, and top up if necessary. Note that the system must be cold before an accurate level is indicated. There is a risk of scalding if the expansion tank cap is removed whilst the system is hot.

*Radiator (and cooling fan) – removal and refitting*
20   Disconnect the battery negative lead.
21   Detach the wiring connectors from the cooling fan and the fan switch located in the radiator (photos).

22   If preferred, the cooling fan unit can be removed separately from the radiator, by undoing the attachment bolts and carefully withdrawing the unit upwards from the vehicle. Take care not to damage the radiator core as it is lifted clear (photo).
23   Drain the cooling system as described earlier in this part of the Section, but note that it will not be necessary to remove the cylinder block drain plug.
24   Undo the retaining screws and remove the front grille panel.
25   Loosen off the retaining clips and detach the upper coolant hose and the expansion hose from the radiator.
26   Note their direction of fitting, then prise free the radiator retaining clips. Carefully lift the radiator from the car.
27   Refitting is a reversal of the removal procedure. Ensure that as the radiator is lowered into position, it engages in the two rubber location grommets.
28   With the radiator (and cooling fan) refitted, top up the cooling system as described earlier in this Section (photo).

*Thermostat – removal and refitting*
**Note:** *A new thermostat cover gasket must be used on refitting.*

29   Drain the cooling system as described earlier in this Section, but note that there is no need to drain the cylinder block.
30   Disconnect the coolant hoses from the thermostat cover (situated at the gearbox end of the cylinder head).
31   Unscrew the two thermostat cover securing bolts, noting that the left-hand bolt may also secure the HT lead bracket, and remove the thermostat/cover assembly. Recover the gasket (photo).
32   If faulty, the thermostat must be renewed complete with the housing as an assembly.
33   If desired the thermostat can be tested as described in Chapter 2.

8C.28 Topping up the radiator coolant level on the 1372 cc ie engine. Note orientation of radiator retaining clip (arrowed)

8C.31 Thermostat unit removal on the 1372 cc ie engine (distributor removed for clarity)

8C.40 Coolant pump/alternator bracket bolt removal

8C.48 Top side view of water pump, alternator and drivebelt

8C.49 Alternator/water pump drivebelt and tensioner viewed from the right-hand wheel arch

8C.52 Fitting a new coolant pump/alternator drivebelt around the pulleys

8C.53 Tightening the alternator adjuster nut

34    Refitting is a reversal of removal, bearing in mind the following points.

35    Clean the mating faces of the thermostat cover and cylinder head, and use a new gasket when refitting the cover.

36    Refill the cooling system as described earlier in this Section.

### Coolant pump – removal and refitting

**Note**: *A new coolant pump gasket must be used on refitting. If the pump is found to be worn it must be renewed as a complete unit, as dismantling and repair is not possible.*

37    Disconnect the battery negative lead.

38    Drain the cooling system as described earlier in this Section.

39    Remove the coolant/alternator drivebelt as described in the next sub-Section.

40    Unscrew the four coolant pump securing bolts, noting that two of the bolts also secure the alternator adjuster bracket, and withdraw the pump from the housing (photo). Recover the gasket.

41    Refitting is a reversal of removal, bearing in mind the following points.

42    Use a new gasket between the pump and the housing.

43    Refit and tension the coolant pump/alternator drivebelt as described in the next sub-Section.

44    On completion, refill the cooling system as described earlier in this Section.

### Coolant pump/alternator drivebelt – checking, renewal and tensioning

45    At the intervals specified in Section 3 or *Routine maintenance* at the beginning of this manual (as applicable), the drivebelt should be checked and if necessary re-tensioned.

46    Access to the drivebelt is made from the underside of the car on the right-hand side. Loosen off the front right-hand roadwheel retaining bolts, then raise and support the car on axle stands at the front. Remove the front roadwheel on the right-hand side.

47    Remove the underwing shield from the right-hand wheel arch by drifting the compression pins out from the retaining clips. Prise free the clips and remove the shield.

48    Additional, though somewhat restricted, access can be obtained from above by removing the air cleaner unit on the non-Turbo ie-engine (photo).

49    Check the full length of the drivebelt for cracks and deterioration. It will be necessary to turn the engine in order to check the portions of the drivebelt in contact with the pulleys. If a drivebelt is unserviceable, renew it as follows (photo).

50    Loosen the alternator mounting and adjuster nuts and bolts and pivot the alternator towards the cylinder block.

51    Slip the drivebelt from the alternator, coolant pump and crankshaft pulleys.

52    Fit the new drivebelt around the pulleys, then lever the alternator away from the cylinder block until the specified belt tension is achieved. Lever the alternator using a wooden or plastic lever at the pulley end to prevent damage. It is helpful to partially tighten the adjuster nut before tensioning the drivebelt (photo).

53    When the specified tension has been achieved, tighten the mounting and adjuster nuts and bolts (photo).

## PART D: HEATER UNIT – LATER MODELS

### Heater unit – removal and refitting

1    The heater unit is removed complete with the facia/control panel. Commence by draining the cooling system as described previously in this Section.

2    Disconnect the battery negative lead.

3    Refer to Section 15 of this Chapter for details and remove the ashtray/cigar lighter and the auxiliary control panel.

4    Undo the upper screw retaining the heater unit to the facia (see Fig. 13.31).

5    Remove the radio from the central facia.

6    Undo the retaining screw on each side at the front of the gear lever console. Prise free the trim cover, undo the retaining screw at the rear of the console. Prise free and release the gear lever gaiter and lift clear the central console.

7    Undo the retaining screws and remove the steering column upper and lower shroud.

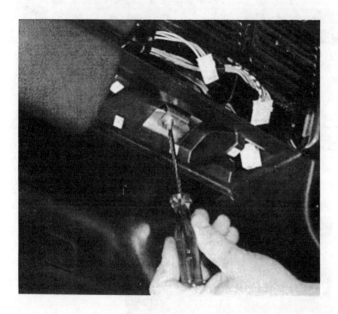

Fig. 13.31 Removing the heater unit-to-facia upper retaining screw (Sec 8D)

Fig. 13.32 Heater unit facia to main facia retaining screw locations (arrowed) (Sec 8D)

8　Detach and remove the lower facia trim on the side of the central facia.

9　Referring to Fig. 13.32, unscrew and remove the four heater facia to main facia retaining screws from the points indicated.

10　Undo the two retaining nuts securing the heater to the body on the driver's side.

11　Undo the retaining screws and remove the pipe shield from the side of the heater unit, then disconnect the coolant supply and return hoses from the heater. As the hoses are detached, be prepared to catch any remaining coolant as it flows from the hoses and heater connections.

12　Undo the remaining two heater unit securing nuts and withdraw the heater unit from the car. As the unit is removed, detach the wiring and position the hoses with their ends pointing upwards to avoid further coolant spillage.

13　Refit in the reverse order of removal. Ensure that the hoses are securely reconnected. Top up the cooling system on completion.

Fig. 13.33 Heater pipe shield securing screw positions on later models (Sec 8D)

### Heater unit – dismantling and reassembly

14　Remove the heater unit as described previously.

15　Pull free the heater/fresh air and blower control knobs (photo).

16　Undo the two retaining screws and withdraw the control panel from the facia. Detach the wiring connectors from the panel illumination lights and remove the panel.

17　Unscrew the retaining bolts and remove the centre panel from the heater unit.

18　Undo the retaining screws and remove the control lever mounting.

19　Loosen off the grub screws and detach the cables from the control levers.

20　Undo the retaining screws and remove the control valve.

21　Undo the two retaining screws and withdraw the heater matrix from the heater housing.

22　To separate the casing halves, drill out the pop rivet securing the mounting bracket, release the retaining clips and unscrew the securing bolts.

23　Reassemble in the reverse order of dismantling. Check that the control cables are correctly adjusted and that the controls operate in a satisfactory manner before refitting the heater unit to the car.

8D.15 Pull free the heater/fresh air and blower control knobs

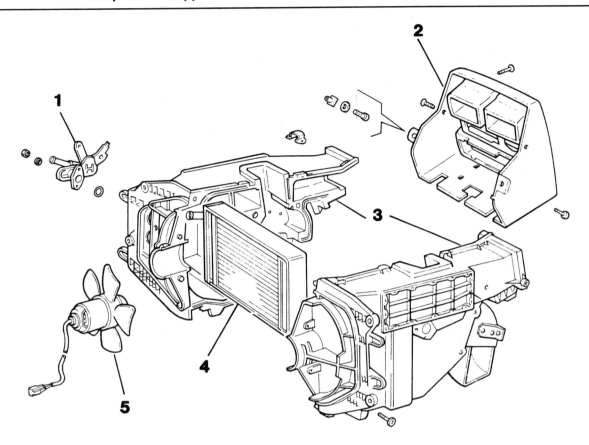

**Fig. 13.34 Heater unit components on later models (Sec 8D)**

| 1 | Coolant inlet tap | 2 | Centre panel | 3 | Side casings | 4 | Heater matrix | 5 | Blower fan |

---

## 9  Fuel and exhaust systems

## PART A: GENERAL

### Unleaded fuel

1  It is possible to use unleaded fuel (minimum 95 RON) in the following models with the indicated serial numbers.

| Engine | Serial number |
| --- | --- |
| 903 cc | 146A.000 |
| | 146A.046 |
| | 146A.048 |
| 999 cc | 156A2.00 |
| 1108 cc | 160A3.000 |
| 1116 cc | 138B.000 |
| | 138B.046 |
| | 146A4.000 |
| | 146A4.048 |
| 1299/1301 cc | 138B2.000 |
| | 138B2.046 |
| | 149A7.000 |
| | 1149A7.000 |
| | 146A2.000 |
| 1372 cc | 146C1.000 |
| | 146A8.000 |
| | 160A1.046 |

2  On all except the 903 cc engine, the use of unleaded fuel is conditional upon the avoidance of constant high speeds and sudden acceleration. Note that on models with catalytic converters **only unleaded** petrol must be used – the use of leaded petrol will destroy the catalyst.

### Air cleaner – modified types

3  The air cleaner on later models is of the automatic temperature-controlled type. The need to move the intake control lever to winter or summer positions is no longer required.

4  The air cleaner on the 999 cc engine is of rectangular shape and the element is removed for renewal after prising back the toggle type clips (photos).

5  To remove this type of air cleaner, disconnect the cold and hot air intake hoses and the large and small breather hoses (photos).

6  Unscrew the nut from the upper casing section and then release the lower toggle type clip and lift the air cleaner from the carburettor (photo). Note the sealing ring between the air cleaner and the carburettor. Unless the ring is in good condition, renew it.

7  If the thermostatically-controlled cold air flap opener in the air cleaner casing is faulty (checked by holding a mirror against the cold air intake when the engine is warm), renew the opener (single fixing screw); no repair is possible (photo).

8  The air cleaner on the 1116 cc and 1299/1301 cc engine is of circular type. Access to the element is obtained by extracting the three cover nuts and lifting off the lid (photos).

9  The air cleaner casing can be removed after unscrewing the four nuts which hold it to the carburettor and the single nut on the camshaft cover bracket. As the casing is withdrawn, disconnect the hoses from it (photos).

10  The thermostatically-controlled cold air flap opener is similar to that described in paragraph 7.

11  The air cleaner on the 1372 cc ie engine is of rectangular shape. The element can be removed after releasing the spring clips at the front of the unit, followed by the two screws from its top face. The air cleaner end cover can then be withdrawn and the element removed. The air cleaner unit on the 1372 cc Turbo ie engine is located in the front right-hand corner of the engine compartment. Prise free the four clips to release the top cover and expose the element.

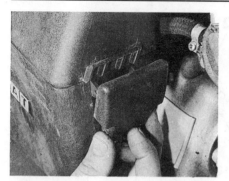

9A.4A Air cleaner toggle clip on the 999 cc model

9A.4B Air cleaner element on the 999 cc model

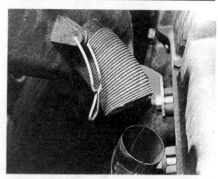

9A.5A Air cleaner hot air intake and lower retaining clip on the 999 cc model

9A.5B Air cleaner cold air intake on the 999 cc model

9A.5C Air cleaner breather hoses on the 999 cc model

9A.6 Air cleaner casing nut on the 999 cc model

9A.7 Air cleaner thermostatic flap opener on the 999 cc model

9A.8A Air cleaner on the 1116 cc, 1299 cc and 1301 cc models

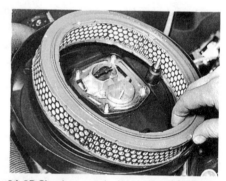

9A.8B Circular type air cleaner element

9A.9A Circular type air cleaner fixing nuts

9A.9B Circular type air cleaner nut on the camshaft cover (arrowed)

## Fuel pump (999 and 1108 cc engines) – description, removal and refitting

12    The fuel pump is mechanically-operated via a pushrod which is in contact with an eccentric cam on the camshaft. The pump is of sealed, disposable type – no repair or cleaning being possible.

13    To remove the pump, disconnect the flexible hoses and unbolt the pump from the cylinder head. Retain the pushrod and the insulator block.

14    Refitting is a reversal of removal, use new gaskets, one on each side of the insulator block.

## Fuel tank (999 and 1108 cc engines)

15    In conjunction with the plastic type fuel tank, the breather and fuel level transmitter unit have been modified as shown in Fig. 13.35.

## PART B: CARBURETTOR MODELS

### Carburettor (Weber 32 TLF) – description

1    This carburettor is used on the 999 cc engine and is of the single venturi downdraught type, with a manually-operated choke (cold start).

2    The unit incorporates an automatic anti-flooding device, a full-power valve and an accelerator pump (photos).

3    The throttle valve block, although incorporating coolant hose stubs, is not in fact coolant-heated.

9B.2A Weber 32 TLF 4/250 carburettor from anti-run-on solenoid valve side

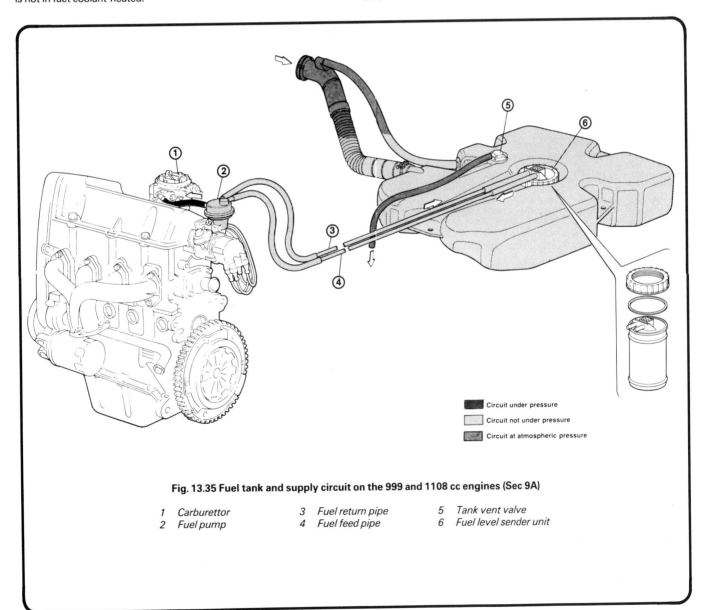

Circuit under pressure

Circuit not under pressure

Circuit at atmospheric pressure

**Fig. 13.35 Fuel tank and supply circuit on the 999 and 1108 cc engines (Sec 9A)**

| | | |
|---|---|---|
| 1   Carburettor | 3   Fuel return pipe | 5   Tank vent valve |
| 2   Fuel pump | 4   Fuel feed pipe | 6   Fuel level sender unit |

9B.2B Weber 32 TLF 4/250 carburettor from choke linkage side

9B.2C Weber 32 TLF 4/250 carburettor from accelerator pump side

9B.2D Weber 32 TLF 4/250 carburettor from throttle linkage side

9B.2E Weber 32 TLF 4/250 carburettor from above

9B.6 Weber 32 TLF 4/250 carburettor idle speed screw (arrowed)

4    A solenoid-operated idle cut-off valve is fitted to prevent running-on (dieseling) when the ignition is switched off.

## Carburettor (Weber 32 TLF) – idle speed and mixture adjustment

5    If the car is not equipped with a rev counter, connect one in accordance with the manufacturer's instructions.
6    Have the engine at normal operating temperature and idling. Turn the idle speed screw on the carburettor until the speed matches that specified (photo).
7    The idle mixture is set in production, and the adjustment screw is sealed with a tamperproof cap. If, however, the idling is not smooth or the engine or carburettor have been extensively overhauled, the mixture may require adjusting.
8    Prise out the tamperproof plug and connect an exhaust gas analyser to the car in accordance with the instrument manufacturer's instructions (photo).
9    With the engine at normal operating temperature and idling at the specified speed, turn the mixture screw until the CO percentage is within the specified tolerance (photo).

10    If an exhaust gas analyser is not available, turn the mixture screw anti-clockwise to obtain maximum idle speed and then turn it clockwise until the speed just starts to drop. Re-adjust the idle speed screw to bring the idle speed to the specified level.
11    Switch off the engine and remove the test instruments. It is advisable to fit a new tamperproof cap to the mixture screw if it is intended to take the vehicle overseas. This is required to meet legislation in certain countries.

## Carburettor (Weber 32 TLF) – removal and refitting

12    Remove the air cleaner.
13    Release the clips and disconnect the fuel hoses from the carburettor. Take extreme care that fuel spillage is contained and that there are no naked flames in the vicinity of the work area. Do not smoke.
14    Disconnect the distributor vacuum hose from the carburettor.
15    Release the clamp screw and pinch-bolt, and disconnect the choke cable.
16    Slacken the throttle cable by releasing the locknut and turning the adjuster sleeve, then slip the cable nipple out of the notch in the throttle spindle quadrant.

9B.8 Weber 32 TLF 4/250 carburettor mixture screw location under tamperproof plug (arrowed)

9B.9 Mixture adjustment – Weber 32 TLF carburettor

9B.18 Removing the Weber 32 TLF carburettor by gripping air cleaner mounting bracket

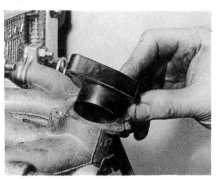

9B.19 Carburettor insulator block

9B.22 Fuel filter removal from the Weber 32 TLF carburettor

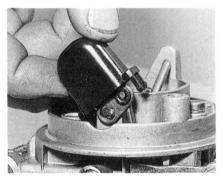

9B.23A Choke linkage cover removal from the Weber 32 TLF carburettor

9B.23B Disconnecting the choke linkage on the Weber 32 TLF carburettor

9B.23C Underside view of the cover on the Weber 32 TLF carburettor

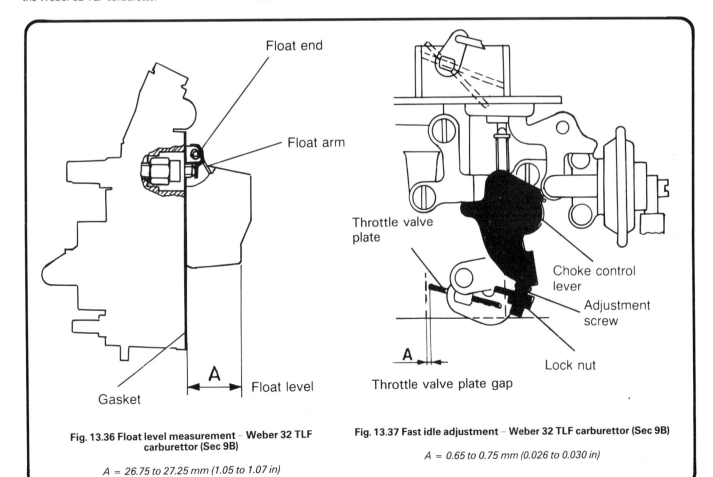

**Fig. 13.36 Float level measurement – Weber 32 TLF carburettor (Sec 9B)**

*A = 26.75 to 27.25 mm (1.05 to 1.07 in)*

**Fig. 13.37 Fast idle adjustment – Weber 32 TLF carburettor (Sec 9B)**

*A = 0.65 to 0.75 mm (0.026 to 0.030 in)*

9B.26A Floats and pivot pin arrangement on the Weber 32 TLF carburettor

9B.26B Fuel inlet valve needle removal from the Weber 32 TLF carburettor

9B.26C Fuel inlet valve body and washer removal from the Weber 32 TLF carburettor

9B.26D Extracting the throttle valve block screws from the Weber 32 TLF carburettor

9B.26E Throttle valve block gasket on the Weber 32 TLF carburettor

9B.26F Main parts of the Weber 32 TLF carburettor

17    Disconnect the lead from the idle cut-off solenoid valve.
18    Unscrew the two long mounting bolts and lift the carburettor from the inlet manifold (photo).
19    Refitting is a reversal of removal, but observe the following points (photo).

   (a)    Use a new flange gasket at each side of the insulator block.
   (b)    Check that the choke cable is fitted so that full choke can be obtained but the choke is fully off when the choke control lever is pushed right in.
   (c)    Adjust the throttle cable so that there is just a slight amount of slackness when the accelerator pedal is released, but when fully depressed, full throttle can be obtained (throttle valve plate quadrant up against its stop).

### Carburettor (Weber 32 TLF) – overhaul

20    It is rare for a carburettor to require complete overhaul and if the unit has seen considerable service and wear is detected in the throttle valve spindle bushes, it is recommended that a new or rebuilt carburettor is obtained.
21    Normally, the following operations are all that will be required to keep the carburettor working perfectly. The unit need not be removed from the manifold unless the throttle block is to be detached; simply remove the air cleaner.
22    Periodically, unscrew the large hexagonal plug adjacent to the fuel inlet pipe, extract the filter and clean it. Refit the filter and plug (photo).
23    Obtain a repair kit for your carburettor which will contain all the necessary replacement gaskets and seals. Extract the top cover and choke diaphragm assembly fixing screws, remove the small plastic cover and push out the bush, then lift the top cover from the carburettor. Discard the gasket (photos).
24    Mop out fuel and sediment from the float chamber.
25    The various jets and calibrated bleeds can then be removed and cleared by blowing them through with air from a tyre pump. **Do not** attempt to clear them by probing with wire, as this will ruin the calibration.
26    Check the tightness of the fuel inlet needle valve. If necessary, remove the float and its pivot pin so that a close-fitting ring spanner can be used on the valve body. Take care to support the pivot pin pedestals

Choke valve plate gap

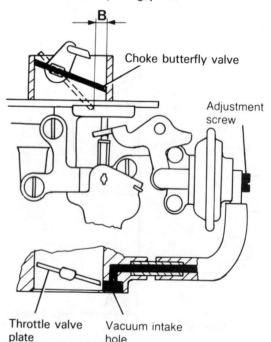

Fig. 13.38 Automatic anti-flooding device adjustment –
Weber 32 TLF carburettor (Sec 9B)

B = 4.5 mm (0.18 in)

9B.34A Weber 30/32 DMTE carburettor from anti-flood device link side

9B.34B Weber 30/32 DMTE carburettor from diaphragm hose side

9B.34C Weber 30/32 DMTE carburettor from choke link side

9B.34D Weber 30/32 DMTE carburettor from throttle link side

9B.34E Weber 30/32 DMTE carburettor from above (with cover removed)

as the pin is tapped out – they are brittle. The throttle valve plate block can be removed after extracting the screws (photos).
27    As reassembly progresses, carry out the following checks and adjustments.

**Float level – checking and adjustment**
28    With the carburettor top cover held vertically so that the float arm just touches the fuel inlet needle valve ball, measure between the float and the surface of the flange gasket as shown in Fig. 13.36. If the dimension is not within the specified tolerance, bend the float tab which bears on the needle valve ball.

**Fast idle – adjustment (requires removal of the carburettor)**
29    Close the choke valve plate by moving the control lever fully. Retain the lever in this position with a rubber band.
30    The throttle valve plate should now be open to give a gap between its edge and the progression holes as specified. Check the gap using a

twist drill of equivalent diameter.
31    If adjustment is required, release the locknut and turn the adjustment screw. Retighten the locknut.

**Automatic anti-flooding device – adjustment**
32    Operate the choke valve plate lever fully.
33    Move the control lever on the automatic anti-flooding device downwards to simulate vacuum pull-down. The choke butterfly should open, leaving a gap (B – Fig 13.38) as specified. Measure the gap with a twist drill of equivalent diameter and make sure that the choke valve plate is in the position shown. If adjustment is required, turn the screw on the diaphragm unit.

*Carburettor (Weber 30/32 DMTE) – general*
34    The carburettor is of twin barrel downdraught type with a

9B.36A Showing idle speed screw (arrowed) and ...

9B.36B ... mixture screw (arrowed) on the Weber 30/32 DMTE carburettor

9B.37A Fuel inlet and return hoses on the Weber 30/32 DMTE carburettor

9B.37B Throttle cable connection on the Weber 30/32 DMTE carburettor

9B.37C Choke cable connection on the Weber 30/32 DMTE carburettor

9B.37D Electrical lead to automatic anti-flood device on the Weber 30/32 DMTE carburettor

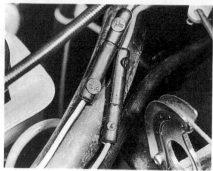

9B.37E Carburettor lead connectors on the Weber 30/32 DMTE carburettor

9B.37F Unscrewing a carburettor fixing nut

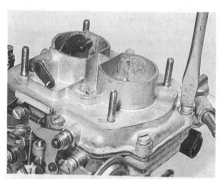

9B.40 Unscrewing a top cover screw from the Weber 30/32 DMTE carburettor

9B.41 Jets on the Weber 30/32 DMTE carburettor (top cover removed)

9B.45 Float pivot arrangement and needle valve on the Weber 30/32 DMTE carburettor

manually-operated choke and an electronic fuel cut-off overrun valve (photos).

35    Periodically, remove the large hexagonal plug from its location at the fuel inlet pipe stubs, and clean any dirt from the filter gauze.

**Idle speed and mixture adjustment**

36    Refer to Chapter 3, Section 7 (photos).

**Removal and refitting**

37    The operations are similar to those described for the Weber 32 TLF earlier in this Supplement, but note that the carburettor is secured by four nuts and additional electrical leads must be disconnected (photos).

*Carburettor (Weber 30/32 DMTE) – overhaul*

38    The carburettor top cover with float may be removed without the need to withdraw the carburettor from the manifold. Other adjustments described in this sub-Section, however, will require removal of the carburettor.

39    Disconnect the short, curved diaphragm hose from the top cover.

40    Extract the top cover screws, lift the cover from the carburettor body, and rotate it in order to release the cranked choke control rod from

its key hole (photo). Mop out the fuel and clean the jets.

41    Check the jet sizes and other components against those listed in the Specifications, in case a previous owner has substituted incorrect components (photo).

42    Overhaul procedures are generally as given in Chapter 3, Section 14 for the Weber 30/32 DMTR, but use the Specifications listed in this Chapter. Additional overhaul procedures are given here.

**Fuel inlet needle valve**

43    If a high float level causing flooding of the carburettor has been evident, first check that the inlet valve housing is tight, and its washer is sealing satisfactorily. A leak here will cause fuel to bypass the inlet valve.

44    If the needle valve is to be renewed, remove it in the following way.

45    Access to the fuel inlet needle valve is obtained by carefully tapping out the float arm pivot pin. Take care, the pivot pin pillars are very brittle (photo).

46    Unscrew the fuel inlet valve body and remove the valve and washer.

9C.5 Electric fuel pump/filter/pressure damper assembly location on a 1301 cc Turbo ie model

47   When refitting the new valve, always use a new sealing washer.
**Float stroke (travel) – see Fig. 3.10**
48   The float stroke should be between 42.5 and 43.5 mm when measured from the top cover gasket. Adjust if necessary by bending the tab on the end of the arm.
**Accelerator pump**
49   Adjustment of the accelerator pump is very rarely required, but if performance is suspect, carry out the following operations.
50   Fill the carburettor float chamber and then operate the throttle valve plate lever several times to prime the pump.
51   Position a test tube under the accelerator pump jet and give ten full strokes of the throttle lever, pausing between each stroke to allow fuel to finish dripping.
52   The total volume of fuel collected should be as specified. Adjust the nut on the pump control if necessary to increase or decrease the volume of fuel ejected.
**General**
53   When the stage is reached where the valve plate spindle bushes have worn, then the carburettor should be renewed complete.
54   When reassembling the carburettor, use new gaskets which can be obtained in a repair pack.

*Carburettor (Weber 32 ICEV 61/250 and DMTE 30/32, DMTE 30/150) – general*
55   These carburettor types are fitted to later models according to engine type. They are similar in structure and operation to their equivalents described in Chapter 3. Reference can therefore be made to that Chapter for the description and any operations concerning them, but refer to Section 2 of this Chapter for their specifications.

*Carburettor (Solex C 30/32-CIC 8) – description*
56   This carburettor is fitted as an alternative to the Weber unit on 1116 cc models produced for certain markets. The removal, refitting and overhaul procedures are essentially the same as described earlier for the Weber carburettors.

## PART C: FUEL INJECTION SYSTEM – 1301 CC TURBO IE ENGINE

*Description*
1   A Bosch LE2-Jetronic fuel injection system is fitted to the 1301 cc Turbo ie model.
2   The fuel injectors are fed at constant pressure in relation to inlet manifold vacuum pressure.
3   The system electronic control unit (ECU) actuates the injectors for variable duration, and so supplies the precise volume of fuel required for any given engine speed and load condition.

4   The ECU also monitors the air induction, air temperature, coolant temperature and throttle opening as additional parameters to compute the required opening of the fuel injectors, giving maximum power with fuel economy.
**Fuel supply system**
5   The fuel supply system consists of an electric pump and primary filter, located adjacent to the fuel tank. A fuel pressure peak damper is located next to the pump (photo).
6   Fuel is then pumped through a secondary filter to the fuel rail and injectors. The injectors are of the solenoid-operated type, actuated from the ECU.
7   Fuel pressure is regulated according to inlet manifold vacuum pressure by a fuel pressure regulator. Excess unpressurised fuel is returned to the fuel tank.
**Airflow meter**
8   This component measures the quantity of air drawn into the engine, and converts this into an electric signal which is transmitted to the ECU.
9   The intake air exerts a force on the floating plate (1) (Fig. 13.39) which is connected to a potentiometer (2).
10   A compensating butterfly valve (3) compensates for any reflux pressure which may occur, and is subject to the braking effect of the damper chamber (4).
11   The idle mixture (air/fuel ratio) is altered by means of the screw (8), which alters the cross-section of the bypass channel (7).
12   An integral-type temperature sensor is fitted, the resistance value of which decreases as the temperature of the intake air increases. This facility is used to correct the mixture strength within a pre-determined air temperature range.
**Throttle valve housing**
13   The housing incorporates a conventional butterfly-type throttle valve, actuated by cables and rods from the accelerator pedal.
14   The idle bypass channel (2) (Fig. 13.40) is fitted with an adjustment screw (3) to vary the idle speed.
15   The other screw (4) and locknut are used to set the closing position of the throttle valve plate.
**Supplementary air valve**
16   This controls the air volume requirement during cold starting. Essentially, the valve is an electrically-heated bi-metallic strip, which rotates the plate (4) (Fig. 13.41) to vary the volume of air being drawn in through the aperture (1), according to the temperature of the engine.
17   The requirement for additional air during cold starting is to dilute the additional fuel, which is injected and controlled by the ECU as a result of monitoring the engine coolant temperature sensor.

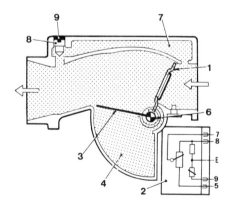

**Fig. 13.39 Sectional view of airflow meter – 1301 cc Turbo ie engine (Sec 9C)**

| | | |
|---|---|---|
| 1 | Floating plate | 6 Spring |
| 2 | Potentiometer | 7 Bypass channel |
| 3 | Compensating | 8 CO adjusting screw |
| | butterfly valve | 9 Tamperproof plug |
| 4 | Damper chamber | |

Terminals:
5, 7, 8   Potentiometer
9   Air temperature sensor
E   Sealed (not to be touched)

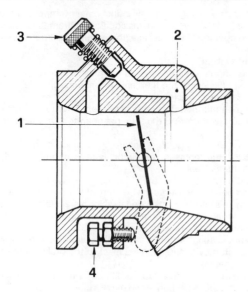

**Fig. 13.40 Sectional view of throttle valve housing – 1301 cc Turbo ie engine (Sec 9C)**

1   Butterfly-type throttle
    valve
2   Idle bypass channel

3   Idle speed adjusting screw
4   Throttle valve plate setting
    screw

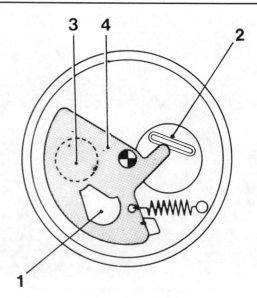

**Fig. 13.41 Supplementary air valve – 1301 cc Turbo ie engine (Sec 9C)**

1   Aperture
2   Bi-metallic strip

3   Passage
4   Rotating plate (closed position)

**Electrical control circuit**
18   The main components of the system are the ECU and the system control relay. The relay incorporates a fuel cut-off facility, which cuts off the fuel supply in the event of engine failure, the vehicle turning over, or a fuel line breaking. The relay energizes the following electrical components.
19   *Coolant temperature sensor,* which signals the coolant temperature to the ECU.
20   *Throttle position switch,* which signals the ECU when the throttle valve plate is closed, in order to actuate the deceleration fuel cut-off device at speeds above 2500 rev/min.
21   The switch also signals the ECU at full throttle, so that the mixture can be enriched to cope with full-power requirements.
22   The system control relay also monitors the engine speed directly from the ignition coil primary winding.

*Maintenance*
23   Regularly check the security of all system hoses, wiring connections and plugs.
24   At the intervals specified in Section 3, renew the secondary fuel filter and the air cleaner element.

*Secondary fuel filter – renewal*
25   This is located within the engine compartment just above the

timing belt cover. Disconnect the fuel hoses, but be prepared for loss of fuel (photo).
26   When fitting the new filter, make sure that the arrow stamped on it is pointing towards the fuel injector rail.

*Air cleaner element – renewal*
27   Prise back the toggle-type clips and take off the air cleaner lid. Remove and discard the element, and wipe any dirt from the inside of the casing (photos).
28   Fit the new element and replace the lid.

*Idle speed and mixture adjustment*
29   Before carrying out any adjustments, the engine must be at operating temperature, the fan having cut in at second speed and then switched off.
30   Release the locknut and turn the main idle speed screw in the throttle valve housing until the engine idles at the specified speed. This should be all that is necessary to obtain the correct idle speed, as the throttle valve plate base setting is set during production. However, if wear has taken place, or incorrect adjustment has been carried out previously, proceed in the following way.
31   Disconnect the intake duct from the throttle valve housing. Release the locknut on the base (small) adjusting screw, and turn the screw until there is a clearance between the lower edge of the throttle valve

9C.25 Secondary fuel filter

9C.27A Removing the air cleaner lid

9C.27B Removing the air cleaner element

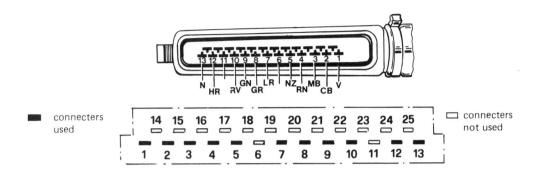

**Fig. 13.42 ECU and component connector plug terminals – 1301 cc Turbo ie engine (Sec 9C)**

*For colour code see main wiring diagrams*

9C.31A Disconnecting the throttle valve housing intake duct

**Fig. 13.43 System control relay connector plug terminals – 1301 cc Turbo ie engine (Sec 9C)**

34    Finally, turn the main (large) adjusting screw to give an idle speed of between 800 and 900 rev/min.

35    It is unlikely that the mixture will require alteration, but if it does, connect an exhaust gas analyzer to the car in accordance with the equipment manufacturer's instructions.

36    With the engine at operating temperature, prise out the tamper-proof cap, and turn the mixture screw, which is located in the airflow meter, until the CO level is as given in the Specifications. Turning the screw clockwise richens the mixture, turning it anti-clockwise weakens the mixture. Use a close-fitting Allen key for the adjustment (photo).

*Fuel injection system – electrical tests*

37    When carrying out checks to trace a fault in the system, an ohmmeter should be used for the following tests.

38    Disconnect the multipin connector from the ECU, and also the one from the system control relay, and apply the probes of the ohmmeter in accordance with the following sequence to check for continuity in the

plate and the throat wall of between 0.05 and 0.1 mm (photos).

32    With the engine still at operating temperature, start the engine, and having released the locknut, turn the main (large) idle speed screw fully clockwise to close the bypass passage.

33    Now turn the base (small) screw until the engine idles at between 700 and 800 rev/min. Tighten the locknut.

9C.31B Idle speed base setting screw (1) and main adjustment screw (2)

9C.31C Checking throttle valve plate opening with a feeler blade

9C.36 Using an Allen key to adjust the mixture (CO level)

cables. The component wiring plug will of course be disconnected for the test.

| ECU connector plug terminal | Component connector plug terminal |
|---|---|
| 1 | 1 of ignition coil |
| 2 | 2 of throttle position switch |
| 3 | 3 of throttle position switch |
| 4 | 50 of ignition switch |
| 5 | Earth |
| 5 | 5 of airflow meter |
| 7 | 7 of airflow meter |
| 8 | 8 of airflow meter |
| 9 | 9 of airflow meter |
| 9 | 9 of throttle position switch |
| 9 | 18 of supplementary air valve |
| 9 | 87 main relay socket |
| 10 | 10 of coolant temperature sensor |
| 12 | Injector terminals |
| 13 | Earth |

| System control relay connector plug terminal | Component connector plug terminal |
|---|---|
| 87 | Injector terminals |
| 87 | 18 of throttle position switch |
| 87 | 9 of ECU multipin socket |
| 31 | Earth |
| 1 | 1 of ignition coil |
| 15 | 15 of ignition switch |
| 50 | 50 of ignition switch |
| 30 | Battery positive |
| 87b | Fuel pump (fused) |

39   Now use the ohmmeter to check the resistance of the following components.
**Supplementary air valve**
40   Resistance between the terminals should be between 40 and 60 ohms at 20°C (68°F).

**Airflow meter**
41   Resistance between terminals 5 and 8 of the potentiometer should be between 330 and 360 ohms at 20°C (68°F).
42   Resistance between terminals 8 and 9 of the internal circuit should be between 190 and 210 ohms at 20°C (68°F) and between 170 and 190 ohms at 60°C (140°F).
**Coolant temperature sensor**
43   At 20°C (68°F) the resistance should be between 2 and 4 k ohms. At 50°C (122°F) the resistance should be between 600 and 900 ohms. At 90°C (194°F) the resistance should be between 100 and 300 ohms.
**Fuel injectors.**
44   The winding resistance should be between 15 and 17 ohms at 20°C (68°F).
**Throttle position switch**
45   With the throttle butterfly valve closed, there should be continuity between terminals 18 and 2, and with the valve fully open, there should be no continuity between terminals 18 and 3.
46   The throttle position switch should not be disturbed unless absolutely necessary. If it has to be removed, then refit it so that the microswitch is heard to click immediately the throttle butterfly is opened.

*Fuel injection system – mechanical tests*
**Fuel pump**
47   To test the pressure of the fuel pump, a pressure gauge will be required, connected into the fuel delivery hose.
48   Remove the multipin plug from the system control relay and bridge terminals 87b and 30.
49   Turn the ignition switch on. The pump should operate and indicate a pressure of between 2.8 and 3.0 bars (40 and 44 lbf/in$^2$).
50   To check the operation of the peak pressure regulator, pinch the fuel return hose. If the fuel pressure increases, the regulator must be faulty, and should be renewed.
51   Check that the fuel pressure increases when, with the engine idling, the accelerator is depressed sharply.

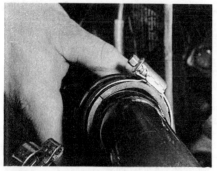
9C.55A Disconnecting the duct from the air cleaner

9C.55B Removing the air cleaner casing upper bracket

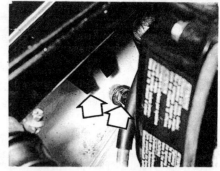
9C.55C Air cleaner casing lower bracket and bolt (arrowed)

9C.55D Air cleaner metal duct over radiator

9C.56 Air intake duct at airflow meter (securing clip arrowed)

9C.57 Air outlet duct securing clip removal from airflow meter

9C.60 Fuel pressure regulator

9C.63 Coolant temperature sensor (arrowed)

### Supplementary air valve

52   With the engine at normal operating temperature and idling, pinch the supplementary air valve hose using a pair of pliers. The engine speed should not drop by more than 50 rev/min. If it does, renew the valve.

## Fuel injection system components – removal and refitting

53   Disconnect the battery before carrying out any of the following operations.

### Air cleaner

54   Remove the cover and filter element as previously described.
55   Disconnect the duct from the air cleaner casing, and then unbolt and remove the casing. Note that the lower bracket bolt need not be completely removed, only unscrewed, due to the design of the bracket. The air cleaner metal duct is routed over the top of the radiator (photos).

### Airflow meter

56   Release the securing clip and disconnect the air intake duct (photo).
57   Release the securing clip and disconnect the air outlet duct (photo).
58   Disconnect the wiring plug.
59   Unscrew the fixing screws and remove the airflow meter from its mounting bracket.

### Fuel pressure regulator

60   Disconnect the vacuum hose from the regulator (photo).
61   Anticipate some loss of pressurised fuel, and then disconnect the fuel hose from the regulator. Unbolt and remove the unit.

### Excessive air pressure switch

62   This is screwed into the end of the inlet manifold. Disconnect the electrical leads and unscrew the switch.

### Coolant temperature sensor

63   This is screwed into the cylinder head (photo). Drain the cooling system before commencing operations.
64   Disconnect the wiring plug and unscrew the sensor.

### Throttle valve housing and inlet manifold

65   Disconnect the air inlet hose from the throttle valve housing, and also the supplementary air valve hose.
66   Disconnect the throttle control cable by swivelling the grooved sector and slipping the cable nipple from its recess.
67   Disconnect the wiring plug from the throttle position (potentiometer) switch.
68   Unbolt the fuel pressure regulator/wiring loom bracket, and also the wiring loom bracket at the other end of the inlet manifold. Move the wiring loom aside.
69   Unbolt and remove the throttle housing support bracket.
70   Disconnect the vacuum servo hose and the fuel pressure regulator vacuum hoses from the inlet manifold (photos).
71   Disconnect the leads from the excessive air pressure switch.
72   Unscrew the inlet manifold fixing nuts. Note that double nuts are used at the ends of the manifold in order to secure the exhaust heat shield (photo). The shield should be released and lowered to rest on the exhaust manifold.
73   Unscrew and remove the remaining two nuts now exposed by lowering the heat shield and lifting the inlet manifold away (photo).
74   If necessary, the injectors and cooling tube can be withdrawn, and the two twin inlet pipe stubs removed. These are retained with the exhaust manifolds using nuts and washers (photo).

### Fuel rail and injectors

75   Disconnect the fuel delivery hose from the fuel rail by unscrewing the union nut (photo). Be prepared for some loss of pressurised fuel.
76   Disconnect the fuel return hose.
77   Unbolt the fuel pressure regulator and the wiring loom brackets (photo).
78   Disconnect the air intake hose from the throttle valve housing, and then unbolt and remove the throttle valve housing support bracket (photo).
79   Disconnect the hose from the injector cooling fan, and also discon-

9C.70A Brake servo vacuum hose connection to inlet manifold

9C.70B Fuel pressure regulator vacuum hose connection at the inlet manifold

9C.72 Double nuts at the end of the inlet manifold

9C.73 Removing the inlet manifold

9C.74 Removing an inlet manifold twin pipe stub

9C.75 Disconnecting the fuel delivery hose union

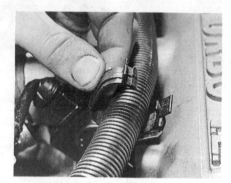

9C.77 Wiring loom clip and bracket

9C.78 Throttle valve housing support bracket

nect the fan thermo-switch on the underside of the injector cooling air duct (photo). Disconnect the injector wiring plugs, and then slide out the injector cooling air duct.

80   The injector retaining plate socket-headed screws may now be removed using an Allen key. Withdraw the fuel injectors and insulators (photos).

81   New injectors, complete with the fuel rail, must be purchased as an assembly. Always use new seals when refitting the injectors and the insulators (photos).

**Electronic control unit (ECU)**

82   The ECU is located under the right-hand side of the facia panel.

83   Pull off the multipin connector plug and extract the fixing screws (photo).

**System control relay**

84   This is located adjacent to the airflow meter. Pull off the multipin connector and release the relay fixing (photo).

**Fuel injector cooling fan**

85   This is located low down on the left-hand side of the radiator (photo).

86   Remove the spiral-wire-wound hose which connects with the injector cooling duct.

87   Pull off the wiring plug, and unbolt and remove the fan.

**Supplementary air valve**

88   Disconnect the hoses and wiring plug from the valve, which is located on the front face of the engine (photos).

89   Unscrew the mounting bracket screws and withdraw the valve.

**Throttle position switch (potentiometer)**

90   This is located on the left side of the throttle valve housing (photo).

91   Disconnect the wiring plug, unscrew the two fixing screws and withdraw the switch.

**Secondary fuel filter**

92   Unscrew the fuel line banjo unions from the filter, which is located in the right-hand rear corner of the engine compartment. Be prepared for some loss of pressurised fuel, and mop it up with rags.

**Fuel pump**

93   The fuel pump can be removed from its location beside the fuel tank after disconnecting the fuel hoses and wiring plug, and then releasing the mounting clamp.

9C.79 Fan thermostatic switch on underside of injector cooling air duct (duct removed for clarity)

9C.80A Extracting a fuel injector screw

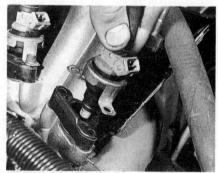

9C.80B Fuel injector removal

9C.81A Fuel injectors attached to fuel rail

9C.81B Fuel injector cooling air duct refitting

9C.81C Injector wiring plug refitting

9C.83 ECU multipin plug

9C.84 Fuel injector system relay

9C.85 Fuel injector cooling fan

9C.88A Disconnecting the supplementary air valve hose from the inlet manifold

9C.88B Supplementary air valve (arrowed)

9C.90 Throttle position switch (wiring plug arrowed)

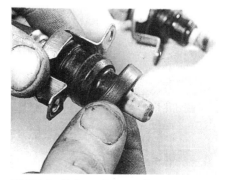

9C.95A Fuel injector large seal

9C.95B Fuel injector small seal

9C.95C Fuel injector insulator seal

9C.95D Inlet pipe stub gasket

9C.99A Throttle cable and end fitting (primary section)

9C.99B Throttle cable (secondary section) and cross-shaft

9C.99C Throttle cable nipple (arrowed) in throttle linkage cut-out

9C.99D Throttle cable balljoint retaining spring clip (arrowed)

9C.101 Fuel tank anti-blow-back compartment (arrowed)

**Refitting – all components**

94   Refitting of all components is a reversal of removal, but observe the following points.

95   Use new seals and gaskets as applicable, noting that three rubber seals are used on each fuel injector and insulator (photos).

96   Adjust the throttle position switch as described in paragraph 46 of this Section.

97   When refitting a new fuel filter, make sure that the arrow marked on it is in the direction of the fuel flow.

98   Apply gasket cement to the threads of the coolant temperature sensor.

*Throttle control linkage – general*

99   This is of the cable and rod type. Adjust the cable by means of the end fitting and nut, to give the slightest play in the cable when the plastic socket is engaged with the ball on the link rod which runs across the camshaft cover (photos).

100   Keep the cross-shaft pivots and return springs lubricated.

*Fuel tank – general*

101   The fuel tank is of metal construction, but note the plastic anti-blow-back compartment between the filler cap and the tank. This is accessible from under the right-hand wheel arch (photo).

# PART D: FUEL INJECTION SYSTEM – 1372 CC IE ENGINE

*Description*

1   The Bosch Mono-Jetronic fuel injection system fitted to the 1372 cc ie engine models is an electronically-controlled single point injection (SPi) system. The SPi system is a compromise between a conventional carburettor fuel supply system and a multi-point fuel injection (MPi) system.

2   Compared with a conventional carburettor, the SPi unit is a rela-tively simple device. Fuel is pumped to the SPi unit and then injected into the inlet system by a single solenoid valve (fuel injector), mounted centrally on top of the unit. The injector is energised by an electrical signal sent from the electronic control unit (ECU), at which point the injector pintle is lifted from its seat and atomized fuel is delivered into the inlet manifold under pressure. The electrical signals take two forms of current; a high current to open the injector and a low current to hold it open for the duration required. At idle speed the injector is pulsed at every other intake stroke rather than with every stroke as during normal operation.

3   The air-to-fuel mixture ratio is regulated by values obtained from the ignition coil (engine speed), engine coolant temperature sensor, throttle position switch, and the Lambda sensor in the exhaust system. No adjustments to the fuel mixture are possible.

4   The throttle position switch enables the ECU to compute both throttle position and its rate of change. Extra fuel can then be provided for acceleration when the throttle is suddenly opened. Throttle position information, together with the idle tracking switch, provide the ECU with the closed throttle position information.

5   The system layout and principal components are shown in Figs. 13.44 and 13.45.

6   The fuel system pump is immersed in the fuel tank and forms a combined unit with the fuel level sender unit. A cartridge type in-line (secondary) fuel filter is fitted to the fuel line, and is located in the engine compartment.

7   The fuel pressure in the system is controlled by a mechanical diaphragm regulator in the injection unit turret. High pressure in the system causes the diaphragm to operate and excess fuel is returned to the fuel tank.

8   The air intake temperature and volume is regulated to ensure the correct mixture ratio under all operating conditions. The temperature of the air passing through the injection unit is measured by a sensor which transmits such information to the ECU for the necessary processing (photo). A conventional paper type air filter element is used and this must be renewed at the specified intervals.

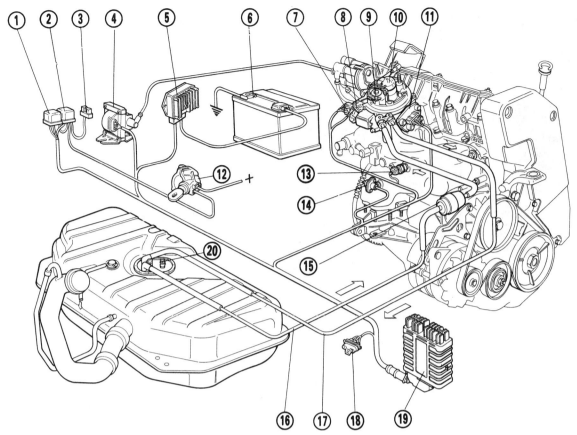

**Fig. 13.44 Bosch Mono-Jetronic fuel injection system components and layout on the 1372 cc ie engine (Sec 9D)**

| | | | | | |
|---|---|---|---|---|---|
| 1 | Fuel pump relay | 6 | Battery | 11 | Throttle position switch |
| 2 | Injection system relay | 7 | Idle speed check actuator | 12 | Ignition switch |
| 3 | Fuel pump fuse | 8 | Injector connector | 13 | Coolant temperature sensor |
| 4 | Ignition coil | 9 | Fuel pressure regulator | 14 | Engine speed and TDC |
| 5 | Digiplex 2 ECU | 10 | Injector | | sensor |
| | | | | 15 | Secondary fuel filter |

| | | |
|---|---|---|
| 16 | Fuel supply pipe |
| 17 | Fuel return pipe |
| 18 | Diagnostic socket |
| 19 | Fuel injection ECU |
| 20 | Fuel pump/level sender unit |

**Fig. 13.45 Mono-Jetronic fuel injection component locations in the engine compartment – 1372 cc ie engine (Sec 9D)**

1  Injector resistor
2  Lambda sensor signal connector
3  Lambda sensor heating connector
4  Secondary fuel filter
5  Fuel return pipe
6  Fuel supply pipe
7  Coolant temperature sensor
8  ECU
9  Injector holder turret
10  Lambda sensor
11  Nut for adjusting accelerator cable
12  Engine speed and TDC sensor connector
13  Ignition control unit
14  Ignition coil
15  Diagnostic socket
16  Fuel pump relay and system relay

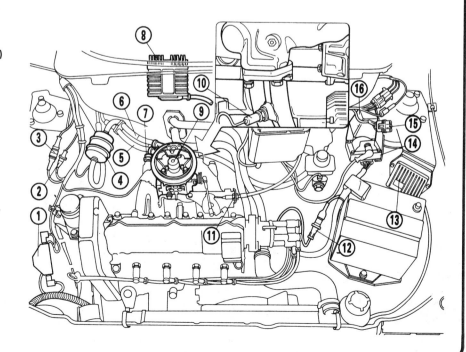

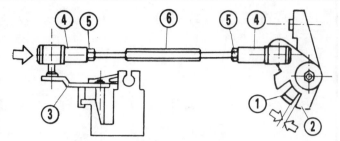

**Fig. 13.46 Accelerator linkage and butterfly control lever –
1372 cc ie engine (Sec 9D)**

| | |
|---|---|
| 1   Butterfly valve lever (fixed) | 4   Linkage ends |
| 2   Throttle valve lever | 5   Locknuts |
| 3   Control pulley | 6   Central adjuster rod |

9D.8 Atmospheric air intake for air temperature sensor (1). Also shown are the supply and return fuel line connections (2 and 3) and the throttle position sensor (4)

9    The ECU is specific to the model type, its function being to control the fuel system under all operating conditions, including starting from cold – it richens the fuel mixture as required but at the same time prevents flooding. As the engine temperature rises, the injection impulses are progressively reduced until the normal operation temperature is reached.

10    An integral emergency system enables the fuel injection system to remain operational in the event of any of the following components malfunctioning. These items are the coolant temperature sensor, the air intake sensor, the Lambda sensor, the idle speed check actuator and the throttle position switch. In the event of the throttle position switch malfunctioning, the fuel system becomes automatically inoperative.

11    The catalytic converter fitted in the exhaust system of the 1.4 ie S model minimises the amount of pollutants which escape into the atmosphere. The Lambda sensor in the exhaust system provides the fuel injection system ECU with constant feedback which enables it to adjust the mixture to provide the best possible conditions for the converter to operate.

### Maintenance

12    Regularly check the condition and security of the system hoses and connections. Also check the system wiring connections for condition and security.

13    At the specified intervals, renew the air cleaner element and the secondary fuel filter.

### Secondary fuel filter – renewal

14    The in-line fuel filter is secured to the right-hand suspension turret in the engine compartment. To remove the filter, first depressurize the fuel in the system as described later in this Part.

15    Undo the retaining strap bolt and withdraw the filter from its

location bracket. Disconnect the inlet and supply hose from the filter. If crimp connectors are fitted they will have to be cut free and new screw type clips fitted (photo).

16    Connect the hoses to the new filter ensuring that the filter is correctly orientated (the arrow mark on the body indicates the direction of fuel flow). Ensure that the hose clips are secure before refitting the filter into the retaining scrap and securing the retaining bolt. When the engine is restarted, check the hose connections to ensure that there is no fuel leakage from them.

### Air cleaner element – renewal

17    Release the spring clip each side at the front of the air cleaner, then unscrew and remove the two screws from the top front face of the housing. Withdraw the end cover and element from the filter unit (photos).

18    Wipe any dirt from within the casing then locate the new element and refit it together with the end cover.

### Idle speed and mixture adjustment

19    No manual idle speed and/or mixture adjustments to this type of fuel system are necessary or possible. Any such adjustments are automatically made by the ECU. If the engine idle speed and/or mixture adjustment is suspect, it must be checked using CO measuring equipment; a task best entrusted to a FIAT dealer or a competent garage. The most probable cause of a malfunction is likely to be a defective sensor or incorrectly adjusted accelerator control cable.

### Accelerator control system – check and adjustment

20    To check the adjustment of the accelerator control system, it is essential that the engine is at its normal operating temperature. This is achieved by running the engine for a period of about fifteen minutes, by which time the cooling fan should have cut into operation several times. At this point, stop the engine, turn the ignition key to the OFF position and proceed as follows.

21    Remove the air cleaner unit.

22    Check that when the accelerator pedal is fully released the control pulley is at the end of its travel and abutting the stop (see Fig. 13.46). In this position the cable should be neither too taut not too slack and there should be no detectable free play at the pedal (photo).

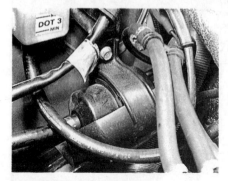

9D.15 Secondary fuel filter element

9D.17A Release the air cleaner end cover retaining clips ...

9D.17B ... remove the cover and extract the element

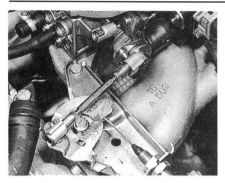

9D.22 Accelerator control rod and cable connections

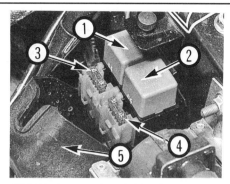

9D.26 Fuel pump relay (1), injection control relay (2), Lambda sensor fuse (3) and pump fuse (4) with cover (5) removed

9D.27 Fuel pump relay removal

23   Open the throttle and using a feeler gauge check that the throttle valve control lever moves 0.2 to 0.5 mm (between items 1 and 2 in Fig. 13.46) before it starts to operate the butterfly valve lever.
24   To make adjustment, loosen off the locknut from each linkage end and turn the central adjuster rod as necessary to achieve the aforementioned setting. Recheck the setting after making adjustment.

### Fuel system – depressurisation
25   The fuel system should always be depressurised whenever any fuel hoses and/or system components are disconnected and/or removed. This can easily be achieved as follows.
26   Loosen off the knurled retaining nut and remove the cover from the fuel pump relay. This is located on the left-hand suspension turret in the engine compartment (photo).
27   Carefully pull free the fuel pump relay, then start the engine and run it until it stops (photo). The fuel system is now depressurised. Turn the ignition off before removing/dismantling any components.
28   Do not refit the fuel pump relay or turn the ignition on until the system is fully reconnected. When the engine is ready to be restarted, refit the relay and its cover, then restart the engine in the normal manner.

### Fuel pump and supply system checks
29   Specialised equipment is required to undertake accurate tests in the fuel supply system and such checks must therefore be entrusted to a FIAT dealer or a fuel injection specialist. If the fuel pump is suspected of malfunction, a basic check can be made by removing the fuel filler cap then listening through the filler pipe, get an assistant to turn on the ignition whilst you listen to hear if the pump is heard to operate in the tank. If the pump fails to operate, check that the pump fuse is sound and that its connection (and also that of the relay) are clean and secure.

9D.30 Test lead connected to relay terminals 30 and 87

30   The pump can be further checked by first depressurising the fuel system as described in the previous sub-Section, then disconnect the fuel supply pipe at the injector unit and locate it in a suitable container. With the fuel pump relay removed, connect up a suitable test lead with a 7.5 amp (10 amp on models with catalyst) fuse, in series, to the relay terminals 30 and 87, and check that fuel flows into the container from the supply pipe (photo). If a suitable pressure gauge is available for connecting into the fuel line between the engine compartment fuel filter and the injection unit, check that the fuel pressure is as specified at the beginning of this Chapter.
31   If the pump fails to operate, check that the battery is in good condition and that the pump wiring connections are clean and secure before condemning the pump. To remove the pump unit from the fuel tank, proceed as described in the following sub-Section.

### Fuel pump – removal and refitting
32   Release the pressure from the fuel system as described previously.
33   Move the front seats forward, then tilt the rear seat cushions forward. Peel back the luggage area floor cover from the right-hand side towards the centre to expose the access cover above the pump/sender unit in the floor. Remove the access cover.
34   Detach the wiring connectors from the pump unit and the fuel level sender unit.
35   Loosen off the hose retaining clips and detach the fuel supply and return hoses from the pump unit connections. Mark the hoses for identity to avoid incorrect attachment during refitting.
36   Unscrew the retaining nuts then carefully lift out and withdraw the fuel pump/level sender unit from the fuel tank.
37   Refitting is a reversal of the removal procedure. A new seal gasket must be used and it is important to ensure that all connections are securely and correctly made.

### Injector unit – removal and refitting
38   Depressurise the fuel system as described previously, then disconnect the battery negative lead.
39   Remove the air cleaner unit and the rubber seal (photo).
40   Disconnect the engine idle speed check actuator lead and the throttle position switch lead from the side faces of the injector unit.
41   Undo the retaining clips and detach the fuel supply and return hose from the injector unit. If crimped type retaining clips are fitted, they will have to be carefully cut free and new screw type clips obtained to replace them. Take care not to cut into the hoses when releasing the crimped type clips.
42   Detach the crankcase ventilation hose from the fuel injector unit.
43   Disconnect the accelerator linkage at the throttle lever on the injector unit.
44   Undo the four retaining screws and lift the injector unit from the inlet manifold. Remove the gasket (photo).
45   Clean the injector unit and the inlet manifold mating faces.
46   Refit in the reverse order of removal.

### Intake air temperature sensor – removal and refitting
47   The air temperature sensor is located in the top of the injector unit. It is basically a resistor which varies its value in accordance with the air temperature entering the induction circuit from the air filter. The sensor can then transmit the registered air temperature at this point to the ECU

9D.39 Removing the filter seal from the injector unit

9D.44 Injector unit retaining screws (arrowed)

9D.49 Fuel injector unit sensor retaining screw (1). Also shown is the intake air temperature sensor (2)

for processing in the management system. To remove the sensor proceed as follows.

48   Remove the air cleaner unit and its mounting bracket in the injector.

49   Disconnect the wiring connector from the air temperature sensor. Undo the retaining screw and remove the sensor from the injector unit (photo).

50   Refit in the reverse order of removal.

### Fuel injector – removal and refitting

51   Depressurise the fuel system as described previously, then disconnect the battery negative lead.

52   Remove the air cleaner unit.

53   Release the injector feed wiring mutliplug and detach it from the injector.

54   Bend over the locking tabs retaining the injector screws, then undo and remove the screws. Withdraw the injector retaining collar, then carefully withdraw the injector (noting its orientation) followed by its seal.

55   Refit in the reverse order of removal. Always use new seals in the unit and the retaining collar and lightly lubricate them with clean engine oil prior to assembly. Take care not to damage the seals when fitting and also when the injector is fitted; check that it engages correctly.

### Fuel injection electronic control unit (ECU) – removal and refitting

56   The control unit is located under the facia on the driver's side of the vehicle. Commence by disconnecting the battery negative lead.

57   To gain access to the control unit, detach and remove the trim panel from the underside of the facia on the driver's side of the car.

58   Disconnect the wiring multiplug from the control unit, then undo the retaining screw and remove the unit from the car (photos).

59   Refit in the reverse order of removal.

### Inlet manifold – removal and refitting

60   Remove the fuel injector unit as described previously.

61   Drain the cooling system as described in Section 8 of this Chapter.

62   Detach the coolant hose and coolant temperature sensor from the inlet manifold.

63   Unbolt and remove the accelerator cable/throttle linkage support bracket from the top of the inlet manifold. The cable can be left attached to the bracket.

64   Detach the brake servo vacuum hose from the connector on the manifold.

65   Unscrew and remove the inlet manifold securing bolts and nuts and remove the manifold from the cylinder head. As they are removed, note the location of the fastenings and their spacers.

66   Remove the gasket and clean the mating faces of the manifold and the cylinder head. The gasket must be renewed when refitting the manifold.

67   Refitting is a reversal of the removal procedure. Ensure that the spacers are correctly located (where applicable) and tighten the retaining bolts and nuts to the specified torque settings.

### Exhaust manifold – removal and refitting

68   Remove the inlet manifold as described previously.

69   Disconnect the Lambda sensor lead (photo).

70   Raise and support the car at the front end on axle stands to allow sufficient clearance to work underneath the car and disconnect the exhaust downpipe from the manifold.

71   Straighten the tab washers, then unscrew and remove the exhaust downpipe-to-manifold retaining nuts (photo). Detach the downpipe from the manifold. Support the downpipe so that the Lambda sensor will not get knocked and/or damaged.

72   Undo the manifold-to-cylinder head securing bolts/nuts and withdraw and remove the manifold and heat shield.

73   Remove the gasket and clean the mating faces of the manifold,

9D.58A Detach the multiplug (arrowed) ...

9D.58B ... for access to the ECU retaining screw (arrowed)

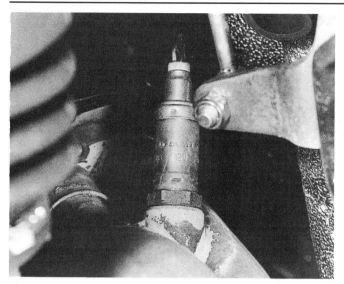

9D.69 Lambda sensor in exhaust downpipe

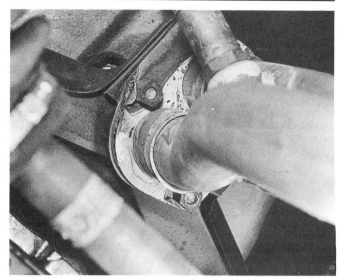

9D.71 Exhaust downpipe to manifold flange connection showing retaining nuts and locktabs

cylinder head and downpipe flange. The gasket must be renewed when refitting the manifold.
74   Refitting is a reversal of the removal procedure. Tighten the retaining bolts/nuts to the specified torque setting.

### Catalytic converter – general information

75   The catalytic converter is a reliable and simple device which needs no maintenance in itself, but there are some facts of which an owner should be aware if the converter is to function properly for its full service life.

(a)   *DO NOT use leaded petrol in a car equipped with a catalytic converter – the lead will coat the previous metals, reducing their converting efficiency and will eventually destroy the converter.*

(b)   *Always keep the ignition and fuel systems well-maintained in accordance with the maintenance schedule – particularly, ensure that the air cleaner filter element, the fuel filter and the spark plugs are renewed at the correct interval – if the intake air/fuel mixture is allowed to become too rich due to neglect, the unburned surplus will enter and burn in the catalytic converter, overheating the element and eventually destroying the converter.*

(c)   *If the engine develops a misfire, do not drive the car at all (or at least as little as possible) until the fault is cured – the misfire will allow unburned fuel to enter the converter, which will result in its overheating, as noted above.*

(d)   *DO NOT push- or tow-start the car – this will soak the catalytic converter in unburned fuel, causing it to overheat when the engine does start – see (b) above.*

(e)   *DO NOT switch off the ignition at high engine speeds – if the ignition is switched off at anything above idle speed, unburned fuel will enter the (very hot) catalytic converter, with the possible risk of its igniting on the element and damaging the converter.*

(f)   *DO NOT use fuel or engine oil additives – these may contain substances harmful to the catalytic converter.*

(g)   *DO NOT continue to use the car if the engine burns oil to the extent of leaving a visible trail of blue smoke – the unburned carbon deposits will clog the converter passages and reduce its efficiency; in severe cases the element will overheat.*

(h)   *Remember that the catalytic converter operates at very high temperatures and the casing will become hot enough to ignite combustible materials which brush against it. DO NOT, therefore, park the car in dry undergrowth, over long grass or piles of dead leaves.*

(i)   *Remember that the catalytic converter is FRAGILE – do not strike it with tools during servicing work, take great care when working on the exhaust system, ensure that the converter is well clear of any jacks or other lifting gear used to raise the car and do not drive the car over rough ground, road humps, etc., in such a way as to 'ground' the exhaust system.*

(j)   *In some cases, particularly when the car is new and/or is used for stop/start driving, a sulphurous smell (like that of rotten eggs) may be noticed from the exhaust. This is common to many catalytic converter-equipped cars and seems to be due to the small amount of sulphur found in some petrols reacting with hydrogen in the exhaust to produce hydrogen sulphide ($H_2S$) gas; while this gas is toxic, it is not produced in sufficient amounts to be a problem. Once the car has covered a few thousand miles the problem should disappear – in the meanwhile a change of driving style or of the brand of petrol used may effect a solution.*

(k)   *The catalytic converter, used on a well-maintained and well-driven car, should last for at least 50 000 miles (80 000 km) or five years – from this point on, careful checks should be made at all specified service intervals on the CO level to ensure that the converter is still operating efficiently – if the converter is no longer effective it must be renewed.*

### PART E: FUEL INJECTION SYSTEM – 1372 CC TURBO IE ENGINE

#### Description

1   A Bosch L3.1-Jetronic fuel injection system is fitted to the 1372 cc Turbo ie engine. The system circuit and main component locations are shown in Figs. 13.47 and 13.48.
2   The L3.1 Jetronic system is a multi-point fuel injection system. It operates in a similar manner to that of the LE2-Jetronic system fitted to the 1301 cc Turbo ie engine described in Part C of this Section. The L3.1 system is more sophisticated and has the ability to provide reasonably efficient engine operation when system sensors malfunction. As with the LE2 system, the fuel and air supply mixture circuits are regulated in accordance with the electronic control unit (ECU), but on the L3.1 system the control unit is attached to the upper part of the airflow meter.
3   The ECU analyses the information passed to it from the system sensors. These signals are then processed and the air/fuel mixture is constantly adjusted as required to provide the optimum engine operating efficiency. In the event of a system sensor malfunction, errors in data passed to the ECU are overcome by an emergency operation, whereby the ECU supplies the injectors with one of two set injection periods independent of the sensors. One period (2.2 ms) is for idle speed and the other (2.5 ms) is for speeds above idle (actuated when the idle speed contact is opened).
4   An injection system relay and a fuel pump relay are fitted and are located in the engine compartment, adjacent to the ECU on the left-hand inner wing panel. In the event of the engine not being started within two seconds of the ignition being switched to the 'ON' position, the fuel pump relay is deactivated. The fuel pump circuit fuse is located in the main fuse block located under the facia within the car. **Note:** *To*

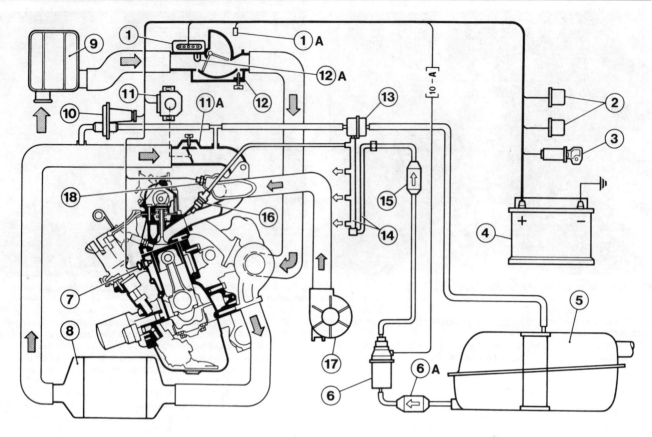

**Fig. 13.47 Bosch L3.1 Jetronic fuel injection system – 1372 cc Turbo ie engine (Sec 9E)**

| | | | |
|---|---|---|---|
| 1 | ECU | 6 | Fuel pump |
| 1A | Diagnostic socket | 6A | Primary fuel filter |
| 2 | Injection system relay | 7 | Coolant temperature sensor |
| | and fuel pump relay | 8 | Intake air cooling radiator |
| 3 | Ignition switch | | (intercooler) |
| 4 | Battery | 9 | Air cleaner |
| 5 | Fuel tank | 10 | Supplementary air valve |

| | | | |
|---|---|---|---|
| 11 | Throttle position switch | 14 | Fuel rail (to injectors) |
| 11A | Throttle housing | 15 | Secondary fuel filter |
| 12 | Airflow meter | 16 | Injectors |
| 12A | Intake air temperature | 17 | Injector cooling fan |
| | sensor | 18 | Thermostatic switch (to |
| 13 | Fuel pressure regulator | | engage injector cooling fan) |

*avoid possible damage to the ECU, it is essential that the ignition is switched off before disconnecting (or connecting) the wiring multi-plug from the ECU.*

## Fuel system – depressurisation

5    The fuel system should always be depressurised whenever any fuel hoses and/or system components are disconnected and/or removed. This can easily be achieved as follows.

6    The fuel pump relay is located next to the ECU and airflow meter in the engine compartment. Carefully pull free the fuel pump relay, then start the engine and run it until it stops. The fuel system is now depressurised. Turn the ignition off before removing/dismantling any components.

7    Do not refit the fuel pump relay or turn the ignition on until the system is fully reconnected. When the engine is ready to be restarted, refit the relay and its cover, then restart the engine in the normal manner.

## Maintenance

8    Regularly check the condition and security of the system hoses and connections. Also check the system wiring connections for condition and security.

9    At the specified intervals, renew the air cleaner element and the secondary fuel filter.

## Secondary fuel filter – renewal

10    This is located in the engine compartment on the right-hand side. Disconnect the fuel inlet and outlet hoses, but be prepared for the loss of fuel. Loosen off the clamp and remove the filter.

11    Reverse the removal procedure to fit the new filter, but ensure that the arrow indicating fuel flow is pointing towards the fuel injector rail.

## Air cleaner element – renewal

12    Prise free the four retaining clips, then remove the cover and the air cleaner element.

13    Wipe clean the inside surfaces of the air cleaner housing, then insert the new element, refit the cover and secure it with the four retaining clips.

## Checks and adjustments
### Engine idle speed and mixture adjustment

14    Before carrying out any adjustments, the engine must be at its normal operating temperature, the cooling fan having cut into operation twice. Also prior to making adjustments ensure that the supplementary air valve pipe is in good condition, with no leaks. Compress the air valve pipe using a pair of grips to prevent incorrect adjustment caused by a defective supplementary air valve.

15    The air cleaner must be connected when checking and/or adjusting the engine idle speed. To adjust, turn the adjuster screw in the required direction to set the engine idle speed to that specified.

16    It is unlikely that the mixture will require adjustment and unless this is proven by measuring the exhaust gases using a CO content analyzer, its setting should not be altered. As with idle speed adjustment, the engine must be at its normal operating temperature when making this check and adjustment. It is also necessary to ensure that the ignition idle advance is as specified. Checking and adjustment must not be made with the engine cooling fan, air conditioning (where fitted) or other related items switched on.

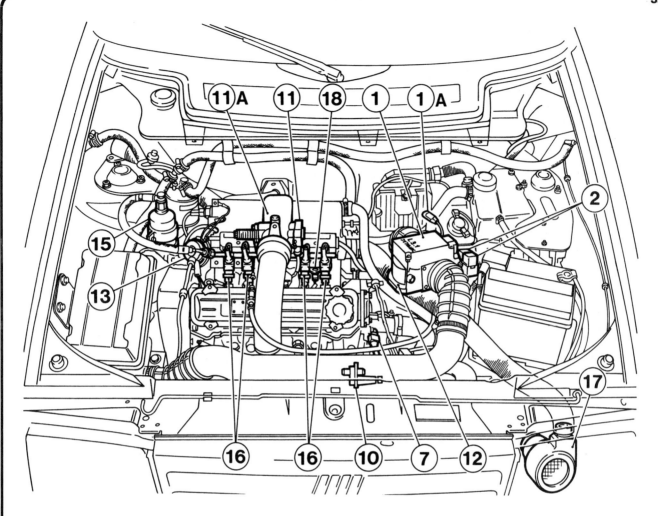

**Fig. 13.48 Fuel injection system components layout in engine compartment on the 1372 cc Turbo ie engine (Sec 9E)**

| | | | |
|---|---|---|---|
| 1 | ECU | 11A Throttle housing | 16 Injectors |
| 1A | Diagnostic socket | 12 Airflow meter | 17 Injector cooling fan |
| 2 | Ignition system relay and fuel pump relay | 13 Fuel pressure regulator | 18 Thermostatic switch (to engage injector cooling fan) |
| 7 | Coolant temperature sensor | 15 Secondary fuel filter | |
| 10 | Supplementary air valve | | |
| 11 | Throttle position switch | | |

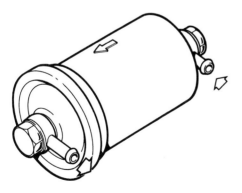

**Fig. 13.49 Secondary fuel filter with arrows indicating direction of flow – 1372 cc Turbo ie engine (Sec 9E)**

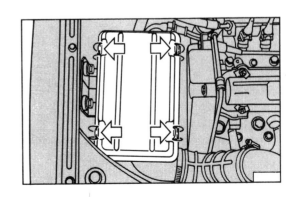

**Fig. 13.50 Air cleaner cover securing clips (arrowed) on the 1372 cc Turbo ie engine (Sec 9E)**

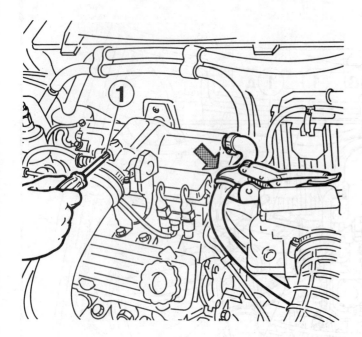

Fig. 13.51 Idle speed adjustment screw (1) on the 1372 cc Turbo ie engine (Sec 9E)

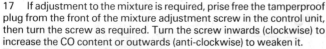

*Note method of compressing the supplementary air valve pipe (arrowed)*

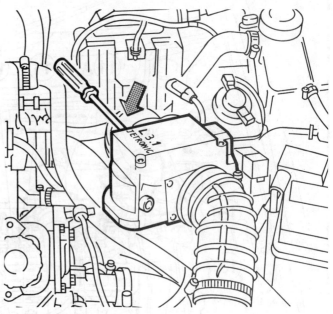

Fig. 13.52 Mixture adjustment screw location on the 1372 cc Turbo ie engine (Sec 9E)

17   If adjustment to the mixture is required, prise free the tamperproof plug from the front of the mixture adjustment screw in the control unit, then turn the screw as required. Turn the screw inwards (clockwise) to increase the CO content or outwards (anti-clockwise) to weaken it.

**Throttle position switch adjustment**
18   This switch will not normally require adjustment having been set during production. The switch should not be loosened off or reset unless absolutely necessary.
19   If a new switch is fitted it can be set by loosely fitting the securing bolts, turning the switch fully anti-clockwise, then clockwise until one of the internal contacts is felt to click into engagement. Hold the switch in this position and tighten the retaining screws. Reconnect the wiring multiplug to the switch.

**Accelerator cable adjustment**
20   If the accelerator cable is removed or detached from the support bracket at the throttle control housing at any time, care must be taken to adjust it correctly. When the inner cable is connected to the throttle quadrant, set the outer cable in the bracket so that the inner cable has a minimal amount of free play, yet does not prevent the throttle valve from fully closing.
21   When the engine is restarted, check that the engine idle speed is as specified and that the action of the accelerator is satisfactory.

**Fuel pump and supply system checks**
22   Although the following basic checks can be made to the fuel pump and fuel supply system, specialised equipment is required to undertake full and accurate tests of the fuel supply system. Such checks must therefore be entrusted to a FIAT dealer or a fuel injection specialist.
23   If the fuel pump is suspected of malfunction, a basic check can be made by turning the ignition on and listening around the area of the pump unit to hear if it is operating. The pump is located on the underside of the car, just forward of the fuel tank. If the pump fails to operate, check that the pump fuse is sound and that its connection (and also that the relay) are clean and secure.
24   The pump can be further checked as described previously for the LE2 fuel injection system fuel pump in Part C of this Section.

**Supplementary air valve – check**
25   With the engine at its normal operating temperature, allow it to idle, then pinch the supplementary air valve hose using suitable pliers as shown in Fig. 13.51 and check to see if the engine speed drops by more than 50 rev/min. If it does, the supplementary air valve is defective and in need of renewal.

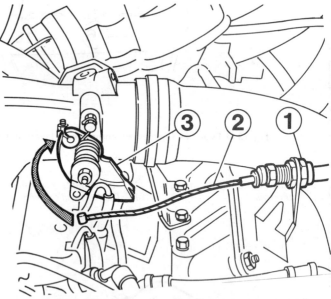

Fig. 13.53 Accelerator cable adjustment on the 1372 cc Turbo ie engine (Sec 9E)

1   Adjuster          3   Quadrant support
2   Inner cable

## Injection system components – removal and refitting

26   With the exception of the items mentioned below, the various components of the fuel injection system are removed in the same manner as that described for the equivalent items in Part C of this Chapter.
27   Disconnect the battery negative lead before carrying out any of the removal and refitting operations. Where fuel lines are to be disconnected it will first be necessary to depressurise the injection system.

**Airflow meter**
28   Release the retaining clips and detach the air intake and outlet ducts from the airflow meter.

Fig. 13.54 Disconnecting the air intake duct and accelerator cable from the throttle housing on the 1372 cc Turbo ie engine (Sec 9E)

Fig. 13.55 Disconnecting the injector air cooling hoses and the supplementary air valve hose on the 1372 cc Turbo ie engine (Sec 9E)

Fig. 13.56 Detach the vacuum pick-up pipes from the points arrowed on the 1372 cc Turbo ie engine (Sec 9E)

Fig. 13.57 Removing the inlet manifold mounting bracket from the cylinder head on the 1372 cc Turbo ie engine (Sec 9E)

29   Ensure that the ignition is switched off, then disconnect the multiplug from the ECU. Unscrew the retaining bolts and remove the airflow meter complete with the ECU.

30   If required, the ECU can be separated from the airflow meter by undoing the securing bolts.

**Throttle valve housing/ inlet manifold**

31   Loosen off the retaining clip and detach the air intake duct from the throttle housing, the air cooling hoses for the injectors and the sup-plementary air valve.

32   Detach the accelerator cable from the throttle linkage.

33   Detach the vacuum pick-up pipes from the points indicated in Fig. 13.56.

34   Detach the wiring connector from the throttle position switch.

35   Unscrew and remove the inlet manifold mounting bracket-to-cylinder head retaining bolt shown in Fig. 13.57.

36   Unscrew and remove the injector cable shield retaining screws. Detach the cables from the injectors.

37   Disconnect the earth leads and the air intake sensor lead shown in Fig. 13.58.

Fig. 13.58 Disconnecting the earth leads (arrowed) on the 1372 cc Turbo ie engine (Sec 9E)

Fig. 13.59 Disconnecting the injector fuel supply pipe and fuel
pressure regulator pipe on the 1372 cc Turbo ie engine (Sec 9E)

Fig. 13.60 Cutting free the hose from an injector on the 1372 cc
Turbo ie engine (Sec 9E)

38   Release and withdraw the injector cable shield from the left-hand
underside of the throttle housing.
39   Unscrew and detach the injector fuel supply pipe and disconnect
the fuel pressure regulator pipe from its inlet manifold union.
40   Disconnect the injector cooling fan thermostatic switch lead.
41   Unscrew the securing bolts and remove the fuel pressure regulator.
42   Unscrew and remove the heat shield-to-exhaust manifold retaining bolts. Unscrew the retaining bolts at the rear and withdraw the heat
shield.
43   Undo the inlet manifold retaining bolts/nuts and carefully withdraw the manifold/throttle housing. Remove the gasket from the mating
face.

**Injectors and fuel rail**
44   Depressurise the system as described previously.
45   Disconnect the fuel supply line from the fuel rail.
46   Disconnect the fuel return line from the base of the fuel pressure
regulator. Unbolt and remove the pressure regulator from the fuel rail.
47   Unscrew and remove the injector cable shield retaining screws.
Detach the cables from the injectors.
48   Disconnect the fuel rail/injector unit and withdraw the fuel rail,
together with the injectors, from the engine.
49   With the injectors and the fuel rail removed, one or more injectors
can be removed and renewed as described below. Note that the
connecting hoses will be destroyed during removal and these together
with the injector seals will therefore need to be renewed.

**Injector(s) and connecting hoses**
50   Remove the injectors and the injector fuel rail as described in the
previous sub-Section and secure the fuel rail in a vice, but do not
overtighten.
51   Cut free the hose between the fuel rail and the injector. Make the
cut in-line with the hose and cut the hose as close as possible to the fuel
rail connection, then pull the hose free from its retaining cap. Once the
hose is detached, the retaining cap is released.
52   Repeat the procedure and release the hose and its retaining cap
from the injector.
53   Whether or not the injector unit itself is to be renewed, the injector
O-ring seals must always be renewed when disturbed.
54   Check that the connections of the fuel rail and the injector are
clean, then push the new injector with retaining cap onto the new hose.
Ensure that the hose is fully located in the retaining cap.

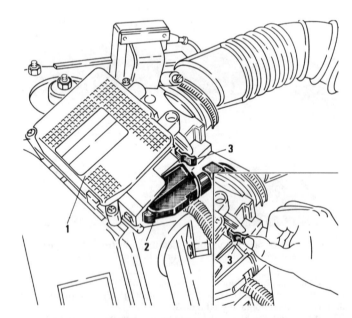

Fig. 13.61 ECU (1) wiring multiplug (2) and tag (3) – 1372 cc Turbo ie
engine (Sec 9E)

55   Check that the fuel rail-to-hose retaining cap is located on the
connector, then push the other end of the injector hose over the fuel rail
connector. Ensure that the hose is fully located in the retaining cap.
56   The interconnecting hose between the fuel rail sections can be
removed and renewed in the same manner as that described above for
the injector hoses.

**Electronic control unit (ECU)**
57   The ECU is mounted on the top face of the airflow meter. Ensure
that the ignition is switched off before disconnecting the multiplug from
the ECU. Disconnect the wiring multiplug connector by compressing
the tag and pulling the connector free from the unit. Undo the retaining
screws and remove the ECU from the airflow meter. Handle the unit

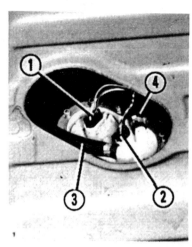

**Fig. 13.62 Fuel pump and sender unit location on the 1372 cc Turbo ie engine (Sec 9E)**

1  Fuel level gauge sender connector
2  Fuel pump connector
3  Fuel return hose
4  Fuel supply hose

with care and if removed for an extensive period, store it in a safe place where it will not get knocked or damaged.

**Fuel pump – removal and refitting**

58  Depressurise the fuel system as described previously.

59  Raise the car at the rear and support it on axle stands. Detach and remove the protective shield to gain access to the pump which is located forward of the fuel tank.

60  Disconnect the fuel hoses and the wiring connector, release the retaining clamp and withdraw the pump unit.

**Refitting – all components**

61  Refitting of all components is a reversal of the removal procedure, but note the following specific points.

62  Ensure that all components are clean prior to refitting and where applicable, use new seals and gaskets. Ensure that all connections are securely and correctly made.

63  Do not reconnect the battery until all the refitting procedures are complete.

64  When the engine is restarted, check around the fuel injection system for any signs of leakage from the fuel supply and return components.

## PART F: FAULT DIAGNOSIS – FUEL INJECTION SYSTEM

| Symptom | Reason(s) |
| --- | --- |
| Difficult starting from cold | Fuel pump fault<br>Blocked fuel pipe or filter<br>Supplementary air valve fault<br>Coolant temperature sensor fault |
| Difficult to start when hot | Choked air cleaner element<br>Fuel pump fault |
| Excessive fuel consumption | Incorrect mixture setting<br>Dirty air cleaner element<br>Coolant temperature sensor fault<br>Airflow sensor fault |
| Uneven idling | Incorrect mixture setting<br>Intake system air leak<br>Throttle position switch out of adjustment<br>Loose ECU connector |

## PART G: TURBOCHARGER SYSTEM

### Description

1  A turbocharger is fitted to certain 1301 and 1372 cc ie engines. The accompanying photographs are all taken from a 1301 cc engine, but the system is much the same for both engine types.

2  The turbocharger is basically a shaft with an exhaust gas-driven turbine at one end, and a compressor located at the other end which draws in outside air and forces it into the inlet manifold. By compressing the incoming air, a larger charge can be let into each cylinder, and greater power output is achieved than with normal aspiration.

3  Lubrication of the turbocharger shaft bearings is provided by pressurised engine oil, and the unit is cooled by the coolant from the engine cooling system.

4  A wastegate valve is incorporated in the turbocharger to divert excessive exhaust gas pressure from the turbine into the exhaust pipe at a predetermined pressure level.

5  A maximum air pressure switch is located in the inlet manifold. Its purpose is to cut the ignition system off when the turbocharger system pressure continues to increase beyond 0.86 bars (12.5 lbf/in$^2$). This would otherwise damage the engine, due to high combustion temperatures and pressures (photo).

6  An intercooler (heat exchanger) is located between the turbocharger and the inlet manifold. Its function is to cool the inlet charge, thus increasing its density, to provide greater power output.

7  A mechanical bypass valve is located between the low-pressure pipe (downstream) and the high-pressure pipe (upstream), which reduces the inherent noise from the turbocharger when the accelerator pedal is released (photo).

8  None of the components of the turbocharger system can be repaired and parts are not available. Any fault will therefore mean that the turbocharger or associated assemblies will have to be renewed complete.

Fig. 13.63 Turbocharger oil supply pipe connection (arrowed) (Sec 9G)

Fig. 13.64 Detach the air hose from the Turbocharger (arrowed) (Sec 9G)

### Precautions

9    The following precautions should be observed when using a turbo-charged vehicle.

   *(a)   Never operate the engine without the air cleaner fitted.*
   *(b)   Never switch off the engine before its speed has dropped to idling. If the car has been driven hard, allow it to idle for a few minutes before switching off. Failure to observe these recommendations can cause damage to the turbocharger due to lack of lubrication.*

10    Always keep the fuel injection system well-maintained and tuned. Operating on a weak mixture can cause overheating of the turbocharger.

### Turbocharger (1301 cc ie engine) – removal and refitting

11    Disconnect and remove the airflow meter as described in Section 9C.
12    Disconnect the spiral-wound hose from the fuel injector cooling duct.
13    Remove the turbocharger air hoses from within the left-hand side of the engine compartment. Note particularly their routing.
14    Remove the throttle housing/inlet manifold as described in Section 9C, also the fuel rail, injectors and inlet manifold branch pipe stubs. Remove the alternator heat shield (photo).
15    Remove the exhaust heat shield.
16    Unscrew the turbocharger-to-exhaust pipe flange nuts (photos).
17    Disconnect the air hoses from the turbocharger (photo).
18    Drain the cooling system, and then disconnect the coolant hoses from the turbocharger (photos).
19    Disconnect the oil feed pipe, which has a banjo-type union (photo).
20    Disconnect the oil return pipe which runs to the engine sump pan (photo).
21    Working underneath the car, disconnect the exhaust manifold support bracket (photo).

Fig. 13.65 Turbocharger mounting bracket bolts (arrowed) (Sec 9G)

9G.5 Maximum air pressure switch (arrowed)

9G.7 Bypass valve

9G.14 Alternator heat shield

9G.16A Turbocharger-to-exhaust flange nut (arrowed)

9G.16B Unscrewing turbocharger-to-exhaust manifold nut

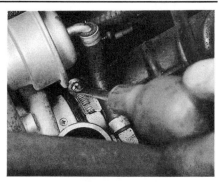

9G.17 Releasing turbocharger air hose clip

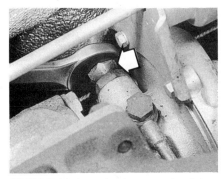

9G.18A Releasing turbocharger coolant inlet union (arrowed)

9G.18B Turbocharger connections:

1   Exhaust connecting nut
2   Oil return hose
3   Coolant pipe union

9G.19 Turbocharger oil feed pipe

22   Unbolt the exhaust manifold and lift it out of the engine compartment, complete with turbocharger.
23   The turbocharger may now be unbolted from the exhaust manifold (photo).
24   Refitting is a reversal of removal, but use new gaskets and seals throughout.

*Turbocharger (1372 cc ie engine) – removal and refitting*
25   Refer to Part E of this Section for details and remove the inlet manifold.

**Fig. 13.66 Disconnect the heat exchanger air hose and the oil return pipe (turbocharger-to-sump) (Sec 9G)**

26   Drain the cooling system as described in Section 8 of this Chapter.
27   Unscrew the union bolt and disconnect the oil supply pipe from the turbocharger.
28   Loosen off the securing clip and detach the air hose from the turbocharger filter.
29   Raise and support the car at the front end on axle stands.
30   Working from underneath the car, unscrew the downpipe-to-exhaust system joint nuts then unscrew the retaining nuts and detach the exhaust downpipe from the turbocharger outlet flange. Remove the downpipe.
31   Unscrew and remove the two turbocharger mounting bracket bolts.
32   Referring to Fig. 13.66, loosen off the retaining clip and detach the air hose from the heat exchanger and the oil return pipe from the turbocharger (to sump).
33   Working from above, undo the turbocharger mounting bracket bolts.
34   Unscrew and remove the coolant pipe-to-pump retaining bolts. The turbocharger can now be removed from above by withdrawing it together with the exhaust manifold from the engine compartment.
35   Locate and support the exhaust manifold in a vice. Fit protector clamps to the jaws of the vice to avoid possible damage to the manifold.
36   Note the orientation and fitted position of the turbocharger mounting bracket, then unscrew the retaining nuts and detach the bracket.
37   Undo the retaining nuts, separate and remove the exhaust manifold from the turbocharger.
38   The turbocharger and wastegate valve are not repairable and must therefore be renewed as a complete unit. This being the case, remove the following ancillary items from the turbocharger unit before renewing it.

(a)   *Loosen off the retaining clip and remove the air outlet hose from turbocharger.*
(b)   *Undo the two retaining bolts and remove the oil return hose union.*
(c)   *Unscrew the union and bolt and coolant inlet pipe.*
(d)   *Undo the retaining nuts and remove the turbocharger-to-exhaust manifold connector.*

9G.20 Turbocharger oil return pipe at sump

9G.21 Exhaust manifold support bracket

9G.23 Exhaust manifold bolts

Fig. 13.67 Turbocharger mounting bracket bolts removal (Sec 9G)

Fig. 13.68 Turbocharger coolant pipe-to-pump bolt location (arrowed) (Sec 9G)

9G.40 Intercooler location (1301 cc engine)

9G.43 Intercooler mounting bolt (arrowed) on 1301 cc engine

39   Where applicable, always use new gaskets and ensure that the mating faces are clean before refitting the ancillary components to the turbocharger.

### Intercooler – removal and refitting

40   The intercooler is mounted behind the left-hand side of the front bumper/spoiler (photo).
41   Disconnect the air ducts from the intercooler.
42   Unscrew the mounting bolts and lift the intercooler from the car.

43   Refitting is a reversal of removal (photo).

### Injector cooling fan – removal and refitting

44   This unit is located on the left-hand side at the front of the car. It can be accessed for removal from above, in the engine compartment.
45   Detach and remove the air intake duct from the air cleaner unit to the ECU/airflow meter.
46   Disconnect and remove the air duct from the air blower unit.
47   Undo the air blower retaining nuts, withdraw the unit and detach its wiring connector.

### Fault diagnosis – turbocharger system

| Symptom | Reason(s) |
| --- | --- |
| Noise or vibration | Worn shaft bearings<br>Lack of lubrication<br>Inlet or exhaust manifold leaking<br>Out-of-balance impeller shaft |
| Power loss/indicated boost pressure too low | Turbocharger leaking, or leak at turbocharger mounting<br>Incorrectly adjusted wastegate valve/wastegate valve not closing<br>Blocked exhaust pipe<br>Clogged air cleaner element<br>Faulty TDC sensor (ignition retarded)<br>Turbo/intercooler connecting hose leaking |
| Indicated boost pressure too high | Faulty wastegate valve<br>Ice forming in exhaust pipe (during very cold weather) |
| Engine 'pinking' | High boost pressure, caused by faulty wastegate valve<br>Fuel octane rating too low<br>Faulty TDC sensor (ignition advanced)<br>Incorrect spark plugs or plug gaps, or spark plugs worn |
| Oil leaks from shaft oil seals, with blue exhaust fumes | Oil return pipe blocked<br>Air cleaner element clogged<br>Worn oil seals |

### 10   Ignition system

#### General

1   The ignition systems dealt with in this Section are all fully electronic and are referred to individually according to type as the 'breakerless', Microplex and Digiplex 2 system. The Microplex system is used on the 1301 and 1372 cc Turbo ie engines, the Digiplex 2 on the 1372 cc ie engine and the 'breakerless' system on all other models.

#### Ignition timing (all later models)

2   The ignition timing check on all systems covered in this Section is made using a stroboscope, connected up in accordance with the manufacturer's instructions and pointed at one of the two positions given below (photos).

  (a)   The timing marks on the crankshaft pulley and the timing cover. The right-hand underwing shield will need to be detached and removed to allow access to view these marks (see photos 7B.27 and 7B.30B in this Chapter).
  (b)   The timing marks on the flywheel and the clutch housing. The rubber plug will need to be extracted for access to these marks.

3   A dwell angle check is not possible on any of these systems.
4   When making the stroboscopic ignition timing check it is necessary to disconnect the vacuum hose from the distributor or inlet manifold to module (as applicable) and plug it. The engine must be at its normal operating temperature and running at the normal specified idle speed when making the check. Refer to the appropriate part of the Specifications at the start of this Chapter for the idle speed and ignition settings.

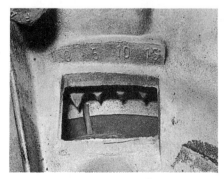

10.2A Flywheel timing marks (999 cc engine)

10.2B Flywheel timing marks (1372 cc ie engine)

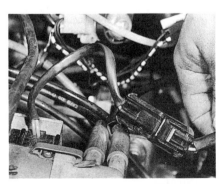

10.16 Distributor LT lead connecting plug

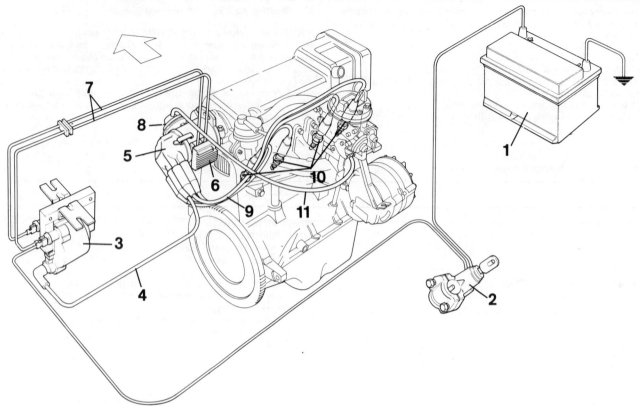

**Fig. 13.69 Breakerless ignition system – 999 and 1108 cc engines (Sec 10)**

| | | | | | | | |
|---|---|---|---|---|---|---|---|
| 1 | Battery | 4 | Coil HT lead | 7 | LT cables | 10 | Spark plugs |
| 2 | Ignition switch | 5 | Distributor | 8 | Vacuum advance unit | 11 | Vacuum hose |
| 3 | Ignition coil | 6 | ECU | 9 | Spark plug HT leads | | |

### Breakerless ignition system – description

5    On 903 cc engines, the distributor is driven from an extension of the oil pump driveshaft which is geared to the camshaft.

6    On 999, 1108 and 1372 cc engines, the distributor is driven from the rear end of the camshaft.

7    On the 1116 and 1299/1301 cc engines, the distributor is driven from an extension of the oil pump driveshaft which is geared to the auxiliary shaft.

8    The distributor contains a reluctor mounted on its shaft, and a magnet and stator fixed to the baseplate.

9    Ignition advance is controlled in the conventional way mechanically by centrifugal weights and a diaphragm unit for vacuum advance.

10    Instead of the conventional method of interrupting the low tension circuit to generate high tension voltage in the coil by means of a mechanical contact breaker, when the electronic ignition is switched on, the switching of the transistors in the electronic control unit (ECU) prevents current flow in the coil primary windings.

11    Once the crankshaft rotates, the reluctor moves through the magnetic field created by the stator and when the reluctor teeth are in alignment with the stator projections a small AC voltage is created. The ECU amplifies this voltage and applies it to switch the transistors and so provide an earth path for the primary circuit.

12    As the reluctor teeth move out of alignment with the stator projections the AC voltage changes, the transistors in the ECU are switched again to interrupt the primary circuit earth path. This causes a high voltage to be induced in the secondary winding.

### Distributor (breakerless type) – removal and refitting

13    Removal of the distributor on the 903, 1116, 1299 and 1301 cc engines is as described in Chapter 4, Section 6.

14    On 999, 1108 and 1372 cc engines, mark the position of the distributor clamp plate in relation to the cylinder head surface.

15    Unclip the distributor cap and move it to one side with the HT leads attached.

16    Disconnect the LT lead plug and, where applicable, the vacuum hose (photo).

**Fig. 13.70 Location of electronic ignition components on early models with breakerless ignition (Sec 10)**

| | | | |
|---|---|---|---|
| 1 | ECU | 4 | Vacuum advance unit |
| 2 | Ignition coil | 5 | Pick-up filter with |
| 3 | Distributor | | calibrated opening for |
| | | | atmospheric pressure |

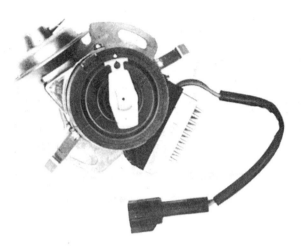

**Fig. 13.71 Rotor aligned with arrow on distributor dust shield – 999 and 1108 cc engines (Sec 10)**

17 Unscrew the distributor fixing nuts and withdraw the unit.
18 The distributor drive is by means of an offset dog – no special procedure is required to refit it. Providing the dog engages in its slot and the distributor body is turned to align the marks made before removal, the timing will automatically be correct.
19 If a new distributor is being fitted (body unmarked), set No 4 piston at TDC (0°) by turning the crankshaft pulley bolt until the timing marks on the crankshaft pulley and engine front cover are in alignment.
20 Align the drive dog and fit the distributor then turn the distributor body until the contact end of the rotor is aligned with the arrow on the distributor dust shield.
21 Tighten the distributor clamp nuts. Refit the cap and disconnected components and then check ignition timing using a stroboscope.

### Distributor (breakerless type) – overhaul
22 It is recommended that a worn out or faulty distributor is renewed. However, individual components such as the cap, rotor, reluctor, magnet/stator/baseplate assembly, vacuum diaphragm unit, and drive gear or dog are available separately.

### Breakerless ignition system components – testing
23 A voltmeter and an ohmmeter will be required for this work.

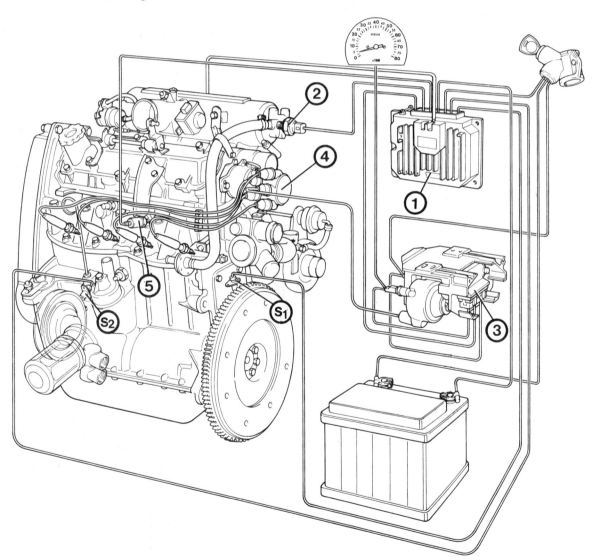

**Fig. 13.72 Microplex ignition system components on the 1301 cc Turbo ie engine (Sec 10)**

| 1 | ECU | 4 | Distributor | S1 | TDC sensor |
| 2 | Safety pressure switch | 5 | Anti-knock sensor | S2 | Engine speed sensor |
| 3 | Ignition unit and coil | | | | |

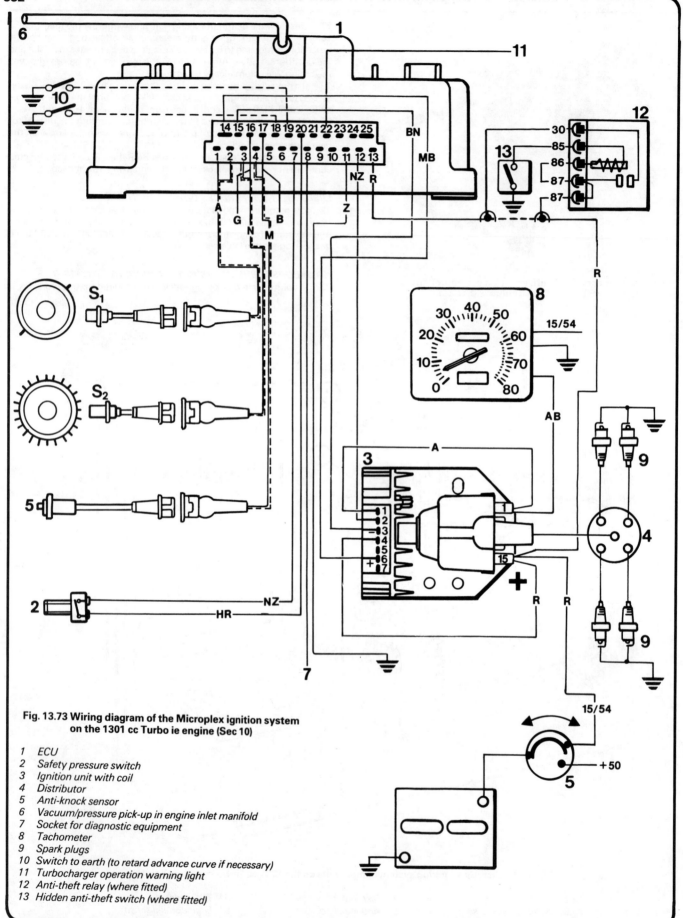

Fig. 13.73 Wiring diagram of the Microplex ignition system
on the 1301 cc Turbo ie engine (Sec 10)

1   ECU
2   Safety pressure switch
3   Ignition unit with coil
4   Distributor
5   Anti-knock sensor
6   Vacuum/pressure pick-up in engine inlet manifold
7   Socket for diagnostic equipment
8   Tachometer
9   Spark plugs
10  Switch to earth (to retard advance curve if necessary)
11  Turbocharger operation warning light
12  Anti-theft relay (where fitted)
13  Hidden anti-theft switch (where fitted)

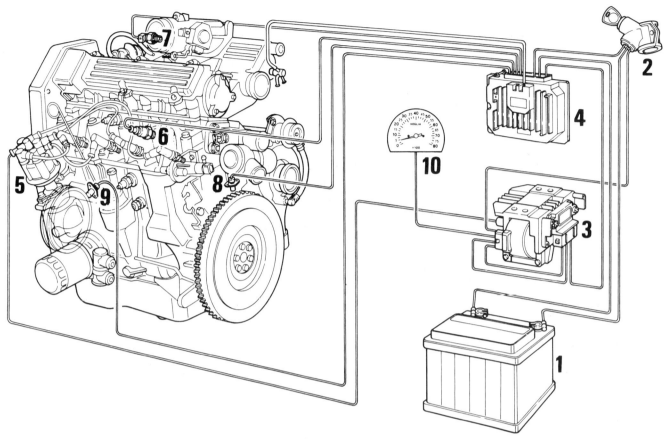

**Fig. 13.74 Microplex ignition system components on the 1372 cc Turbo ie engine (Sec 10)**

| | | | |
|---|---|---|---|
| 1 | Battery | 3 | Ignition coil with control |
| 2 | Ignition switch | | unit |
| | | 4 | ECU |

| | | | |
|---|---|---|---|
| 5 | Distributor | 8 | Engine speed sensor |
| 6 | Anti-knock sensor | 9 | TDC sensor |
| 7 | Air pressure switch | 10 | Tachometer |

**Primary circuit voltage**

24   Turn on the ignition, and using a voltmeter check the voltage at the ignition coil LT terminals. Any deviation from battery voltage will indicate a faulty connection, or if these are satisfactory, then the coil is unserviceable.

**Magnetic impulse generator winding**

25   Remove the distributor and ECU and disconnect their connecting leads.

26   Connect an ohmmeter to the impulse generator terminals and note the reading. The resistance should be as given in the Specifications at the beginning of this Chapter.

27   Now check between one of the impulse generator terminals and the metal body of the distributor. Infinity should be indicated on the ohmmeter. If it is not, renew the impulse generator carrier plate. **Note:** *When carrying out this test, it is imperative that the connections are re-made as originally observed. Also ensure that there is no possibility of the ECU supply (red) cable and earth cable making contact in service.*

**Ignition coil winding resistance**

28   Check the resistance using an ohmmeter between the coil LT terminals. Refer to the Specifications for the expected coil resistance.

29   Now check the resistance between the LT lead socket on the coil and each of the LT terminals. Refer to the Specifications for the expected coil resistance.

30   The rotor arm resistance should be approximately 5000 ohms.

*Microplex ignition system – description*

31   This system is fitted to the 1301 and 1372 cc Turbo ie models, and comprises the following components.

**Electro-magnetic sensors**

32   Two sensors are used to pick up engine speed and TDC position directly from the crankshaft.

**Pressure and vacuum sensor**

33   This converts inlet manifold vacuum pressure into an electrical signal for use by the electronic control unit (ECU).

**Anti-knock sensor**

34   This converts 'pinking' detonations which occur within the combustion chambers into an electrical signal for use by the ECU (photo).

10.34 Anti-knock sensor

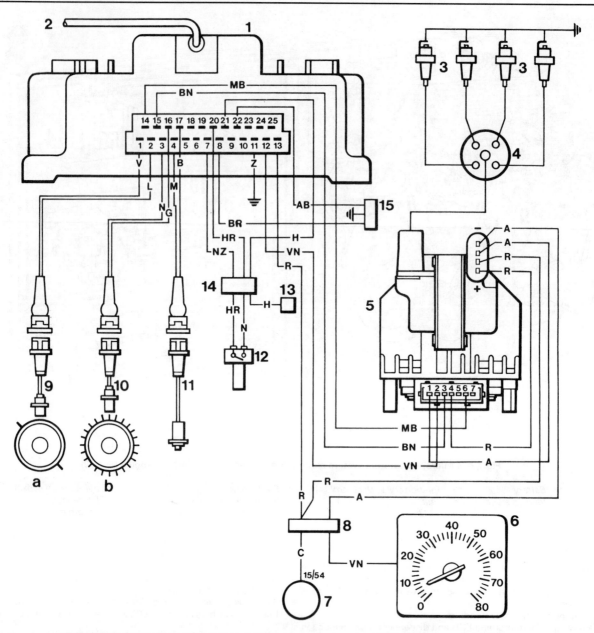

**Fig. 13.75 Wiring diagram of the Microplex ignition system on the 1372 cc Turbo ie engine (Sec 10)**

| | | | |
|---|---|---|---|
| 1 | ECU | 5 | Ignition coil (with control unit) |
| 2 | Pipe (pressure/vacuum in inlet manifold to control unit) | 6 | Tachometer |
| 3 | Spark plugs | 7 | Ignition switch |
| 4 | Distributor | 8 | Connector |
| | | 9 | TDC sensor |

| | |
|---|---|
| 10 | Engine speed |
| 11 | Anti-knock sensor |
| 12 | Air pressure safety switch |
| 13 | Speedometer signal for electronic injection |

| | |
|---|---|
| 14 | Connector |
| 15 | Diagnostic socket |
| a | Crankshaft pulley |
| b | Flywheel |

### Electronic control unit (ECU)

35    This computes the optimum ignition advance angle from the sensor signals received, and controls the action of the ignition unit (photo).

### Ignition unit

36    This comprises four elements (photo).

(a)    *Power module – receives the ignition advance command and controls the conduction angle of the primary current and energy stored in the coil.*

(b)    *Dissipator plate – eliminates the heat which is generated by the high volume of current.*

(c)    *Ignition coil – with low primary resistance.*

(d)    *Distributor – a means of distributing high tension to the spark plugs. The rotor is driven in an anti-clockwise direction (viewed from transmission) by a dog on the end of the camshaft.*

37    The system incorporates a safety pressure switch, which cuts out the ignition if the turbocharging pressure exceeds a value of between 0.84 and 0.93 bars (12.2 and 13.5 lbf/in$^2$) above atmospheric pressure.

### Distributor (Microplex) – removal and refitting

38    Remove the distributor cap and place it to one side, complete with spark plug leads (photo).

39    Turn the crankshaft by means of the pulley nut, or by raising and turning a front wheel with top gear engaged, until No 4 piston is on its firing stroke. This will be indicated when the contact end of the rotor arm is aligned with the mark on the distributor body rim, and the lug on the crankshaft pulley is aligned with the timing pointer on the engine. The right-hand underwing shield will have to be removed in order to see the marks (photo).

10.35 Ignition ECU on rear bulkhead (1301 cc Turbo ie engine)

10.36 Ignition coil (1) and power module (2) on 1301 cc Turbo ie engine

10.38 Removing the distributor cap

10.39 Crankshaft pulley timing marks (arrowed)

10.41A Distributor body showing elongated slots in the mounting lugs

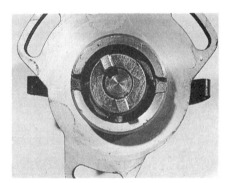

10.41B Distributor drive dog

40    Unscrew the distributor fixing nuts and withdraw the distributor.
41    When fitting the distributor, the offset drive dog will automatically locate the distributor rotor in its correct position, but the distributor body may require rotating in order to align the rim mark with the rotor. The elongated slots for the fixing studs are to permit initial alignment, not for subsequent adjustment, as advance angle alterations are carried out automatically by the system ECU (photos).
42    Tighten the nuts and refit the cap with leads.
43    Unless a stroboscope and a vacuum pressure gauge are available, it will not be possible to check the advance values with the engine

running. Where these instruments are available, connect the vacuum gauge to the inlet manifold, and the stroboscope in accordance with the equipment manufacturer's instructions. Refer to Fig. 13.78 according to the inlet manifold vacuum pressure indicated.

### Microplex ignition system components – testing
44    An ohmmeter and a voltmeter will be required for these tests.
45    Remove the multipin plug from the ECU.
**Engine speed sensor**
46    Insert the probes of an ohmmeter between terminals 3 and 16 of the multipin connector; 618 to 748 ohms (1301 cc) or 578 to 782 ohms (1372 cc) should be indicated.

Fig. 13.76 Crankshaft pulley timing mark aligned with timing pointer – Microplex ignition system (Sec 10)

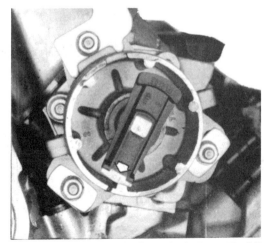

Fig. 13.77 Rotor aligned with distributor body rim mark – Microplex ignition system (Sec 10)

1    TDC sensor

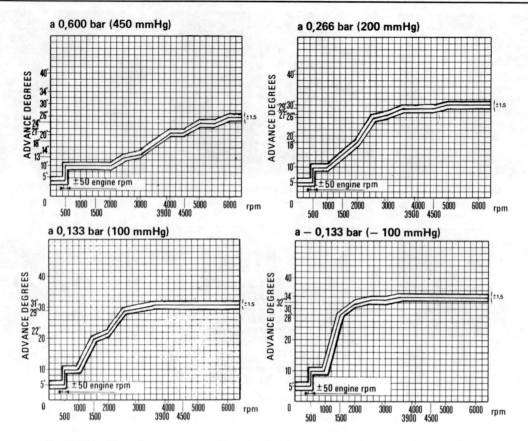

**Fig. 13.78 Ignition advance curves – Microplex ignition system on the 1301 cc Turbo ie (Sec 10)**

47    If necessary, carry out a check of the gap between the sensor and flywheel teeth as described in Chapter 4, Section 10.
**TDC sensor**
48    Insert the probes of the ohmmeter between terminals 1 and 2 of the multipin connector; 618 to 748 ohms (1301 cc) or 578 to 782 ohms (1372 cc) should be indicated.
49    If necessary, carry out a check of the gap between the sensor and the crankshaft pulley, as described in Chapter 4, Section 10.
**ECU supply**
50    Switch on the ignition, and then insert the probes of a voltmeter between terminals 13 and 11 of the multipin connector. Battery voltage should be indicated. If not, check the battery earth, ignition switch or intermediate connector plug for security.
**Power module supply (1301 cc)**
51    Pull the multipin plug from the power module, and connect the probes of a voltmeter between terminal 4 of the connector and earth. If the reading is less than battery voltage, check the security of all connections between the ignition switch and terminal + 15 of the ignition coil.
52    Reconnect the multipin connector to the ECU, but have the one

from the power module disconnected, and then switch on the ignition.
53    Connect the voltmeter between terminals 4 and 2 of the power module multipin connector. If the indicated voltage is less than battery voltage, check the security of all connections between the ignition switch and terminal + 15 of the ignition coil, and the battery earth. If all are satisfactory, check for continuity between terminals 11 and 12. If continuity is broken, renew the ECU.
**Power module (1372 cc)**
54    Proceed as described in paragraph 53.
**Anti-knock sensor**
55    If 'pinking' occurs, or loss of power is noticed, test the sensor by substitution of a new one.

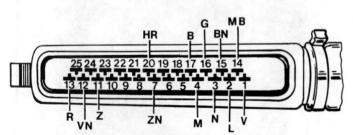

**Fig. 13.79 Microplex ignition system ECU multipin connector (Sec 10)**

*For colour code, see main wiring diagrams*

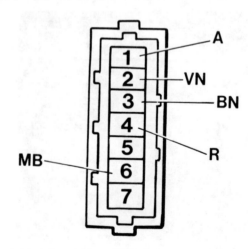

**Fig. 13.80 Microplex ignition system control unit connector (Sec 10)**

*For colour code, see main wiring diagrams*

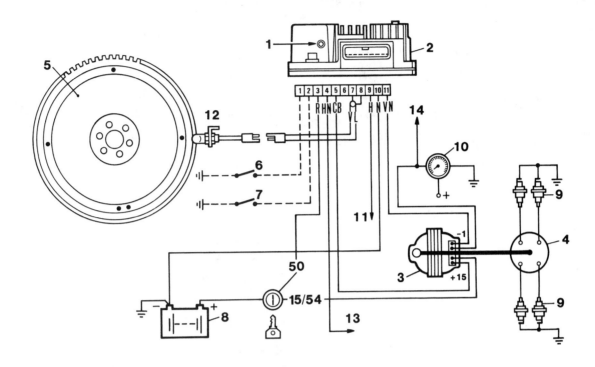

**Fig. 13.81 Digiplex 2 ignition system wiring circuits and components (Sec 10)**

| | | | |
|---|---|---|---|
| 1 | Connection point (lines connected to the intake manifold) | 4 | Distributor |
| | | 5 | Engine flywheel (with five pins) |
| 2 | ECU | 6 | On/off switch (if fitted) for advance reduction |
| 3 | Ignition coil | | |

| | | | |
|---|---|---|---|
| 7 | On/off switch 2 (if fitted) for curves | 11 | Diagnostic socket |
| 8 | Battery | 12 | Engine speed and TDC sensor |
| 9 | Spark plugs | 13 | To check actuator idle speed |
| 10 | Tachometer | 14 | To terminal no. 1 of injection control unit (rpm signal) |

### Ignition coil

56   Disconnect the leads from terminals 1 and 15 on the coil before testing.

57   Using the ohmmeter, check the resistance of the primary winding. This should be between 0.31 and 0.37 ohms (1301 cc) or 0.40 to 0.49 ohms (1372 cc), at an ambient temperature of 20°C (68°F).

58   The secondary winding resistance should be between 3330 and 4070 ohms (1301 cc) or 4320 to 5280 ohms (1372 cc), at an ambient temperature of 20°C (68°F).

### Distributor

59   Check the resistance of the rotor arm, which should be between 800 and 1200 ohms.

60   Where all the foregoing tests have proved satisfactory, then any

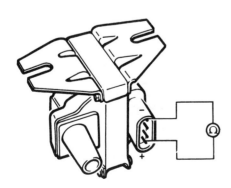

**Fig. 13.82 Test connections for ignition coil primary windings check – Digiplex 2 ignition system (Sec 10)**

problem must be due to a fault in either the power module or the ECU. These components can only be checked by the substitution of a new unit – power module first, then the ECU.

### Safety pressure switch

61   The device protects the engine from excessive turbocharging pressure, cutting off the ignition by earthing the Microplex ECU. Testing is not possible without a special pressure pump, so the easiest way to check a suspected fault is to fit a new unit.

### Digiplex 2 ignition system – description

62   This system operates in a similar manner to that of the earlier type described in Chapter 4, but the circuit layout differs to suit the Mono-Jetronic fuel injection system. In operation, the main difference is that the Digiplex 2 system has a greater number of advance points than the earlier system. Comparison of Fig. 13.81 with Fig. 4.2 illustrates the difference in layout. Note that the distributor is mounted on the rear end of the cylinder head and is driven by the camshaft.

63   When working on the Digiplex 2 ignition system or associated components, the precautionary notes outlined in Section 9 of Chapter 4 must be adhered to.

64   As with the earlier system, test procedures possible on the Digiplex 2 system are restricted due to the need for specialised testing equipment. The following checks are possible, however, using a conventional test meter.

### Ignition coil check

65   To check the resistance of the coil's primary windings, connect the probes of an ohmmeter between the positive terminal and the negative terminal as shown in Fig. 13.82, and check that the resistance reading at 18 to 28°C is 0.45 ohms ± 10% (photo).

66   To check the resistance of the coil's secondary windings, connect the probes of an ohmmeter between the positive terminal and the HT lead terminal as shown in Fig. 13.83. Check that the resistance reading at 18 to 28°C (64 to 82°F) is 4800 ohms ± 10%.

10.65 Ignition coil and connections on the 1372 cc ie engine

10.68 ECU location on the 1372 cc ie engine

10.70 Ignition distributor and HT lead connections on the 1372 cc ie engine

**Ignition timing check**

67    Refer to paragraph 2 in this Section.

**Engine speed and TDC sensor check**

68    To check the resistance between the sensor and the ECU, detach the wiring connector (photo). Connect the probes of an ohmmeter to the connector terminals and check that the resistance reading is between 600 and 760 ohms at 20°C (68°F). If the reading is not as specified, the sensor must be renewed.

69    The gap between the sensor and the pins on the rear face of the flywheel must be between 0.2 and 0.8 mm (0.0078 and 0.0314 in). Any deviation outside of this clearance will be due to mechanical damage to the sensor and necessitates its renewal. The sensor is accurately positioned during manufacture and secured with tamperproof screws; it does not require any adjustment during servicing. If it is necessary to renew the sensor, a special gap setting tool is required and the task is therefore best entrusted to a FIAT dealer.

*Distributor (Digiplex 2) – removal and refitting*

70    Proceed as described in paragraphs 14 to 21. When refitting the distributor, ensure that the engine is still set at the TDC position. Engage the rotor arm into position on the shaft so that its lug engages in the slot in the top end of the drive spindle. Align the rotor arm with the reference slot on the edge of the distributor housing as shown in Fig. 13.84, then fit the distributor into position and secure with the retaining nuts (photo). As previously mentioned, the fine timing is made automatically through the ECU.

*Spark plugs and HT leads – general*

71    Copper-cored spark plugs are now fitted to all models. The recommended types are given in the Specifications Section of this Supplement.

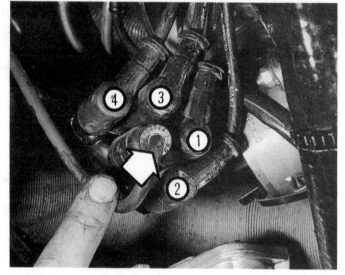

10.72 HT lead connecting sequence on the 1301 cc Turbo ie engine

72    The HT lead connection sequence to the distributor cap on the 999 and 1108 cc engines is shown in Fig. 13.85. That for the 1301 cc Turbo ie is as shown (photo).

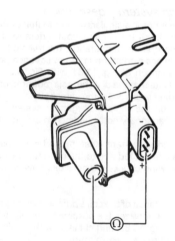

Fig. 13.83 Test connections for ignition coil secondary windings check – Digiplex 2 ignition system (Sec 10)

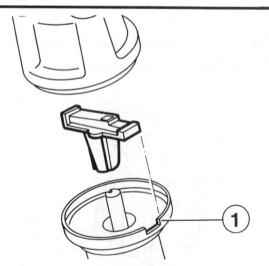

Fig. 13.84 Rotor arm must align with slot (1) in distributor housing when refitting distributor – Digiplex 2 ignition system (Sec 10)

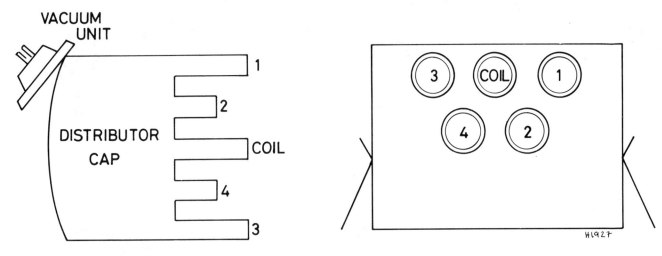

Fig. 13.85 HT lead connections on distributor cap of the 999 and 1108 cc engines (Sec 10)

*Fault diagnosis – Microplex ignition system*

| Symptom | Reason(s) |
|---|---|
| Starter motor turns but engine will not start | Excessive TDC sensor gap<br>Engine speed or TDC sensors short-circuited<br>Faulty ECU<br>ECU multipin contacts corroded<br>Defective ignition coil<br>Defective ignition switch<br>ECU terminal 8 cable faulty |
| Engine firing on three cylinders | Faulty spark plug<br>Distributor cap cracked<br>Faulty HT cable |
| Loss of power, excessive fuel consumption | TDC sensor incorrectly located<br>Fault in ECU advance angle facility |

### 11 Clutch

*Clutch pedal – adjustment (cable clutch)*
1    The method of adjusting the clutch has been revised.
2    Fully depress the clutch pedal two or three times.
3    Using a suitable measuring stick placed in contact with the floor panel (carpet peeled back), measure dimension 'X' in Fig. 13.86. This dimension must be taken between the centre of the pedal pad and the floor, first with the pedal in the fully depressed position, and then in the fully released position.
4    The dimension measured should fall within the range quoted in the Specifications for this Supplement.
5    Any adjustment which may be required should be carried out by slackening the locknut on the cable at the release lever (on top of the gearbox) and turning the adjusting nut. Tighten the locknut on completion.

*Hydraulic clutch – description*
6    Some later models are fitted with an hydraulically operated clutch in place of the cable operated type. The main components of the system are a master cylinder, with separate hydraulic fluid reservoir, and the operating cylinder. The master cylinder is mounted in-line with and just forward of the clutch pedal. The operating cylinder is mounted within a housing on top of the transmission. The fluid reservoir is located in the engine compartment and is mounted on the left-hand side near the bulkhead. No settings or specific procedures are given by the manufacturer at the time of writing.

*Maintenance (hydraulic clutch)*
7    Periodically check the fluid level in the reservoir. If the level has dropped, top it up with the specified fluid. The fluid level must not be

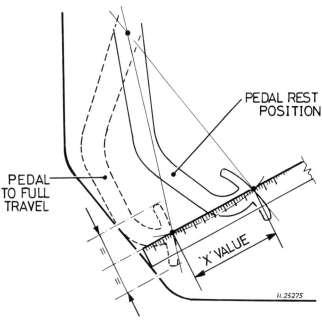

Fig. 13.86 Clutch pedal adjustment diagram – cable clutch (Sec 11)

*For dimension 'X', refer to Specifications*

11.7A Clutch hydraulic fluid reservoir showing MIN and MAX markings

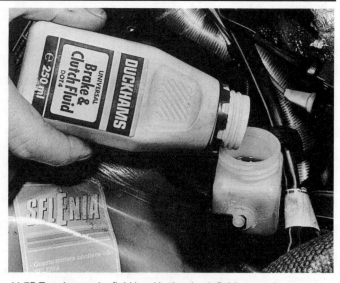

11.7B Topping up the fluid level in the clutch fluid reservoir

allowed to drop below the MIN level mark on the side of the reservoir (photos). If the fluid level drops by a significant amount, it is indicative of a leak in the hydraulic circuit and this must therefore be traced and repaired at the earliest opportunity.
8    Inspect the fluid lines and connections for security and any signs of leaks.

### Clutch master cylinder – removal, overhaul and refitting
9    If the cylinder is to be dismantled, it will first be necessary to obtain a cylinder repair kit. Start by detaching and removing the trim panel from the underside of the facia on the driver's side.
10    Place a suitable covering over the floor carpet to prevent staining in the event of fluid spillage. Clamp the fluid supply hose at the master

cylinder end, then unscrew the retaining clip and detach the hose from the cylinder. Position the hose out of the way and with its end pointing up.
11    Detach the operating rod clevis from the brake pedal.
12    Unscrew and detach the hydraulic pipe to the operating cylinder from the master cylinder (photo).
13    Undo the two retaining nuts and withdraw the master cylinder.
14    To dismantle the cylinder, prise free and pull back the dust boot, extract the retainer and withdraw the operating rod.
15    Invert the cylinder and shake free the piston and seal assembly. If it is stuck inside the cylinder, apply moderate air pressure (from a foot pump) into the tail end and catch the assembly in a clean cloth as it is ejected.

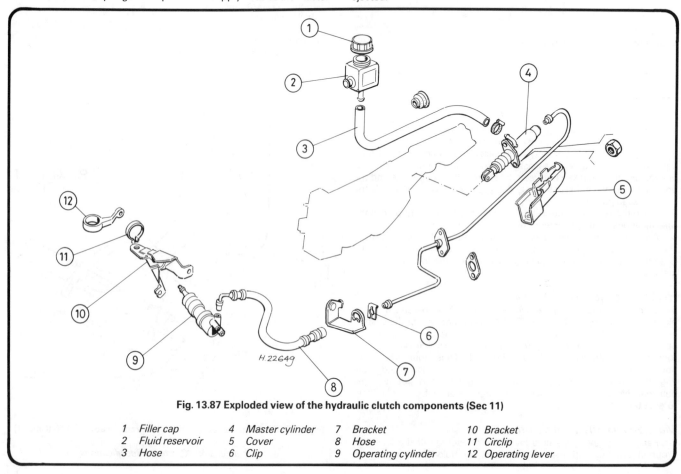

**Fig. 13.87 Exploded view of the hydraulic clutch components (Sec 11)**

| | | | |
|---|---|---|---|
| 1 Filler cap | 4 Master cylinder | 7 Bracket | 10 Bracket |
| 2 Fluid reservoir | 5 Cover | 8 Hose | 11 Circlip |
| 3 Hose | 6 Clip | 9 Operating cylinder | 12 Operating lever |

11.12 Clutch master cylinder and hydraulic pipe connections

11.25 Clutch operating cylinder showing hydraulic line connection and bleed nipple (arrowed)

11.26 Clutch operating lever (A) and operating cylinder bracket-to-transmission housing bolt (B)

16    Remove the seals noting their orientation. Clean all components in methylated spirits or new hydraulic fluid. If the cylinder is damaged, scored or badly worn it must be renewed. The seals must always be renewed once they are removed.

17    Assemble the new seals to the piston and lubricate the cylinder, seals and piston assembly with new hydraulic fluid (of the specified type) before assembling them. Ensure that the seals are fitted the correct way round (as noted during removal).

18    Renew the dust boot, fit and secure the operating rod into position with the retainer, then refit the dust boot over the cylinder.

19    If the intake pipe connector was removed, this must be refitted using a new seal.

20    Refit the cylinder in the reverse order of removal. Connect and hand tighten the hydraulic pipe to the operating cylinder before fully tightening the cylinder securing nuts. The hydraulic pipe can then be fully tightened.

21    Reconnect the fluid supply hose to the cylinder and tighten the retaining clip to secure. Release the clamp.

22    Top up the clutch fluid level in the reservoir then bleed the system as described later in this Section.

### Clutch operating cylinder – removal, overhaul and refitting

23    If the cylinder is to be dismantled once it is removed, it will first be necessary to obtain a cylinder repair kit. Access is much improved by first detaching the appropriate ducts and hoses from the areas directly above the cylinder, on top of the transmission/clutch housing.

24    To avoid excessive fluid loss when the hydraulic line is detached from the operating cylinder, remove the filler cap from the reservoir, place a clean piece of polythene sheet over the filler neck and refit the reservoir cap.

25    Unscrew the union nut and detach the hydraulic fluid line from the operating cylinder (photo).

26    Undo the cylinder/mounting bracket retaining bolts and lift clear the cylinder together with the bracket (photo). Release the retaining clip and separate the cylinder from the bracket.

27    To dismantle the cylinder, prise free and pull back the dust boot, withdrawing it together with the operating rod.

28    Invert the cylinder and shake free the piston and seal assembly. If it is stuck inside the cylinder, remove the bleed screw then apply moderate air pressure (from a foot pump) into the bleed port and catch the cylinder in a clean cloth as it is ejected.

29    Remove the seals noting their orientation. Clean all components in methylated spirits or new hydraulic fluid. If the cylinder is damaged, scored or badly worn it must be renewed. The seals must always be renewed once they are removed.

30    Assemble the new seals to the piston and lubricate the cylinder, seals and piston assembly with new hydraulic fluid (of the specified type) before assembling them. Ensure that the seals are fitted the correct way round (as noted during removal).

31    Renew the dust boot, fit and secure the operating rod into position then refit the dust boot over the cylinder. If removed, refit the bleed screw.

32    Reconnect the cylinder to the mounting bracket and refit the combined assembly to the vehicle in the reverse order of removal. Ensure the hydraulic union is clean and take care not to damage the threads as it is reconnected.

33    Remove the polythene seal from the hydraulic reservoir filler neck, top up the fluid level and bleed the system as described below.

### Clutch hydraulic system – bleeding

34    The clutch hydraulic circuit is bled in much the same manner to that described for a brake circuit. Refer to Section 12 in Chapter 8 and proceed as described, but note that the bleed screw for the clutch circuit is located in the end of the operating cylinder (see photo 11.25). The clutch hydraulic circuit reservoir is mounted in the engine compartment on the left-hand side near the bulkhead and is separate from the master cylinder. As the system is being bled, ensure that the fluid level in the reservoir is maintained between the MIN and MAX level marks. Do not allow the fluid level to drop below the MIN level mark otherwise air will enter the system and greatly lengthen the operation. Wipe clean any fluid spillage from the paintwork or adjacent components as it has a corrosive effect if left.

---

### 12    Transmission

## PART A: 1301 CC TURBO IE ENGINE

### Description

1    The transmission is of five-speed type, based on that used in the Fiat Strada 105 TC.

2    For all practical purposes, the operations described in Chapter 6 apply, but observe the following differences.

### Gearchange linkage – removal and refitting

3    This is of two-rod type.

4    Remove the gaiter and disconnect the rods at the gear lever end as described in Chapter 6, Section 3.

5    Disconnect the rods at the transmission end by unscrewing the nuts and bolts which connect the linkage rods to the selector rods (photo).

6    Extract the spring clip which retains the end of the short link rod (photo).

### Gearchange linkage (Antiskid models) – general

7    The gearchange linkage and internal selector arrangement has been modified, as shown in Fig. 13.88.

### Final drive output shafts – description and oil seal renewal

8    The output shafts on this transmission incorporate a flange on the left-hand side, to which a coupling flange on the driveshaft is bolted. On the right-hand side, an intermediate shaft (see Section 13) is splined directly into the differential side gear.

9    A leaking oil seal may be renewed on the left-hand side of the final drive casing after first disconnecting the driveshaft. Then using two levers, prise out the flange/stub shaft against the tension of its retaining circlip.

10    Unbolt and remove the bearing cover. When refitting the cover, make sure that the O-ring is in good condition.

11    To renew the oil seal on the right-hand side, first remove the intermediate driveshaft, and then prise the defective seal out of the final drive housing using a suitable tool.

12A.5 Gearchange rod connections at transmission
(1301 cc Turbo ie engine)

12A.6 Gearchange link rod spring clip (arrowed) on
the 1301 cc Turbo ie engine

12    Apply grease to the new seal lips before refitting the intermediate
shaft or the stub shaft. Tighten all bolts to the specified torque.

## PART B: 1372 CC IE AND 1372 CC TURBO IE ENGINES
### Description
1    The transmission is of five-speed type, based on that used in the
FIAT Tipo. The transmission is mounted in-line with the engine and is
located in the left-hand side of the engine compartment. Drive from the
clutch is transferred through the input shaft and the mainshaft to the
integrally-located final drive unit. The inboard end of each driveshaft
locates in the differential. All helical gear clusters are in constant mesh,
with the fifth gear assembly located on an intermediate plate mounted
on the rear end of the gearbox. Gear engagement is made by sliding
synchromesh hubs. Gearchanges are made via a central floor-mounted
gear lever.

### Maintenance
2    Maintenance is limited to periodically checking the oil level, topping
up as required, renewing the oil, and visually inspecting the trans-

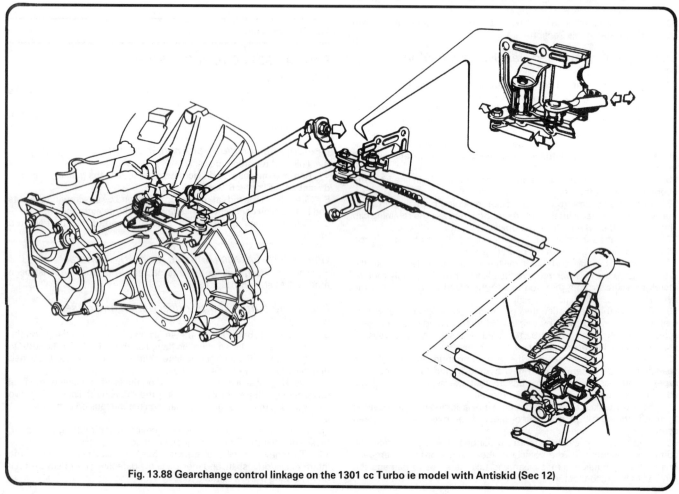

Fig. 13.88 Gearchange control linkage on the 1301 cc Turbo ie model with Antiskid (Sec 12)

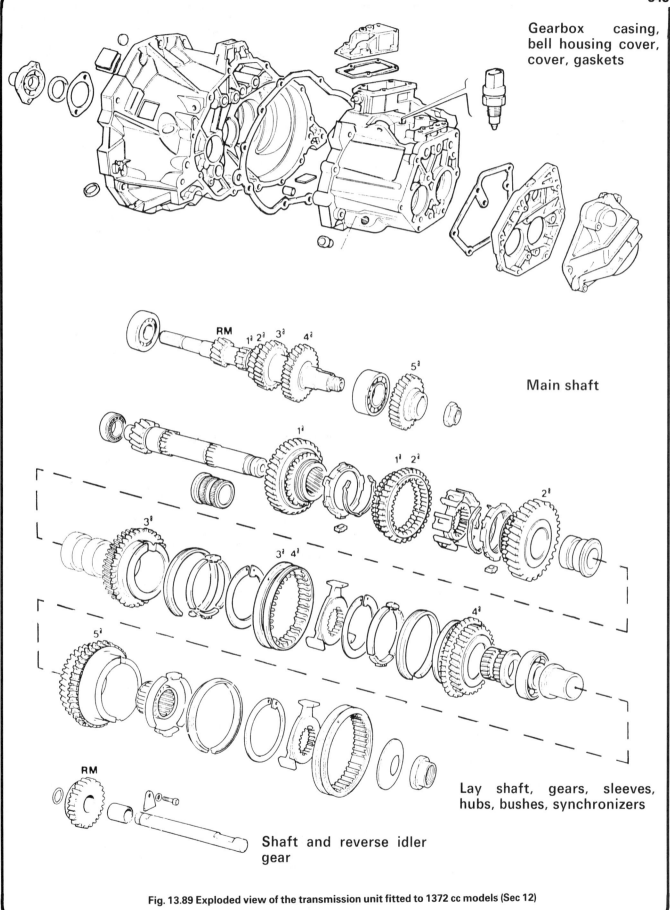

Gearbox casing, bell housing cover, cover, gaskets

Main shaft

Lay shaft, gears, sleeves, hubs, bushes, synchronizers

Shaft and reverse idler gear

**Fig. 13.89 Exploded view of the transmission unit fitted to 1372 cc models (Sec 12)**

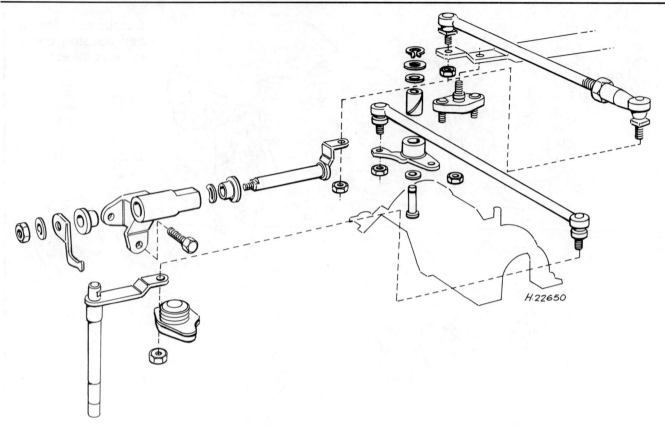

**Fig. 13.90 Exploded view of the gear selector lever, rod and linkage components on 1372 cc models (Sec 12)**

mission for oil leaks. The most likely source of an oil leak will be from the driveshaft seals.

### Oil level checking

3    For improved access, jack up the vehicle and support it on axle stands. Note that the vehicle must be level in order to carry out this check.

4    If the transmission is hot due to the car having been driven recently, allow it to cool before making the check; oil foams when hot and can produce a false level reading. Wipe the area around the filler plug then unscrew and remove the plug from its location in the front of the casing. The oil should be level with the base of the filler plug hole.

5    If necessary, top up with oil of the specified grade.

6    On completion refit the filler plug, wipe clean any oil spillage, then lower the car to the ground.

### Oil – renewal

7    The transmission oil should ideally be drained when hot (directly after the vehicle has been used). For improved access, jack up the vehicle and support it on axle stands. Note that the vehicle must be level to ensure a correct level reading when topping up.

8    Wipe clean the area around the filler plug on the front face of the transmission casing, then unscrew and remove the plug.

9    Position a suitable container underneath the drain plug (located at the left-hand end of the transmission). Unscrew the plug and allow the oil to drain into the container. Oil will start to drain before the plug is fully withdrawn so take precautions against scalding. Wait about ten minutes to allow the oil to drain fully.

10    When the oil has finished draining, clean around the threads of the drain plug and its location in the transmission casing, then refit the plug and tighten it.

11    Refill the transmission with the specified quantity and grade of oil through the filler/lever plug hole. With the vehicle level and the transmission cold check the oil level as described above, then refit and tighten the plug. Lower the vehicle to complete.

### Gearlever and linkages – general

12    The component parts of the gearchange and selector assemblies are shown in Figs. 13.90 and 13.91. They do not normally require

maintenance other than general inspection for wear in the linkage joints. If excessive wear is found in any of the joints, they can be individually detached and renewed.

13    Access to the control rods is eased by detaching and lowering the exhaust system from the exhaust manifold.

14    If a new adjustable control rod is to be fitted, remove the original rod as a unit, but do not alter its adjustment for length. The new rod can then (if required) be set to the same length as the original in order to maintain the original setting. Do so by loosening off the locknut and turning the balljoint as required; ensure that the angle of the joint is correct before tightening the locknut.

15    Access to the gear lever/main connecting rod joint from above is made by prising back the gear lever gaiter from the centre console. Access from underneath can be made by raising and supporting the car on axle stands. Working from the underside of the lever, undo the retaining nuts and remove the inspection plate from the floor (photos).

16    Any adjustment to the gear linkage should be entrusted to a FIAT dealer.

### Transmission – removal and refitting

17    The transmission can be removed together with the engine and then separated as described in Section 7, or on its own (as described below), leaving the engine in position in the car. Before starting to remove the transmission, it should be noted that suitable equipment will be required to support the engine during this procedure.

18    Disconnect the battery negative lead.

19    Remove the bonnet as described in Chapter 12.

20    Refer to Section 11 in this Chapter for details and detach the clutch operating cylinder together with its mounting bracket from the top of the transmission, but do not disconnect the hydraulic fluid hose from the cylinder connection. Leave the cylinder attached to the bracket. Tie the cylinder and bracket up to support them out of the way.

21    Reaching down between the transmission and the bulkhead, unscrew the knurled retaining nut and withdraw the speedometer cable from the transmission.

22    Remove the front roadwheel trims, then loosen off the front wheel retaining bolts. Raise the vehicle and support it on axle stands at a suitable height to allow working underneath and eventual transmission removal from under the front end.

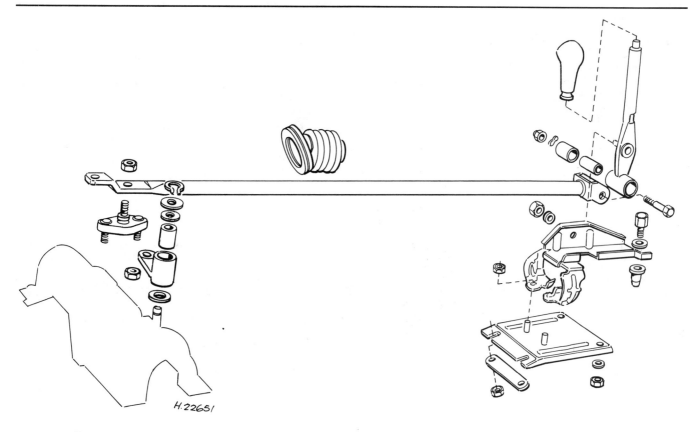

**Fig. 13.91 Exploded view of the gear selector and control rod assembly components fitted to 1372 cc models (Sec 12)**

23  Drain the transmission oil as described previously in this Section.
24  Disconnect and remove the starter motor (photos).
25  Detach the reversing light switch lead connector.
26  Undo the retaining bolt and detach the earth lead from the rear end of the transmission (see photo 7C.33). Refit the bolt once the lead has been disconnected.
27  The engine must now be supported at its left-hand end. If the engine/transmission lift bracket is unbolted it can be attached at another suitable position on the engine and the lift sling/tool attached to it, but take care not to attach it to a weak fixing point.
28  The engine will need to be supported using an engine lift beam/support bar of the type shown in Fig. 13.92. A strong wood or metal beam resting on blocks in the front wing drain channels will suffice, or alternatively use an engine lift hoist and sling.
29  Refer to Section 13 in this Chapter and Section 2 in Chapter 7 for details and remove the front driveshaft each side.
30  Prise back the tabs of the retaining washers, then undo the retaining nuts and detach the exhaust downpipe from the manifold. Detach the exhaust mounting bracket (where applicable) and lower the exhaust to allow access to the gearchange linkages.
31  Disconnect the gearchange control and selector link rod balljoints (photo). Do not alter their lengths or the adjustment setting will be affected.
32  Using a small diameter pin punch, drive the retaining pins from the retaining clips which secure the left-hand side underwing shield. Prise free the clips and detach the shield.
33  Undo the retaining bolts and remove the lower cover plate from the flywheel housing (photo).
34  Position a trolley jack under the transmission, with an interposed block of wood to protect the casing and spread the load. Raise the jack to support the weight of the transmission.
35  Check that the weight of the engine is securely supported, then unbolt and detach the front engine mounting unit, then the rear engine mounting unit.
36  Unscrew and remove the remaining bolts securing the transmission to the engine. As they are removed, note the position of any brackets or additional fixings secured by these bolts (photo).
37  Check around the transmission to ensure that all fixings are detached from it and out of the way, then carefully pull the transmission

free from the engine dowel pins. If possible engage the aid of an assistant to help in guiding or lowering the unit as it is removed. As the unit is withdrawn from the engine, take care not to place any strain on the input shaft. Once the input shaft is clear of the clutch, the transmission can be lowered and manoeuvred from underneath the car. If available, lower the unit onto a suitable crawler board to ease its withdrawal from under the front end of the car.
38  Dismantling and overhaul of this transmission is not recommended. If the transmission has covered a high mileage it is likely that

**Fig. 13.92 FIAT lift beam/support bar in place to support the weight of the engine. Inset shows lift hook engagement point – 1372 cc models (Sec 12)**

12B.15A Gear lever connection to the main connecting rod on the 1372 cc engine

12B.15B Access cover to gear lever lower connection to rod on the 1372 cc engine

12B.24A Starter motor electrical connections ...

12B.24B ... and retaining bolts (arrowed) on the 1372 cc ie engine

12B.31 Gear control and selector link rod joints

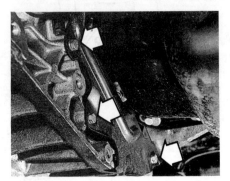

12B.33 Lower cover plate and retaining bolts (arrowed)

12B.36 Transmission upper retaining bolts. Note bracket under the left-hand bolt

several internal components are in need of renewal. The cumulative cost of renewing all worn and defective components will almost certainly make overhaul uneconomical when compared with the cost of a new or service exchange transmission from a FIAT dealer or transmission specialist.

39   Refitting is a reversal of the removal procedure, but note the following special points.

   (a)   Ensure that the engine and transmission mating surfaces and the dowel pins are clean and that all clutch components are in good condition.
   (b)   Apply a thin smear of molybdenum disulphide grease to the

splines of the input shaft. Do not over-lubricate though or the grease may work its way onto the clutch friction surfaces and cause clutch slip.
   (c)   Raise the transmission so that it is in-line with the engine, engage the end of the input shaft into the clutch driven plate hub and align the splines of each to enable the transmission to be pushed home. It may well be necessary to turn the flywheel a fraction so that the splines align for re-engagement.
   (d)   Do not fully tighten the engine and transmission retaining bolts until all are attached.
   (e)   Tighten all retaining bolts and nuts to the specified torque wrench settings (where given).
   (f)   Refer to Section 13 in this Chapter for details on refitting the driveshafts.
   (g)   Refill the transmission with the specified quantity and grade of oil before lowering the car to the ground (see paragraph 11).

---

### 13   Driveshafts

#### Inboard joint boots (non-Turbo models, September 1987 on) – modification

1   Modified boots have been fitted to the differential ends of the driveshafts on non-Turbo models produced after September 1987.
2   The new boots incorporate a seal/bearing assembly, and it is very important when a boot is being fitted to the driveshaft that it is located as shown in Fig. 13.93.
3   The boot retaining band must be crimped using suitable pinchers at the highest point on the boot.

#### Intermediate driveshaft (Turbo ie models)
**Description**
4   On these models, an intermediate driveshaft is fitted between the final drive of the transmission and the flange of the right-hand driveshaft.

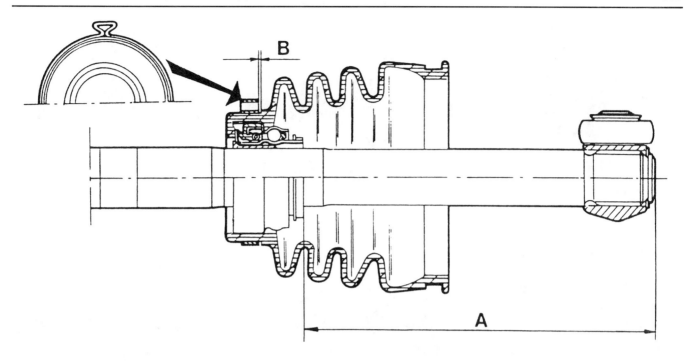

**Fig. 13.93 Driveshaft boot positioning diagram – later non-Turbo models (Sec 13)**

*Left-hand shaft*
*With 4-speed transmission, A = 143.0 mm (5.63 in)*
*With 5-speed transmission, A = 133.0 mm (5.24 in)*

*Right-hand shaft:*
*With 4-speed transmission, A = 123.0 mm (4.84 in)*
*With 5-speed transmission, A = 108.9 mm (4.25 in)*

*B = 0 to 1 mm (0 to 0.04 in)*

**Fig. 13.94 Crimping the driveshaft boot securing band (Sec 13)**

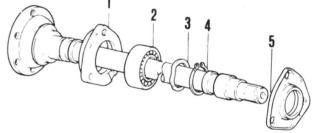

**Fig. 13.95 Components of the intermediate driveshaft –
Turbo ie models (Sec 13)**

| | | | |
|---|---|---|---|
| *1* | *Bearing retaining plate* | *4* | *Circlip* |
| *2* | *Ball bearing* | *5* | *Bearing cap* |
| *3* | *Wave washer* | | |

5    A support bearing assembly for the intermediate shaft is bolted to the engine crankcase. The bearing carrier also acts as the alternator bracket.

**Removal**

6    Drain the transmission oil. Disconnect the right-hand driveshaft from the intermediate shaft flange, move the driveshaft aside, and support it.

7    Unscrew and remove the bolts which hold the intermediate shaft retainer plate to the crankcase support bracket.

8    Withdraw the intermediate shaft from the final drive housing. The shaft assembly, complete with bearing, will pass through the crankcase support bracket until the bearing retainer and flexible boot can be slipped off the shaft.

**Bearing renewal**

9    The bearing on the intermediate shaft can be renewed after removing the plate, circlip and washer, and pressing the shaft out of the bearing.

10    When fitting the new bearing, apply pressure only to the inner track, and do not apply any heat.

**Refitting**

11    This is a reversal of removal. Tighten all bolts to the specified torque and replenish the transmission oil.

*Inboard CV joints (Turbo ie models) – overhaul*

12    A worn joint is best renewed, but it may be necessary to dismantle it for cleaning, if replacement of a split boot has been neglected.

13    Disconnect the boot securing clip and pull the boot up the shaft. Wipe away the old grease.

14    Extract the joint securing circlip and pull the joint from the shaft.

15    Renew the joint complete if it is worn or damaged.

16    Before dismantling the joint, align the housing and ball cage marks 'A' and 'B' (Fig. 13.97).

17    Tap the joint from its backplate.

18    Turn the ball/cage assembly through 90°, mark its relative position to the outer track and withdraw it (photo).

19    The balls are a light snap fit in the cage. Once they are removed,

13.18 Removing inboard CV joint ball/cage assembly from outer track

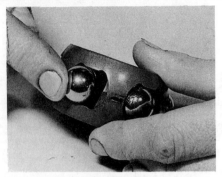

13.19A CV joint balls and cage

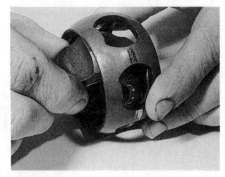

13.19B Separating inner and outer cage members

13.19C Components of CV joint

13.21 Outer track reference groove

13.24 Right-hand driveshaft damper weight

the inner and outer cage members can be separated; again, mark the side of the cages in relation to the outer track (photos).

20   When reassembling, pack the joint with special FIAT Tutela MRM2 lubricant; if this is not available, use molybdenum disulphide grease.

21   The reference groove on the outer track must be assembled so that it is towards the final drive when refitted (photo).

22   Pack the joint and the inside of the boot liberally with the specified grease.

23   If a new joint is being fitted to the shaft, make sure that the joint and shaft colour codes match.

| Shaft colour | Joint colour |
| --- | --- |
| Blue | Blue or white |
| Red | Red or white |

Fig. 13.96 Extracting the CV joint circlip – Turbo ie models (Sec 13)

Fig. 13.97 CV joint housing and ball cage alignment marks (A and B) – Turbo ie models (Sec 13)

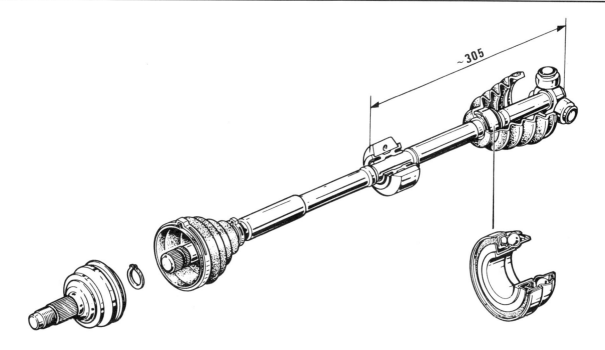

**Fig. 13.98 Correct position of driveshaft damper weight on 1108 cc and 1372 cc ie models (Sec 13)**

*Dimensions in mm*

*Right-hand driveshaft damper weight
(1108 cc and 1372 cc ie models) – removal and refitting*

24    A damper weight is fitted to the longer, right-hand driveshaft to reduce vibration (photo).

25    It should not be necessary to remove the damper weight unless the driveshaft is to be renewed, or the weight has been damaged.

26    The weight is in two halves, and can be removed by simply unscrewing the two clamp bolts securing the two halves to the driveshaft. Note that the weight locates on a rubber mounting which is split along its length, and can simply be pulled from the driveshaft for renewal if necessary.

27    Refitting is a reversal of removal, but ensure that the damper weight is positioned exactly as shown in Fig. 13.98.

---

**14    Braking system**

## PART A: BRAKING SYSTEM – GENERAL

*Front brake pads – all later models*

1    The front brake pads have modified anti-vibration plates and a wire spring fitted to prevent them from vibrating and knocking in operation.

2    On some models the clip securing the disc pad locking block is located on the inboard end, rather than the outer end (shown in Chapter 8). To ensure correct reassembly, check the location of the original block retaining clip before dismantling the brake unit. The alternative fixing arrangement is shown in the accompanying photos, in this instance on a 1372 cc ie model (photos).

14A.2A Front brake pad locking block is secured by a clip on the inboard end of the brake unit on certain models

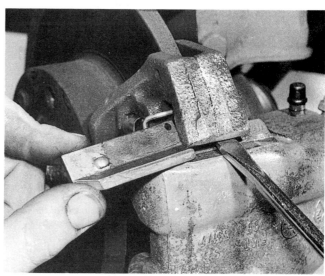

14A.2B Front brake locking block orientation with inboard retaining clip

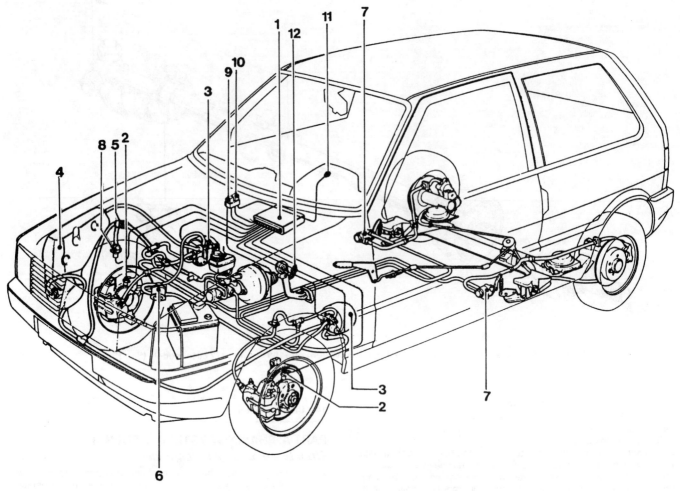

**Fig. 13.99 Braking system on Turbo ie Antiskid models (Sec 14)**

| | | | |
|---|---|---|---|
| *1* | *Electronic control unit (ECU)* | *7* | *Load proportioning (pressure* |
| *2* | *Roadwheel speed sensors* | | *regulating) valves* |
| *3* | *Pressure modulators* | *8* | *Vacuum switch* |
| *4* | *Vacuum reservoir* | *9* | *ECU relay* |
| *5* | *Check valve* | *10* | *System fault warning lamp* |
| *6* | *Air cleaner* | | *relay* |
| | | *11* | *System fault warning lamp* |
| | | *12* | *Brake stop lamp switch* |

## PART B: BRAKING SYSTEM – TURBO IE MODELS

### Description
1    Disc brakes are fitted to all four wheels on the Turbo ie models. The front disc brakes are of different design from those used on other models, in that the wear in the pads can be checked without the need to remove the caliper cylinder housing.

### Front disc pads – renewal
2    Raise the front of the car and remove the roadwheels.
3    Check the thickness of the friction material on the pads through the aperture in the caliper cylinder body. If the thickness of the material is 1.5 mm (0.06 in) or less, then the pads on both sides must be renewed (photo).
4    Using a ring spanner and an open-ended spanner, unscrew and remove the caliper cylinder housing lower guide bolt (photo). Release the upper bolt, but do not remove it.
5    Swivel the cylinder housing upwards and tie it up out of the way. There is no need to disconnect the hydraulic hose. The sensor wiring plug will have to be disconnected (where fitted).
6    Remove the pads, complete with anti-rattle springs (photo).
7    Clean away all dust and dirt, taking care not to inhale it as it may be injurious to health.
8    The caliper piston must now be fully depressed to accommodate the new, thicker, pads. Do this using a G-clamp or lever, but anticipate a

rise in the brake fluid reservoir level by syphoning out some of the fluid using a clean syringe.
9    Fit the new pads, which must be of the same type as the originals, complete with anti-rattle springs.
10    Locate the cylinder body. The fixing bolts are of self-locking type, and should be renewed whenever they are loosened or removed. If new ones are not available, clean the threads of the old ones thoroughly and apply thread-locking fluid (photo). Tighten the bolts to the specified torque. Check that the rubber dust excluders are in good condition.
11    Reconnect the sensor wiring plug.
12    Renew the pads on the other front wheel.
13    Refit the roadwheels, and then apply the footbrake several times to position the pads against the discs.
14    Top up the brake fluid reservoir if necessary (photo).

### Front disc caliper – removal and refitting
15    Raise the front of the car and remove the appropriate roadwheel.
16    Using a ring spanner and an open-ended spanner, unscrew and remove the cylinder housing fixing bolts.
17    Withdraw the cylinder housing, and then, holding it firmly, release the flexible hydraulic hose union. Unscrew the cylinder body from the end of the flexible hose, and then cap the end of the hose to prevent loss of fluid.
18    If required, the disc pads can be removed and the caliper support bracket unbolted and removed.

14B.3 Front disc pads (arrowed) on Turbo ie model

14B.4 Unscrewing the caliper cylinder housing lower guide bolt

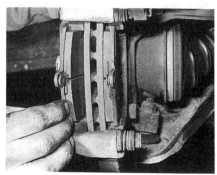

14B.6 Disc pad and anti-rattle spring removal

14B.10 Applying thread-locking fluid to the bolt threads

14B.14 Topping up the brake fluid reservoir (1301 cc Turbo ie model)

19   Refitting is a reversal of removal, but use new fixing bolts.
20   Bleed the front hydraulic circuit.

### Front disc caliper – overhaul

21   The operations are as described in Chapter 8, Section 5, paragraphs 6 to 13.

### Front brake disc – inspection, renovation or renewal

22   The operations are as described in Chapter 8, Section 6, but the caliper fixing bolts are secured with thread-locking fluid; lockplates are not used.

### Rear disc pads – renewal

23   Any wear in the disc pads can be observed through the aperture in the caliper cylinder body, once the car has been jacked up and the roadwheels removed (photo).
24   If the thickness of the pad friction material is less than 1.5 mm (0.06 in), renew the pads on both sides in the following way.

25   Using a ring spanner and an open-ended spanner, unscrew the caliper cylinder body fixing bolts.
26   Withdraw the caliper and remove the disc pads, complete with anti-rattle springs (photo).
27   Clean away all dust and dirt, but avoid inhaling it, as it may be injurious to health.
28   Fully retract the caliper piston in order to accommodate the new, thicker, pads. To do this, rotate the piston clockwise, using a suitable tool engaged in the handbrake sectors (photo). Anticipate a rise in the brake fluid reservoir level by syphoning out some fluid, using a clean syringe.
29   Fit the new pads, complete with anti-rattle springs (photo).
30   Refit the caliper using new self-locking bolts, or if not available, apply thread-locking fluid to clean threads of the original bolts. Tighten the bolts to the specified torque.
31   Apply the brake pedal several times to bring the disc pads up against the disc.
32   Top up the brake fluid reservoir if necessary.
33   Check the adjustment of the handbrake.
34   Refit the roadwheels and lower the car to the ground.

14B.23 Rear brake pad inspection aperture

14B.26 Withdrawing the rear brake caliper

14B.28 Rotating a rear caliper piston

14B.29 Rear disc pad

14B.36 Disconnecting the handbrake cable from the caliper lever

14B.42 Unscrewing a rear caliper bracket bolt

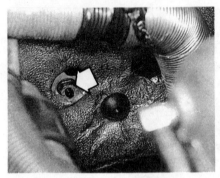

14B.45 Brake pedal cross-shaft fixed nut (arrowed) on engine compartment rear bulkhead

14B.46 Left-hand end of brake pedal cross-shaft

14B.47 Right-hand end of brake pedal cross-shaft

### Rear disc caliper – removal, overhaul and refitting

35   Carry out the operations described in paragraphs 25 to 27.

36   Disconnect the handbrake cable from the caliper. To do this, grip the cable nipple and pull it until the cable can be slipped out of its lever groove (photo). If necessary, slacken the cable adjustment.

37   Using a pair of pliers or similar tool, turn the piston in an anti-clockwise direction until it can be removed from the cylinder.

38   Having obtained a repair kit, renew the seal and dust excluder.

39   Reassemble the piston to the cylinder, turning it clockwise as far as it will go.

40   Reconnect the handbrake cable.

41   Carry out the operations described in paragraphs 30 to 32.

### Rear brake disc – inspection, renovation or renewal

42   The operations are as described in Chapter 8, Section 6, but the caliper bracket fixing bolts are of the socket-headed type and thread-locking fluid is used, not lockplates (photo).

### Pressure regulating valve

43   The valve renewal and adjustment operations are described in Chapter 8, Section 10, but the luggage compartment should be loaded with 45 kg (99 lb), and the load applied to the bracket eye should be 11 kg (24 lb).

### Brake pedal – removal and refitting

44   The brake master cylinder and vacuum servo are mounted on the left-hand side of the engine compartment rear bulkhead. in consequence, the brake pedal on right-hand drive cars operates through a cross-shaft, which is located underneath the facia panel inside the car.

45   The cross-shaft is supported in two brackets, whose mounting nuts can be reached through cut-outs in the insulation on the engine compartment rear bulkhead (photo).

46   To remove the cross-shaft, working inside the car, take off the cover from the left-hand end of the shaft, and then disconnect the servo pushrod from the crankarm on the cross-shaft (photo).

47   Disconnect the brake pedal from the right-hand crankarm on the cross-shaft (photo).

48   Disconnect the accelerator pedal by extracting the split pin which secures its pivot spindle.

49   The cross-shaft may now be removed after extracting the cotter pin from the left-hand end of the shaft.

50   Push the shaft first to the right, and then to the left, to release it from its brackets.

51   Alternatively, the cross-shaft, complete with brackets, may be removed as an assembly if the bulkhead nuts are unscrewed.

52   Removal of the brake and clutch pedals is described in Chapter 5, Section 4, but note that on hydraulic clutch models, the master cylinder will also require removal as described in Section 11 of this Chapter.

53   Refitting is a reversal of the removal procedure.

### Vacuum servo unit and master cylinder – general

54   Access to the vacuum servo unit and the master cylinder can only

14B.54 Master cylinder/vacuum servo located next to the coolant expansion tank (1301 cc Turbo ie model)

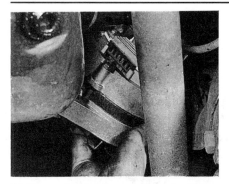

15.4 Removing the alternator from the 999 cc engine

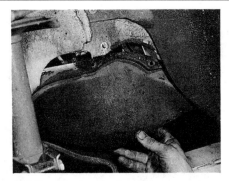

15.8 Remove the wheel arch lower guard panel for access to the alternator

15.12A Alternator air cooling hose

15.12B Alternator rear cover and fixing nut

15.13 Driveshaft bracket swivelled downwards

15.14 Withdrawing the alternator

be obtained after the cooling system expansion tank has been released and moved aside (photo).

### Antiskid system – description

55    This system is available as an option on the Turbo ie models only.
56    The purpose of the system is to prevent the wheel(s) locking during heavy brake applications. This is achieved by automatic release of the brake on a roadwheel which is about to lock up, after which the brake is re-applied. This cycle is carried out many times per second under heavy braking, retaining full steering control to avoid any hazards.
57    The main components of the system are shown in Fig. 13.99. The control module processes the signals received from the sensors, and compares them with deceleration values of the roadwheel and the slip values of the tyre, which are stored in the module memory.
58    When reference values are exceeded and wheel lock is imminent, the control module signals the pressure modulators, which in turn decrease the brake hydraulic pressure.
59    Vehicle road speeds are also taken into account by the module's electronic circuits.
60    In order to retain optimum system performance, the tyres and wheels should always be of the type originally fitted by the vehicle manufacturer.
61    Maintenance of the system should be limited to checking the security of all electrical and hydraulic connections. Individual components are not repairable, and must be renewed complete if faulty.

### 15   Electrical system

### Alternator (999 and 1108 cc models – removal and refitting

1    To remove the alternator from 999 cc engine models, disconnect the leads from the terminals on its rear face.
2    Extract the screws and remove the plastic drivebelt guard.
3    Slacken the mounting and adjuster bolts, push the alternator in towards the engine and remove the drivebelt.

4    Remove the mounting and adjuster bolts, and withdraw the alternator downwards through the gap between the right-hand driveshaft and the engine sump pan (photo).
5    Refitting is a reversal of removal; re-tension the drivebelt.

### Alternator (later models) – removal and refitting

6    Disconnect the battery negative lead.
7    Loosen off the right-hand front roadwheel bolts, then raise and support the car at the front end on axle stands. Remove the right-hand roadwheel.
8    Remove the wheel arch underwing shield by driving the compression pins from the centre of the retaining clips (using a 2 mm drift), then prise free the panel retaining clips and remove the shield. Keep the pins and clips in a safe place and renew any that may have been damaged during removal (photo).
9    Detach the wiring connector from the alternator.
10    Release the alternator mounting and belt adjuster link bolts, and take off the drivebelt.
11    Take out the alternator top and bottom mounting bolts.
12    Disconnect the air cooling hose from the rear cover of the alternator, and then unscrew the fixing nuts and take off the rear cover with hose spout. Mark the position of the cover on the alternator before removing it, so that the spout will be correctly positioned when refitted (photos).
13    Unbolt the driveshaft bearing support/alternator bracket from the engine crankcase, and swivel the support downwards to provide space for withdrawal of the alternator (photo).
14    Withdraw the alternator from under the right-hand front wing (photo).
15    Refit in the reverse order of removal. Refit the drivebelt and ensure correct engagement with the pulleys, then set the drivebelt tension and tighten the alternator retaining nuts.

### Alternator brushes – renewal

16    Depending on model, the brush holder is secured by two screws, which should be extracted and the brush holder removed (photos).
17    New brushes and the holder are supplied as an assembly.

15.16A Extracting the alternator brush holder screw

15.16B Removing the alternator brush holder

### *Starter motor (999 cc models) – removal and refitting*

18   To remove the starter motor from 999 and 1108 cc models, first disconnect the leads from the starter motor terminals.
19   Release the washer fluid reservoir flexible bag from the engine compartment rear bulkhead and move it to the left-hand side.
20   Unscrew the starter motor mounting bolts, withdraw the starter from the flywheel bellhousing, and then lift it out of the left-hand side of the engine compartment (photo).
21   Refitting is a reversal of removal.

### *Starter motor (1301 cc Turbo ie, 1372 cc ie, 1372 cc Turbo ie) – removal and refitting*

22   Disconnect the battery. Working from under the front end of the car, unscrew the starter motor mounting bolts and disconnect the electrical leads.
23   Withdraw the starter motor downwards. On Turbo models, there is just enough clearance, if the oil cooler hose and the oil pressure switch lead are deflected carefully aside (photos).
24   Refit by reversing the removal operations.

### *Starter motor brushes (later models) – renewal*

25   When renewing the starter motor brushes on later models, the old brushes will need to be crushed (in a vice or with a hammer) and their leads then soldered to the new brushes.

### *Fuses – later models*

26   The fuse arrangement is slightly different on later models, but the circuits protected are still identified by a symbol. Refer to the Specifications Section for full details. Note also the terminal block with plastic cover, which can be used to isolate the battery from the electrical system by disconnecting the leads from the terminals (photos).

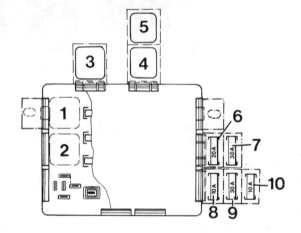

**Fig. 13.100 Auxiliary fuses and relays on 1301 cc Turbo ie models (Sec 15)**

| | |
|---|---|
| 1   Horn relay | 6   Foglamps fuse |
| 2   Heated rear screen relay | 7   Radiator fan second speed fuse |
| 3   Foglamps relay | 8   Fuel injector fan fuse |
| 4   Radiator fan relay | 9   Electric windows fuse |
| 5   Electric windows relay | 10   Electric fuel pump fuse |

15.20 Starter motor removal from the 999 cc engine

15.23A Starter motor removal from the 1301 cc Turbo ie engine

15.23B Starter motor and wiring connections on the 1372 cc ie engine

15.26A Fuse block on the 1301 cc Turbo ie model

15.26B Battery lead terminal block on the 1301 cc Turbo ie model

### Relays (Turbo ie models) – general

27   On Turbo ie models, the relays mounted in the fuse block are as shown in Fig. 13.100. Additional relays are located as follows:

  *Headlamp relay – on lead under main fuse block*
  *Fuel injection system main control relay – adjacent to airflow meter*

### Headlamps – later models

28   The headlamp units fitted on later models differ according to model, but the bulb and unit replacement details are generally the same as described for previous models in Chapter 9. Note that the rubber cover can only be fitted with the tab to the top as shown (photo).

### Headlamp beam adjusters for load compensation – later models

29   Some later models are fitted with headlamp beam adjusters which allow temporary resetting to be made (such as when the car is fully loaded). Access to these adjusters is made by lifting the bonnet (photo).
30   Turn the adjusters anti-clockwise to lower the beam to the normal level or clockwise to raise the beam (when the car is unloaded). Repeat the procedure on the opposite headlamp unit an equal amount.
31   Other later models have separate horizontal and vertical beam adjusters, positioned as shown (photos). A load compensating lever is attached to the adjusters to enable temporary resetting of the headlamp beams, without changing the normal adjustment. Turn the lever to the

15.28 Headlamp unit fitted to the 1372 cc ie model

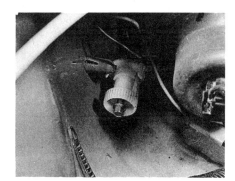

15.29 Headlamp beam adjuster on the 1301 cc Turbo ie model

15.31A Headlamp horizontal beam alignment adjuster screw on a 1372 cc ie model

15.31B Headlamp vertical beam alignment adjuster screw on a 1372 cc ie model. Note the load compensator lever which is set in the 'O' (normal load) setting position

15.34 Headlamp dim-dip transformer

15.37A Undo the retaining bolts ...

15.37B ... and withdraw the front fog lamp unit ...

15.38 ... remove the rear cover ...

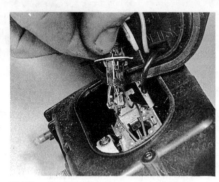

15.39 ... detach the wires, extract the bulb

15.43 Horn location

appropriate side (right or left) to make the adjustment as required. The normal setting adjustment procedures are the same as those outlined for the previous model units in Chapter 9, but ensure that the load compensation lever is turned to the 'O' (normal load setting) position before making any adjustments.

### Headlamp unit removal – later models

32    The removal and refitting procedures described in Chapter 9 also apply to the later headlamp type, but note that later units are secured in position by three retaining screws.

### Headlamp dim-dip system – description

33    On later models, the wiring circuit has been modified to prevent the car being driven on parking lamps only in built-up areas.
34    Headlamp intensity is reduced by the transformer located at the front of the engine compartment (photo).
35    Any attempt to start the car with parking lamps only on will automatically cause the headlamps to switch on with a low-intensity dipped beam. Dipped and main beam function normally.
36    The headlamp dim-dip system is a legal requirement for all UK models registered after April 1st, 1987.

### Front fog lamps – bulb/unit removal and refitting and beam adjustment

37    Ensure that the front fog lamps are switched off, then unscrew the two retaining screws and withdraw the lamp unit from the underside of the front bumper (photos).
38    Undo the retaining screw and remove the access cover from the unit (photo).
39    Disconnect the wiring connector from the bulb, release the clips and withdraw the bulb from the lamp (photo).
40    Refit in the reverse order of removal. Check the light for satisfactory operation and if the beam requires resetting, turn the adjustment screw in the required direction.
41    To adjust the beam, position the car 5 m (16.4 ft) from, and square on to, a wall or similar.
42    Measure the height of the centre of the lamp lens from the ground and mark the position on the wall. Switch on the lamp. The demarcation line (cut-off) of the light should be below the mark on the wall by 50 mm (2 in) plus one-third of the ground-to-lamp centre measurement. Adjust the beam as required using the long centre screw.

### Horn – relocation

43    The single horn, on applicable models, is now located behind the grille, bolted on a bracket attached to the top rail (photo).

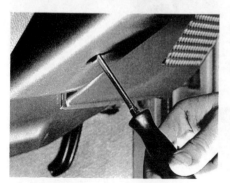

15.45A Undo the retaining screws ...

15.45B ... then remove the upper ...

15.45C ... and the lower column shroud ...

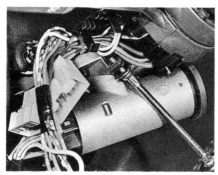

15.47A Undo the retaining screw ...

15.47B ... and remove the column switch

### Steering column combination switches (later models) – removal and refitting

44   Disconnect the battery negative lead.

45   Undo the retaining screws and remove the steering column shrouds (photos).

46   Remove the steering wheel as described in Chapter 10.

47   Loosen off the switch-to-column clamp screw, disconnect the wiring connectors to the switch and withdraw the switch from the column (photos).

48   Refit in the reverse order of removal, but ensure that the lug of the switch aligns with the slot in the column as it is fitted into position. Check for satisfactory operation of the switches on completion.

### Instrument panel (Turbo ie models) – removal and refitting

49   The instrument panel on these models incorporates an engine oil pressure gauge and a turbo boost gauge. The latter is connected directly to the inlet manifold.

50   Apart from disconnecting the boost gauge rubber hose, the instrument panel removal and refitting procedure is as described in Chapter 9 for the 1301 cc model or from paragraph 57 in this Section for the 1372 cc model.

51   A digital electronic instrument panel is available as an option on Turbo ie models. The removal and refitting procedures differ from analogue instrument panels in respect of the electrical connections – a speedometer drive cable is not used.

### Facia-mounted switches (1301 cc Turbo ie model) – removal and refitting

52   Disconnect the battery.

53   Insert a thin-bladed screwdriver into the joint between the switch block and the switch block housing, to depress the plastic retaining tabs. Do this carefully, otherwise the switch block or casing will be damaged.

54   Withdraw the switch block. Individual switches can now be pushed out of the block. Fibre optics are used to illuminate some switches, these simply pull out of their sockets (photos).

55   The switch housing can be removed after extracting the fixing screws (photos).

56   Refitting is a reversal of removal.

### Instrument panel (later models) – removal and refitting

57   Disconnect the battery negative lead.

58   Unscrew and remove the two instrument panel-to-facia retaining screws (photo).

59   Remove the lower facia trim panel, which is secured by two screws and a nut. Reach up to the rear of the instrument panel to disconnect the speedometer cable, then push the panel from its recess in the facia. Disconnect the multi-connectors from the rear face of the panel and withdraw it (photo).

60   Refit in the reverse order of removal. Ensure that the speedometer cable is fully engaged as the unit is refitted into position.

### Auxiliary control panel (later models) – removal and refitting

61   Disconnect the battery negative lead.

62   Insert the flat of a screwdriver under the trim piece at the end of the auxiliary panel as shown and prise it free. Repeat the procedure and remove the trim piece at the other end of the panel (photo).

15.54A Switch block withdrawal on the 1301 cc Turbo ie model

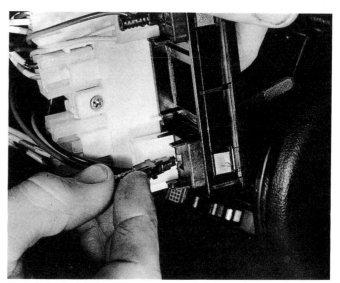

15.54B Disconnecting a fibre optic cable from its holder on the 1301 cc Turbo ie model

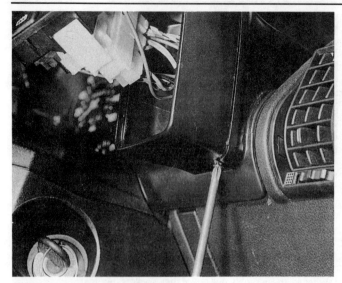

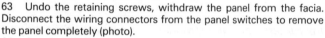
15.55A Facia switch housing lower screw removal on the 1301 cc Turbo ie model

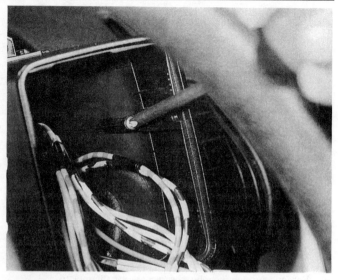
15.55B Facia switch housing inner screw removal on the 1301 cc Turbo ie model

63   Undo the retaining screws, withdraw the panel from the facia. Disconnect the wiring connectors from the panel switches to remove the panel completely (photo).
64   A switch bulb can be renewed by untwisting the holder and removing the holder and bulb.
65   A switch unit can be removed from the panel by unscrewing the four retaining screws.
66   Refitting is a reversal of the removal procedure. Ensure that the wiring connections are securely made and check for satisfactory operation of the switches on completion.

### Heater control panel (later models) – removal and refitting
67   Disconnect the battery negative lead.
68   Pull free the heater/fresh air and blower control knobs (photo).
69   Undo the two retaining screws and withdraw the control panel from the facia (photos). Detach the wiring connectors from the panel illumination lights and remove the panel.
70   Refitting is a reversal of the removal procedure. Ensure that the wiring connections are securely made and on completion check that the operation of the controls is satisfactory.

15.58 Remove the retaining screws ...

15.59A ... withdraw the instrument panel ...

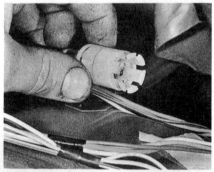
15.59B ... and disconnect the speedometer cable

15.62 Prise free the trim covers for access to retaining screws ...

15.63 ... and withdraw the auxiliary control panel

15.68 Remove the control knobs ...

15.69A ... undo the retaining screws (arrowed)

15.69B ... and withdraw the heater control panel

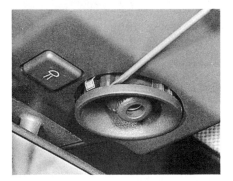

15.80A Prising free the roof-mounted spotlamp

15.80B Roof-mounted spotlamp bulb removal

15.81 Roof-mounted spotlamp switch removal

## Trip master

71    This electronic instrument is fitted into the check panel of 1100SL and 1300SL models from 1986.

72    The device provides information on fuel consumption, range, speed and elapsed time.

73    With the ignition key turned to MAR, figures are displayed in respect of the last journey – average fuel consumption, average speed and elapsed time (up to switching off the ignition).

74    As soon as the engine is started, the instrument processes the current values to include fuel consumption, range and the actual time.

75    Fuel consumption is only displayed when the roadspeed exceeds 8.0 km/h (5.0 mph).

76    The fuel range is only displayed after a roadspeed of between 25.0 and 70.0 km/h (15.0 to 44.0 mph) has been maintained for at least 90 seconds or at higher speeds for 22 seconds.

77    A reset button is provided, also a display change button (from instant to average or total values). Should the instrument reading exceed 99 hours, 59 minutes or 1000 km (622 miles) depressing the display change button will display all zeros. Depress button E to resume normal function.

78    Refer to the end of the manual for a wiring diagram of the check panel, incorporating the trip master.

## Interior roof mounted spotlamp, switch and/or clock – removal and refitting

79    Disconnect the battery negative lead.

80    Prise free the lamp unit from its aperture in the roof panel using a thin-bladed screwdriver. The lamp bulb can be inspected by untwisting the holder and withdrawing it from the rear of the unit (photos). Extract the bulb from the holder if it requires renewal.

81    To remove the lamp switch from the panel, reach through the lamp aperture and press it free from the roof panel (photo). Detach the wiring connectors.

82    To remove the clock, reach through the lamp aperture and undo the retaining screws (photo). Withdraw the clock and detach the wiring connectors.

83    Refitting is a reversal of the removal procedure. Reset the clock on completion.

## Central door locking system

84    Certain later models, equipped with a central door locking system, have an infra-red remote control for opening the door locks.

85    It is important that the battery used in the hand control is renewed when necessary with one of identical type (Duracell 7H34). This is only available as a FIAT spare part (No 7595393).

86    The remote control door lock receiver unit can be removed by carefully prising it free from the roof panel and disconnecting the wiring connector (photo).

87    If either this unit or the hand control are renewed at any time, recoding will be necessary and this is a task best entrusted to a FIAT dealer.

15.82 Roof-mounted clock retaining screw removal

15.86 Remote control receiver unit removal

15.91 Prising free the window regulator switch from the armrest

### Cigar lighter (later models) – removal and refitting

88    Pivot back the cover and lift out the ashtray.
89    Undo the retaining screws and remove the trim together with the lighter unit. Detach the wiring connector and release the lighter unit from the panel.
90    Refit in the reverse order of removal.

### Electrically operated window switches – removal and refitting

91    The window regulator switches on later models are located in the door pull trim. To remove a switch, prise it free from the trim by inserting a thin-bladed screwdriver under the switch flange, then lever it free from its aperture (photo). Take care not to damage the trim. Detach the wiring connector to fully remove the switch.

92    Refit in the reverse order of removal and then check the operation of the switch.

### Windscreen wiper motor (later models) – removal and refitting

93    Disconnect the battery negative lead.
94    Remove the bonnet as described in Chapter 12.
95    Remove the wiper arm and blade as described in Chapter 9, then unscrew and remove the pivot nut (photo).
96    Undo the air inlet grille retaining screws noting that two are not fitted with washers. Where applicable, remove the washer reservoir filler cap from the reservoir neck protruding through the grille. Carefully prise free and lift the air inlet grille clear of the body. As it is lifted, invert it and detach the washer hose from the washer nozzle (photos).

15.95 Unscrewing the wiper pivot nut

15.96A Release the air grille from its fixing points ...

15.96B ... and detach the windscreen washer hose

15.98A Remove the wiper motor retaining screws ...

15.98B ... separate the wiper motor from its cover ...

15.98C ... and detach the wiring connector

15.106 Tailgate wiper motor – later model

15.108A Pillar upper screws for aerial

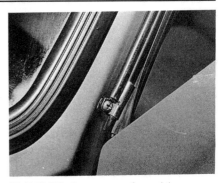

15.108B Pillar lower screw for aerial

97    Where applicable, detach and remove the washer reservoir from the recess in the front of the windscreen to allow access to the wiper motor.

98    Unscrew and remove the two wiper motor retaining screws. Lower and withdraw the unit, then detach the cover from the motor. Disconnect the wiring from the wiper motor and withdraw it from the car (photos).

99    Refit in the reverse order of removal. Check for satisfactory operation of the wiper and washer on completion.

### Windscreen washer reservoir (Turbo ie models) – removal and refitting

100    Disconnect the battery negative lead.

101    Remove the bonnet as described in Chapter 12.

102    Remove the wiper arm and blade as described in Chapter 9, then unscrew and remove the pivot nut.

103    Undo the air inlet grille retaining screws noting that two are not fitted with washers. Where applicable, remove the washer reservoir filler cap from the reservoir neck protruding through the grille. Carefully prise free and lift the air inlet grille clear of the body. As it is lifted, invert it and detach the washer hose from the washer nozzle.

104    Syphon any remaining washer fluid from the reservoir, then disconnect it and partially withdraw it from the recess in front of the windscreen so that the wiring connection and the washer supply hoses (to the windscreen washer and the rear screen washer nozzles) can be detached from the pump unit. Remove the reservoir from the vehicle.

105    Refit in the reverse order of removal. If the washer pump unit was detached from the reservoir, use a new seal washer when refitting it. Top up the reservoir and check the screen washers for satisfactory operation before refitting the grille panel and the wiper arm/blade.

### Tailgate wiper motor (later models) – removal and refitting

106    Although the tailgate wiper motor differs in appearance, its removal and refitting procedures are much the same as those described for the earlier models in Section 27 of Chapter 9 (photo).

### Radio

107    All later models are now equipped with power supply and speaker leads for radio installation.

108    Installation of the standard FIAT aerial mounted on the windscreen pillar is shown (photos).

### Check control system sensors – description

109    The locations of the sensors referred to in Chapter 9, Section 34 are given in the following paragraphs, and their construction differs according to their individual function.

**Brake fluid level sensor**

110    This is mounted in the master cylinder fluid reservoir cap, and comprises a pair of reed switches in a glass bulb, and a magnet at the end of a float.

111    When the fluid level is correct, the magnetic flux closes the switches. In the event of a leak in the system, the magnet moves away, the switches open and the warning lamp comes on.

**Brake disc pad wear sensor**

112    This is basically a circuit wire embedded in the pad friction material. As the pad wears, the wire is eventually exposed and contacts the disc, whereupon the warning lamp comes on to indicate that pad renewal is necessary.

**Coolant level sensor**

113    This is located in the cooling system expansion tank, and is of the reed switch type, which operates in a similar way to that described for the brake fluid sensor.

**Engine oil level sensor**

114    This is located at the end of the dipstick, and comprises a pair of switches at the end of a bi-metallic strip, heated by electrical resistance.

115    The heat is dissipated by the immersion of the dipstick in the engine oil, so preventing the bi-metallic strip from curving so much that the switches would open.

116    If the oil level drops, the heat is no longer dissipated, the switches open, and the warning lamp comes on.

**Door closure sensor**

117    The sensor consists of a microswitch within the lock. The switch actuates the warning lamp according to whether the lock is in the open or closed mode.

### Check control system sensors – testing

**Brake fluid level sensor**

118    With the fluid level correct, switch on the ignition and depress the centre of the reservoir cap. If the sensor switches are working correctly, then 'FAULT' should be indicated on the check panel.

**Coolant level sensor**

119    With the coolant level in the expansion tank correct, switch on the ignition and then pull the wiring plug from the sensor. 'FAULT' should be indicated on the check panel. If it is not, then it is the panel which is faulty.

120    An ohmmeter should be used to check for continuity, holding the float in both the full and low level positions.

**Engine oil level sensor**

121    With the oil level correct, disconnect the wiring plug from the dipstick, and then bridge the plug terminals (not dipstick side) with a 12 ohm resistor. Switch on the ignition.

122    If the red light on the check panel goes out, then the fault is due to the sensor.

123    If the light stays on, then it is the check panel module which is faulty.

**Door closure sensor**

124    Any fault in the lock microswitch can best be detected using an ohmmeter.

---

### 16    Suspension

### Front anti-roll bar – removal and refitting

1    A front anti-roll bar is fitted to the 1372 cc ie , 1301 cc and 1372 cc Turbo ie engined models. Removal of the bar on all models is as follows. Firstly loosen off the front roadwheel bolts, then raise the front of the car, securely support it on axle stands and remove the front roadwheels.

2    Disconnect the two gearchange rods from the transmission.

3    Unbolt and disconnect the anti-roll bar insulating clamps from the floorpan (photo).

4    Unbolt the end links from the track control arms and withdraw the anti-roll bar (photo).

5    Refitting is a reversal of removal, but only tighten the nuts and bolts to the specified torque with the car parked on level ground, with four passengers and 40 kg (88 lb) of luggage inside.

16.3 Anti-roll bar clamp

16.4 Anti-roll bar fixing nuts (arrowed)

16.7 Suspension strut upper mounting nuts, showing bracket and cable clip on the 1372 cc ie model

## Suspension strut – later models

6    The suspension strut upper mounting nuts on later models also secure the brackets for the mounting of ancillary components such as the fuel filter, fuel system relays and fuses, etc. (depending on model).

7    When removing the suspension strut units, it will therefore be necessary to detach and support these brackets and their fittings (photo).

## 17   Bodywork

### Plastic components

1    With the use of more and more plastic body components by the vehicle manufacturers (eg bumpers, spoilers, and in some cases major body panels), rectification of more serious damage to such items has become a matter of either entrusting repair work to a specialist in this field, or renewing complete components. Repair of such damage by the DIY owner is not really feasible owing to the cost of the equipment and materials required for effecting such repairs. The basic technique involves making a groove along the line of the crack in the plastic using a rotary burr in a power drill. The damaged part is then welded back together by using a hot air gun to heat up and fuse a plastic filler rod into the groove. Any excess plastic is then removed and the area rubbed down to a smooth finish. It is important that a filler rod of the correct plastic is used, as body components can be made of a variety of different types (eg polycarbonate, ABS, polypropylene). Damage of a less serious nature (abrasions, minor cracks, etc.) can be repaired by the DIY owner using a two-part epoxy filler repair material, like Holts Body + Plus or Holts No Mix which can be used directly from the tube. Once mixed in equal proportions (or applied direct from the tube in the case of Holts No Mix), this is used in similar fashion to the bodywork filler used on metal panels. The filler is usually cured in twenty to thirty minutes, ready for sanding and painting.

2    If the owner is renewing a complete component himself, or if he has repaired it with epoxy filler, he will be left with the problem of finding a suitable paint for finishing which is compatible with the type of plastic used. At one time the use of a universal paint was not possible owing to the complex range of plastics encountered in body component applications. Standard paints, generally speaking, will not bond to plastic or rubber satisfactorily, but Holts Professional Spraymatch paints to match any plastic or rubber finish can be obtained from dealers. However, it is now possible to obtain a plastic body parts finishing kit which consists of a pre-primer treatment, a primer and coloured top coat. Full instructions are normally supplied with a kit, but basically the

17.4 Interior mirror base

17.5 Interior mirror mounting plate

17.7A Exterior mirror trim plate

17.7B Withdrawing the exterior mirror

17.8 Extracting the mirror balljoint screw

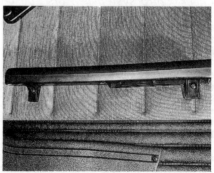

17.9 Door armrest

17.13 Tailgate handle link rod (arrowed)

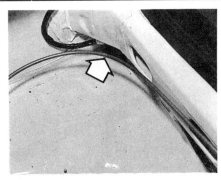

17.15 Tailgate release cable (arrowed)

17.17 Tailgate wiper motor

17.19A Extracting a radiator grille screw

17.19B Prising down a radiator grille clip

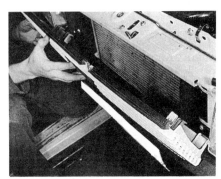

17.20 Removing the radiator grille from a 1301 cc Turbo ie model

method of use is to first apply the pre-primer to the component concerned and allow it to dry for up to 30 minutes. Then the primer is applied and left to dry for about an hour before finally applying the special coloured top coat. The result is a correctly coloured component where the paint will flex with the plastic or rubber, a property that standard paint does not normally possess.

### Rear view mirrors

**Interior**

3   The mirror is of safety type, 'breaking' off its ball fixing upon impact from a front seat occupant.

4   To remove the mirror, grip the head and push it towards the windscreen; the ball socket will release (photo).

5   Extract the screws from the mounting plate (photo).

6   When refitting the mirror, engage the front of the socket on the ball and then twist the mirror rearwards and upwards.

**Exterior**

7   On models without remotely-controlled type exterior mirrors, the balljointed mirror is held in position by the two self-tapping screws which secure the triangular trim plate inside the car (photos).

8   To dismantle the mirror, extract the balljoint fixing screw, but take care as considerable force is exerted by the interior coil spring (photo).

### Door armrest

9   A redesigned armrest is used on some models. This is simply secured by two self-tapping screws (photo).

### Tailgate (Turbo ie model) – component removal and refitting

10   The tailgate on these models is of plastic injection-moulded type, with a bonded window glass.

11   Renewal of the glass or repair of the tailgate should be entrusted to your FIAT dealer or a specialist repairer, due to the need for special products and techniques.

12   To remove the tailgate lock and handle, open the tailgate and extract the lock handle screws.

13   Prise off the link rod socket from the ball-pin (photos). Unbolt and remove the handle and lock.

14   A remote type of tailgate release is fitted, with a control handle located by the driver's seat. Access to the handle can be obtained by removing the seat and sill trim, and peeling back the carpet.

15   If a new cable is to be fitted, disconnect it from the tailgate latch,

tape the new cable to the old one, and draw it carefully around the side panel and sill trim (photo).

16   To remove the tailgate wiper motor, first take off the wiper arm and blade.

17   Extract the plastic clips and take off the wiper motor protective cover. Disconnect, unbolt, and remove the wiper motor (photo).

18   Refitting of all components is a reversal of removal.

### Radiator grille (1301 cc Turbo ie model) – removal and refitting

19   The grille is secured by a central screw and two upper clips. Use a screwdriver to prise the tabs on the upper clips downwards (photos).

20   Lift the grille upwards and forwards to disengage its lower mountings (photo).

21   Refitting is a reversal of removal.

17.22 Radiator grille screw removal on a 1372 cc SX ie model

17.24 Front bumper upper mounting screw (arrowed)

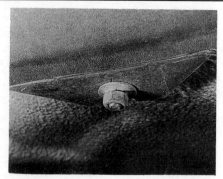

17.28 Rear bumper lower mounting nut

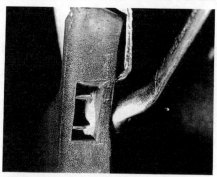

17.29 Unscrewing a bumper end fixing nut

### *Radiator grille (1372 cc ie and 1372 cc Turbo ie models) – removal and refitting*

22    The radiator grille on these models is secured by screws at the top edge (photo). Raise and support the bonnet. Undo the retaining screws, then lift the grille clear.
23    Refit in the reverse order of removal.

### *Bumpers (1301 cc Turbo ie, 1372 cc ie and 1372 cc Turbo ie models) – removal and refitting*

**Removal – front**
24    Remove the radiator grille as previously described, to provide access to the bumper upper mounting screws (photo).
25    The ends of the bumpers are secured with bolts and captive nuts, but to reach them, the underwing shields must be released and pulled away.
26    Disconnect the leads from the auxiliary lamps which are mounted in the spoiler, and then lift the bumper/spoiler from the car.
**Removal – rear**
27    Open the tailgate to provide access to the bumper upper mounting screws.
28    Disconnect the leads from the rear number plate lamp. Unscrew the lower mounting nuts (photo).
29    Disconnect the bumper end fixings, which are accessible under the rear wing edges (photo).
**Refitting – front and rear**
30    Refitting either front or rear bumpers is a reversal of removal.

17.31 Rear window toggle-type catch

### *Rear hinged windows – removal and refitting*

31    These have toggle-type catches and hinges bolted directly through the glass (photo).
32    To remove the window glass, have as assistant support it, and then unscrew the cross-head hinge screws and the toggle catch anchor plate screws. Lift the glass away. If the toggle catch must be removed from the glass, first drive out the handle pivot pin and then, using a pin

wrench or circlip pliers, unscrew the ring nut which secures the handle to the glass.
33    When refitting the screws or ring nut to the glass, make sure that the insulating washers are in good condition to prevent metal-to-glass contact.

### *Door trim panel (Turbo ie model) – removal and refitting*

34    The operations are similar to those described in Chapter 12, Section 11, except that electric windows are fitted instead of a conventional mechanical regulator and handle. Before the trim panel can be withdrawn, the window control switches must be disconnected from the wiring plug, and the plug fed through the panel aperture (photos).

17.34A Armrest electric window switches

17.34B Disconnecting an electric window regulator switch plug

17.34C Door interior showing electric window motor (arrowed)

**Component key for wiring diagrams on pages 367 to 383**

**Note:** *Not all the items listed will be fitted to all models*

| No | Description |
|---|---|
| 00200 | Alternator with built-in regulator |
| 00500 | Battery |
| 01001 | Starter motor |
| 01202 | Rear front electric window motor |
| 01203 | Left front electric window motor |
| 01206 | Windscreen wiper motor |
| 01207 | Rear screen wiper motor |
| 01252 | Right front door locking motor |
| 01253 | Left front door locking motor |
| 01254 | Right rear door locking motor |
| 01255 | Left rear door locking motor |
| 01400 | Windscreen washer pump |
| 01401 | Rear screen washer pump |
| 01420 | Electric fuel pump |
| 01500 | Engine cooling fan |
| 01502 | Injector cooling fan |
| 01504 | Ventilation fan |
| 02001 | Engine cut-out solenoid on injection pump |
| 02010 | Fuel injector |
| 02011 | Fuel injector |
| 02012 | Fuel injector |
| 02013 | Fuel injector |
| 02015 | Supplementary air valve |
| 02210 | Accelerator pump outlet cut-out solenoid on carburettor |
| 02215 | Supplementary air valve |
| 02400 | Ignition coil |
| 02405 | Ignition coil with electronic control unit |
| 02490 | Static advance ignition control unit |
| 02492 | Microplex ignition system control unit |
| 03000 | Insufficient engine oil pressure switch |
| 03002 | Right front door ajar switch |
| 03003 | Left front door ajar switch |
| 03004 | Right rear door ajar switch |
| 03005 | Left rear door ajar switch |
| 03006 | Handbrake 'on' warning switch |
| 03007 | Brake stop-lamp switch |
| 03008 | Reversing light switch |
| 03028 | Radiator thermostatic switch |
| 03029 | Coolant overheating warning light thermostatic switch |
| 03034 | Injector cooling fan thermostatic switch |
| 03035 | Accelerator pump outlet cut-out solenoid thermostatic switch |
| 03036 | Radiator thermostatic switch with two operating ranges |
| 03053 | Map reading light switch |
| 03059 | Foglamps switch |
| 03060 | Rear foglamp switch |
| 03110 | Heated rear screen switch |
| 03114 | Ventilation fan switch |
| 03123 | Air pressure switch |
| 03142 | Choke warning light switch |
| 03144 | Reset switch |
| 03145 | Display switch |
| 03305 | Right front door open light push button |

| No | Description |
|---|---|
| 03306 | Left front door open light push button |
| 03319 | Horn push button |
| 03500 | Ignition switch |
| 03505 | Butterfly valve cut-off switch |
| 03506 | Throttle position switch |
| 03530 | Right front electric window switch |
| 03531 | Left front electric window switch |
| 03546 | Rear screen wash/wipe switch |
| 03550 | Hazard warning lights switch |
| 04010 | Steering column switch unit, direction indicators |
| 04022 | Steering column switch unit, headlamps, main beam and dipped, side lights |
| 04032 | Steering column switch unit, windscreen wash/wipe |
| 04214 | Fuel injection system control relay |
| 04215 | Antiskid system failure relay |
| 04225 | Radiator fan 2nd speed engagement relay feed |
| 04241 | Foglamps relay feed |
| 04260 | Electric windows motor relay feed |
| 04283 | Antiskid system relay |
| 04291 | Horn relay feed |
| 04292 | Heated rear screen relay feed |
| 04441 | Dim-dip cut-out |
| 04600 | Ignition distributor |
| 04700 | Coolant temperature sender unit |
| 04701 | Electronic injection coolant temperature sender unit |
| 04720 | Oil pressure sender unit |
| 05008 | Right headlamp, main beam and dipped with side light |
| 05009 | Left headlamp, main beam and dipped with side light |
| 05013 | Abnormal fuel consumption sensor |
| 05015 | Right foglamp |
| 05016 | Left foglamp |
| 05410 | Right front direction indicator |
| 05411 | Left front direction indicator |
| 05412 | Right front side direction indicator |
| 05413 | Left front side direction indicator |
| 05640 | Rear number plate lamp |
| 05690 | Right rear light cluster, sidelight, direction indicator, brake light, rear foglamp |
| 05691 | Left rear light cluster; side light, direction indicator, brake light, rear foglamp |
| 06000 | Centre courtesy light |
| 06026 | Map reading light |
| 06076 | Ideogram fibre optic light |
| 06080 | Heater controls light |
| 06084 | Instrument panel light |
| 06300 | Sidelights warning light |
| 06305 | Main beam headlamps warning light |
| 06310 | Rear foglamps warning light |
| 06311 | Foglamps warning light |
| 06315 | Hazard warning lights warning light |
| 06320 | Direction indicators warning light |
| 06335 | Insufficient brake fluid level warning light |
| 06336 | Handbrake 'on' warning light |

**Component key for wiring diagrams on pages 367 to 383 (continued)**

| No | Description |
|----|-------------|
| 06343 | Insufficient engine oil pressure warning light |
| 06344 | Insufficient brake fluid level warning light |
| 06345 | Fuel reserve warning light |
| 06350 | Coolant overheating warning light |
| 06355 | Battery charging warning light |
| 06365 | Choke warning light |
| 06368 | Antiskid system failure lamp |
| 06385 | Heated rear screen warning light |
| 06800 | Horn |
| 06801 | Right horn |
| 06802 | Left horn |
| 07000 | Coolant level sensor |
| 07001 | Engine oil level sensor |
| 07003 | Brake fluid level sensor |
| 07015 | Right front brake pad wear sensor |
| 07016 | Left front brake pad wear sensor |
| 07020 | Engine speed sensor |
| 07021 | TDC sensor |
| 07022 | Anti-knock sensor |
| 07023 | Diagnostic socket |
| 07037 | Butterfly valve (cut-off) switch |
| 07050 | Fuel gauge |
| 07051 | Instant fuel consumption gauge (econometer) |
| 07052 | Airflow meter |
| 07060 | Idle cut-off device |
| 07107 | Roadwheel speed sensors |
| 07109 | Vacuum switch |

| No | Description |
|----|-------------|
| 07191 | Absolute pressure sensor |
| 07192 | Vacuum switch |
| 07400 | Fuel gauge |
| 07410 | Engine oil temperature gauge |
| 07415 | Coolant temperature gauge |
| 07420 | Engine oil pressure gauge |
| 07430 | Tachometer |
| 07460 | Clock |
| 07461 | Digital clock |
| 08051 | Ignition coil condenser |
| 09000 | Dim-dip transformer |
| 09008 | Radiator cooling fan 1st speed resistor |
| 09100 | Heated rear screen |
| 10022 | Cut-off device electronic control unit |
| 10500 | Control (fuse) box |
| 10515 | Electronic injection control unit |
| 10571 | Central locking control unit |
| 10584 | Antiskid system ECU |
| 10586 | Pressure modulators |
| 59000 | Cigar lighter |
| 60000 | Instrument panel |
| 60204 | Four place fusebox |
| 70090 | General earth |
| 70091 | General earth |
| 70092 | Earth plate |
| M | Electronic control unit |

**Wire colour codes**

**Example of two-colour wire: BN (White/Black)**

| | | | | |
|---|---|---|---|---|
| A | Light blue | | M | Brown |
| B | White | | N | Black |
| C | Orange | | R | Red |
| G | Yellow | | S | Pink |
| H | Grey | | V | Green |
| L | Blue | | Z | Violet |

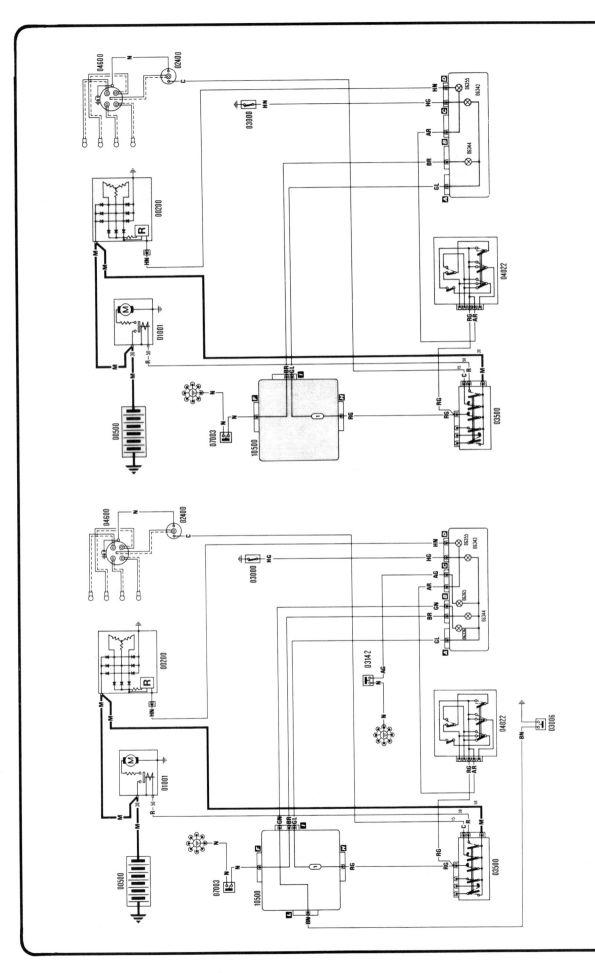

Wiring diagram – starting, charging, oil pressure and low brake fluid
(Comfort and ES models)

Wiring diagram – starting, ignition, charging, oil pressure, low brake fluid, choke
warning light and handbrake 'on' (S and SX models)

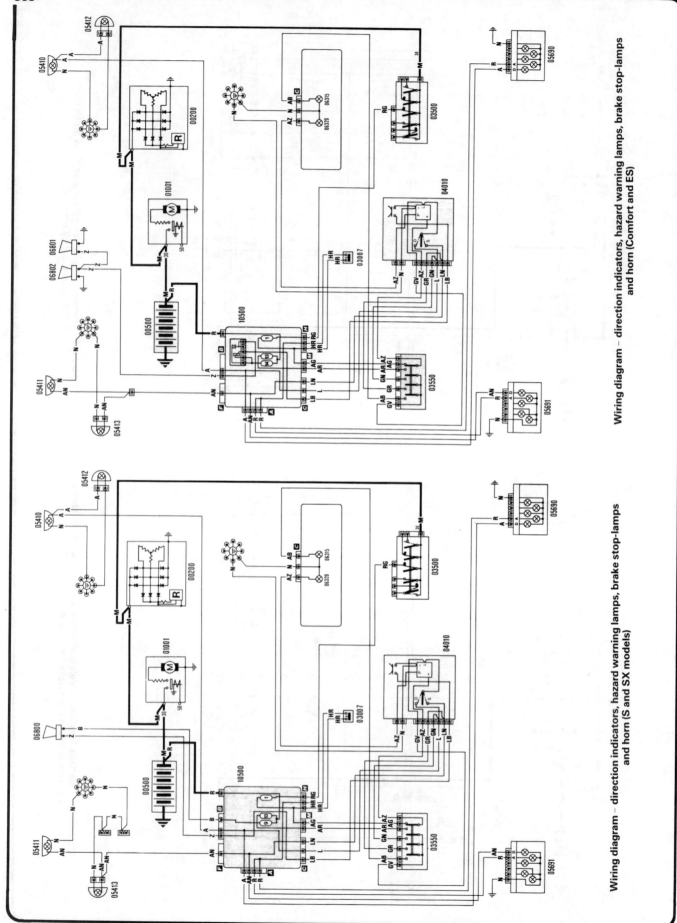

Wiring diagram – direction indicators, hazard warning lamps, brake stop-lamps and horn (Comfort and ES)

Wiring diagram – direction indicators, hazard warning lamps, brake stop-lamps and horn (S and SX models)

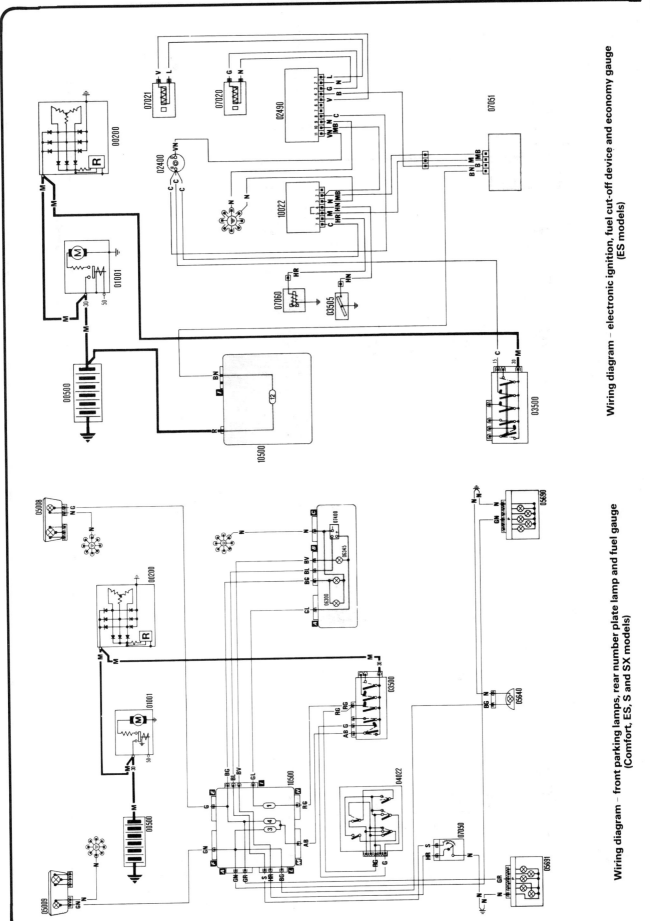

Wiring diagram – electronic ignition, fuel cut-off device and economy gauge (ES models)

Wiring diagram – front parking lamps, rear number plate lamp and fuel gauge (Comfort, ES, S and SX models)

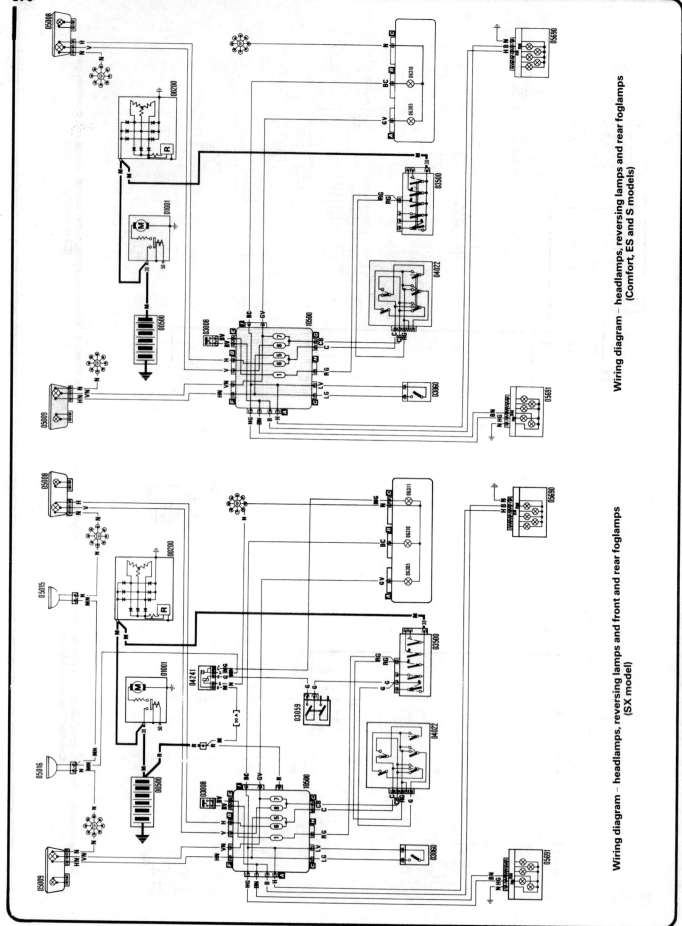

**Wiring diagram – headlamps, reversing lamps and rear foglamps (Comfort, ES and S models)**

**Wiring diagram – headlamps, reversing lamps and front and rear foglamps (SX model)**

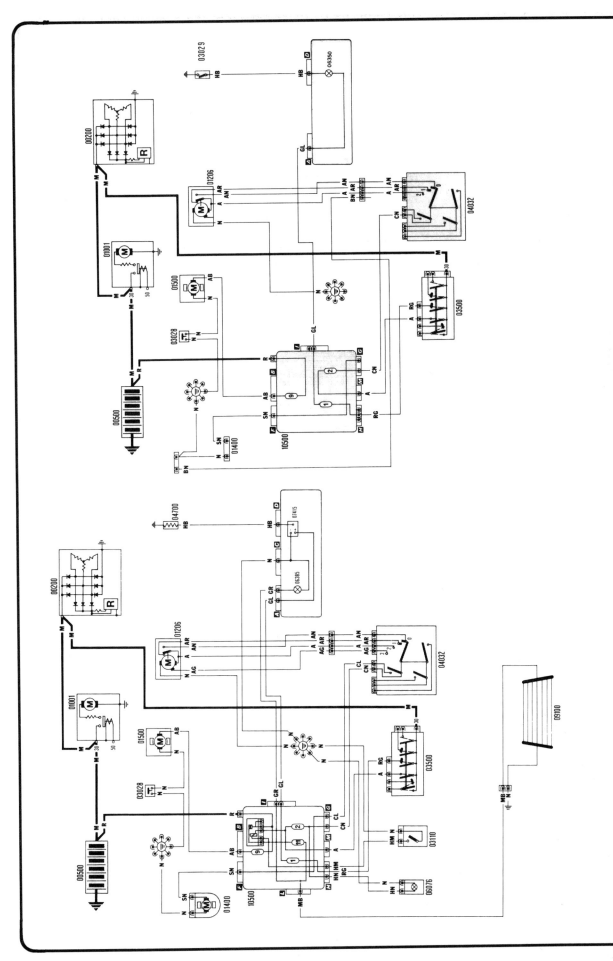

Wiring diagram – windscreen wash/wipe, radiator fan and coolant temperature sensor (Comfort and ES models)

Wiring diagram – windscreen wash/wipe, radiator fan, coolant temperature sensor, heated rear screen and instrument panel illumination

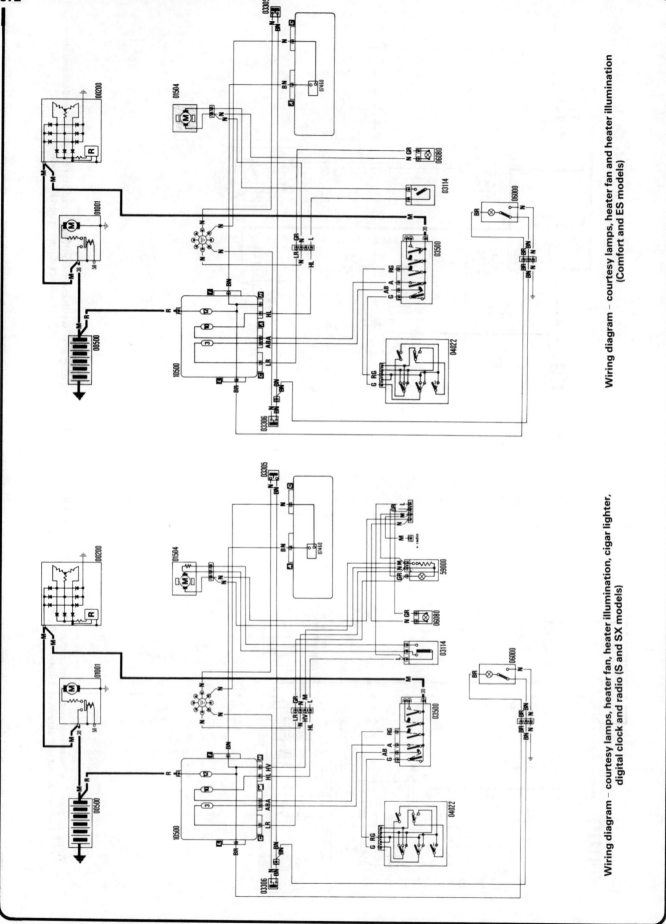

Wiring diagram – courtesy lamps, heater fan and heater illumination
(Comfort and ES models)

Wiring diagram – courtesy lamps, heater fan, heater illumination, cigar lighter,
digital clock and radio (S and SX models)

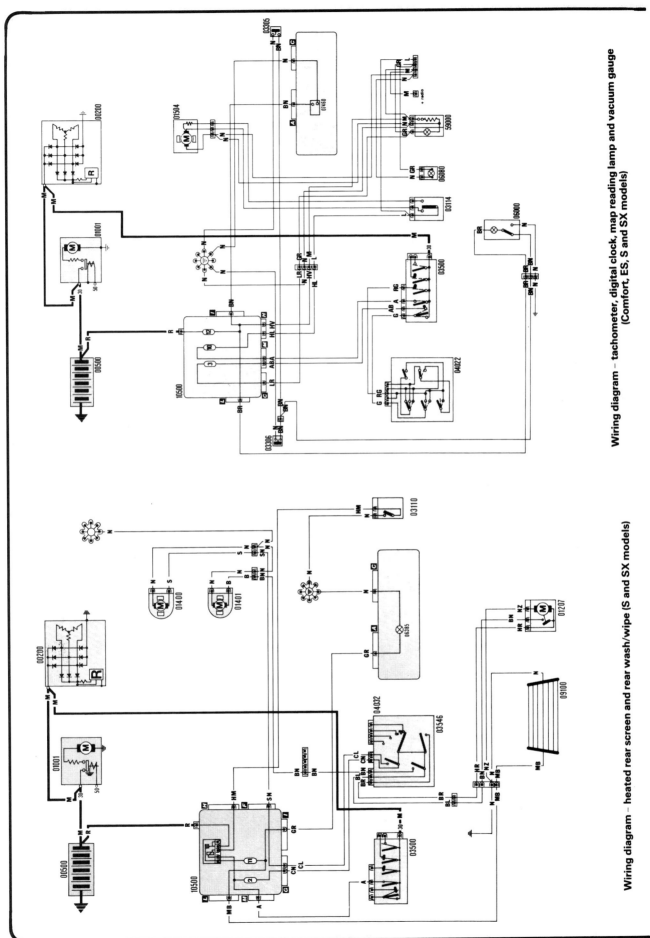

**Wiring diagram – tachometer, digital clock, map reading lamp and vacuum gauge (Comfort, ES, S and SX models)**

**Wiring diagram – heated rear screen and rear wash/wipe (S and SX models)**

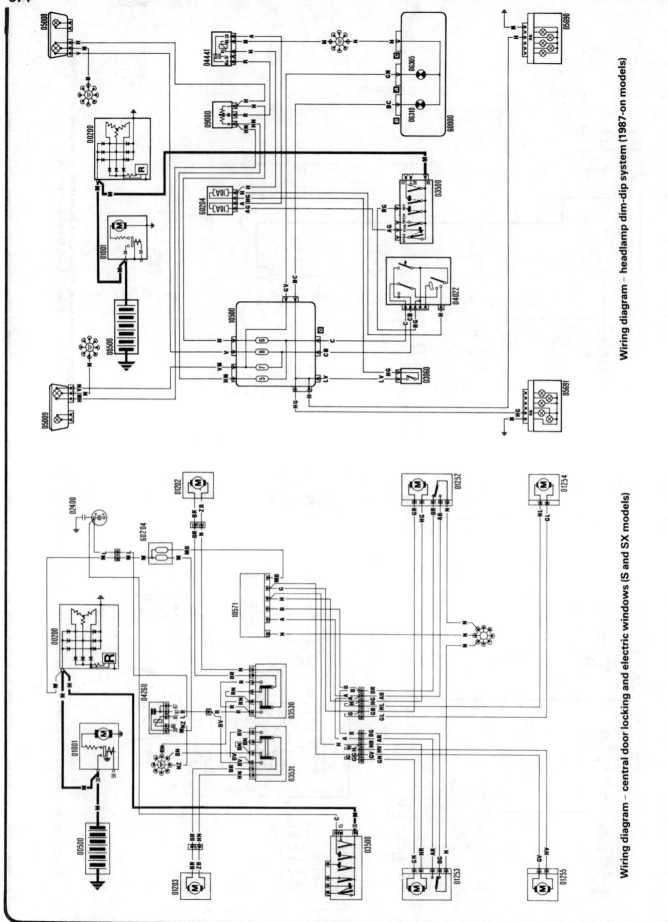

**Wiring diagram – headlamp dim-dip system (1987-on models)**

**Wiring diagram – central door locking and electric windows (S and SX models)**

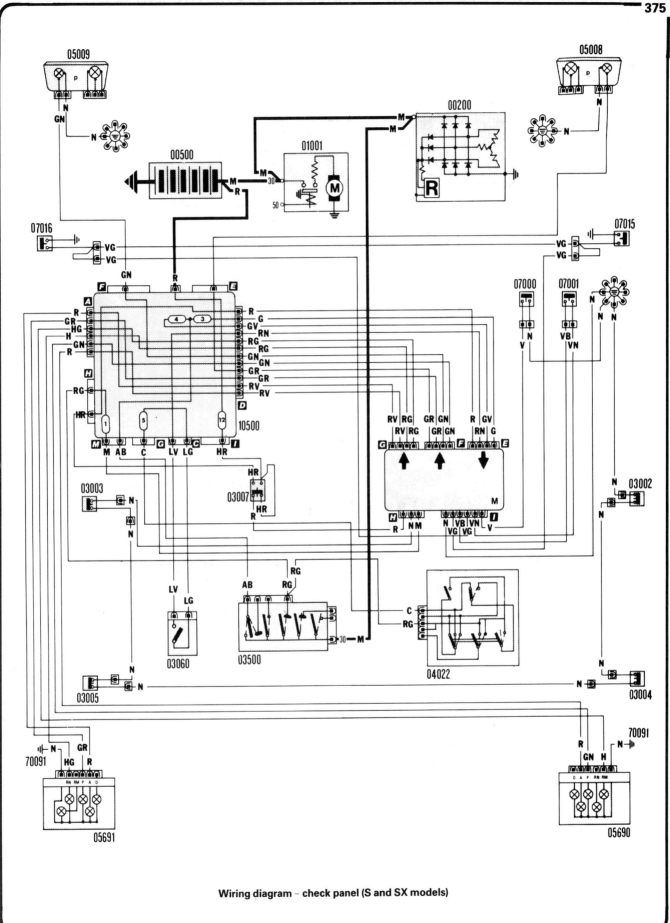

**Wiring diagram – check panel (S and SX models)**

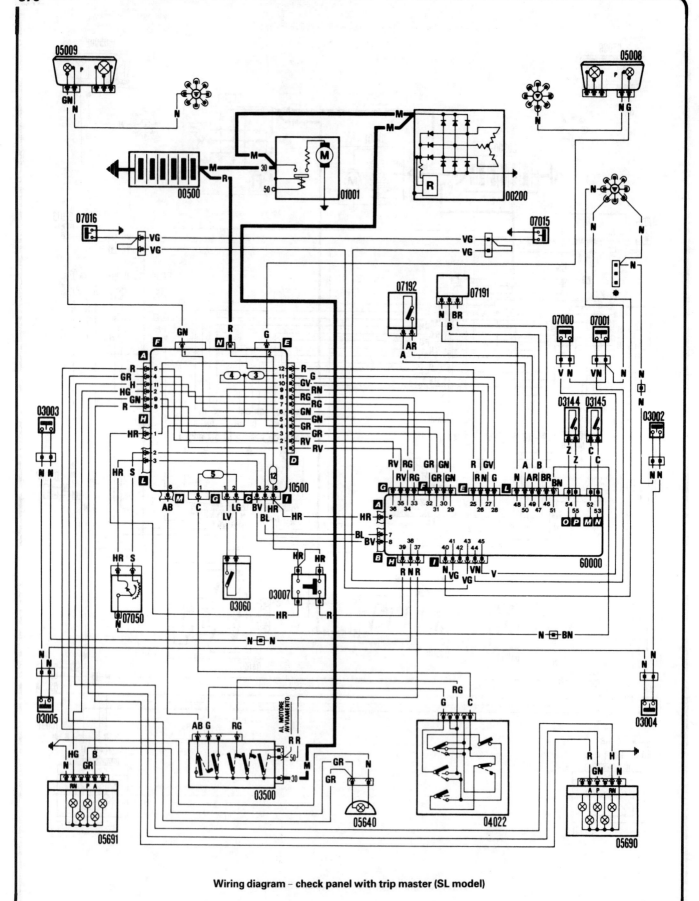

**Wiring diagram – check panel with trip master (SL model)**

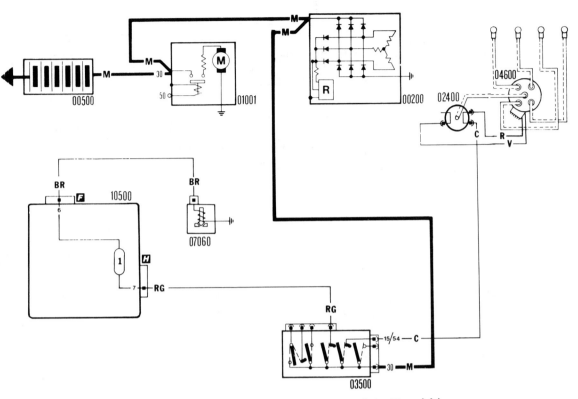

**Wiring diagram – ignition and idle cut-out (later 45 models)**

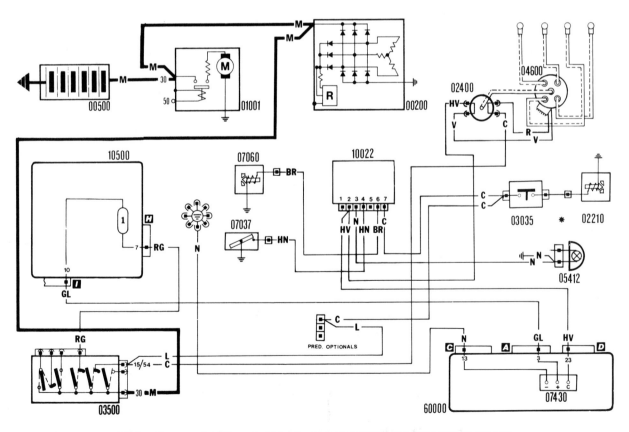

**Wiring diagram – ignition cut-off device, tachometer and accelerator pump cut-out
(60 and 70 models)**

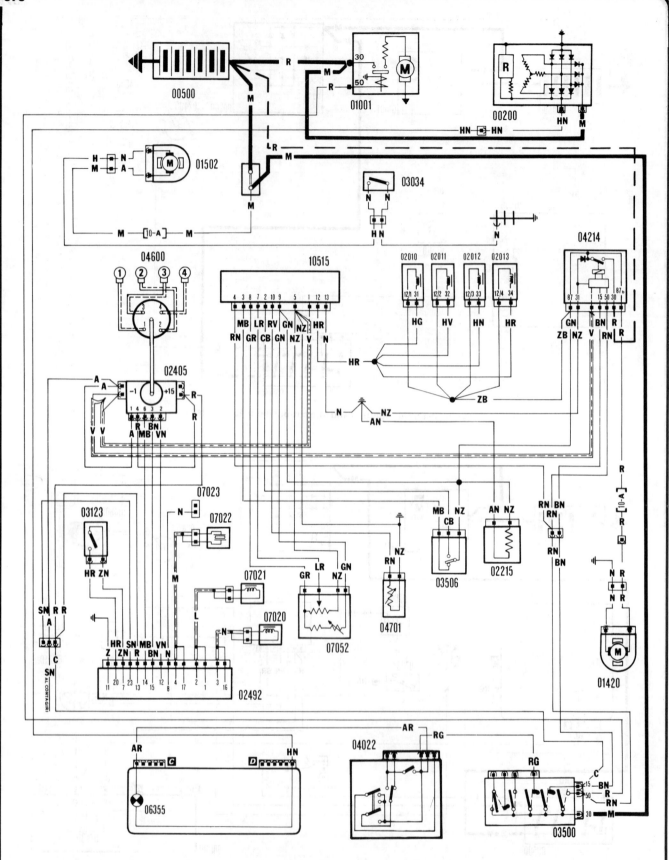

**Wiring diagram – starting, charging, Microplex ignition, LE-2 Jetronic fuel injection, fuel pump and fuel injector cooling fan (1301 cc Turbo ie model)**

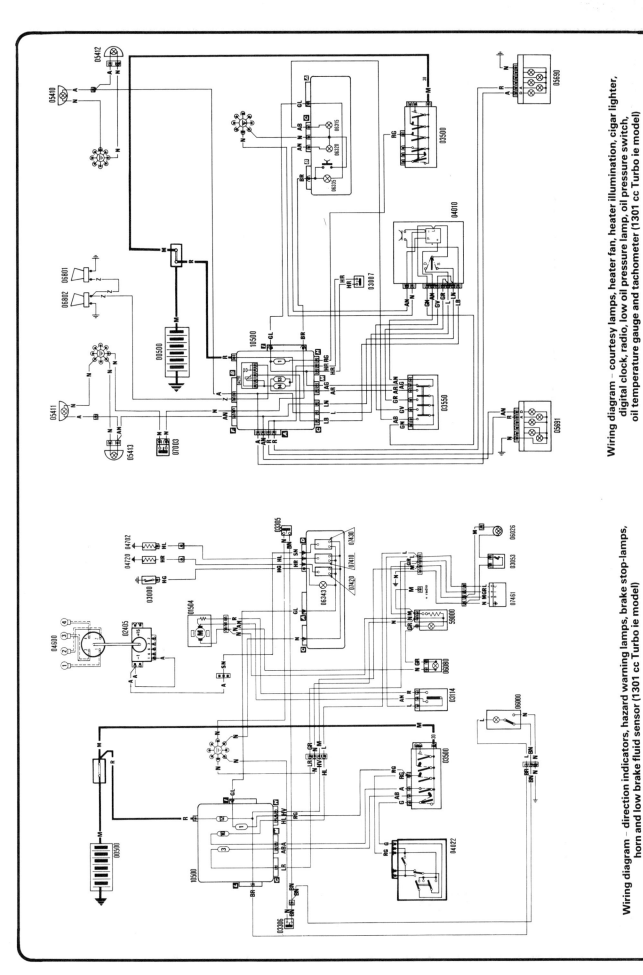

**379**

Wiring diagram – courtesy lamps, heater fan, heater illumination, cigar lighter, digital clock, radio, low oil pressure lamp, oil pressure switch, oil temperature gauge and tachometer (1301 cc Turbo ie model)

Wiring diagram – direction indicators, hazard warning lamps, brake stop-lamps, horn and low brake fluid sensor (1301 cc Turbo ie model)

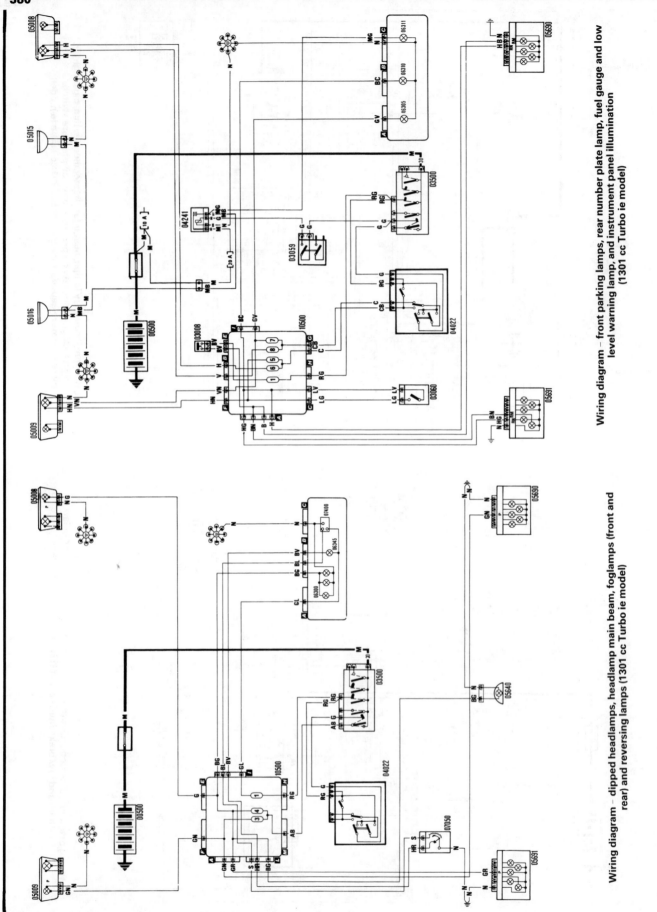

Wiring diagram — front parking lamps, rear number plate lamp, fuel gauge and low level warning lamp, and instrument panel illumination (1301 cc Turbo ie model)

Wiring diagram — dipped headlamps, headlamp main beam, foglamps (front and rear) and reversing lamps (1301 cc Turbo ie model)

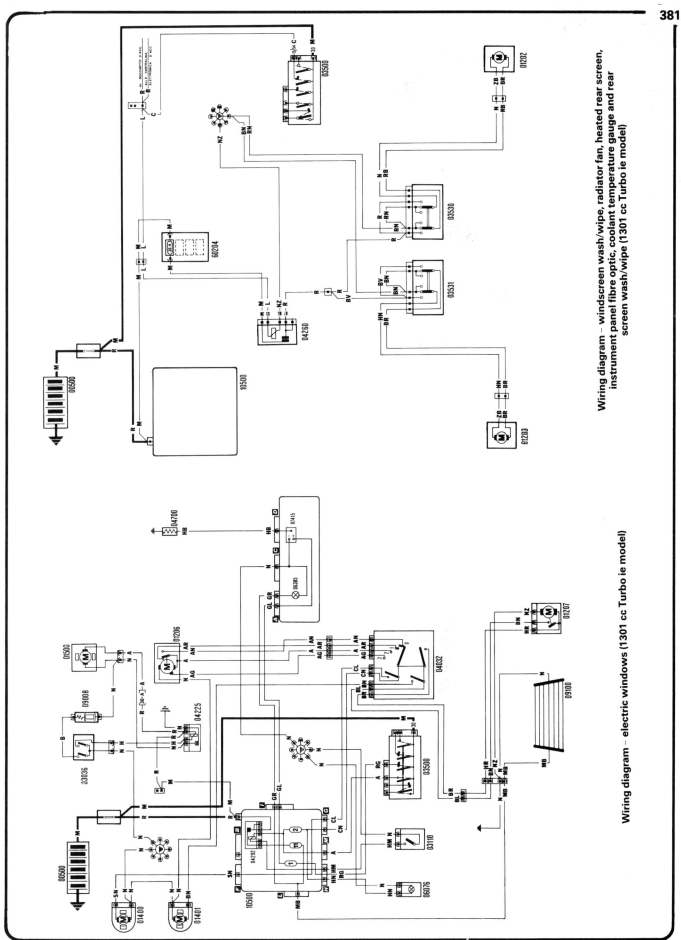

Wiring diagram – windscreen wash/wipe, radiator fan, heated rear screen,
instrument panel fibre optic, coolant temperature gauge and rear
screen wash/wipe (1301 cc Turbo ie model)

Wiring diagram – electric windows (1301 cc Turbo ie model)

**Wiring diagram – check panel (1301 cc Turbo ie model)**

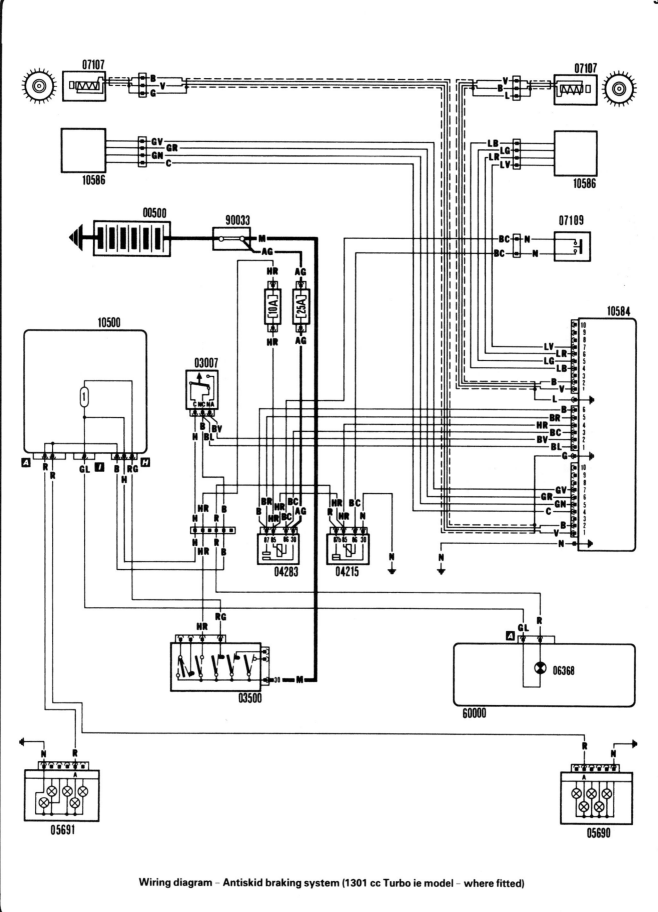

**Wiring diagram – Antiskid braking system (1301 cc Turbo ie model – where fitted)**

## Component key for wiring diagrams on pages 386 to 408

**Note:** *Not all the items listed will be fitted to all models*

| No | Description |
|---|---|
| 1 | Injector cooling fan |
| 2 | Left front light cluster |
| 3 | Left foglamp |
| 4 | Left front engine compartment earth |
| 5 | Radiator cooling fan |
| 6 | Double contact thermostatic switch on engine radiator |
| 6A | Thermostatic switch on engine radiator |
| 7 | Left horn |
| 8 | Right horn |
| 9 | Resistor for engaging radiator fan 1st speed |
| 10 | Right front light cluster |
| 11 | Right foglamp |
| 12 | Right front engine compartment earth |
| 13 | Battery |
| 14 | Ignition coil |
| 15 | Ignition distributor with magnetic impulse generator |
| 16 | Left front side direction indicator |
| 17 | Ignition power module |
| 18 | MPi electronic injection control unit |
| 19 | Join between injection/ignition cables in engine compartment |
| 20 | Battery cables join in engine compartment |
| 21 | Antiskid braking system wiring join |
| 22 | Starting go-ahead relay |
| 23 | Earth for battery |
| 24 | Radiator coolant temperature sender unit for electronic injection |
| 25 | Anti-knock sensor |
| 26 | Injection system diagnostic socket |
| 27 | Switch signalling insufficient engine oil pressure |
| 28 | Radiator coolant temperature sender unit |
| 29 | Engine oil temperature sender unit |
| 30 | Engine oil pressure sender unit |
| 31 | Right front side direction indicator |
| 32 | Engine oil temperature sender unit cable join |
| 33 | Battery recharging signal cable join |
| 34 | Windscreen washer pump |
| 35 | Rear screen washer pump |
| 36 | Reversing switch |
| 37 | Fuel injectors relay feed |
| 38 | Insufficient brake fluid level sensor |
| 39 | Left brake pad wear sensor |
| 40 | Microplex electronic ignition control unit |
| 41 | Injection cables join in engine compartment |
| 42 | Ignition cables join in engine compartment |
| 43 | Join between battery cable and injection cables |
| 44 | Join between engine cable and battery cables |
| 45 | Left front brake pad cables join |
| 46 | Starter motor |
| 47 | Windscreen wiper motor |
| 48 | Headlamp washer pump |
| 49 | Fuel injector |
| 50 | Fuel injector |
| 51 | Fuel injector |
| 52 | Fuel injector |
| 53 | Supplementary air valve |
| 54 | Spark plug |
| 55 | Spark plug |
| 56 | Spark plug |
| 57 | Spark plug |
| 58 | Excess supercharging pressure switch |
| 59 | Throttle position switch |
| 60 | Engine speed sensor |
| 61 | Ignition diagnostic socket |
| 62 | Connector block |
| 63 | Connector block |
| 64 | Alternator |
| 65 | Thermostatic switch for injector cooling fan |
| 66 | Right brake pad wear sensor |
| 67 | TDC sensor |
| 68 | Connector block |

| No | Description |
|---|---|
| 69 | Connector block |
| 70 | Connector block |
| 71 | Connector block |
| 72 | Join with right brake pad cables |
| 73 | Electronic earth |
| 74 | Power earth |
| 75 | Brake stop-lamp switch |
| 76 | 20 A fuse for central locking |
| 77 | 10 A fuse for electric fuel pump |
| 78 | 30 A fuse for radiator cooling fan |
| 79 | 30 A fuse for electric windows |
| 80 | 10 A fuse for injector cooling fan |
| 81 | 20 A fuse for headlamp wash/wipe |
| 82 | 20 A fuse for foglamps |
| 83 | Junction box with fuses and relays: |
| E1 | Horn relay (for single tone horns bridge between 86 and 87) |
| E2 | Heated rear screen relay |
| E3 | Heater (bridge between 85 and 30) |
| 84 | Join between front cable and rear cables |
| 85 | Join between front cable and door ajar sensor cables |
| 86 | Earth on dashboard, left hand side |
| 87 | Earth on dashboard, right hand side |
| 88 | Choke warning light switch |
| 89 | Ignition switch |
| 90 | Hazard warning lights switch |
| 91 | Steering column switch unit |
| A | Rear screen wash/wipe switch |
| B | Horn button |
| C | Direction indicators switch |
| D | Windscreen wiper intermittent speed selector switch |
| E | Windscreen/headlamp washer control switch |
| F | Rear foglamps/headlamp washer intermittent device switch |
| G | Headlamp dip switch |
| H | External lights switch |
| I | Flasher switch |
| 92 | Foglamp relay |
| 93 | Electric fuel pump relay |
| 94 | Electric windows relay feed |
| 95 | Headlamp wash/wipe intermittent device |
| 96 | Direction indicators/hazard warning lights flasher unit |
| 97 | Central locking receiver |
| 98 | Central locking control unit |
| 99 | Join with brake pad cables |
| 100 | Join between engine cable and dashboard cables |
| 101 | Automatic heater cable join |
| 102 | Instrument panel |
| A | Foglamps warning light |
| B | Main beam headlamps warning light |
| C | Side lights warning light |
| D | Rear foglamps warning light |
| E | Heated rear screen warning light |
| F | Hazard warning lights warning light |
| G | Direction indicators warning light |
| H | Handbrake applied and insufficient brake fluid level warning light |
| I | Choke warning light |
| K | Instrument panel light bulbs |
| L | Battery recharging warning light |
| M | Insufficient engine oil pressure warning light |
| O | Antiskid braking system failure warning light |
| P | Maximum turbocharging pressure warning light |
| Q | Brake pad wear warning light |
| R | Door ajar warning light |
| U | Fuel level gauge |
| V | Engine oil pressure gauge |
| W | Engine oil temperature gauge |
| Y | Tachometer |
| Z | Coolant temperature gauge |

## Component key for wiring diagrams on pages 386 to 408 (continued)

| No | Description | No | Description |
|----|-------------|----|-------------|
| 103 | Join with remote control central locking cables | 172 | Mixed air temperature sensor |
| 104 | Cigar lighter | 173 | Air mixture flap electrical control motor |
| 105 | Radio receiver | 174 | Diagnostic socket for automatic heater |
| 106 | Heater unit | 175 | Connector block |
| 107 | Switch unit | 176 | Connector block |
| | A  Heated rear screen switch | 177 | Join with cables for automatic heater |
| | B  Rear foglamps switch | 178 | Radiator coolant circulation solenoid valve |
| | C  Switch unit light bulb | 179 | Automatic heater unit: |
| | D  Rear screen wiper switch | | A  Temperature control potentiometer |
| | E  Foglamps switch | | B  Fan speed control potentiometer |
| | F  Clock | | C  Heater controls light bulbs |
| 108 | Left front electric window motor | | D  Ideogram signalling automatic function engaged |
| 109 | Left front central locking geared motor | | E  Automatic function engaged switch |
| 110 | Switch signalling left front door ajar | 180 | Horn |
| 111 | Push button on left front pillar for centre courtesy light | 181 | Check Panel: |
| 112 | Front electric windows switch panel, driver's side | | A  Insufficient engine oil level warning light |
| 113 | Join between dashboard cable and adjustable map reading light cables | | B  Insufficient coolant level warning light |
| 114 | Join with left front electric window cables | | C  Failure with side lights/rear foglamp/rear number plate light/braking lights warning light |
| 115 | Join between dashboard cable and rear cables | | D  Insufficient brake fluid level warning light |
| 116 | Join between rear cable and courtesy light cables | | E  Door ajar warning light |
| 117 | Left front speaker | | F  Brake pad wear warning light |
| 118 | Handbrake 'on' switch | 182 | Earth on dashboard |
| 119 | Centre courtesy light bulb | 183 | Join with cables for central locking |
| 119A | Adjustable map reading light on rear view mirror | 184 | Join with cables for central locking |
| 120 | Right front electric window motor | 185 | Left rear central locking geared motor |
| 121 | Right front central locking geared motor | 186 | Right rear central locking geared motor |
| 122 | Switch signalling right front door ajar | 187 | Contact on choke lever |
| 123 | Push button on right front pillar for centre courtesy light | 188 | Resistor for inlet manifold heating |
| 124 | Electric windows control panel, passenger side | 189 | Pre-heating thermal switch |
| 125 | Fuel level gauge | 191 | Heated Lambda sensor |
| 126 | Join with right front electric window cables | 192 | Lambda sensor protective fuse |
| 127 | Join between engine cable and dashboard cables | 193 | Silicon diode |
| 128 | Right front speaker | 194 | Join between front cable and injection cable |
| 129 | Left rear light cluster | 197 | Connector block |
| 130 | Join between rear cable and luggage compartment courtesy light | 198 | Rear cable join |
| 131 | Windscreen washer pump wiring join | 199 | Insufficient engine oil level sensor |
| 132 | Rear screen washer pump wiring join | 200 | Insufficient coolant level sensor |
| 133 | Left rear earth | 201 | Switch signalling left rear door ajar |
| 134 | Rear screen wiper motor | 202 | Switch signalling right rear door ajar |
| 135 | Electric fuel pump | 203 | Switch on gear selector |
| 136 | Rear number plate lamp | 204 | Light for gear selector panel signalling gear engaged |
| 137 | Heated rear screen | 205 | Parking signal not on |
| 138 | Right rear light cluster | 206 | Connector block |
| 139 | Rear foglamp go-ahead switch | 207 | Join in engine compartment with injection cables |
| 140 | Join between front cable and antiskid brakes cables | 208 | Petrol vapour cut out-solenoid valve |
| 141 | Join between front cable and antiskid brakes cables | 209 | Petrol vapour cut out-solenoid valve |
| 142 | 25 A fuse for antiskid brakes | 210 | Airflow meter |
| 143 | Antiskid braking system control unit | 211 | Speedometer relay |
| 144 | Left modulator for antiskid brakes | 212 | LE2 Jetronic electronic injection control unit |
| 145 | Right modulator for antiskid brakes | 213 | Connector block |
| 146 | Sensor on left front wheel | 214 | Connector block |
| 147 | Sensor on right front wheel | 215 | Connector block |
| 148 | 10 A fuse for antiskid braking system | 216 | Ignition cable join |
| 149 | Vacuum switch for antiskid braking system | 217 | Join between front cable and emission control cable |
| 150 | Antiskid braking system engagement relay | 218 | Join between front cable and battery cable |
| 151 | Antiskid braking system failure signalling switch | 219 | Injection system air temperature sensor |
| 152 | Digiplex electronic ignition control unit | 220 | Ignition control unit relay feed |
| 153 | Bosch SPi Mono-Jetronic injection system control unit | 225 | Front cable join |
| 155 | Join between engine cable and injection cables | 226 | Front cable join |
| 156 | Join between engine cable and rear cables for SPi system | 227 | Dim-dip circuit cut out switch |
| 157 | Idle adjustment actuator | 228 | Dim-dip circuit resistance |
| 158 | Throttle position switch | 229 | Dim-dip circuit 7.5 A protective fuse |
| 159 | Injector current restriction resistor (SPi) | 230 | Driver's side seat heated pad |
| 162 | Engine cut-out solenoid | 231 | Driver's seat backrest heated pad |
| 163 | Idle cut-out solenoid valve | 232 | 10 A protective fuse for driver's seat heated pads |
| 168 | Tachometer electro-magnetic sensor | 233 | Foglamps go-ahead switch |
| 169 | Automatic heater control unit | 234 | Driving lights cut out switch |
| 170 | Heater fan | 235 | Dipped headlamps relay |
| 171 | Outside temperature sensor | 236 | Main beam headlamps relay |
| | | 237 | Join between engine cable and dashboard cables |

*For wire colour codes, see page 369*

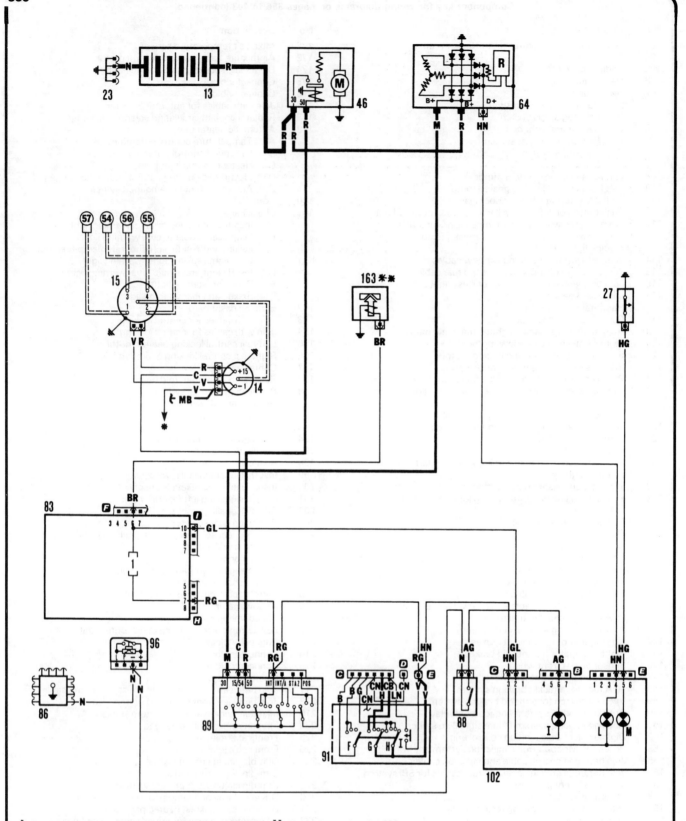

* To the rev counter (Only for the 999 SX - 1108 SX)     ** Non existent for the 903

Wiring diagram – starting, charging, ignition, low oil pressure and choke warning lamps (1990-on 45, and 55 models)

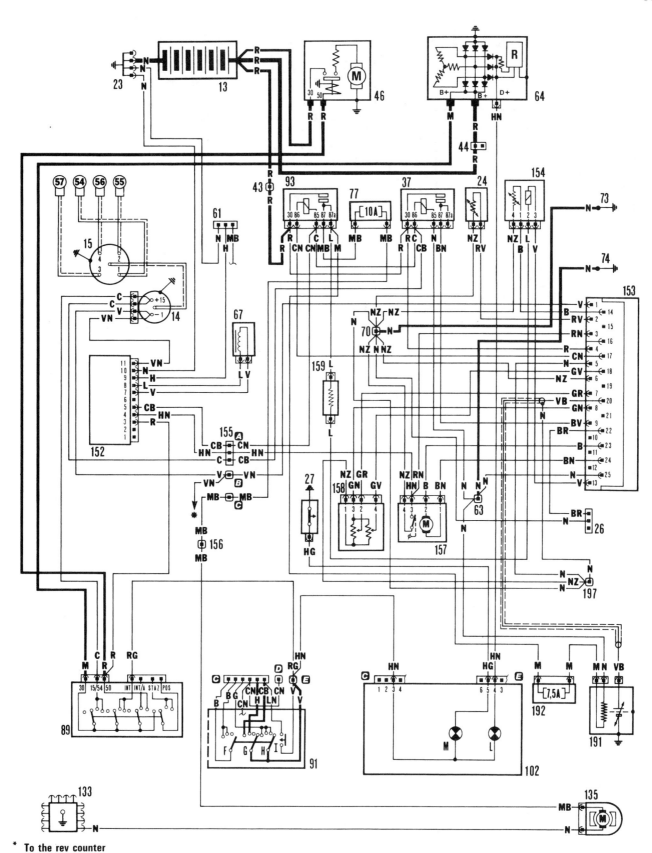

* To the rev counter

**Wiring diagram – starting, charging, Digiplex 2 ignition, SPi fuel injection, fuel pump and low oil pressure (1990-on 70 SX and 1.4 models)**

388

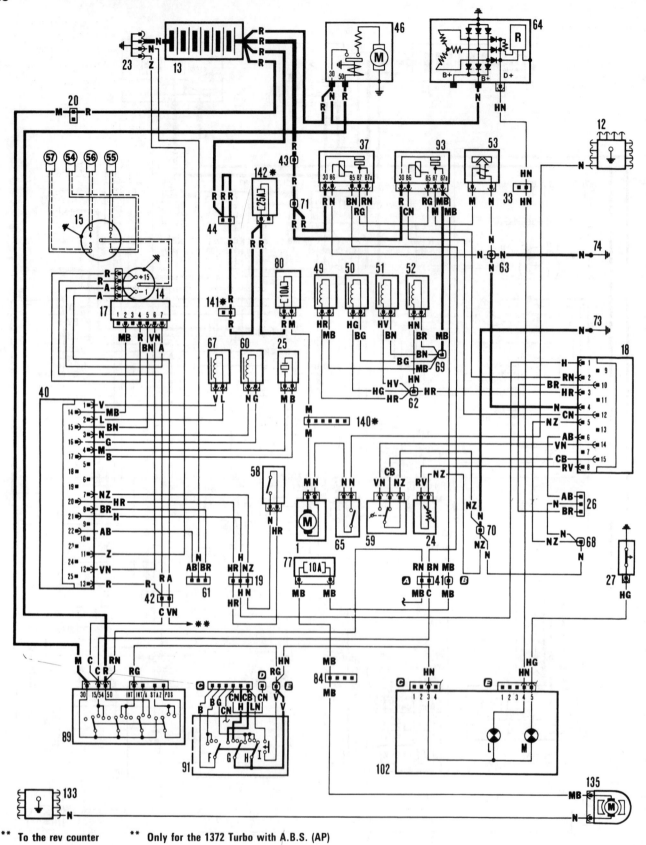

** To the rev counter     ** Only for the 1372 Turbo with A.B.S. (AP)

**Wiring diagram** – starting, charging, Microplex ignition, MPi fuel injection, fuel pump and low oil pressure
(1372 cc Turbo ie model)

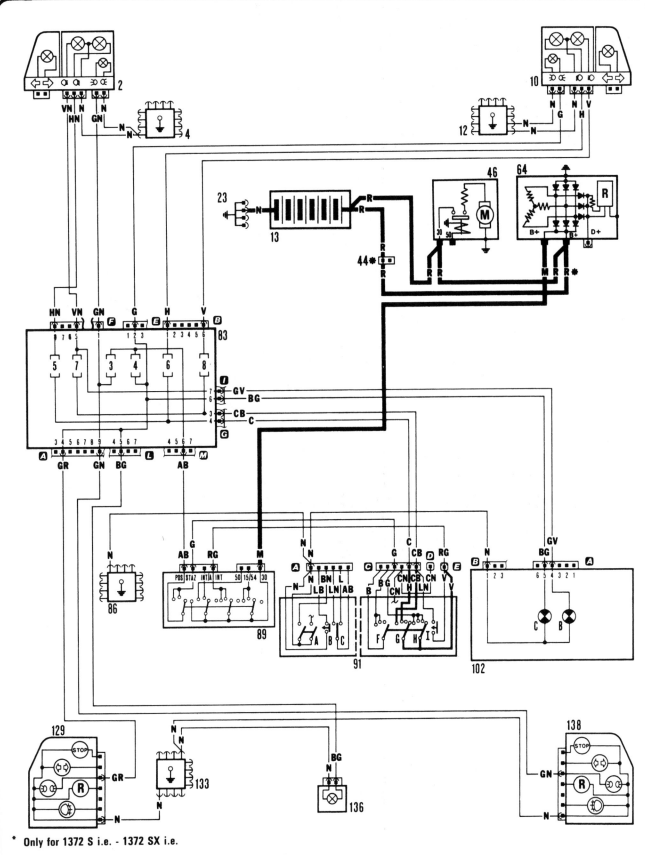

**Wiring diagram – parking lamps, main/dipped headlamps, headlamp flasher and rear number plate lamp**
**(1990-on 45, 55, 70 and 1.4 models)**

\* Only for 1372 S i.e. - 1372 SX i.e.

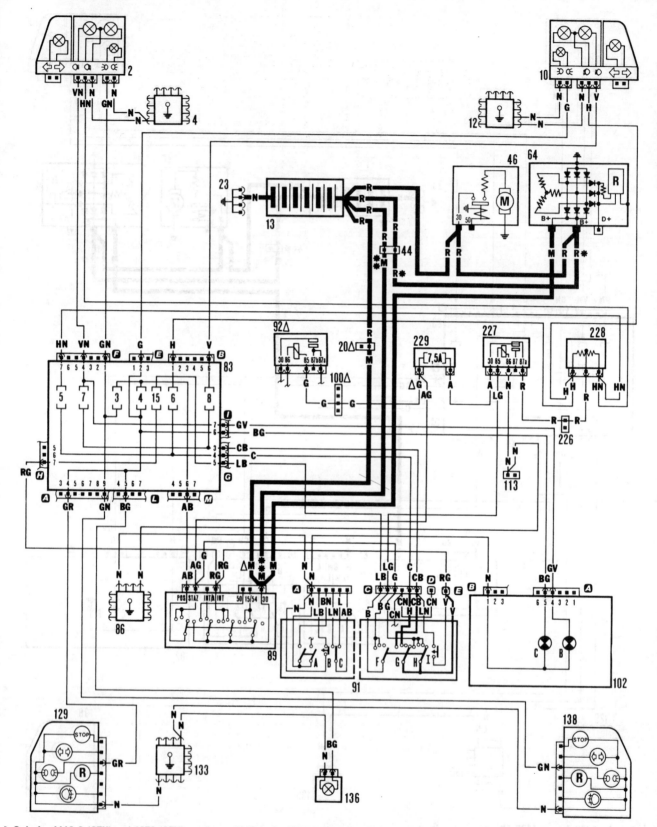

* Only for 1116 S (CTX) and 1372 (CTX) versions - ** Only for 1116 S (CTX) version - ** Only for 1372 Turbo i.e. version

Wiring diagram – parking lamps, main/dipped headlamps, headlamp flasher and rear number plate lamp
(1372 cc Turbo ie models)

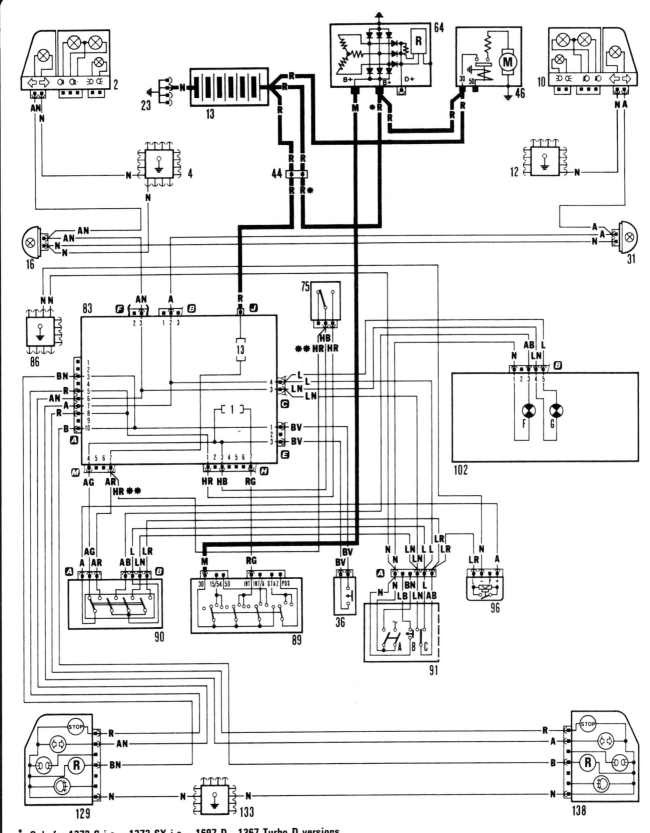

* Only for 1372 S i.e. - 1372 SX i.e. - 1697 D - 1367 Turbo D versions.
** Only for 903 - 999 - 999 S - 1108 S - 1372 S i.e - 1301 D - 1697 D versions.

**Wiring diagram – direction indicators, hazard warning lamps, reversing lamps and brake stop-lamps
(1990-on 45, 55, 70 and 1.4 models)**

**Wiring diagram – direction indicators, hazard warning lamps, reversing lamps and brake stop-lamps (1372 cc Turbo ie model)**

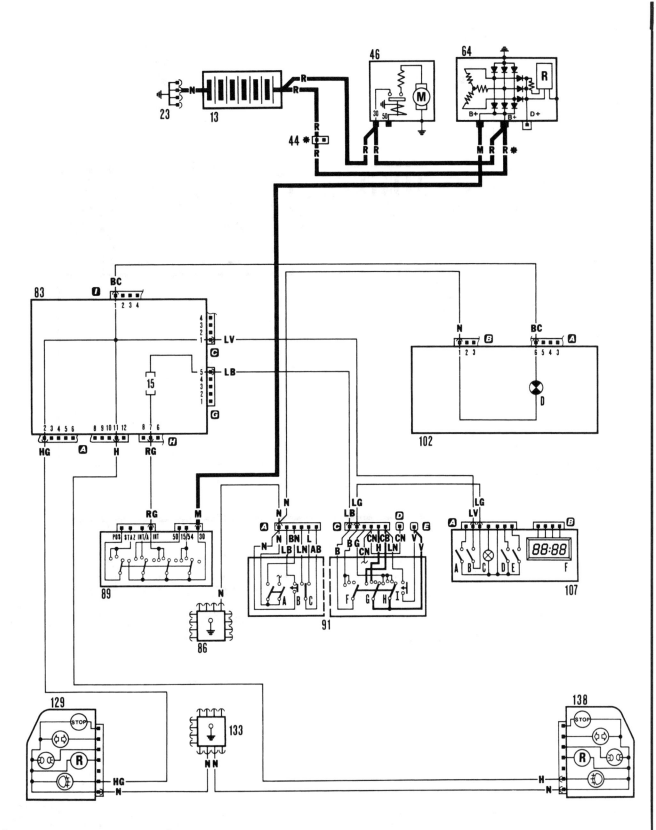

* Only for 1372 S i.e. - 1697 D versions

Wiring diagram – rear foglamps (1990-on 45 and 55 models)

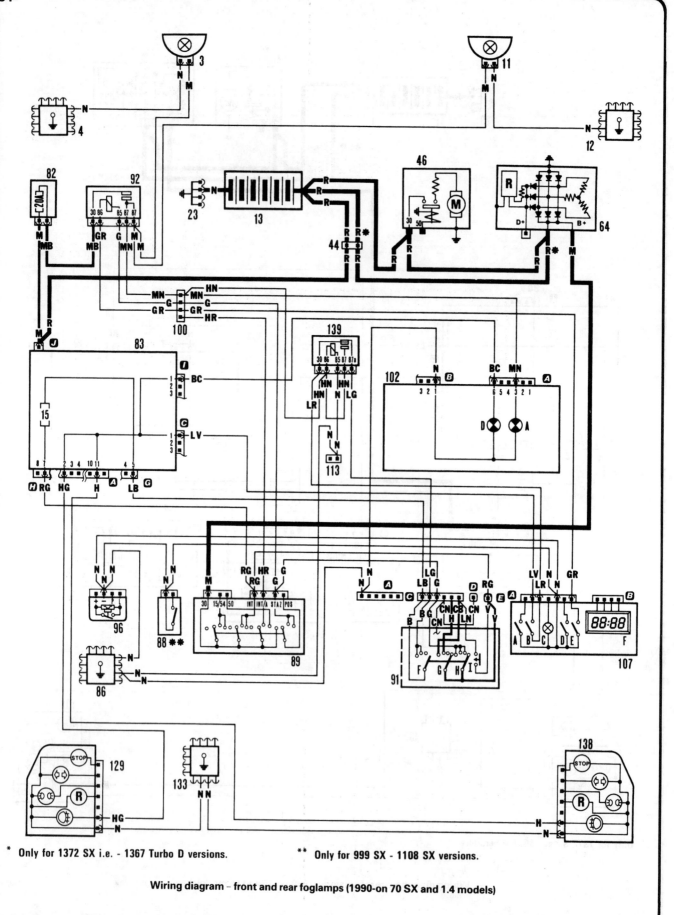

* Only for 1372 SX i.e. - 1367 Turbo D versions.     ** Only for 999 SX - 1108 SX versions.

**Wiring diagram – front and rear foglamps (1990-on 70 SX and 1.4 models)**

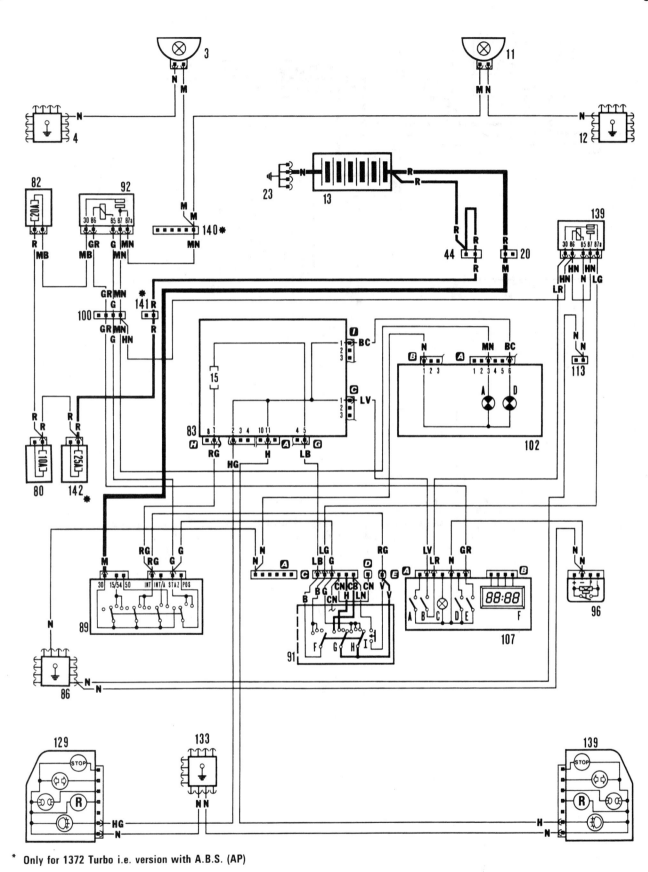

* Only for 1372 Turbo i.e. version with A.B.S. (AP)

Wiring diagram – front and rear foglamps (1372 cc Turbo ie model)

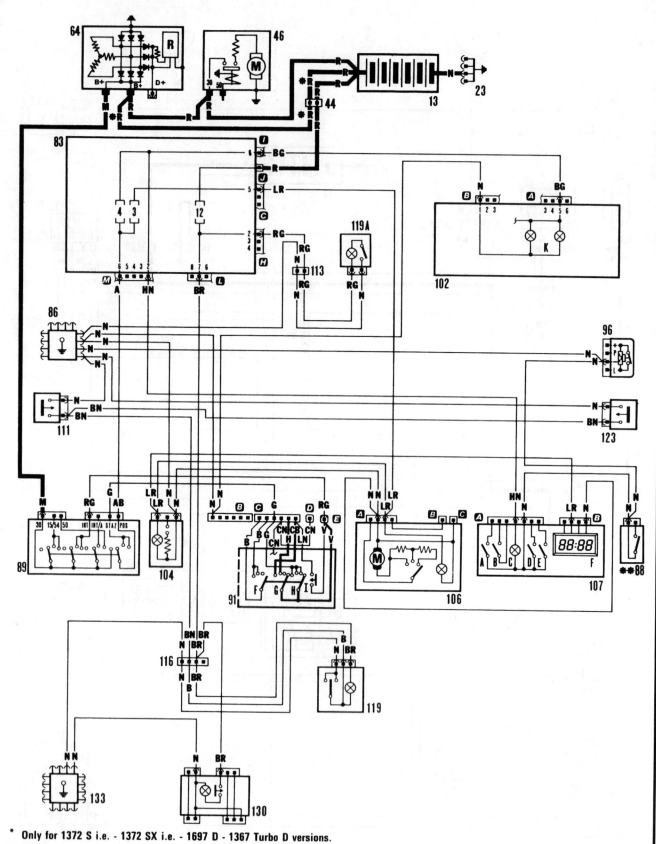

* **Only for 1372 S i.e. - 1372 SX i.e. - 1697 D - 1367 Turbo D versions.**

** **Only for 903 - 999 - 1108 S - 1108 SX versions**

**Wiring diagram – courtesy lamps and instrument panel lamps (1990-on 45, 55, 70 and 1.4 models)**

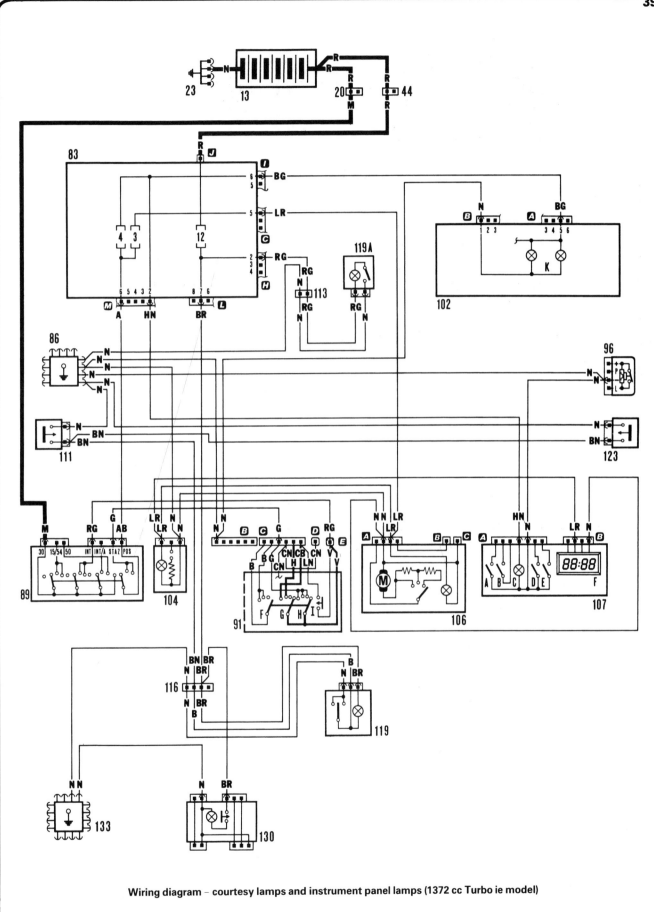

Wiring diagram – courtesy lamps and instrument panel lamps (1372 cc Turbo ie model)

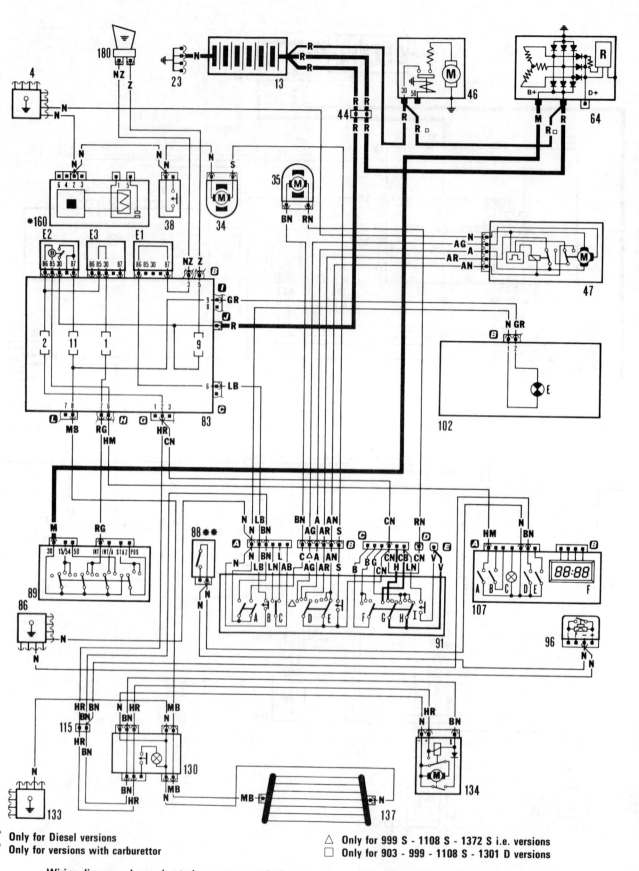

* **Only for Diesel versions**
** **Only for versions with carburettor**

△ **Only for 999 S - 1108 S - 1372 S i.e. versions**
□ **Only for 903 - 999 - 1108 S - 1301 D versions**

**Wiring diagram – horns, heated rear screen and windscreen/rear screen wash/wipe (1990-on 45 and 55 models)**

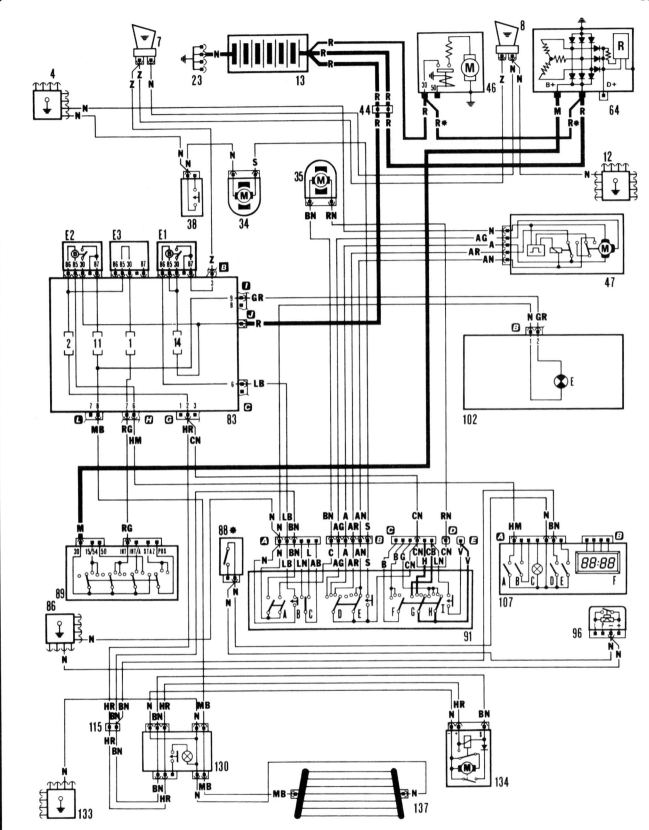

* Only for 999 SX - 1108 SX versions

**Wiring diagram – horns, heated rear screen and windscreen/rear screen wash/wipe (1990-on 70 SX and 1.4 models)**

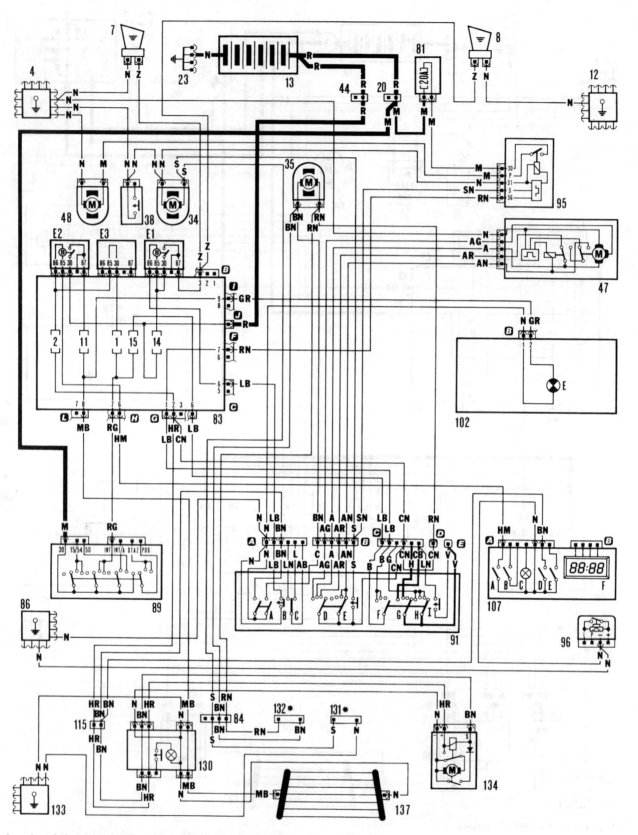

* Location of electric pumps Nos. 34 and 35 if optional headlamp washer is connected.

**Wiring diagram – horns, heated rear screen, windscreen/rear screen wash/wipe and headlamp wash/wipe**
**(1372 cc Turbo ie model)**

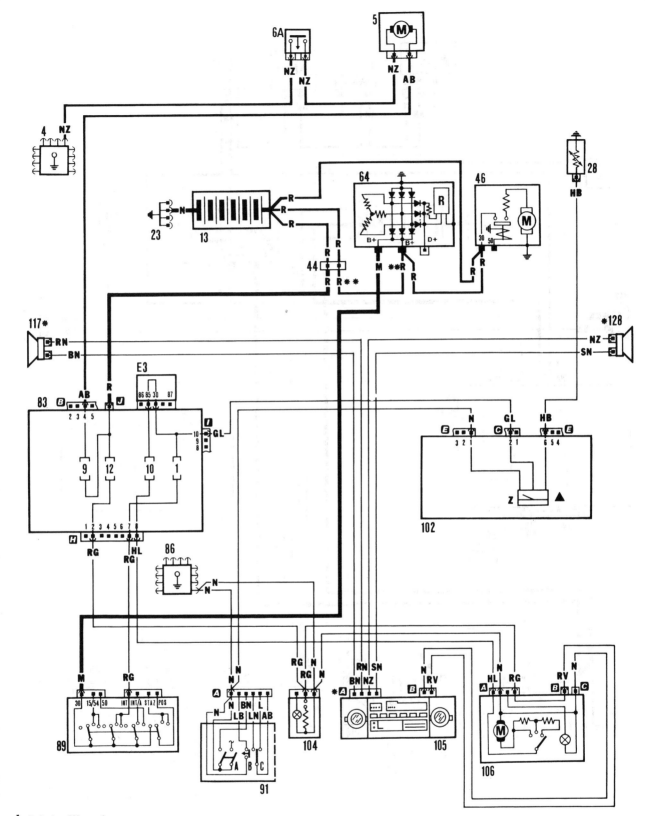

* Only for SX versions
** Only for 1372 S i.e. - 1372 SX i.e. versions
▲ For standard versions with 903 and 999 engines warning light only

Wiring diagram – radiator cooling fan, heater, radio and cigar lighter (1990-on 45, 55, 70 and 1.4 models)

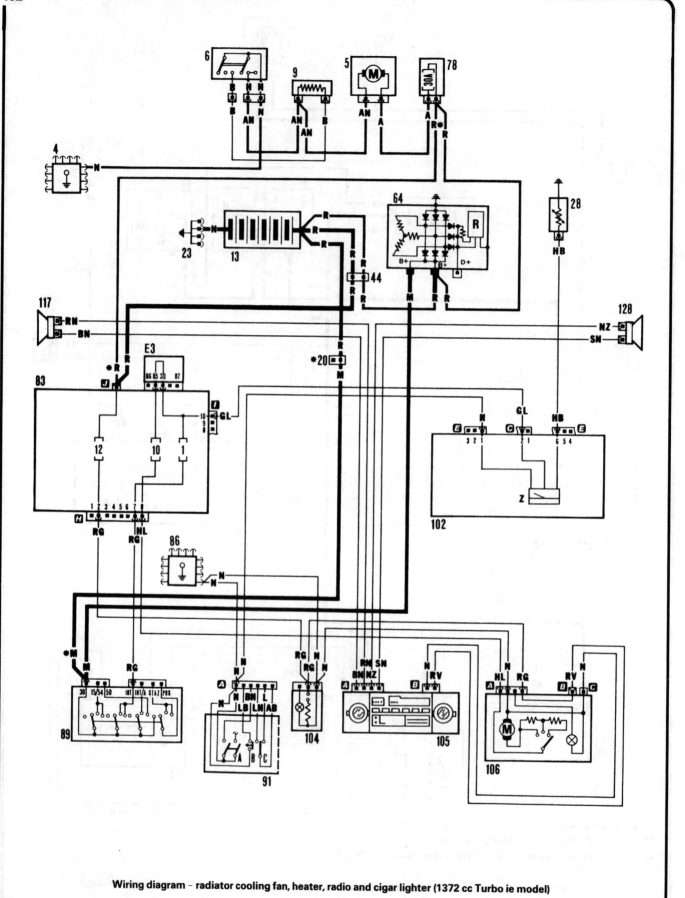

**Wiring diagram – radiator cooling fan, heater, radio and cigar lighter (1372 cc Turbo ie model)**

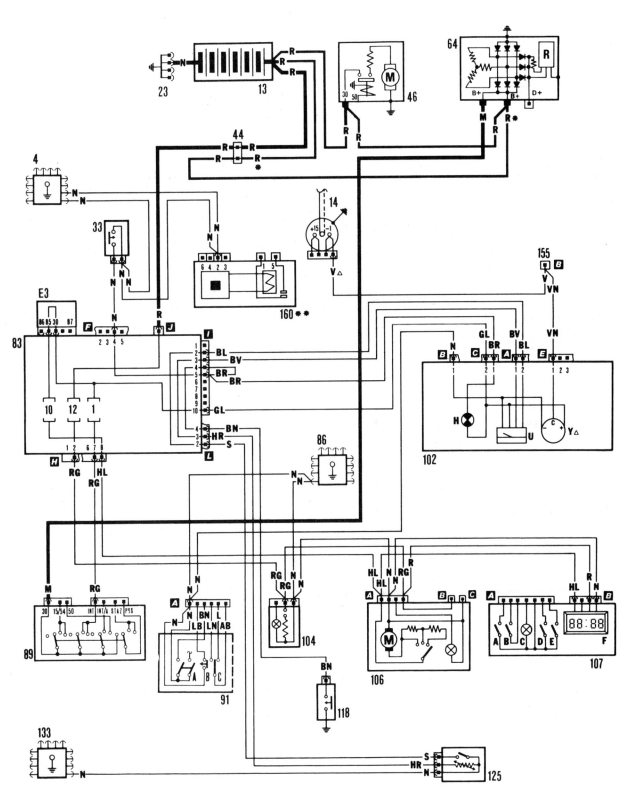

* Only for 1372 S i.e. - 1372 SX i.e. - 1697 D
** Only for D versions
▲ Only for SX versions

**Wiring diagram – fuel gauge, tachometer, digital clock, and brake fluid and handbrake warning lamp
(1990-on 45, 55, 70 and 1.4 models)**

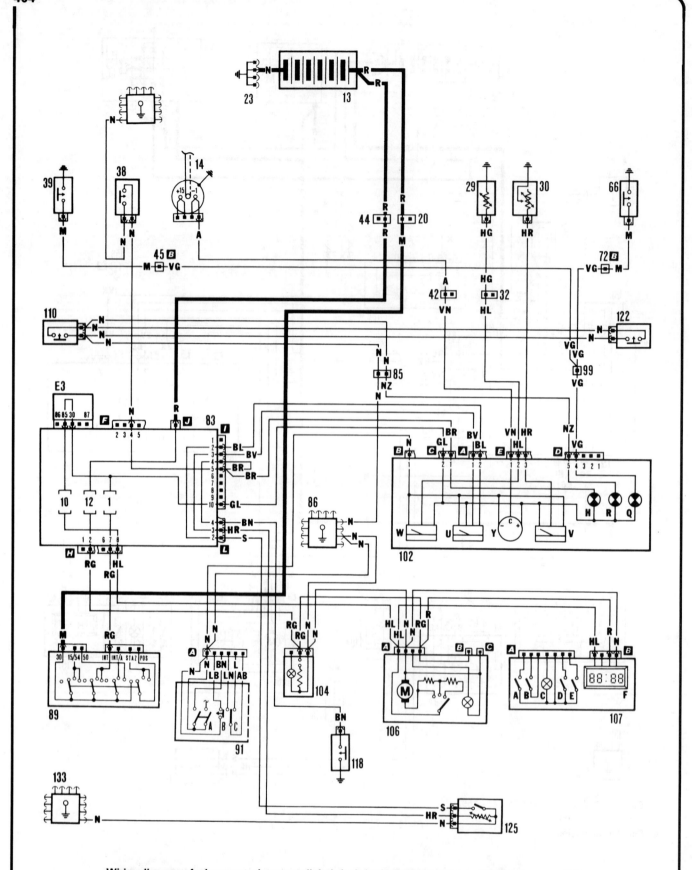

**Wiring diagram** – fuel gauge, tachometer, digital clock, brake fluid level sensor, handbrake-on switch, brake pad wear sensor, door ajar switch and oil pressure/temperature sender units (1372 cc Turbo ie model)

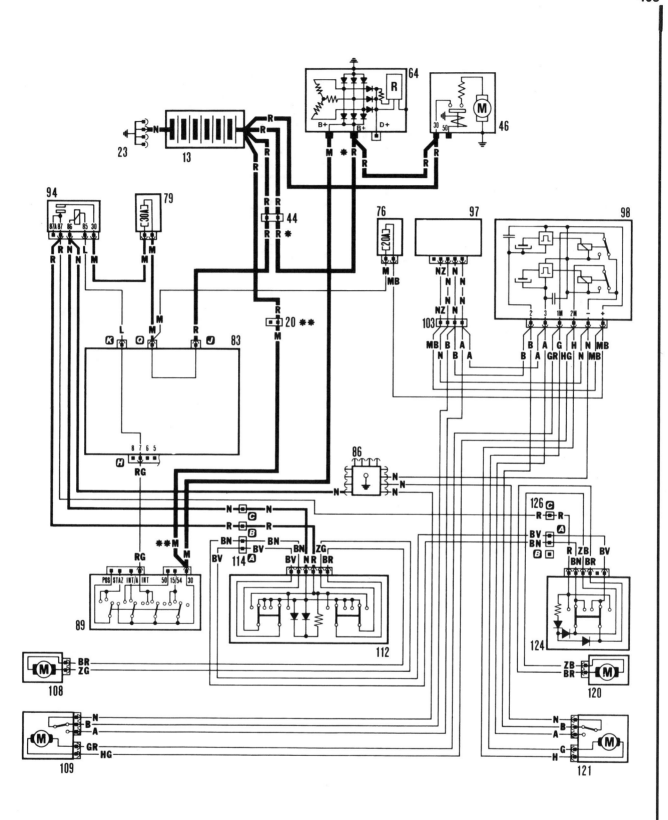

Wiring diagram – electric windows and central locking (1990-on 3-door models)

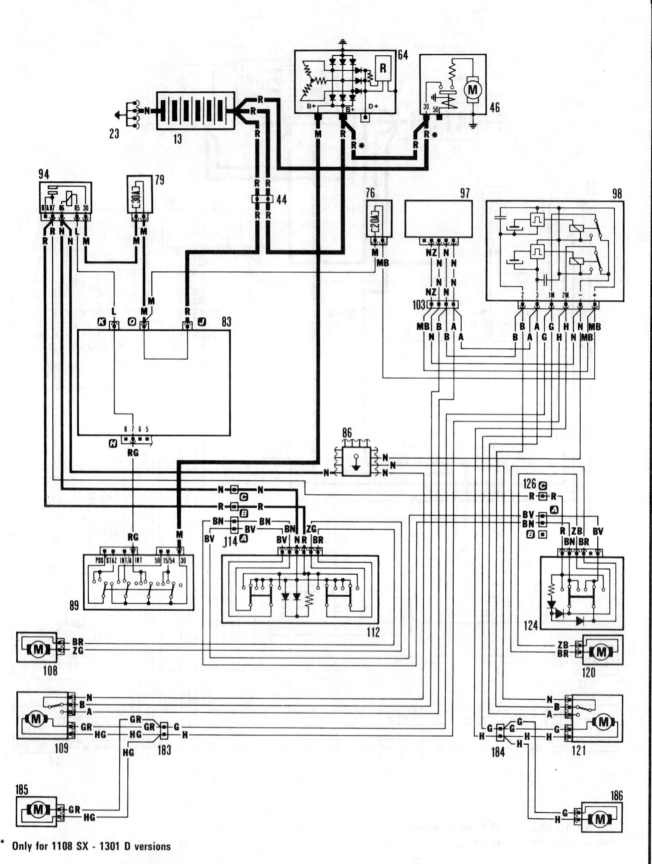

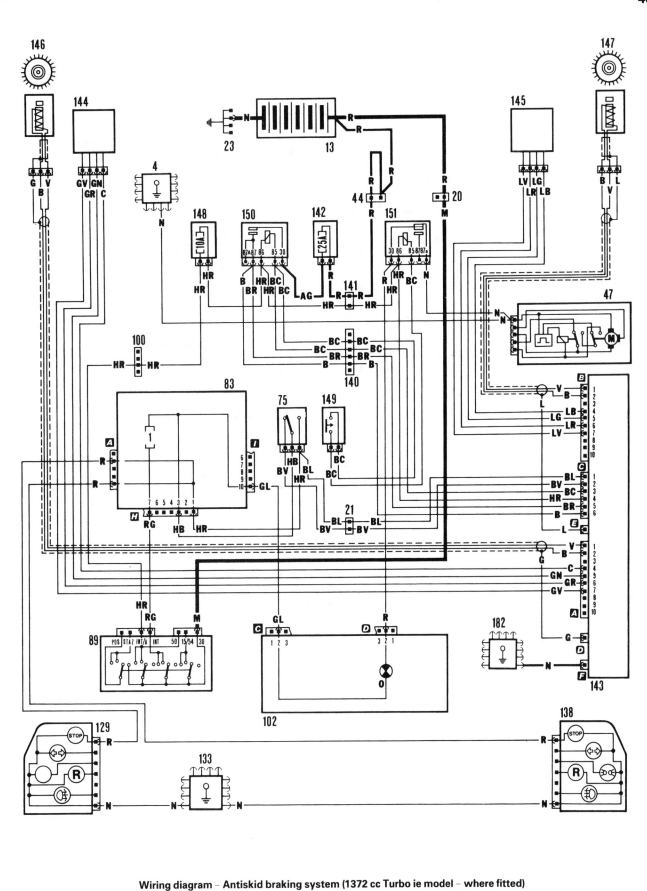

**Wiring diagram – Antiskid braking system (1372 cc Turbo ie model – where fitted)**

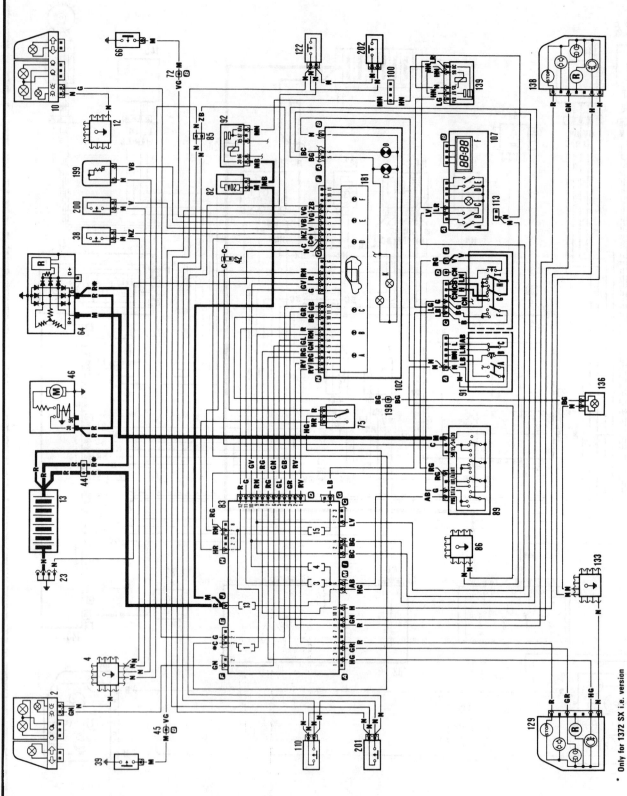

Wiring diagram – check panel (1990-on 5-door models (3 door similar))

* Only for 1372 SX i.e. version

# Index